Berkeley DB

Contents At a Glance

I   Reference Guide

1   Introduction

2   A Simple Access Method Tutorial

3   Access Method Configuration

4   Access Method Operations

5   Access Method Wrap-Up

6   Berkeley DB Architecture

7   Berkeley DB Environment

8   Berkeley DB Concurrent Data Store Applications

9   Berkeley DB Transactional Data Store Applications

10 XA Resource Manager

11 Programmer Notes

12 Locking Subsystem

13 Logging Subsystem

14 Memory Pool Subsystem

15 Transaction Subsystem

16 PC Client/Server

17 Java API

18 Tcl API

19   Dumping and Reloading Databases

20   Debugging Applications

21   Building Berkeley DB for UNIX
     and QNX Systems

22   Building Berkeley DB for Win32
     Platforms

23   Building Berkeley DB for VxWorks
     Systems

24   Upgrading Berkeley DB
     Applications

25   Test Suite

26   Distribution

27   Additional References

II   API Manual

28   C API

29   C++ API

30   Java API

31   Tcl API

32   Supporting Utilities

Berkeley DB

Sleepycat™ Software, Inc.

New Riders

www.newriders.com

201 West 103rd Street, Indianapolis, Indiana 46290
An Imprint of Pearson Education
Boston • Indianapolis • London • Munich • New York • San Francisco

Berkeley DB

Trademarks

Warning and Disclaimer

Publisher
David Dwyer

Associate Publisher
Al Valvano

Executive Editor
Stephanie Wall

Acquisitions Editor
Ann Quinn

Managing Editor
Gina Brown

Development Editor
Nancy E. Sixsmith

Product Marketing Manager
Stephanie Layton

Publicity Manager
Susan Petro

Indexer
Cheryl Lenser

Technical Reviewers
Joshua McDonald
Christopher Small

Manufacturing Coordinator
Jim Conway

Book Designer
Louisa Klucznik

Cover Designer
Brainstorm Design, Inc.

Cover Production
Aren Howell

Proofreader
Debbie Williams

Composition
Amy Parker

Table of Contents

I   Reference Guide   1

1   Introduction   3
Mapping the Terrain: Theory and Practice   4
What Is Berkeley DB?   8
What Is Berkeley DB Not?   11
Do You Need Berkeley DB?   14
What Other Services Does Berkeley DB Provide?   15
What Does the Berkeley DB Distribution Include?   16
Where Does Berkeley DB Run?   16
Sleepycat Software's Berkeley DB Products   16

2   Getting Started: A Simple Tutorial   19
Key/Data Pairs   20
Object Handles   20
Error Returns   20
Opening a Database   21
Adding Elements to a Database   22
Retrieving Elements from a Database   25
Removing Elements from a Database   26
Closing a Database   28

3   Access Method Configuration   31
Selecting an Access Method   32
Logical Record Numbers   34
Selecting a Page Size   35
Selecting a Cache Size   36
Selecting a Byte Order   37
Non-Local Memory Allocation   37

Btree Comparison   37

Btree Prefix Comparison   39

Minimum Keys Per Page   40

Retrieving Btree Records by Number   40

Page Fill Factor   41

Specifying a Database Hash   41

Hash Table Size   42

Managing Record-Based Databases   42

Selecting a Queue Extent Size   43

Flat-Text Backing Files   43

Logically Renumbering Records   44

4 Access Method Operations   47

Opening a Database   47

Opening Multiple Databases in a Single File   48

Upgrading Databases   49

Retrieving Records   50

Storing Records   50

Deleting Records   50

Flushing the Database Cache   51

Database Statistics   51

Closing a Database   51

Database Cursors   52

Retrieving Records with a Cursor   52

Storing Records with a Cursor   53

Deleting Records with a Cursor   54

Duplicating a Cursor   54

Logical Join   54

Data Item Count   58

Closing a Cursor   58

Cursor Stability   58

Database Verification and Salvage   59

5 Access Method Wrap-Up 61
Retrieved Key/Data Permanence for C/C++ 61
Database Limits 62
Disk Space Requirements 62
Partial Record Storage and Retrieval 65
Error Support 67

6 Berkeley DB Architecture 69
Programming Model 72
Programmatic APIs 72
Scripting Languages 74
Supporting Utilities 74

7 Berkeley DB Environment 77
Creating a Database Environment 78
File Naming 79
Filename Resolution in Berkeley DB 80
Security 82
Shared Memory Regions 83
Remote Filesystems 84
Opening Databases Within the
Environment 84
Error Support 85

**8 Berkeley DB Concurrent Data Store
Applications 87**

**9 Berkeley DB Transactional
Data Store Applications 91**
Why Transactions? 92
Terminology 92
Application Structure 93
Opening the Environment 95
Opening the Databases 98
Recoverability and Deadlock Avoidance 100
Atomicity 103
Repeatable Reads 106
Transactional Cursors 107
Nested Transactions 110
Environment Infrastructure 111

Deadlock Detection   111

Performing Checkpoints   113

Database and Log File Archival Procedures   115

Log File Removal   117

Recovery Procedures   119

Recovery and Filesystem Operations   120

Berkeley DB Recoverability   121

Transaction Throughput   123

10   XA Resource Manager   127

Configuring Berkeley DB with the Tuxedo
System   128

Frequently Asked Questions   129

11   Programmer Notes   131

Error Returns to Applications   132

Environmental Variables   134

Building Multithreaded Applications   134

Berkeley DB Handles   135

Name Spaces   136

Library Version Information   138

Compatibility with Historic UNIX
Interfaces   138

Recovery Implementation   139

Application-Specific Logging and Recovery   139

Run-Time Configuration   144

12   The Locking Subsystem   147

Page Locks   149

Standard Lock Modes   150

Locking Without Transactions   151

Locking with Transactions: Two-Phase
Locking   151

Access Method Locking Conventions   152

Berkeley DB Concurrent Data Store Locking
Conventions   154

Deadlocks and Deadlock Avoidance   155

Configuring Locking   156

Locking and Non-Berkeley DB
Applications   158

13 **The Logging Subsystem**   161
Configuring Logging   162
Log File Limits   162

14 **The Memory Pool Subsystem**   165
Configuring the Memory Pool   166

15 **The Transaction Subsystem**   167
Transaction Limits   168
Configuring Transactions   169
Transactions and Non-Berkeley DB
Applications   170

16 **RPC/Client Server**   173
Client Program   174
Server Program   175

17 **Java API**   177
Compatibility   178
Java Programming Notes   179
Java FAQ   180

18 **Tcl API**   181
Loading Berkeley DB with Tcl   181
Using Berkeley DB with Tcl   182
Tcl API Programming Notes   183
Tcl Error Handling   183
Tcl FAQ   185

19 **Dumping and Reloading Databases**   187
The db_dump and db_load Utilities   187
Dump Output Formats   188
Loading Text into Databases   189

20 **Debugging Applications**   191
Compile-time Configuration   192
Run-time Error Information   193
Reviewing Berkeley DB Log Files   193
Common Errors   197

21 Building Berkeley DB for UNIX and QNX Systems   201

Building for UNIX   201

Configuring Berkeley DB   202

Changing Compile or Load Options   205

Installing Berkeley DB   206

Dynamic Shared Libraries   207

Running the Test Suite Under UNIX   208

Architecture-Independent FAQs   209

AIX   212

FreeBSD   213

HP-UX   214

IRIX   215

Linux   216

OSF/1   216

SCO   216

Solaris   216

SunOS   218

Ultrix   218

22 Building Berkeley DB for Win32 Platforms   219

Building for Win32   219

Running the Test Suite Under Windows   222

Windows Notes   223

Windows FAQ   224

23 Building Berkeley DB for VxWorks Systems   225

VxWorks Notes   227

VxWorks FAQ   228

24 Upgrading Berkeley DB Applications   231

Upgrading Berkeley DB Installations   231

25   **Test Suite   235**
Running the Test Suite   235
Test Suite FAQ   237

26   **Distribution   239**

27   **Additional References   241**
Technical Papers on Berkeley DB   241
Background on Berkeley DB Features   242
Database Systems Theory   242

II   **API Manual   243**

28   **C API   245**

29   **C++ API   373**

30   **Java API   489**

31   **Tcl API   591**

32   **Supporting Utilities   617**

About the Author

Sleepycat™ Software, Inc. develops, and supports Berkeley DB.
Berkeley DB was originally written by Keith Bostic, Mike Olson, Margo
Seltzer, and Ozan Yigit in the early 1990s. Keith Bostic, one of the principal
developers of the University of California's 4.4BSD UNIX releases,
approached Seltzer and Yigit to write an Open Source implementation of the
UNIX C library dbm hash package for inclusion in 4.4BSD. They agreed, and
created a general-purpose hashing library. Later, Bostic enlisted Olson to add
a Btree access method to the package. These two projects were integrated and
became the first Berkeley DB release, which was included in the 4.4BSD
UNIX and related Net/2 releases.

In the years that followed, Berkeley DB was adopted by an enormous number
of both proprietary and Open Source projects. Its high performance, ready
availability, and easy-to-use interfaces made it a natural tool for a wide variety
of applications.

In 1996, there were enough commercial users of the software to justify the
formation of a company to enhance and support it. Bostic and Seltzer formed
Sleepycat Software to do this. They spent a year adding critical features to the
academic code (most notably, transactions, support for concurrent users, and
recoverability), and version 2.0 of Berkeley DB was released by Sleepycat
Software in 1997.

Since that initial release, Berkeley DB has been deployed in network switches,
email clients, wireless communication systems, mission-critical site-monitor-
ing software, and many other applications.

Sleepycat is an Open Source company, and it is committed to the development
and distribution of Berkeley DB as an Open Source product. Sleepycat's license
for Berkeley DB permits its use at no charge in Open Source applications.

About the Technical Reviewer

This reviewer contributed his considerable hands-on expertise to the entire development process for *Berkeley DB*. As the book was being written, this dedicated professional reviewed all the material for technical content, organization, and flow. His feedback was critical to ensuring that *Berkeley DB* fits our readers' need for the highest-quality technical information.

Joshua MacDonald is currently a graduate student at UC Berkeley, where he studies computer science. His research interests include filesystems and version control, and he is especially interested in applying transaction-processing techniques to these systems. He has used Berkeley DB for a number of projects, including several original filesystem prototypes. His activities in the Open Source community include Xdelta and the Project Revision Control System (PCRS). His advice for you is to "Kill your RDBMS"!

Acknowledgments

As with any software project of this scale, there are many people to thank. The University of California, Berkeley and Harvard University supported development of the first versions of this work. Nathan Goodman reviewed early versions of the Berkeley DB interfaces. Ozan Yigit was the co-developer of the hash access method, Jeremy Rassen redesigned large portions of the hash access method, and Steve Rozen wrote the first logging subsystem. Paul Marquess wrote Berkeley DB's Perl modules and has been our link to the Perl community. Netscape Communications Corp. supported development of Berkeley DB's transactional model. David Boreham and Tim Howes were early adopters at Netscape who provided the much needed "application perspective" and suggested many of the features now found in Berkeley DB. And special thanks to the millions of Berkeley DB users around the world who have reported bugs, suggested features, and made Sleepycat a rewarding and fun place to work.

Tell Us What You Think

As the reader of this book, you are the most important critic and commentator. We value your opinion and want to know what we're doing right, what we could do better, what areas you'd like to see us publish in, and any other words of wisdom you're willing to pass our way.

As an Executive Editor for the Web Development team at New Riders Publishing, I welcome your comments. You can fax, email, or write me directly to let me know what you did or didn't like about this book—as well as what we can do to make our books stronger.

Please note that I cannot help you with technical problems related to the topic of this book, and that due to the high volume of mail I receive, I might not be able to reply to every message.

When you write, please be sure to include this book's title and author as well as your name and phone or fax number. I will carefully review your comments and share them with the author and editors who worked on the book.

Fax: 317-581-4663
Email: stephanie.wall@newriders.com
Mail: Stephanie Wall
            Executive Editor
            New Riders Publishing
            201 West 103rd Street
            Indianapolis, IN 46290 USA

If you have technical comments or problems regarding Berkeley DB, contact:
support@sleepycat.com

Introduction

For many programmers, the word "database" instantly calls to mind a complex client/server relational engine from an established commercial vendor. Over the last couple of decades, database management has become big business, and some businesses have become very big indeed, providing products and services for storing information.

With the advent of the Internet, the miniaturization of computing components, and the explosion in data storage capacity of disks and memory systems, computers are being deployed in places and used in ways that were unthinkable just a decade ago. With that shift, the one-size-fits-all philosophy of the big relational products has become outdated. Applications today demand a wide range of data management services: from palmtop devices that need robust, simple single-user record lookup to high-end Internet servers that deliver terabytes of data to thousands of concurrent users. Programmers today need to be able to choose a database manager that delivers exactly the services that their applications demand, and to leave out the complexity and management overhead that their users can't tolerate.

Berkeley DB is an embedded database system. It links directly into the address space of the application that uses it, and provides a simple function-call API for storing and retrieving data. It can run in single-user mode, or provide high-concurrency, transaction-protected, fully recoverable access to records that it stores. Programmers embed it in their applications, and end users are generally unaware that they're using a database at all. There is no separate server to install and administer, no ongoing manual maintenance required, and no complex query language to master.

This book gives detailed information on the design and implementation of Berkeley DB, and how to use it in applications. The book will help you decide whether you need an embedded database at all, and how your application should use Berkeley DB to get the best performance and greatest reliability from it.

What's Inside?

Berkeley DB is organized into two main parts: the Reference Guide and the API Manual. The first section of the Reference Guide has a tutorial, which explains what Berkeley DB is and gives a straightforward example of how it's used in application code. Programmers should be able to read this section and understand how Berkeley DB works generally. The application is a good starting point for developers who need to build applications of their own, and want some code that they can modify.

The Reference Guide gives much more detailed information on the design and implementation of Berkeley DB. This section should help you understand the performance and behavior of your Berkeley DB application. It includes advice on how and when to use particular features, and explains the internals of the library so that you know how it really works.

Part II, the API Manual, provides manual-page style information on the Berkeley DB API. Programmers can use this section to be sure that they're calling Berkeley DB functions with the correct arguments, and to refresh their memories on return types and values and any side effects of individual functions.

Who Is this Book For?

This book is intended for experienced programmers who write applications that need data management services. Applications can be written in C, C++, Java, Perl, Python, Tcl, or PHP; but familiarity with the C programming language will help you get the most out of the book. Berkeley DB is written in C.

You need not be familiar with SQL-based client/server relational systems. If you are, the section that compares Berkeley DB to such systems will help you understand what Berkeley DB is (and is not).

Who Is this Book Not For?

The book is not intended for end users who need a simple GUI-based query tool for their data. Berkeley DB is an embedded database system that requires application code to store and fetch records. Although it's possible to build a GUI-based query tool for a Berkeley DB database, the library, as distributed by Sleepycat Software, does not include that support. The overriding design goal of Berkeley DB is to do one job well: high-performance data management. Extraneous features such as GUI tools, query languages, and relational interfaces are not a part of the core product.

Conventions Used in this Book

Throughout the book, sample code looks like this:

```
compare_dbt(dbp, a, b)
```

Several of the examples span more than one section. The first time any piece of code is presented, it's in boldface, like this:

../dist/configure

> **Note**
> Notes present interesting pieces of information related to the discussion at hand. Notes look like this:

> **Warning**
> Warnings advise you about potential problems and help you steer clear of disaster. Warnings look like this:

I

Reference Guide

1   Introduction

2   A Simple Access Method Tutorial

3   Access Method Configuration

4   Access Method Operations

5   Access Method Wrap-Up

6   Berkeley DB Architecture

7   Berkeley DB Environment

8   Berkeley DB Concurrent Data Store Applications

9   Berkeley DB Transactional Data Store Applications

10   XA Resource Manager

11   Programmer Notes

12   Locking Subsystem

13   Logging Subsystem

14   Memory Pool Subsystem

15   Transaction Subsystem

16   PC Client/Server

17   Java API

18   Tcl API

19   Dumping and Reloading Databases

20   Debugging Applications

21   Building Berkeley DB for UNIX and QNX Systems

22   Building Berkeley DB for Win32 Platforms

23   Building Berkeley DB for VxWorks Systems

24   Upgrading Berkeley DB Applications

25   Test Suite

26   Distribution

27   Additional References

1

Introduction

INEXPENSIVE, POWERFUL COMPUTING AND NETWORKING have created countless new applications that could not exist a decade ago. The advent of the World Wide Web and its influence in driving the Internet into homes and businesses is one obvious example. Equally important, though, is the movement from large general-purpose desktop and server computers toward smaller special-purpose devices with built-in processing and communications services.

As computer hardware has spread into virtually every corner of our lives, software has followed. Software developers today are building applications not just for conventional desktop and server environments, but also for hand-held computers, home appliances, networking hardware, cars and trucks, factory floor automation systems, and more.

Although these operating environments are diverse, the problems that software engineers must solve in them are often strikingly similar. Most systems must deal with the outside world, whether that means communicating with users or controlling machinery. As a result, most need some sort of I/O system. Even a simple single-function system generally needs to handle multiple tasks, so it needs some kind of operating system to schedule and manage control threads. Also, many computer systems must store and retrieve data to track history, record configuration settings, or manage access.

Data management can be very simple. In some cases, just recording configuration in a flat text file is enough. More often, though, programs need to store and search a large amount of data or structurally complex data. Database management systems are tools that programmers can use to do this work quickly and efficiently using off-the-shelf software.

Of course, database management systems have been around for a long time. Data storage is a problem dating back to the earliest days of computing. Software developers can choose from hundreds of good commercially available database systems. The problem is selecting the one that best solves the problems that their particular applications create.

Mapping the Terrain: Theory and Practice

The first step of selecting a database system is to figure out what the choices are. Decades of research and real-world deployment have produced countless systems. We need to organize them somehow to reduce the number of options.

One obvious way to group systems is to use the common labels that vendors apply to them. The buzzwords here include *network, relational, object-oriented,* and *embedded*; with some cross-fertilization such as *object-relational* and *embedded network*. Understanding the buzzwords is important. Each has some grounding in theory, but has also evolved into a practical label for categorizing systems that work in a certain way.

All database systems, regardless of the buzzwords that apply to them, provide a few common services. All of them store data, for example. We begin by exploring the common services that all systems provide; we then examine the differences between the various systems.

Data Access and Data Management

Fundamentally, database systems provide two services. The first service is *data access*, which means adding new data to the database (inserting), finding data of interest (searching), changing data already stored (updating), and removing data from the database (deleting). All databases provide these services. How they work varies from category to category, and depends on the record structure that the database supports.

Each record in a database is a collection of values. For example, the record for a Web site customer might include a name, an email address, a shipping address, and payment information. Records are usually stored in tables, and each table holds records of the same kind. For example, the **customer** table at an e-commerce Web site might store the customer records for every person who shopped at the site. Often, database records have a different structure from the structures or instances supported by the programming language in which an application is written. As a result, working with records can mean

- using database operations such as searches and updates on records.
- converting between programming language structures and database record types in the application.

The second service is *data management*. Data management is more complicated than data access. Providing good data management services is the hard part of building a database system. When you choose a database system to use in an application you build, making sure that it supports the data management services you need is critical.

Data management services include allowing multiple users to work on the database simultaneously (concurrency), allowing multiple records to be changed instantaneously (transactions), and surviving application and system crashes (recovery). Different database systems offer different data management services. Data management services are entirely independent of the data access services listed previously. For example, nothing about relational database theory requires that the system support transactions, but most commercial relational systems do.

Concurrency means that multiple users can operate on the database at the same time. Support for concurrency ranges from none (single-user access only) to complete (many readers and writers working simultaneously).

Transactions permit users to make multiple changes appear at once. For example, a transfer of funds between bank accounts needs to be a transaction because the balance in one account is reduced and the balance in the other increases. If the reduction happens before the increase, a poorly timed system crash can leave the customer poorer; if the bank uses the opposite order, the same system crash can make the customer richer. Obviously, both the customer and the bank are best served if both operations happen at the same instant.

Transactions have well-defined properties in database systems. They are *atomic*, so the changes happen all at once or not at all. They are *consistent*, so the database is in a legal state when the transaction begins and when it ends. They are typically *isolated*, which means that any other users in the database cannot interfere with them while they are in progress. And they are *durable*, so if the system or application crashes after a transaction finishes, the changes are not lost. Together, the properties of *atomicity*, *consistency*, *isolation*, and *durability* are known as the *ACID* properties.

As in the case for concurrency, support for transactions varies among databases. Some offer atomicity without making guarantees about durability. Some ignore isolatability, especially in single-user systems; there's no need to isolate other users from the effects of changes when there are no other users.

Another important management service is recovery. Strictly speaking, *recovery* is a procedure that the system carries out when it starts up. The purpose of recovery is to guarantee that the database is complete and usable. This is most important after a system or application crash, when the database may be damaged. The recovery process guarantees that the internal structure of the database is good. Recovery usually means that any completed transactions are checked, and any lost changes are reapplied to the database. At the end of the recovery process, applications can use the database as if there were no interruption in service.

Finally, there are a number of data management services that permit the copying of data. For example, most database systems are able to import data from other sources and to export it for use elsewhere. Also, most systems provide some way to back up databases and to restore them in the event of a system failure. Many commercial systems allow *hot backups* that allow users to back up databases while they are in use. Many applications must run without interruption, and cannot be shut down for backups.

A particular database system may provide other data management services. Some provide browsers that show database structure and contents. Some include tools that enforce data integrity rules, such as the rule that no employee can have a negative salary. These data management services are not common to all systems, however. Concurrency, recovery, and transactions are the data management services that most database vendors support.

Deciding what kind of database to use means understanding the data access and data management services that your application needs. Berkeley DB is an embedded database that supports a fairly simple data model with a rich set of data management services. To highlight its strengths and weaknesses, we can compare it to other database system categories.

Relational Databases

Relational databases are probably the best-known database variant because of the success of companies such as Oracle. Relational databases are based on the mathematical field of set theory. Those operations define the relational data model. The term *relation* is really just a synonym for *set*—a relation is just a set of records or, in our terminology, a table. One of the main innovations in early relational systems was to insulate the programmer from the physical organization of the database. Rather than walking through arrays of records or traversing pointers, programmers make statements about tables in a high-level language, and the system executes those statements.

Relational databases operate on *tuples*, or records, which are composed of values of several different data types, including integers, character strings, and others. Operations include searching for records whose values satisfy some criteria, updating records, and so on.

Virtually all relational databases use Structured Query Language, or SQL. This language permits people and computer programs to work with the database by writing simple statements. The database engine reads those statements and determines how to satisfy them on the tables in the database.

SQL is the main practical advantage of relational database systems. Rather than writing a computer program to find records of interest, the relational system user can just type a query in a simple syntax and let the engine do the work. This gives users enormous flexibility; they do not need to decide in advance what kind of searches they want to do, and they do not need expensive programmers to find the data they need. Learning SQL requires some effort, but it's much simpler than a full-blown high-level programming language for most purposes. And there are a lot of programmers who have already learned SQL.

Object-Oriented Databases

Object-oriented databases are less common than relational systems, but are still fairly widespread. Most object-oriented databases were originally conceived as persistent storage systems closely wedded to particular high-level programming languages like C++. With the spread of Java, most now support more than one programming language, but object-oriented databases fundamentally provide the same class and method abstractions as object-oriented programming languages.

Many object-oriented systems allow applications to operate on objects uniformly, whether they are in memory or on disk. These systems create the illusion that all objects are in memory all the time. The advantage to object-oriented programmers who simply want object storage and retrieval is clear: They need never be aware of whether an object is in memory or not. The application simply uses objects, and the database system moves them between disk and memory transparently. All the operations on an object and all its behavior are determined by the programming language.

Object-oriented databases aren't nearly as widely deployed as relational systems. To attract developers who understand relational systems, many of the object-oriented systems have added support for query languages very much like SQL. In practice, though, object-oriented databases are mostly used for the persistent storage of objects in C++ and Java programs.

Network Databases

The *network model* is a fairly old technique for managing and navigating application data. Network databases are designed to make pointer traversal very fast. Every record stored in a network database is allowed to contain pointers to other records. These pointers are generally physical addresses, so fetching the referenced record just means reading it from disk by its disk address.

Network database systems generally permit records to contain integers, floating point numbers, and character strings, as well as references to other records. An application can search for records of interest. After retrieving a record, the application can quickly fetch any referenced record.

Pointer traversal is fast because most network systems use physical disk addresses as pointers. When the application wants to fetch a record, the database system uses the address to fetch exactly the right string of bytes from the disk. This requires only a single disk access in all cases. Other systems, by contrast, often must do more than one disk read to find a particular record.

The key advantage of the network model is also its main drawback. The fact that pointer traversal is so fast means that applications that do it will run well. On the other hand, storing pointers all over the database makes it very hard to reorganize the database. In effect, once you've stored a pointer to a record, it is difficult to move that record elsewhere. Some network databases handle this by leaving forwarding pointers behind, but this defeats the speed advantage of doing a single disk access in the first place. Other network databases find and fix all the pointers to a record when it moves, but this makes reorganization very expensive. Reorganization is often necessary in databases because adding and deleting records over time will consume space that cannot be reclaimed without reorganizing. Without periodic reorganization to compact databases, they can end up with a considerable amount of wasted space.

Clients and Servers

Database vendors have two choices for system architecture. They can build a server to which remote clients connect and do all the database management inside the server. Alternatively, they can provide a module that links directly into the application and does all database management locally. In either case, the application developer needs some way of communicating with the database (generally, an Application Program Interface, or API, that does work in the process or communicates with a server to get work done).

Almost all commercial database products are implemented as servers, and applications connect to them as clients. Servers have several features that make them attractive. First, because all the data is managed by a separate process, possibly on a separate machine, it's easy to isolate the database server from bugs and crashes in the application.

Second, because some database products (particularly relational engines) are quite large, splitting them off as separate server processes keeps applications small, which uses less disk space and memory. Relational engines include code to parse SQL statements, to analyze them and produce plans for execution, to optimize the plans, and to execute them.

Finally, by storing all the data in one place and managing it with a single server, it's easier for organizations to back up, protect, and set policies on their databases. The enterprise databases for large companies often have several full-time administrators caring for them, making certain that applications run quickly, granting and denying access to users, and making backups.

However, centralized administration can be a disadvantage in some cases. In particular, if a programmer wants to build an application that uses a database for storage of important information, shipping and supporting the application is much harder. The end user needs to install and administer a separate database server, and the programmer must support not just one product, but two. Adding a server process to the application creates new opportunity for installation mistakes and run-time problems.

What is Berkeley DB?

So far, we discussed database systems in general terms. It's time now to consider Berkeley DB in particular and see how it fits into the framework we have introduced. The key question is this: Which kinds of applications should use Berkeley DB?

Berkeley DB is an open source embedded database library that provides scalable, high-performance, transaction-protected data management services to applications. It provides a simple function-call API for data access and management.

By *open source*, we mean that Berkeley DB is distributed under a license that conforms to the Open Source Definition. This license guarantees that Berkeley DB is freely available for use and redistribution in other open source products. Although Sleepycat Software sells commercial licenses for redistribution in proprietary applications, the complete source code for Berkeley DB is freely available for download and use in all cases.

Berkeley DB is embedded because it links directly into the application, and it runs in the same address space as the application. As a result, no interprocess communication, either over the network or between processes on the same machine, is required for database operations. Berkeley DB provides a simple function-call API for a number of programming languages, including C, C++, Java, Perl, Tcl, Python, and PHP. All database operations happen inside the library. Multiple processes or multiple threads in a single process can all use the database at the same time each uses the Berkeley DB library. Low-level services such as locking, transaction logging, shared buffer management, memory management, and so on are all handled transparently by the library.

The library is extremely portable. It runs under almost all UNIX and Linux variants, Windows, and a number of embedded real-time operating systems. It runs on both 32-bit and 64-bit systems. It has been deployed in high-end Internet servers, desktop machines, palmtop computers, set-top boxes, network switches, and elsewhere. After Berkeley DB is linked into the application, the end user generally does not know that there's a database present at all.

Berkeley DB is scalable in a number of respects. The database library itself is quite compact (fewer than 300 kilobytes of text space on common architectures), but it can manage databases up to 256 terabytes in size. It also supports high concurrency, with thousands of users operating on the same database at the same time. Berkeley DB is small enough to run in tightly constrained embedded systems, but can take advantage of gigabytes of memory and terabytes of disk on high-end server machines.

Berkeley DB generally outperforms relational and object-oriented database systems in embedded applications for a couple of reasons. First, because the library runs in the same address space, no interprocess communication is required for database operations. The cost of communicating between processes on a single machine or among machines on a network is much higher than the cost of making a function call. Second, because Berkeley DB uses a simple function-call interface for all operations, there is no query language to parse, and no execution plan to produce.

Data Access Services

Berkeley DB applications can choose the storage structure that best suits the application. Berkeley DB supports hash tables, Btrees, simple record-number-based storage, and persistent queues. Programmers can create tables using any of these storage structures, and can mix operations on different kinds of tables in a single application.

Hash tables are generally good for very large databases that need predictable search and update times for random-access records. Hash tables allow users to ask, "Does this key exist?" or to fetch a record with a known key. Hash tables do not allow users to ask for records with keys that are close to a known key.

Btrees are better for range-based searches (when the application needs to find all records with keys between some starting and ending value, for example). Btrees also do a better job of exploiting *locality of reference*. If the application is likely to touch keys near each other at the same time, the Btrees work well. The tree structure keeps keys that are close together near one another in storage, so fetching nearby values usually doesn't require disk access.

Record-number-based storage is natural for applications that need to store and fetch records, but do not have a simple way to generate keys of their own. In a record-number table, the record number is the key for the record. Berkeley DB will can generate these record numbers automatically.

Queues are well-suited for applications that create records and then must deal with those records in creation order. A good example is an online purchasing system. Although orders can enter the system at any time, they should usually be filled in the order in which they were placed.

Data Management Services

Berkeley DB offers important data management services, including concurrency, transactions, and recovery. These services work on all the storage structures.

Many users can work on the same database concurrently. Berkeley DB handles locking transparently, ensuring that two users working on the same record do not interfere with each other.

The library provides strict ACID transaction semantics. Some systems allow the user to relax. Berkeley DB ensures that all applications can see only committed updates.

Multiple operations can be grouped into a single transaction, and can be committed or rolled back atomically. Berkeley DB uses a technique called *two-phase locking* to be sure that concurrent transactions are isolated from one another; and uses a technique called *write-ahead logging* to guarantee that committed changes survive application, system, or hardware failures.

When an application starts up, it can ask Berkeley DB to run recovery. Recovery restores the database to a clean state with all committed changes present, even after a crash. The database is guaranteed to be consistent, and all committed changes are guaranteed to be present when recovery completes.

When it starts up, an application can specify which data management services it will use. Some applications may need fast, single-user, nontransactional Btree data storage. In that case, the application can disable the Locking and Transaction systems, and will not incur the overhead of locking or logging. If an application needs to support multiple concurrent users, but doesn't need transactions, it can turn on locking without transactions. Applications that need concurrent, transaction-protected database access can enable all the subsystems.

In all these cases, the application uses the same function-call API to fetch and update records.

Design

Berkeley DB was designed to provide industrial-strength database services to application developers, without requiring them to become database experts. It is a classic C-library-style *toolkit*, providing a broad base of functionality to application writers. Berkeley DB was designed by programmers, for programmers: Its modular design surfaces simple orthogonal interfaces to core services, and it provides mechanism (for example, good thread support) without imposing policy (for example, the use of threads is not required). Just as importantly, Berkeley DB allows developers to balance performance against the need for crash recovery and concurrent use. An application can use the storage structure that provides the fastest access to its data, and can request only the degree of logging and locking that it needs.

Because of the tool-based approach and separate interfaces for each Berkeley DB subsystem, you can support a complete transaction environment for other system operations. Berkeley DB even allows you to wrap transactions around the standard UNIX file read/write operations! Further, Berkeley DB was designed to interact correctly with the native system's toolset, a feature no other database package offers. For example, Berkeley DB supports *hot backups* (database backups while the database is in use) using the standard UNIX tools: dump, tar, cpio, pax, or even cp.

Finally, because scripting language interfaces are available for Berkeley DB (notably Tcl and Perl), application writers can build incredibly powerful database engines with little effort. You can build transaction-protected database applications using your favorite scripting languages, an increasingly important feature in a world using CGI scripts to deliver HTML.

What is Berkeley DB Not?

In contrast with most other database systems, Berkeley DB provides relatively simple data access services. Records in Berkeley DB are (*key, value*) pairs. Berkeley DB supports only a few logical operations on records, as follows:

- Inserting a record in a table.
- Deleting a record from a table.
- Finding a record in a table by looking up its key.
- Updating a record that has already been found.

Notice that Berkeley DB never operates on the value part of a record. Values are simply payload to be stored with keys and reliably delivered back to the application on demand.

Both keys and values can be arbitrary bit strings, either fixed-length or variable-length. As a result, programmers can put native programming language data structures into the database without converting them to a foreign record format first. Storage and retrieval are very simple, but the application needs to know what the structure of a key and a value is in advance. It cannot ask Berkeley DB because Berkeley DB doesn't know.

This is an important feature of Berkeley DB, and one worth considering more carefully. On the one hand, Berkeley DB cannot provide the programmer with any information on the contents or structure of the values that it stores. The application must understand the keys and values that it uses. On the other hand, there is literally no limit to the data types that can be stored in a Berkeley DB database. The application never needs to convert its own program data into the data types that Berkeley DB supports. Berkeley DB is able to operate on any data type the application uses, no matter how complex.

Because both keys and values can be up to four gigabytes in length, a single record can store images, audio streams, or other large data values. Large values are not treated in a special way in Berkeley DB. They are simply broken into page-sized chunks and then reassembled on demand when the application needs them. Unlike some other database systems, Berkeley DB offers no special support for *binary large objects* (*BLOBs*).

Not a Relational Database

Berkeley DB is not a relational database. First, Berkeley DB does not support SQL queries. All access to data is through the Berkeley DB API. Developers must learn a new set of interfaces in order to work with Berkeley DB. Although the interfaces are fairly simple, they are nonstandard.

SQL support is a double-edged sword. One big advantage of relational databases is that they allow users to write simple declarative queries in a high-level language. The database system knows everything about the data and can carry out the command. This means that it's simple to search for data in new ways and to ask new questions of the database. No programming is required.

On the other hand, if a programmer can predict in advance how an application will access data, writing a low-level program to get and store records can be faster. It eliminates the overhead of query parsing, optimization, and execution. The programmer must understand the data representation, and must write the code to do the work; after that's done, however, the application can be very fast.

Second, Berkeley DB has no notion of schema in the way that relational systems do. *Schema* is the structure of records in tables and the relationships among the tables in the database. In a relational system, for example, the programmer can create a record from a fixed menu of data types. Because the record types are declared to the system, the relational engine can reach inside records and examine individual values in them. In addition, programmers can use SQL to declare relationships among tables and create indexes on tables. Relational engines usually maintain these relationships and indexes automatically.

In Berkeley DB, the key and value in a record are opaque to Berkeley DB. They may have a rich internal structure, but the library is unaware of it. As a result, Berkeley DB cannot decompose the value part of a record into its constituent parts, and cannot use those parts to find values of interest. Only the application, which knows the data structure, can do that.

Berkeley DB does allow programmers to create indexes on tables, and to use those indexes to speed up searches. However, the programmer has no way to tell the library how different tables and indexes are related. The application needs to make sure that they all stay consistent. In the case of indexes in particular, if the application puts a new record into a table, it must also put a new record in the index for it. It's generally simple to write a single function to make the required updates, but it is work that relational systems do automatically.

Berkeley DB is not a relational system. Relational database systems are semantically rich and offer high-level database access. Compared to such systems, Berkeley DB is a high-performance, transactional library for record storage. It's possible to build a relational system on top of Berkeley DB. In fact, the popular MySQL relational system uses Berkeley DB for transaction-protected table management, and takes care of all the SQL parsing and execution. It uses Berkeley DB for the storage level, and provides the semantics and access tools.

Not an Object-Oriented Database

Object-oriented databases are designed for very tight integration with object-oriented programming languages. Berkeley DB is written entirely in the C programming language. It includes language bindings for C++, Java, and other languages, but the library has no information about the objects created in any object-oriented application. Berkeley DB never makes method calls on any application object. It has no idea what methods are defined on user objects, and cannot see the public or private members of any instance. The key and value part of all records are opaque to Berkeley DB.

Berkeley DB cannot automatically page in referenced objects, as some object-oriented databases do. The object-oriented application programmer must decide which records are required, and must fetch them by making method calls on Berkeley DB objects.

Not a Network Database

Berkeley DB does not support network-style navigation among records, as network databases do. Records in a Berkeley DB table may move around over time, as new records are added to the table and old ones are deleted. Berkeley DB can do fast searches for records based on keys, but there is no way to create a persistent physical pointer to a record. Applications can refer to records only by key, not by address.

Not a Database Server

Berkeley DB is not a standalone database server. It is a library, and it runs in the address space of the application that uses it. If more than one application links in Berkeley DB, all can use the same database at the same time; the library handles coordination among the applications, and guarantees that they do not interfere with one another.

Recent releases of Berkeley DB allow programmers to compile the library as a standalone process, and to use RPC stubs to connect to it and to carry out operations. However, there are some important limitations to this feature. The RPC stubs provide exactly the same API that the library itself does. There is no higher-level access provided by the standalone process. Tuning the standalone process is difficult because Berkeley DB does no threading in the library (applications can be threaded, but the library never creates a thread on its own).

It is possible to build a server application that uses Berkeley DB for data management. For example, many commercial and open source Lightweight Directory Access Protocol (LDAP) servers use Berkeley DB for record storage. LDAP clients connect to these servers over the network. Individual servers make calls through the Berkeley DB API to find records and return them to clients. On its own, however, Berkeley DB is not a server.

Do You Need Berkeley DB?

Berkeley DB is an ideal database system for applications that need fast, scalable, and reliable embedded database management. For applications that need different services, however, it can be a poor choice.

First, do you need the ability to access your data in ways you cannot predict in advance? If your users want to be able to enter SQL queries to perform complicated searches that you cannot program into your application to begin with, you should consider a relational engine instead. Berkeley DB requires a programmer to write code in order to run a new kind of query.

On the other hand, if you can predict your data access patterns up front—and in particular if you need fairly simple key/value lookups—Berkeley DB is a good choice. The queries can be coded up once, and will then run very quickly because there is no SQL to parse and execute.

Second, are there political arguments for or against a standalone relational server? If you're building an application for your own use and have a relational system installed with administrative support already, it may be simpler to use that than to build and learn Berkeley DB. On the other hand, if you'll be shipping many copies of your application to customers, and don't want your customers to have to buy, install, and manage a separate database system, then Berkeley DB may be a better choice.

Third, are there any technical advantages to an embedded database? If you're building an application that will run unattended for long periods of time or for end users who are not sophisticated administrators, a separate server process may be too big a burden. It will require separate installation and management, and if it creates new ways for the application to fail or new complexities to master in the field, Berkeley DB may be a better choice.

The fundamental question is the following: How closely do your requirements match the Berkeley DB design? Berkeley DB was conceived and built to provide fast, reliable, transaction-protected record storage. The library itself was never intended to provide interactive query support, graphical reporting tools, or similar services that some other database systems provide. We have tried always to err on the side of minimalism and simplicity. By keeping the library small and simple, we create fewer opportunities for bugs to creep in, and we guarantee that the database system stays fast because there is very little code to execute. If your application needs that set of features, Berkeley DB is almost certainly the best choice for you.

What Other Services Does Berkeley DB Provide?

Berkeley DB also provides core database services to developers. These services include the following:

- **Page cache management.** The page cache provides fast access to a cache of database pages, handling the I/O associated with the cache to ensure that dirty pages are written back to the filesystem and that new pages are allocated on demand. Applications may use the Berkeley DB shared memory buffer manager to serve their own files and pages.

- **Transactions and logging.** The Transaction and Logging systems provide recoverability and atomicity for multiple database operations. The Transaction system uses two-phase locking and write-ahead logging protocols to ensure that database operations may be undone or redone in the case of application or system failure. Applications may use Berkeley DB Transaction and Logging subsystems to protect their own data structures and operations from application or system failure.

- **Locking.** The Locking system provides multiple reader or single writer access to objects. The Berkeley DB access methods use the Locking system to acquire the right to read or write database pages. Applications may use the Berkeley DB Locking subsystem to support their own locking needs.

By combining the Page Cache, Transaction, Locking, and Logging systems, Berkeley DB provides the same services found in much larger, more complex, and more expensive database systems. Berkeley DB supports multiple simultaneous readers and writers, and guarantees that all changes are recoverable, even in the case of a catastrophic hardware failure during a database update.

Developers may select some or all of the core database services for any access method or database. Therefore, it is possible to choose the appropriate storage structure and the right degrees of concurrency and recoverability for any application. In addition, some of the systems (for example, the Locking subsystem) can be called separately from the Berkeley DB access method. As a result, developers can integrate non-database objects into their transactional applications using Berkeley DB.

What Does the Berkeley DB Distribution Include?

The Berkeley DB distribution includes complete source code for the Berkeley DB library, including all three Berkeley DB products and their supporting utilities, as well as complete documentation in HTML format.

The distribution does not include prebuilt binaries or libraries, or hard-copy documentation. Prebuilt libraries and binaries for some architecture/compiler combinations are available as part of Sleepycat Software's Berkeley DB support services.

Where Does Berkeley DB Run?

Berkeley DB requires only underlying IEEE/ANSI Std 1003.1 (POSIX) system calls, and can be ported easily to new architectures by adding stub routines to connect the native system interfaces to the Berkeley DB POSIX-style system calls.

Berkeley DB autoconfigures and runs on almost any modern UNIX system, and even on most historical UNIX platforms. See "Building Berkeley DB for UNIX and QNX Systems" for more information.

The Berkeley DB distribution includes support for QNX Neutrino. See "Building Berkeley DB for UNIX and QNX Systems" for more information.

The Berkeley DB distribution includes support for VxWorks via a workspace and project files for Tornado 2.0. See "Building Berkeley DB for VxWorks Systems" for more information.

The Berkeley DB distribution includes support for Windows 95, Windows 98, Windows NT and Windows 2000 via the MSVC 5 and 6 development environments. See "Building Berkeley DB for Win32 Platforms" for more information.

Sleepycat Software's Berkeley DB Products

Sleepycat Software licenses three different products that use the Berkeley DB technology, and each product offers a distinct level of database support. It is not possible to mix and match products; that is, each application or group of applications must use the same Berkeley DB product.

All three products are included in the single Open Source distribution of Berkeley DB from Sleepycat Software, and building that distribution automatically builds all three products. Each product adds services and new interfaces to the product that precedes it in the list. As a result, developers can download Berkeley DB and build an application that does only single-user, read-only database access; later, they can add support for more users and more complex database access patterns.

Users who distribute Berkeley DB must ensure that they are licensed for the Berkeley DB interfaces they use. Information on licensing is available directly from Sleepycat Software.

Berkeley DB Data Store

The Berkeley DB Data Store product is an embeddable, high-performance data store. It supports multiple concurrent threads of control to read information managed by Berkeley DB. When updates are required, only a single process may be using the database. That process may be multithreaded, but only one thread of control should be allowed to update the database at any time. The Berkeley DB Data Store does no locking, so it provides no guarantees of correct behavior if more than one thread of control is updating the database at a time.

The Berkeley DB Data Store product includes the **db_create** interface, the DB handle methods, and the methods returned by **DB→cursor**.

The Berkeley DB Data Store is intended for use in single-user or read-only applications that can guarantee that no more than one thread of control will ever update the database at any time.

Berkeley DB Concurrent Data Store

The Berkeley DB Concurrent Data Store product adds multiple-reader, single writer capabilities to the Berkeley DB Data Store product, supporting applications that need concurrent updates and do not want to implement their own locking protocols. The additional interfaces included with the Berkeley DB Concurrent Data Store product are **db_env_create**, the **DBENV→**open method (using the DB_INIT_CDB flag), and the **DBENV→close** method.

Berkeley DB Concurrent Data Store is intended for applications that require occasional write access to a database that is largely used for reading.

Berkeley DB Transactional Data Store

The Berkeley DB Transactional Data Store product adds full transactional support and recoverability to the Berkeley DB Data Store product. This product includes all the interfaces in the Berkeley DB library.

Berkeley DB Transactional Data Store is intended for applications that require industrial-strength database services, including good performance under high-concurrency workloads with a mixture of readers and writers; the capability to commit or roll back multiple changes to the database at a single instant; and the guarantee that even in the event of a catastrophic system or hardware failure, any committed database changes will be preserved.

2

Getting Started:
A Simple Tutorial

As AN INTRODUCTION TO BERKELEY DB, WE WILL PRESENT A FEW Berkeley DB
programming concepts and then a simple database application.

The programming concepts are the following:

- Key/data pairs
- Object handles
- Error returns

This database application will do the following:

- Create a simple database
- Store items
- Retrieve items
- Remove items
- Close the database

The introduction will be presented using the programming language C. The complete
source of the final version of the example program is included in the Berkeley DB
distribution.

Key/Data Pairs

Berkeley DB uses key/data pairs to identify elements in the database. That is, whenever you call a Berkeley DB interface, you present a key to identify the key/data pair on which you intend to operate.

For example, you might store the key/data pairs as follows:

Key	Data
fruit	apple
sport	cricket
drink	water

In each case, the first element of the pair is the key, and the second is the data. To store the first of these key/data pairs into the database, you call the Berkeley DB interface to store items with `fruit` as the key and `apple` as the data. At some future time, you could then retrieve the data item associated with fruit, and the Berkeley DB retrieval interface would return `apple` to you. Although there are many variations and some subtleties, all accesses to data in Berkeley DB come down to key/data pairs.

Both key and data items are stored in simple structures (called DBTs) that contain a reference to memory and a length, counted in bytes. (*DBT* is an acronym for *database thang*, chosen because nobody could think of a sensible name that wasn't already in use somewhere else.) Key and data items can be arbitrary binary data of practically any length, including 0 bytes. There is a single data item for each key item by default, but databases can be configured to support multiple data items for each key item.

Object Handles

With a few minor exceptions, Berkeley DB functionality is accessed by creating a structure and then calling functions that are fields in that structure. This is, of course, similar to object-oriented concepts—of instances and methods on them. For simplicity, we will often refer to these structure fields as *methods of the handle*.

The manual pages will show these methods as C structure references. For example, the open-a-database method for a database handle is represented as **DB→open**.

Error Returns

The Berkeley DB interfaces always return a value of 0 on success. If the operation does not succeed for any reason, the return value will be non-zero.

If a system error occurred (for example, Berkeley DB ran out of disk space, permission to access a file was denied, or an illegal argument was specified to one of the interfaces), Berkeley DB returns an **errno** value. All the possible values of **errno** are greater than 0.

If the operation didn't fail due to a system error, but wasn't successful either, Berkeley DB returns a special error value. For example, if you tried to retrieve the data item associated with the key fruit, and there was no such key/data pair in the database, Berkeley DB would return DB_NOTFOUND, a special error value that means the requested key does not appear in the database. All the possible special error values are less than 0.

Berkeley DB also offers programmatic support for displaying error return values. First, the db_strerror interface returns a pointer to the error message corresponding to any Berkeley DB error return, which is similar to the ANSI C strerror interface, but can handle both system error returns and Berkeley DB-specific return values.

Second, there are two error functions: **DB→err** and **DB→errx**. These functions work like the ANSI C printf interface, taking a printf-style format string and argument list, and optionally appending the standard error string to a message constructed from the format string and other arguments.

Opening a Database

Opening a database is done in two steps. First, a DB handle is created using the Berkeley DB **db_create** interface and then the actual database is opened using the **DB→open** function.

The **db_create** interface takes three arguments:

- dbp: A location to store a reference to the created structure.
- environment: A location to specify an enclosing Berkeley DB environment; not used in our example.
- flags: A placeholder for flags; not used in our example.

The **DB→open** interface takes five arguments:

- file: The name of the database file to be opened.
- database: The optional database name; not used in this example.
- type: The type of database to open. This value will be one of the four access methods Berkeley DB supports: DB_BTREE, DB_HASH, DB_QUEUE, or DB_RECNO; or the special value DB_UNKNOWN, which allows you to open an existing file without knowing its type.
- flags: Various flags that modify the behavior of **DB→open**. In our simple case, the only interesting flag is DB_CREATE. This flag behaves similarly to the IEEE/ANSI Std 1003.1 (POSIX) O_CREATE flag to the open system call, causing Berkeley DB to create the underlying database if it does not yet exist.
- mode: The file mode of any underlying files that **DB→open** will create. The mode behaves as the IEEE/ANSI Std 1003.1 (POSIX) mode argument does to the open system call; and specifies file read, write, and execute permissions. Of course, only the read and write permissions are relevant to Berkeley DB.

Here's what code to create a handle and then call **DB→open** looks like:

```
#include <sys/types.h>
#include <stdio.h>
#include <db.h>

#define DATABASE "access.db"

int
main()
{
    DB *dbp;
    int ret;

    if ((ret = db_create(&dbp, NULL, 0)) != 0) {
            fprintf(stderr, "db_create: %s\n", db_strerror(ret));
            exit (1);
    }
    if ((ret = dbp→open(
        dbp, DATABASE, NULL, DB_BTREE, DB_CREATE, 0664)) != 0) {
            dbp→err(dbp, ret, "%s", DATABASE);
            goto err;
    }
```

If the call to **db_create** is successful, the variable **dbp** will contain a database handle that will be used to configure and access an underlying database.

As you see, the program opens a database named **access.db**, and the underlying database is a Btree. Because the DB_CREATE flag was specified, the file will be created if it does not already exist. The mode of any created files will be 0664 (that is, readable and writable by the owner and the group, and readable by everyone else).

One additional function call is used in this code sample: **DB→err**. This method works like the ANSI C printf interface. The second argument is the error return from a Berkeley DB function, and the rest of the arguments are a printf-style format string and argument list. The error message associated with the error return will be appended to a message constructed from the format string and other arguments. In the previous code, if the **DB→open** call were to fail, the message it would display would be something like the following:

```
access.db: Operation not permitted
```

Adding Elements to a Database

The simplest way to add elements to a database is the **DB→put** interface, which takes five arguments:

- db: The database handle returned by **db_create**.
- txnid: A transaction handle. In our simple case, we aren't expecting to recover the database after an application or system crash, so we aren't using transactions and will leave this argument NULL.

- key: The key item for the key/data pair that we want to add to the database.
- data: The data item for the key/data pair that we want to add to the database.
- flags: Optional flags that modify the underlying behavior of the **DB→put** interface.

Here's what the code to call **DB→put** looks like:

```
#include <sys/types.h>
#include <stdio.h>
#include <db.h>

#define DATABASE "access.db"

int main()
{
        DB *dbp;
        DBT key, data;
        int ret;

        if ((ret = db_create(&dbp, NULL, 0)) != 0) {
                fprintf(stderr, "db_create: %s\n", db_strerror(ret));
                exit (1);
        }
        if ((ret = dbp→open(
            dbp, DATABASE, NULL, DB_BTREE, DB_CREATE, 0664)) != 0) {
                dbp→err(dbp, ret, "%s", DATABASE);
                goto err;
        }
        memset(&key, 0, sizeof(key));
        memset(&data, 0, sizeof(data));
        key.data = "fruit";
        key.size = sizeof("fruit");
        data.data = "apple";
        data.size = sizeof("apple");

        if ((ret = dbp→put(dbp, NULL, &key, &data, 0)) == 0)
                printf("db: %s: key stored.\n", (char *)key.data);
        else {
                dbp→err(dbp, ret, "DB→put");
                goto err;
        }
```

The first thing to notice about this new code is that we clear the **DBT** structures that we're about to pass as arguments to Berkeley DB functions. This is very important, and will result in fewer errors in your programs. All Berkeley DB structures instantiated in the application and handed to Berkeley DB should be cleared before use—without exception. This is necessary so future versions of Berkeley DB may add additional fields to the structures. If applications clear the structures before use, it will be possible for Berkeley DB to change those structures without requiring that the applications be rewritten to be aware of the changes.

Notice also that we're storing the trailing nul byte found in the C strings "fruit" and "apple" in both the key and data items. That is, the trailing nul byte is part of the stored key, and therefore has to be specified in order to access the data item. There is no requirement to store the trailing nul byte; it simply makes it easier for us to display strings that we stored in programming languages that use nul bytes to terminate strings.

In many applications, it is important not to overwrite existing data. For example, we might not want to store the key/data pair fruit/apple if it already existed; for example, if someone previously stored the key/data pair fruit/cherry into the database.

This is easily accomplished by adding the DB_NOOVERWRITE flag to the **DB→put** call:

```
if ((ret =
        dbp→put(dbp, NULL, &key, &data, DB_NOOVERWRITE)) == 0)
                    printf("db: %s: key stored.\n", (char *)key.data);
else {
        dbp→err(dbp, ret, "DB→put");
        goto err;
}
```

This flag causes the underlying database functions to not overwrite any previously existing key/data pair. (Note that the value of the previously existing data doesn't matter in this case. The only question is whether a key/data pair already exists where the key matches the key we are trying to store.)

Specifying DB_NOOVERWRITE opens up the possibility of a new Berkeley DB return value from the **DB→put** function DB_KEYEXIST, which means it could not add the key/data pair to the database because the key already existed in the database. The previous sample code simply displays a message in this case:

```
DB→put: DB_KEYEXIST: Key/data pair already exists
```

The following code shows an explicit check for this possibility:

```
switch (ret =
        dbp→put(dbp, NULL, &key, &data, DB_NOOVERWRITE) {
case 0:
        printf("db: %s: key stored.\n", (char *)key.data);
        break;
case DB_KEYEXIST:
        printf("db: %s: key previously stored.\n",
        (char *)key.data);
        break;
default:
        dbp→err(dbp, ret, "DB→put");
        goto err;
}
```

Retrieving Elements from a Database

The simplest way to retrieve elements from a database is using the **DB→get** interface. It takes the same five arguments as the **DB→put** interface:

- db: The database handle returned by **db_create**.
- txnid: A transaction ID. In our simple case, we don't expect to recover the database after an application or system crash, so we aren't using transactions and will leave this argument NULL.
- key: The key item for the key/data pair that we want to retrieve from the database.
- data: The data item for the key/data pair that we want to retrieve from the database.
- flags: Optional flags that modify the underlying behavior of the **DB→get** interface.

Here's what the code to call **DB→get** looks like:

```
#include <sys/types.h>
#include <stdio.h>
#include <db.h>

#define DATABASE "access.db"

int
main()
{
        DB *dbp;
        DBT key, data;
        int ret;

        if ((ret = db_create(&dbp, NULL, 0)) != 0) {
                fprintf(stderr, "db_create: %s\n", db_strerror(ret));
                exit (1);
        }
        if ((ret = dbp->open(
            dbp, DATABASE, NULL, DB_BTREE, DB_CREATE, 0664)) != 0) {
                dbp->err(dbp, ret, "%s", DATABASE);
                goto err;
        }

        memset(&key, 0, sizeof(key));
        memset(&data, 0, sizeof(data));
        key.data = "fruit";
        key.size= sizeof("fruit");
        data.data = "apple";
        data.size = sizeof("apple");
```

```
if ((ret = dbp→put(dbp, NULL, &key, &data, 0)) == 0)
        printf("db: %s: key stored.\n", (char *)key.data);
else {
        dbp→err(dbp, ret, "DB→put");
        goto err;
}
if ((ret = dbp→get(dbp, NULL, &key, &data, 0)) == 0)
        printf("db: %s: key retrieved: data was %s.\n",
            (char *)key.data, (char *)data.data);
else {
        dbp→err(dbp, ret, "DB→get");
        goto err;
}
```

It is not usually necessary to clear the **DBT** structures passed to the Berkeley DB functions between calls. This is not always true when some of the less commonly used flags for those structures are used; the **DBT** manual page should be consulted for details in those cases.

It is possible, of course, to distinguish between system errors and the key/data pair simply not existing in the database. There are three possible returns from **DB→get**:

- The call might be successful and the key found; the return value will be 0.
- The call might be successful, but the key not found; the return value will be DB_NOTFOUND.
- The call might not be successful; the return value with be a system error.

Removing Elements from a Database

The simplest way to remove elements from a database is using the **DB→del** interface, which takes four of the same five arguments that the **DB→get** and **DB→put** interfaces take (the difference is that there is no need to specify a data item because the delete operation is only interested in the key that you want to remove), as follows:

- db: The database handle returned by **db_create**.
- txnid: A transaction ID. In our simple case, we don't expect to recover the database after an application or system crash, so we aren't using transactions and will leave this argument unspecified.
- key: The key item for the key/data pair that we want to delete from the database.
- flags: Optional flags that modify the underlying behavior of the **DB→del** interface. There are currently no available flags for this interface, so the flags argument should always be set to 0.

Here's what the code to call **DB→del** looks like:

```
#include <sys/types.h>
#include <stdio.h>
#include <db.h>

#define DATABASE "access.db"

int
main()
{
        DB *dbp;
        DBT key, data;
        int ret;

        if ((ret = db_create(&dbp, NULL, 0)) != 0) {
                fprintf(stderr, "db_create: %s\n", db_strerror(ret));
                exit (1);
        }
        if ((ret = dbp→open(
            dbp, DATABASE, NULL, DB_BTREE, DB_CREATE, 0664)) != 0) {
                dbp→err(dbp, ret, "%s", DATABASE);
                goto err;
        }

        memset(&key, 0, sizeof(key));
        memset(&data, 0, sizeof(data));
        key.data = "fruit";
        key.size = sizeof("fruit");
        data.data = "apple";
        data.size = sizeof("apple");

        if ((ret = dbp→put(dbp, NULL, &key, &data, 0)) == 0)
                printf("db: %s: key stored.\n",\ (char *)key.data);
        else {
                dbp→err(dbp, ret, "DB→put");
                goto err;
        }

        if ((ret = dbp→get(dbp, NULL, &key, &data, 0)) == 0)
                printf("db: %s: key retrieved: data was %s.\n",
                    (char *)key.data, (char *)data.data);
        else {
                dbp→err(dbp, ret, "DB→get");
                goto err;
        }

        if ((ret = dbp→del(dbp, NULL, &key, 0)) == 0)
                printf("db: %s: key was deleted.\n", (char *)key.data);
        else {
                dbp→err(dbp, ret, "DB→del");
                goto err;
        }
```

After the **DB→del** call returns, the entry referenced by the key **fruit** has been removed from the database.

Closing a Database

The only other operation that we need for our simple example is to close the database and clean up the DB handle.

It is necessary that the database be closed because Berkeley DB runs on top of an underlying buffer cache. If the modified database pages are never explicitly flushed to disk and the database is never closed, changes made to the database may never make it out to disk because they are held in the Berkeley DB cache. Because the default behavior of the close function is to flush the Berkeley DB cache, closing the database will update the on-disk information.

The **DB→close** interface takes two arguments:

- db: The database handle returned by **db_create**.

- flags: Optional flags that modify the underlying behavior of the **DB→close** interface.

Here's what the code to call **DB→close** looks like:

```
#include <sys/types.h>
#include <stdio.h>
#include <db.h>

#define DATABASE "access.db"

int
main()
{
        DB *dbp;
        DBT key, data;
        int ret, t_ret;

        if ((ret = db_create(&dbp, NULL, 0)) != 0) {
                fprintf(stderr, "db_create: %s\n", db_strerror(ret));
                exit (1);
        }
        if ((ret = dbp->open(
            dbp, DATABASE, NULL, DB_BTREE, DB_CREATE, 0664)) != 0) {
                dbp->err(dbp, ret, "%s", DATABASE);
                goto err;
        }
        memset(&key, 0, sizeof(key));
        memset(&data, 0, sizeof(data));
        key.data = "fruit";
        key.size = sizeof("fruit");
        data.data = "apple";
        data.size = sizeof("apple");
```

```
        if ((ret = dbp→put(dbp, NULL, &key, &data, 0)) == 0)
                printf("db: %s: key stored.\n", (char *)key.data);
        else {
                dbp→err(dbp, ret, "DB→put");
                goto err;
        }

        if ((ret = dbp→get(dbp, NULL, &key, &data, 0)) == 0)
                printf("db: %s: key retrieved: data was %s.\n",
                        (char *)key.data, (char *)data.data);
        else {
                dbp→err(dbp, ret, "DB→get");
                goto err;
        }

        if ((ret = dbp→del(dbp, NULL, &key, 0)) == 0)
                printf("db: %s: key was deleted.\n", (char *)key.data);
        else {
                dbp→err(dbp, ret, "DB→del");
                goto err;
        }

        if ((ret = dbp→get(dbp, NULL, &key, &data, 0)) == 0)
                printf("db: %s: key retrieved: data was %s.\n",
                        (char *)key.data, (char *)data.data);
        else
                dbp→err(dbp, ret, "DB→get");
err:    if ((t_ret = dbp→close(dbp, 0)) != 0 && ret == 0)
                ret = t_ret;

        exit(ret);
}
```

Note that we do not necessarily overwrite the **ret** variable because it may contain
error return information from a previous Berkeley DB call.

3

Access Method Configuration

Berkeley DB currently offers four access methods: Btree, Hash, Queue, and Recno. Each is discussed in the following sections.

Btree

The Btree access method is an implementation of a sorted, balanced tree structure. Searches, insertions, and deletions in the tree all take O(log base_b N) time, where base_b is the average number of keys per page, and N is the total number of keys stored. Often, inserting ordered data into Btree implementations results in pages that are only half-full. Berkeley DB makes ordered (or inverse-ordered) insertion the best case, resulting in nearly full-page space utilization.

Hash

The Hash access method data structure is an implementation of Extended Linear Hashing, as described in "Linear Hashing: A New Tool for File and Table Addressing," by Witold Litwin in the *Proceedings of the 6th International Conference on Very Large Databases (VLDB)*, 1980.

Queue

The Queue access method stores fixed-length records with logical record numbers as keys. It is designed for fast inserts at the tail, and has a special cursor consume operation that deletes and returns a record from the head of the queue. The Queue access method uses record-level locking.

Recno

The Recno access method stores both fixed- and variable-length records with logical record numbers as keys, optionally backed by a flat text (byte stream) file.

Selecting an Access Method

The Berkeley DB access method implementation unavoidably interacts with each application's data set, locking requirements, and data access patterns. For this reason, one access method may result in a dramatically better performance for an application than another one. Applications whose data can be stored using more than one access method may want to benchmark their performance using the different candidates.

One of the strengths of Berkeley DB is that it provides multiple access methods with nearly identical interfaces to the different access methods. This means that it is simple to modify an application to use a different access method. Applications can easily benchmark the different Berkeley DB access methods against each other for their particular data set and access pattern.

Most applications choose between using the Btree or Hash access methods, or between using the Queue and Recno access methods because each of the two pairs offer similar functionality.

Hash or Btree?

The Hash and Btree access methods should be used when logical record numbers are not the primary key used for data access. (If logical record numbers are a secondary key used for data access, the Btree access method is a possible choice because it supports simultaneous access by a key and a record number.)

Keys in Btrees are stored in sorted order, and the relationship between them is defined by that sort order. For this reason, the Btree access method should be used when there is locality of reference among keys. *Locality of reference* means that accessing one particular key in the Btree implies that the application is more likely to access keys near the key being accessed, where *near* is defined by the sort order. For example, if keys are timestamps, and it is likely that a request for an 8 a.m. timestamp will be followed by a request for a 9 a.m. timestamp, the Btree access method is generally the right choice. Or, if the keys are names, for example, and the application wants to review all entries with the same last name, the Btree access method is again a good choice.

There is little difference in performance between the Hash and Btree access methods on small data sets in which all or most of the data set fits into the cache. However, when a data set is large enough that significant numbers of data pages no longer fit into the cache, the Btree locality of reference described previously becomes important for performance reasons. For example, there is no locality of reference for the Hash access method, so key "AAAAA" is as likely to be stored on the same database page with key "ZZZZZ" as with key "AAAAB." In the Btree access method, key "AAAAA" is far more likely to be near key "AAAAB" than key "ZZZZZ" because items are sorted. So, if the application exhibits locality of reference in its data requests, the Btree page read into the cache to satisfy a request for key "AAAAA" is much more likely to be useful to satisfy subsequent requests from the application than the Hash page read into the cache to satisfy the same request. This means that for applications with locality of reference, the cache is generally much more effective for the Btree access method than the Hash access method, and the Btree access method will make many fewer I/O calls.

However, when a data set becomes even larger, the Hash access method can outperform the Btree access method because Btrees contain more metadata pages than Hash databases. The data set can grow so large that metadata pages begin to dominate the cache for the Btree access method. If this happens, the Btree can be forced to do an I/O for each data request because the probability that any particular data page is already in the cache becomes quite small. Because the Hash access method has fewer metadata pages, its cache stays "hotter" longer in the presence of large data sets. In addition, once the data set is so large that both the Btree and Hash access methods are almost certainly doing an I/O for each random data request, the fact that Hash does not have to walk several internal pages as part of a key search becomes a performance advantage for the Hash access method.

Application data access patterns strongly affect all of these behaviors. For example, accessing the data by walking a cursor through the database will greatly mitigate the large data set behavior described previously because each I/O into the cache will satisfy a fairly large number of subsequent data requests.

In the absence of information on application data and data access patterns, either the Btree or Hash access methods will suffice for small data sets. For data sets larger than the cache, we normally recommend using the Btree access method. If you have truly large data, the Hash access method may be a better choice. The **db_stat** utility is a useful tool for monitoring how well your cache is performing.

Queue or Recno?

The Queue or Recno access methods should be used when logical record numbers are the primary key used for data access. The advantage of the Queue access method is that it performs record-level locking; for this reason, it supports significantly higher levels of concurrency than the Recno access method. The advantage of the Recno access method is that it supports a number of additional features beyond those supported by the Queue access method, such as variable-length records and support for backing flat-text files.

Logical record numbers can be mutable or fixed: Mutable where logical record numbers can change as records are deleted or inserted, and fixed where record numbers never change, regardless of the database operation. It is possible to store and retrieve records based on logical record numbers in the Btree access method. However, those record numbers are always mutable, and the logical record number for other records in the database will change as records are deleted or inserted. The Queue access method always runs in fixed mode, and logical record numbers never change, regardless of the database operation. The Recno access method can be configured to run in either mutable or fixed mode.

In addition, the Recno access method provides support for databases whose permanent storage is a flat text file, and the database is used as a fast temporary storage area while the data is being read or modified.

Logical Record Numbers

The Berkeley DB Btree, Queue, and Recno access methods can operate on logical record numbers. Logical record numbers are 1-based, not 0-based; that is, the first record in the database is record number 1. In all cases for the Queue and Recno access methods (and when calling the Btree access method using the **DB→get** and **DBcursor→c_get** functions with the DB_SET_RECNO flag specified), the **data** field of the key must be a pointer to a memory location of type **db_recno_t**, as typedef'd in the standard Berkeley DB include file. This type is a 32-bit unsigned type, which limits the number of logical records in a Queue or Recno database; and the maximum logical record, which may be directly retrieved from a Btree database, to 4,294,967,296. The **size** field of the key should be the size of that type (for example, **sizeof(db_recno_t** in the C programming language). In the case of Btree supporting duplicate data items, the logical record number refers to a key and all of its data items.

Record numbers in Recno databases can be configured to run in either mutable or fixed mode: *mutable*, in which logical record numbers change as records are deleted or inserted; and *fixed*, in which record numbers never change, regardless of the database operation. Record numbers in Queue databases are always fixed and never change, regardless of the database operation. Record numbers in Btree databases are always mutable, and as records are deleted or inserted, the logical record number for other records in the database can change. See "Logically Renumbering Records" for more information.

Configuring Btree databases to support record numbers can severely limit the throughput of applications with multiple concurrent threads writing the database because locations used to store record counts often become hot spots that many different threads all need to update.

Selecting a Page Size

The size of the pages used in the underlying database can be specified by calling the **DB→set_pagesize** function. The minimum page size is 512 bytes, and the maximum page size is 64K bytes and must be a power of two. If no page size is specified by the application, a page size is selected based on the underlying filesystem I/O block size. (A page size selected in this way has a lower limit of 512 bytes and an upper limit of 16K bytes.) There are four issues to consider when selecting a page size: overflow record sizes, locking, I/O efficiency, and recoverability.

First, the page size implicitly sets the size of an overflow record. *Overflow records* are key or data items that are too large to fit on a normal database page because of their size, and are therefore stored in overflow pages. *Overflow pages* are pages that exist outside of the normal database structure. For this reason, there is often a significant performance penalty associated with retrieving or modifying overflow records. Selecting a page size that is too small and forces the creation of large numbers of overflow pages can seriously impact the performance of an application.

Second, in the Btree, Hash, and Recno access methods, the finest-grained lock that Berkeley DB acquires is for a page. (The Queue access method generally acquires record-level locks rather than page-level locks.) Selecting a page size that is too large and causes threads or processes to wait because other threads of control are accessing or modifying records on the same page can impact the performance of your application.

Third, the page size specifies the granularity of I/O from the database to the operating system. Berkeley DB gives a page-sized unit of bytes to the operating system to be scheduled for writing to the disk. For many operating systems, there is an internal **block size** that is used as the granularity of I/O from the operating system to the disk. If the page size is smaller than the block size, the operating system may be forced to read a block from the disk, copy the page into the buffer it read, and then write out the block to disk. Obviously, it will be much more efficient for Berkeley DB to write filesystem-sized blocks to the operating system and for the operating system to write those same blocks to the disk. Selecting a page size that is too small and causes the operating system to coalesce or otherwise manipulate Berkeley DB pages can impact the performance of your application. Alternatively, selecting a page size that is too large may cause Berkeley DB and the operating system to write more data than is strictly necessary.

Fourth, when using the Berkeley DB Transactional Data Store product, the page size may affect the errors from which your database can recover. See "Berkeley DB Recoverability" for more information.

Selecting a Cache Size

The size of the cache used for the underlying database can be specified by calling the **DB→set_cachesize** function. Choosing a cache size is, unfortunately, an art. Your cache must be at least large enough for your working set plus some overlap for unexpected situations.

When using the Btree access method, you must have a cache big enough for the minimum working set for a single access. This includes a root page, one or more internal pages (depending on the depth of your tree), and a leaf page. If your cache is any smaller than that, each new page will force out the least-recently-used page, and Berkeley DB will reread the root page of the tree anew on each database request.

If your keys are of moderate size (a few tens of bytes), and your pages are on the order of 4K to 8K, most Btree applications will be only three levels. For example, using 20 byte keys with 20 bytes of data associated with each key, an 8KB page can hold roughly 400 keys and 200 key/data pairs. Thus, a fully populated three-level Btree holds 32 million key/data pairs, and a tree with only a 50% page-fill factor still holds 16 million key/data pairs. We rarely expect trees to exceed five levels, although Berkeley DB supports trees up to 255 levels.

The rule-of-thumb is that cache is good and more cache is better. Generally, applications benefit from increasing the cache size up to a point when the performance will stop improving as the cache size increases. When this point is reached, one of two things have happened: either the cache is large enough that the application is almost never having to retrieve information from disk; or your application is doing truly random accesses, so increasing the size of the cache doesn't significantly increase the odds of finding the next requested information in the cache. The latter is fairly rare—almost all applications show some form of locality of reference.

That said, it is important not to increase your cache size beyond the capabilities of your system because it will result in reduced performance. Under many operating systems, tying down enough virtual memory will cause your memory and potentially your program to be swapped. This is especially likely on systems without unified OS buffer caches and virtual memory spaces because the buffer cache was allocated at boot time and so cannot be adjusted based on application requests for large amounts of virtual memory.

For example, even if accesses are truly random within a Btree, your access pattern will favor internal pages to leaf pages, so your cache should be large enough to hold all internal pages. In the steady state, this requires at most one I/O per operation to retrieve the appropriate leaf page.

You can use the **db_stat** utility to monitor the effectiveness of your cache. The following output is excerpted from the output of that utility's **-m** option:

```
prompt: db_stat -m
131072  Cache size (128K).
4273    Requested pages found in the cache (97%).
134     Requested pages not found in the cache.
18      Pages created in the cache.
```

```
116     Pages read into the cache.
93      Pages written from the cache to the backing file.
5       Clean pages forced from the cache.
13      Dirty pages forced from the cache.
0       Dirty buffers written by trickle-sync thread.
130     Current clean buffer count.
4       Current dirty buffer count.
```

The statistics for this cache say that there have been 4,273 requests of the cache, and only 116 of those requests required an I/O from disk. This means that the cache is working well, yielding a 97% cache hit rate. The **db_stat** utility will present these statistics both for the cache as a whole and for each file within the cache separately.

Selecting a Byte Order

Database files created by Berkeley DB can be created in either little- or big-endian formats. The byte order used for the underlying database is specified by calling the **DB→set_lorder** function. If no order is selected, the native format of the machine on which the database is created will be used.

Berkeley DB databases are architecture-independent, and any format database can be used on a machine with a different native format. In this case, each page that is read into or written from the cache must be converted to or from the host format, and databases with non-native formats will incur a performance penalty for the run-time conversion.

It is important to note that the Berkeley DB access methods do no data conversion for application-specified data. Key/data pairs written on a little-endian format architecture will be returned to the application exactly as they were written when retrieved on a big-endian format architecture.

Non-Local Memory Allocation

Berkeley DB can allocate memory for returned key/data pairs, which then become the responsibility of the application. See DB_DBT_MALLOC or DB_DBT_REALLOC for further information.

On systems where there may be multiple library versions of malloc (notably Windows NT), the Berkeley DB library could allocate memory from a different heap than the application will use to free it. To avoid this problem, the allocation routine to be used for allocating such key/data items can be specified by calling the **DB→set_malloc** or **DB→set_realloc** functions. If no allocation function is specified, the underlying C library functions are used.

Btree Comparison

The Btree data structure is a sorted, balanced tree structure storing associated key/data pairs. By default, the sort order is lexicographical, with shorter keys collating before longer keys. The user can specify the sort order for the Btree by using the **DB→set_bt_compare** function.

Sort routines are passed pointers to keys as arguments. The keys are represented as **DBT** structures. The routine must return an integer less than, equal to, or greater than zero if the first argument is considered to be respectively less than, equal to, or greater than the second argument. The only fields that the routines may examine in the **DBT** structures are the **data** and **size** fields.

An example routine that might be used to sort integer keys in the database is as follows:

```
int
compare_int(dbp, a, b)
        DB *dbp;
        const DBT *a, *b;
{
        int ai, bi;

        /*
         * Returns:
         *      < 0 if a < b
         *      = 0 if a = b
         *      > 0 if a > b
         */
        memcpy(&ai, a→data, sizeof(int));
        memcpy(&bi, b→data, sizeof(int));
        return (ai - bi);
}
```

Note that the data must first be copied into memory that is appropriately aligned because Berkeley DB does not guarantee any kind of alignment of the underlying data, including for comparison routines. When writing comparison routines, remember that databases created on machines of different architectures may have different integer byte orders, for which your code may need to compensate.

An example routine that might be used to sort keys based on the first five bytes of the key (ignoring any subsequent bytes) is as follows:

```
int
compare_dbt(dbp, a, b)
        DB *dbp;
        const DBT *a, *b;
{
        u_char *p1, *p2;

        /*
         * Returns:
         * < 0 if a < b
         * = 0 if a = b
         * > 0 if a > b
         */
        for (p1 = a→data, p2 = b→data, len = 5; len—; ++p1, ++p2)
                if (*p1 != *p2)
                        return ((long)*p1 - (long)*p2);
        return (0);
}
```

All comparison functions must cause the keys in the database to be well-ordered. The most important implication of being well-ordered is that the key relations must be transitive; that is, if key A is less than key B and key B is less than key C, the comparison routine must also return that key A is less than key C. In addition, comparisons will be able to return 0 only when comparing full-length keys; partial key comparisons must always return a result less than or greater than 0.

Btree Prefix Comparison

The Berkeley DB Btree implementation maximizes the number of keys that can be stored on an internal page by storing only as many bytes of each key as are necessary to distinguish it from adjacent keys. The prefix comparison routine is what determines this minimum number of bytes (that is, the length of the unique prefix) that must be stored. A prefix comparison function for the Btree can be specified by calling **DB→set_bt_prefix**.

The prefix comparison routine must be compatible with the overall comparison function of the Btree because what distinguishes any two keys depends entirely on the function used to compare them. This means that if a prefix comparison routine is specified by the application, a compatible overall comparison routine must also have been specified.

Prefix comparison routines are passed pointers to keys as arguments. The keys are represented as **DBT** structures. The prefix comparison function must return the number of bytes of the second key argument that are necessary to determine if it is greater than the first key argument. If the keys are equal, the length of the second key should be returned. The only fields that the routines may examine in the **DBT** structures are **data** and **size** fields.

An example prefix comparison routine follows:

```
u_int32_t
compare_prefix(dbp, a, b)
        DB *dbp;
        const DBT *a, *b;
{
        size_t cnt, len;
        u_int8_t *p1, *p2;

        cnt = 1;
        len = a→size > b→size ? b→size : a→size;
        for (p1 =
                a-&gt;data, p2 = b→data; len--; ++p1, ++p2, ++cnt)
                        if (*p1 != *p2)
                                return (cnt);
        /*
         * They match up to the smaller of the two sizes.
         * Collate the longer after the shorter.
         */
        if (a→size < b→size)
                return (a→size + 1);
```

```
        if (b→size < a→size)
                return (b→size + 1);
        return (b→size);
}
```

The usefulness of this functionality is data-dependent, but in some datasets, it can produce significantly reduced tree sizes and faster search times.

Minimum Keys Per Page

The number of keys stored on each page affects the size of a Btree and how it is maintained. Therefore, it also affects the retrieval and search performance of the tree. For each Btree, Berkeley DB computes a maximum key and data size. This size is a function of the page size and the fact that at least two key/data pairs must fit on any Btree page. Whenever key or data items exceed the calculated size, they are stored on overflow pages instead of in the standard Btree leaf pages.

Applications may use the **DB→set_bt_minkey** function to change the minimum number of keys that must fit on a Btree page from two to another value. Altering this value in turn alters the on-page maximum size, and can be used to force key and data items that would normally be stored in the Btree leaf pages onto overflow pages.

Some data sets can benefit from this tuning. For example, consider an application using large page sizes, with a data set almost entirely consisting of small key and data items, but with a few large items. By setting the minimum number of keys that must fit on a page, the application can force the outsized items to be stored on overflow pages. That in turn can potentially keep the tree more compact; that is, with fewer internal levels to traverse during searches.

The following calculation is similar to the one performed by the Btree implementation. (The **minimum_keys** value is multiplied by 2 because each key/data pair requires two slots on a Btree page.)

```
    maximum_size = page_size / (minimum_keys * 2)
```

Using this calculation, if the page size is 8KB and the default **minimum_keys** value of 2 is used, any key or data items larger than 2KB will be forced to an overflow page. If an application were to specify a **minimum_key** value of 100, any key or data items larger than roughly 40 bytes would be forced to overflow pages.

It is important to remember that accesses to overflow pages do not perform as well as accesses to the standard Btree leaf pages, so setting the value incorrectly can result in overusing overflow pages and decreasing the application's overall performance.

Retrieving Btree Records by Number

The Btree access method optionally supports retrieval by logical record numbers. To configure a Btree to support record numbers, call the **DB→set_flags** function with the DB_RECNUM flag.

Configuring a Btree for record numbers should not be done lightly. Although often useful, it requires that storing items into the database be single-threaded, which can severely impact application throughput. Generally, it should be avoided in trees with a need for high write concurrency.

To determine a key's record number, use the DB_GET_RECNO flag to the **DBcursor→c_get** function. To retrieve by record number, use the DB_SET_RECNO flag to the **DB→get** and **DBcursor→c_get** functions.

Page Fill Factor

The density, or *page fill factor*, is an approximation of the number of keys allowed to accumulate in any one bucket, determining when the hash table grows or shrinks. If you know the average sizes of the keys and data in your dataset, setting the fill factor can enhance performance. A reasonable rule to use to compute fill factor is the following:

```
(pagesize - 32) / (average_key_size + average_data_size + 8)
```

The desired density within the hash table can be specified by calling the **DB→set_h_ffactor** function. If no density is specified, one will be selected dynamically as pages are filled.

Specifying a Database Hash

The database hash determines in which bucket a particular key will reside. The goal of hashing keys is to distribute keys equally across the database pages; therefore, it is important that the hash function work well with the specified keys so that the resulting bucket usage is relatively uniform. A hash function that does not work well can effectively turn into a sequential list.

No hash performs equally well on all possible datasets. It is possible that applications may find that the default hash function performs poorly with a particular set of keys. The distribution resulting from the hash function can be checked using the **db_stat** utility. By comparing the number of hash buckets and the number of keys, one can decide if the entries are hashing in a well-distributed manner.

The hash function for the hash table can be specified by calling the **DB→set_h_hash** function. If no hash function is specified, a default function will be used. Any application-specified hash function must take a reference to a DB object, a pointer to a byte string and its length as arguments, and return an unsigned 32-bit hash value.

Hash Table Size

When setting up the hash database, knowing the expected number of elements that will be stored in the hash table is useful. This value can be used by the Hash access method implementation to more accurately construct the necessary number of buckets that the database will eventually require.

The anticipated number of elements in the hash table can be specified by calling the **DB→set_h_nelem** function. If not specified or set too low, hash tables will expand gracefully as keys are entered, although a slight performance degradation may be noticed. In order for the estimated number of elements to be a useful value to Berkeley DB, the **DB→set_h_ffactor** function must also be called to set the page fill factor.

Managing Record-Based Databases

When using fixed- or variable-length record-based databases, particularly with flat-text backing files, there are several items that the user can control. The Recno access method can be used to store either variable- or fixed-length data items. By default, the Recno access method stores variable-length data items. The Queue access method can store only fixed-length data items.

Record Delimiters

When using the Recno access method to store variable-length records, records read from any backing source file are separated by a specific byte value that marks the end of one record and the beginning of the next. This delimiting value is ignored except when reading records from a backing source file; that is, records may be stored into the database that include the delimiter byte. However, if such records are written out to the backing source file and the backing source file is subsequently read into a database, the records will be split where delimiting bytes were found.

For example, UNIX text files can usually be interpreted as a sequence of variable-length records separated by ASCII newline characters. This byte value (ASCII 0x0a) is the default delimiter. Applications may specify a different delimiting byte using the **DB→set_re_delim** interface. If no backing source file is being used, there is no reason to set the delimiting byte value.

Record Length

When using the Recno or Queue access methods to store fixed-length records, the record length must be specified. Because the Queue access method always uses fixed-length records, the user must always set the record length prior to creating the database. Setting the record length is what causes the Recno access method to store fixed-length records, not variable-length records.

The length of the records is specified by calling the **DB→set_re_len** function. The default length of the records is 0 bytes. Any record read from a backing source file or otherwise stored in the database that is shorter than the declared length will automatically be padded, as described for the **DB→set_re_pad** function. Any record stored that is longer than the declared length results in an error. For further information on backing source files, see "Flat-Text Backing Files."

Record Padding Byte Value

When storing fixed-length records in a Queue or Recno database, a pad character may be specified by calling the **DB→set_re_pad** function. Any record read from the backing source file or otherwise stored in the database that is shorter than the expected length will automatically be padded with this byte value. If fixed-length records are specified but no pad value is specified, a space character (0x20 in the ASCII character set) will be used. For further information on backing source files, see "Flat-Text Backing Files."

Selecting a Queue Extent Size

In Queue databases, records are allocated sequentially and directly mapped to an offset within the file storage for the database. As records are deleted from the queue, pages will become empty and will not be reused in normal queue operations. To facilitate the reclamation of disk space, a queue may be partitioned into extents, and each extent is kept in a separate physical file. Extent files are automatically created as needed and destroyed when they are emptied of records.

The extent size specifies the number of pages that make up each extent. By default, if no extent size is specified, the queue resides in a single file and disk space is not reclaimed. In choosing an extent size, there is a tradeoff between the amount of disk space used and the overhead of creating and deleting files. If the extent size is too small, the system will pay a performance penalty—creating and deleting files frequently. In addition, if the active part of the queue spans many files, all those files will need to be open at the same time, consuming system and process file resources.

Flat-Text Backing Files

It is possible to back any Recno database (either fixed- or variable-length) with a flat-text source file. This provides fast read (and potentially write) access to databases that are normally created and stored as flat-text files. The backing source file may be specified by calling the **DB→set_re_source** function.

The backing source file will be read to initialize the database. In the case of variable length records, the records are assumed to be separated, as described for the **DB→set_re_delim** function interface. For example, standard UNIX byte stream files can be interpreted as a sequence of variable length records separated by ASCII newline characters. This is the default.

When cached data would normally be written back to the underlying database file (for example, **DB→close** or **DB→sync** functions are called), the in-memory copy of the database will be written back to the backing source file.

The backing source file must already exist (but may be zero-length) when **DB→open** is called. By default, the backing source file is read lazily; that is, records are not read from the backing source file until they are requested by the application. If multiple processes (not threads) are accessing a Recno database concurrently and either inserting or deleting records, the backing source file must be read in its entirety before more than a single process accesses the database, and only that process should specify the backing source file as part of the **DB→open** call. This can be accomplished by calling the **DB→set_flags** function with the DB_SNAPSHOT flag.

Reading and writing the backing source file cannot be transactionally protected because it involves filesystem operations that are not part of the Berkeley DB transaction methodology. For this reason, if a temporary database is used to hold the records (a NULL was specified as the file argument to **DB→open**), it is possible to lose the contents of the backing source file if the system crashes at the right instant. If a permanent file is used to hold the database (a filename was specified as the file argument to **DB→open**), normal database recovery on that file can be used to prevent information loss. It is still possible that the contents of the backing source file itself will be corrupted or lost if the system crashes.

For all of these reasons, the backing source file is generally used to specify databases that are read-only for Berkeley DB applications, and that are either generated on-the-fly by software tools or modified using a different mechanism such as a text editor.

Logically Renumbering Records

Records stored in the Queue and Recno access methods are accessed by logical record number. In all cases in Btree databases, and optionally in Recno databases (see the **DB→set_flags** function and the DB_RENUMBER flag for more information), record numbers are mutable. This means that the record numbers may change as records are added to and deleted from the database. The deletion of record number 4 causes any records numbered 5 and higher to be renumbered downward by 1; the addition of a new record after record number 4 causes any records numbered 5 and higher to be renumbered upward by 1. In all cases in Queue databases, and by default in Recno databases, record numbers are not mutable, and the addition or deletion of records to the database will not cause already-existing record numbers to change. For this reason, new records cannot be inserted between already-existing records in databases with immutable record numbers.

Cursors pointing into a Btree database or a Recno database with mutable record numbers maintain a reference to a specific record rather than a record number; that is, the record they reference does not change as other records are added or deleted. For example, if a database contains three records with the record numbers 1, 2, and 3; and the data items "A", "B", and "C", respectively, the deletion of record number 2 ("B") will cause the record "C" to be renumbered downward to record number 2. A cursor positioned at record number 3 ("C") will be adjusted and continue to point to "C" after the deletion. Similarly, a cursor previously referencing the now deleted record number 2 will be positioned between the new record numbers 1 and 2, and an insertion using that cursor will appear between those records. In this manner, records can be added and deleted to a database without disrupting the sequential traversal of the database by a cursor.

Only cursors created using a single DB handle can adjust each other's position in this way, however. If multiple DB handles have a renumbering Recno database open simultaneously (as when multiple processes share a single database environment), a record referred to by one cursor could change underfoot if a cursor created using another DB handle inserts or deletes records into the database. For this reason, applications using Recno databases with mutable record numbers will usually make all accesses to the database using a single DB handle and cursors created from that handle, or will otherwise single-thread access to the database (for example, by using the Berkeley DB Concurrent Data Store product).

In any Queue or Recno databases, creating new records will cause the creation of multiple records if the record number being created is more than one greater than the largest record currently in the database. For example, creating record number 28 when record 25 was previously the last record in the database will implicitly create records 26 and 27, as well as 28. All first, last, next, and previous cursor operations will automatically skip over these implicitly created records. So, if record number 5 is the only record the application has created, implicitly creating records 1 through 4, the **DBcursor→c_get** interface with the DB_FIRST flag will return record number 5, not record number 1. Attempts to explicitly retrieve implicitly created records by their record number will result in a special error return, DB_KEYEMPTY.

In any Berkeley DB database, attempting to retrieve a deleted record using a cursor positioned on the record results in a special error return, DB_KEYEMPTY. In addition, when using Queue databases or Recno databases with immutable record numbers, attempting to retrieve a deleted record by its record number will also result in the DB_KEYEMPTY return.

4

Access Method Operations

O NCE A DATABASE HANDLE HAS BEEN CREATED USING **db_create**, there are several standard access method operations. Each of these operations is performed using a method that is referenced from the returned handle. The operations are as follows:

- **DB→close**   Close the database.
- **DB→cursor**   Open a cursor into the database.
- **DB→del**   Delete a record.
- **DB→get**   Retrieve a record.
- **DB→open**   Open a database.
- **DB→put**   Store a record.
- **DB→stat**   Return statistics about the database.
- **DB→sync**   Flush the underlying cache.
- **DB→upgrade**   Upgrade a database.

Opening a Database

The **DB→open** function, the standard interface for opening a database, takes the following arguments:

- file   The name of the file to be opened.
- database   An optional database name.

- type   The type of database to open. This value will be one of the four access methods Berkeley DB supports: DB_BTREE, DB_HASH, DB_QUEUE, or DB_RECNO; or the special value DB_UNKNOWN, which allows you to open an existing file without knowing its type.

- mode   The permissions to give to any created file.

There are a few flags that you can set to customize open:

- DB_CREATE   Create the underlying database and any necessary physical files.

- DB_NOMMAP   Do not map this database into process memory.

- DB_RDONLY   Treat the data base as read-only.

- DB_THREAD   The returned handle is free-threaded; that is, it can be used simultaneously by multiple threads within the process.

- DB_TRUNCATE   Physically truncate the underlying database file, discarding all databases it contained. Underlying filesystem primitives are used to implement this flag. For this reason, it is applicable only to the physical file, and cannot be used to discard individual databases from within physical files.

- DB_UPGRADE   Upgrade the database format as necessary.

Opening Multiple Databases in a Single File

Applications may create multiple databases within a single physical file. This is useful when the databases are both numerous and reasonably small, when you want to avoid creating a large number of underlying files, or when it is desirable to include secondary index databases in the same file as the primary index database. Multiple databases are an administrative convenience, and using them is unlikely to affect database performance. To open or create a file that will include more than a single database, specify a database name when calling the **DB→open** method.

Physical files do not need to be comprised of a single type of database, and databases in a file may be of any type (Btree, Hash, or Recno) except Queue databases. Queue databases must be created one per file and cannot share a file with any other database type. There is no limit on the number of databases that may be created in a single file other than the standard Berkeley DB file size and disk space limitations.

It is an error to attempt to open a second database in a file that was not initially created using a database name; that is, the file must initially be specified as capable of containing multiple databases for a second database to be created in it.

Although it is not an error to open a file that contains multiple databases without specifying a database name, the database type should be specified as DB_UNKNOWN, and the database must be opened read-only. The handle that is returned from such a call is a handle on a database whose key values are the names of the databases stored in the database file and whose data values are opaque objects. No keys or data values may be modified or stored using this database handle.

Storing multiple databases in a single file is almost identical to storing each database in its own separate file. The one crucial difference is how locking and the underlying memory pool services must to be configured. As an example, consider two databases instantiated in two different physical files. If access to each separate database is single-threaded, there is no reason to perform locking of any kind, and the two databases may be read and written simultaneously. Further, there would be no requirement to create a shared database environment in which to open the databases. Because multiple databases in a file exist in a single physical file, opening two databases in the same file requires that locking be enabled unless access to the databases is known to be single-threaded; that is, only one of the databases is ever accessed at a time. (Because the locks for the two databases can conflict only during page allocation, this additional locking is unlikely to affect performance.) Further, the databases must share an underlying memory pool so per-physical-file information is updated correctly.

Upgrading Databases

When upgrading to a new release of Berkeley DB, it may be necessary to upgrade the on-disk format of already-created database files. Berkeley DB database upgrades are done in place, so are potentially destructive. This means that if the system crashes during the upgrade procedure, or if the upgrade procedure runs out of disk space, the databases may be left in an inconsistent and unrecoverable state. To guard against failure, the procedures outlined in "Upgrading Berkeley DB Applications" should be carefully followed. If you are not performing catastrophic archival as part of your application upgrade process, you should at least copy your database to archival media, verify that your archival media is error-free and readable, and ensure that copies of your backups are stored off-site!

The actual database upgrade is done by using the **DB→upgrade** method, or by dumping the database using the old version of the Berkeley DB software and reloading it using the current version.

After an upgrade, Berkeley DB applications must be recompiled to use the new Berkeley DB library before they can access an upgraded database. There is no guarantee that applications compiled against previous releases of Berkeley DB will work correctly with an upgraded database format. Nor is there any guarantee that applications compiled against newer releases of Berkeley DB will work correctly with the previous database format. We do guarantee that any archived database may be upgraded using a current Berkeley DB software release and the **DB→upgrade** method, and there is no need to step-wise upgrade the database using intermediate releases of Berkeley DB. Sites should consider archiving appropriate copies of their application or application sources if they may need to access archived databases without first upgrading them.

Retrieving Records

The **DB→get** function is the standard interface for retrieving records from the database. In general, **DB→get** takes a key and returns the associated data from the database.

There are a few flags that you can set to customize retrieval:

- DB_GET_BOTH   Search for a matching key and data item; that is, only return success if both the key and the data items match those stored in the database.
- DB_RMW   Read-modify-write: Acquire write locks instead of read locks during retrieval. This can enhance performance in threaded applications by reducing the chance of deadlock.
- DB_SET_RECNO   If the underlying database is a Btree and was configured so it is possible to search it by logical record number, retrieve a specific record.

If the database has been configured to support duplicate records, **DB→get** will always return the first data item in the duplicate set.

Storing Records

The **DB→put** function is the standard interface for storing records into the database. In general, **DB→put** takes a key and stores the associated data into the database.

There are a few flags that you can set to customize storage:

- DB_APPEND   Simply append the data to the end of the database, treating the database much like a simple log. This flag is valid only for the Queue and Recno access methods.
- DB_NOOVERWRITE   Store the data item only if the key does not already appear in the database.

If the database was configured to support duplicate records, the **DB→put** function will add the new data value at the end of the duplicate set. If the database supports sorted duplicates, the new data value is inserted at the correct sorted location.

Deleting Records

The **DB→del** function is the standard interface for deleting records from the database. In general, **DB→del** takes a key and deletes the data item associated with it from the database.

If the database was configured to support duplicate records, the **DB→del** function will remove all the duplicate records. To remove individual duplicate records, you must use a Berkeley DB cursor interface.

Flushing the Database Cache

The **DB→sync** function is the standard interface for flushing all modified records from the database cache to disk.

It is important to understand that flushing cached information to disk only minimizes the window of opportunity for corrupted data; it does not eliminate the possibility.

Although unlikely, it is possible for database corruption to happen if a system or application crash occurs while writing data to the database. To ensure that database corruption never occurs, applications must do either of the following:

- Use transactions and logging with automatic recovery.
- Use logging and application-specific recovery.
- Edit a copy of the database, and use system operations (for example, the POSIX rename system call) to atomically replace the original database with the updated copy after all applications using the database have successfully called **DB→close**.

Database Statistics

The **DB→stat** function is the standard interface for obtaining database statistics. Generally, **DB→stat** returns a set of statistics about the underlying database (for example, the number of key/data pairs in the database, how the database was originally configured, and so on).

There are two flags that you can set to customize the returned statistics:

- DB_CACHED_COUNTS   Request an approximate key and key/data pair count. Because obtaining an exact count can be very performance-intensive for large databases, it is possible to request a previously cached count. Obviously, the cached count is only an approximate count, and it may be out-of-date.
- DB_RECORDCOUNT   If the database is a Queue or Recno database, or a Btree database that was configured so that it is possible to search it by logical record number, return only a count of the records in the database.

Closing a Database

The **DB→close** function is the standard interface for closing the database. By default, **DB→close** also flushes all modified records from the database cache to disk. There is one flag that you can set to customize **DB→close**:

- DB_NOSYNC   Do not flush cached information to disk.

It is important to understand that flushing cached information to disk only minimizes the window of opportunity for corrupted data; it does not eliminate the possibility.

Database Cursors

A *database cursor* is a reference to a single key/data pair in the database. It supports traversal of the database, and is the only way to access individual duplicate data items. Cursors are used for operating on collections of records, for iterating over a database, and for saving handles to individual records, so they can be modified after they have been read.

The **DB→cursor** function is the standard interface for opening a cursor into a database. Upon return, the cursor is uninitialized; positioning occurs as part of the first cursor operation.

After a database cursor has opened, there are a set of access method operations that can be performed. Each of the following operations is performed using a method referenced from the returned cursor handle.

- **DBcursor→c_close**   Close the cursor.
- **DBcursor→c_del**   Delete a record.
- **DBcursor→c_dup**   Duplicate a cursor.
- **DBcursor→c_get**   Retrieve a record.
- **DBcursor→c_put**   Store a record.

Retrieving Records with a Cursor

The **DBcursor→c_get** function is the standard interface for retrieving records from the database with a cursor. The **DBcursor→c_get** function takes a flag that controls how the cursor is positioned within the database, and returns the key/data item associated with that positioning. Similar to **DB→get**, **DBcursor→c_get** may also take a supplied key and retrieve the data associated with that key from the database. There are several flags that you can set to customize retrieval:

Cursor Position Flags

- DB_FIRST, DB_LAST   Return the first (last) record in the database.
- DB_NEXT, DB_PREV   Return the next (previous) record in the database.
- DB_NEXT_DUP   Return the next record in the database if it is a duplicate data item for the current key.
- DB_NEXT_NODUP, DB_PREV_NODUP   Return the next (previous) record in the database that is not a duplicate data item for the current key.
- DB_CURRENT   Return the record from the database currently referenced by the cursor.

Retrieving Specific Key/Data Pairs

- DB_SET   Return the record from the database that matches the supplied key. In the case of duplicates, the first duplicate is returned and the cursor is positioned at the beginning of the duplicate list. The user can then traverse the duplicate entries for the key.

- DB_SET_RANGE   Return the smallest record in the database greater than or equal to the supplied key. This functionality permits partial key matches and range searches in the Btree access method.

- DB_GET_BOTH   Return the record from the database that matches both the supplied key and data items. This is particularly useful when there are large numbers of duplicate records for a key because it allows the cursor to easily be positioned at the correct place for traversal of some part of a large set of duplicate records.

Retrieving Based on Record Numbers

- DB_SET_RECNO   If the underlying database is a Btree, and was configured to be searched by logical record number, retrieve a specific record based on a record number argument.

- DB_GET_RECNO   If the underlying database is a Btree, and was configured to be searched by logical record number, return the record number for the record referenced by the cursor.

Special-Purpose Flags

- DB_CONSUME   Read-and-delete: The first record (the head) of the queue is returned and deleted. The underlying database must be a Queue.

- DB_RMW   Read-modify-write: Acquire write locks instead of read locks during retrieval. This can enhance performance in threaded applications by reducing the chance of deadlock.

In all cases, the cursor is repositioned by a **DBcursor→c_get** operation to point to the newly returned key/data pair in the database.

Storing Records with a Cursor

The **DBcursor→c_put** function is the standard interface for storing records into the database with a cursor. In general, **DBcursor→c_put** takes a key and inserts the associated data into the database at a location controlled by a specified flag.

There are several flags that you can set to customize storage:

- DB_AFTER   Create a new record immediately after the record currently referenced by the cursor.
- DB_BEFORE   Create a new record immediately before the record currently referenced by the cursor.
- DB_CURRENT_PUT   Replace the data part of the record currently referenced by the cursor.
- DB_KEYFIRST   Create a new record as the first of the duplicate records for the supplied key.
- DB_KEYLAST   Create a new record as the last of the duplicate records for the supplied key.

In all cases, the cursor is repositioned by a **DBcursor→c_put** operation to point to the newly inserted key/data pair in the database.

Deleting Records with a Cursor

The **DBcursor→c_del** function is the standard interface for deleting records from the database using a cursor. The **DBcursor→c_del** function deletes the record currently referenced by the cursor. In all cases, the cursor position is unchanged after a delete.

Duplicating a Cursor

After a cursor has been initialized (for example, by a call to **DBcursor→c_get**), it can be thought of as identifying a particular location in a database. The **DBcursor→c_dup** function permits an application to create a new cursor that has the same locking and transactional information as the cursor from which it is copied, and which optionally refers to the same position in the database.

In order to maintain a cursor position when an application is using locking, locks are maintained on behalf of the cursor until the cursor is closed. In cases when an application is using locking without transactions, cursor duplication is often required to avoid self-deadlocks. For further details, refer to "Access Method Locking Conventions."

Logical Join

A *logical join* is a method of retrieving data from a primary database using criteria stored in a set of secondary indexes. A logical join requires that your data be organized as a primary database, which contains the primary key, the primary data field, and a set of secondary indexes. Each of the secondary indexes is indexed by a different secondary key, and there is a set of duplicate data items that matches the primary keys in the primary database for each key in a secondary index.

For example, let's assume the need for an application that will return the names of stores in which one can buy fruit of a given color. We would first construct a primary database that lists types of fruit as the key item and the store where you can buy them as the data item:

Primary Key	Primary Data
apple	Convenience Store
blueberry	Farmer's Market
peach	Shopway
pear	Farmer's Market
raspberry	Shopway
strawberry	Farmer's Market

We would then create a secondary index with the key **color**, and use the names of fruits of different colors as the data items.

Secondary Key	Secondary Data
blue	blueberry
red	apple
red	raspberry
red	strawberry
yellow	peach
yellow	pear

This secondary index would allow an application to look up a color and then use the data items to look up the stores in which the colored fruit could be purchased. For example, by first looking up **blue**, the data item **blueberry** could be used as the lookup key in the primary database, returning **Farmer's Market**.

Your data must be organized in the following manner in order to use the **DB→join** function:

1. The actual data should be stored in the database represented by the DB object used to invoke this function. Generally, this DB object is called the *primary*.

2. Secondary indexes should be stored in separate databases, whose keys are the values of the secondary indexes and whose data items are the primary keys corresponding to the records having the designated secondary key value. It is acceptable (and expected) that there may be duplicate entries in the secondary indexes.

These duplicate entries should be sorted for performance reasons, although it is not required. For more information, see the DB_DUPSORT flag to the **DB→set_flags** function.

What the **DB→join** function does is review a list of secondary keys, and when it finds a data item that appears as a data item for all of the secondary keys, it uses that data item as a lookup into the primary database, and returns the associated data item.

If there were a another secondary index that had as its key the **cost** of the fruit, a similar lookup could be done on stores in which inexpensive fruit could be purchased:

Secondary Key	Secondary Data
expensive	blueberry
expensive	peach
expensive	pear
expensive	strawberry
inexpensive	apple
inexpensive	pear
inexpensive	raspberry

The **DB→join** function provides logical join functionality. Although not strictly cursor functionality because it is not a method off a cursor handle, it is more closely related to the cursor operations than to the standard DB operations.

It is also possible to do lookups based on multiple criteria in a single operation (for example, it is possible to look up fruits that are both red and expensive in a single operation). If the same fruit appeared as a data item in both the color and expense indexes, that fruit name would be used as the key for retrieval from the primary index and would then return the store where expensive red fruit could be purchased.

Example

Consider the following three databases:

personnel

- key = SSN
- data = record containing name, address, phone number, job title

lastname

- key = lastname
- data = SSN

jobs

- key = job title
- data = SSN

Consider the following query:

```
Return the personnel records of all people named smith with the job title
manager.
```

This query finds all the records in the primary database (personnel) for whom the criteria **lastname=smith** and job **title=manager** are true.

Assume that all databases have been properly opened and have the handles: pers_db, name_db, job_db. We also assume that we have an active transaction referenced by the handle txn.

```
DBC *name_curs, *job_curs, *join_curs;
DBC *carray[3];
DBT key, data;
int ret, tret;

name_curs = NULL;
job_curs = NULL;
memset(&key, 0, sizeof(key));
memset(&data, 0, sizeof(data));

if ((ret =
    name_db→cursor(name_db, txn, &name_curs)) != 0)
        goto err;
key.data = "smith";
key.size = sizeof("smith");
if ((ret =
    name_curs→c_get(name_curs, &key, &data, DB_SET)) != 0)
        goto err;

if ((ret = job_db→cursor(job_db, txn, &job_curs)) != 0)
        goto err;
key.data = "manager";
key.size = sizeof("manager");
if ((ret =
    job_curs→c_get(job_curs, &key, &data, DB_SET)) != 0)
        goto err;

carray[0] = name_curs;
carray[1] = job_curs;
carray[2] = NULL;

if ((ret =
    pers_db→join(pers_db, carray, &join_curs, 0)) != 0)
        goto err;
while ((ret =
    join_curs→c_get(join_curs, &key, &data, 0)) == 0) {
        /* Process record returned in key/data. */
}

/*
 * If we exited the loop because we ran out of records,
 * then it has completed successfully.
 */
if (ret == DB_NOTFOUND)
        ret = 0;
```

```
err:
if (join_curs != NULL &&
    (tret = join_curs→c_close(join_curs)) != 0 && ret == 0)
        ret = tret;
if (name_curs != NULL &&
    (tret = name_curs→c_close(name_curs)) != 0 && ret == 0)
        ret = tret;
if (job_curs != NULL &&
    (tret = job_curs→c_close(job_curs)) != 0 && ret == 0)
        ret = tret;

return (ret);
```

The name cursor is positioned at the beginning of the duplicate list for **smith** and the job cursor is placed at the beginning of the duplicate list for **manager**. The join cursor is returned from the logical join call. This code then loops over the join cursor and gets the personnel records of each one until there are no more.

Data Item Count

After a cursor has been initialized to reference a particular key in the database, it can be used to determine the number of data items that are stored for any particular key. The **DBcursor→c_count** method returns this number of data items. The returned value is always one unless the database supports duplicate data items; it then may be any number of items.

Closing a Cursor

The **DBcursor→c_close** function is the standard interface for closing a cursor, after which the cursor may no longer be used. Although cursors are implicitly closed when the database they point to is closed, it is good programming practice to explicitly close cursors. In addition, cursors may not exist outside of a transaction in transactional systems, so they must be explicitly closed.

Cursor Stability

In the absence of locking, no guarantees are made about the stability of cursors in different threads of control. However, the Btree, Queue, and Recno access methods guarantee that cursor operations, interspersed with any other operation in the same thread of control, will always return keys in order and will return each non-deleted key/data pair exactly once. Because the Hash access method uses a dynamic hashing algorithm, it cannot guarantee any form of stability in the presence of inserts and deletes unless locking is performed.

If locking was specified when the Berkeley DB environment was opened, but transactions are not in effect, the access methods provide repeatable reads with respect to the cursor. That is, a DB_CURRENT call on the cursor is guaranteed to return the same record as was returned on the last call to the cursor.

With the exception of the Queue access method, in the presence of transactions, all access method calls between a call to **txn_begin** and a call to **txn_abort** or **txn_commit** provide degree 3 consistency (serializable transactions).

The Queue access method permits phantom records to appear between calls. That is, deleted records are not locked, so another transaction may replace a deleted record between two calls to retrieve it. The record would not appear in the first call, but would be seen by the second call.

For all access methods, a cursor scan of the database performed within the context of a transaction is guaranteed to return each key/data pair once and only once, except in the following case. If, while performing a cursor scan using the Hash access method, the transaction performing the scan inserts a new pair into the database, it is possible that duplicate key/data pairs will be returned.

Database Verification and Salvage

The **DB→verify** method is the standard interface for verifying that a file and any databases it may contain are uncorrupted. In addition, the method may optionally be called with a file stream argument to which all key/data pairs found in the database are output. There are two modes for finding key/data pairs to be output:

1. If the DB_SALVAGE flag is specified, the key/data pairs in the database are output. When run in this mode, the database is assumed to be largely uncorrupted. For example, the **DB→verify** method will search for pages that are no longer linked into the database, and will output key/data pairs from such pages. However, key/data items that have been marked as deleted in the database will not be output because the page structures are generally trusted in this mode.

2. If both the DB_SALVAGE and DB_AGGRESSIVE flags are specified, all possible key/data pairs are output. When run in this mode, the database is assumed to be seriously corrupted. For example, key/data pairs that have been deleted will reappear in the output. In addition, because pages may have been subsequently reused and modified during normal database operations after the key/data pairs were deleted, it is not uncommon for apparently corrupted key/data pairs to be output in this mode, even when there is no corruption in the underlying database. The output will almost always have to be edited by hand or other means before the data is ready for reload into another database. We recommend that DB_SALVAGE be tried first, and DB_AGGRESSIVE tried only if the output from that first attempt is obviously missing data items or the data is sufficiently valuable that human review of the output is preferable to any kind of data loss.

5

Access Method Wrap-Up

T HE BERKELEY DB ACCESS METHODS PROVIDE NO GUARANTEES about byte alignment for returned key/data pairs or callback functions that take **DBT** references as arguments, and applications are responsible for arranging any necessary alignment. The DB_DBT_MALLOC, DB_DBT_REALLOC, and DB_DBT_USERMEM flags may be used to store returned items in memory of arbitrary alignment.

Retrieved Key/Data Permanence for C/C++

When using the non-cursor Berkeley DB calls to retrieve key/data items under the C/C++ APIs (for example, **DB→get**), the memory referenced by the pointer stored into the **DBT** is valid only until the next call to Berkeley DB using the DB handle. (This includes any use of the returned DB handle, including by another thread of control within the process. For this reason, when multiple threads are using the returned DB handle concurrently, one of the DB_DBT_MALLOC, DB_DBT_REALLOC, or DB_DBT_USERMEM flags must be specified with any non-cursor **DBT** used for key or data retrieval.)

When using the cursor Berkeley DB calls to retrieve key/data items under the C/C++ APIs (for example, **DBcursor→c_get**), the memory referenced by the pointer into the **DBT** is valid only until the next call to Berkeley DB using the DBC handle returned by **DB→cursor**.

Database Limits

The largest database file that Berkeley DB can handle depends on the page size selected by the application. Berkeley DB stores database file page numbers as unsigned 32-bit numbers and database file page sizes as unsigned 16-bit numbers. Using the maximum database page size of 65536, this results in a maximum database file size of 2^{48} (256 terabytes). The minimum database page size is 512 bytes, which results in a minimum maximum database size of 2^{41} (2 terabytes).

The largest database file Berkeley DB can support is potentially further limited if the host system does not have filesystem support for files larger than 2^{32}, including the capability to seek to absolute offsets within those files.

The largest key or data item that Berkeley DB can support is largely limited by available memory. Specifically, although key and data byte strings may be of essentially unlimited length, any one of them must fit into available memory so that it can be returned to the application. Because some of the Berkeley DB interfaces return both key and data items to the application, those interfaces will require that any key/data pair fits simultaneously into memory. Further, because the access methods may need to compare key and data items with other key and data items, it may be a requirement that any two key or two data items fit into available memory. Finally, when writing applications supporting transactions, it may be necessary to have an additional copy of any data item in memory for logging purposes.

The maximum Btree depth is 255.

Disk Space Requirements

It is possible to estimate the total database size based on the size of the data. The following calculations are an estimate of how many bytes you will need to hold a set of data and then how many pages it will take to actually store it on disk.

Space freed by deleting key/data pairs from a Btree or Hash database is never returned to the filesystem, although it is reused where possible. This means that the Btree and Hash databases are grow-only. If enough keys are deleted from a database that shrinking the underlying file is desirable, you should create a new database and copy the records from the old one into it.

These are rough estimates at best. For example, they do not take into account overflow records; filesystem metadata information; large sets of duplicate data items (in which the key is only stored once); or real-life situations in which the sizes of key and data items are wildly variable, and the page-fill factor changes over time.

Btree

The formulas for the Btree access method are as follows:

```
useful-bytes-per-page = (page-size - page-overhead) * page-fill-factor

bytes-of-data = n-records * (bytes-per-entry + page-overhead-for-two-
entries)
```

```
n-pages-of-data = bytes-of-data / useful-bytes-per-page
```

```
total-bytes-on-disk = n-pages-of-data * page-size
```

The *useful-bytes-per-page* is a measure of the bytes on each page that will actually hold the application data. It is computed as the total number of bytes on the page that are available to hold application data, corrected by the percentage of the page that is likely to contain data. The reason for this correction is that the percentage of a page that contains application data can vary from close to 50% after a page split to almost 100% if the entries in the database were inserted in sorted order. Obviously, the *page-fill-factor* can drastically alter the amount of disk space required to hold any particular data set. The page-fill factor of any existing database can be displayed using the **db_stat** utility.

As an example, using an 8K page size with an 85% page-fill factor, there are 6941 bytes of useful space on each page:

```
6941 = (8192 - 26) * .85
```

The total *bytes-of-data* is an easy calculation: It is the number of key/data pairs plus the overhead required to store each pair on a page. The overhead to store a single item on a Btree page is 5 bytes. So, assuming 60,000,000 key/data pairs, each of which is 8 bytes long, there are 1440000000 bytes, or roughly 1.34GB of total data:

```
1560000000 = 60000000 * ((8 * 2) + (5 * 2))
```

The total pages of data, *n-pages-of-data*, is the bytes-of-data divided by the *useful-bytes-per-page*. In the example, there are 224751 pages of data.

```
224751 = 1560000000 / 6941
```

The total bytes of disk space for the database is *n-pages-of-data* multiplied by the *page-size*. In the example, the result is 1841160192 bytes, or roughly 1.71GB.

```
1841160192 = 224751 * 8192
```

Hash

The formulas for the Hash access method are as follows:

```
useful-bytes-per-page = (page-size - page-overhead)
```

```
bytes-of-data = n-records *
    (bytes-per-entry + page-overhead-for-two-entries)
```

```
n-pages-of-data = bytes-of-data / useful-bytes-per-page
```

```
total-bytes-on-disk = n-pages-of-data * page-size
```

The *useful-bytes-per-page* is a measure of the bytes on each page that will actually hold the application data. It is computed as the total number of bytes on the page that are available to hold application data. If the application has explicitly set a page-fill factor, pages will not necessarily be kept full. For databases with a preset fill factor, see the following calculation. The page-overhead for Hash databases is 26 bytes and the page-overhead-for-two-entries is 6 bytes.

As an example, using an 8K page size, there are 8166 bytes of useful space on each page:

```
8166 = (8192 - 26)
```

The total *bytes-of-data* is an easy calculation: It is the number of key/data pairs plus the overhead required to store each pair on a page. In this case, that's 6 bytes per pair. So, assuming 60,000,000 key/data pairs, each of which is 8 bytes long, there are 1320000000 bytes, or roughly 1.23GB of total data:

```
1320000000 = 60000000 * (16 + 6)
```

The total pages of data, *n-pages-of-data*, is the *bytes-of-data* divided by the *useful-bytes-per-page*. In this example, there are 161646 pages of data.

```
161646 = 1320000000 / 8166
```

The total bytes of disk space for the database is *n-pages-of-data* multiplied by the *page-size*. In the example, the result is 1324204032 bytes, or roughly 1.23GB.

```
1324204032 = 161646 * 8192
```

Now, let's assume that the application specified a fill factor explicitly. The *fill factor* indicates the target number of items to place on a single page (a fill factor might reduce the utilization of each page, but it can be useful for avoiding splits and preventing buckets from becoming too large. Using our previous estimates, each item is 22 bytes (16 + 6), and there are 8166 useful bytes on a page (8192–26). That means that, on average, you can fit 371 pairs per page.

```
371 = 8166 / 22
```

However, let's assume that the application designer knows that although most items are 8 bytes, they can sometimes be as large as 10; and it's very important to avoid overflowing buckets and splitting. Then, the application might specify a fill factor of 314.

```
314 = 8166 / 26
```

With a fill factor of 314, then the formula for computing database size is the following

```
n-pages-of-data = npairs / pairs-per-page
```

or 191082.

```
191082 = 60000000 / 314
```

At 191082 pages, the total database size would be 1565343744 or 1.46GB.

```
1565343744 = 191082 * 8192
```

There are a few additional caveats with respect to Hash databases. This discussion assumes that the hash function does a good job of evenly distributing keys among hash buckets. If the function does not do this, you may find your table growing significantly larger than you expected. Second, in order to provide support for Hash databases coexisting with other databases in a single file, pages within a Hash database are allocated in power-of-two chunks. That means that a Hash database with 65 buckets will take up as much space as a Hash database with 128 buckets; each time the Hash database grows beyond its current power-of-two number of buckets, it allocates space for the next power-of-two buckets. This space may be sparsely allocated in the filesysem, but the files will appear to be their full size. Finally, because of this need for contiguous allocation, overflow pages and duplicate pages can be allocated only at specific points in the file, and this can lead to sparse hash tables.

Partial Record Storage and Retrieval

It is possible to both store and retrieve parts of data items in all Berkeley DB access methods. This is done by setting the DB_DBT_PARTIAL flag in the **DBT** structure passed to the Berkeley DB interface.

The DB_DBT_PARTIAL flag is based on the values of two fields of the **DBT** structure: **dlen** and **doff**. The value of **dlen** is the number of bytes of the record in which the application is interested. The value of **doff** is the offset from the beginning of the data item where those bytes start.

For example, if the data item were **ABCDEFGHIJKL**, a **doff** value of 3 would indicate that the bytes of interest started at **D**, and a **dlen** value of 4 would indicate that the bytes of interest were **DEFG**.

When retrieving a data item from a database, the **dlen** bytes starting **doff** bytes from the beginning of the record are returned, as if they comprised the entire record. If any or all of the specified bytes do not exist in the record, the retrieval is still successful, and any existing bytes (and nul bytes for any non-existent bytes) are returned.

When storing a data item into the database, the **dlen** bytes starting **doff** bytes from the beginning of the specified key's data record are replaced by the data specified by the **data** and **size** fields. If **dlen** is smaller than size, the record will grow, and if **dlen** is larger than **size**, the record will shrink. If the specified bytes do not exist, the record will be extended using nul bytes as necessary, and the store call will still succeed.

The following are various examples of the put case for the DB_DBT_PARTIAL flag. In all examples, the initial data item is 20 bytes in length:

ABCDEFGHIJ0123456789

1. ```
   size = 20
   doff = 0
   dlen = 20
   data = abcdefghijabcdefghij
   ```

   Result: The 20 bytes at offset 0 are replaced by the 20 bytes of data; that is, the entire record is replaced.

   ABCDEFGHIJ0123456789 → abcdefghijabcdefghij

2. ```
   size = 10
   doff = 20
   dlen = 0
   data = abcdefghij
   ```

   Result: The 0 bytes at offset 20 are replaced by the 10 bytes of data; that is, the record is extended by 10 bytes.

   ABCDEFGHIJ0123456789 → ABCDEFGHIJ0123456789abcdefghij

3. `size = 10`
   `doff = 10`
   `dlen = 5`
   `data = abcdefghij`

   Result: The 5 bytes at offset 10 are replaced by the 10 bytes of data.

   ABCDEFGHIJ0123456789 → ABCDEFGHIJabcdefghij56789

4. `size = 10`
   `doff = 10`
   `dlen = 0`
   `data = abcdefghij`

   Result: The 0 bytes at offset 10 are replaced by the 10 bytes of data; that is, 10 bytes are inserted into the record.

   ABCDEFGHIJ0123456789 → ABCDEFGHIJabcdefghij0123456789

5. `size = 10`
   `doff = 2`
   `dlen = 15`
   `data = abcdefghij`

   Result: The 15 bytes at offset 2 are replaced by the 10 bytes of data.

   ABCDEFGHIJ0123456789 → ABabcdefghij789

6. `size = 10`
   `doff = 0`
   `dlen = 0`
   `data = abcdefghij`

   Result: The 0 bytes at offset 0 are replaced by the 10 bytes of data; that is, the 10 bytes are inserted at the beginning of the record.

   ABCDEFGHIJ0123456789 → abcdefghijABCDEFGHIJ0123456789

7. `size = 0`
   `doff = 0`
   `dlen = 10`
   `data = ""`

   Result: The 10 bytes at offset 0 are replaced by the 0 bytes of data; that is, the first 10 bytes of the record are discarded.

   ABCDEFGHIJ0123456789 → 0123456789

8. `size = 10`
   `doff = 25`
   `dlen = 0`
   `data = abcdefghij`

   Result: The 0 bytes at offset 25 are replaced by the 10 bytes of data; that is, 10 bytes are inserted into the record past the end of the current data (\0 represents a nul byte).

   ABCDEFGHIJ0123456789 → ABCDEFGHIJ0123456789\0\0\0\0\0abcdefghij

Error Support

Berkeley DB offers programmatic support for displaying error return values.

The **db_strerror** interface returns a pointer to the error message corresponding to any Berkeley DB error return, similar to the ANSI C strerror interface, but is able to handle both system error returns and Berkeley DB-specific return values.

For example:

```
int ret;
if ((ret = dbp→put(dbp, NULL, &key, &data, 0)) != 0) {
        fprintf(stderr, "put failed: %s\n", db_strerror(ret));
        return (1);
}
```

There are also two additional error interfaces, **DB→err** and **DB→errx**. These interfaces work like the ANSI C X3.159-1989 (ANSI C) printf interface, taking a printf-style format string and argument list, and writing a message constructed from the format string and arguments.

The **DB→err** function appends the standard error string to the constructed message; the **DB→errx** function does not. These interfaces provide simpler ways of displaying Berkeley DB error messages. For example, if your application tracks session IDs in a variable called session_id, it can include that information in its error messages:

Error messages can additionally be configured to always include a prefix (for example, the program name) using the **DB→set_errpfx** interface.

```
#define DATABASE "access.db"
int ret;
dbp→errpfx(dbp, argv0);
if ((ret =
        dbp→open(dbp, DATABASE, DB_BTREE, DB_CREATE, 0664)) != 0) {
        dbp→err(dbp, ret, "%s", DATABASE);
        dbp→errx(dbp,
                "contact your system administrator: session ID was %d",
                session_id);
        return (1);
}
```

For example, if the program were called my_app and the open call returned an EACCESS system error, the error messages shown would appear as follows:

```
my_app: access.db: Permission denied.
my_app: contact your system administrator: session ID was 14
```

6

Berkeley DB Architecture

THE PREVIOUS CHAPTERS IN THIS *REFERENCE GUIDE* DESCRIBED APPLICATIONS that use the Berkeley DB Access Methods for fast data storage and retrieval. The applications described in the following chapters are similar in nature to the Access Methods applications, but they are also threaded and/or recoverable in the face of application or system failure.

Application code that uses only the Berkeley DB Access Methods might appear as follows:

```
switch (ret = dbp→put(dbp, NULL, &key, &data, 0)) {
case 0:
        printf("db: %s: key stored.\n", (char *)key.data);
        break;
default:
        dbp→err(dbp, ret, "dbp→put");
        exit (1);
}
```

The underlying Berkeley DB architecture that supports this is shown in Figure 6.1.

As you can see from this diagram, the application makes calls into the Access Methods, and the Access Methods use the underlying shared memory buffer cache to hold recently used file pages in main memory.

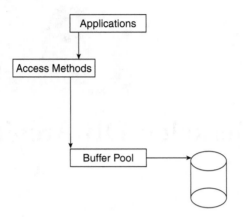

Figure 6.1   Underlying Berkeley DB architecture.

When applications require recoverability, their calls to the Access Methods must be wrapped in calls to the Transaction subsystem. The application must inform Berkeley DB where to begin and end transactions, and must be prepared for the possibility that an operation may fail at any particular time, causing the transaction to abort.

An example of transaction-protected code might appear as follows:

```
retry:  if ((ret = txn_begin(dbenv, NULL, &tid)) != 0) {
                dbenv→err(dbenv, ret, "txn_begin");
                exit (1);
        }
        switch (ret = dbp→put(dbp, tid, &key, &data, 0)) {
        case DB_LOCK_DEADLOCK:
                (void)txn_abort(tid);
                goto retry;
        case 0:
                printf("db: %s: key stored.\n", (char *)key.data);
                break;
        default:
                dbenv→err(dbenv, ret, "dbp→put");
                exit (1);
        }

        if ((ret = txn_commit(tid)) != 0) {
                dbenv→err(dbenv, ret, "txn_commit");
                exit (1);
        }
```

In this example, the same operation is being done as before; however, it is wrapped in transaction calls. The transaction is started with **txn_begin** and finished with **txn_commit**. If the operation fails due to a deadlock, the transaction is aborted using **txn_abort**, after which the operation may be retried.

There are actually five major subsystems in Berkeley DB, as follows:

- **Access Methods**   The *Access Methods* subsystem provides general-purpose support for creating and accessing database files formatted as Btrees, Hashed files, and Fixed- and Variable-length records. These modules are useful in the absence of transactions for applications that need fast formatted file support. See **DB→open** and **DB→cursor** for more information. These functions were already discussed in detail in the previous chapters.

- **Memory Pool (Buffer Pool)**   The *Memory Pool*, or *Buffer Pool*, subsystem is the general-purpose shared memory buffer pool used by Berkeley DB. This is the shared memory cache that allows multiple processes and threads within processes to share access to databases. This module is useful outside of the Berkeley DB package for processes that require portable, page-oriented, cached, shared file access.

- **Transaction**   The *Transaction* subsystem allows a group of database changes to be treated as an atomic unit so that either all of the changes are done, or none of the changes are done. The Transaction subsystem implements the Berkeley DB transaction model. This module is useful outside of the Berkeley DB package for processes that want to transaction-protect their own data modifications.

- **Locking**   The *Locking* subsystem is the general-purpose lock manager used by Berkeley DB. This module is useful outside of the Berkeley DB package for processes that require a portable, fast, configurable lock manager.

- **Logging**   The *Logging* subsystem is the write-ahead logging used to support the Berkeley DB transaction model. It is largely specific to the Berkeley DB package, and unlikely to be useful elsewhere except as a supporting module for the Berkeley DB Transaction subsystem.

Figure 6.2 shows a more complete picture of the Berkeley DB library.

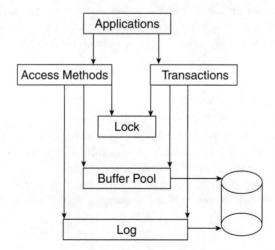

Figure 6.2   Berkeley DB library.

In this model, the application makes calls to the Access Methods and Transaction subsystems. The Access Methods and Transaction subsystems in turn make calls into the Memory Pool, Locking, and Logging subsystems on behalf of the application.

The underlying subsystems can be used independently by applications. For example, the Memory Pool subsystem can be used apart from the rest of Berkeley DB by applications simply wanting a shared memory buffer pool, or the Locking subsystem may be called directly by applications that are doing their own locking outside of Berkeley DB. However, this usage is not common, and most applications will either use only the Access Methods subsystem or the Access Methods subsystem wrapped in calls to the transaction interfaces.

Programming Model

The Berkeley DB distribution is a database library, in which the library is linked into the address space of the application using it. The code using Berkeley DB may be a standalone application or it may be a server providing functionality to many clients via inter-process or remote-process communication (IPC/RPC).

In the standalone application model, one or more applications link the Berkeley DB library directly into their address spaces. There may be many threads of control in this model because Berkeley DB supports locking for both multiple processes and for multiple threads within a process. This model provides significantly faster access to the database functionality, but implies trust among all threads of control sharing the database environment because they will have the capability to read, write, and potentially corrupt each other's data.

In the client-server model, developers write a database server application that accepts requests via some form of IPC/RPC, and issues calls to the Berkeley DB interfaces based on those requests. In this model, the database server is the only application linking the Berkeley DB library into its address space. The client-server model trades performance for protection because it does not require that the applications share a protection domain with the server, but IPC/RPC is slower than a function call. Of course, this model also greatly simplifies the creation of network client-server applications.

Programmatic APIs

The Berkeley DB subsystems can be accessed through interfaces from multiple languages. The standard library interface is ANSI C. Applications can also use Berkeley DB via C++ or Java, as well as from scripting languages. Environments can be shared among applications written by using any of these APIs. For example, you might have a local server written in C or C++, a script for an administrator written in Perl or Tcl, and a Web-based user interface written in Java—all sharing a single database environment.

C

The Berkeley DB library is written entirely in ANSI C. C applications use a single include file:

```
#include <db.h>
```

C++

The C++ classes provide a thin wrapper around the C API, with the major advantages being improved encapsulation and an optional exception mechanism for errors. C++ applications use a single include file:

```
#include <db_cxx.h>
```

The classes and methods are named in a fashion that directly corresponds to structures and functions in the C interface. Likewise, arguments to methods appear in the same order as the C interface, except to remove the explicit **this** pointer. The #defines used for flags are identical between the C and C++ interfaces.

As a rule, each C++ object has exactly one structure from the underlying C API associated with it. The C structure is allocated with each constructor call and deallocated with each destructor call. Thus, the rules the user needs to follow in allocating and deallocating structures are the same between the C and C++ interfaces.

To ensure portability to many platforms, both new and old, Berkeley DB makes as few assumptions as possible about the C++ compiler and library. For example, it does not expect STL, templates, or namespaces to be available. The newest C++ feature used is exceptions, which are used liberally to transmit error information. Even the use of exceptions can be disabled at runtime.

Java

The Java classes provide a layer around the C API that is almost identical to the C++ layer. The classes and methods are, for the most part identical to the C++ layer. Berkeley DB constants and #defines are represented as "static final int" values. Error conditions are communicated as Java exceptions.

As in C++, each Java object has exactly one structure from the underlying C API associated with it. The Java structure is allocated with each constructor or open call, but is deallocated only by the Java garbage collector. Because the timing of garbage collection is not predictable, applications should take care to do a close when finished with any object that has a close method.

Dbm/Ndbm, Hsearch

Berkeley DB supports the standard UNIX interfaces **dbm/ndbm**, and **hsearch**. After including a new header file and recompiling, programs will run orders of magnitude faster, and underlying databases can grow as large as necessary. Also, historic **dbm** and **ndbm** applications can fail after some number of entries are inserted into the database, in which the number depends on the effectiveness of the internal hashing function on the particular data set. This is not a problem with Berkeley DB.

Scripting Languages

The following sections describe the Berkeley DB scripting languages.

Perl

Two Perl APIs are distributed with the Berkeley DB release. The Perl interface to Berkeley DB version 1.85 is called DB_File. The Perl interface to Berkeley DB version 2 is called BerkeleyDB. See "Using Berkeley DB with Perl" for more information.

Tcl

A Tcl API is distributed with the Berkeley DB release. See "Using Berkeley DB with Tcl" for more information.

Supporting Utilities

The following are the standalone utilities that provide supporting functionality for the Berkeley DB environment:

- **berkeley_db_svc** The **berkeley_db_svc** utility is the Berkeley DB RPC server that provides standard server functionality for client applications.
- **db_archive** The **db_archive** utility supports database backup and archival, and log file administration. It facilitates log reclamation and the creation of database snapshots. Generally, some form of log archival must be done if a database environment has been configured for logging or transactions.
- **db_checkpoint** The **db_checkpoint** utility runs as a daemon process, monitoring the database log and periodically issuing checkpoints. It facilitates log reclamation and the creation of database snapshots. Generally, some form of database checkpointing must be done if a database environment has been configured for transactions.
- **db_deadlock** The **db_deadlock** utility runs as a daemon process, periodically traversing the database lock structures and aborting transactions when it detects a deadlock. Generally, some form of deadlock detection must be done if a database environment has been configured for locking.
- **db_dump** The **db_dump** utility writes a copy of the database to a flat-text file in a portable format.

- **db_load**   The **db_load** utility reads the flat-text file produced by **db_dump** and loads it into a database file.

- **db_printlog**   The **db_printlog** utility displays the contents of Berkeley DB log files in a human-readable and parsable format.

- **db_recover**   The **db_recover** utility runs after an unexpected Berkeley DB or system failure to restore the database to a consistent state. Generally, some form of database recovery must be done if databases are being modified.

- **db_stat**   The **db_stat** utility displays statistics for databases and database environments.

- **db_upgrade**   The **db_upgrade** utility provides a command-line interface for upgrading underlying database formats.

- **db_verify**   The **db_verify** utility provides a command-line interface for verifying the database format.

All of the functionality implemented for these utilities is also available as part of the standard Berkeley DB API. This means that threaded applications can easily create a thread that calls the same Berkeley DB functions as do the utilities. This often simplifies an application environment by removing the necessity for multiple processes to negotiate database and database environment creation and shutdown.

Berkeley DB Environment

A BERKELEY DB ENVIRONMENT IS AN ENCAPSULATION OF ONE OR MORE databases, log files, and shared information about the database environment, such as shared memory buffer cache pages.

The simplest way to administer a Berkeley DB application environment is to create a single **home** directory that stores the files for the applications that will share the environment. The environment home directory must be created before any Berkeley DB applications are run. Berkeley DB itself never creates the environment home directory. The environment can then be identified by the name of that directory.

An environment may be shared by any number of processes, as well as by any number of threads within those processes. It is possible for an environment to include resources from other directories on the system, and applications often choose to distribute resources to other directories or disks for performance or other reasons. However, by default, the databases, shared regions (the Locking, Logging, Memory Pool, and Transaction shared memory areas), and log files will be stored in a single directory hierarchy.

It is important to realize that all applications sharing a database environment implicitly trust each other. They have access to each other's data as it resides in the shared regions, and they will share resources such as buffer space and locks. At the same time, any applications using the same databases must share an environment if consistency is to be maintained between them.

Creating a Database Environment

The Berkeley DB environment is created and described by the **db_env_create** and **DBENV→open** interfaces. In situations where customization is desired, such as storing log files on a separate disk drive or selecting particular cache size, applications must describe the customization by either creating an environment configuration file in the environment home directory or by arguments passed to other DB_ENV handle methods.

Once an environment has been created, database files specified using relative pathnames will be named relative to the home directory. Using pathnames relative to the home directory allows the entire environment to be easily moved, simplifying restoration and recovery of a database in a different directory or on a different system.

Applications first obtain an environment handle using the **db_env_create** function and then calling the **DBENV→open** function, which creates or joins the database environment. There are a number of options you can set to customize **DBENV→open** for your environment. These options fall into four broad categories:

- **Subsystem initialization**   These flags indicate which Berkeley DB subsystems will be initialized for the environment, and what operations will happen automatically when databases are accessed within the environment. The flags include DB_JOINENV, DB_INIT_CDB, DB_INIT_LOCK, DB_INIT_LOG, DB_INIT_MPOOL, and DB_INIT_TXN. The DB_INIT_CDB flag does initialization for Berkeley DB Concurrent Data Store applications. (See "Building Berkeley DB Concurrent Data Store Applications" for more information.) The rest of the flags initialize a single subsystem; that is, when DB_INIT_LOCK is specified, applications reading and writing databases opened in this environment will be using locking to ensure that they do not overwrite each other's changes.

- **Recovery options**   These flags, which include DB_RECOVER and DB_RECOVER_FATAL, indicate what recovery is to be performed on the environment before it is opened for normal use.

- **Naming options**   These flags, which include DB_USE_ENVIRON and DB_USE_ENVIRON_ROOT, modify how file naming happens in the environment.

- **Miscellaneous**   Finally, there are a number of miscellaneous flags (for example, DB_CREATE) that causes underlying files to be created as necessary. See the **DBENV→open** manual pages for further information.

Most applications either specify only the DB_INIT_MPOOL flag or they specify all four subsystem initialization flags (DB_INIT_MPOOL, DB_INIT_LOCK, DB_INIT_LOG, and DB_INIT_TXN). The former configuration is for applications that simply want to use the basic Access Method interfaces with a shared underlying buffer pool, but don't care about recoverability after application or system failure. The latter is for applications that need recoverability. There are situations in which other combinations of the initialization flags make sense, but they are rare.

The DB_RECOVER flag is specified by applications that want to perform any necessary database recovery when they start running. That is, if there was a system or application failure the last time they ran, they want the databases to be made consistent before they start running again. It is not an error to specify this flag when no recovery needs to be done.

The DB_RECOVER_FATAL flag is more special-purpose. It performs catastrophic database recovery, and normally requires that some initial arrangements be made; that is, archived log files be brought back into the filesystem. Applications should not normally specify this flag. Instead, under these rare conditions, the **db_recover** utility should be used.

File Naming

One of the most important tasks of the database environment is to structure file naming within Berkeley DB.

Each of the Locking, Logging, Memory Pool, and Transaction subsystems of Berkeley DB require shared memory regions, backed by the filesystem. Further, cooperating applications (or multiple invocations of the same application) must agree on the location of the shared memory regions and other files used by the Berkeley DB subsystems, the log files used by the Logging subsystem, and, of course, the data files. Although it is possible to specify full pathnames to all Berkeley DB functions, this is cumbersome and requires that applications be recompiled when database files are moved.

Applications are normally expected to specify a single directory home for their database. This can be done easily in the call to **DBENV→open** by specifying a value for the **db_home** argument. There are more complex configurations in which it may be desirable to override **db_home** or provide supplementary path information.

Specifying File Naming to Berkeley DB

The following list describes the possible ways in which file naming information may be specified to the Berkeley DB library. The specific circumstances and order in which these ways are applied are described in a subsequent paragraph.

- **db_home**   If the **db_home** argument to **DBENV→open** is non-NULL, its value may be used as the database home, and files named relative to its path.

- **DB_HOME**   If the DB_HOME environment variable is set when **DBENV→open** is called, its value may be used as the database home, and files named relative to its path.

  The DB_HOME environment variable is intended to permit users and system administrators to override application and installation defaults. For example:

  ```
  env DB_HOME=/database/my_home application
  ```

Application writers are encouraged to support the **-h** option found in the supporting Berkeley DB utilities to let users specify a database home.

- **DB_ENV methods**   There are three DB_ENV methods that affect file naming. The **DBENV→set_data_dir** function specifies a directory to search for database files. The **DBENV→set_lg_dir** function specifies a directory in which to create logging files. The **DBENV→set_tmp_dir** function specifies a directory in which to create backing temporary files. These methods are intended to permit applications to customize a file location for a database. For example, an application writer can place data files and log files in different directories or instantiate a new log directory each time the application runs.

- **DB_CONFIG**   The same information specified to the DB_ENV methods may also be specified using a configuration file. If an environment home directory has been specified (either by the application specifying a non-NULL **db_home** argument to **DBENV→open**, or by the application setting the DB_USE_ENVIRON or DB_USE_ENVIRON_ROOT flags and the DB_HOME environment variable being set), any file named **DB_CONFIG** in the database home directory will be read for lines of the format **NAME VALUE**.

  The characters delimiting the two parts of the entry may be one or more whitespace characters, and trailing whitespace characters are discarded. All empty lines or lines whose first character is a whitespace or hash (#) character will be ignored. Each line must specify both the NAME and the VALUE of the pair. The specific NAME VALUE pairs are documented in the manual **DBENV→set_data_dir**, **DBENV→set_lg_dir**, and **DBENV→set_tmp_dir** pages.

  The DB_CONFIG configuration file is intended to permit systems to customize file location for an environment independent of applications using that database. For example, a database administrator can move the database log and data files to a different location without application recompilation.

Filename Resolution in Berkeley DB

The following list describes the specific circumstances and order in which the different ways of specifying file naming information are applied. Berkeley DB filename processing proceeds sequentially through the following steps:

- **Absolute pathnames**   If the filename specified to a Berkeley DB function is an *absolute pathname*, that filename is used without modification by Berkeley DB.

  On UNIX systems, an absolute pathname is defined as any pathname that begins with a leading slash (/).

  On Windows systems, an absolute pathname is any pathname that begins with a leading slash or leading backslash (\); or any pathname beginning with a single alphabetic character, a colon, and a leading slash or backslash (for example, **C:/tmp**).

- **DB_ENV methods, DB_CONFIG**   If a relevant configuration string (for example, set_data_dir), is specified either by calling a DB_ENV method or as a line in the DB_CONFIG configuration file, the VALUE from the **NAME VALUE** pair is prepended to the filename. If the resulting filename is an absolute pathname, the filename is used without further modification by Berkeley DB.

- **db_home**   If the application specified a non-NULL **db_home** argument to **DBENV→open**, its value is prepended to the filename. If the resulting filename is an absolute pathname, the filename is used without further modification by Berkeley DB.

- **DB_HOME**   If the **db_home** argument is NULL, the DB_HOME environment variable was set, and the application has set the appropriate DB_USE_ENVIRON or DB_USE_ENVIRON_ROOT environment variable, its value is prepended to the filename. If the resulting filename is an absolute pathname, the filename is used without further modification by Berkeley DB.

- **default**   Finally, all filenames are interpreted relative to the current working directory of the process.

The common model for a Berkeley DB environment is one in which only the DB_HOME environment variable or the **db_home** argument is specified. In this case, all data filenames are relative to that directory, and all files created by the Berkeley DB subsystems will be created in that directory.

The more complex model for a transaction environment might be one in which a database home is specified, using either the DB_HOME environment variable or the **db_home** argument to **DBENV→open**; and then the data directory and logging directory are set to the relative pathnames of directories underneath the environment home.

Examples

Store all files in the directory **/a/database**:

```
DBENV→open(DBENV, "/a/database", ...);
```

Create temporary backing files in **/b/temporary**, and all other files in **/a/database**:
```
DBENV→set_tmp_dir(DBENV, "/b/temporary");
DBENV→open(DBENV, "/a/database", ...);
```

Store data files in **/a/database/datadir**, log files in **/a/database/logdir**, and all other files in the directory **/a/database**:
```
DBENV→set_lg_dir("logdir");
DBENV→set_data_dir("datadir");
DBENV→open(DBENV, "/a/database", ...);
```

Store data files in **/a/database/data1** and **/b/data2**, and all other files in the directory **/a/database**. Any data files that are created will be created in **/b/data2** because
it is the first DB_DATA_DIR directory specified:

```
DBENV→set_data_dir(DBENV, "/b/data2");
DBENV→set_data_dir(DBENV, "data1");
DBENV→open(DBENV, "/a/database", ...);
```

Security

The following are security issues that should be considered when writing Berkeley
DB applications:

Database environment permissions

The directory used as the Berkeley DB database environment should have its permissions set to ensure that files in the environment are not accessible to users without
appropriate permissions. Applications that add to the user's permissions (for example,
UNIX setuid or setgid applications) must be carefully checked to not permit illegal
use of those permissions such as general file access in the environment directory.

Environment variables

Setting the DB_USE_ENVIRON and DB_USE_ENVIRON_ROOT flags, and
allowing the use of environment variables during file naming can be dangerous.
Setting those flags in Berkeley DB applications with additional permissions (for example, UNIX setuid or setgid applications) could potentially allow users to read and
write databases to which they would not normally have access.

File permissions

By default, Berkeley DB always creates files readable and writable by the owner and
the group (that is, S_IRUSR, S_IWUSR, S_IRGRP, and S_IWGRP; or octal mode
0660 on historic UNIX systems). The group ownership of created files is based on the
system and directory defaults, and is not further specified by Berkeley DB.

Temporary backing files

If an unnamed database is created and the cache is too small to hold the database in
memory, Berkeley DB will create a temporary physical file to enable it to page the
database to disk, as needed. In this case, environment variables such as **TMPDIR** may
be used to specify the location of that temporary file. Although temporary backing
files are created readable and writable by the owner only (S_IRUSR and S_IWUSR,
or octal mode 0600 on historic UNIX systems), some filesystems may not sufficiently
protect temporary files created in random directories from improper access. To be

absolutely safe, applications storing sensitive data in unnamed databases should use the **DBENV→set_tmp_dir** method to specify a temporary directory with known permissions.

Shared Memory Regions

Each of the Berkeley DB subsystems within an environment is described by one or more regions. The regions contain all of the per-process and per-thread shared information, including mutexes, that comprise a Berkeley DB environment. These regions are created in one of three areas, depending on the flags specified to the **DBENV→open** function:

1. If the DB_PRIVATE flag is specified to **DBENV→open**, regions are created in per-process heap memory; that is, memory returned by **malloc(3)**. In this case, the Berkeley DB environment may only be accessed by a single process, although that process may be multithreaded.

2. If the DB_SYSTEM_MEM flag is specified to **DBENV→open**, regions are created in system memory. When regions are created in system memory, the Berkeley DB environment may be accessed by both multiple processes and multiple threads within processes.

   The system memory used by Berkeley DB is potentially useful past the lifetime of any particular process. Therefore, additional cleanup may be necessary after an application fails because there may be no way for Berkeley DB to ensure that system resources backing the shared memory regions are returned to the system. The system memory that is used is architecture-dependent. For example, on systems supporting X/Open-style shared memory interfaces, such as UNIX systems, the **shmget**(2) and related System V IPC interfaces are used. Additionally, VxWorks systems use system memory. In these cases, an initial segment ID must be specified by the application to ensure that applications do not overwrite each other's database environments, so that the number of segments created does not grow without bounds. See the **DBENV→set_shm_key** function for more information.

3. If no memory-related flags are specified to **DBENV→open**, memory backed by the filesystem is used to store the regions. On UNIX systems, the Berkeley DB library will use the POSIX mmap interface. If mmap is not available, the UNIX shmget interfaces will be used, assuming they are available.

Any files created in the filesystem to back the regions are created in the environment home directory specified to the **DBENV→open** call. These files are named __db.###, (for example, __db.001, __db.002, and so on). When region files are backed by the filesystem, one file per region is created. When region files are backed by system memory, a single file will still be created because there must be a well-known name in the filesystem so that multiple processes can locate the system shared memory that is being used by the environment.

Statistics about the shared memory regions in the environment can be displayed using the **-e** option to the **db_stat** utility.

Remote Filesystems

When regions are backed by the filesystem, it is a common error to attempt to create Berkeley DB environments backed by remote filesystems such as the Network File System (NFS) or the Andrew File System (AFS). Remote filesystems rarely support mapping files into process memory, and even more rarely support correct semantics for mutexes after the attempt succeeds. For this reason, we strongly recommend that the database environment directory reside in a local filesystem.

For remote filesystems that do allow system files to be mapped into process memory, home directories accessed via remote filesystems cannot be used simultaneously from multiple clients. None of the commercial remote filesystems available today implement coherent, distributed shared memory for remote-mounted files. As a result, different machines will see different versions of these shared regions, and the system behavior is undefined.

Databases, log files, and temporary files may be placed on remote filesystems as long as the remote filesystem fully supports standard POSIX filesystem semantics (although the application may incur a performance penalty for doing so). Obviously, NFS-mounted databases cannot be accessed from more than one Berkeley DB environment at a time (and therefore from more than one system) because no Berkeley DB database may be accessed from more than one Berkeley DB environment at a time.

Linux Note

Some Linux releases are known to not support complete semantics for the POSIX fsync call on NFS-mounted filesystems. No Berkeley DB files should be placed on NFS-mounted filesystems on these systems.

Opening Databases Within the Environment

Once the environment has been created, database handles may be created and then opened within the environment. This is done by calling the **db_create** interface and specifying the appropriate environment as an argument.

File naming, database operations, and error-handling are done as specified for the environment. For example, if the DB_INIT_LOCK or DB_INIT_CDB flags were specified when the environment was created or joined, database operations automatically perform all necessary locking operations for the application.

Error Support

Berkeley DB offers programmatic support for displaying error return values. The
db_strerror interface returns a pointer to the error message corresponding to any
Berkeley DB error return. This is similar to the ANSI C strerror interface, but it can
handle both system error returns and Berkeley DB-specific return values.

For example:

```
int ret;
if ((ret = dbenv→set_cachesize(dbenv, 0, 32 * 1024)) != 0) {
        fprintf(stderr, "set_cachesize failed: %s\n", db_strerror(ret));
        return (1);
}
```

There are also two additional error functions: **DBENV→err** and **DBENV→errx**.
These functions work like the ANSI C printf interface, taking a printf-style format
string and argument list, and writing a message constructed from the format string and
arguments.

The **DBENV→err** function appends the standard error string to the constructed
message; the DBENV→errx function does not.

Error messages can be configured always to include a prefix (for example, the
program name) using the **DBENV→set_errpfx** interface.

These functions provide simpler ways of displaying Berkeley DB error messages:

```
int ret;
dbenv→set_errpfx(dbenv, argv0);
if ((ret = dbenv→open(dbenv, home, NULL,
    DB_CREATE | DB_INIT_LOG | DB_INIT_TXN | DB_USE_ENVIRON))
    != 0) {
        dbenv→err(dbenv, ret, "open: %s", home);
        dbenv→errx(dbenv,
            "contact your system administrator: session ID was %d",
            session_id);
        return (1);
}
```

For example, if the program was called "my_app", it tried to open an environment
home directory in "/tmp/home", and the open call returned a permission error, the
error messages shown would look like this:

```
my_app: open: /tmp/home: Permission denied.
my_app: contact your system administrator: session ID was 2
```

Berkeley DB Concurrent Data Store Applications

I T IS OFTEN DESIRABLE TO HAVE CONCURRENT READ–WRITE ACCESS to a database when there is no need for full recoverability or transaction semantics. For this class of applications, Berkeley DB provides an interface supporting deadlock-free, multiple-reader/single-writer access to the database. This means that at any instant in time, there may be either multiple readers accessing data or a single writer modifying data. The application is entirely unaware of which is happening, and Berkeley DB implements the necessary locking and blocking to ensure this behavior.

To create Berkeley DB Concurrent Data Store applications, you must first initialize an environment by calling **DBENV→open**. You must specify the DB_INIT_CDB and DB_INIT_MPOOL flags to that interface. It is an error to specify any of the other **DBENV→open** subsystem or recovery configuration flags; for example, DB_INIT_LOCK, DB_INIT_TXN, or DB_RECOVER. All databases must, of course, be created in this environment by using the **db_create** interface or **Db** constructor, and specifying the environment as an argument.

Berkeley DB performs appropriate locking in its interface so that safe enforcement of the deadlock-free, multiple-reader/single-writer semantic is transparent to the application. However, a basic understanding of Berkeley DB Concurrent Data Store locking behavior is helpful when writing Berkeley DB Concurrent Data Store applications.

Berkeley DB Concurrent Data Store avoids deadlocks without the need for a deadlock detector by performing all locking on an entire database at once (or on an entire environment in the case of the DB_CDB_ALLDB flag), and by ensuring that at any given time only one thread of control is allowed to simultaneously hold a read (shared) lock and attempt to acquire a write (exclusive) lock.

All open Berkeley DB cursors hold a read lock, which serves as a guarantee that the database will not change beneath them; likewise, all non-cursor **DB→get** operations temporarily acquire and release a read lock that is held during the actual traversal of the database. Because read locks will not conflict with each other, any number of cursors in any number of threads of control may be open simultaneously, and any number of **DB→get** operations may be concurrently in progress.

To enforce the rule that only one thread of control at a time can attempt to upgrade a read lock to a write lock, however, Berkeley DB must forbid multiple cursors from attempting to write concurrently. This is done using the DB_WRITECURSOR flag to the **DB→cursor** interface. This is the only difference between access method calls in Berkeley DB Concurrent Data Store and in the other Berkeley DB products. The DB_WRITECURSOR flag causes the newly created cursor to be a "write" cursor; that is, a cursor capable of performing writes as well as reads. Only cursors thus created are permitted to perform write operations (either deletes or puts), and only one such cursor can exist at any given time.

Any attempt to create a second write cursor or to perform a non-cursor write operation while a write cursor is open will block until that write cursor is closed. Read cursors may open and perform reads without blocking while a write cursor is extant. However, any attempts to actually perform a write, either using the write cursor or directly using the **DB→put** or **DB→del** methods, will block until all read cursors are closed. This is how the multiple-reader/single-writer semantic is enforced, and prevents reads from seeing an inconsistent database state that may be an intermediate stage of a write operation.

With these behaviors, Berkeley DB can guarantee deadlock-free concurrent database access, so that multiple threads of control are free to perform reads and writes without needing to handle synchronization themselves or having to run a deadlock detector. Because Berkeley DB has no knowledge of which cursors belong to which threads, however, some care must be taken to ensure that applications do not inadvertently block themselves, causing the application to hang and be unable to proceed. Some common mistakes include the following:

1. Keeping a cursor open while issuing a **DB→put** or **DB→del** access method call.

2. Attempting to open a write cursor while a write cursor is already being held open by the same thread of control. Note that it is correct operation for one thread of control to attempt to open a write cursor or to perform a non-cursor write (**DB→put** or **DB→del**) while a write cursor is already active in another

thread. It is only a problem if these things are done within a single thread of control—in which case that thread will block and never be able to release the lock that is blocking it.

3. Keeping a write cursor open for an extended period of time.

4. Not testing Berkeley DB error return codes (if any cursor operation returns an unexpected error, that cursor must still be closed).

5. By default, Berkeley DB Concurrent Data Store does locking on a per-database basis. For this reason, accessing multiple databases in different orders in different threads or processes, or leaving cursors open on one database while accessing another database, can cause an application to hang. If this behavior is a requirement for the application, Berkeley DB should be configured to do locking on an environment-wide basis. See the DB_CDB_ALLDB flag of the **DBENV→set_flags** function for more information.

9

Berkeley DB Transactional
Data Store Applications

I T IS DIFFICULT TO WRITE A USEFUL TRANSACTIONAL TUTORIAL AND STILL keep within reasonable bounds of documentation; that is, without writing a book on transactional programming. We have two goals in this section: to familiarize readers with the transactional interfaces of Berkeley DB and to provide code building blocks that will be useful for creating applications.

We have not attempted to present this information using a real-world application. First, transactional applications are often complex and time-consuming to explain. Also, one of our goals is to give you an understanding of the wide variety of tools Berkeley DB makes available to you, and no single application would use most of the interfaces included in the Berkeley DB library. For these reasons, we have chosen to simply present the Berkeley DB data structures and programming solutions, using examples that differ from page to page. All the examples are included in a standalone program you can examine, modify, and run; and from which you will be able to extract code blocks for your own applications. Fragments of the program will be presented throughout this chapter, and the complete text of the example program for IEEE/ANSI Std 1003.1 (POSIX) standard systems is included in the Berkeley DB distribution.

Why Transactions?

Perhaps the first question to answer is "Why transactions?" There are a number of reasons to include transactional support in your applications. The most common ones are the following:

- **Recoverability** Applications often need to ensure that no matter how the system or application fails, previously saved data is available the next time the application runs.

- **Deadlock avoidance** When multiple threads of control change the database at the same time, there is usually the possibility of deadlock; that is, each of the threads of control owns a resource that another thread wants, so no thread is able to make forward progress—all waiting for a resource. Deadlocks are resolved by having one of the operations involved release the resources it controls so the other operations can proceed. (The operation releasing its resources usually just tries again later.) Transactions are necessary so that any changes that were already made to the database can be undone as part of releasing the held resources.

- **Atomicity** Applications often need to make multiple changes to one or more databases, but want to ensure that either all of the changes happen, or none of them happens. Transactions guarantee that a group of changes are atomic; that is, if the application or system fails, either all the changes to the databases will appear when the application next runs, or none of them will appear.

- **Repeatable reads** Applications sometimes need to ensure that while doing a group of operations on a database, the value returned as a result of a database retrieval doesn't change; that is, if you retrieve the same key more than once, the data item will be the same each time. Transactions guarantee this behavior.

Terminology

The following are some definitions that will be helpful for understanding transactions:

- **Thread of control** Berkeley DB is indifferent to the type or style of threads being used by the application; or, for that matter, if threads are being used at all—because Berkeley DB supports multiprocess access. In the Berkeley DB documentation, any time we refer to a *thread of control*, it can be read as a true thread (one of many in an application's address space) or a process.

- **Free-threaded** A Berkeley DB handle that can be used by multiple threads simultaneously without any application-level synchronization is called *free-threaded*.

- **Transaction** A *transaction* is one or more operations on one or more databases that should be treated as a single unit of work. For example, changes to a set of databases, in which either all of the changes must be applied to the database(s) or none of them should. Applications specify when each transaction starts, what database operations are included in it, and when it ends.

- **Transaction abort/commit**   Every transaction ends by *committing* or *aborting*. If a transaction commits, Berkeley DB guarantees that any database changes included in the transaction will never be lost, even after system or application failure. If a transaction aborts, or is uncommitted when the system or application fails, then the changes involved will never appear in the database.

- **System or application failure**   *System or application failure* is the phrase that we use to describe something bad happening near your data. It can be an application dumping core, being interrupted by a signal, the disk filling up, or the entire system crashing. In any case, for whatever reason, the application can no longer make forward progress, and its databases are left in an unknown state.

- **Recovery**   Whenever system or application failure occurs, the application must run recovery. *Recovery* is what makes the database consistent; that is, the recovery process includes a review of log files and databases to ensure that the changes from each committed transaction appear in the database, and that no changes from an unfinished (or aborted) transaction do.

- **Deadlock**   In its simplest form, deadlock happens when one thread of control owns resource A, but needs resource B; whereas another thread of control owns resource B, but needs resource A. Neither thread of control can make progress, and so one has to give up and release all its resources, at which time the remaining thread of control can make forward progress.

Application Structure

When building transactionally protected applications, there are some special issues that must be considered. The most important one is that if any thread of control exits for any reason while holding Berkeley DB resources, recovery must be performed to do the following:

- Recover the Berkeley DB resources.

- Release any locks or mutexes that may have been held to avoid starvation as the remaining threads of control convoy behind the failed thread's locks.

- Clean up any partially completed operations that may have left a database in an inconsistent or corrupted state.

Complicating this problem is the fact that the Berkeley DB library itself cannot determine whether recovery is required; the application itself must make that decision. A further complication is that recovery *must* be single-threaded; that is, one thread of control or process must perform recovery before any other thread of control or processes attempts to create or join the Berkeley DB environment.

There are two approaches to handling this problem. The first is the hard way. An application can track its own state carefully enough that it knows when recovery needs to be performed. Specifically, the rule to use is that recovery must be performed before using a Berkeley DB environment any time the threads of control previously using the Berkeley DB environment did not shut the environment down cleanly before exiting the environment for any reason (including application or system failure).

Requirements for shutting down the environment cleanly differ, depending on the type of environment created. If the environment is public and persistent (that is, the DB_PRIVATE flag was not specified to the **DBENV→open** function), recovery must be performed if any transaction was not committed or aborted, or **DBENV→close** function was not called for any open DB_ENV handle.

If the environment is private and temporary (that is, the DB_PRIVATE flag was specified to the **DBENV→open** function), recovery must be performed if any transaction was not committed or aborted, or **DBENV→close** function was not called for any open DB_ENV handle. In addition, at least one transaction checkpoint must be performed after all existing transactions have been committed or aborted.

The second method is the easy way. It greatly simplifies matters that recovery may be performed regardless of whether recovery strictly needs to be performed; that is, it is not an error to run recovery on a database in which no recovery is necessary. Because of this fact, it is almost invariably simpler to ignore the previous rules about shutting an application down cleanly, and simply run recovery each time a thread of control accessing a database environment fails for any reason, as well as before accessing any database environment after system reboot.

There are two common ways to build transactionally protected Berkeley DB applications. The most common way is as a single, usually multithreaded, process. This architecture is simplest because it requires no monitoring of other threads of control. When the application starts, it opens and potentially creates the environment, runs recovery (whether it was needed or not), and then opens its databases. From then on, the application can create new threads of control as it chooses. All threads of control share the open Berkeley DB DB_ENV and DB handles. In this model, databases are rarely opened or closed when more than a single thread of control is running; that is, they are opened when only a single thread is running, and closed after all threads but one have exited. The last thread of control to exit closes the databases and the environment.

An alternative way to build Berkeley DB applications is as a set of cooperating processes, which may or may not be multithreaded. This architecture is more complicated.

First, this architecture requires that the order in which threads of control are created and subsequently access the Berkeley DB environment be controlled because recovery must be single-threaded. The first thread of control to access the environment must run recovery, and no other thread should attempt to access the environment until recovery is complete. (Note that this ordering requirement does not apply to environment creation without recovery. If multiple threads attempt to create a Berkeley DB environment, only one will perform the creation and the others will join the already existing environment.)

Second, this architecture requires that threads of control be monitored. If any thread of control that owns Berkeley DB resources exits without first cleanly discarding those resources, recovery is usually necessary. Before running recovery, all threads using the Berkeley DB environment must relinquish all of their Berkeley DB resources (it does not matter if they do so gracefully or because they are forced to exit). Then, recovery can be run and the threads of control continued or restarted.

We have found that the safest way to structure groups of cooperating processes is to first create a single process (often a shell script) that opens/creates the Berkeley DB environment and runs recovery, and that then creates the processes or threads that will actually perform work. The initial thread has no further responsibilities other than to monitor the threads of control it has created, to ensure that none of them unexpectedly exits. If one exits, the initial process then forces all of the threads of control using the Berkeley DB environment to exit, runs recovery, and restarts the working threads of control.

If it is not practical to have a single parent for the processes sharing a Berkeley DB environment, each process sharing the environment should log its connection to and exit from the environment in some fashion that permits a monitoring process to detect whether a thread of control may have potentially acquired Berkeley DB resources and never released them.

Obviously, it is important that the monitoring process in either case be as simple and well-tested as possible because there is no recourse if it fails.

Opening the Environment

Creating transaction-protected applications using the Berkeley DB library is quite easy. Applications first use **DBENV→open** to initialize the database environment. Transaction-protected applications normally require all four Berkeley DB subsystems, so the DB_INIT_MPOOL, DB_INIT_LOCK, DB_INIT_LOG, and DB_INIT_TXN flags should be specified.

Once the application has called **DBENV→open**, it opens its databases within the environment. Once the databases are opened, the application makes changes to the databases inside of transactions. Each set of changes that entails a unit of work should be surrounded by the appropriate **txn_begin**, **txn_commit**, and **txn_abort** calls. The Berkeley DB access methods will make the appropriate calls into the Locking, Logging and Memory Pool subsystems in order to guarantee transaction semantics. When the application is ready to exit, all outstanding transactions should have been committed or aborted.

Databases accessed by a transaction must not be closed during the transaction. Once all outstanding transactions are finished, all open Berkeley DB files should be closed. When the Berkeley DB database files have been closed, the environment should be closed by calling **DBENV→close**.

The following code fragment creates the database environment directory and then opens the environment, running recovery. Our DB_ENV database environment handle is declared to be free-threaded using the DB_THREAD flag, and so may be used by any number of threads that we may subsequently create.

```
#include <sys/types.h>
#include <sys/stat.h>

#include <errno.h>
#include <pthread.h>
#include <stdarg.h>
#include <stdlib.h>
#include <string.h>
#include <unistd.h>

#include <db.h>
#define ENV_DIRECTORY "TXNAPP"

void env_dir_create(void);
void env_open(DB_ENV **);

int
main(int argc, char *argv)
{
        extern char *optarg;
        extern int optind;
        DB *db_cats, *db_color, *db_fruit;
        DB_ENV *dbenv;
        pthread_t ptid;
        int ch;

        while ((ch = getopt(argc, argv, "")) != EOF)
                switch (ch) {
                case '?':
                default:
                        usage();
                }
        argc -= optind;
        argv += optind;

        env_dir_create();
        env_open(&dbenv);

        return (0);
}

void
env_dir_create()
{
        struct stat sb;
```

```
        /*
         * If the directory exists, we're done. We do not further check
         * the type of the file, DB will fail appropriately if it's the
         * wrong type.
         */
        if (stat(ENV_DIRECTORY, &sb) == 0)
                return;

        /* Create the directory, read/write/access owner only. */
        if (mkdir(ENV_DIRECTORY, S_IRWXU) != 0) {
                fprintf(stderr,
                    "txnapp: mkdir: %s: %s\n", ENV_DIRECTORY, strerror(errno));
                exit (1);
        }
}

void
env_open(DB_ENV **dbenvp)
{
        DB_ENV *dbenv;
        int ret;

        /* Create the environment handle. */
        if ((ret = db_env_create(&dbenv, 0)) != 0) {
                fprintf(stderr,
                    "txnapp: db_env_create: %s\n", db_strerror(ret));
                exit (1);
        }
        /* Set up error handling. */
        dbenv→set_errpfx(dbenv, "txnapp");

        /*
         * Open a transactional environment:
         * create if it doesn't exist
         * free-threaded handle
         * run recovery
         * read/write owner only
         */
        if ((ret = dbenv→open(dbenv, ENV_DIRECTORY,
            DB_CREATE | DB_INIT_LOCK | DB_INIT_LOG |
            DB_INIT_MPOOL | DB_INIT_TXN | DB_RECOVER | DB_THREAD,
            S_IRUSR | S_IWUSR)) != 0) {
                dbenv→err(dbenv, ret, "dbenv→open: %s", ENV_DIRECTORY);
                exit (1);
        }
        *dbenvp = dbenv;
}
```

After running this initial program, we can use the **db_stat** utility to display the contents of the environment directory:

```
prompt> db_stat -e -h TXNAPP
3.2.1   Environment version.
120897  Magic number.
```

```
0       Panic value.
1       References.
6       Locks granted without waiting.
0       Locks granted after waiting.
=.=.=.=.=.=.=.=.=.=.=.=.=.=.=.=.=.=.=.=.=.=.=
Mpool Region: 4.
264KB   Size (270336 bytes).
-1      Segment ID.
1       Locks granted without waiting.
0       Locks granted after waiting.
=.=.=.=.=.=.=.=.=.=.=.=.=.=.=.=.=.=.=.=.=.=.=
Log Region: 3.
96KB    Size (98304 bytes).
-1      Segment ID.
3       Locks granted without waiting.
0       Locks granted after waiting.
=.=.=.=.=.=.=.=.=.=.=.=.=.=.=.=.=.=.=.=.=.=.=
Lock Region: 2.
240KB   Size (245760 bytes).
-1      Segment ID.
1       Locks granted without waiting.
0       Locks granted after waiting.
=.=.=.=.=.=.=.=.=.=.=.=.=.=.=.=.=.=.=.=.=.=.=
Txn Region: 5.
8KB     Size (8192 bytes).
-1      Segment ID.
1       Locks granted without waiting.
0       Locks granted after waiting.
```

Opening the Databases

Next, we open three databases ("color," "fruit," and "cats") in the database environment. Again, our DB database handles are declared to be free-threaded using the DB_THREAD flag, and so may be used by any number of threads we subsequently create.

```
int
main(int argc, char *argv)
{
        extern char *optarg;
        extern int optind;
        DB *db_cats, *db_color, *db_fruit;
        DB_ENV *dbenv;
        pthread_t ptid;
        int ch;

        while ((ch = getopt(argc, argv, "")) != EOF)
                switch (ch) {
                case '?':
                default:
                        usage();
                }
        argc -= optind;
        argv += optind;
```

```
        env_dir_create();
        env_open(&dbenv);

        /* Open database: Key is fruit class; Data is specific type. */
        db_open(dbenv, &db_fruit, "fruit", 0);

        /* Open database: Key is a color; Data is an integer. */
        db_open(dbenv, &db_color, "color", 0);

        /*
         * Open database:
         *      Key is a name; Data is: company name, address, cat breeds.
         */
        db_open(dbenv, &db_cats, "cats", 1);

        return (0);
}

void
db_open(DB_ENV *dbenv, DB **dbp, char *name, int dups)
{
        DB *db;
        int ret;

        /* Create the database handle. */
        if ((ret = db_create(&db, dbenv, 0)) != 0) {
                dbenv→err(dbenv, ret, "db_create");
                exit (1);
        }

        /* Optionally, turn on duplicate data items. */
        if (dups && (ret = db→set_flags(db,DB_DUP)) != 0) {
                dbenv→err(dbenv, ret, "db→set_flags: DB_DUP");
                exit (1);
        }

        /*
         * Open a database in the environment:
         *      create if it doesn't exist
         *      free-threaded handle
         *      read/write owner only
         */
        if ((ret = db→open(db, name, NULL,
            DB_BTREE, DB_CREATE | DB_THREAD, S_IRUSR | S_IWUSR)) != 0) {
                dbenv→err(dbenv, ret, "db→open: %s", name);
                exit (1);
        }

        *dbp = db;
}
```

There is no reason to wrap database opens inside of transactions. All database opens are transaction-protected internally to Berkeley DB, and applications using transaction-protected environments can simply rely on files either being successfully re-created in a recovered environment or not appearing at all.

After running this initial code, we can use the **db_stat** utility to display information about a database we have created:

```
prompt> db_stat -h TXNAPP -d color
53162   Btree magic number.
8       Btree version number.
Flags:
2       Minimum keys per-page.
8192    Underlying database page size.
1       Number of levels in the tree.
0       Number of unique keys in the tree.
0       Number of data items in the tree.
0       Number of tree internal pages.
0       Number of bytes free in tree internal pages (0% ff).
1       Number of tree leaf pages.
8166    Number of bytes free in tree leaf pages (0.% ff).
0       Number of tree duplicate pages.
0       Number of bytes free in tree duplicate pages (0% ff).
0       Number of tree overflow pages.
0       Number of bytes free in tree overflow pages (0% ff).
0       Number of pages on the free list.
```

Recoverability and Deadlock Avoidance

The first reason listed for using transactions was recoverability. Any logical change to a database may require multiple changes to underlying data structures. For example, modifying a record in a Btree may require leaf and internal pages to split, so a single **DB→put** method call can potentially require that multiple physical database pages be written. If only some of those pages are written and then the system or application fails, the database is left inconsistent and cannot be used until it has been recovered; that is, until the partially completed changes have been undone.

Write-ahead-logging is the term that describes the underlying implementation that Berkeley DB uses to ensure recoverability. What it means is that before any change is made to a database, information about the change is written to a database log. During recovery, the log is read, and databases are checked to ensure that changes described in the log for committed transactions appear in the database. Changes that appear in the database but are related to aborted or unfinished transactions in the log are undone from the database.

For recoverability after application or system failure, operations that modify the database must be protected by transactions. More specifically, operations are not recoverable unless a transaction is begun and each operation is associated with the transaction via the Berkeley DB interfaces, and then the transaction successfully committed. This is true even if logging is turned on in the database environment.

Here is an example function that updates a record in a database in a transactionally protected manner. The function takes a key and data items as arguments and then attempts to store them into the database.

```
int
main(int argc, char *argv)
{
```

```
        extern char *optarg;
        extern int optind;
        DB *db_cats, *db_color, *db_fruit;
        DB_ENV *dbenv;
        pthread_t ptid;
        int ch;

        while ((ch = getopt(argc, argv, "")) != EOF)
                switch (ch) {
                case '?':
                default:
                        usage();
                }
        argc -= optind;
        argv += optind;

        env_dir_create();
        env_open(&dbenv);

        /* Open database: Key is fruit class; Data is specific type. */
        db_open(dbenv, &db_fruit, "fruit", 0);

        /* Open database: Key is a color; Data is an integer. */
        db_open(dbenv, &db_color, "color", 0);

        /*
         * Open database:
         *      Key is a name; Data is: company name, address, cat breeds.
         */
        db_open(dbenv, &db_cats, "cats", 1);

        add_fruit(dbenv, db_fruit, "apple", "yellow delicious");

        return (0);
}

void
add_fruit(DB_ENV *dbenv, DB *db, char *fruit, char *name)
{
        DBT key, data;
        DB_TXN *tid;
        int ret;

        /* Initialization. */
        memset(&key, 0, sizeof(key));
        memset(&data, 0, sizeof(data));
        key.data = fruit;
        key.size = strlen(fruit);
        data.data = name;
        data.size = strlen(name);
```

```
for (;;) {
        /* Begin the transaction. */
        if ((ret = txn_begin(dbenv, NULL, &tid, 0)) != 0) {
                dbenv→err(dbenv, ret, "txn_begin");
                exit (1);
        }

        /* Store the value. */
        switch (ret = db→put(db, tid, &key, &data, 0)) {
        case 0:
                /* Success: commit the change. */
                if ((ret = txn_commit(tid, 0)) != 0) {
                        dbenv→err(dbenv, ret, "txn_commit");
                        exit (1);
                }
                return;
        case DB_LOCK_DEADLOCK:
                /* Deadlock: retry the operation. */
                if ((ret = txn_abort(tid)) != 0) {
                        dbenv→err(dbenv, ret, "txn_abort");
                        exit (1);
                }
                break;
        default:
                /* Error: run recovery. */
                dbenv→err(dbenv, ret, "dbc→put: %s/%s", fruit, name);
                exit (1);
        }
    }
}
```

The second reason listed for using transactions was deadlock avoidance. Each database operation (that is, any call to a function underlying the handles returned by **DB→open** and **DB→cursor**) is normally performed on behalf of a unique locker. If multiple calls on behalf of the same locker are desired within a single thread of control, transactions must be used. For example, consider the case in which a cursor scan locates a record and then accesses some other item in the database, based on that record. If these operations are done using the default lockers for the handle, they may conflict. If the application wishes to guarantee that the operations do not conflict, locks must be obtained on behalf of a transaction, instead of the default locker ID; and a transaction must be specified to subsequent **DB→cursor** and other Berkeley DB calls.

There is a new error return in this function that you may not have seen before. In Transactional (not Concurrent Data Store) applications supporting both readers and writers, or just multiple writers, Berkeley DB functions have an additional possible error return: DB_LOCK_DEADLOCK. This return means that our thread of control was deadlocked with another thread of control, and our thread was selected to discard all its Berkeley DB resources in order to resolve the problem. In the sample code, any time the **DB→put** function returns DB_LOCK_DEADLOCK, the transaction is aborted (by calling **txn_abort**, which releases the transaction's Berkeley DB resources and undoes any partial changes to the databases) and then the transaction is retried from the beginning.

There is no requirement that the transaction be attempted again, but that is a common course of action for applications. Applications may want to set an upper boundary on the number of times an operation will be retried because some operations on some data sets may simply be unable to succeed. For example, updating all the pages on a large Web site during prime business hours may simply be impossible because of the high access rate to the database.

Atomicity

The third reason listed for using transactions is atomicity. Consider an application suite in which multiple threads of control (multiple processes or threads in one or more processes) are changing the values associated with a key in one or more databases. Specifically, they are taking the current value, incrementing it, and then storing it back into the database.

Such an application requires atomicity. Because we want to change a value in the database, we must make sure that after we read it, no other thread of control modifies it. For example, assume that both thread #1 and thread #2 are doing similar operations in the database, where thread #1 is incrementing records by 3, and thread #2 is incrementing records by 5. We want to increment the record by a total of 8. If the operations interleave in the right (well, wrong) order, that is not what will happen:

```
thread #1   read record: the value is 2

thread #2   read record: the value is 2

thread #2   write record + 5 back into the database (new value 7)

thread #1   write record + 3 back into the database (new value 5)
```

As you can see, instead of incrementing the record by a total of 8, we've incremented it only by 3 because thread #1 overwrote thread #2's change. By wrapping the operations in transactions, we ensure that this cannot happen. In a transaction, when the first thread reads the record, locks are acquired that will not be released until the transaction finishes, guaranteeing that all other readers and writers will block, waiting for the first thread's transaction to complete (or to be aborted).

Here is an example function that does transaction-protected increments on database records to ensure atomicity:

```
int
main(int argc, char *argv)
{
        extern char *optarg;
        extern int optind;
        DB *db_cats, *db_color, *db_fruit;
        DB_ENV *dbenv;
```

```
            pthread_t ptid;
            int ch;


            while ((ch = getopt(argc, argv, "")) != EOF)
                    switch (ch) {
                    case '?':
                    default:
                            usage();
                    }
            argc -= optind;
            argv += optind;

            env_dir_create();
            env_open(&dbenv);

            /* Open database: Key is fruit class; Data is specific type. */
            db_open(dbenv, &db_fruit, "fruit", 0);

            /* Open database: Key is a color; Data is an integer. */
            db_open(dbenv, &db_color, "color", 0);

            /*
             * Open database:
             *      Key is a name; Data is: company name, address, cat breeds.
             */
            db_open(dbenv, &db_cats, "cats", 1);

            add_fruit(dbenv, db_fruit, "apple", "yellow delicious");

            add_color(dbenv, db_color, "blue", 0);
            add_color(dbenv, db_color, "blue", 3);

            return (0);
    }

    void
    add_color(DB_ENV *dbenv, DB *dbp, char *color, int increment)
    {
            DBT key, data;
            DB_TXN *tid;
            int original, ret;
            char buf64;

            /* Initialization. */
            memset(&key, 0, sizeof(key));
            key.data = color;
            key.size = strlen(color);
            memset(&data, 0, sizeof(data));
            data.flags = DB_DBT_MALLOC;
```

```
for (;;) {
      /* Begin the transaction. */
      if ((ret = txn_begin(dbenv, NULL, &tid, 0)) != 0) {
            dbenv→err(dbenv, ret, "txn_begin");
            exit (1);
      }

      /*
       * Get the key. If it exists, we increment the value. If it
       * doesn't exist, we create it.
       */
      switch (ret = dbp→get(dbp, tid, &key, &data, 0)) {
      case 0:
            original = atoi(data.data);
            break;
      case DB_LOCK_DEADLOCK:
            /* Deadlock: retry the operation. */
            if ((ret = txn_abort(tid)) != 0) {
                  dbenv→err(dbenv, ret, "txn_abort");
                  exit (1);
            }
            continue;
      case DB_NOTFOUND:
            original = 0;
            break;
      default:
            /* Error: run recovery. */
            dbenv→err(
                dbenv, ret, "dbc→get: %s/%d", color, increment);
            exit (1);
      }
      if (data.data != NULL)
            free(data.data);

      /* Create the new data item. */
      (void)snprintf(buf, sizeof(buf), "%d", original + increment);
      data.data = buf;
      data.size = strlen(buf) + 1;

      /* Store the new value. */
      switch (ret = dbp→put(dbp, tid, &key, &data, 0)) {
      case 0:
            /* Success: commit the change. */
            if ((ret = txn_commit(tid, 0)) != 0) {
                  dbenv→err(dbenv, ret, "txn_commit");
                  exit (1);
            }
            return;
      case DB_LOCK_DEADLOCK:
            /* Deadlock: retry the operation. */
            if ((ret = txn_abort(tid)) != 0) {
                  dbenv→err(dbenv, ret, "txn_abort");
                  exit (1);
```

```
                    }
                    break;
            default:
                    /* Error: run recovery. */
                    dbenv→err(
                        dbenv, ret, "dbc→put: %s/%d", color, increment);
                    exit (1);
            }
        }
    }
```

Any number of operations on any number of databases can be included in a single transaction to ensure the atomicity of the operations. There is, however, a trade-off between the number of operations included in a single transaction and both throughput and the possibility of deadlock. The reason for this is because transactions acquire locks throughout their lifetime, and do not release the locks until commit or abort time. So, the more operations included in a transaction, the more likely it is that a transaction will block other operations and that deadlock will occur. However, each transaction commit requires a synchronous disk I/O, so grouping multiple operations into a transaction can increase overall throughput. (There is one exception to this. The DB_TXN_NOSYNC option causes transactions to exhibit the ACI (atomicity, consistency and isolation) properties, but not D (durability); avoiding the synchronous disk I/O on transaction commit and greatly increasing transaction throughput for some applications.

When applications do create complex transactions, they often avoid having more than one complex transaction at a time because simple operations such as a single **DB→put** are unlikely to deadlock with each other or the complex transaction; whereas multiple complex transactions are likely to deadlock with each other because they will both acquire many locks over their lifetime. Alternatively, complex transactions can be broken up into smaller sets of operations, and each of those sets may be encapsulated in a nested transaction. Because nested transactions may be individually aborted and retried without causing the entire transaction to be aborted, this allows complex transactions to proceed even in the face of heavy contention, repeatedly trying the suboperations until they succeed.

It is also helpful to order operations within a transaction; that is, access the databases and items within the databases in the same order, to the extent possible, in all transactions. Accessing databases and items in different orders greatly increases the likelihood of operations being blocked and failing due to deadlocks.

Repeatable Reads

The fourth reason listed for using transactions is *repeatable reads*. Generally, most applications do not need to place reads inside a transaction for performance reasons. The problem is that a transactionally protected cursor, reading each key/data pair in a database, will acquire a read lock on most of the pages in the database, and so will gradually block all write operations on the databases until the transaction commits or aborts. Note, however, that if there are update transactions present in the application, the reading transactions must still use locking, and should be prepared to repeat any operation (possibly closing and reopening a cursor) that fails with a return value of DB_LOCK_DEADLOCK.

The exceptions to this rule are when the application is doing a read-modify-write operation and so requires atomicity, and when an application requires the ability to repeatedly access a data item knowing that it will not have changed. A repeatable read simply means that, for the life of the transaction, every time a request is made by any thread of control to read a data item, it will be unchanged from its previous value; that is, that the value will not change until the transaction commits or aborts.

Transactional Cursors

Berkeley DB cursors may be used inside a transaction, exactly as any other DB method. The enclosing transaction ID must be specified when the cursor is created, but it does not then need to be further specified on operations performed using the cursor. One important point to remember is that a cursor must be closed before the enclosing transaction is committed or aborted.

The following code fragment uses a cursor to store a new key in the cats database with four associated data items. The key is a name. The data items are a company name, an address, and a list of the breeds of cat owned. Each of the data entries is stored as a duplicate data item. In this example, transactions are necessary to ensure that either all or none of the data items appear in case of system or application failure:

```
int
main(int argc, char *argv)
{
        extern char *optarg;
        extern int optind;
        DB *db_cats, *db_color, *db_fruit;
        DB_ENV *dbenv;
        pthread_t ptid;
        int ch;

        while ((ch = getopt(argc, argv, "")) != EOF)
                switch (ch) {
                case '?':
                default:
                        usage();
                }
        argc -= optind;
        argv += optind;

        env_dir_create();
        env_open(&dbenv);

        /* Open database: Key is fruit class; Data is specific type. */
        db_open(dbenv, &db_fruit, "fruit", 0);
```

```
        /* Open database: Key is a color; Data is an integer. */
        db_open(dbenv, &db_color, "color", 0);

        /*
         * Open database:
         * Key is a name; Data is: company name, address, cat breeds.
         */
        db_open(dbenv, &db_cats, "cats", 1);

        add_fruit(dbenv, db_fruit, "apple", "yellow delicious");

        add_color(dbenv, db_color, "blue", 0);
        add_color(dbenv, db_color, "blue", 3);

        add_cat(dbenv, db_cats,
                "Amy Adams",
                "Sleepycat Software",
                "394 E. Riding Dr., Carlisle, MA 01741, USA",
                "abyssinian",
                "bengal",
                "chartreaux",
                NULL);

        return (0);
}

  void
add_cat(DB_ENV *dbenv, DB *db, char *name, ...)
{
        va_list ap;
        DBC *dbc;
        DBT key, data;
        DB_TXN *tid;
        int ret;
        char *s;

        /* Initialization. */
        memset(&key, 0, sizeof(key));
        memset(&data, 0, sizeof(data));
        key.data = name;
        key.size = strlen(name);

retry:  /* Begin the transaction. */
        if ((ret = txn_begin(dbenv, NULL, &tid, 0)) != 0) {
                dbenv→err(dbenv, ret, "txn_begin");
                exit (1);
        }

        /* Delete any previously existing item. */
        switch (ret = db→del(db, tid, &key, 0)) {
        case 0:
```

```
case DB_NOTFOUND:
        break;
case DB_LOCK_DEADLOCK:
        /* Deadlock: retry the operation. */
        if ((ret = txn_abort(tid)) != 0) {
                dbenv→err(dbenv, ret, "txn_abort");
                exit (1);
        }
        goto retry;
default:
        dbenv→err(dbenv, ret, "db→del: %s", name);
        exit (1);
}


/* Create a cursor. */
if ((ret = db→cursor(db, tid, &dbc, 0)) != 0) {
        dbenv→err(dbenv, ret, "db→cursor");
        exit (1);
}


/* Append the items, in order. */
va_start(ap, name);
while ((s = va_arg(ap, char *)) != NULL) {
        data.data = s;
        data.size = strlen(s);
        switch (ret = dbc→c_put(dbc, &key, &data, DB_KEYLAST)) {
        case 0:
                break;
        case DB_LOCK_DEADLOCK:
                va_end(ap);

                /* Deadlock: retry the operation. */
                if ((ret = dbc→c_close(dbc)) != 0) {
                        dbenv→err( dbenv, ret, "dbc→c_close");
                        exit (1);
                }
                if ((ret = txn_abort(tid)) != 0) {
                        dbenv→err(dbenv, ret, "txn_abort");
                        exit (1);
                }
                goto retry;
        default:
                /* Error: run recovery. */
                dbenv→err(dbenv, ret, "dbc→put: %s/%s", name, s);
                exit (1);
        }
}
va_end(ap);
```

```
                    /* Success: commit the change. */
                    if ((ret = dbc→c_close(dbc)) != 0) {
                            dbenv→err(dbenv, ret, "dbc→c_close");
                            exit (1);
                    }
                    if ((ret = txn_commit(tid, 0)) != 0) {
                            dbenv→err(dbenv, ret, "txn_commit");
                            exit (1);
                    }
            }
```

Nested Transactions

Berkeley DB provides support for nested transactions. Nested transactions allow an application to decompose a large or long-running transaction into smaller units that may be independently aborted.

Normally, when beginning a transaction, the application will pass a NULL value for the parent argument to **txn_begin**. If, however, the parent argument is a DB_TXN handle, the newly created transaction will be treated as a nested transaction within the parent. Transactions may nest arbitrarily deeply. For the purposes of this discussion, transactions created with a parent identifier will be called *child transactions*.

Once a transaction becomes a parent, as long as any of its child transactions are unresolved (that is, they have neither committed nor aborted), the parent may not issue any Berkeley DB calls except to begin more child transactions, or to commit or abort. For example, it may not issue any access method or cursor calls. After all of a parent's children have committed or aborted, the parent may again request operations on its own behalf.

The semantics of nested transactions are as follows. When a child transaction is begun, it inherits all the locks of its parent. This means that the child will never block waiting on a lock held by its parent. Further, locks held by two children of the same parent will also conflict. To make this concrete, consider the following set of transactions and lock acquisitions.

Transaction T1 is the parent transaction. It acquires a write lock on item A and then begins two child transactions: C1 and C2. C1 also wishes to acquire a write lock on A; this succeeds. If C2 attempts to acquire a write lock on A, it will block until C1 releases the lock, at which point it will succeed. Now, let's say that C1 acquires a write lock on B. If C2 now attempts to obtain a lock on B, it will block. However, let's now assume that C1 commits. Its locks are anti-inherited, which means they are given to T1, so T1 will now hold a lock on B. At this point, C2 would be unblocked and would then acquire a lock on B.

Child transactions are entirely subservient to their parent transaction. They may abort, undoing their operations regardless of the eventual fate of the parent. However, even if a child transaction commits, if its parent transaction is eventually aborted, the child's changes are undone and the child's transaction is effectively aborted. Any child transactions that are not yet resolved when the parent commits or aborts are resolved based on the parent's resolution—committing if the parent commits and aborting if the parent aborts. Any child transactions that are not yet resolved when the parent prepares are also prepared.

Environment Infrastructure

When building transactional applications, it is usually necessary to build an administrative infrastructure around the database environment. There are five components to this infrastructure, and each is supported by the Berkeley DB package in two different ways: a standalone utility and one or more library interfaces.

- Deadlock detection: **db_deadlock, lock_detect, DBENV→set_lk_detect**
- Checkpoints: **db_checkpoint, txn_checkpoint**
- Database and log file archival: **db_archive, log_archive**
- Log file removal: **db_archive, log_archive**
- Recovery procedures: **db_recover, DBENV→open**

When writing multithreaded server applications and/or applications intended for download from the Web, it is usually simpler to create local threads that are responsible for administration of the database environment because scheduling is often simpler in a single-process model, and only a single binary need be installed and run. However, the supplied utilities can be generally useful tools even when the application is responsible for doing its own administration because applications rarely offer external interfaces to database administration. The utilities are required when programming to a Berkeley DB scripting interface because the scripting APIs do not always offer interfaces to the administrative functionality.

Deadlock Detection

The first component of the infrastructure, *deadlock detection*, is not so much a requirement specific to transaction-protected applications, but instead is necessary for almost all applications in which more than a single thread of control will be accessing the database at one time. Although Berkeley DB automatically handles database locking, it is normally possible for deadlock to occur. It is not required by all transactional applications, but exceptions are rare.

When the deadlock occurs, two (or more) threads of control each request additional locks that can never be granted because one of the threads of control waiting holds the requested resource.

For example, consider two processes: A and B. Let's say that A obtains an exclusive lock on item X, and B obtains an exclusive lock on item Y. Then, A requests a lock on Y, and B requests a lock on X. A will wait until resource Y becomes available and B will wait until resource X becomes available. Unfortunately, because both A and B are waiting, neither will release the locks they hold and neither will ever obtain the resource on which it is waiting. In order to detect that deadlock has happened, a separate process or thread must review the locks currently held in the database. If deadlock has occurred, a victim must be selected, and that victim will then return the error DB_LOCK_DEADLOCK from whatever Berkeley DB call it was making.

Berkeley DB provides a separate UNIX-style utility that can be used to perform this deadlock detection, named **db_deadlock**. Alternatively, applications can create their own deadlock utility or thread using the underlying **lock_detect** function, or specify that Berkeley DB run the deadlock detector internally whenever there is a conflict over a lock (see **DBENV→set_lk_detect** for more information). The following code fragment does the latter:

```
void
env_open(DB_ENV **dbenvp)
{
        DB_ENV *dbenv;
        int ret;


        /* Create the environment handle. */
        if ((ret = db_env_create(&dbenv, 0)) != 0) {
                fprintf(stderr,
                    "txnapp: db_env_create: %s\n", db_strerror(ret));
                exit (1);
        }

        /* Set up error handling. */
        dbenv→set_errpfx(dbenv, "txnapp");

        /* Do deadlock detection internally. */
        if ((ret = dbenv→set_lk_detect(dbenv, DB_LOCK_DEFAULT)) != 0) {
                dbenv→err(dbenv, ret, "set_lk_detect:DB_LOCK_DEFAULT");
                exit (1);
        }

        /*
         * Open a transactional environment:
         *      create if it doesn't exist
         *      free-threaded handle
         *      run recovery
         *      read/write owner only
         */
        if ((ret = dbenv→open(dbenv, ENV_DIRECTORY,
            DB_CREATE | DB_INIT_LOCK | DB_INIT_LOG |
            DB_INIT_MPOOL | DB_INIT_TXN | DB_RECOVER | DB_THREAD,
            S_IRUSR | S_IWUSR)) != 0) {
                dbenv >err(dbenv, ret, "dbenv→open: %s", ENV_DIRECTORY);
                exit (1);
        }

        *dbenvp = dbenv;
}
```

Deciding how often to run the deadlock detector and which of the deadlocked transactions will be forced to abort when the deadlock is detected is a common tuning parameter for Berkeley DB applications.

Performing Checkpoints

The second component of the infrastructure is performing checkpoints of the log files. As transactions commit, change records are written into the log files, but the actual changes to the database are not necessarily written to disk. When a checkpoint is performed, the changes to the database that are part of committed transactions are written into the backing database file.

Performing checkpoints is necessary for two reasons. First, you can remove the Berkeley DB log files from your system only after a checkpoint. Second, the frequency of your checkpoints is inversely proportional to the amount of time it takes to run database recovery after a system or application failure.

Once the database pages are written, log files can be archived and removed from the system because they will never be needed for anything other than catastrophic failure. In addition, recovery after system or application failure has to redo or undo changes only since the last checkpoint because changes before the checkpoint have all been flushed to the filesystem.

Berkeley DB provides a separate utility, **db_checkpoint**, which can be used to perform checkpoints. Alternatively, applications can write their own checkpoint utility using the underlying **txn_checkpoint** function. The following code fragment checkpoints the database environment every 60 seconds:

```
int
main(int argc, char *argv)
{
        extern char *optarg;
        extern int optind;
        DB *db_cats, *db_color, *db_fruit;
        DB_ENV *dbenv;
        pthread_t ptid;
        int ch;

        while ((ch = getopt(argc, argv, "")) != EOF)
                switch (ch) {
                case '?':
                default:
                        usage();
                }
        argc -= optind;
        argv += optind;

        env_dir_create();
        env_open(&dbenv);
```

```
        /* Start a checkpoint thread. */
        if ((errno = pthread_create(
            &ptid, NULL, checkpoint_thread, (void *)dbenv)) != 0) {
                fprintf(stderr,
                    "txnapp: failed spawning checkpoint thread: %s\n",
                    strerror(errno));
                exit (1);
        }

        /* Open database: Key is fruit class; Data is specific type. */
        db_open(dbenv, &db_fruit, "fruit", 0);

        /* Open database: Key is a color; Data is an integer. */
        db_open(dbenv, &db_color, "color", 0);

        /*
         * Open database:
         *      Key is a name; Data is: company name, address, cat breeds.
         */
        db_open(dbenv, &db_cats, "cats", 1);

        add_fruit(dbenv, db_fruit, "apple", "yellow delicious");

        add_color(dbenv, db_color, "blue", 0);
        add_color(dbenv, db_color, "blue", 3);

        add_cat(dbenv, db_cats,
                "Amy Adams",
                "Sleepycat Software",
                "118 Tower Rd., Lincoln, MA 01741, USA",
                "abyssinian",
                "bengal",
                "chartreaux",
                NULL);

        return (0);
}

void *
checkpoint_thread(void *arg)
{
        DB_ENV *dbenv;
        int ret;

        dbenv = arg;
        dbenv→errx(dbenv, "Checkpoint thread: %lu", (u_long)pthread_self());

        /* Checkpoint once a minute. */
        for (;; sleep(60))
                switch (ret = txn_checkpoint(dbenv, 0, 0, 0)) {
                case 0:
```

```
        case DB_INCOMPLETE:
             break;
        default:
             dbenv→err(dbenv, ret, "checkpoint thread");
             exit (1);
        }

    /* NOTREACHED */
}
```

Because checkpoints can be quite expensive, choosing how often to perform a checkpoint is a common tuning parameter for Berkeley DB applications.

Database and Log File Archival Procedures

The third component of the administrative infrastructure, archival for catastrophic recovery, concerns the recoverability of the database in the face of catastrophic failure. Recovery after catastrophic failure is intended to minimize data loss when physical hardware has been destroyed—for example, loss of a disk that contains databases or log files. Although the application may still experience data loss in this case, it is possible to minimize it.

First, you may want to periodically create snapshots (that is, backups) of your databases to make it possible to recover from catastrophic failure. These snapshots are either a standard backup, which creates a consistent picture of the databases as of a single instant in time; or an online backup (also known as a *hot* backup), which creates a consistent picture of the databases as of an unspecified instant during the period of time when the snapshot was made. The advantage of a hot backup is that applications may continue to read and write the databases while the snapshot is being taken. The disadvantage of a hot backup is that more information must be archived, and recovery based on a hot backup is to an unspecified time between the start of the backup and when the backup is completed.

Second, after taking a snapshot, you should periodically archive the log files being created in the environment. It is often helpful to think of database archival in terms of full and incremental filesystem backups. A snapshot is a full backup, whereas the periodic archival of the current log files is an incremental backup. For example, it might be reasonable to take a full snapshot of a database environment weekly or monthly, and archive additional log files daily. Using both the snapshot and the log files, a catastrophic crash at any time can be recovered to the time of the most recent log archival; a time long after the original snapshot.

To create a standard backup of your database that can be used to recover from catastrophic failure, take the following steps:

1. Commit or abort all ongoing transactions.

2. Force an environment checkpoint (see **db_checkpoint** for more information).

3. Stop writing your databases until the backup has completed. Read-only operations are permitted, but no write operations and no filesystem operations may be performed (for example, the **DBENV→remove** and **DB→open** functions may not be called).

4. Run **db_archive -l** to identify all the log files, and copy the last one (that is, the one with the highest number) to a backup device such as a CD-ROM, alternate disk, or tape.

5. Run **db_archive -s** to identify all the database data files, and copy them to a backup device such as a CD-ROM, alternate disk, or tape.

   If the database files are stored in a separate directory from the other Berkeley DB files, it may be simpler to archive the directory itself instead of the individual files (see **DBENV→set_data_dir** for additional information). Note: if any of the database files did not have an open DB handle during the lifetime of the current log files, db_archive will not list them in its output! This is another reason it may be simpler to use a separate database file directory and archive the entire directory, instead of archiving only the files listed by **db_archive**.

To create a *hot* backup of your database that can be used to recover from catastrophic failure, take the following steps:

1. Archive your databases, as described in the previous step 4. You do not have to halt ongoing transactions or force a checkpoint. In the case of a hot backup, the utility you use to copy the databases must read database pages atomically (as described in "Berkeley DB Recoverability").

2. When performing a hot backup, you must additionally archive the active log files. Note that the order of these two operations is required, and the database files must be archived before the log files. This means that if the database files and log files are in the same directory, you cannot simply archive the directory; you must make sure that the correct order of archival is maintained.

   To archive your log files, run the **db_archive** utility using the -l option to identify all the database log files, and copy them to your backup media. If the database log files are stored in a separate directory from the other database files, it may be simpler to archive the directory itself instead of the individual files (see the **DBENV→set_lg_dir** function for more information).

Once these steps are completed, your database can be recovered from catastrophic failure (see "Recovery Procedures" for more information).

To update your snapshot so that recovery from catastrophic failure is possible up to a new point in time, repeat step 2 under the hot backup instructions—copying all existing log files to a backup device. This is applicable to both standard and hot backups; that is, you can update snapshots made either way. Each time both the database and log files are copied to backup media, you may discard all previous database snapshots and saved log files. Archiving additional log files does not allow you to discard either previous database snapshots or log files.

The time to restore from catastrophic failure is a function of the number of log records that have been written since the snapshot was originally created. Perhaps more importantly, the more separate pieces of backup media you use, the more likely it is that you will have a problem reading from one of them. For these reasons, it is often best to make snapshots on a regular basis.

Obviously, the reliability of your archive media will affect the safety of your data. For archival safety, ensure that you have multiple copies of your database backups, verify that your archival media is error-free and readable, and that copies of your backups are stored offsite!

The functionality provided by the **db_archive** utility is also available directly from the Berkeley DB library. The following code fragment prints out a list of log and database files that need to be archived:

```
void
log_archlist(DB_ENV *dbenv)
{
        int ret;
        char **begin, **list;

        /* Get the list of database files. */
        if ((ret = log_archive(dbenv,
            &list, DB_ARCH_ABS | DB_ARCH_DATA, NULL)) != 0) {
                dbenv→err(dbenv, ret, "log_archive: DB_ARCH_DATA");
                exit (1);
        }
        if (list != NULL) {
                for (begin = list; *list != NULL; ++list)
                        printf("database file: %s\n", *list);
                free (begin);
        }

        /* Get the list of log files. */
        if ((ret = log_archive(dbenv,
            &list, DB_ARCH_ABS | DB_ARCH_LOG, NULL)) != 0) {
                dbenv→err(dbenv, ret, "log_archive: DB_ARCH_LOG");
                exit (1);
        }
        if (list != NULL) {
                for (begin = list; *list != NULL; ++list)
                        printf("log file: %s\n", *list);
                free (begin);
        }
}
```

Log File Removal

The fourth component of the infrastructure, log file removal, concerns the ongoing disk consumption of the database log files. Depending on the rate at which the application writes to the databases and the available disk space, the number of log files may increase quickly enough so that disk space will be a resource problem. For this reason, you will periodically want to remove log files in order to conserve disk space. This procedure is distinct from database and log file archival for catastrophic recovery, and you cannot remove the current log files simply because you have created a database snapshot or copied log files to archival media.

Log files may be removed at any time, as long as

- the log file is not involved in an active transaction.
- at least two checkpoints have been written subsequent to the log file's creation.
- the log file is not the only log file in the environment.

Obviously, if you are preparing for catastrophic failure, you will want to copy the log files to archival media before you remove them.

To remove log files, take the following steps:

1. If you are concerned with catastrophic failure, first copy the log files to backup media, as described in "Archival for Catastrophic Recovery."

2. Run **db_archive** without options to identify all the log files that are no longer in use (for example, no longer involved in an active transaction).

3. Remove those log files from the system.

The functionality provided by the **db_archive** utility is also available directly from the Berkeley DB library. The following code fragment removes log files that are no longer needed by the database environment:

```
int
main(int argc, char *argv)
{
    ...


        /* Start a logfile removal thread. */
        if ((errno = pthread_create(
            &ptid, NULL, logfile_thread, (void *)dbenv)) != 0) {
                fprintf(stderr,
                    "txnapp: failed spawning log file removal thread: %s\n",
                    strerror(errno));
                exit (1);
        }

    ...

}

void *
logfile_thread(void *arg)
{
        DB_ENV *dbenv;
        int ret;
        char **begin, **list;
```

```
        dbenv = arg;
        dbenv→errx(dbenv,
            "Log file removal thread: %lu", (u_long)pthread_self());

        /* Check once every 5 minutes. */
        for (;; sleep(300)) {
                /* Get the list of log files. */
                if ((ret = log_archive(dbenv, &list, DB_ARCH_ABS, NULL)) != 0) {
                        dbenv→err(dbenv, ret, "log_archive");
                        exit (1);
                }

                /* Remove the log files. */
                if (list != NULL) {
                        for (begin = list; *list != NULL; ++list)
                                if ((ret = remove(*list)) != 0) {
                                        dbenv→err(dbenv,
                                                ret, "remove %s", *list);
                                        exit (1);
                                }
                        free (begin);
                }
        }
        /* NOTREACHED */
}
```

Recovery Procedures

The fifth component of the infrastructure, recovery procedures, concerns the recoverability of the database. After any application or system failure, there are two possible approaches to database recovery:

1. There is no need for recoverability, and all databases can be re-created from scratch. Although these applications may still need transaction protection for other reasons, recovery usually consists of removing the Berkeley DB environment home directory and all files it contains, and then restarting the application.

2. It is necessary to recover information after system or application failure. In this case, recovery processing must be performed on any database environments that were active at the time of the failure. Recovery processing involves running the **db_recover** utility or calling the **DBENV→open** function with the DB_RECOVER or DB_RECOVER_FATAL flags. During recovery processing, all database changes made by aborted or unfinished transactions are undone, and all database changes made by committed transactions are redone, as necessary. Database applications must not be restarted until recovery completes. After recovery finishes, the environment is properly initialized so that applications may be restarted.

If you intend to do recovery, there are two possible types of recovery processing:

- *Catastrophic recovery.* A failure that requires catastrophic recovery is a failure in which either the database or log files are destroyed or corrupted. For example, catastrophic failure includes the case where the disk drive on which either the database or logs are stored has been physically destroyed, or when the system's normal filesystem recovery on startup cannot bring the database and log files to a consistent state. This is often difficult to detect, and is perhaps the most common sign of the need for catastrophic recovery is when the normal recovery procedures fail.

To restore your database environment after catastrophic failure, take the following steps:

1. Restore the most recent snapshots of the database and log files from the backup media into the system directory where recovery will be performed.

2. If any log files were archived since the last snapshot was made, they should be restored into the Berkeley DB environment directory where recovery will be performed. Make sure that you restore them in the order in which they were written. The order is important because it's possible that the same log file appears on multiple backups, and you want to run recovery using the most recent version of each log file.

3. Run the **db_recover** utility, specifying its -c option; or call the **DBENV→open** function, specifying the DB_RECOVER_FATAL flag. The catastrophic recovery process will review the logs and database files to bring the environment databases to a consistent state as of the time of the last uncorrupted log file that is found. It is important to realize that only transactions committed before that date will appear in the databases. It is possible to re-create the database in a location different from the original by specifying appropriate pathnames to the **-h** option of the **db_recover** utility. In order for this to work properly, it is important that your application reference files by names relative to the database home directory or the pathname(s) specified in calls to **DBENV→set_data_dir**, instead of using full path names.

- *Non-catastrophic* or *normal recovery*. If the failure is non-catastrophic and the database files and log are both accessible on a stable filesystem, run the **db_recover** utility without the -c option or call the **DBENV→open** function specifying the DB_RECOVER flag. The normal recovery process will review the logs and database files to ensure that all changes associated with committed transactions appear in the databases, and that all uncommitted transactions do not appear.

Recovery and Filesystem Operations

When running in a transaction-protected environment, database creation and deletion are logged as standalone transactions internal to Berkeley DB. That is, for each such operation, a new transaction is begun and aborted or committed internally, so that they will be recovered during recovery.

The Berkeley DB API supports removing and renaming files. Renaming files is supported by the **DB→rename** method, and removing files is supported by the **DB→remove** method. Berkeley DB does not permit specifying the DB_TRUNCATE flag when opening a file in a transaction-protected environment. This is an implicit file deletion, but one that does not always require the same operating system file permissions as deleting and creating a file do.

If you changed the name of a file or deleted it outside of the Berkeley DB library (for example, you explicitly removed a file using your normal operating system utilities), then it is possible that recovery will not be able to find a database referenced in the log. In this case, **db_recover** will produce a warning message, saying it was unable to locate a file it expected to find. This message is only a warning because the file may have been subsequently deleted as part of normal database operations before the failure occurred, so it is not necessarily a problem.

Generally, any filesystem operations that are performed outside the Berkeley DB interface should be performed at the same time as making a snapshot of the database. To perform filesystem operations correctly, do the following:

1. Cleanly shut down database operations.

    To shut down database operations cleanly, all applications accessing the database environment must be shut down and a transaction checkpoint must be taken. If the applications are not implemented so they can be shut down gracefully (that is, closing all references to the database environment), recovery must be performed after all applications have been killed to ensure that the underlying databases are consistent on disk.

2. Perform the filesystem operations; for example, remove or rename one or more files.

3. Make an archival snapshot of the database.

    Although this step is not strictly necessary, it is strongly recommended. If this step is not performed, recovery from catastrophic failure will require that recovery first be performed up to the time of the filesystem operations, the filesystem operations be redone, and then recovery be performed from the filesystem operations forward.

4. Restart the database applications.

Berkeley DB Recoverability

Berkeley DB recovery is based on write-ahead logging. This means that when a change is made to a database page, a description of the change is written into a log file. This description in the log file is guaranteed to be written to stable storage before the database pages that were changed are written to stable storage. This is the fundamental feature of the logging system that makes durability and rollback work.

If the application or system crashes, the log is reviewed during recovery. Any database changes described in the log that were part of committed transactions and that were never written to the actual database itself are written to the database as part of recovery. Any database changes described in the log that were never committed and that were written to the actual database itself are backed out of the database as part of recovery. This design allows the database to be written lazily, and only blocks from the log file have to be forced to disk as part of transaction commit.

There are two interfaces that are a concern when considering Berkeley DB recoverability:

- The interface between Berkeley DB and the operating system/filesystem.

- The interface between the operating system/filesystem and the underlying stable storage hardware.

Berkeley DB uses the operating system interfaces and its underlying filesystem when writing its files. This means that Berkeley DB can fail if the underlying filesystem fails in some unrecoverable way. Otherwise, the interface requirements here are simple: The system call that Berkeley DB uses to flush data to disk (normally **fsync**(2)) must guarantee that all the information necessary for a file's recoverability has been written to stable storage before it returns to Berkeley DB, and that no possible application or system crash can cause that file to be unrecoverable.

In addition, Berkeley DB implicitly uses the interface between the operating system and the underlying hardware. The interface requirements here are not as simple.

First, it is necessary to consider the underlying page size of the Berkeley DB databases. The Berkeley DB library performs all database writes using the page size specified by the application. These pages are not checksummed, and Berkeley DB assumes that they are written atomically. This means that if the operating system performs filesystem I/O in blocks of different sizes than the database page size, it may increase the possibility for database corruption. For example, assume that Berkeley DB is writing 32KB pages for a database, and the operating system does filesystem I/O in 16KB blocks. If the operating system writes the first 16KB of the database page successfully, but crashes before being able to write the second 16KB of the database, the database has been corrupted and this corruption will not be detected during recovery. For this reason, it may be important to select database page sizes that will be written as single block transfers by the underlying operating system.

Second, it is necessary to consider the behavior of the system's underlying stable storage hardware. For example, consider a SCSI controller that has been configured to cache data and return to the operating system that the data has been written to stable storage, when, in fact, it has only been written into the controller RAM cache. If power is lost before the controller is able to flush its cache to disk, and the controller cache is not stable (that is, the writes will not be flushed to disk when power returns), the writes will be lost. If the writes include database blocks, there is no loss because recovery will correctly update the database. If the writes include log file blocks, it is possible that transactions that were already committed may not appear in the recovered database, although the recovered database will be coherent after a crash.

If the underlying hardware can fail in any way so that only part of the block was written, the failure conditions are the same as those described previously for an operating system failure that writes only part of a logical database block.

For these reasons, it is important to select hardware that does not do partial writes and does not cache data writes (or does not return that the data has been written to stable storage until it has either been written to stable storage or the actual writing of all of the data is guaranteed, barring catastrophic hardware failure—that is, your disk drive exploding). You should also be aware that Berkeley DB does not protect against all cases of stable storage hardware failure, nor does it protect against hardware misbehavior.

If the disk drive on which you are storing your databases explodes, you can perform normal Berkeley DB catastrophic recovery because it requires only a snapshot of your databases plus all of the log files you have archived since those snapshots were taken. In this case, you will lose no database changes at all. If the disk drive on which you are storing your log files explodes, you can still perform catastrophic recovery, but you will lose any database changes that were part of transactions committed since your last archival of the log files. For this reason, storing your databases and log files on different disks should be considered a safety measure as well as a performance enhancement.

Finally, if your hardware misbehaves (for example, if a SCSI controller writes incorrect data to the disk), Berkeley DB will not detect it, and your data may be corrupted.

Transaction Throughput

Generally, the speed of a database system is measured by the *transaction throughput*, expressed as the number of transactions per second. The two gating factors for Berkeley DB performance in a transactional system are usually the underlying database files and the log file. Both are factors because they require disk I/O, which is slow relative to other system resources such as CPU.

In the worst-case scenario:

- Database access is truly random and the database is too large to fit into the cache, resulting in a single I/O per requested key/data pair.
- Both the database and the log are on a single disk.

This means that for each transaction, Berkeley DB is potentially performing several filesystem operations:

- Disk seek to database file
- Database file read
- Disk seek to log file
- Log file write

- Flush log file information to disk
- Disk seek to update log file metadata (for example, inode information)
- Log metadata write
- Flush log file metadata to disk

There are a number of ways to increase transactional throughput, all of which attempt to decrease the number of filesystem operations per transaction:

- Tune the size of the database cache. If the Berkeley DB key/data pairs used during the transaction are found in the database cache, the seek and read from the database are no longer necessary, resulting in two fewer filesystem operations per transaction. To determine whether your cache size is too small, see "Selecting a Cache Size."

- Put the database and the log files on different disks. This allows reads and writes to the log files and the database files to be performed concurrently.

- Set the filesystem configuration so that file access and modification times are not updated. Note that although the file access and modification times are not used by Berkeley DB, they may affect other programs—so be careful.

- Upgrade your hardware. When considering the hardware on which to run your application, however, it is important to consider the entire system. The controller and bus can have as much to do with the disk performance as the disk itself. It is also important to remember that throughput is rarely the limiting factor, and that disk seek times are normally the true performance issue for Berkeley DB.

- Turn on the DB_TXN_NOSYNC flag. This changes the Berkeley DB behavior so that the log files are not flushed when transactions are committed. Although this change will greatly increase your transaction throughput, it means that transactions will exhibit the ACI (atomicity, consistency, and isolation) properties, but not D (durability). Database integrity will be maintained, but it is possible that some of the most recently committed transactions may be undone during recovery instead of being redone.

If you are bottlenecked on logging, the following test will help you confirm that the number of transactions per second that your application does is reasonable for the hardware on which you're running. Your test program should repeatedly perform the following operations:

- Seek to the beginning of a file.
- Write to the file.
- Flush the file write to disk.

The number of times that you can perform these three operations per second is a rough measure of the number of transactions per second of which the hardware is capable. This test simulates the operations applied to the log file. (As a simplifying assumption in this experiment, we assume that the database files are either on a separate disk; or that they fit, with some few exceptions, into the database cache.) We do not have to directly simulate updating the log file directory information because it will normally be updated and flushed to disk as a result of flushing the log file write to disk.

Running this test program, in which we write 256 bytes for 1000 operations on reasonably standard commodity hardware (Pentium II CPU, SCSI disk), returned the following results:

```
% testfile -b256 -o1000
running: 1000 ops
Elapsed time: 16.641934 seconds
1000 ops:    60.09 ops per second
```

Note that the number of bytes being written to the log as part of each transaction can dramatically affect the transaction throughput. The test run used 256, which is a reasonable size log write. Your log writes may be different. To determine your average log write size, use the **db_stat** utility to display your log statistics.

As a quick sanity check, the average seek time is 9.4 msec for this particular disk, and the average latency is 4.17 msec. That results in a minimum requirement for a data transfer to the disk of 13.57 msec, or a maximum of 74 transfers per second. This is close enough to the previous 60 operations per second (which wasn't done on a quiescent disk) that the number is believable.

An implementation of the previous example test program for IEEE/ANSI Std 1003.1 (POSIX) standard systems is included in the Berkeley DB distribution.

10

XA Resource Manager

BERKELEY DB CAN BE USED AS AN XA-COMPLIANT RESOURCE MANAGER. The XA implementation is known to work with the Tuxedo™ transaction manager.

The XA support is encapsulated in the Resource Manager switch db_xa_switch, which defines the following functions:

__db_xa_close	Close the resource manager.
__db_xa_commit	Commit the specified transaction.
__db_xa_complete	Wait for asynchronous operations to complete.
__db_xa_end	Disassociate the application from a transaction.
__db_xa_forget	Forget about a transaction that was heuristically completed. (Berkeley DB does not support heuristic completion.)
__db_xa_open	Open the resource manager.
__db_xa_prepare	Prepare the specified transaction.
__db_xa_recover	Return a list of prepared, but not yet committed transactions.
__db_xa_rollback	Abort the specified transaction.
__db_xa_start	Associate the application with a transaction.

The Berkeley DB resource manager does not support the following optional XA features:

- Asynchronous operations
- Transaction migration

The Tuxedo System is available from BEA Systems, Inc.

For additional information on Tuxedo, see *Building Client/Server Applications Using Tuxedo*, by Hall (John Wiley & Sons, Inc.)

For additional information on XA Resource Managers, see Open CAE Specification *Distributed Transaction Processing: The XA Specification*, X/Open Document Number: XO/CAE/91/300.

For additional information on *The Tuxedo System*, see The Tuxedo System, by Andrade, Carges, Dwyer and Felts (Addison Wesley Longman).

Configuring Berkeley DB with the Tuxedo System

This information assumes that you have already installed the Berkeley DB library.

First, you must update the Resource Manager file in Tuxedo. For the purposes of this discussion, assume that the Tuxedo home directory is in

```
/home/tuxedo
```

In that case, the resource manager file will be located in

```
/home/tuxedo/udataobj/RM
```

Edit the resource manager file, adding the line

```
BERKELEY-DB:db_xa_switch:-L${DB_INSTALL}/lib -ldb \
        -lsocket -ldl -lm
```

where ${DB_INSTALLHOME} is the directory into which you installed the Berkeley DB library.

Note that the previous load options are for a Sun Microsystems Solaris 5.6 Sparc installation of Tuxedo, and may not be correct for your system.

Next, you must build the transaction manager server. To do this, use the Tuxedo **buildtms**(1) utility. The buildtms utility will create the Berkeley DB resource manager in the directory from which it was run. The parameters to buildtms should be

```
buildtms -v -o DBRM -r BERKELEY-DB
```

This will create an executable transaction manager server, DBRM, which is called by Tuxedo to process begins, commits, and aborts.

Finally, you must make sure that your TUXCONFIG environment variable identifies an ubbconfig file that properly identifies your resource managers. In the GROUPS section of the ubb file, you should identify the group's LMID and GRPNO, as well as the transaction manager server name "TMSNAME=DBRM."

You must also specify the OPENINFO parameter, setting it equal to the string

```
rm_name:dir
```

where `rm_name` is the resource name specified in the RM file (that is, BERKELEY-DB) and `dir` is the directory for the Berkeley DB home environment (see **DBENV→open** for a discussion of Berkeley DB environments).

Because Tuxedo Resource Manager startup accepts only a single string for configuration, any environment customization that might have been done via the config parameter to **DBENV→open** must instead be done by placing a DB_CONFIG file in the Berkeley DB environment directory. See "File Naming" in Chapter 7, "Berkeley DB Environment," for further information.

Consider the following configuration. We have built a transaction manager server, as described previously. We want the Berkeley DB environment to be **/home/dbhome**, our database files to be maintained in **/home/datafiles**, our log files to be maintained in **/home/log**, and we want a duplexed server.

The GROUPS section of the ubb file might look like the following:

```
group_tm LMID=myname GRPNO=1 TMSNAME=DBRM TMSCOUNT=2 \
         OPENINFO="BERKELEY-DB:/home/dbhome"
```

There would be a DB_CONFIG configuration file in the directory **/home/dbhome** that contained the following two lines:

```
DB_DATA_DIR    /home/datafiles
DB_LOG_DIR     /home/log
```

Finally, the ubb file must be translated into a binary version using Tuxedo's **tmloadcf**(1) utility, and then the pathname of that binary file must be specified as your TUXCONFIG environment variable.

At this point, your system is properly initialized to use the Berkeley DB resource manager.

See **db_create** for further information on accessing data files using XA.

Frequently Asked Questions

1. **Does converting an application to run within XA change any of the already existing C/C++ API calls it does?**

   When converting an application to run under XA, the application's Berkeley DB calls are unchanged, with two exceptions:

   - The application must use specify the DB_XA_CREATE flag to the **db_create** interface.
   - The application should never explicitly call **txn_commit**, **txn_abort**, or **txn_begin** because those calls are replaced by calls into the Tuxedo transaction manager. For the same reason, the application will always specify a transaction argument of NULL to the Berkeley DB functions that take transaction arguments (for example, **DB→put** or **DB→cursor**).

   Otherwise, your application should be unchanged.

2. **Is it possible to mix XA and non-XA transactions?**

   Yes. It is also possible for XA and non-XA transactions to coexist in the same Berkeley DB environment. To do this, specify the same environment to the non-XA **DBENV→open** calls as was specified in the Tuxedo configuration file.

3. **How does Berkeley DB recovery interact with recovery by the transaction manager?**

   When the Tuxedo recovery calls the Berkeley DB recovery functions, the standard Berkeley DB recovery procedures occur for all operations that are represented in the Berkeley DB log files. This includes any non-XA transactions that were performed in the environment. Of course, this means that you can't use the standard Berkeley DB utilities (for example, **db_recover**) to perform recovery.

   Also, standard log file archival and catastrophic recovery procedures should occur independently of XA operation.

11

Programmer Notes

Application signal handling: When applications using Berkeley DB receive signals, it is important that they exit gracefully, discarding any Berkeley DB locks that they may hold. This is normally done by setting a flag when a signal arrives and then checking for that flag periodically within the application. Because Berkeley DB is not re-entrant, the signal handler should not attempt to release locks and/or close the database handles itself. Re-entering Berkeley DB is not guaranteed to work correctly, and the results are undefined.

If an application exits holding a lock, the situation is no different than if the application crashed, and all applications participating in the database environment must be shut down and then recovery must be performed. If this is not done, databases may be left in an inconsistent state, or locks the application held may cause unresolveable deadlocks inside the environment, causing applications to hang.

Error Returns to Applications

Except for the historic **dbm**, **ndbm**, and **hsearch** interfaces, Berkeley DB does not use the global variable **errno** to return error values. The return values for all Berkeley DB functions are grouped into the following three categories:

- 0   A return value of 0 indicates that the operation was successful.

- > 0   A return value that is greater than 0 indicates that there was a system error. The **errno** value returned by the system is returned by the function; for example, when a Berkeley DB function is unable to allocate memory, the return value from the function will be ENOMEM.

- < 0   A return value that is less than 0 indicates a condition that was not a system failure, but was not an unqualified success, either. For example, a routine to retrieve a key/data pair from the database may return DB_NOTFOUND when the key/data pair does not appear in the database; as opposed to the value of 0, which would be returned if the key/data pair were found in the database.

All values returned by Berkeley DB functions are less than 0 in order to avoid conflict with possible values of **errno**. Specifically, Berkeley DB reserves all values from -30,800 to -30,999 to itself as possible error values. There are a few Berkeley DB interfaces where it is possible for an application function to be called by a Berkeley DB function and subsequently fail with an application-specific return. Such failure returns will be passed back to the function that originally called a Berkeley DB interface. To avoid ambiguity about the cause of the error, error values separate from the Berkeley DB error name space should be used.

Although possible error returns are specified by each individual function's manual page, there are a few error returns that deserve special mention:

DB_NOTFOUND and DB_KEYEMPTY

There are two special return values that are similar in meaning and are returned in similar situations, and therefore might be confused: DB_NOTFOUND and DB_KEYEMPTY.

The DB_NOTFOUND error return indicates that the requested key/data pair did not exist in the database or that start-of- or end-of-file has been reached by a cursor.

The DB_KEYEMPTY error return indicates that the requested key/data pair logically exists but was never explicitly created by the application (the Recno and Queue access methods will automatically create key/data pairs under some circumstances; see **DB→open** for more information), or that the requested key/data pair was deleted and never re-created. In addition, the Queue access method will return DB_KEYEMPTY for records that were created as part of a transaction that was later aborted and never re-created.

DB_LOCK_DEADLOCK

When multiple threads of control are modifying the database, there is normally the potential for deadlock. In Berkeley DB, *deadlock* is signified by an error return from the Berkeley DB function of the value DB_LOCK_DEADLOCK. Whenever a Berkeley DB function returns DB_LOCK_DEADLOCK, the enclosing transaction should be aborted.

Any Berkeley DB function that attempts to acquire locks can potentially return DB_LOCK_DEADLOCK. Practically speaking, the safest way to deal with applications that can deadlock is to handle a DB_LOCK_DEADLOCK return from any Berkeley DB access method call.

DB_LOCK_NOTGRANTED

When multiple threads of control are modifying the database, there is normally the potential for deadlock. In order to avoid deadlock, applications may specify—on a per-transaction basis—that if a lock is unavailable, the Berkeley DB operation should return immediately instead of waiting on the lock. The error return in this case will be DB_LOCK_NOTGRANTED. Whenever a Berkeley DB function returns DB_LOCK_NOTGRANTED, the enclosing transaction should be aborted.

DB_RUNRECOVERY

There exists a class of errors that Berkeley DB considers fatal to an entire Berkeley DB environment. An example of this type of error is a corrupted database or a log write failure because the disk is out of free space. The only way to recover from these failures is to have all threads of control exit the Berkeley DB environment, run recovery of the environment, and re-enter Berkeley DB. (It is not strictly necessary that the processes exit, although that is the only way to recover system resources, such as file descriptors and memory, allocated by Berkeley DB.)

When this type of error is encountered, the error value DB_RUNRECOVERY is returned. This error can be returned by any Berkeley DB interface. Once DB_RUNRECOVERY is returned by any interface, it will be returned from all subsequent Berkeley DB calls made by any threads of control participating in the environment.

Optionally, applications may also specify a fatal-error callback function using the **DBENV→set_paniccall** function. This callback function will be called with two arguments: a reference to the DB_ENV structure associated with the environment and the errno value associated with the underlying **error** that caused the problem.

Applications can handle such fatal errors in one of two ways: by checking for DB_RUNRECOVERY as part of their normal Berkeley DB error return checking, similarly to DB_LOCK_DEADLOCK or any other error, or by simply exiting the application when the callback function is called in applications that have no cleanup processing of their own.

Environmental Variables

The Berkeley DB library uses the following environmental variables:

- DB_HOME   If the environmental variable DB_HOME is set, it is used as part of file naming. Note: For the DB_HOME variable to take effect, either the DB_USE_ENVIRON or DB_USE_ENVIRON_ROOT flags must be specified to **DBENV→open**.

- TMPDIR, TEMP, TMP, TempFolder   The TMPDIR, TEMP, TMP, and TempFolder environmental variables are all checked as locations in which to create temporary files. See **DBENV→set_tmp_dir** for more information.

Building Multithreaded Applications

Berkeley DB fully supports multithreaded applications. The Berkeley DB library is not itself multithreaded because it was deliberately architected to not use threads internally because of the portability problems it would introduce. Environmental and database object handles returned from Berkeley DB library functions are free-threaded. No other object handles returned from the Berkeley DB library are free-threaded. The following rules should be observed when using threads to access the Berkeley DB library:

1. The DB_THREAD flag must be specified to the **DBENV→open** and **DB→open** functions if the Berkeley DB handles returned by those interfaces will be used in the context of more than one thread. Setting the DB_THREAD flag inconsistently may result in database corruption.

    Threading is assumed in the Java API, so no special flags are required; and Berkeley DB functions will always behave as if the DB_THREAD flag was specified.

    Only a single thread may call the **DBENV→close** or **DB→close** functions for a returned environment or database handle.

    No other Berkeley DB handles are free-threaded; for example, cursors and trans-actions may not span threads because their returned handles are not free-threaded.

2. When using the non-cursor Berkeley DB calls to retrieve key/data items (for example, **DB→get**), the memory referenced by the pointer stored into the Dbt is valid only until the next call using the DB handle returned by **DB→open**. This includes **any** use of the returned DB handle, including by another thread within the process.

    For this reason, if the DB_THREAD handle was specified to the **DB→open** function, either DB_DBT_MALLOC, DB_DBT_REALLOC, or DB_DBT_USERMEM must be specified in the **DBT** when performing any non-cursor key or data retrieval.

3. The DB_CURRENT, DB_NEXT, and DB_PREV flags to the **log_get** function may not be used by a free-threaded handle. If such calls are necessary, a thread should explicitly create a unique environment handle by separately calling **DBENV→open** without specifying DB_THREAD.

4. Transactions may not span threads. Each transaction must begin and end in the same thread, and each transaction may be used only by a single thread.

   Cursors may not span transactions or threads. Each cursor must be allocated and deallocated within the same transaction and within the same thread.

5. User-level synchronization mutexes must have been implemented for the compiler/architecture combination. Attempting to specify the DB_THREAD flag will fail if fast mutexes are not available.

   If blocking mutexes are available (for example, POSIX pthreads), they will be used. Otherwise, the Berkeley DB library will make a system call to pause for some amount of time when it is necessary to wait on a lock. This may not be optimal, especially in a thread-only environment, in which it will be more efficient to explicitly yield the processor to another thread.

   It is possible to specify a yield function on an per-application basis. See **db_env_set_func_yield** for more information.

   It is possible to specify the number of attempts that will be made to acquire the mutex before waiting. See **db_env_set_tas_spins** for more information.

Berkeley DB Handles

The Berkeley DB library has a number of object handles. The following table lists those handles, their scope, and whether they are free-threaded (that is, whether multiple threads within a process can share them).

- DB_ENV   The DB_ENV handle, created by the **db_env_create** function, references a Berkeley DB database environment—a collection of databases and Berkeley DB subsystems. DB_ENV handles are free-threaded if the DB_THREAD flag is specified to the **DBENV→open** function when the environment is opened. The handle should not be closed while any other handle remains open that is using it as a reference (for example, DB or DB_TXN). Once either the **DBENV→close** or **DBENV→remove** functions are called, the handle may not be accessed again, regardless of the function's return.

- DB_TXN   The DB_TXN handle, created by the **txn_begin** function, references a single transaction. The handle is not free-threaded; and transactions may not span threads, nor may transactions be used by more than a single thread. Once the **txn_abort** or **txn_commit** functions are called, the handle may not be accessed again, regardless of the function's return. In addition, parent transactions may not issue any Berkeley DB operations while it has active child transactions (child transactions that have not yet been committed or aborted) except for **txn_begin**, **txn_abort**, and **txn_commit**.

- DB_MPOOLFILE   The DB_MPOOLFILE handle references an open file in the shared memory buffer pool of the database environment. The handle is not free-threaded. Once the **memp_fclose** function is called, the handle may not be accessed again, regardless of the function's return.

- DB   The DB handle, created by the **db_create** function, references a single Berkeley DB database, which may or may not be part of a database environment. DB handles are free-threaded if the DB_THREAD flag is specified to the **DB→open** function when the database is opened or if the database environment in which the database is opened is free-threaded. The handle should not be closed while any other handle that references the database is in use; for example, database handles must not be closed while cursor handles into the database remain open, or transactions that include operations on the database have not yet been committed or aborted. Once the **DB→close**, **DB→remove**, or **DB→rename** functions are called, the handle may not be accessed again, regardless of the function's return.

- DBC   The DBC handle references a cursor into a Berkeley DB database. The handle is not free-threaded, and cursors may not span threads; nor may cursors be used by more than a single thread. If the cursor is to be used to perform operations on behalf of a transaction, the cursor must be opened and closed within the context of that single transaction. Once **DBcursor→c_close** has been called, the handle may not be accessed again, regardless of the function's return.

Name Spaces

C Language Name Space

The Berkeley DB library is careful to avoid C language programmer name spaces, but there are a few potential areas for concern, mostly in the Berkeley DB include file db.h. The db.h include file defines a number of types and strings. Where possible, all of these types and strings are prefixed with "DB_" or "db_". There are a few notable exceptions.

The Berkeley DB library uses a macro named "__P" to configure for systems that do not provide ANSI C function prototypes. This could potentially collide with other systems using a "__P" macro for similar or different purposes.

The Berkeley DB library needs information about specifically sized types for each architecture. If they are not provided by the system, they are typedef'd in the db.h include file. The types that may be typedef'd by db.h include the following: u_int8_t, int16_t, u_int16_t, int32_t, u_int32_t, u_char, u_short, u_int, and u_long.

The Berkeley DB library declares a number of external routines. All these routines are prefixed with the strings "db_", "lock_", "log_", "memp_" or "txn_". All internal routines are prefixed with the strings "__db_", "__lock_," "__log_", "__memp_", or "__txn_".

Filesystem Name Space

Berkeley DB environments create or use some number of files in environment home directories. These files are named DB_CONFIG, "log.NNNNNNNNNN" (for example, log.0000000003), or with the string prefix "__db" (for example, __db.001). Database files that match these names should not be created in the environment directory.

Copying Databases

Because file identification cookies (for example, filenames, device and inode numbers, volume and file IDs, and so on) are not necessarily unique or maintained across system reboots, each Berkeley DB database file contains a 20-byte file identification bytestring that is stored in the first page of the database, starting with the fifty-third byte on the page. When multiple processes or threads open the same database file in Berkeley DB, it is this bytestring that is used to ensure that the same underlying pages are updated in the shared memory buffer pool, no matter which Berkeley DB handle is used for the operation.

It is usually a bad idea to physically copy a database to a new name. In the few cases in which copying is the best solution for your application, you must guarantee that there are never two different databases with the same file identification bytestring in the memory pool at the same time. Copying databases is further complicated by the fact that the shared memory buffer pool does not discard all cached copies of pages for a database when the database is logically closed; that is, when **DB→close** is called. Nor is there a Berkeley DB interface to explicitly discard pages from the shared memory buffer pool for any particular database.

Before copying a database, you must ensure that all modified pages have been written from the memory pool cache to the backing database file. This is done using the **DB→sync** or **DB→close** interfaces.

Before using a copy of a database from Berkeley DB, you must ensure that all pages from any database with the same bytestring have been removed from the memory pool cache. If the environment in which you intend to open the copy of the database potentially has pages from files with identical bytestrings to the copied database (which is likely to be the case), there are a few possible solutions:

1. Remove the environment, either explicitly or by calling **DBENV→remove**. Note that this will not allow you to access both the original and copy of the database at the same time.

2. Create a new file that will have a new bytestring. The simplest way to create a new file that will have a new bytestring is to call the **db_dump** utility to dump out the contents of the database and then use the **db_load** utility to load the dumped output into a new filename. This allows you to access both the original and copy of the database at the same time.

3. If your database is too large to be copied, overwrite the bytestring in the copied database with a new bytestring. This allows you to access both the original and copy of the database at the same time.

Library Version Information

Each release of the Berkeley DB library has a major version number, a minor version number, and a patch number.

The *major version number* changes only when major portions of the Berkeley DB functionality have been changed. In this case, it may be necessary to significantly modify applications in order to upgrade them to use the new version of the library.

The *minor version number* changes when Berkeley DB interfaces have changed, and the new release is not entirely backward-compatible with previous releases. To upgrade applications to the new version, they must be recompiled and minor modifications may be made (for example, the order of arguments to a function might have changed).

The *patch number* changes on each release. If only the patch number has changed in a release, applications do not need to be recompiled, and they can be upgraded to the new version by installing the new version of a shared library or by relinking the application to the new version of a static library.

Internal Berkeley DB interfaces may change at any time and during any release, without warning. This means that the library must be entirely recompiled and reinstalled when upgrading to new releases of the library because there is no guarantee that modules from the current version of the library will interact correctly with modules from a previous release.

To retrieve the Berkeley DB version information, applications should use the **db_version** interface. In addition to the previous information, the **db_version** interface returns a string encapsulating the version information, suitable for display to a user.

Compatibility with Historic UNIX Interfaces

The Berkeley DB version 2 library provides backward-compatible interfaces for the historic UNIX **dbm**, **ndbm**, and **hsearch** interfaces. It also provides a backward-compatible interface for the historic Berkeley DB 1.85 release.

Berkeley DB version 2 does not provide database compatibility for any of the previous interfaces, and existing databases must be converted manually. To convert existing databases from the Berkeley DB 1.85 format to the Berkeley DB version 2 format, review the **db_dump185** and **db_load** information. No utilities are provided to convert UNIX **dbm**, **ndbm**, or **hsearch** databases.

Recovery Implementation

The physical recovery process works as follows: First, find the last checkpoint that completed. Because the system may have crashed while writing a checkpoint, this implies finding the second-to-last checkpoint in the log files. Read forward from this checkpoint, opening any database files for which modifications are found in the log.

Then, read backward from the end of the log. For each commit record encountered, record its transaction ID. For every other data update record, find the transaction ID of the record. If that transaction ID appears in the list of committed transactions, do nothing; if it does not appear in the committed list, call the appropriate recovery routine to undo the operation.

In the case of catastrophic recovery, this roll-backward pass continues through all the present log files. In the case of normal recovery, this pass continues until we find a checkpoint written before the second-to-last checkpoint described previously.

When the roll-backward pass is complete, the roll-forward pass begins at the point where the roll-backward pass ended. Each record is read, and if its transaction ID is in the committed list, the appropriate recovery routine is called to redo the operation if necessary.

In a distributed transaction environment, there may be transactions that are prepared, but not yet committed. If these transactions are XA transactions, they are rolled forward to their current state; and an active transaction corresponding to it is entered in the transaction table so that the XA transaction manager may call either transaction abort or commit, depending on the outcome of the overall transaction. If the transaction is not an XA transaction, it is aborted as any other transactions would be.

Application-Specific Logging and Recovery

Berkeley DB includes tools to assist in the development of application-specific logging and recovery. Specifically, given a description of the information to be logged, these tools will automatically create logging functions (functions that take the values as parameters and construct a single record that is written to the log), read functions (functions that read a log record and unmarshall the values into a structure that maps onto the values you chose to log), a print function (for debugging), templates for the recovery functions, and automatic dispatching to your recovery functions.

Defining Application-Specific Operations

Log records are described in files named XXX.src, where "XXX" is a unique prefix. The prefixes currently used in the Berkeley DB package are btree, crdel, db, hash, log, qam, and txn. These files contain interface definition language descriptions for each type of log record that is supported.

All lines beginning with a hash character in **.src** files are treated as comments.

The first non-comment line in the file should begin with the keyword PREFIX, followed by a string that will be prepended to every function. Frequently, the PREFIX is either identical or similar to the name of the **.src** file.

The rest of the file consists of one or more log record descriptions. Each log record description begins with the line

```
BEGIN RECORD_NAME RECORD_NUMBER
```

and ends with the line

```
END
```

The RECORD_NAME variable should be replaced with a unique record name for this log record. Record names must be unique within **.src** files.

The RECORD_NUMBER variable should be replaced with a record number. Record numbers must be unique for an entire application; that is, both application-specific and Berkeley DB log records must have unique values. Further, because record numbers are stored in log files, which often must be portable across application releases, no record number should ever be reused. The record number space below 10,000 is reserved for Berkeley DB itself; applications should choose record number values equal to or greater than 10,000.

Between the BEGIN and END keywords there should be one line for each data item that will be logged in this log record. The format of these lines is as follows:

```
ARG ¦ DBT ¦ POINTER    variable_name    variable_type    printf_format
```

The keyword ARG indicates that the argument is a simple parameter of the type specified. The keyword DBT indicates that the argument is a DBT containing a length and pointer to a byte string. The keyword PTR indicates that the argument is a pointer to the data type specified, and the entire type should be logged.

The variable name is the field name within the structure that will be used to reference this item. The variable type is the C type of the variable, and the printf format should be "s" for string, "d" for signed integral type, or "u" for unsigned integral type.

Automatically Generated Functions

For each log record description found in the file, the following structure declarations and #defines will be created in the file PREFIX_auto.h:

```
#define DB_PREFIX_RECORD_TYPE        /* Integer ID number */


typedef struct _PREFIX_RECORD_TYPE_args {
  /*
   * These three fields are generated for every record.
   */
  u_int32_t type; /* Record type used for dispatch. */

  /*
```

```
     * Transaction handle that identifies the transaction on whose
     * behalf the record is being logged.
     */
    DB_TXN *txnid;

    /*
     * The log sequence number returned by the previous call to log_put
     * for this transaction.
     */
    DB_LSN *prev_lsn;

    /*
     * The rest of the structure contains one field for each of
     * the entries in the record statement.
     */
};
```

The DB_PREFIX_RECORD_TYPE should be described as an offset from the library provided DB_user_BEGIN #define (this is the value of the first identifier available to users outside of the Berkeley DB library).

In addition to the PREFIX_auto.h file, a file named PREFIX_auto.c is created, containing the following functions for each record type.

Log Function

The log function has the following parameters:

- dbenv The environment handle returned by **db_env_create**.
- txnid   The transaction identifier for the transaction handle returned by **txn_begin**.
- lsnp   A pointer to storage for a log sequence number into which the log sequence number of the new log record will be returned.
- syncflag   A flag indicating whether the record must be written synchronously. Valid values are 0 and DB_FLUSH.

The log function marshalls the parameters into a buffer, and calls **log_put** on that buffer returning 0 on success and non-zero on failure.

Read Function

The read function has the following parameters:

- recbuf   A buffer.
- argp   A pointer to a structure of the appropriate type.

The read function takes a buffer and unmarshalls its contents into a structure of the appropriate type. It returns 0 on success and non-zero on error. After the fields of the structure have been used, the pointer returned from the read function should be freed.

Recovery Function

The recovery function has the following parameters:

- dbenv   The handle returned from the **db_env_create** call, which identifies the environment in which recovery is running.
- rec   The **rec** parameter is the record being recovered.
- lsn   The log sequence number of the record being recovered.
- op   A parameter of type db_recops, which indicates what operation is being run (DB_TXN_OPENFILES, DB_TXN_ABORT, DB_TXN_BACK-WARD_ROLL, DB_TXN_FORWARD_ROLL).
- info   A structure passed by the dispatch function. It is used to contain a list of committed transactions and information about files that may have been deleted.

The recovery function is called on each record read from the log during system recovery or transaction abort.

The recovery function is created in the file PREFIX_rtemp.c because it contains templates for recovery functions. The actual recovery functions must be written manually, but the templates usually provide a good starting point.

Print Function

The print function takes the same parameters as the recover function, so it is simple to dispatch both to simple print functions as well as to the actual recovery functions. This is useful for debugging purposes, and is used by the **db_printlog** utility to produce a human-readable version of the log. All parameters except the **rec** and **lsnp** parameters are ignored. The **rec** parameter contains the record to be printed.

Initialization Function

One additional function, an initialization function, is created for each **.src** file. It has the following parameters:

- dbenv   The environment handle returned by **db_env_create**.

The recovery initialization function registers each log record type declared with the recovery system, so the appropriate function is called during recovery.

Using Automatically Generated Routines

Applications use the automatically generated functions, as follows:

1. When the application starts, call the **DBENV→set_recovery_init** with your recovery initialization function so that the initialization function is called at the appropriate time.
2. Issue a **txn_begin** call before any operations you wish to be transaction-protected.

3. Before accessing any data, issue the appropriate lock call to lock the data (either for reading or writing).

4. Before modifying any data that is transaction-protected, issue a call to the appropriate log function.

5. Issue a **txn_commit** to save all the changes, or a **txn_abort** to cancel all of the modifications.

The recovery functions (described as follows) can be called in two cases:

- From the recovery daemon upon system failure, with op set to DB_TXN_FORWARD_ROLL or DB_TXN_BACKWARD_ROLL.

- From **txn_abort** if it is called to abort a transaction, with op set to DB_TXN_ABORT.

For each log record type you declare, you must write the appropriate function to undo and redo the modifications. The shell of these functions will be generated for you automatically, but you must fill in the details.

Your code should be able to detect whether the described modifications have been applied to the data. The function will be called with the "op" parameter set to DB_TXN_ABORT when a transaction that wrote the log record aborts, and with DB_TXN_FORWARD_ROLL and DB_TXN_BACKWARD_ROLL during recovery. The actions for DB_TXN_ABORT and DB_TXN_BACKWARD_ROLL should generally be the same.

For example, each page in the access methods contains the log sequence number of the most recent log record that describes a modification to the page. When the access method changes a page, it writes a log record describing the change and including the log sequence number (LSN) that was on the page before the change. This LSN is referred to as the previous LSN. The recovery functions read the page described by a log record, and compare the LSN on the page to the LSN they were passed. If the page LSN is less than the passed LSN and the operation is an undo, no action is necessary (because the modifications have not been written to the page). If the page LSN is the same as the previous LSN and the operation is a redo, the actions described are reapplied to the page. If the page LSN is equal to the passed LSN and the operation is an undo, the actions are removed from the page; if the page LSN is greater than the passed LSN and the operation is a redo, no further action is necessary. If the action is a redo and the LSN on the page is less than the previous LSN in the log record, it is an error because it could happen only if some previous log record was not processed.

Please refer to the internal recovery functions in the Berkeley DB library (found in files named XXX_rec.c) for examples of the way recovery functions should work.

Nonconformant Logging

If your application cannot conform to the default logging and recovery structure, you will have to create your own logging and recovery functions explicitly.

First, you must decide how you will dispatch your records. Encapsulate this algorithm in a dispatch function that is passed to **DBENV→open**. The arguments for the dispatch function are as follows:

- dbenv   The environment handle returned by **db_env_create**.
- rec   The record being recovered.
- lsn   The log sequence number of the record to be recovered.
- op   Indicates what operation of recovery is needed (openfiles, abort, forward roll, or backward roll).
- info   An opaque value passed to your function during system recovery.

When you abort a transaction, **txn_abort** reads the last log record written for the aborting transaction and then calls your dispatch function. It continues looping, calling the dispatch function on the record whose LSN appears in the lsn parameter of the dispatch call (until a NULL LSN is placed in that field). The dispatch function will be called with the op set to DB_TXN_ABORT.

Your dispatch function can do any processing necessary. See the code in db/db_dispatch.c for an example dispatch function (that is based on the assumption that the transaction ID, previous LSN, and record type appear in every log record written).

If you do not use the default recovery system, you need to construct your own recovery process based on the recovery program provided in db_recover/db_recover.c. Note that your recovery functions need to correctly process the log records produced by calls to **txn_begin** and **txn_commit**.

Run-Time Configuration

There are a few interfaces that support run-time configuration of Berkeley DB. First is a group of interfaces that allow applications to intercept Berkeley DB requests for underlying library or system call functionality:

```
db_env_set_func_close
db_env_set_func_dirfree
db_env_set_func_dirlist
db_env_set_func_exists
db_env_set_func_free
db_env_set_func_fsync
db_env_set_func_ioinfo
db_env_set_func_malloc
db_env_set_func_map
db_env_set_func_open
db_env_set_func_read
db_env_set_func_realloc
db_env_set_func_seek
db_env_set_func_sleep
db_env_set_func_unlink
db_env_set_func_unmap
db_env_set_func_write
db_env_set_func_yield
```

These interfaces are available only from the Berkeley DB C language API.

In addition, there are a few interfaces that allow applications to reconfigure Berkeley DB behaviors on an application-wide basis.

DBENV→set_mutexlocks
db_env_set_pageyield
db_env_set_panicstate
db_env_set_region_init
db_env_set_tas_spins

These interfaces are available from all the Berkeley DB programmatic APIs.

A not-uncommon problem for applications is the new API in Solaris 2.6 for manipulating large files. Because this API was not part of Solaris 2.5, it is difficult to create a single binary that takes advantage of the large file functionality in Solaris 2.6, but still runs on Solaris 2.5. Example code that supports this is included in the Berkeley DB distribution.

12

The Locking Subsystem

THE LOCKING SUBSYSTEM PROVIDES INTERPROCESS and intraprocess concurrency control mechanisms. Although the Locking system is used extensively by the Berkeley DB Access Methods and Transaction system, it may also be used as a standalone subsystem to provide concurrency control to any set of designated resources.

The Locking subsystem is created, initialized, and opened by calls to **DBENV→open** with the DB_INIT_LOCK or DB_INIT_CDB flags specified.

The **lock_detect** function provides the programmatic interface to the Berkeley DB deadlock detector. Whenever two threads of control issue lock requests that are not carefully ordered or that require upgrading locks (obtaining write locks on objects that are already read-locked), the possibility for deadlock arises. A deadlock occurs when two or more threads of control are blocked, waiting for actions that another one of these blocked threads must take. For example, assume that threads one and two have each obtained read locks on object A. Now, suppose that both threads wish to obtain write locks on object A. Neither thread can be granted its write lock (because of the other thread's read lock). Both threads block and will never unblock because the event for which they are waiting can never happen.

The deadlock detector examines all the locks held in the environment, and identifies situations where no thread can make forward progress. It then selects one of the participants in the deadlock (according to the argument that was specified to **DBENV→set_lk_detect**), and forces it to return the value DB_LOCK_DEAD-LOCK, which indicates that a deadlock occurred. The thread receiving such an error should abort its current transaction or simply release all its locks if it is not running in a transaction, and retry the operation.

The **lock_vec** interface is used to acquire and release locks. The **lock_vec** function performs any number of lock operations atomically. It also provides the capability to release all locks held by a particular locker and release all the locks on a particular object. Performing multiple lock operations atomically is useful in performing Btree traversals—you want to acquire a lock on a child page and, once acquired, immediately release the lock on its parent (this is traditionally referred to as *lock-coupling*).

Two additional interfaces, **lock_get** and **lock_put**, are provided. These interfaces are simpler front-ends to the **lock_vec** functionality, where **lock_get** acquires a lock, and **lock_put** releases a lock that was acquired using **lock_get** or **lock_vec**. Using **lock_vec** instead of separate calls to **lock_put** and **lock_get** reduces the synchronization overhead between multiple threads or processes.

The application must specify lockers and lock objects appropriately. When used with the Berkeley DB Access Methods, these lockers and objects are handled completely internally, but an application using the lock manager directly must either use the same conventions as the access methods or define its own convention to which it adheres. If the application is using the access methods with locking at the same time that it is calling the lock manager directly, the application must follow a convention that is compatible with the access methods' use of the Locking subsystem. See "Access Method Locking Conventions" for more information.

The **lock_id** function returns a unique ID that may safely be used as the locker parameter to the **lock_vec** interface. The access methods use **lock_id** to generate unique lockers for the cursors associated with a database.

The following three interfaces are fully compatible, and may be used interchangeably: **lock_get**, **lock_put**, and **lock_vec**.

All locks explicitly requested by an application should be released via calls to **lock_put** or **lock_vec**.

The **lock_stat** function returns information about the status of the Locking subsystem. It is the programmatic interface used by the **db_stat** utility.

The Locking subsystem is closed by the call to **DBENV→close**.

Finally, the entire Locking subsystem may be discarded using the DBENV→remove interface.

Page Locks

With the exception of the Queue access method, the access methods use page-level locking. The size of pages a database has may be set when the database is created by calling the **DB→set_pagesize** function. If not specified by the application, Berkeley DB selects a page size that will provide the best I/O performance by setting the page size equal to the block size of the underlying file system. Selecting a smaller page size can result in increased concurrency for some applications.

In the Btree access method, Berkeley DB uses a technique called lock-coupling to improve concurrency. The traversal of a Btree requires reading a page, searching that page to determine which page to search next, and then repeating this process on the next page. Once a page has been searched, it will never be accessed again for this operation, unless a page split is required. To improve concurrency in the tree, once the next page to read/search has been determined, that page is locked and then the original page lock is released atomically (that is, without relinquishing control of the lock manager).

Because the Recno access method is built upon Btree, it also uses lock-coupling for read operations. However, because the Recno access method must maintain a count of records on its internal pages, it cannot lock-couple during write operations. Instead, it retains write locks on all internal pages during every update operation. For this reason, it is not possible to have high concurrency in the Recno access method in the presence of write operations.

The Queue access method uses only short-term page locks. That is, a page lock is released prior to requesting another page lock. Record locks are used for transaction isolation. The provides a high degree of concurrency for write operations. A metadata page is used to keep track of the head and tail of the queue. This page is never locked during other locking or I/O operations.

The Hash access method does not have such traversal issues, but it must always refer to its metadata while computing a hash function because it implements dynamic hashing. This metadata is stored on a special page in the hash database. This page must therefore be read-locked on every operation. Fortunately, it needs be write-locked only when new pages are allocated to the file, which happens in three cases: 1) a hash bucket becomes full and needs to split, 2) a key or data item is too large to fit on a normal page, and 3) the number of duplicate items for a fixed key becomes so large that they are moved to an auxiliary page. In this case, the access method must obtain a write lock on the metadata page, thus requiring that all readers be blocked from entering the tree until the update completes.

Standard Lock Modes

The Berkeley DB locking protocol is described by a conflict matrix. *A conflict matrix* is an NxN array in which N is the number of different lock modes supported, and the (i, j)th entry of the array indicates whether a lock of mode i conflicts with a lock of mode j. In addition, Berkeley DB defines the type **db_lockmode_t**, which is the type of a lock mode within a conflict matrix.

The Berkeley DB library has a standard conflict matrix. This is a conflict matrix that includes the intent lock modes (for example, intent-to-read, intent-to-write) used for multigranularity locking, as well as a wait lock mode:

- DB_LOCK_NG   Not granted (always 0)
- DB_LOCK_READ   Read (shared)
- DB_LOCK_WRITE   Write (exclusive)
- DB_LOCK_WAIT   Wait
- DB_LOCK_IWRITE   Intention to write (shared)
- DB_LOCK_IREAD   Intention to read (shared)
- DB_LOCK_IWR   Intention to read and write (shared)

The default access method locking within the library uses only the first three of these modes: not-granted (DB_LOCK_NG), read (DB_LOCK_READ), and write (DB_LOCK_WRITE). The Queue access method's blocking interface also uses the wait (DB_LOCK_WAIT) lock mode.

In a conflict matrix, the rows indicate the lock that is held, and the columns indicate the lock that is requested. A 1 represents a conflict (do not grant the lock if the indicated lock is held), and a 0 indicates that it is OK to grant the lock.

	Notheld	**Read**	**Write**	**Wait**	**IWrite**	**IRead**	**IRW**
Notheld	0	0	0	0	0	0	0
Read*	0	0	1	0	1	0	1
Write**	0	1	1	1	1	1	1
Wait	0	0	0	0	0	0	0
Intent Write	0	1	1	0	0	0	0
Intent Read	0	0	1	0	0	0	0
Intent RW	0	1	1	0	0	0	0

* In this case, suppose that there is a read lock held on an object. A new request for a read lock would be granted, but a request for a write lock would not.

** In this case, suppose that there is a write lock held on an object. A new request for either a read or write lock would be denied.

Locking Without Transactions

If an application runs with locking specified, but not transactions (for example, **DBENV→open** is called with DB_INIT_LOCK or DB_INIT_CDB specified, but not DB_INIT_TXN), locks are normally acquired during each Berkeley DB operation and released before the operation returns to the caller. The only exception is in the case of cursor operations. Cursors identify a particular position in a file. For this reason, cursors must retain read locks across cursor calls to make sure that the position is uniquely identifiable during a subsequent cursor call, and so that an operation using DB_CURRENT will always reference the same record as a previous cursor call. Such cursor locks cannot be released until the cursor is either repositioned using the DB_GET_BOTH, DB_SET, DB_SET_RANGE, DB_KEYFIRST, or DB_KEYLAST functionality, in which case a new cursor lock is established or the cursor is closed. As a result, application designers are encouraged to close cursors as soon as possible.

Concurrent applications that use locking must ensure that two concurrent threads do not block each other. However, because Btree and Hash access method page splits can occur at any time, there is virtually no way to guarantee that an application that writes the database cannot deadlock. Applications running without the protection of transactions may deadlock, and can leave the database in an inconsistent state when they do so. Applications that need concurrent access, but not transactions, are more safely implemented using the Berkeley DB Concurrent Data Store Product.

Locking with Transactions: Two-Phase Locking

Berkeley DB uses a locking protocol called *two-phase locking (2PL)*. This is the traditional protocol used in conjunction with lock-based transaction systems.

In a two-phase locking (2PL) system, transactions are broken up into two distinct phases. During the first phase, the transaction only acquires locks; during the second phase, the transaction only releases locks. More formally, once a transaction releases a lock, it may not acquire any additional locks. Practically, this translates into a system in which locks are acquired as they are needed throughout a transaction and retained until the transaction ends, either by committing or aborting. In Berkeley DB, locks are released during **txn_abort** or **txn_commit**. The only exception to this protocol occurs when we use lock-coupling to traverse a data structure. If the locks are held only for traversal purposes, it is safe to release locks before transactions commit or abort.

For applications, the implications of 2PL are that long-running transactions will hold locks for a long time. When designing applications, lock contention should be considered. In order to reduce the probability of deadlock and achieve the best level of concurrency possible, the following guidelines are helpful:

1. When accessing multiple databases, design all transactions so that they access the files in the same order.

2. If possible, access your most hotly contested resources last (so that their locks are held for the shortest time possible).

3. If possible, use nested transactions to protect the parts of your transaction most likely to deadlock.

Access Method Locking Conventions

All Berkeley DB access methods follow the same conventions for locking database objects. Applications that do their own locking and also do locking via the access methods must be careful to adhere to these conventions.

Whenever a Berkeley DB database is opened, the DB handle is assigned a unique locker ID. Unless transactions are specified, that ID is used as the locker for all calls that the Berkeley DB methods make to the Locking subsystem. In order to lock a file, pages in the file, or records in the file, we must create a unique ID that can be used as the object to be locked in calls to the lock manager. Under normal operation, that object is a 28-byte value created by the concatenation of a unique file identifier, a page or record number, and an object type (page or record).

In a transaction-protected environment, database create and delete operations are recoverable and single-threaded. This single-threading is achieved using a single lock for the entire environment that must be acquired before beginning a create or delete operation. In this case, the object on which Berkeley DB will lock is a 32-bit unsigned integer with a value of 0.

If applications are using the Locking subsystem directly while they are also using locking via the access methods, they must take care not to inadvertently lock objects that happen to be equal to the unique file IDs used to lock files. This is most easily accomplished by using a locker ID with a length different from the values used by Berkeley DB.

All the access methods other than Queue use a simple multiple-reader/single-writer page-locking scheme. The standard read/write locks (**DB_LOCK_READ** and **DB_LOCK_WRITE**) and conflict matrix (as described in "Standard Lock Modes") are used. An operation that returns data (for example, **DB→get, DBcursor→c_get**) obtains a read lock on all the pages accessed while locating the requested record. When an update operation is requested (for example, **DB→put, DBcursor→c_del**), the page containing the updated (or new) data is write-locked. As read-modify-write cycles are quite common and are deadlock-prone under normal circumstances, the Berkeley DB interfaces allow the application to specify the DB_RMW flag, which causes operations to immediately obtain a write lock, even though they are only reading the data. Although this may reduce concurrency somewhat, it reduces the probability of deadlock.

The Queue access method does not hold long-term page locks. Instead, page locks are held only long enough to locate records or to change metadata on a page, and record locks are held for the appropriate duration. In the presence of transactions, record locks are held until transaction commit. For Berkeley DB operations, record locks are held until operation completion; for DBC operations, record locks are held until subsequent records are returned or the cursor is closed.

Under non-transaction operations, the access methods do not normally hold locks across calls to the Berkeley DB interfaces. The one exception to this rule is when cursors are used. Because cursors maintain a position in a file, they must hold locks across calls; in fact, they will hold locks until the cursor is closed. Furthermore, each cursor is assigned its own unique locker ID when it is created, so cursor operations can conflict with one another. (Each cursor is assigned its own locker ID because Berkeley DB handles may be shared by multiple threads of control. The Berkeley DB library cannot identify which operations are performed by which threads of control, and it must ensure that two different threads of control are not simultaneously modifying the same data structure. By assigning each cursor its own locker, two threads of control sharing a handle cannot inadvertently interfere with each other.)

This has important implications. If a single thread of control opens two cursors or uses a combination of cursor and non-cursor operations, these operations are performed on behalf of different lockers. Conflicts that arise between these different lockers may not cause actual deadlocks, but can, in fact, permanently block the thread of control. For example, assume that an application creates a cursor and uses it to read record A. Now, assume that a second cursor is opened, and the application attempts to write record A using the second cursor. Unfortunately, the first cursor has a read lock, so the second cursor cannot obtain its write lock. However, that read lock is held by the same thread of control, so the read lock can never be released if we block waiting for the write lock. This might appear to be a deadlock from the application's perspective, but Berkeley DB cannot identify it as such because it has no knowledge of which lockers belong to which threads of control. For this reason, application designers are encouraged to close cursors as soon as they are done with them.

Complicated operations that require multiple cursors (or combinations of cursor and non-cursor operations) can be performed in two ways. First, they may be performed within a transaction, in which case all operations lock on behalf of the designated transaction. Alternatively, the **DBcursor→c_dup** function duplicates a cursor, using the same locker ID as the originating cursor. There is no way to achieve this duplication functionality through the DB handle calls, but any DB call can be implemented by one or more calls through a cursor.

When the access methods use transactions, many of these problems disappear. The transaction ID is used as the locker ID for all operations performed on behalf of the transaction. This means that the application may open multiple cursors on behalf of the same transaction and these cursors will all share a common locker ID. This is safe because transactions cannot span threads of control, so the library knows that two cursors in the same transaction cannot modify the database concurrently.

As mentioned earlier, most of the Berkeley DB access methods use page-level locking. During Btree traversal, lock-coupling is used to traverse the tree. Note that the tree traversal that occurs during an update operation can also use lock-coupling; it is not necessary to retain locks on internal Btree pages, even if the item finally referenced will be updated. Even in the presence of transactions, locks obtained on internal pages of the Btree may be safely released as the traversal proceeds. This greatly improves concurrency. The only time when internal locks become crucial is when internal pages are split or merged. When traversing duplicate data items for a key, the lock on the key value also acts as a lock on all duplicates of that key. Therefore, two conflicting threads of control cannot access the same duplicate set simultaneously.

The Recno access method uses a Btree as its underlying data representation and follows similar locking conventions. However, because the Recno access method must keep track of the number of children for all internal pages, it must obtain write locks on all internal pages during read and write operations. In the presence of transactions, these locks are not released until transaction commit.

Berkeley DB Concurrent Data Store Locking Conventions

The Berkeley DB Concurrent Data Store product has a different set of conventions for locking. It provides multiple-reader/single-writer semantics, but not per-page locking or transaction recoverability. As such, it does its locking entirely at the interface to the access methods.

The object it locks is the file, identified by its unique file number. The locking matrix is not one of the two standard lock modes; instead, we use a four-lock set, consisting of the following:

- DB_LOCK_NG   Not granted (always 0)
- DB_LOCK_READ   Read (shared)
- DB_LOCK_WRITE   Write (exclusive)
- DB_LOCK_IWRITE   Intention-to-write (shared with NG and READ, but conflicts with WRITE and IWRITE)

The IWRITE lock is used for cursors that will be used for updating (IWRITE locks are implicitly obtained for write operations through the Berkeley DB handles—for example, **DB→put, DB→del**). While the cursor is reading, the IWRITE lock is held; but as soon as the cursor is about to modify the database, the IWRITE is upgraded to a WRITE lock. This upgrade blocks until all readers have exited the database. Because only one IWRITE lock is allowed at any one time, no two cursors can ever try to upgrade to a WRITE lock at the same time, and therefore deadlocks are prevented, which is essential because Berkeley DB Concurrent Data Store does not include deadlock detection and recovery.

Applications that need to lock compatibly with Berkeley DB Concurrent Data Store must obey the following rules:

1. Use only lock modes DB_LOCK_NG, DB_LOCK_READ, DB_LOCK_WRITE, DB_LOCK_IWRITE.

2. Never attempt to acquire a WRITE lock on an object that is already locked with a READ lock.

Deadlocks and Deadlock Avoidance

Practically any application that uses locking may deadlock. In order to recover from a deadlock, in nearly all cases, transactions must be used so that an operation that deadlocks midway through can be undone, leaving the database in a consistent state. Because the access methods may perform updates on multiple pages during a single API call, transactions are necessary even when the application makes only single update calls into the database. The only exception to this rule is when all the threads of control accessing the database are read-only or when the Berkeley DB Concurrent Data Store product is used; this product guarantees deadlock-free operation at the expense of reduced concurrency. Because deadlocks cannot be prevented, Berkeley DB provides the capability to detect deadlocks and recover from them gracefully.

Deadlocks occur when two or more threads of control are blocked, waiting for each other's forward progress. Consider two transactions, each of which wants to modify items A and B. Assume that transaction 1 modifies first A and then B, but transaction 2 modifies B and then A. Now, assume that transaction 1 obtains its write lock on A, but before it obtains its write lock on B, it is descheduled and transaction 2 runs. Transaction 2 successfully acquires its write lock on B, but then blocks when it tries to obtain its write lock on A because transaction 1 already holds a write lock on it. This is a deadlock. Transaction 1 cannot make forward progress until Transaction 2 releases its lock on B, but Transaction 2 cannot make forward progress until Transaction 1 releases its lock on A.

The **db_deadlock** utility performs deadlock detection by calling **lock_detect** at regular intervals. The **lock_detect** function runs the Berkeley DB deadlock detector. When a deadlock exists in the system, all the threads of control involved in the deadlock are, by definition, waiting on a lock. The deadlock detector examines the state of the lock manager and identifies a deadlock, and selects one of the participants to abort. (See "Configuring Locking" for a discussion of the way a participant is selected). The **lock_get** or **lock_vec** call for which the selected participant is waiting then returns a DB_LOCK_DEADLOCK error. When using the Berkeley DB access methods, this error return is propagated back through the Berkeley DB interface to the calling application.

When an application receives a DB_LOCK_DEADLOCK return, the correct action is to abort the enclosing transaction and optionally retry it. Transaction support is necessary for recovery from deadlocks. When a deadlock occurs, the database may be left in an inconsistent or corrupted state, and any database changes already accomplished must be undone before the application can proceed further.

The deadlock detector identifies deadlocks by looking for a cycle in what is commonly referred to as its "waits-for" graph. More precisely, the deadlock detector reads through the lock table, and reviews each lock object currently locked. Each object has lockers that currently hold locks on the object and possibly a list of lockers waiting for a lock on the object. Each object's list of waiting lockers defines a partial ordering. That is, for a particular object, every waiting locker comes after every holding locker because that holding locker must release its lock before the waiting locker can make forward progress. Conceptually, after each object has been examined, the partial orderings are topologically sorted. If this topological sort reveals any cycles, the lockers forming the cycle are involved in a deadlock. One of the lockers is selected for abortion.

It is possible that aborting a single transaction involved in a deadlock is not enough to allow other transactions to make forward progress. Unfortunately, at the time a transaction is selected for abortion, there is not enough information available to determine whether aborting that single transaction will allow forward progress or not. Because most applications have few deadlocks, Berkeley DB takes the conservative approach, aborting as few transactions as may be necessary to resolve the existing deadlocks. In particular, for each unique cycle found in the waits-for graph described in the previous paragraph, only one transaction is selected for abortion. However, if there are multiple cycles, one transaction from each cycle is selected for abortion. Only after the aborting transactions have received the deadlock return and aborted their transactions can it be determined whether it is necessary to abort additional transactions in order to allow forward progress.

Configuring Locking

The **DBENV→set_lk_detect** function specifies that the deadlock detector should be run whenever a lock blocks. This option provides for rapid detection of deadlocks at the expense of potentially frequent invocations of the deadlock detector. On a fast processor with a highly contentious application where response time is critical, this is a good choice. An argument to the **DBENV→set_lk_detect** function indicates which transaction to abort when a deadlock is detected. It can take on any one of the following values:

- DB_LOCK_YOUNGEST   Abort the most recently started transaction.
- DB_LOCK_OLDEST   Abort the longest-lived transaction.
- DB_LOCK_RANDOM   Abort whatever transaction the deadlock detector happens to find first.
- DB_LOCK_DEFAULT   Use the default policy (currently DB_RANDOM).

In general, DB_LOCK_DEFAULT is probably the correct choice. If an application has long-running transactions, DB_LOCK_YOUNGEST will guarantee that transactions eventually complete, but it may do so at the expense of a large number of aborts.

The alternative to using the **DBENV→set_lk_detect** interface is to run the deadlock detector manually using the Berkeley DB **lock_detect** interface.

The **DBENV→set_lk_conflicts** function allows you to specify your own locking conflicts matrix. This is an advanced configuration option, and is rarely necessary.

Configuring Locking: Sizing the System

The Locking system is sized using the following three functions:

```
DBENV→set_lk_max_locks
DBENV→set_lk_max_lockers
DBENV→set_lk_max_objects
```

The **DBENV→set_lk_max_locks**, **DBENV→set_lk_max_lockers**, and **DBENV→set_lk_max_objects** functions specify the maximum number of locks, lockers, and locked objects supported by the Locking subsystem, respectively. The maximum number of locks is the number of locks that can be simultaneously requested in the system. The maximum number of lockers is the number of lockers that can simultaneously request locks in the system. The maximum number of lock objects is the number of objects that can simultaneously be locked in the system. Selecting appropriate values requires an understanding of your application and its databases. If the values are too small, requests for locks in an application will fail. If the values are too large, the Locking subsystem will consume more resources than is necessary. It is better to err in the direction of allocating too many locks, lockers, and objects because increasing the number of locks does not require large amounts of additional resources.

The recommended algorithm for selecting the maximum number of locks, lockers, and lock objects is to run the application under stressful conditions and then review the Locking system's statistics to determine the maximum number of locks, lockers, and lock objects that were used. Then, double these values for safety. However, in some large applications, finer granularity of control is necessary in order to minimize the size of the Locking subsystem.

The maximum number of lockers can be estimated as follows:

- If the database environment is configured to use transactions, the maximum number of lockers needed is the number of simultaneously active transactions and child transactions (where a child transaction is active until its parent commits or aborts, not until it commits or aborts).

- If the database environment is not configured to use transactions, the maximum number of lockers needed is the number of simultaneous non-cursor operations plus an additional locker for every simultaneously open cursor.

The maximum number of lock objects needed can be estimated as follows:

- For Btree and Recno access methods, you will need one lock object per level of the database tree at a minimum. (Unless keys are quite large with respect to the page size, neither Recno nor Btree database trees should ever be deeper than five levels.) Then, you will need one lock object for each leaf page of the database tree that will be simultaneously accessed.

- For the Queue access method, you will need one lock object per record that is simultaneously accessed. To this, add one lock object per page that will be simultaneously accessed. (Because the Queue access method uses fixed-length records and the database page size is known, it is possible to calculate the number of pages—and, therefore, the lock objects—required.) Deleted records skipped by a DB_NEXT or DB_PREV operation do not require a separate lock object. Further, if your application is using transactions, no database operation will ever use more than three lock objects at any time.

- For the Hash access method, you need only a single lock object.

For all access methods, you should then add an additional lock object per database for the database's metadata page.

The maximum number of locks required by an application cannot be easily estimated. It is possible to calculate a maximum number of locks by multiplying the maximum number of lockers, times the maximum number of lock objects, times two (two for the two possible lock modes for each object, read and write). However, this is a pessimal value, and real applications are unlikely to actually need that many locks. Reviewing the Locking subsystem statistics is the best way to determine this value.

Locking and Non-Berkeley DB Applications

The Locking subsystem is useful outside the context of Berkeley DB. It can be used to manage concurrent access to any collection of either ephemeral or persistent objects. That is, the lock region can persist across invocations of an application, so it can be used to provide long-term locking (for example, conference-room scheduling).

In order to use the Locking subsystem in such a general way, the applications must adhere to a convention for identifying objects and lockers. Consider a conference room scheduling problem, in which there are three conference rooms scheduled in half-hour intervals. The scheduling application must then select a way to identify each conference room/time slot combination. In this case, we could describe the objects being locked as bytestrings consisting of the conference room name, the date when it is needed, and the beginning of the appropriate half-hour slot.

Lockers are 32-bit numbers, so we might choose to use the User ID of the individual running the scheduling program. To schedule half-hour slots, all the application needs to do is issue a **lock_get** call for the appropriate locker/object pair. To schedule a longer slot, the application needs to issue a **lock_vec** call, with one **lock_get** operation per half-hour—up to the total length. If the **lock_vec** call fails, the application would have to release the parts of the time slot that were obtained.

To cancel a reservation, the application would make the appropriate **lock_put** calls. To reschedule a reservation, the **lock_get** and **lock_put** calls could all be made inside of a single **lock_vec** call. The output of **lock_stat** could be post-processed into a human-readable schedule of conference room use.

13

The Logging Subsystem

THE LOGGING SUBSYSTEM IS THE LOGGING FACILITY used by Berkeley DB. It is largely Berkeley DB-specific, although it is potentially useful outside of the Berkeley DB package for applications wanting write-ahead logging support. Applications wanting to use the log for purposes other than logging file modifications based on a set of open file descriptors will almost certainly need to make source code modifications to the Berkeley DB code base.

A log can be shared by any number of threads of control. The **DBENV→open** interface is used to open a log. When the log is no longer in use, it should be closed using the **DBENV→close** interface.

Individual log entries are identified by log sequence numbers. Log sequence numbers are stored in an opaque object, a **DB_LSN**.

The **log_put** interface is used to append new log records to the log. Optionally, the DB_CHECKPOINT flag can be used to output a checkpoint log record (indicating that the log is consistent to that point, and recoverable after a system or application failure), as well as open-file information. The **log_get** interface is used to retrieve log records from the log.

There are additional interfaces for integrating the Logging subsystem with a transaction processing system:

- **log_register** and **log_unregister**   These interfaces associate files with identification numbers. These identification numbers are logged so that transactional recovery correctly associates log records with the appropriate files.
- **log_flush**   Flushes the log up to a particular log sequence number.
- **log_compare**   Allows applications to compare any two log sequence numbers.
- **log_file**   Maps a log sequence number to the specific log file that contains it.
- **log_archive**   Returns various sets of log file names. These interfaces are used for database administration; for example, to determine whether log files may safely be removed from the system.
- **log_stat**   The display **db_stat** utility uses the **log_stat** interface to display statistics about the log.
- **DBENV→remove**   The log meta-information (but not the log files themselves) may be removed using the **DBENV→remove** interface.

Configuring Logging

The two aspects of logging that may be configured are the size of log files on disk and the size of the log buffer in memory. The **DBENV→set_lg_max** interface specifies the individual log file size for all the applications sharing the Berkeley DB environment. Setting the log file size is largely a matter of convenience and a reflection of the application's preferences in backup media and frequency. However, setting the log file size too low can potentially cause problems because it would be possible to run out of log sequence numbers, which requires a full archival and application restart to reset. See "Log File Limits" for more information.

The **DBENV→set_lg_bsize** interface specifies the size of the in-memory log buffer, in bytes. Log information is stored in memory until the buffer fills up or transaction commit forces the buffer to be written to disk. Larger buffer sizes can significantly increase throughput in the presence of long-running transactions, highly concurrent applications, or transactions producing large amounts of data. By default, the buffer is 32KB.

Log File Limits

Log filenames and sizes impose a limit on how long databases may be used in a Berkeley DB database environment. It is quite unlikely that an application will reach this limit; however, if the limit is reached, the Berkeley DB environment's databases must be dumped and reloaded.

The log filename consists of **log**, followed by 10 digits, with a maximum of 2,000,000,000 log files. Consider an application performing 6000 transactions per second for 24 hours a day, logged into 10MB log files, in which each transaction is logging approximately 500 bytes of data. The following calculation indicates that the system will run out of log filenames in roughly 221 years:

```
(10 * 2^20 * 2000000000)/(6000 * 500 * 365 * 60 * 60 * 24) = ~221
```

There is no way to reset the log filename space in Berkeley DB. If your application is reaching the end of its log filename space, you must do the following:

1. Archive your databases as if to prepare for catastrophic failure (see **db_archive** for more information).

2. Dump and reload all your databases (see **db_dump** and **db_load** for more information).

3. Remove all of the log files from the database environment. Note: This is the only situation in which all the log files are removed from an environment; in all other cases, at least a single log file is retained.

4. Restart your application.

14

The Memory Pool Subsystem

T HE MEMORY POOL SUBSYSTEM IS THE GENERAL-PURPOSE SHARED memory buffer pool used by Berkeley DB. This module is useful outside of the Berkeley DB package for processes that require page-oriented, cached, shared-file access.

A memory pool is a memory cache shared among any number of threads of control. The DB_INIT_MPOOL flag to the **DBENV→open** interface opens, optionally creating a memory pool. When that pool is no longer in use, it should be closed using the **DBENV→close** interface.

The **memp_fopen** interface returns a DB_MPOOLFILE handle on an underlying file within the memory pool. When that handle is no longer in use, it should be closed using the **memp_fclose** interface. The **memp_fget** interface is used to retrieve pages from files in the pool. All retrieved pages must be subsequently returned using the **memp_fput** interface. At the time pages are returned, they may be marked **dirty**, which causes them to be written to the underlying file before being discarded from the pool. If there is insufficient room to bring a new page in the pool, a page is selected to be discarded from the pool using a least-recently-used algorithm. Pages in files may also be explicitly marked clean or dirty using the **memp_fset** interface. All dirty pages in the pool may be flushed using the **memp_sync** interface. All dirty pages in the pool from a single underlying file may be flushed using the **memp_fsync** interface.

There are additional interfaces related to the memory pool:

- It is possible to gradually flush buffers from the pool in order to maintain a consistent percentage of clean buffers in the pool using the **memp_trickle** interface.

- The **db_stat** utility uses the **memp_stat** interface to display statistics about the efficiency of the pool.

- Because some processing may be necessary when pages are read or written (for example, endian conversion), the **memp_register** function allows applications to specify automatic input and output processing in these cases.

- Although the **memp_sync** interface can be used to simply flush the entire pool, it also takes an argument that is specific to database systems. This argument allows the pool to be flushed up to a specified log sequence number.

- Finally, the entire pool may be discarded using the **DBENV→remove** interface.

Configuring the Memory Pool

There are two issues to consider when configuring the memory pool. The first issue, the most important tuning parameter for Berkeley DB applications, is the size of the memory pool. There are two ways to specify the pool size. First, calling the **DBENV→set_cachesize** function specifies the pool size for all of the applications sharing the Berkeley DB environment. Second, the **DB→set_cachesize** function only specifies a pool size for the specific database. Note: It is meaningless to call **DB→set_cachesize** for a database opened inside of a Berkeley DB environment because the environment pool size will override any pool size specified for a single database. For information on tuning the Berkeley DB cache size, see "Selecting a Cache Size."

The second memory pool configuration issue is the maximum size an underlying file can be and still be mapped into the process address space (instead of reading the file's pages into the cache). Mapping files into the process address space can result in better performance because available virtual memory is often much larger than the local cache, and page faults are faster than page copying on many systems. However, in the presence of limited virtual memory, it can cause resource starvation; and in the presence of large databases, it can result in immense process sizes. In addition, because of the requirements of the Berkeley DB transactional implementation, only read-only files can be mapped into process memory.

To specify that no files are to be mapped into the process address space, specify the DB_NOMMAP flag to the **DBENV→set_flags** interface. To specify that any individual file should not be mapped into the process address space, specify the DB_NOMMAP flag to the **memp_fopen** interface. To limit the size of files mapped into the process address space, use the **DBENV→set_mp_mmapsize** function.

15

The Transaction Subsystem

THE TRANSACTION SUBSYSTEM MAKES OPERATIONS ATOMIC, CONSISTENT, isolated, and durable in the face of system and application failures. The subsystem requires that the data be properly logged and locked in order to attain these properties. Berkeley DB contains all the components necessary to transaction-protect the Berkeley DB access methods, and other forms of data may be protected if they are logged and locked appropriately.

The Transaction subsystem is created, initialized, and opened by calls to **DBENV→open** with the DB_INIT_TXN flag specified. Note that enabling transactions automatically enables logging, but does not enable locking because a single thread of control that needed atomicity and recoverability would not require it.

The **txn_begin** function starts a transaction, returning an opaque handle to a transaction. If the parent parameter to **txn_begin** is non-NULL, the new transaction is a child of the designated parent transaction.

The **txn_abort** function ends the designated transaction and causes all updates performed by the transaction to be undone. The end result is that the database is left in a state identical to the state that existed prior to the **txn_begin**. If the aborting transaction has any child transactions associated with it (even ones that have already been committed), they are also aborted. Any transactions that are unresolved (neither committed nor aborted) when the application or system fails are aborted during recovery.

The **txn_commit** function ends the designated transaction and makes all the updates performed by the transaction permanent, even in the face of application or system failure. If this is a parent transaction committing, all child transactions that individually committed or had not been resolved are also committed.

Transactions are identified by 32-bit unsigned integers. The ID associated with any transaction can be obtained using the **txn_id** function. If an application is maintaining information outside of Berkeley DB that it wishes to transaction-protect, it should use this transaction ID as the locking ID.

The **txn_checkpoint** function causes a transaction checkpoint. A checkpoint is performed using to a specific log sequence number (LSN), referred to as the checkpoint LSN. When a checkpoint completes successfully, it means that all data buffers whose updates are described by LSNs less than the checkpoint LSN have been written to disk. This, in turn, means that the log records less than the checkpoint LSN are no longer necessary for normal recovery (although they would be required for catastrophic recovery if the database files were lost), and all log files containing only records prior to the checkpoint LSN may be safely archived and removed.

It is possible that in order to complete a transaction checkpoint, it will be necessary to write a buffer that is currently in use (that is, it is actively being read or written by some transaction). In this case, **txn_checkpoint** will not be able to write the buffer because doing so might cause an inconsistent version of the page to be written to disk, and will return with an error code of DB_INCOMPLETE instead of completing successfully. In such cases, the checkpoint can simply be retried after a short delay.

The time required to run normal recovery is proportional to the amount of work done between checkpoints. If a large number of modifications happen between checkpoints, many updates recorded in the log may not have been written to disk when failure occurred, and recovery may take longer to run. Generally, if the interval between checkpoints is short, data may be being written to disk more frequently, but the recovery time will be shorter. Often, the checkpoint interval is tuned for each specific application.

The **txn_stat** function returns information about the status of the Transaction subsystem. It is the programmatic interface used by the **db_stat** utility.

The Transaction system is closed by a call to **DBENV→close**.

Finally, the entire Transaction system may be removed using the **DBENV→remove** interface.

Transaction Limits

Transactions are identified uniquely by 32-bit unsigned integers. The high-order bit of the transaction ID is reserved (and defined to be 1), resulting in just over two billion unique transaction IDs. Each time that recovery is run, the beginning transaction ID is reset with new transactions being numbered, starting from 1. This means that recovery must be run at least once every two billion transactions.

It is possible that some environments may need to be aware of this limitation. Consider an application performing 600 transactions a second for 15 hours a day. The transaction ID space will run out in roughly 66 days:

```
2^31 / (600 * 15 * 60 * 60) = 66
```

Doing only 100 transactions a second exhausts the transaction ID space in roughly one year.

The transaction ID name space is initialized each time a database environment is created or recovered. If you reach the end of the transaction ID name space, it must be handled as if an application or system failure occurred. The most recently allocated transaction ID is the **st_last_txnid** value in the transaction statistics information, and is displayed by the **db_stat** utility.

Cursors

When using transactions, cursors are localized to a single transaction. That is, a cursor may not span transactions, and must be opened and closed within a single transaction. In addition, intermingling transaction-protected cursor operations and non-transaction-protected cursor operations on the same database in a single thread of control is practically guaranteed to deadlock because the locks obtained for transactions and non-transactions can conflict.

Multiple Threads of Control

Because transactions must hold all their locks until commit, a single transaction may accumulate a large number of long-term locks during its lifetime. As a result, when two concurrently running transactions access the same database, there is strong potential for conflict. Although Berkeley DB allows an application to have multiple outstanding transactions active within a single thread of control, great care must be taken to ensure that the transactions do not block each other (for example, attempt to obtain conflicting locks on the same data). If two concurrently active transactions in the same thread of control do encounter a lock conflict, the thread of control will deadlock so that the deadlock detector cannot detect the problem. In this case, there is no true deadlock, but because the transaction on which a transaction is waiting is in the same thread of control, no forward progress can be made.

Configuring Transactions

There is only a single parameter used in configuring transactions: the DB_TXN_NOSYNC flag. Setting the DB_TXN_NOSYNC flag to **DBENV→set_flags** when opening a transaction region changes the behavior of transactions to not synchronously flush the log during transaction commit.

This change will significantly increase application transactional throughput. However, it means that although transactions will continue to exhibit the ACI (atomicity, consistency, and isolation) properties, they will not have D (durability). Database integrity will be maintained, but it is possible that some number of the most recently committed transactions may be undone during recovery instead of being redone.

The application may also change the number of simultaneous outstanding transactions supported by the Berkeley DB environment by calling the **DBENV→set_tx_max** function. When this number is reached, additional calls to **txn_begin** will fail until some active transactions complete.

Transactions and Non–Berkeley DB Applications

It is possible to use the Locking, Logging and Transaction subsystems of Berkeley DB to provide transaction semantics on objects other than those described by the Berkeley DB access methods. In these cases, the application will need more explicit customization of the subsystems, as well as the development of appropriate data-structure-specific recovery functions.

For example, consider an application that provides transaction semantics on data stored in plain UNIX files accessed using the POSIX read and write system calls. The operations for which transaction protection is desired are bracketed by calls to **txn_begin** and **txn_commit**.

Before data are referenced, the application must make a call to the lock manager, **lock_get**, for a lock of the appropriate type (for example, read) on the object being locked. The object might be a page in the file, a byte, a range of bytes, or some key. It is up to the application to ensure that appropriate locks are acquired. Before a write is performed, the application should acquire a write lock on the object by making an appropriate call to the lock manager, **lock_get**. Then, the application should make a call to the log manager, **log_put**, to record enough information to redo the operation in case of failure after commit and to undo the operation in case of abort.

When designing applications that will use the Logging subsystem, it is important to remember that the application is responsible for providing any necessary structure to the log record. For example, the application must understand what part of the log record is an operation code, what part identifies the file being modified, what part is redo information, and what part is undo information.

After the log message is written, the application may issue the write system call. After all requests are issued, the application may call **txn_commit**. When **txn_commit** returns, the caller is guaranteed that all necessary log writes have been written to disk.

At any time, the application may call **txn_abort**, which will result in restoration of the database to a consistent pretransaction state. (The application may specify its own recovery function for this purpose using the **DBENV→set_tx_recover** function. The recovery function must be able to either reapply or undo the update, depending on the context, for each different type of log record.)

If the application crashes, the recovery process uses the log to restore the database to a consistent state.

The **txn_prepare** function provides the core functionality to implement distributed transactions, but it does not manage the notification of distributed transaction managers. The caller is responsible for issuing **txn_prepare** calls to all sites participating in the transaction. If all responses are positive, the caller can issue a **txn_commit**. If any of the responses are negative, the caller should issue a **txn_abort**. In general, the **txn_prepare** call requires that the transaction log be flushed to disk.

16

RPC/Client Server

BERKELEY DB INCLUDES A BASIC IMPLEMENTATION OF A CLIENT-SERVER protocol using Sun Microsystem's Remote Procedure Call Protocol. RPC support is available only for UNIX systems, and is not included in the Berkeley DB library by default, but it must be enabled during configuration. See "Configuring Berkeley DB" for more information. For more information on RPC itself, see your UNIX system documentation or *RPC: Remote Procedure Call Protocol Specification, RFC1831, Sun Microsystems, Inc., USC-ISI.*

Only some of the complete Berkeley DB functionality is available when using RPC. The following functionality is available:

1. The **db_env_create** interface and the DB_ENV handle methods.
2. The **db_create** interface and the DB handle methods.
3. The **txn_begin**, **txn_commit**, and **txn_abort** interfaces.

The RPC client/server code does not support any of the user-defined comparison or allocation functions; for example, an application using the RPC support may not specify its own Btree comparison function. If your application requires only those portions of Berkeley DB, then using RPC is fairly simple. If your application requires other Berkeley DB functionality, such as direct access to locking, logging or shared memory buffer memory pools, then your application cannot use the RPC support.

The Berkeley DB RPC code requires that the client and server programs be running the exact same version numbers. The Berkeley DB RPC protocol version number is tied to the Berkeley DB major and minor release numbers. As such, the server program will reject requests from clients using a different version number.

The Berkeley DB RPC support does not provide any security or authentication of any kind. Sites needing any kind of data security measures must modify the client and server code to provide whatever level of security they require.

One particularly interesting use of the RPC support is for debugging Berkeley DB applications. The seamless nature of the interface means that with very minor application code changes, an application can run outside of the Berkeley DB address space, making it far easier to track down many types of errors—such as memory misuse.

Using the RPC mechanisms in Berkeley DB involves two basic steps:

1. Modify your Berkeley DB application to act as a client and call the RPC server.

2. Run the **berkeley_db_svc** server program on the system where the database resides.

Client Program

Changing a Berkeley DB application to remotely call a server program requires only a few changes on the client side:

1. The client application must create and use a Berkeley DB environment; that is, it cannot simply call the **db_create** interface, but must first call the **db_env_create** interface to create an environment in which the database will live.

2. The client application must call **db_env_create** using the DB_CLIENT flag.

3. The client application must call the additional DB_ENV method **DBENV→set_server** to specify the database server. This call must be made before opening the environment with the **DBENV→open** call.

The client application provides three pieces of information to Berkeley DB as part of the **DBENV→set_server** call:

- The hostname of the server. The hostname format is not specified by Berkeley DB, but must be in a format acceptable to the local network support—specifically, the RPC clnt_create interface.

- The client timeout. This is the number of seconds the client will wait for the server to respond to its requests. A default is used if this value is zero.

- The server timeout. This is the number of seconds the server will allow client resources to remain idle before releasing those resources. The resources this applies to are transactions and cursors because those objects hold locks; and if a client dies, the server needs to release those resources in a timely manner. This value is really a hint to the server because the server may choose to override this value with its own.

The only other item of interest to the client is the home directory that is given to the **DBENV→open** call. The server is started with a list of allowed home directories. The client must use one of those names (where a name is the last component of the home directory). This allows the pathname structure on the server to change without client applications needing to be aware of it.

Once the **DBENV→set_server** call has been made, the client is connected to the server, and all subsequent Berkeley DB operations will be forwarded to the server. The client does not need to be otherwise aware that it is using a database server rather than accessing the database locally.

It is important to realize that the client portion of the Berkeley DB library acts as a simple conduit, forwarding Berkeley DB interface arguments to the server without interpretation. This has two important implications. First, all pathnames must be specified relative to the server. For example, the home directory and other configuration information passed by the application when creating its environment or databases must be pathnames for the server, not the client system. In addition, because there is no logical bundling of operations at the server, performance is usually significantly less than when Berkeley DB is embedded within the client's address space, even if the RPC is to a local address.

Server Program

The Berkeley DB server utility, **berkeley_db_svc**, handles all the client application requests.

Currently, the **berkeley_db_svc** utility is single-threaded, limiting the number of requests that it can handle. Modifying the server implementation to run in multithread or multiprocess mode requires modification of the server code automatically generated by the rpcgen program.

There are two different types of timeouts used by **berkeley_db_svc**. The first timeout (which can be modified within some constraints by the client application), is the resource timeout. When clients use transactions or cursors, those resources hold locks in Berkeley DB across calls to the server. If a client application dies or loses its connection to the server while holding those resources, it prevents any other client from acquiring them. Therefore, it is important to detect that a client has not used a resource for some period of time and release them. In the case of transactions, the server aborts the transaction. In the case of cursors, the server closes the cursor.

The second timeout is an idle timeout. A client application may remain idle with an open handle to an environment and a database. Doing so simply consumes some memory; it does not hold locks. However, the Berkeley DB server may want to eventually reclaim resources if a client dies or remains disconnected for a long period of time, so there is a separate idle timeout for open Berkeley DB handles.

The list of home directories specified to **berkeley_db_svc** are the only ones client applications are allowed to use. When **berkeley_db_svc** is started, it is given a list of pathnames. Clients are expected to specify the name of the home directory (defined as the last component in the directory pathname) as the database environment they are opening. In this manner, clients need to know only the name of their home environment; not its full pathname on the server machine. This means, of course, that only one environment of a particular name is allowed on the server at any given time.

17

Java API

BUILDING THE BERKELEY DB JAVA CLASSES, THE EXAMPLES and the native support
library is integrated into the normal build process. See—enable-java and "Building for
Win32" for more information.

We expect that you already installed the Java JDK or equivalent on your system.
For the sake of discussion, we assume that it is in a directory called db-VERSION;
for example, you extracted Berkeley DB version 2.3.12, and you did not change the
top-level directory name. The files related to Java are in two subdirectories of db-
VERSION: java (the java source files) and libdb_java (the C++ files that provide
the "glue" between java and Berkeley DB). The directory tree looks like this:

```
    db-VERSION
        /            \
      java        libdb_java
        |             |
      src           ...
        |
      com
        |
   sleepycat
    /       \
   db      examples
   |          |
  ...        ...
```

This naming conforms to the emerging standard for naming java packages. When the java code is built, it is placed into a **classes** subdirectory that is parallel to the **src** subdirectory.

For your application to use Berkeley DB successfully, you must set your CLASS-PATH environment variable to include db-VERSION/java/classes, as well as the classes in your java distribution. On UNIX, CLASSPATH is a colon-separated list of directories; on Windows, it is separated by semicolons. Alternatively, you can set your CLASSPATH to include db-VERSION/java/classes/db.jar, which is created as a result of the build. The db.jar file contains the classes in com.sleepycat.db; it does not contain any classes in com.sleepycat.examples.

On Windows, you will want to set your PATH variable to include

```
db-VERSION\build_win32\Release
```

On UNIX, you will want to set the LD_LIBRARY_PATH environment variable to include the Berkeley DB library installation directory. Of course, the standard install directory may have been changed for your site; see your system administrator for details. Regardless, if you get the following exception when you run, you probably do not have the library search path configured correctly:

```
java.lang.UnsatisfiedLinkError
```

Different Java interpreters provide different error messages if the CLASSPATH value is incorrect; a typical error is the following:

```
java.lang.NoClassDefFoundError
```

To ensure that everything is running correctly, you may want to try a simple test from the example programs in

```
db-VERSION/java/src/com/sleepycat/examples
```

For example, the following sample program will prompt for text input lines, which are then stored in a Btree database named "access.db" in your current directory:

```
% java com.sleepycat.examples.AccessExample
```

Try giving it a few lines of input text and then end-of-file. Before it exits, you should see a list of the lines you entered display with data items. This is a simple check to make sure that the fundamental configuration is working correctly.

Compatibility

The Berkeley DB Java API has been tested with the Sun Microsystems JDK 1.1.3 on SunOS 5.5; and Sun's JDK 1.1.7, JDK 1.2.2, and JDK 1.3.0 on Linux and Windows/NT. It should work with any JDK 1.1-, 1.2-, or 1.3-compatible environment (the latter two are known as Java 2). IBM's VM 1.3.0 has also been tested on Linux.

The primary requirement of the Berkeley DB Java API is that the target Java environment must support JNI (Java Native Interface) rather than another method for allowing native C/C++ code to interface to Java. The JNI was new in JDK 1.1, but is the most likely interface to be implemented across multiple platforms. However, using the JNI means that Berkeley DB will not be compatible with Microsoft Visual J++.

Java Programming Notes

The Java API closely parallels the Berkeley DB C++ and C interfaces. If you are currently using either of those APIs, there will be very little to surprise you in the Java API. We have even taken care to make the names of classes, constants, methods and arguments identical where possible, across all three APIs.

1. The Java runtime does not automatically close Berkeley DB objects on finalization. There are several reasons for this. One is that finalization is generally run only when garbage collection occurs, and there is no guarantee that this occurs at all, even on exit. Allowing specific Berkeley DB actions to occur in ways that cannot be replicated seems wrong. Second, finalization of objects may happen in an arbitrary order, so we would have to do extra bookkeeping to make sure that everything was closed in the proper order. The best word of advice is to always do a close() for any matching open() call. Specifically, the Berkeley DB package requires that you explicitly call close on each individual **Db** and **Dbc** object that you opened. Your database activity may not be synchronized to disk unless you do so.

2. Some methods in the Java API have no return type, and throw a **DbException** when an severe error arises. There are some notable methods that do have a return value, and can also throw an exception. **Db.get** and **Dbc.get** both return 0 when a get succeeds, return DB_NOTFOUND when the key is not found, and throw an error when there is a severe error. This approach allows the programmer to check for typical data-driven errors by watching return values without special casing exceptions.

    An object of type **DbDeadlockException** is thrown when a deadlock would occur.

    An object of type **DbMemoryException** is thrown when the system cannot provide enough memory to complete the operation (the ENOMEM system error on UNIX).

    An object of type **DbRunRecoveryException**, a subclass of **DbException**, is thrown when there is an error that requires a recovery of the database using **db_recover**.

3. There is no class corresponding to the C++ DbMpoolFile class in the Berkeley DB Java API. There is a subset of the memp_XXX methods in the **DbEnv** class. This has been provided to allow you to perform certain administrative actions on underlying memory pools opened as a consequence of **DbEnv.open**. Direct access to other memory pool functionality is not appropriate for the Java environment.

4. Berkeley DB always turns on the DB_THREAD flag because threads are expected in Java.

5. If there are embedded null strings in the **curslist** argument for **Db.join**, they will be treated as the end of the list of cursors, even if you may have allocated a longer array. Fill in all the strings in your array unless you intend to cut it short.

6. The callback installed for **DbEnv.set_errcall** will run in the same thread as the caller to **DbEnv.set_errcall**. Make sure that thread remains running until your application exits or until **DbEnv.close** is called.

Java FAQ

1. **During one of the first calls to the Berkeley DB Java API, a DbException is thrown with a "Bad file number" or "Bad file descriptor" message.**

   There are known large-file support bugs under JNI in various releases of the JDK. Please upgrade to the latest release of the JDK, and, if that does not help, disable big file support using the —disable-bigfile configuration option.

18

Tcl API

BERKELEY DB INCLUDES A DYNAMICALLY LOADABLE TCL API, which requires that Tcl/Tk 8.1 or later already be installed on your system. We recommend that you install later releases of Tcl/Tk than 8.1 if possible, especially on Windows platforms, because we found that we had to make local fixes to the 8.1 release in a few cases. You can download a copy of Tcl from the Ajuba Solutions corporate Web site.

Loading Berkeley DB with Tcl

This document assumes that you already configured Berkeley DB for Tcl support, and you built and installed everything where you want it to be. If you have not done so, see "Configuring Berkeley DB" or "Building for Win32" for more information.

Installing as a Tcl Package

Once enabled, the Berkeley DB shared library for Tcl is automatically installed as part of the standard installation process. However, if you wish to be able to dynamically load it as a Tcl package into your script, there are several steps that must be performed:

1. Run the Tcl shell in the install directory.
2. Append this directory to your auto_path variable.
3. Run the pkg_mkIndex proc, giving the name of the Berkeley DB Tcl library.

For example:
```
# tclsh8.1
% lappend auto_path /usr/local/BerkeleyDB/lib
% pkg_mkIndex /usr/local/BerkeleyDB/lib libdb_tcl-3.2.so libdb-3.2.so
```

Note that your Tcl and Berkeley DB version numbers may differ from the example, so your tclsh and library names may be different.

Loading Berkeley DB with Tcl

The Berkeley DB package may be loaded into the user's interactive Tcl script (or wish session) via the **load** command. For example:
```
load /usr/local/BerkeleyDB/lib/libdb_tcl-3.2.so
```

Note that your Berkeley DB version numbers may differ from the example, so the library name may be different.

If you installed your library to run as a Tcl package, Tcl application scripts should use the **package** command to indicate to the Tcl interpreter that it needs the Berkeley DB package and where to find it. For example:
```
lappend auto_path "/usr/local/BerkeleyDB/lib"
package require Db_tcl
```

No matter which way the library gets loaded, it creates a command named **berkdb**. All the Berkeley DB functionality is accessed via this command and additional commands it creates on behalf of the application. A simple test to determine whether everything is loaded and ready is to display the library version:
```
berkdb version -string
```

This should return you the Berkeley DB version in a string format.

Using Berkeley DB with Tcl

All commands in the Berkeley DB Tcl interface are in the following form:
```
command_handle operation options
```

The *command handle* is **berkdb** or one of the additional commands that may be created. The *operation* is what you want to do to that handle, and the *options* apply to the operation. Commands that get created on behalf of the application have their own sets of operations. Generally, any calls in DB that result in new object handles will translate into a new command handle in Tcl. Then, the user can access the operations of the handle via the new Tcl command handle.

Newly created commands are named with an abbreviated form of their objects, followed by a number. Some created commands are subcommands of other created commands and will be the first command, followed by a period (.), and then followed by the new subcommand. For example, suppose that you have a database already existing called my_data.db. The following example shows the commands created when you open the database and when you open a cursor:

```
# First open the database and get a database command handle
% berkdb open my_data.db
db0
#Get some data from that database
% db0 get my_key
{{my_key my_data0}{my_key my_data1}}
#Open a cursor in this database, get a new cursor handle
% db0 cursor
db0.c0
#Get the first data from the cursor
% db0.c0 get -first
{{first_key first_data}}
```

All commands in the library support a special option -? that will list the correct operations for a command or the correct options.

A list of commands and operations can be found in the **Tcl Interface** documentation.

Tcl API Programming Notes

The Tcl API closely parallels the Berkeley DB programmatic interfaces. If you are already familiar with one of those interfaces, there will not be many surprises in the Tcl API.

Several pieces of Berkeley DB functionality are not available in the Tcl API. Any of the functions that require a user-provided function are not supported via the Tcl API. For example, there is no equivalent to the **DB→set_dup_compare** or the **DBENV→set_errcall** methods.

The Berkeley DB Tcl API always turns on the DB_THREAD flag for environments and databases, making no assumptions about the existence or lack thereof of threads support in current or future releases of Tcl.

Tcl Error Handling

The Tcl interfaces to Berkeley DB generally return TCL_OK on success and throw a Tcl error on failure, using the appropriate Tcl interfaces to provide the user with an informative error message. There are some "expected" failures, however, for which no Tcl error will be thrown and for which Tcl commands will return TCL_OK. These failures include times when a searched-for key is not found, a requested key/data pair was previously deleted, or a key/data pair cannot be written because the key already exists.

These failures can be detected by searching the Berkeley DB error message that is returned. For example, use the following to detect that an attempt to put a record into the database failed because the key already existed:

```
% berkdb open -create -btree a.db
db0
% db0 put dog cat
0
% set ret [db0 put -nooverwrite dog newcat]
DB_KEYEXIST: Key/data pair already exists
% if { [string first DB_KEYEXIST $ret] != -1 } {
        puts "This was an error; the key existed"
}
This was an error; the key existed
% db0 close
0
% exit
```

To simplify parsing, it is recommended that the initial Berkeley DB error name be checked; for example, DB_KEYEXIST in the previous example. To ensure that Tcl scripts are not broken by upgrading to new releases of Berkeley DB, these values will not change in future releases of Berkeley DB. There are currently only three such "expected" error returns:

```
DB_NOTFOUND: No matching key/data pair found
DB_KEYEMPTY: Non-existent key/data pair
DB_KEYEXIST: Key/data pair already exists
```

Finally, sometimes Berkeley DB will output additional error information when a Berkeley DB error occurs. By default, all Berkeley DB error messages will be prefixed with the created command in whose context the error occurred (for example, "env0", "db2", and so on). There are several ways to capture and access this information.

First, if Berkeley DB invokes the error callback function, the additional information will be placed in the error result returned from the command and in the errorInfo backtrace variable in Tcl.

Also, the two calls to open an environment and open a database take an option, **–errfile filename**, which sets an output file to which these additional error messages should be written.

Additionally, the two calls to open an environment and open a database take an option, **–errpfx string**, which sets the error prefix to the given string. This option may be useful in circumstances where a more descriptive prefix is desired or where a constant prefix indicating an error is desired.

Tcl FAQ

1. **I have several versions of Tcl installed. How do I configure Berkeley DB to use a particular version?**

   To compile the Tcl interface with a particular version of Tcl, use the —with-tcl option to specify the Tcl installation directory that contains the tclConfig.sh file.

   See "Changing Compile or Load Options" for more information.

2. **Berkeley DB was configured using —enable-tcl or —with-tcl and fails to build.**

   The Berkeley DB Tcl interface requires Tcl version 8.1 or greater. You can download a copy of Tcl from the Ajuba Solutions corporate Web site.

3. **Berkeley DB was configured using —enable-tcl or —with-tcl, and fails to build.**

   If the Tcl installation was moved after it was configured and installed, try reconfiguring and reinstalling Tcl.

   Also, some systems do not search for shared libraries by default, do not search for shared libraries named the way the Tcl installation names them, or are searching for a different kind of library from those in your Tcl installation. For example, Linux systems often require linking libtcl.a to libtcl#.#.a, whereas AIX systems often require adding the -brtl flag to the linker. A simpler solution that almost always works on all systems is to create a link from libtcl.#.#.a or libtcl.so (or whatever you happen to have) to libtcl.a, and reconfigure.

4. **Loading the Berkeley DB library into Tcl on AIX causes a core dump.**

   In some versions of Tcl, the tclConfig.sh autoconfiguration script created by the Tcl installation does not work properly under AIX. To build a working Berkeley DB Tcl API when this happens, use the —enable-tcl flag to configure Berkeley DB (rather than —with-tcl). In addition, you will have to specify any necessary include and library paths and linker flags needed to build with Tcl by setting the CPPFLAGS, LIBS, and LDFLAGS environmental variables before running configure.

19

Dumping and Reloading Databases

THERE ARE THREE UTILITIES USED FOR DUMPING and loading Berkeley DB databases: **db_dump**, **db_dump185**, and **db_load**.

The db_dump and db_load Utilities

The **db_dump** and **db_dump185** utilities dump Berkeley DB databases into a flat-text representation of the data that can be read by **db_load**. The only difference between them is that **db_dump** reads Berkeley DB version 2 and greater database formats, whereas **db_dump185** reads Berkeley DB version 1.85 and 1.86 database formats.

The **db_load** utility reads either the output format used by the dump utilities or (optionally) a flat-text representation created using other tools, and stores it into a Berkeley DB database.

Dumping and reloading Hash databases that use user-defined hash functions will result in new databases that use the default hash function. Although using the default hash function may not be optimal for the new database, it will continue to work correctly.

Dumping and reloading Btree databases that use user-defined prefix or comparison functions will result in new databases that use the default prefix and comparison functions. In this case, it is quite likely that applications will be unable to retrieve records, and it is possible that the load process itself will fail.

The only available workaround for either Hash or Btree databases is to modify the sources for the **db_load** utility to load the database using the correct hash, prefix, and comparison functions.

Dump Output Formats

There are two output formats used by **db_dump** and **db_dump185**. In both output formats, the first few lines of the output contain header information describing the underlying access method, filesystem page size, and other bookkeeping information.

The header information starts with a single line, VERSION=N, where N is the version number of the dump output format.

The header information is then output in name=value pairs, where name may be any of the keywords listed in the **db_load** manual page, and value will be its value. Although this header information can be manually edited before the database is reloaded, there is rarely any reason to do so because all this information can also be specified or overridden by command-line arguments to **db_load**.

The header information ends with single line HEADER=END.

Following the header information are the key/data pairs from the database. If the database being dumped is a Btree or Hash database, or if the **-k** option was specified, the output will be paired lines of text where the first line of the pair is the key item, and the second line of the pair is its corresponding data item. If the database being dumped is a Queue or Recno database, and the **-k** has not been specified, the output will be lines of text where each line is the next data item for the database. Each of these lines will be preceded by a single space.

If the **-p** option to **db_dump** or **db_dump185** was specified, the key/data lines will consist of single characters representing any characters from the database that are *printing characters*, and backslash (\) escaped characters for any that were not. Backslash characters appearing in the output mean one of two things: if the backslash character precedes another backslash character, it means that a literal backslash character occurred in the key or data item. If the backslash character precedes any other character, the next two characters must be interpreted as a hexadecimal specification of a single character; for example, \0a is a newline character in the ASCII character set.

Although some care should be exercised, it is perfectly reasonable to use standard text editors and tools to edit databases dumped using the **-p** option before reloading them using the **db_load** utility.

Note that the definition of a printing character may vary from system to system, so database representations created using the **-p** option may be less portable than those created without it.

If the **-p** option to **db_dump** or **db_dump185** is not specified, each output line will consist of paired hexadecimal values; for example, the line **726f6f74** is the string **root** in the ASCII character set.

In all output formats, the key and data items are ended by a single line DATA= END.

Where multiple databases have been dumped from a file, the overall output will repeat; that is, a new set of headers and a new set of data items.

Loading Text into Databases

The **db_load** utility can be used to load text into databases. The **-T** option permits nondatabase applications to create flat-text files that are then loaded into databases for fast, highly-concurrent access. For example, the following command loads the standard UNIX **/etc/passwd** file into a database, with the login name as the key item and the entire password entry as the data item:

```
awk -F: '{print $1; print $0}' < /etc/passwd | \
      sed 's/\\/\\\\/g' | db_load -T -t hash passwd.db
```

Note that backslash characters naturally occurring in the text are escaped to avoid interpretation as escape characters by **db_load**.

20

Debugging Applications

BECAUSE BERKELEY DB IS AN EMBEDDED LIBRARY, DEBUGGING applications that use Berkeley DB is both harder and easier than debugging a separate server. Debugging can be harder because when a problem arises, it is not always readily apparent whether the problem is in the application, is in the database library, or is a result of an unexpected interaction between the two. Debugging can be easier because it is simpler to track down a problem when you can review a stack trace rather than deciphering interprocess communication messages. This chapter is intended to assist you with debugging applications and with reporting bugs to us so that we can provide you with the correct answer or fix as quickly as possible.

When you encounter a problem, there are a few general actions you can take:

- **Review the Berkeley DB error output** If an error output mechanism has been configured in the Berkeley DB environment, additional run-time error messages are made available to the applications. If you are not using an environment, it is well worth modifying your application to create one so that you can get more detailed error messages. See "Run-time Error Information" for more information on configuring Berkeley DB to output these error messages.

- **Review DBENV→set_verbose** Check the list of flags for the **DBENV→set_verbose** function, and see if any of them will produce additional information that might help understand the problem.

- **Add run-time diagnostics**   You can configure and build Berkeley DB to perform run-time diagnostics. (By default, these checks are not done because they can seriously impact performance.) See "Compile-time Configuration" for more information.

- **Apply all available patches**   Before reporting a problem to Sleepycat Software, please upgrade to the latest Sleepycat Software release of Berkeley DB, if possible, or at least make sure you have applied any updates available for your release from the Sleepycat Software Web site.

- **Run the test suite**   If you see repeated failures or failures of simple test cases, run the Berkeley DB test suite to determine whether the distribution of Berkeley DB you are using was built and configured correctly.

Compile-time Configuration

There are three compile-time configuration options that assist with debugging Berkeley DB and Berkeley DB applications:

- —enable-debug   If you want to build Berkeley DB with **-g** as the C and C++ compiler flag, enter —enable-debug as an argument to configure. This will create Berkeley DB with debugging symbols, as well as load various Berkeley DB routines that can be called directly from a debugger to display database page content, cursor queues, and so forth. (Note that the **-O** optimization flag will still be specified. To compile with only the **-g**, explicitly set the **CFLAGS** environment variable before configuring.)

- —enable-diagnostic   If you want to build Berkeley DB with debugging run-time sanity checks and with DIAGNOSTIC #defined during compilation, enter —enable-diagnostic as an argument to configure. This will cause a number of special checks to be performed when Berkeley DB is running. This flag should not be defined when configuring to build production binaries because it degrades performance.

- —enable-umrw   When compiling Berkeley DB for use in run-time memory consistency checkers (in particular, programs that look for reads and writes of uninitialized memory), use —enable-umrw as an argument to configure. This guarantees, among other things, that Berkeley DB will completely initialize allocated pages rather than initializing only the minimum necessary amount.

In addition, when compiling Berkeley DB for use in run-time memory consistency checkers (in particular, programs that look for reads and writes of uninitialized memory), use —enable-diagnostic as an argument to configure. This guarantees that Berkeley DB will completely initialize allocated pages rather than initializing only the minimum necessary amount.

Run-time Error Information

Normally, when an error occurs in the Berkeley DB library, an integer value (either a Berkeley DB-specific value or a system **errno** value) is returned by the function. In some cases, however, this value may be insufficient to completely describe the cause of the error, especially during initial application debugging.

There are four interfaces intended to provide applications with additional run-time error information: **DBENV→set_errcall**, **DBENV→set_errfile**, **DBENV→set_errpfx**, and **DBENV→set_verbose**.

If the environment is configured with these interfaces, many Berkeley DB errors will result in additional information being written to a file or passed as an argument to an application function.

The Berkeley DB error-reporting facilities do not slow performance or significantly increase application size, and may be run during normal operation as well as during debugging. Where possible, we recommend that these options always be configured and the output saved in the filesystem. We have found that that this often saves time when debugging installation or other system-integration problems.

In addition, there are three routines to assist applications with displaying their own error messages: **db_strerror**, **DBENV→err**, and **DBENV→errx**. The first is a superset of the ANSI C strerror interface, and returns a descriptive string for any error return from the Berkeley DB library. The **DBENV→err** and **DBENV→errx** functions use the error message configuration options described previously to format and display error messages to appropriate output devices.

Reviewing Berkeley DB Log Files

If you are running with transactions and logging, the **db_printlog** utility can be a useful debugging aid. The **db_printlog** utility will display the contents of your log files in a human readable (and machine-processable) format.

The **db_printlog** utility will attempt to display any and all log files present in a designated db_home directory. For each log record, **db_printlog** will display a line with the following form:

```
[22][28]db_big: rec: 43 txnid 80000963 prevlsn [21][10483281]
```

The opening numbers in square brackets are the *log sequence numbers* (*LSNs*) of the log record being displayed. The first number indicates the log file in which the record appears, and the second number indicates the offset in that file of the record.

The first character string identifies the particular log operation being reported. The log records corresponding to particular operations are described following. The rest of the line consists of name/value pairs.

The rec field indicates the record type (this is used to dispatch records in the log to appropriate recovery functions).

The txnid field identifies the transaction for which this record was written. A txnid of 0 means that the record was written outside the context of any transaction. You will see these most frequently for checkpoints.

Finally, the prevlsn contains the LSN of the last record for this transaction. By following prevlsn fields, you can accumulate all the updates for a particular transaction. During normal abort processing, this field is used to quickly access all the records for a particular transaction.

After the initial line identifying the record type, each field of the log record is displayed, one item per line. There are several fields that appear in many different records and a few fields that appear only in some records.

The following table presents each log record type currently produced, with a brief description of the operation it describes.

Table 20.1 **Berkeley DB Log Record Types**

Log Record Type	Description
bam_adj	Used when we insert/remove an index into/from the page header of a Btree page.
bam_cadjust	Keeps track of record counts in a Btree or Recno database.
bam_cdel	Used to mark a record on a page as deleted.
bam_curadj	Used to adjust a cursor location when a nearby record changes in a Btree database.
bam_pg_alloc	Indicates that we allocated a page to a Btree.
bam_pg_free	Indicates that we freed a page in the Btree (freed pages are added to a freelist and reused).
bam_rcuradj	Used to adjust a cursor location when a nearby record changes in a Recno database.
bam_repl	Describes a replace operation on a record.
bam_root	Describes an assignment of a root page.
bam_rsplit	Describes a reverse page split.
bam_split	Describes a page split.
crdel_delete	Describes the removal of a Berkeley DB file.
crdel_fileopen	Describes a Berkeley DB file create attempt.
crdel_metapage	Describes the creation of a metadata page for a new file.
crdel_metasub	Describes the creation of a metadata page for a subdatabase.
crdel_rename	Describes a file rename operation.
db_addrem	Add or remove an item from a page of duplicates.
db_big	Add an item to an overflow page (*overflow pages* contain items too large to place on the main page).
db_debug	Log debugging message.
db_noop	Marks an operation that did nothing but update the LSN on a page.
db_ovref	Increment or decrement the reference count for a big item.

Log Record Type	Description
db_relink	Fix prev/next chains on duplicate pages because a page was added or removed.
ham_chgpg	Used to adjust a cursor location when a Hash page is removed and its elements are moved to a different Hash page.
ham_copypage	Used when we empty a bucket page, but there are overflow pages for the bucket; one needs to be copied back into the actual bucket.
ham_curadj	Used to adjust a cursor location when a nearby record changes in a Hash database.
ham_groupalloc	Allocate some number of contiguous pages to the Hash database.
ham_insdel	Insert/delete an item on a Hash page.
ham_metagroup	Update the metadata page to reflect the allocation of a sequence of contiguous pages.
ham_newpage	Add or remove overflow pages from a Hash bucket.
ham_replace	Handle updates to records that are on the main page.
ham_splitdata	Record the page data for a split.
log_register	Record an open of a file (mapping the file name to a log-id that is used in subsequent log operations).
qam_add	Describe the actual addition of a new record to a Queue.
qam_del	Delete a record in a Queue.
qam_delext	Delete a record in a Queue with extents.
qam_delete	Remove a Queue extent file.
qam_inc	Increments the maximum record number allocated in a Queue, indicating that we allocated another space in the file.
qam_incfirst	Increments the record number that refers to the first record in the database.
qam_mvptr	Indicates that we changed the reference to either or both of the first and current records in the file.
qam_rename	Rename a Queue extent file.
txn_child	Commit a child transaction.
txn_ckp	Transaction checkpoint.
txn_regop	Logs a regular (non-child) transaction commit.
txn_xa_regop	Logs a prepare message.

Augmenting the Log for Debugging

When debugging applications, it is sometimes useful to log not only the actual operations that modify pages, but also the underlying Berkeley DB functions being executed. This form of logging can add significant bulk to your log, but can permit debugging application errors that are almost impossible to find any other way. To turn on these log messages, specify the —enable-debug_rop and —enable-debug_wop configuration options when configuring Berkeley DB. See "Configuring Berkeley DB" for more information.

Extracting Committed Transactions and Transaction Status

Sometimes, it is useful to use the human-readable log output to determine which transactions committed and aborted. The awk script, commit.awk (found in the db_printlog directory of the Berkeley DB distribution) allows you to do just that. The following command, where log_output is the output of db_printlog, will display a list of the transaction IDs of all committed transactions found in the log:

```
awk -f commit.awk log_output
```

If you need a complete list of both committed and aborted transactions, the script status.awk will produce it. The syntax is as follows:

```
awk -f status.awk log_output
```

Extracting Transaction Histories

Another useful debugging aid is to print out the complete history of a transaction. The awk script txn.awk allows you to do that. The following command line, where log_output is the output of **db_printlog** and txnlist is a comma-separated list of transaction IDs, will display all log records associated with the designated transaction ids:

```
awk -f txn.awk TXN=txnlist log_output
```

Extracting File Histories

The awk script fileid.awk allows you to extract all log records that affect particular files. The syntax for the fileid.awk script is the following, where log_output is the output of db_printlog and fids is a comma-separated list of fileids:

```
awk -f fileid.awk PGNO=fids log_output
```

The script will output all log records that reference the designated file.

Extracting Page Histories

The awk script pgno.awk allows you to extract all log records that affect particular pages. As currently designed, however, it will extract records of all files with the designated page number, so this script is most useful in conjunction with the fileid script. The syntax for the pgno.awk script is the following, where log_output is the output of db_printlog, and pgnolist is a comma-separated list of page numbers:

```
awk -f pgno.awk PGNO=pgnolist log_output
```

The script will output all log records that reference the designated page numbers.

Other Log-Processing Tools

The awk script count.awk prints out the number of log records encountered that belonged to some transaction (that is the number of log records excluding those for checkpoints and non-transaction-protected operations).

The script range.awk will extract a subset of a log. This is useful when the output of **db_printlog** is too large to be reasonably manipulated with an editor or other tool.

The syntax for range.awk is the following, where **sf** and **so** represent the log sequence number (LSN) of the beginning of the sublog you wish to extract, and **ef** and **eo** represent the LSN of the end of the sublog you wish to extract:

```
awk -f range.awk START_FILE=sf START_OFFSET=so END_FILE=ef END_OFFSET=eo
log_output
```

Common Errors

This page outlines some of the most common problems that people encounter and some suggested courses of action.

- **Symptom:** Core dumps or garbage returns from random Berkeley DB operations.

  Possible Cause: Failure to zero out DBT structure before issuing request.

  Fix: Before using a **DBT**, you must initialize all its elements to 0 and then set the ones you are using explicitly.

- **Symptom:** Random crashes and/or database corruption.

  Possible Cause: Running multiple threads, but did not specify DB_THREAD to **DB→open** or **DBENV→open**.

  Fix: Any time you are sharing a handle across multiple threads, you must specify DB_THREAD when you open that handle.

- **Symptom: DBENV→open** returns EINVAL.

  Possible Cause: The environment home directory is a remote mounted filesystem.

  Fix: Use a locally mounted filesystem instead.

- **Symptom: DB→get** calls are returning EINVAL.

  Possible Cause: The application is running with threads, but did not specify the DB_DBT_MALLOC, DB_DBT_REALLOC, or DB_DBT_USERMEM flags in the **DBT** structures used in the call.

  Fix: When running with threaded handles (that is, specifying DB_THREAD to **DBENV→open** or **DB→open**), you must specify one of those flags for all **DBT** structures in which Berkeley DB is returning data.

- **Symptom:** Running multiple threads or processes, and the database appears to be getting corrupted.

  Possible Cause: Locking is not enabled.

  Fix: Make sure that you are acquiring locks in your access methods. You must specify DB_INIT_LOCK to your **DBENV→open** call and then pass that environment to **DB→open**.

- **Symptom:** Locks are accumulating, or threads and/or processes are deadlocking, even though there is no concurrent access to the database.

  Possible Cause: Failure to close a cursor.

  Fix: Cursors retain locks between calls. Everywhere the application uses a cursor, the cursor should be explicitly closed as soon as possible after it is used.

- **Symptom:** The system locks up.

  Possible Cause: Application not checking for DB_LOCK_DEADLOCK.

  Fix: Unless you are using the Concurrent Data Store product, whenever you have multiple threads and/or processes and at least one of them is writing, you have the potential for deadlock. As a result, you must test for the DB_LOCK_DEADLOCK return on every Berkeley DB call. In general, updates should take place in a transaction, or you might leave the database in an inconsistent state. Reads may take place outside the context of a transaction under common conditions.

Whenever you get a DB_LOCK_DEADLOCK return, you should do the following:

1. If you are running in a transaction, abort the transaction after first closing any cursors opened in the transaction.

2. If you are not running in a transaction, simply close the cursor that got the DB_LOCK_DEADLOCK (if it was a cursor operation), and retry.

See "Recoverability and Deadlock Avoidance" for further information.

- **Symptom:** An inordinately high number of deadlocks.

  Possible Cause: Read-Modify-Write pattern without using the RMW flag.

  Fix: If you frequently read a piece of data, modify it, and then write it, you may be inadvertently causing a large number of deadlocks. Try specifying the DB_RMW flag on your get calls.

  Or, if the application is doing a large number of updates in a small database, turning off Btree splits may help (see DB_REVSPLITOFF for more information.)

- **Symptom:** I run recovery and it exits cleanly, but my database changes are missing.

  Possible Cause: Failure to enable logging and transactions in the database environment; failure to specify DB_ENV handle when creating a DB handle; transaction handle not passed to Berkeley DB interface; failure to commit transaction.

  Fix: Make sure that the environment and database handles are properly created, the application passes the transaction handle returned by **txn_begin** to the appropriate Berkeley DB interfaces, and each transaction is eventually committed.

- **Symptom:** Recovery fails.

  Possible Cause: A database was updated in a transactional environment, both with and without transactional handles.

  Fix: If any database write operation is done using a transaction handle, every write operation must be done in the context of a transaction.

- **Symptom:** A database environment locks up, sometimes gradually.

  Possible Cause: A thread of control exited unexpectedly, holding Berkeley DB resources.

  Fix: Whenever a thread of control exits holding Berkeley DB resources, all threads of control must exit the database environment, and recovery must be run.

- **Symptom:** A database environment locks up, sometimes gradually.

  Possible Cause: Cursors are not being closed before transaction abort.

  Fix: Before an application aborts a transaction, any cursors opened within the context of that transaction must be closed.

- **Symptom:** Transaction abort or recovery fail, or database corruption occurs.

  Possible Cause: Log files were removed before it was safe.

  Fix: Do not remove any log files from a database environment until Berkeley DB declares it safe.

21

Building Berkeley DB for UNIX and QNX Systems

THE BERKELEY DB DISTRIBUTION BUILDS UP TO FOUR SEPARATE libraries: the base C API Berkeley DB library, and the optional C++, Java, and Tcl API libraries. For portability reasons, each library is standalone and contains the full Berkeley DB support necessary to build applications; that is, the C++ API Berkeley DB library does not require any other Berkeley DB libraries to build and run C++ applications.

Building for UNIX

The Berkeley DB distribution uses the Free Software Foundation's autoconf and libtool tools to build on UNIX platforms. In general, the standard configuration and installation options for these tools apply to the Berkeley DB distribution.

To perform the default UNIX build of Berkeley DB, first change to the **build_unix** directory and then enter the following two commands:

```
../dist/configure
make
```

This will build the Berkeley DB library.

To install the Berkeley DB library, enter the following command:

```
make install
```

To rebuild Berkeley DB, enter the following:

```
make clean
make
```

If you change your mind about how Berkeley DB is to be configured, you must start from scratch by entering the following:

```
make realclean
../dist/configure
make
```

To build multiple UNIX versions of Berkeley DB in the same source tree, create a new directory at the same level as the build_unix directory, and configure and build in that directory, as described previously.

If you have trouble with any of these commands, please send email to the addresses found in the Sleepycat Software contact information. In that email, please provide a complete copy of the commands that you entered and any output, along with a copy of any **config.log** or **config.cache** files created during configuration.

Configuring Berkeley DB

There are several options that you can specify when configuring Berkeley DB. Although only the Berkeley DB-specific ones are described here, most of the standard GNU autoconf options are available and supported. To see a complete list of the options, specify the —help flag to the configure program.

The Berkeley DB specific options are as follows:

- —disable-bigfile   Some systems, notably versions of HP/UX and Solaris, require special compile-time options in order to create files larger than 2^32 bytes. These options are automatically enabled when Berkeley DB is compiled. For this reason, binaries built on current versions of these systems may not run on earlier versions of the system because the library and system calls necessary for large files are not available. To disable building with these compile-time options, enter —disable-bigfile as an argument to configure.

- —enable-compat185   To compile or load Berkeley DB 1.85 applications against this release of the Berkeley DB library, enter —enable-compat185 as an argument to configure. This will include Berkeley DB 1.85 API compatibility code in the library.

- —enable-cxx   To build the Berkeley DB C++ API, enter —enable-cxx as an argument to configure.

- —enable-debug   To build Berkeley DB with **-g** as a compiler flag and with **DEBUG** #defined during compilation, enter —enable-debug as an argument to configure. This will create a Berkeley DB library with debugging symbols, as well as load various routines that can be called from a debugger to display pages, cursor queues, and so forth. This option shouldn't be specified when configuring to build production binaries, although there shouldn't be any significant performance degradation.

- —enable-debug_rop   To build Berkeley DB to output log records for read operations, enter —enable-debug_rop as an argument to configure. This option should not be specified when configuring to build production binaries because you will lose a significant amount of performance.

- —enable-debug_wop   To build Berkeley DB to output log records for write operations, enter —enable-debug_wop as an argument to configure. This option should not be specified when configuring to build production binaries because you will lose a significant amount of performance.

- —enable-diagnostic   To build Berkeley DB with debugging run-time sanity checks, enter —enable-diagnostic as an argument to configure. This will cause a number of special checks to be performed when Berkeley DB is running. This option should not be specified when configuring to build production binaries because you will lose a significant amount of performance.

- —enable-dump185   To convert Berkeley DB 1.85 (or earlier) databases to this release of Berkeley DB, enter —enable-dump185 as an argument to configure. This will build the **db_dump185** utility, which can dump Berkeley DB 1.85 and 1.86 databases in a format readable by the Berkeley DB **db_load** utility.

  The system libraries with which you are loading the **db_dump185** utility must already contain the Berkeley DB 1.85 library routines for this to work because the Berkeley DB distribution does not include them. If you are using a non-standard library for the Berkeley DB 1.85 library routines, you will have to change the Makefile that the configuration step creates to load the **db_dump185** utility with that library.

- —enable-dynamic   To build a dynamic shared library version of Berkeley DB, instead of the default static library, specify —enable-dynamic. Dynamic libraries are built using the GNU Project's Libtool distribution, which supports shared library builds on many (although not all) systems.

  Berkeley DB can be configured to build either a static or a dynamic library, but not both at once. You should not attempt to build both library types in the same directory because they have incompatible object file formats. To build both static and dynamic libraries, create two separate build directories, and configure and build them separately.

- —enable-java   To build the Berkeley DB Java API, enter —enable-java as an argument to configure. To build Java, you must also configure the option —enable-dynamic. Before configuring, you must set your PATH environment variable to include javac. Note that it is not sufficient to include a symbolic link to javac in your PATH because the configuration process uses the location of javac to determine the location of the Java include files (for example, jni.h). On some systems, additional include directories may be needed to process jni.h; see "Changing Compile or Load Options" for more information.

- —enable-posixmutexes   To force Berkeley DB to use the POSIX pthread mutex interfaces for underlying mutex support, enter —enable-posixmutexes as an argument to configure. The Berkeley DB library requires that the POSIX pthread implementation support mutexes shared between multiple processes, as described for the pthread_condattr_setpshared and pthread_mutexattr_setpshared interfaces. In addition, this configuration option requires that Berkeley DB be linked with the -lpthread library. On systems where POSIX mutexes are the preferred mutex support (for example, HP-UX), they will be selected automatically.

- —enable-rpc   To build the Berkeley DB RPC client code and server utility, enter —enable-rpc as an argument to configure. The —enable-rpc option requires that RPC libraries already be installed on your system.

- —enable-shared   The —enable-shared configure argument is an alias for —enable-dynamic.

- —enable-tcl   To build the Berkeley DB Tcl API, enter —enable-tcl as an argument to configure. This configuration option expects to find Tcl's tclConfig.sh file in the **/usr/local/lib** directory. See the —with-tcl option for instructions on specifying a non-standard location for the Tcl installation. See "Loading Berkeley DB with Tcl" for information on sites from which you can download Tcl and which Tcl versions are compatible with Berkeley DB. To configure the Berkeley DB Tcl API, you must also specify the —enable-dynamic option.

- —enable-test   To build the Berkeley DB test suite, enter —enable-test as an argument to configure. To run the Berkeley DB test suite, you must also specify the —enable-dynamic and —enable-tcl options.

- —enable-uimutexes   To force Berkeley DB to use the UNIX International (UI) mutex interfaces for underlying mutex support, enter —enable-uimutexes as an argument to configure. This configuration option requires that Berkeley DB be linked with the -lthread library. On systems where UI mutexes are the preferred mutex support (for example, SCO's UnixWare 2), they will be selected automatically.

- —enable-umrw   Rational Software's Purify product and other run-time tools complain about uninitialized reads/writes of structure fields whose only purpose is padding, as well as when heap memory that was never initialized is written to disk. Specify the —enable-umrw option during configuration to mask these errors. This option should not be specified when configuring to build production binaries because you will lose a significant amount of performance.

- —with-tcl=DIR   To build the Berkeley DB Tcl API, enter —with-tcl=DIR, replacing DIR with the directory in which the Tcl tclConfig.sh file may be found. See "Loading Berkeley DB with Tcl" for information on sites from which you can download Tcl and which Tcl versions are compatible with Berkeley DB. To configure the Berkeley DB Tcl API, you must also specify the —enable-dynamic option.

Changing Compile or Load Options

You can specify compiler and/or compile and load time flags by using environment variables during Berkeley DB configuration. For example, if you want to use a specific compiler, specify the CC environment variable before running configure:

```
prompt: env CC=gcc ../dist/configure
```

Using anything other than the native compiler will almost certainly mean that you'll want to check the flags specified to the compiler and loader, too.

To specify debugging and optimization options for the C compiler, use the CFLAGS environment variable:

```
prompt: env CFLAGS=-O2 ../dist/configure
```

To specify header file search directories and other miscellaneous options for the C preprocessor and compiler, use the CPPFLAGS environment variable:

```
prompt: env CPPFLAGS=-I/usr/contrib/include ../dist/configure
```

To specify debugging and optimization options for the C++ compiler, use the CXXFLAGS environment variable:

```
prompt: env CXXFLAGS=-Woverloaded-virtual ../dist/configure
```

To specify miscellaneous options or additional library directories for the linker, use the LDFLAGS environment variable:

```
prompt: env LDFLAGS="-N32 -L/usr/local/lib" ../dist/configure
```

If you want to specify additional libraries, set the LIBS environment variable before running configure. For example, the following would specify two additional libraries to load: "posix" and "socket":

```
prompt: env LIBS="-lposix -lsocket" ../dist/configure
```

Make sure that you prepend –L to any library directory names, and that you prepend –I to any include file directory names! Also, if the arguments you specify contain blank or tab characters, be sure to quote them as shown previously; that is, with single or double quotes around the values you're specifying for LIBS.

The env command, which is available on most systems, simply sets one or more environment variables before running a command. If the env command is not available to you, you can set the environment variables in your shell before running configure. For example, in sh or ksh, you could do the following:

```
prompt: LIBS="-lposix -lsocket" ../dist/configure
```

In csh or tcsh, you could do the following:

```
prompt: setenv LIBS "-lposix -lsocket"
prompt: ../dist/configure
```

See your command shell's manual page for further information.

Installing Berkeley DB

Berkeley DB installs the following files into the following locations, with the following default values, as shown in Table 21.1:

Table 21.1 **Installing Berkeley DB**

Configuration variable	Default value
—prefix	/usr/local/BerkeleyDB.**Major**.**Minor**
—exec_prefix	$(prefix)
—bindir	$(exec_prefix)/bin
—includedir	$(prefix)/include
—libdir	$(exec_prefix)/lib
docdir	$(prefix)/docs
Files	**Default location**
include files	$(includedir)
libraries	$(libdir)
utilities	$(bindir)
documentation	$(docdir)

With one exception, this follows the GNU Autoconf and GNU Coding Standards installation guidelines; please see that documentation for more information and rationale.

The single exception is the Berkeley DB documentation. The Berkeley DB documentation is provided in HTML format, not in UNIX-style man or GNU info format. For this reason, Berkeley DB configuration does not support **—infodir** or **—mandir**. To change the default installation location for the Berkeley DB documentation, modify the Makefile variable, **docdir**.

To move the entire installation tree to somewhere besides **/usr/local**, change the value of **prefix**.

To move the binaries and libraries to a different location, change the value of **exec_prefix**. The values of **includedir** and **libdir** may be similarly changed.

Any of the following values except for **docdir** may be set as part of the configuration:

```
prompt: ../dist/configure —bindir=/usr/local/bin
```

Any of the following values, including **docdir**, may be changed when doing the install itself:

```
prompt: make prefix=/usr/contrib/bdb install
```

The Berkeley DB installation process will attempt to create any directories that do not already exist on the system.

Dynamic Shared Libraries

The Berkeley DB dynamic shared libraries are created with the name libdb-**major**.**minor**.so, where **major** is the major version number and **minor** is the minor version number. Other shared libraries are created if Java and Tcl support are enabled—specifically, libdb_java-**major**.**minor**.so and libdb_tcl-**major**.**minor**.so.

On most UNIX systems, when any shared library is created, the linker stamps it with a "SONAME". In the case of Berkeley DB, the SONAME is libdb-**major**.**minor**.so. It is important to realize that applications linked against a shared library remember the SONAMEs of the libraries they use, and not the underlying names in the filesystem.

When the Berkeley DB shared library is installed, links are created in the install lib directory so that libdb-**major**.**minor**.so, libdb-**major**.so, and libdb.so all reference the same library. This library will have an SONAME of libdb-**major**.**minor**.so.

Any previous versions of the Berkeley DB libraries that are present in the install directory (such as libdb-2.7.so or libdb-2.so) are left unchanged. (Removing or moving old shared libraries is one drastic way to identify applications that have been linked against those vintage releases.)

Once you have installed the Berkeley DB libraries, unless they are installed in a directory where the linker normally looks for shared libraries, you will need to specify the installation directory as part of compiling and linking against Berkeley DB. Consult your system manuals or system administrator for ways to specify a shared library directory when compiling and linking applications with the Berkeley DB libraries. Many systems support environment variables (for example, LD_LIBRARY_PATH, LD_RUN_PATH), or system configuration files (for example, /etc/ld.so.conf) for this purpose.

We recommend that applications link against libdb.so (for example, using -ldb). Even though the linker uses the file named libdb.so, the executable file for the application remembers the library's SONAME (libdb-**major**.**minor**.so). This has the effect of marking the applications with the versions they need at link time. Because applications locate their needed SONAMEs when they are executed, all previously linked applications will continue to run using the library they were linked with, even when a new version of Berkeley DB is installed and the file **libdb.so** is replaced with a new version.

Warning

Some UNIX installations may have an already existing **/usr/lib/libdb.so**, and this library may be an incompatible version of Berkeley DB.

Warning

The information in this section is intended to be generic and is likely to be correct for most UNIX systems. Unfortunately, dynamic shared libraries are not standard between UNIX systems, so there may be information here that is not correct for your system. If you have problems, consult your compiler and linker manual pages, or your system administrator.

Applications that know they are using features specific to a particular Berkeley DB release can be linked to that release. For example, an application wanting to link to Berkeley DB major release "3" can link using -ldb-3, and applications that know about a particular minor release number can specify both major and minor release numbers; for example, -ldb-3.5.

If you want to link with Berkeley DB before performing library installation, the "make" command will have created a shared library object in the **.libs** subdirectory of the build directory, such as **build_unix/.libs/libdb-major.minor.so**. If you want to link a file against this library, with, for example, a major number of "3" and a minor number of "5", you should be able to do something like the following:

```
cc -L BUILD_DIRECTORY/.libs -o testprog testprog.o -ldb-3.5
env LD_LIBRARY_PATH="BUILD_DIRECTORY/.libs:$LD_LIBRARY_PATH" ./testprog
```

BUILD_DIRECTORY is the full directory path to the directory where you built Berkeley DB.

The libtool program (which is configured in the build_unix directory) can be used to set the shared library path and run a program. For example, the following runs the gdb debugger on the db_dump utility after setting the appropriate paths:

```
libtool gdb db_dump
```

Libtool may not know what to do with arbitrary commands (it is hard-wired to recognize "gdb" and some other commands). If it complains, the mode argument will usually resolve the problem:

```
libtool —mode=execute my_debugger db_dump
```

On most systems, using libtool in this way is exactly equivalent to setting the LD_LIBRARY_PATH environment variable and then executing the program. On other systems, using libtool has the virtue of knowing about any other details on systems that don't behave in this typical way.

Running the Test Suite Under UNIX

The Berkeley DB test suite is built if you specify —enable-test as an argument when configuring Berkeley DB.

Before running the tests for the first time, you may need to edit the **include.tcl** file in your build directory. The Berkeley DB configuration assumes that you intend to use the version of the tclsh utility included in the Tcl installation with which Berkeley DB was configured to run the test suite, and further assumes that the test suite will be run with the libraries prebuilt in the Berkeley DB build directory. If either of these assumptions are incorrect, you will need to edit the **include.tcl** file and change the following line to correctly specify the full path to the version of tclsh with which you are going to run the test suite:

```
set tclsh_path ...
```

You may also need to change the following line to correctly specify the path from the directory where you are running the test suite to the location of the Berkeley DB Tcl API library you built:

```
set test_path ...
```

It may not be necessary that this be a full path if you have configured your system's dynamic shared library mechanisms to search the directory where you built or installed the Tcl library.

All Berkeley DB tests are run from within **tclsh**. After starting tclsh, you must source the file **test.tcl** in the test directory. For example, if you built in the **build_unix** directory of the distribution, this would be done using the following command:

```
% source ../test/test.tcl
```

Once you have executed that command and the "%" prompt has returned without errors, you are ready to run tests in the test suite.

Architecture-Independent FAQs

1. **When compiling with gcc, I get unreferenced symbols; for example, the following:**

```
symbol __muldi3: referenced symbol not found
symbol __cmpdi2: referenced symbol not found
```

On systems where they're available (HP-UX, Solaris), Berkeley DB uses 64-bit integral types. As far as we can tell, some versions of gcc don't support these types. The simplest workaround is to reconfigure Berkeley DB using the —disable-bigfile configuration option and then rebuild.

2. **My C++ program traps during a failure in a DB call on my gcc-based system.**

We believe there are some severe bugs in the implementation of exceptions for some gcc compilers. Exceptions require some interaction between compiler, assembler, and runtime libraries. We're not sure exactly what is at fault, but one failing combination is gcc 2.7.2.3 running on SuSE Linux 6.0. The problem on this system can be seen with a rather simple test case of an exception thrown from a shared library and caught in the main program.

A variation of this problem seems to occur on AIX, although we believe it does not necessarily involve shared libraries on that platform.

If you see a trap that occurs when an exception might be thrown by the DB runtime, we suggest that you use static libraries instead of dynamic (shared) libraries. See the documentation for configuration. If this doesn't work and you have a choice of compilers, try using a more recent gcc- or a non-gcc-based compiler to build Berkeley DB.

Finally, you can disable the use of exceptions in the C++ runtime for Berkeley DB by using the DB_CXX_NO_EXCEPTIONS flag with db_env_create or db_create. When this flag is on, all C++ methods fail by returning an error code rather than throwing an exception.

3. **I get unexpected results and database corruption when running threaded programs.**

   I get error messages that mutex (for example, pthread_mutex_XXX or mutex_XXX) functions are undefined when linking applications with Berkeley DB.

   On some architectures, the Berkeley DB library uses the ISO POSIX standard pthreads and UNIX International (UI) threads interfaces for underlying mutex support; for example, Solaris and HP-UX. You can specify compilers or compiler flags, or link with the appropriate thread library when loading your application to resolve the undefined references:

   ```
   cc ... -lpthread ...
   cc ... -lthread ...
   xlc_r ...
   cc ... -mt ...
   ```

   See the appropriate architecture-specific Reference Guide pages for more information.

   On systems where more than one type of mutex is available, it may be necessary for applications to use the same threads package from which Berkeley DB draws its mutexes. For example, if Berkeley DB was built to use the POSIX pthreads mutex calls for mutex support, the application may need to be written to use the POSIX pthreads interfaces for its threading model. This is only conjecture at this time, and although we know of no systems that actually have this requirement, it's not unlikely that some exist.

   In a few cases, Berkeley DB can be configured to use specific underlying mutex interfaces. You can use the —enable-posixmutexes and —enable–uimutexes configuration options to specify the POSIX and UNIX International (UI) threads packages. This should not, however, be necessary in most cases.

   In some cases, it is vitally important to make sure that you load the correct library. For example, on Solaris systems, there are POSIX pthread interfaces in the C library, so applications can link Berkeley DB using only C library and not see any undefined symbols. However, the C library POSIX pthread mutex support is insufficient for Berkeley DB, and Berkeley DB cannot detect that fact. Similar errors can arise when applications (for example, tclsh) use dlopen to dynamically load Berkeley DB as a library.

If you are seeing problems in this area after you confirm that you're linking with the correct libraries, there are two other things you can try. First, if your platform supports interlibrary dependencies, we recommend that you change the Berkeley DB Makefile to specify the appropriate threads library when creating the Berkeley DB dynamic library, as an interlibrary dependency. Second, if your application is using dlopen to dynamically load Berkeley DB, specify the appropriate thread library on the link line when you load the application itself.

4. **I get core dumps when running programs that fork children.**

   Berkeley DB handles should not be shared across process forks; each forked child should acquire its own Berkeley DB handles.

5. **I get reports of uninitialized memory reads and writes when running software analysis tools (for example, Rational Software Corp.'s Purify tool).**

   For performance reasons, Berkeley DB does not write the unused portions of database pages or fill in unused structure fields. To turn off these errors when running software analysis tools, build with the —enable-umrw configuration option.

6. **Berkeley DB programs or the test suite fail unexpectedly.**

   The Berkeley DB architecture does not support placing the shared memory regions on remote filesystems—for example, the Network File System (NFS) or the Andrew File System (AFS). For this reason, the shared memory regions (normally located in the database home directory) must reside on a local filesystem. See "Shared Memory Regions" for more information.

   With respect to running the test suite, always check to make sure that TEST-DIR is not on a remote mounted filesystem.

7. **The db_dump185 utility fails to build.**

   The **db_dump185** utility is the utility that supports the conversion of Berkeley DB 1.85 and earlier databases to current database formats. If the errors look something like the following, it means that the Berkeley DB 1.85 code was not found in the standard libraries:

   ```
   cc -o db_dump185 db_dump185.o
   ld:
   Unresolved:
   dbopen
   ```

To build **db_dump185**, the Berkeley DB version 1.85 code must have already been built and installed on the system. If the Berkeley DB 1.85 header file is not found in a standard place, or if the library is not part of the standard libraries used for loading, you will need to edit your Makefile, and change the following lines:

```
DB185INC=
DB185LIB=
```

The system Berkeley DB 1.85 header file and library are found; for example:

```
DB185INC=/usr/local/include
DB185LIB=-ldb185
```

AIX

1. **I can't compile and run multithreaded applications.**

   Special compile-time flags are required when compiling threaded applications on AIX. If you are compiling a threaded application, you must compile with the _THREAD_SAFE flag and load with specific libraries; for example, "-lc_r". Specifying the compiler name with a trailing "_r" usually performs the right actions for the system.

   ```
   xlc_r ...
   cc -D_THREAD_SAFE -lc_r ...
   ```

   The Berkeley DB library will automatically build with the correct options.

2. **I can't run using the DB_SYSTEM_MEM option to DBENV→open.**

   AIX 4.1 allows applications to map only 10 system shared memory segments. In AIX 4.3, this has been raised to 256K segments, but only if you set the environment variable "export EXTSHM=ON".

3. **I can't create database files larger than 1GB on AIX.**

   By default, Berkeley DB does not include large-file support for AIX systems. Sleepycat Software has been told that the following changes will add large-file support on the AIX 4.2 and later releases, but we have not tested them ourselves.

   Add the following lines to the **db_config.h** file in your build directory:

   ```
   #ifdef      HAVE_FILE_OFFSET_BITS
   #define     _LARGE_FILES                    /* AIX specific. */
   #endif
   ```

   Change the source code for **os/os_open.c** to always specify the **O_LARGEFILE** flag to the **open**(2) system call.

   Recompile Berkeley DB from scratch.

Note that the documentation for the IBM Visual Age compiler states that it does not support the 64-bit filesystem APIs necessary for creating large files; the ibm-cxx product must be used instead. We have not heard whether the GNU gcc compiler supports the 64-bit APIs or not.

Finally, to create large files under AIX, the filesystem has to be configured to support large files and the system-wide user hard-limit for file sizes has to be greater than 1GB.

FreeBSD

1. **I can't compile and run multithreaded applications.**

   Special compile-time flags are required when compiling threaded applications on FreeBSD. If you are compiling a threaded application, you must compile with the _THREAD_SAFE and -pthread flags:

   ```
   cc -D_THREAD_SAFE -pthread ...
   ```

   The Berkeley DB library will automatically build with the correct options.

2. **I get occasional failures when running RPC-based programs under FreeBSD clients.**

   There is a known bug in the XDR implementation in the FreeBSD C library from version 2.2 up to version 4.0-RELEASE that causes certain-sized messages to fail and return a zero-filled reply to the client. A bug report (#16028) has been filed with FreeBSD. The following patch is the FreeBSD fix:

   ```
   *** /usr/src/lib/libc/xdr/xdr_rec.c.orig        Mon Jan 10 10:20:42 2000
   --- /usr/src/lib/libc/xdr/xdr_rec.c     Wed Jan 19 10:53:45 2000
   ***************
   *** 558,564 ****
               * but we don't have any way to be certain that they aren't
               * what the client actually intended to send us.
               */
   !         if ((header & (~LAST_FRAG)) == 0)
                       return(FALSE);
             rstrm→fbtbc = header & (~LAST_FRAG);
             return (TRUE);
   --- 558,564 ----
               * but we don't have any way to be certain that they aren't
               * what the client actually intended to send us.
               */
   !         if (header == 0)
                       return(FALSE);
             rstrm→fbtbc = header & (~LAST_FRAG);
             return (TRUE);
   ```

HP-UX

1. **I can't specify the DB_SYSTEM_MEM flag to DBENV→open.**

   The **shmget**(2) interfaces are not always used on HP-UX, even though they exist, because anonymous memory allocated using shmget(2) cannot be used to store the standard HP-UX msemaphore semaphores. For this reason, it may not be possible to specify the DB_SYSTEM_MEM flag on some versions of HP-UX. (We have seen this problem only on HP-UX 10.XX, so the simplest workaround may be to upgrade your HP-UX release.)

2. **I can't specify both the DB_PRIVATE and DB_THREAD flags to DBENV→open.**

   It is not possible to store the standard HP-UX msemaphore semaphores in memory returned by **malloc**(3) in some versions of HP-UX. For this reason, it may not be possible to specify both the DB_PRIVATE and DB_THREAD flags on some versions of HP-UX. (We have seen this problem only on HP-UX 10.XX, so the simplest workaround may be to upgrade your HP-UX release.)

3. **During configuration, I see a message that large file support has been turned off.**

   Some HP-UX system include files redefine "open" when big-file support (the HAVE_FILE_OFFSET_BITS and _FILE_OFFSET_BITS #defines) is enabled. This causes problems when compiling for C++, where "open" is a legal identifier, used in the Berkeley DB C++ API. For this reason, we automatically turn off big-file support when Berkeley DB is configured with a C++ API. This should not be a problem for applications unless there is a need to create databases larger than 2GB.

4. **I can't compile and run multithreaded applications.**

   Special compile-time flags are required when compiling threaded applications on HP-UX. If you are compiling a threaded application, you must compile with the _REENTRANT flag:

   ```
   cc -D_REENTRANT ...
   ```

   The Berkeley DB library will automatically build with the correct options.

5. **An ENOMEM error is returned from DBENV→open or DBENV→remove.**

   Due to the constraints of the PA-RISC memory architecture, HP-UX does not allow a process to map a file into its address space multiple times. For this reason, each Berkeley DB environment may be opened only once by a process on HP-UX; that is, calls to **DBENV→open** will fail if the specified Berkeley DB environment has been opened and not subsequently closed.

6. **When compiling with gcc, I see the following error:**

   ```
   #error "Large Files (ILP32) not supported in strict ANSI mode."
   ```

   We believe this is an error in the HP-UX include files, but we don't really understand it. The only workaround we have found is to add -D__STDC_EXT__ to the C preprocessor defines as part of compilation.

7. **When using the Tcl or Perl APIs (including running the test suite), I see the error "Can't shl_load() a library containing Thread Local Storage".**

   This problem happens when HP-UX has been configured to use pthread mutex locking, and an attempt is made to call Berkeley DB using the Tcl or Perl APIs. We have never found any way to fix this problem as part of the Berkeley DB build process. To work around the problem, rebuild tclsh or perl, and modify its build process to explicitly link it against the HP-UX pthread library (currently /usr/lib/libpthread.a).

8. **When running an executable that has been dynamically linked against the Berkeley DB library, I see the error "Can't find path for shared library", even though I correctly set the SHLIB_PATH environment variable.**

   By default, some versions of HP-UX ignore the dynamic library search path specified by the SHLIB_PATH environment variable. To work around this, specify the "+s" flag to ld when linking, or run the following on the executable that is not working:

   ```
   chatr +s enable -l /full/path/to/libdb-3.2.sl ...
   ```

IRIX

1. **I can't compile and run multithreaded applications.**

   Special compile-time flags are required when compiling threaded applications on IRIX. If you are compiling a threaded application, you must compile with the _SGI_MP_SOURCE flag:

   ```
   cc -D_SGI_MP_SOURCE ...
   ```

   The Berkeley DB library will automatically build with the correct options.

Linux

1. **I can't compile and run multithreaded applications.**

   Special compile-time flags are required when compiling threaded applications on Linux. If you are compiling a threaded application, you must compile with the _REENTRANT flag:

   ```
   cc -D_REENTRANT ...
   ```

   The Berkeley DB library will automatically build with the correct options.

OSF/1

1. **I can't compile and run multithreaded applications.**

   Special compile-time flags are required when compiling threaded applications on OSF/1. If you are compiling a threaded application, you must compile with the _REENTRANT flag:

   ```
   cc -D_REENTRANT ...
   ```

   The Berkeley DB library will automatically build with the correct options.

SCO

1. **If I build with gcc, programs such as db_dump and db_stat core dump immediately when invoked.**

   We suspect gcc or the runtime loader may have a bug, but we haven't tracked it down. If you want to use gcc, we suggest building static libraries.

Solaris

1. **I can't compile and run multithreaded applications.**

   Special compile-time flags and additional libraries are required when compiling threaded applications on Solaris. If you are compiling a threaded application, you must compile with the D_REENTRANT flag and link with the libpthread.a or libthread.a libraries:

   ```
   cc -mt ...
   cc -D_REENTRANT ... -lthread
   cc -D_REENTRANT ... -lpthread
   ```

   The Berkeley DB library will automatically build with the correct options.

2. **I've installed gcc on my Solaris system, but configuration fails because the compiler doesn't work.**

   On some versions of Solaris, there is a cc executable in the user's path, but all it does is display an error message and fail:

   ```
   % which cc
   /usr/ucb/cc
   % cc
   /usr/ucb/cc: language optional software package not installed
   ```

   Because Berkeley DB always uses the native compiler in preference to gcc, this is a fatal error. If the error message you're seeing is the following, this may be the problem you're seeing:

   ```
   checking whether the C compiler (cc -O ) works... no
   configure: error: installation or configuration problem: C compiler cannot
   create executables.
   ```

   The simplest workaround is to set your CC environment variable to the system compiler and reconfigure; for example:

   ```
   env CC=gcc ../dist/configure
   ```

   If you are using the —configure-cxx option, you may also want to specify a C++ compiler, for example, the following:

   ```
   env CC=gcc CCC=g++ ../dist/configure
   ```

3. **I get the error "libc internal error: _rmutex_unlock: rmutex not held", followed by a core dump when running threaded or JAVA programs.**

   This is a known bug in Solaris 2.5 and it is fixed by Sun patch 103187-25.

4. **I get error reports of nonexistent files, corrupted metadata pages, and core dumps.**

   Solaris 7 contains a bug in the threading libraries (-lpthread, -lthread), which causes the wrong version of the pwrite routine to be linked into the application if the thread library is linked in after the the C library. The result will be that the pwrite function is called rather than the pwrite64. To work around the problem, use an explicit link order when creating your application.

   Sun Microsystems is tracking this problem with Bug Id's 4291109 and 4267207, and patch 106980-09 to Solaris 7 fixes the problem:

   ```
   Bug Id: 4291109
   Duplicate of: 4267207
   Category: library
   Subcategory: libthread
   State: closed
   Synopsis: pwrite64 mapped to pwrite
   Description:
   When libthread is linked after libc, there is a table of functions in
   libthread that gets "wired into" libc via _libc_threads_interface().
   The table in libthread is wrong in both Solaris 7 and on28_35 for the
   TI_PWRITE64 row (see near the end).
   ```

5. **During configuration, I see a message that large file support has been turned off.**

The Solaris 8 system include files redefine "open" when big-file support (the HAVE_FILE_OFFSET_BITS and _FILE_OFFSET_BITS #defines) is enabled. This causes problems when compiling for C++, where "open" is a legal identifier used in the Berkeley DB C++ API. For this reason, we automatically turn off big-file support when Berkeley DB is configured with a C++ API. This should not be a problem for applications unless there is a need to create databases larger than 2GB.

SunOS

1. **I can't specify the DB_SYSTEM_MEM flag to DBENV→open.**

The **shmget**(2) interfaces are not used on SunOS releases prior to 5.0, even though they apparently exist, because the distributed include files did not allow them to be compiled. For this reason, it will not be possible to specify the DB_SYSTEM_MEM flag those versions of SunOS.

Ultrix

1. **Configuration complains that mmap(2) interfaces aren't being used.**

The **mmap**(2) interfaces are not used on Ultrix, even though they exist, because they are known to not work correctly.

Building Berkeley DB for Win32 Platforms

T HE BUILD_WIN32 DIRECTORY IN THE BERKELEY DB DISTRIBUTION contains project files for both MSVC 5.0 and 6.0:

Project File	Description
Berkeley_DB.dsw	Visual C++ 5.0 project (compatible with 6.0)
*.dsp	Visual C++ 5.0 subprojects (compatible with 6.0)

Building for Win32

These project files can be used to build Berkeley DB for any Win32 platform: Windows 2000, Windows NT, Windows 98, and Windows 95.

Building with Visual C++ 6.0

Open the file **Berkeley_DB.dsw**. You will be told that the project was generated by a previous version of Developer Studio, and asked if you want to convert the project. Select Yes, and all projects will be converted. Then, continue with the instructions for building with Visual C++ 5.0.

Note that when you build a release version, you may receive a warning about an unknown compiler option /Ob2. This is apparently a flaw in the project conversion for Visual C++ and can be ignored.

Each release of Berkeley DB is built and tested with this procedure using Microsoft Visual C++ 6.0, Standard Edition.

Building with Visual C++ 5.0

Open the file **Berkeley_DB.dsw**. This workspace includes a number of subprojects needed to build Berkeley DB.

First, you'll need to set the include directories. To do this, select *Options…* from the *Tools* pull-down menu. At this point, a tabbed dialog should appear. In this new window, choose the *Directories* tab. For the *Platform*, select *Win32* and for *Show directories for*, select *Include files*. Below these options, you should add two directories to the list of directories: the full pathname of the *build_win32* subdirectory of Berkeley DB, followed by the full pathname of the *include* subdirectory of Berkeley DB. Then, click OK.

Select *Active Project Configuration* under the *Build* pull-down menu. For a debug version of the libraries, tools, and examples, select *db_buildall—Win32 Debug*. Results from this build are put into **build_win32/Debug**. For a release version, select *db_buildall—Win32 Release*; results are put into **build_win32/Release**. For a debug version that has all tools and examples built with static libraries, select *db_buildall—Win32 Debug Static*; results are put into **build_win32/Debug_static**. For a release version of the same, select *db_buildall—Win32 Release Static*; results are put into **build_win32/Release_static**. Finally, to build, select *Build db_buildall.exe* under the *Build* pull-down menu.

When building your application, you should normally use compile options "debug multithreaded dll" and link against **build_win32/Debug/libdb32d.lib**. If you want to link against a static (non-DLL) version of the library, use the "debug multithreaded" compile options and link against **build_win32/Debug_static/libdb32sd.lib**. You can also build using a release version of the libraries and tools, which will be placed in **build_win32/Release/libdb32.lib**. The static version will be in **build_win32/Release_static/libdb32s.lib**.

Each release of Berkeley DB is maintained, built, and tested using Microsoft Visual C++ 5.0 and 6.0.

Including the C++ API

C++ support is built automatically on Win32.

Including the Java API

Java support is not built automatically. The following instructions assume that you installed the Sun Java Development Kit in **d:/java**. Of course, if you installed elsewhere or have different Java software, you will need to adjust the pathnames accordingly. First, use the previous instructions for Visual C++ 5.0 or 6.0 to open the Tools/Options tabbed dialog for adding include directories. In addition to the directories specified previously, add **d:/java/include** and **d:/java/include/win32**. These are the directories needed when including **jni.h**. Now, before clicking OK, choose *Executable files* under *Show directories for*. Add **d:/java/bin**. That directory is needed to find javac. Now, select OK.

Select *Active Project Configuration* under the *Build* pull-down menu. Choose *db_java—Win32 Release*. To build, select *Build libdb_java32.dll* under the *Build* pull-down menu. This builds the Java support library for Berkeley DB and compiles all the java files, placing the class files in the **java/classes** subdirectory of Berkeley DB. Set your environment variable CLASSPATH to include this directory, set your environment variable PATH to include the **build_win32/Release** subdirectory, and try running the command as a test:

```
java com.sleepycat.examples.AccessExample
```

Including the Tcl API

Tcl support is not built automatically. See "Loading Berkeley DB with Tcl" for information on sites from which you can download Tcl and which Tcl versions are compatible with Berkeley DB.

The Tcl library must be built as the same build type as the Berkeley DB library (both Release or both Debug). We found that the binary release of Tcl can be used with the Release configuration of Berkeley DB, but you will need to build Tcl from sources for the Debug configuration. Before building Tcl, you will need to modify its makefile to make sure that you are building a debug version, including thread support. This is because the set of DLLs linked into the Tcl executable must match the corresponding set of DLLs used by Berkeley DB.

These notes assume that Tcl is installed as **d:/tcl**, but you can change that if you wish. If you run using a version of Tcl different from the one currently being used by Sleepycat Software, you will need to change the name of the Tcl library used in the build (for example, tcl83d.lib) to the appropriate name. See Projects→Settings→Link in the db_tcl subproject.

Use the previous instructions for Visual C++ 5.0 or 6.0 to open the *Tools/Options* tabbed dialog for adding include directories. In addition to the directories specified previously, add **d:/tcl/include**. This is the directory that contains **tcl.h**. Then, in that same dialog, show directories for "Library Files". Add **d:/tcl/lib** (or whatever directory contains **tcl83d.lib** in your distribution) to the list. Now, select OK.

Select *Active Project Configuration* under the *Build* pull-down menu. Choose *db_tcl—Win32 Release*. To build, select *Build libdb_tcl32.dll* under the *Build* pull-down menu. This builds the Tcl support library for Berkeley DB, placing the result into **build_win32/Release/libdb_tcl32.dll**. Selecting an Active Configuration of *db_tcl—Win32 Debug* will build a debug version, placing the result into **build_win32/Debug/libdb_tcl32d.dll**.

Running the Test Suite Under Windows

To build the test suite on Win32 platforms, you will need to configure Tcl support. You will also need sufficient main memory (at least 64MB) and disk (around 100MB of disk will be sufficient). For main memory, 32MB is too small; we recommend at least 64MB.

Building the Software Needed by the Tests

There are bugs in some versions of Tcl that may cause the test suite to hang on Windows/NT 4.0. Tcl version 8.4 (currently available as an alpha release) has fixed the problem, or there are patches available for Tcl 8.3.2 (see bug #119188 in the Tcl SourceForge database). Note that if you want to run the test suite against a Debug version of Berkeley DB, you need to build a Debug version of Tcl. This involves building Tcl from its source.

To build, perform the following steps. Note that steps #1, #4, and #5 are part of the normal build process for building Berkeley DB; #2, #3 are part of including the Tcl API.

1. Open the **build_win32/Berkeley_DB.dsw** workspace.

2. Add the pathname for the Tcl include subdirectory to your include path. To do this, under the *Tools* menu item, select *Options*. In the dialog, select the *Directories* tab, and choose directories for *Include Files*. Add **d:/tcl/include** (or whatever directory contains **tcl.h** in your distribution) to the list.

3. Add the pathname for the Tcl library subdirectory to your library path. To do this, select *Options* under the *Tools* menu item. In the dialog, select the *Directories* tab, and choose directories for *Library Files*. Add **d:/tcl/lib** (or whatever directory contains **tcl83d.lib** in your distribution) to the list.

4. Set the active configuration to db_test—Debug. To set an active configuration, select *Set Active Configuration* under the *Build* menu item in the IDE. Then, choose *db_test—Debug*.

5. Build. The IDE menu for this is called "build dbkill.exe", even though dbkill is just one of the things that is built. This step builds the base Berkeley DB .dll, tcl support, and various tools that are needed by the test suite.

Running the Test Suite Under Windows

Before running the tests for the first time, you must edit the file **include.tcl** in your build directory and change the line that reads:

```
set tclsh_path SET_YOUR_TCLSH_PATH
```

You will want to use the location of the **tclsh** program. For example, if Tcl is installed as **d:/tcl**, this line should be the following:

```
set tclsh_path d:/tcl/bin/tclsh83d.exe
```

Then, in a shell of your choice enter the following commands:

1. cd build_win32
2. run **d:/tcl/bin/tclsh83d.exe**, or the equivalent name of the Tcl shell for your distribution.

   You should get a "%" prompt.
3. % source ../test/test.tcl.

   You should get a "%" prompt with no errors.

Windows Notes

- Various Berkeley DB interfaces take a **mode** argument, which is intended to specify the underlying file permissions for created files. Berkeley DB currently ignores this argument on Windows systems.

  It would be possible to construct a set of security attributes to pass to **CreateFile** that accurately represents the mode. In the worst case, this would involve looking up user and all group names, and creating an entry for each. Alternatively, we could call the **_chmod** (partial emulation) function after file creation, although this leaves us with an obvious race.

  Practically speaking, however, these efforts would be largely meaningless on FAT, the most common filesystem, which only has a "readable" and "writeable" flag, applying to all users.

- When using the DB_SYSTEM_MEM flag, Berkeley DB shared regions are created without ACLs, which means that the regions are only accessible to a single user. If wider sharing is appropriate (for example, both user applications and Windows/NT service applications need to access the Berkeley DB regions), the Berkeley DB code will need to be modified to create the shared regions with the correct ACLs. Alternatively, by not specifying the DB_SYSTEM_MEM flag, filesystem-backed regions will be created instead, and the permissions on those files may be directly specified through the **DBENV→open** interface.

- On Windows/9X, files opened by multiple processes do not share data correctly. For this reason, the DB_SYSTEM_MEM flag is implied for any application that does not specify the DB_PRIVATE flag, causing the system paging file to be used for sharing data. However, paging file memory is freed on last close, implying that multiple processes sharing an environment must arrange for at least one process to always have the environment open, or, alternatively, that any process joining the environment be prepared to re-create it. If a shared environment is closed by all processes, a subsequent open without specifying the DB_CREATE flag will result in the return of a system EAGAIN error code.

Windows FAQ

1. **My Win* C/C++ application crashes in the Berkeley DB library when Berkeley DB calls fprintf (or some other standard C library function).**

   You should be using the "Debug Multithreaded DLL" compiler option in your application when you link with the build_win32/Debug/libdb32d.lib library (this .lib file is actually a stub for libdb32d.DLL). To check this setting in Visual C++, choose the *Project/Settings* menu item and select *Code Generation* under the tab marked *C/C++*, and see the box marked *Use runtime library*. This should be set to *Debug Multithreaded DLL*. If your application is linked against the static library, build_win32/Debug/libdb32sd.lib; then, you will want to set *Use runtime library* to *Debug Multithreaded*.

   Setting this option incorrectly can cause multiple versions of the standard libraries to be linked into your application (one on behalf of your application, and one on behalf of the Berkeley DB library). That violates assumptions made by these libraries, and traps can result.

2. **Why are the build options for DB_DLL marked as "Use MFC in a Shared DLL"? Does Berkeley DB use MFC?**

   Berkeley DB does not use MFC at all. It does however, call malloc and free and other facilities provided by the Microsoft C runtime library. We found in our work that many applications and libraries are built assuming MFC, and specifying this for Berkeley DB solves various interoperation issues, and guarantees that the right runtime libraries are selected. Note that because we do not use MFC facilities, the MFC library DLL is not marked as a dependency for libdb.dll, but the appropriate Microsoft C runtime is.

23

Building Berkeley DB for VxWorks Systems

T HE BUILD_VXWORKS DIRECTORY IN THE BERKELEY DB DISTRIBUTION contains a workspace and project files for Tornado 2.0.

Table 23.1 **Files and Descriptions**

File	Description
Berkeley DB.wsp	Berkeley DB Workspace file
Berkeley DB.wpj	Berkeley DB Project file
ex_*/*.wpj	Example programs project files

Building with Tornado 2.0

Open the workspace **Berkeley DB.wsp**. The list of projects in this workspace will be shown. These projects were created for the x86 BSP for VxWorks.

The remainder of this document assumes that you already have a VxWorks target and a target server, both up and running.

First, you need to set the include directories. To do this, go to the *Builds* tab for the workspace. Open up *Berkeley DB Builds*. You will see several different builds, containing different configurations. All of the projects in the Berkeley DB workspace are created to be downloadable applications.

Table 23.2 **Builds and Descriptions**

Build	Description
PENTIUM_RPCdebug	x86 BSP with RPC and debugging
PENTIUM_RPCnodebug	x86 BSP with RPC no debugging
PENTIUM_debug	x86 BSP no RPC with debugging
PENTIUM_nodebug	x86 BSP no RPC no debugging
SIMSPARCSOLARISgnu	VxSim BSP no RPC with debugging

You have to add a new build specification if you use a different BSP or want to customize further. For instance, if you have the Power PC (PPC) BSP, you need to add a new build for the PPC tool chain. To do so, select the Builds tab, select the Berkeley DB project name, and right-click. Choose the *New Build…* selection and create the new build target. For your new build target, you need to decide whether you want it configured to support RPC and whether it should be built for debugging. See the properties of the Pentium builds for ways to configure for each case. After you add this build, you still need to correctly configure the include directories, as described in the sections that follow.

If you are running on a host that is not Solaris or with a different BSP, you should remove the build specifications that do not apply to your hardware. We recommend that you do this after you configure any new build specifications first. The Tornado tools will get confused if you have a SIMSPARCSOLARISgnu build specification on a Windows NT host, for instance.

Select the build you are interested in, and right-click. Choose the *Properties…* selection. At this point, a tabbed dialog should appear. In this new window, choose the *C/C++ compiler* tab. In the edit box, you need to modify the full pathname of the *build_vxworks* subdirectory of Berkeley DB, followed by the full pathname of the *include* subdirectory of Berkeley DB. Then, click OK.

If the architecture for this new build has the most significant byte first, you also need to edit the *db_config.h* file in the build directory and define **WORDS_BIGENDIAN**.

To build and download the Berkeley DB downloadable application for the first time requires several steps:

1. Select the build you are interested in, and right-click. Choose the *Set… as Active Build* selection.

2. Select the build you are interested in, and right-click. Choose the *Dependencies…* selection. Run dependencies over all files in the Berkeley DB project.

3. Select the build you are interested in, and right-click. Choose the *Rebuild All (Berkeley DB.out)* selection.

4. Select the Berkeley DB project name, and right-click. Choose the *Download 'Berkeley DB.out'* selection.

You need to repeat this procedure for all builds you are interested in building, as well as for all of the example project builds you want to run.

VxWorks Notes

Berkeley DB currently disallows the DB_TRUNC flag to **DB→open**. The operations that this flag represents are not fully supported under VxWorks 5.4.

The memory on VxWorks is always resident and fully shared among all tasks running on the target. For this reason, the DB_SYSTEM_MEM flag is implied for any application that does not specify the DB_PRIVATE flag. Additionally, applications must use a segment ID to ensure that different applications do not overwrite each other's database environments. See the **DBENV→set_shm_key** function for more information. Also, the DB_LOCKDOWN flag has no effect.

The **DB→sync** function is implemented using an ioctl call into the filesystem driver with the FIOSYNC command. Most, but not all filesystem drivers support this call. Berkeley DB requires the use of a filesystem supporting FIOSYNC.

Building and Running the Example Programs

Each example program can be downloaded and run by calling the function equivalent to the example's name. You may have to edit the pathname to the environments and database names in the examples' sources. The examples included are shown in the following table:

Table 23.3 **Example Programs and Descriptions**

Name	Description
ex_access	Simple access method example.
ex_btrec	Example using Btree and record numbers.
ex_dbclient	Example running an RPC client. Takes a hostname as an argument; for example, *ex_dbclient "myhost"*.
ex_env	Example using an environment.
ex_mpool	Example using mpools.
ex_tpcb	Example using transactions. This example requires two invocations, both taking an integer identifier as an argument. This identifier allows for multiple sets of databases to be used within the same environment. The first is to initialize the databases; for example, *ex_tpcb_init 1*. The second is to run the program on those databases; or example, *ex_tpcb 1*.

VxWorks FAQ

1. **Can I run the test suite under VxWorks?**

   The test suite requires the Berkeley DB Tcl library. In turn, this library requires Tcl 8.1 or greater. In order to run the test suite, you would need to port Tcl 8.1 or greater to VxWorks. The Tcl shell included in *windsh* is not adequate, for two reasons. First, it is based on Tcl 8.0. Second, it does not include the necessary Tcl components for adding a Tcl extension.

2. **Are all Berkeley DB features available for VxWorks?**

   All Berkeley DB features are available for VxWorks, with the exception of the DB_TRUNCATE flag for **DB→open**. The underlying mechanism needed for that flag is not available consistently across different filesystems for VxWorks.

3. **Are there any constraints using particular filesystem drivers?**

   There are constraints using the dosFs filesystems with Berkeley DB. Namely, you must configure your dosFs filesystem to support long filenames if you are using Berkeley DB logging in your application. The VxWorks' dosFs 1.0 filesystem, by default, uses the old MS-DOS 8.3 file-naming constraints, restricting to 8-character filenames with a 3-character extension. If you have configured with VxWorks' dosFs 2.0, you should be compatible with Windows FAT32 filesystems that support long filenames.

4. **Are there any dependencies on particular filesystem drivers?**

   There is one dependency on specifics of filesystem drivers in the port of Berkeley DB to VxWorks. Berkeley DB synchronizes data using the FIOSYNC function to ioctl() (another option would have been to use the FIOFLUSH function instead). The FIOSYNC function was chosen because the NFS client driver, nfsDrv, only supports it and doesn't support FIOFLUSH. All local filesystems, as of VxWorks 5.4, support FIOSYNC—with the exception of rt11fsLib, which only supports FIOFLUSH. To use rt11fsLib, you will need to modify the os/os_fsync.c file to use the FIOFLUSH function; note that rt11fsLib cannot work with NFS clients.

5. **Are there any known filesystem problems?**

   During the course of our internal testing, we came across two problems with the dosFs 2.0 filesystem that warranted patches from Wind River Systems. You should ask Wind River Systems for the patches to these problems if you encounter them.

   The first problem is that files will seem to disappear. You should look at **SPR 31480** in the Wind River Systems' Support pages for a more detailed description of this problem.

The second problem is a semaphore deadlock within the dosFs filesystem code. Looking at a stack trace via CrossWind, you will see two or more of your application's tasks waiting in semaphore code within dosFs. The patch for this problem is under **SPR 33221** at Wind River Systems.

6. **Are there any filesystems I cannot use?**

The Target Server File System (TSFS) uses the netDrv driver. This driver does not support any ioctl that allows flushing to the disk, and therefore cannot be used with Berkeley DB.

7. **Why aren't the utility programs part of the project?**

The utility programs, in their UNIX-style form, are not ported to VxWorks. The reasoning is that the utility programs are essentially wrappers for the specific Berkeley DB interface they call. Their interface and generic model are not the appropriate paradigm for VxWorks. It is most likely that specific applications will want to spawn tasks that call the appropriate Berkeley DB function to perform the actions of some utility programs, using VxWorks native functions. For example, an application that spawns several tasks that all may operate on the same database would also want to spawn a task that calls **lock_detect** for deadlock detection, but specific to the environment used for that application.

8. **What VxWorks primitives are used for mutual exclusion in Berkeley DB?**

Mutexes inside of Berkeley DB use the basic binary semaphores in VxWorks. The mutexes are created using the FIFO queue type.

24

Upgrading Berkeley DB Applications

T HE FOLLOWING INFORMATION DESCRIBES THE GENERAL PROCESS of upgrading Berkeley DB installations. There are three issues to be considered when upgrading Berkeley DB applications and database environments: the application API; the underlying database formats; and, in the case of transactional database environments, the log files. The issues that need to be considered depend on whether or not the release is a major or minor release (in which either the major or minor number of the version changed), or a patch release (in which only the patch number in the version changed).

Upgrading Berkeley DB Installations

Berkeley DB major and minor releases may optionally include changes to the Berkeley DB application API, log files, and database formats that are not backward-compatible with previous releases. Each Berkeley DB major or minor release has information in this chapter of the Reference Guide, describing how to upgrade to the new release. The section describes any API changes made in the release. Application maintainers should review the API changes, update their applications as necessary, and then recompile using the new release. In addition, each section includes a page specifying whether the log file format or database formats changed in non-backward-compatible ways as part of the release. Because there are several underlying Berkeley DB database formats, and they do not all necessarily change in the same release, changes to a database format in a release may not affect any particular application.

A Berkeley DB patch release will never modify the Berkeley DB API, log file, or database formats in non-backward-compatible ways, and so applications need only be relinked (or, in the case of a shared library, pointed at the new version of the shared library) to upgrade to a new release.

Note that internal Berkeley DB interfaces may change at any time and in any release (including patch releases) without warning. This means the library must be entirely recompiled and reinstalled when upgrading to new releases of the library because there is no guarantee that modules from one version of the library will interact correctly with modules from another release.

If the release is a patch release, do the following:

1. Shut down the old version of the application.

2. Install the new version of the application by relinking or installing a new version of the Berkeley DB shared library.

3. Restart the application.

Otherwise, if the application does not have a Berkeley DB transactional environment, the application may be installed in the field using the following steps:

1. Shut down the old version of the application.

2. Remove any Berkeley DB environment using the **DBENV→remove** function or an appropriate system utility.

3. Recompile and install the new version of the application.

4. If the database format has changed, upgrade the application's databases. See "Upgrading Databases" for more information.

5. Restart the application.

Otherwise, if the application has a Berkeley DB transactional environment, but neither the log file nor database formats have changed, the application may be installed in the field using the following steps:

1. Shut down the old version of the application.

2. Run recovery on the database environment using the **DBENV→open** function or the **db_recover** utility.

3. Remove any Berkeley DB environment using the **DBENV→remove** function or an appropriate system utility.

4. Recompile and install the new version of the application.

5. Restart the application.

If the application has a Berkeley DB transactional environment, and the log file format has changed, but the database formats have not, the application may be installed in the field using the following steps:

1. Shut down the old version of the application.
2. Run recovery on the database environment using the **DBENV→open** function or the **db_recover** utility.
3. Remove any Berkeley DB environment using the **DBENV→remove** function or an appropriate system utility.
4. Archive the database environment for catastrophic recovery. See "Archival Procedures" for more information.
5. Recompile and install the new version of the application.
6. Restart the application.

Otherwise, if the application has a Berkeley DB transactional environment and the database format has changed, the application may be installed in the field using the following steps:

1. Shut down the old version of the application.
2. Run recovery on the database environment using the **DBENV→open** function or the **db_recover** utility.
3. Remove any Berkeley DB environment using the **DBENV→remove** function or an appropriate system utility.
4. Archive the database environment for catastrophic recovery. See "Archival Procedures" for more information.
5. Recompile and install the new version of the application.
6. Upgrade the application's databases. See "Upgrading Databases" for more information.
7. Archive the database for catastrophic recovery again (using different media than before, of course).
8. Restart the application.

Note

This archival is not strictly necessary. However, if you have to perform catastrophic recovery after restarting the application, that recovery must be done based on the last archive you have made. If you make this second archive, you can use it as the basis of that catastrophic recovery. If you do not make this second archive, you have to use the archive you made in step 4 as the basis of your recovery, and you have to do a full upgrade on it before you can apply log files created after the upgrade to it.

25

Test Suite

ONCE YOU HAVE STARTED TCLSH AND HAVE LOADED THE test.tcl source file (see "Running the Test Suite Under UNIX" and "Running the Test Suite Under Windows" for more information), you are ready to run the test suite. At the tclsh prompt, to run the entire test suite, enter the following:

```
% run_std
```

Running the Test Suite

Running all the tests can take from several hours to a few days to complete, depending on your hardware. For this reason, the output from this command is redirected to a file in the current directory named **ALL.OUT**. Periodically, a line will be written to the standard output, indicating what test is being run. When the suite has finished, a single message indicating that the test suite completed successfully or that it failed will be written. If the run failed, you should review the file **ALL.OUT** to determine which tests failed. Errors will appear in that file as output lines, beginning with the string: FAIL.

It is also possible to run specific tests or tests for a particular subsystem:

```
% r archive
% r btree
% r env
% r frecno
% r hash
% r join
% r join
% r lock
% r log
% r mpool
% r mutex
% r queue
% r rbtree
% r recno
% r rrecno
% r subdb
% r txn
```

Or to run a single, individual test:

```
% test001 btree
```

It is also possible to modify the test run based on arguments on the command line. For example, the following command will run a greatly abbreviated form of test001, doing 10 operations instead of 10,000:

```
% test001 btree 10
```

In all cases, when not running the entire test suite as described previously, a successful test run will return you to the tclsh prompt (%). On failure, a message is displayed indicating what failed.

Tests are run, by default, in the directory **TESTDIR**. However, the test files are often very large. To use a different directory for the test directory, edit the file include.tcl in your build directory, and change the following line to a more appropriate value for your system:

```
set testdir ./TESTDIR
```

For example, change it to the following::

```
set testdir /var/tmp/db.test
```

Alternatively, you can create a symbolic link named TESTDIR in your build directory to an appropriate location for running the tests. Regardless of where you run the tests, the TESTDIR directory should be on a local filesystem; using a remote filesystem (for example, NFS) will almost certainly cause spurious test failures.

Test Suite FAQ

1. **The test suite has been running for over a day. What's wrong?**

   The test suite can take anywhere from some number of hours to several days to run, depending on your hardware configuration. As long as the run is making forward progress and new lines are being written to the **ALL.OUT** file, everything is probably fine.

2. **The test suite hangs.**

   The test suite requires Tcl 8.1 or greater, preferably at least Tcl 8.3. If you are using an earlier version of Tcl, the test suite may simply hang at some point.

26

Distribution

THE FOLLOWING TABLE LISTS THE DIRECTORIES WITH THEIR DESCRIPTIONS.

Table 26.1 **Source Code Layout**

Directory	Description
LICENSE	Berkeley DB Copyright
btree	Btree access method source code
build_unix	UNIX build directory
build_vxworks	VxWorks build directory
build_win32	Windows build directory
clib	C library replacement functions
common	Common Berkeley DB functions
cxx	C++ API
db	Berkeley DB database interfaces
db185	Berkeley DB version 1.85 compatibility API
db_archive	The db_archive utility
db_checkpoint	The db_checkpoint utility
db_deadlock	The db_deadlock utility
db_dump	The db_dump utility
db_dump185	The db_dump185 utility
db_load	The db_load utility

db_printlog	The db_printlog debugging utility
db_recover	The db_recover utility
db_stat	The db_stat utility
db_upgrade	The db_upgrade utility
db_verify	The db_verify utility
dbm	The dbm/ndbm compatibility APIs
dist	Berkeley DB administration/distribution tools
docs	Documentation
env	Berkeley DB environment interfaces
examples_c	C API example programs
examples_cxx	C++ API example programs
examples_java	Java API example programs
hash	Hash access method
hsearch	The hsearch compatibility API
include	Include files
java	Java API
libdb_java	The libdb_java shared library
lock	Lock manager
log	Log manager
mp	Shared memory buffer pool
mutex	Mutexes
os	POSIX 1003.1 operating system- specific functionality
os_vxworks	VxWorks operating system-specific functionality
os_win32	Windows operating system-specific functionality
perl.BerkeleyDB	BerkeleyDB Perl module
perl.DB_File	DB_File Perl module
qam	Queue access method source code
rpc_client	RPC client interface
rpc_server	RPC server utility
tcl	Tcl API
test	Test suite
txn	Transaction manager
xa	X/Open Distributed Transaction Processing XA interface

27

Additional References

FOR MORE INFORMATION ON BERKELEY DB OR ON DATABASE SYSTEMS theory in general, we recommend the following sources:

Technical Papers on Berkeley DB

- *Berkeley DB*, by Michael Olson, Keith Bostic, and Margo Seltzer, Proceedings of the 1999 Summer Usenix Technical Conference, Monterey, California, June 1999. This paper describes recent commercial releases of Berkeley DB, its most important features, the history of the software, and Sleepycat's Open Source licensing policies.

- *Challenges in Embedded Database System Administration*, by Margo Seltzer and Michael Olson, First Workshop on Embedded Systems, Cambridge, Massachusetts, March 1999. This paper describes the challenges that face embedded systems developers, and how Berkeley DB has been designed to address them.

- *LIBTP: Portable Modular Transactions for UNIX*, by Margo Seltzer and Michael Olson, USENIX Conference Proceedings, Winter 1992. This paper describes an early prototype of the transactional system for Berkeley DB.

- *A New Hashing Package for UNIX*, by Margo Seltzer and Oz Yigit, USENIX Conference Proceedings, Winter 1991. This paper describes the Extended Linear Hashing techniques used by Berkeley DB.

Background on Berkeley DB Features

These papers, although not specific to Berkeley DB, give a good overview of the way different Berkeley DB features were implemented.

- *The Art of Computer Programming Vol. 3: Sorting and Searching*, by D.E. Knuth, 1968, pp. 471–480.

- *Document Processing in a Relational Database System*, by Michael Stonebraker, Heidi Stettner, Joseph Kalash, Antonin Guttman, Nadene Lynn, Memorandum No. UCB/ERL M82/32, May 1982.

- *Dynamic Hash Tables*, by Per-Ake Larson, Communications of the ACM, April 1988.

- *Linear Hashing: A New Tool for File and Table Addressing*, by Witold Litwin, Proceedings of the 6th International Conference on Very Large Databases (VLDB), 1980

- *Operating System Support for Database Management*, by Michael Stonebraker, Communications of the ACM 24(7), 1981, pp. 412–418.

- *Prefix B-trees*, by Bayer and Unterauer, ACM Transactions on Database Systems, Vol. 2, 1 (March 1977), pp. 11–26.

- *The Ubiquitous B-tree*, by Douglas Comer, ACM Comput. Surv. 11, 2 (June 1979), pp. 121–138.

Database Systems Theory

These publications are standard reference works on the design and implementation of database systems. Berkeley DB uses many of the ideas they describe.

- *Concurrency Control and Recovery in Database Systems* by Bernstein, Goodman, Hadzilaco. Currently out of print, but available from http://research.microsoft.com/pubs/ccontrol/.

- *An Introduction to Database Systems, Volume 1* by C. J. Date, Addison Wesley Longman Publishers. In the 5th Edition, we recommend chapters 1, 2, 3, 16 and 17.

- *Transaction Processing Concepts and Techniques* by Jim Gray and Andreas Reuter, Morgan Kaufmann Publishers. We recommend chapters 1, 4 (skip 4.6, 4.7, 4.9, 4.10 and 4.11), 7, 9, 10.3, and 10.4.

II

API Manual

28   C API

29   C++ API

30   Java API

31   Tcl API

32   Supporting Utilities

28

C API

DB→close

```
#include <db.h>
int
DB→close(DB *db, u_int32_t flags);
```

Description

The DB→close function flushes any cached database information to disk, closes any open cursors, frees any allocated resources, and closes any underlying files. Because key/data pairs are cached in memory, failing to sync the file with the DB→close or **DB→sync** function may result in inconsistent or lost information.

The **flags** parameter must be set to 0 or the following value:

- DB_NOSYNC   Do not flush cached information to disk. The DB_NOSYNC flag is a dangerous option. It should be set only if the application is doing logging (with trans-actions) so that the database is recoverable after a system or application crash, or if the database is always generated from scratch after any system or application crash.

It is important to understand that flushing cached information to disk only minimizes the window of opportunity for corrupted data. Although unlikely, it is possible for data-base corruption to happen if a system or application crash occurs while writing data to the database. To ensure that database corruption never occurs, applications must either use transactions and logging with automatic recovery, use logging and application-specific recovery, or edit a copy of the database; and, once all applications using the database have successfully called DB→close, atomically replace the original database with the updated copy.

When multiple threads are using the Berkeley DB handle concurrently, only a single thread may call the DB→close function.

Once DB→close has been called, regardless of its return, the DB handle may not be accessed again.

The DB→close function returns a non-zero error value on failure, 0 on success, and returns DB_INCOMPLETE if the underlying database still has dirty pages in the cache. (The only reason to return DB_INCOMPLETE is if another thread of control were writing pages in the underlying database file at the same time as the DB→close function was called. For this reason, a return of DB_INCOMPLETE can normally be ignored, or, in cases where it is a possible return value, the DB_NOSYNC option should probably have been specified.)

Errors

The DB→close function may fail and return a non-zero error for errors specified for other Berkeley DB and C library or system functions. If a catastrophic error has occurred, the DB→close function may fail and return DB_RUNRECOVERY, in which case all subsequent Berkeley DB calls will fail in the same way.

DB→cursor

```
#include <db.h>

int
DB→cursor(DB *db,
    DB_TXN *txnid, DBC **cursorp, u_int32_t flags);
```

Description

The DB→cursor function creates a cursor and copies a pointer to it into the memory referenced by **cursorp**.

If the operation is to be transaction-protected, the **txnid** parameter is a transaction handle returned from **txn_begin**; otherwise, NULL.

To transaction-protect cursor operations, cursors must be opened and closed within the context of a transaction, and the **txnid** parameter specifies the transaction context in which the cursor may be used.

The **flags** value must be set to 0 or by bitwise inclusively **OR**'ing together one or more of the following values:

- DB_WRITECURSOR   Specify that the cursor will be used to update the database. This flag should **only** be set when the DB_INIT_CDB flag was specified to **DBENV→open**.

The DB→cursor function returns a non-zero error value on failure and 0 on success.

Errors

The DB→cursor function may fail and return a non-zero error for the following conditions:

- EINVAL   An invalid flag value or parameter was specified.

The DB→cursor function may fail and return a non-zero error for errors specified for other Berkeley DB and C library or system functions. If a catastrophic error has occurred, the DB→cursor function may fail and return DB_RUNRECOVERY, in which case all subsequent Berkeley DB calls will fail in the same way.

DB→del

```
#include <db.h>

int
DB→del(DB *db, DB_TXN *txnid, DBT *key, u_int32_t flags);
```

Description

The DB→del function removes key/data pairs from the database. The key/data pair associated with the specified **key** is discarded from the database. In the presence of duplicate key values, all records associated with the designated key will be discarded.

If the operation is to be transaction-protected, the **txnid** parameter is a transaction handle returned from **txn_begin**; otherwise, NULL.

The **flags** parameter is currently unused, and must be set to 0.

The DB→del function returns a non-zero error value on failure, 0 on success, and DB_NOTFOUND if the specified **key** did not exist in the file.

Errors

The DB→del function may fail and return a non-zero error for the following conditions:

- DB_LOCK_DEADLOCK   The operation was selected to resolve a deadlock.
- EACCES   An attempt was made to modify a read-only database.
- EINVAL   An invalid flag value or parameter was specified.

The DB→del function may fail and return a non-zero error for errors specified for other Berkeley DB and C library or system functions. If a catastrophic error has occurred, the DB→del function may fail and return DB_RUNRECOVERY, in which case all subsequent Berkeley DB calls will fail in the same way.

DB→fd

```
#include <db.h>

int
DB→fd(DB *db, int *fdp);
```

Description

The DB→fd function copies a file descriptor representative of the underlying database into the memory referenced by **fdp**. A file descriptor referencing the same file will be returned to all processes that call **DB→open** with the same **file** argument. This file descriptor may be safely used as an argument to the **fcntl**(2) and **flock**(2) locking functions. The file descriptor is not necessarily associated with any of the underlying files actually used by the access method.

The DB→fd function only supports a coarse-grained form of locking. Applications should use the lock manager where possible.

The DB→fd function returns a non-zero error value on failure and 0 on success.

Errors

The DB→fd function may fail and return a non-zero error for errors specified for other Berkeley DB and C library or system functions. If a catastrophic error has occurred, the DB→fd function may fail and return DB_RUNRECOVERY, in which case all subsequent Berkeley DB calls will fail in the same way.

DB→get

```
#include <db.h>

int
DB→get(DB *db,
    DB_TXN *txnid, DBT *key, DBT *data, u_int32_t flags);
```

Description

The DB→get function retrieves key/data pairs from the database. The address and length of the data associated with the specified **key** are returned in the structure referenced by **data**.

In the presence of duplicate key values, DB→get will return the first data item for the designated key. Duplicates are sorted by insert order, except where this order has been overridden by cursor operations. Retrieval of duplicates requires the use of cursor operations. See **DBcursor→c_get** for details.

If the operation is to be transaction-protected, the **txnid** parameter is a transaction handle returned from **txn_begin**; otherwise, NULL.

The **flags** parameter must be set to 0 or one of the following values:

- DB_CONSUME   Return the record number and data from the available record closest to the head of the queue, and delete the record. The cursor will be positioned on the deleted record. The record number will be returned in **key**, as described in **DBT**. The data will be returned in the **data** parameter. A record is available if it is not deleted and is not currently locked. The underlying database must be of type Queue for DB_CONSUME to be specified.

- DB_CONSUME_WAIT   The DB_CONSUME_WAIT flag is the same as the DB_CONSUME flag, except that if the Queue database is empty, the thread of control will wait until there is data in the queue before returning. The underlying database must be of type Queue for DB_CONSUME_WAIT to be specified.

- DB_GET_BOTH   Retrieve the key/data pair only if both the key and data match the arguments.

- DB_SET_RECNO   Retrieve the specified numbered key/data pair from a database. Upon return, both the **key** and **data** items will have been filled in, not just the data item as is done for all other uses of the DB→get function.

  The **data** field of the specified **key** must be a pointer to a logical record number (that is, a **db_recno_t**). This record number determines the record to be retrieved.

  For DB_SET_RECNO to be specified, the underlying database must be of type Btree, and it must have been created with the DB_RECNUM flag.

In addition, the following flag may be set by bitwise inclusively **OR**'ing it into the **flags** parameter:

- DB_RMW   Acquire write locks instead of read locks when doing the retrieval. Setting this flag can eliminate deadlock during a read-modify-write cycle by acquiring the write lock during the read part of the cycle so that another thread of control acquiring a read lock for the same item, in its own read-modify-write cycle, will not result in deadlock.

  Because the DB→get interface will not hold locks across Berkeley DB interface calls in non-transactional environments, the DB_RMW flag to the DB→get call is meaningful only in the presence of transactions.

If the database is a Queue or Recno database and the requested key exists, but was never explicitly created by the application or was later deleted, the DB→get function returns DB_KEYEMPTY.

Otherwise, if the requested key is not in the database, the DB→get function returns DB_NOTFOUND.

Otherwise, the DB→get function returns a non-zero error value on failure and 0 on success.

Errors

The DB→get function may fail and return a non-zero error for the following conditions:

- DB_LOCK_DEADLOCK   The operation was selected to resolve a deadlock.
- ENOMEM   There was insufficient memory to return the requested item.
- EINVAL   An invalid flag value or parameter was specified.

A record number of 0 was specified.

The DB_THREAD flag was specified to the **DB→open** function and none of the DB_DBT_MALLOC, DB_DBT_REALLOC or DB_DBT_USERMEM flags were set in the **DBT**.

The DB→get function may fail and return a non-zero error for errors specified for other Berkeley DB and C library or system functions. If a catastrophic error has occurred, the DB→get function may fail and return DB_RUNRECOVERY, in which case all subsequent Berkeley DB calls will fail in the same way.

DB→get_byteswapped

```
#include <db.h>

int
DB→get_byteswapped(DB *db);
```

Description

The DB→get_byteswapped function returns 0 if the underlying database files were created on an architecture of the same byte order as the current one, and 1 if they were not (that is, big-endian on a little-endian machine, or vice versa). This field may be used to determine whether application data needs to be adjusted for this architecture or not.

DB→get_type

```
#include <db.h>

DBTYPE
DB→get_type(DB *db);
```

Description

The DB→get_type function returns the type of the underlying access method (and file format). It returns one of DB_BTREE, DB_HASH, DB_RECNO, or DB_QUEUE. This value may be used to determine the type of the database after a return from **DB→open** with the **type** argument set to DB_UNKNOWN.

DB→join

```
#include <db.h>

int
DB→join(DB *primary, DBC **curslist,
    DBC **dbcp, u_int32_t flags);
```

Description

The DB→join function creates a specialized cursor for use in performing joins on secondary indexes. For information on how to organize your data to use this functionality, see "Logical Join."

The **primary** argument contains the DB handle of the primary database, which is keyed by the data values found in entries in the **curslist**.

The **curslist** argument contains a NULL terminated array of cursors. Each cursor must have been initialized to reference the key on which the underlying database should be joined. Typically, this initialization is done by a **DBcursor→c_get** call with the DB_SET flag specified. Once the cursors have been passed as part of a **curslist**, they should not be accessed or modified until the newly created join cursor has been closed, or else inconsistent results may be returned.

Joined values are retrieved by doing a sequential iteration over the first cursor in the **curslist** argument, and a nested iteration over each secondary cursor in the order they are specified in the **curslist** argument. This requires database traversals to search for the current datum in all the cursors after the first. For this reason, the best join performance normally results from sorting the cursors from the one that references the least number of data items to the one that references the most. By default, DB→join does this sort on behalf of its caller.

The **flags** parameter must be set to 0 or the following value:

- DB_JOIN_NOSORT   Do not sort the cursors based on the number of data items they reference. If the data are structured so that cursors with many data items also share many common elements, higher performance will result from listing those cursors before cursors with fewer data items; that is, a sort order other than the default. The DB_JOIN_NOSORT flag permits applications to perform join optimization prior to calling DB→join.

A newly created cursor is returned in the memory location referenced by **dbcp** and supports only the **DBcursor→c_get** and **dbc_close** cursor functions:

- **DBcursor→c_get**   Iterates over the values associated with the keys to which each item in **curslist** was initialized. Any data value that appears in all items specified by the **curslist** argument is then used as a key into the **primary**, and the key/data pair found in the **primary** is returned.

The **flags** parameter must be set to 0 or the following value:

- DB_JOIN_ITEM   Do not use the data value found in all the cursors as a lookup key for the **primary**, but simply return it in the key parameter instead. The data parameter is left unchanged.

In addition, the following flag may be set by bitwise inclusively **OR**'ing it into the **flags** parameter:

- DB_RMW   Acquire write locks instead of read locks when doing the retrieval. Setting this flag can eliminate deadlock during a read-modify-write cycle by acquiring the write lock during the read part of the cycle so that another thread of control acquiring a read lock for the same item, in its own read-modify-write cycle, will not result in deadlock.

- **DBcursor→c_close**   Close the returned cursor and release all resources. (Closing the cursors in **curslist** is the responsibility of the caller.)

For the returned join cursor to be used in a transaction- protected manner, the cursors listed in **curslist** must have been created within the context of the same transaction.

The DB→join function returns a non-zero error value on failure and 0 on success.

Errors

The DB→join function may fail and return a non-zero error for the following conditions:

- EINVAL   An invalid flag value or parameter was specified.

  Cursor functions other than **DBcursor→c_get** or **DBcursor→c_close** were called.

The DB→join function may fail and return a non-zero error for errors specified for other Berkeley DB and C library or system functions. If a catastrophic error has occurred, the DB→join function may fail and return DB_RUNRECOVERY, in which case all subsequent Berkeley DB calls will fail in the same way.

DB→key_range

```
#include <db.h>

int
DB→key_range(DB *db, DB_TXN *txnid,
      DBT *key, DB_KEY_RANGE *key_range, u_int32_t flags);
```

Description

The DB→key_range function returns an estimate of the proportion of keys that are less than, equal to, and greater than the specified key. The underlying database must be of type Btree.

The information is returned in the **key_range** argument, which contains three elements of type double: **less**, **equal**, and **greater**. Values are in the range of 0 to 1; for example, if the field **less** is 0.05, 5% of the keys in the database are less than the key argument. The value for **equal** will be zero if there is no matching key, and will be non-zero otherwise.

If the operation is to be transaction-protected, the **txnid** parameter is a transaction handle returned from **txn_begin**; otherwise, NULL. The DB→key_range function does not retain the locks it acquires for the life of the transaction, so estimates may not be repeatable.

The **flags** parameter is currently unused, and must be set to 0.

The DB→key_range function returns a non-zero error value on failure and 0 on success.

Errors

The DB→key_range function may fail and return a non-zero error for the following conditions:

- DB_LOCK_DEADLOCK   The operation was selected to resolve a deadlock.
- EINVAL   An invalid flag value or parameter was specified.

  The underlying database was not of type Btree.

The DB→key_range function may fail and return a non-zero error for errors specified for other Berkeley DB and C library or system functions. If a catastrophic error has occurred, the DB→key_range function may fail and return DB_RUNRECOVERY, in which case all subsequent Berkeley DB calls will fail in the same way.

DB→open

```
#include <db.h>

int
DB→open(DB *db, const char *file,
    const char *database, DBTYPE type, u_int32_t flags, int mode);
```

Description

The currently supported Berkeley DB file formats (or *access methods*) are Btree, Hash, Queue, and Recno. The Btree format is a representation of a sorted, balanced tree structure. The Hash format is an extensible, dynamic hashing scheme. The Queue format supports fast access to fixed-length records accessed sequentially or by logical record number. The Recno format supports fixed- or variable-length records, accessed sequentially or by logical record number, and optionally backed by a flat text file.

Storage and retrieval for the Berkeley DB access methods are based on key/data pairs; see "DBT" for more information.

The DB→open interface opens the database represented by the **file** and **database** arguments for both reading and writing. The **file** argument is used as the name of an underlying file that will be used to back the database. The **database** argument is optional, and allows applications to have multiple databases in a single file. Although no **database** argument needs to be specified, it is an error to attempt to open a second database in a **file** that was not initially created using a **database** name. Further, the **database** argument is not supported by the Queue format.

In-memory databases never intended to be preserved on disk may be created by setting both the **file** and **database** arguments to NULL. Note that in-memory databases can only ever be shared by sharing the single database handle that created them, in circumstances where doing so is safe.

The **type** argument is of type DBTYPE, and must be set to one of DB_BTREE, DB_HASH, DB_QUEUE, DB_RECNO, or DB_UNKNOWN. If **type** is DB_UNKNOWN, the database must already exist and DB→open will automatically determine its type. The **DB→get_type** function may be used to determine the underlying type of databases opened using DB_UNKNOWN.

The **flags** and **mode** arguments specify how files will be opened and/or created if they do not already exist.

The **flags** value must be set to 0 or by bitwise inclusively **OR**'ing together one or more of the following values.

- DB_CREATE   Create any underlying files, as necessary. If the files do not already exist and the DB_CREATE flag is not specified, the call will fail.

- DB_EXCL   Return an error if the file already exists. Underlying filesystem primitives are used to implement this flag. For this reason, it is only applicable to the file and cannot be used to test whether a database in a file already exists. The DB_EXCL flag is only meaningful when specified with the DB_CREATE flag.

- DB_NOMMAP   Do not map this database into process memory (see the description of the **DBENV→set_mp_mmapsize** function for further information).

- DB_RDONLY   Open the database for reading only. Any attempt to modify items in the database will fail, regardless of the actual permissions of any underlying files.

- DB_THREAD   Cause the DB handle returned by DB→open to be *free-threaded*; that is, usable by multiple threads within a single address space.

- DB_TRUNCATE   Physically truncate the underlying file, discarding all previous databases it might have held. Underlying filesystem primitives are used to implement this flag. For this reason, it is only applicable to the file and cannot be used to discard databases within a file. The DB_TRUNCATE flag cannot be transaction-protected, and it is an error to specify it in a transaction-protected environment.

On UNIX systems or in IEEE/ANSI Std 1003.1 (POSIX) environments, all files created by the access methods are created with mode **mode** (as described in **chmod**(2)) and modified by the process' umask value at the time of creation (see **umask**(2)). The group ownership of created files is based on the system and directory defaults, and is not further specified by Berkeley DB. If **mode** is 0, files are created readable and writable by both owner and group. On Windows systems, the mode argument is ignored.

Calling DB→open is a reasonably expensive operation, and maintaining a set of open databases will normally be preferable to repeatedly opening and closing the database for each new query.

The DB→open function returns a non-zero error value on failure and 0 on success.

Environment Variables

- DB_HOME   If the **dbenv** argument to **db_create** was initialized using **DBENV→open**, the environment variable **DB_HOME** may be used as the path of the database environment home. Specifically, DB→open is affected by the configuration value DB_DATA_DIR.

- TMPDIR   If the **file** and **dbenv** arguments to DB→open are NULL, the environment variable **TMPDIR** may be used as a directory in which to create a temporary backing file.

Errors

The DB→open function may fail and return a non-zero error for the following conditions:

- DB_OLD_VERSION   The database cannot be opened without being first upgraded.

- EEXIST   DB_CREATE and DB_EXCL were specified and the file exists.

- EINVAL   An invalid flag value or parameter was specified (for example, unknown database type, page size, hash function, pad byte, byte order) or a flag value or parameter that is incompatible with the specified database.

    The DB_THREAD flag was specified, and spinlocks are not implemented for this architecture.

    The DB_THREAD flag was specified to DB→open, but was not specified to the **DBENV→open** call for the environment in which the DB handle was created.

    A backing flat text file was specified with either the DB_THREAD flag or the provided database environment supports transaction processing.

- ENOENT   A non-existent **re_source** file was specified.

The DB→open function may fail and return a non-zero error for errors specified for other Berkeley DB and C library or system functions. If a catastrophic error has occurred, the DB→open function may fail and return DB_RUNRECOVERY, in which case all subsequent Berkeley DB calls will fail in the same way.

DB→put

```
#include <db.h>

int
DB→put(DB *db,
    DB_TXN *txnid, DBT *key, DBT *data, u_int32_t flags);
```

Description

The DB→put function stores key/data pairs in the database. The default behavior of the DB→put function is to enter the new key/data pair, replacing any previously existing key if duplicates are disallowed, or adding a duplicate data item if duplicates are allowed. If the database supports duplicates, the DB→put function adds the new data value at the end of the duplicate set. If the database supports sorted duplicates, the new data value is inserted at the correct sorted location.

If the operation is to be transaction-protected, the **txnid** parameter is a transaction handle returned from **txn_begin**; otherwise, NULL.

The **flags** parameter must be set to 0 or one of the following values:

- DB_APPEND   Append the key/data pair to the end of the database. For the DB_APPEND flag to be specified, the underlying database must be a Queue or Recno database. The record number allocated to the record is returned in the specified **key**.

There is a minor behavioral difference between the Recno and Queue access methods for the DB_APPEND flag. If a transaction enclosing a DB→put operation with the DB_APPEND flag aborts, the record number may be decremented (and later reallocated by a subsequent DB_APPEND operation) by the Recno access method, but will not be decremented or reallocated by the Queue access method.

- DB_NODUPDATA   In the case of the Btree and Hash access methods, enter the new key/data pair only if it does not already appear in the database. If the key/data pair already appears in the database, DB_KEYEXIST is returned. The DB_NODUPDATA flag may only be specified if the underlying database has been configured to support sorted duplicates.

  The DB_NODUPDATA flag may not be specified to the Queue or Recno access methods.

- DB_NOOVERWRITE   Enter the new key/data pair only if the key does not already appear in the database. If the key already appears in the database, DB_KEYEXIST is returned. Even if the database allows duplicates, a call to DB→put with the DB_NOOVERWRITE flag set will fail if the key already exists in the database.

Otherwise, the DB→put function returns a non-zero error value on failure and 0 on success.

Errors

The DB→put function may fail and return a non-zero error for the following conditions:

- DB_LOCK_DEADLOCK   The operation was selected to resolve a deadlock.
- EACCES   An attempt was made to modify a read-only database.
- EINVAL   An invalid flag value or parameter was specified.

  A record number of 0 was specified.

  An attempt was made to add a record to a fixed-length database that was too large to fit.

  An attempt was made to do a partial put.

- ENOSPC   A btree exceeded the maximum btree depth (255).

The DB→put function may fail and return a non-zero error for errors specified for other Berkeley DB and C library or system functions. If a catastrophic error has occurred, the DB→put function may fail and return DB_RUNRECOVERY, in which case all subsequent Berkeley DB calls will fail in the same way.

DB→remove

```
#include <db.h>

int
DB→remove(DB *db,
      const char *file, const char *database, u_int32_t flags);
```

Description

The DB→remove interface removes the database specified by the **file** and **database** arguments. If no **database** is specified, the underlying file represented by **file** is removed, incidentally removing all databases that it contained.

Applications should not remove databases that are currently in use. If an underlying file is being removed and logging is currently enabled in the database environment, no database in the file may be open when the DB→remove function is called. In particular, some architectures do not permit the removal of files with open handles. On these architectures, attempts to remove databases that are currently in use by any thread of control in the system will fail.

The **flags** parameter is currently unused, and must be set to 0.

Once DB→remove has been called, regardless of its return, the DB handle may not be accessed again.

The DB→remove function returns a non-zero error value on failure and 0 on success.

Environment Variables

- DB_HOME   If the **dbenv** argument to **db_create** was initialized using **DBENV→open**, the environment variable **DB_HOME** may be used as the path of the database environment home. Specifically, DB→remove is affected by the configuration value DB_DATA_DIR.

Errors

The DB→remove function may fail and return a non-zero error for the following conditions:

- EINVAL   A database in the file is currently open.

The DB→remove function may fail and return a non-zero error for errors specified for other Berkeley DB and C library or system functions. If a catastrophic error has occurred, the DB→remove function may fail and return DB_RUNRECOVERY, in which case all subsequent Berkeley DB calls will fail in the same way.

DB→rename

```
#include <db.h>

int
DB→rename(DB *db, const char *file,
    const char *database, const char *newname, u_int32_t flags);
```

Description

The DB→rename interface renames the database specified by the **file** and **database** arguments to **newname**. If no **database** is specified, the underlying file represented by **file** is renamed, incidentally renaming all databases that it contained.

Applications should not rename databases that are currently in use. If an underlying file is being renamed and logging is currently enabled in the database environment, no database in the file may be open when the DB→rename function is called. In particular, some architectures do not permit renaming files with open handles. On these architectures, attempts to rename databases that are currently in use by any thread of control in the system will fail.

The **flags** parameter is currently unused, and must be set to 0.

Once DB→rename has been called, regardless of its return, the DB handle may not be accessed again.

The DB→rename function returns a non-zero error value on failure and 0 on success.

Environment Variables

- DB_HOME   If the **dbenv** argument to **db_create** was initialized using **DBENV→open**, the environment variable **DB_HOME** may be used as the path of the database environment home. Specifically, DB→rename is affected by the configuration value DB_DATA_DIR.

Errors

The DB→rename function may fail and return a non-zero error for the following conditions:

- EINVAL   A database in the file is currently open.

The DB→rename function may fail and return a non-zero error for errors specified for other Berkeley DB and C library or system functions. If a catastrophic error has occurred, the DB→rename function may fail and return DB_RUNRECOVERY, in which case all subsequent Berkeley DB calls will fail in the same way.

DB→set_append_recno

```
#include <db.h>

int
DB→set_append_recno(DB *,
    int (*db_append_recno_fcn)(DB *dbp, DBT *data, db_recno_t recno));
```

Description

When using the DB_APPEND option of the **DB→put** method, it may be useful to modify the stored data based on the generated key. If a callback function is specified using the DB→set_append_recno function, it will be called after the record number has been selected, but before the data has been stored. The callback function must return 0 on success and **errno** or a value outside of the Berkeley DB error name space on failure.

The called function must take three arguments: a reference to the enclosing database handle, the data **DBT** to be stored, and the selected record number. The called function may then modify the data **DBT**.

The DB→set_append_recno interface may only be used to configure Berkeley DB before the **DB→open** interface is called.

The DB→set_append_recno function returns a non-zero error value on failure and 0 on success.

DB→set_bt_compare

```
#include <db.h>

int
DB→set_bt_compare(DB *db,
    int (*bt_compare_fcn)(DB *, const DBT *, const DBT *));
```

Description

Set the Btree key comparison function. The comparison function is called when it is necessary to compare a key specified by the application with a key currently stored in the tree. The first argument to the comparison function is the **DBT** representing the application supplied key; the second is the current tree's key.

The comparison function must return an integer value less than, equal to, or greater than zero if the first key argument is considered to be respectively less than, equal to, or greater than the second key argument. In addition, the comparison function must cause the keys in the database to be *well-ordered*. The comparison function must correctly handle any key values used by the application (possibly including zero-length keys). In addition, when Btree key prefix comparison is being performed (see **DB→set_bt_prefix** for more information), the comparison routine may be passed a prefix of any database key. The **data** and **size** fields of the **DBT** are the only fields that may be used for the purposes of this comparison, and no particular alignment of the memory referenced by the **data** field may be assumed.

If no comparison function is specified, the keys are compared lexically, with shorter keys collating before longer keys. The same comparison method must be used each time a particular Btree is opened.

The DB→set_bt_compare interface may only be used to configure Berkeley DB before the **DB→open** interface is called.

The DB→set_bt_compare function returns a non-zero error value on failure and 0 on success.

Errors

- EINVAL   An invalid flag value or parameter was specified.

  Called after **DB→open** was called.

DB→set_bt_minkey

```
#include <db.h>

int
DB→set_bt_minkey(DB *db, u_int32_t bt_minkey);
```

Description

Set the minimum number of keys that will be stored on any single Btree page.

This value is used to determine which keys will be stored on overflow pages; that is, if a key or data item is larger than the underlying database page size divided by the **bt_minkey** value, it will be stored on overflow pages instead of within the page itself. The **bt_minkey** value specified must be at least 2; if **bt_minkey** is not explicitly set, a value of 2 is used.

The DB→set_bt_minkey interface may only be used to configure Berkeley DB before the **DB→open** interface is called.

The DB→set_bt_minkey function returns a non-zero error value on failure and 0 on success.

Errors

- EINVAL   An invalid flag value or parameter was specified.

  Called after **DB→open** was called.

DB→set_bt_prefix

```
#include <db.h>

int
DB→set_bt_prefix(DB *db,
    size_t (*bt_prefix_fcn)(DB *, const DBT *, const DBT *));
```

Description

Set the Btree prefix function. The prefix function must return the number of bytes of the second key argument that would be required by the Btree key comparison function to determine the second key argument's ordering relationship with respect to the first key argument. If the two keys are equal, the key length should be returned. The prefix function must correctly handle any key values used by the application (possibly including zero-length keys). The **data** and **size** fields of the **DBT** are the only fields that may be used for the purposes of this determination, and no particular alignment of the memory referenced by the **data** field may be assumed.

The prefix function is used to determine the amount by which keys stored on the Btree internal pages can be safely truncated without losing their uniqueness. See the "Btree Prefix Comparison" section of the *Reference Guide* for more details about how this works. The usefulness of this is data- dependent, but can produce significantly reduced tree sizes and search times in some data sets.

If no prefix function or key comparison function is specified by the application, a default lexical comparison function is used as the prefix function. If no prefix function is specified and a key comparison function is specified, no prefix function is used. It is an error to specify a prefix function without also specifying a key comparison function.

The DB→set_bt_prefix interface may only be used to configure Berkeley DB before the **DB→open** interface is called.

The DB→set_bt_prefix function returns a non-zero error value on failure and 0 on success.

Errors

- EINVAL   An invalid flag value or parameter was specified.

  Called after **DB→open** was called.

DB→set_cachesize

```
#include <db.h>

int
DB→set_cachesize(DB *db,
    u_int32_t gbytes, u_int32_t bytes, int ncache);
```

Description

Set the size of the database's shared memory buffer pool—that is, the cache—to **gbytes** gigabytes plus **bytes**. The cache should be the size of the normal working data set of the application, with some small amount of additional memory for unusual situations. (Note, the working set is not the same as the number of simultaneously referenced pages, and should be quite a bit larger!)

The default cache size is 256KB, and may not be specified as less than 20KB. Any cache size less than 500MB is automatically increased by 25% to account for buffer pool overhead; cache sizes larger than 500MB are used as specified. For information on tuning the Berkeley DB cache size, see "Selecting a Cache Size."

It is possible to specify caches to Berkeley DB that are large enough so that they cannot be allocated contiguously on some architectures. For example, some releases of Solaris limit the amount of memory that may be allocated contiguously by a process. If **ncache** is 0 or 1, the cache will be allocated contiguously in memory. If it is greater than 1, the cache will be broken up into **ncache** equally sized separate pieces of memory.

Because databases opened within Berkeley DB environments use the cache specified to the environment, it is an error to attempt to set a cache in a database created within an environment.

The DB→set_cachesize interface may only be used to configure Berkeley DB before the **DB→open** interface is called.

The DB→set_cachesize function returns a non-zero error value on failure and 0 on success.

Errors

- EINVAL   An invalid flag value or parameter was specified.

   The specified cache size was impossibly small.

DB→set_dup_compare

```
#include <db.h>

int
DB→set_dup_compare(DB *db,
    int (*dup_compare_fcn)(DB *, const DBT *, const DBT *));
```

Description

Set the duplicate data item comparison function. The comparison function is called when it is necessary to compare a data item specified by the application with a data item currently stored in the tree. The first argument to the comparison function is the **DBT** representing the application's data item; the second is the current tree's data item.

The comparison function must return an integer value less than, equal to, or greater than zero if the first data item argument is considered to be respectively less than, equal to, or greater than the second data item argument. In addition, the comparison function must cause the data items in the set to be *well-ordered*. The comparison function must correctly handle any data item values used by the application (possibly including zero-length data items). The **data** and **size** fields of the **DBT** are the only fields that may be used for the purposes of this comparison, and no particular alignment of the memory referenced by the **data** field may be assumed.

If no comparison function is specified, the data items are compared lexically, with shorter data items collating before longer data items. The same duplicate data item comparison method must be used each time a particular Btree is opened.

The DB→set_dup_compare interface may only be used to configure Berkeley DB before the **DB→open** interface is called.

The DB→set_dup_compare function returns a non-zero error value on failure and 0 on success.

Errors

- EINVAL   An invalid flag value or parameter was specified.

DB→set_errcall

```
#include <db.h>

void
DB→set_errcall(DB *,
    void (*db_errcall_fcn)(const char *errpfx, char *msg));
```

Description

When an error occurs in the Berkeley DB library, a Berkeley DB error or an error return value is returned by the function. In some cases, however, the **errno** value may be insufficient to completely describe the cause of the error, especially during initial application debugging.

The DB→set_errcall function is used to enhance the mechanism for reporting error messages to the application. In some cases, when an error occurs, Berkeley DB will call **db_errcall_fcn** with additional error information. The function must be declared with two arguments; the first will be the prefix string (as previously set by **DB→set_errpfx** or **DBENV→set_errpfx**); the second will be the error message string. It is up to the **db_errcall_fcn** function to display the error message in an appropriate manner.

Alternatively, you can use the **DB→set_errfile** or **DBENV→set_errfile** functions to display the additional information via a C library FILE *.

This error-logging enhancement does not slow performance or significantly increase application size, and may be run during normal operation as well as during application debugging.

For DB handles opened inside of Berkeley DB environments, calling the DB→set_errcall function affects the entire environment and is equivalent to calling the **DBENV→set_errcall** function.

The DB→set_errcall interface may be used to configure Berkeley DB at any time during the life of the application.

DB→set_errfile

```
#include <db.h>

void
DB→set_errfile(DB *db, FILE *errfile);
```

Description

When an error occurs in the Berkeley DB library, a Berkeley DB error or an error return value is returned by the function. In some cases, however, the **errno** value may be insufficient to completely describe the cause of the error, especially during initial application debugging.

The DB→set_errfile function is used to enhance the mechanism for reporting error messages to the application by setting a C library FILE * to be used for displaying additional Berkeley DB error messages. In some cases, when an error occurs, Berkeley DB will output an additional error message to the specified file reference.

The error message will consist of the prefix string and a colon (":") (if a prefix string was previously specified using **DB→set_errpfx** or **DBENV→set_errpfx**), an error string, and a trailing <newline> character.

This error-logging enhancement does not slow performance or significantly increase application size, and may be run during normal operation as well as during application debugging.

For DB handles opened inside of Berkeley DB environments, calling the DB→set_errfile function affects the entire environment and is equivalent to calling the **DBENV→set_errfile** function.

The DB→set_errfile interface may be used to configure Berkeley DB at any time during the life of the application.

DB→set_errpfx

```
#include <db.h>

void
DB→set_errpfx(DB *db, const char *errpfx);
```

Description

Set the prefix string that appears before error messages issued by Berkeley DB.

The DB→set_errpfx function does not copy the memory referenced by the **errpfx** argument; rather, it maintains a reference to it. This allows applications to modify the error message prefix at any time without repeatedly calling DB→set_errpfx, but means that the memory must be maintained until the handle is closed.

For DB handles opened inside of Berkeley DB environments, calling the DB→set_errpfx function affects the entire environment and is equivalent to calling the **DBENV→set_errpfx** function.

The DB→set_errpfx interface may be used to configure Berkeley DB at any time during the life of the application.

DB→set_feedback

```
#include <db.h>

int
DB→set_feedback(DB *,
    void (*db_feedback_fcn)(DB *dbp, int opcode, int pct));
```

Description

Some operations performed by the Berkeley DB library can take non-trivial amounts of time. The DB→set_feedback function can be used by applications to monitor progress within these operations.

When an operation is likely to take a long time, Berkeley DB will call the specified callback function. This function must be declared with three arguments: the first will be a reference to the enclosing database handle; the second will be a flag value; and the third will be the percent of the operation that has been completed, specified as an integer value between 0 and 100. It is up to the callback function to display this information in an appropriate manner.

The **opcode** argument may take on any of the following values:

- DB_UPGRADE   The underlying database is being upgraded.
- DB_VERIFY   The underlying database is being verified.

The DB→set_feedback interface may be used to configure Berkeley DB at any time during the life of the application.

The DB→set_feedback function returns a non-zero error value on failure and 0 on success.

DB→set_flags

```
#include <db.h>

int
DB→set_flags(DB *db, u_int32_t flags);
```

Description

Calling DB→set_flags is additive; there is no way to clear flags.

The **flags** value must be set to 0 or by bitwise inclusively **OR**'ing together one or more of the following values.

Btree

The following flags may be specified for the Btree access method:

- DB_DUP   Permit duplicate data items in the tree; that is, insertion when the key of the key/data pair being inserted already exists in the tree will be successful. The ordering of duplicates in the tree is determined by the order of insertion, unless the ordering is otherwise specified by use of a cursor operation. It is an error to specify both DB_DUP and DB_RECNUM.

- DB_DUPSORT   Permit duplicate data items in the tree; that is, insertion when the key of the key/data pair being inserted already exists in the tree will be successful. The ordering of duplicates in the tree is determined by the duplicate comparison function. If the application does not specify a comparison function using the **DB→set_dup_compare** function, a default lexical comparison will be used. It is an error to specify both DB_DUPSORT and DB_RECNUM.

- DB_RECNUM   Support retrieval from the Btree using record numbers. For more information, see the DB_GET_RECNO flag to the **DB→get** and **DBcursor→c_get** methods.

  Logical record numbers in Btree databases are mutable in the face of record insertion or deletion. See the DB_RENUMBER flag in the Recno access method information for further discussion.

  Maintaining record counts within a Btree introduces a serious point of contention, namely the page locations where the record counts are stored. In addition, the entire tree must be locked during both insertions and deletions, effectively single-threading the tree for those operations. Specifying DB_RECNUM can result in serious performance degradation for some applications and data sets.

  It is an error to specify both DB_DUP and DB_RECNUM.

- DB_REVSPLITOFF   Turn off reverse splitting in the Btree. As pages are emptied in a database, the Berkeley DB Btree implementation attempts to coalesce empty pages into higher-level pages in order to keep the tree as small as possible and minimize tree search time. This can hurt performance in applications with cyclical data demands; that is, applications where the database grows and shrinks repeatedly. For example, because Berkeley DB does page-level locking, the maximum level of concurrency in a database of two pages is far smaller than that in a database of 100 pages, so a database that has shrunk to a minimal size can cause severe deadlocking when a new cycle of data insertion begins.

Hash

The following flags may be specified for the Hash access method:

- DB_DUP   Permit duplicate data items in the tree; that is, insertion when the key of the key/data pair being inserted already exists in the tree will be successful. The ordering of duplicates in the tree is determined by the order of insertion, unless the ordering is otherwise specified by use of a cursor operation. It is an error to specify both DB_DUP and DB_RECNUM.

- DB_DUPSORT Permit duplicate data items in the tree; that is, insertion when the key of the key/data pair being inserted already exists in the tree will be successful. The ordering of duplicates in the tree is determined by the duplicate comparison function. If the application does not specify a comparison function using the **DB→set_dup_ compare** function, a default lexical comparison will be used. It is an error to specify both DB_DUPSORT and DB_RECNUM.

Queue

There are no additional flags that may be specified for the Queue access method.

Recno

The following flags may be specified for the Recno access method:

- DB_RENUMBER Specifying the DB_RENUMBER flag causes the logical record numbers to be mutable, and change as records are added to and deleted from the database. For example, the deletion of record number 4 causes records numbered 5 and greater to be renumbered downward by one. If a cursor was positioned to record number 4 before the deletion, it will reference the new record number 4, if any such record exists, after the deletion. If a cursor was positioned after record number 4 before the deletion, it will be shifted downward one logical record, continuing to reference the same record as it did before.

  Using the **DB→put** or **DBcursor→c_put** interfaces to create new records will cause the creation of multiple records if the record number is more than one greater than the largest record currently in the database. For example, creating record 28, when record 25 was previously the last record in the database, will create records 26 and 27 as well as 28. Attempts to retrieve records that were created in this manner will result in an error return of DB_KEYEMPTY.

  If a created record is not at the end of the database, all records following the new record will be automatically renumbered upward by one. For example, the creation of a new record numbered 8 causes records numbered 8 and greater to be renumbered upward by one. If a cursor was positioned to record number 8 or greater before the insertion, it will be shifted upward one logical record, continuing to reference the same record as it did before.

  For these reasons, concurrent access to a Recno database with the DB_RENUMBER flag specified may be largely meaningless, although it is supported.

- DB_SNAPSHOT This flag specifies that any specified **re_source** file be read in its entirety when **DB→open** is called. If this flag is not specified, the **re_source** file may be read lazily.

The DB→set_flags interface may only be used to configure Berkeley DB before the **DB→open** interface is called.

The DB→set_flags function returns a non-zero error value on failure and 0 on success.

Errors

- EINVAL An invalid flag value or parameter was specified.

DB→set_h_ffactor

```
#include <db.h>

int
DB→set_h_ffactor(DB *db, u_int32_t h_ffactor);
```

Description

Set the desired density within the hash table.

The density is an approximation of the number of keys allowed to accumulate in any one bucket, determining when the hash table grows or shrinks. If you know the average sizes of the keys and data in your dataset, setting the fill factor can enhance performance. A reasonable rule computing fill factor is to set it to the following:

```
(pagesize - 32) / (average_key_size + average_data_size + 8)
```

If no value is specified, the fill factor will be selected dynamically as pages are filled.

The DB→set_h_ffactor interface may only be used to configure Berkeley DB before the **DB→open** interface is called.

The DB→set_h_ffactor function returns a non-zero error value on failure and 0 on success.

Errors

- EINVAL   An invalid flag value or parameter was specified.

    Called after **DB→open** was called.

DB→set_h_hash

```
#include <db.h>

int
DB→set_h_hash(DB *db,
u_int32_t (*h_hash_fcn)(DB *, const void *bytes, u_int32_t length));
```

Description

Set a user-defined hash method; if no hash method is specified, a default hash method is used. Because no hash method performs equally well on all possible data, the user may find that the built-in hash method performs poorly with a particular data set. User-specified hash functions must take a pointer to a byte string and a length as arguments, and return a value of type **u_int32_t**. The hash function must handle any key values used by the application (possibly including zero-length keys).

If a hash method is specified, **DB→open** will attempt to determine whether the hash method specified is the same as the one with which the database was created, and will fail if it detects that it is not.

The DB→set_h_hash interface may only be used to configure Berkeley DB before the **DB→open** interface is called.

The DB→set_h_hash function returns a non-zero error value on failure and 0 on success.

Errors

- EINVAL   An invalid flag value or parameter was specified.

    Called after **DB→open** was called.

DB→set_h_nelem

```
#include <db.h>

int
DB→set_h_nelem(DB *db, u_int32_t h_nelem);
```

Description

Set an estimate of the final size of the hash table.

If not set or set too low, hash tables will still expand gracefully as keys are entered, although a slight performance degradation may be noticed.

The DB→set_h_nelem interface may only be used to configure Berkeley DB before the **DB→open** interface is called.

The DB→set_h_nelem function returns a non-zero error value on failure and 0 on success.

Errors

- EINVAL   An invalid flag value or parameter was specified.

    Called after **DB→open** was called.

DB→set_lorder

```
#include <db.h>

int
DB→set_lorder(DB *db, int lorder);
```

Description

Set the byte order for integers in the stored database metadata. The number should represent the order as an integer; for example, big-endian order is the number 4,321, and little-endian order is the number 1,234. If **lorder** is not explicitly set, the host order of the machine where the Berkeley DB library was compiled is used.

The value of **lorder** is ignored except when databases are being created. If a database already exists, the byte order it uses is determined when the database is opened.

The access methods provide no guarantees about the byte ordering of the application data stored in the database, and applications are responsible for maintaining any necessary ordering.

The DB→set_lorder interface may only be used to configure Berkeley DB before the **DB→open** interface is called.

The DB→set_lorder function returns a non-zero error value on failure and 0 on success.

Errors

- EINVAL An invalid flag value or parameter was specified.

DB→set_malloc

```
#include <db.h>

int
DB→set_malloc(DB *db, void *(*db_malloc)(size_t size));
```

Description

Set the allocation function used by the DB methods to allocate memory in which to return key/data items to the application.

The DB_DBT_MALLOC flag, when specified in the **DBT** object, will cause the DB methods to allocate and reallocate memory, which then becomes the responsibility of the calling application. See **DBT** for more information.

On systems in which there may be multiple library versions of malloc (notably Windows NT), specifying the DB_DBT_MALLOC flag will fail because the DB library will allocate memory from a different heap than the application will use to free it. To avoid this problem, the DB→set_malloc function can be used to pass Berkeley DB a reference to the application's allocation routine, in which case it will be used to allocate the memory returned when the DB_DBT_MALLOC flag is set.

The function specified must match the calling conventions of the ANSI C X3.159-1989 (ANSI C) library routine of the same name.

The DB→set_malloc interface may only be used to configure Berkeley DB before the **DB→open** interface is called.

The DB→set_malloc function returns a non-zero error value on failure and 0 on success.

Errors

- EINVAL An invalid flag value or parameter was specified.

DB→set_pagesize

```
#include <db.h>

int
DB→set_pagesize(DB *db, u_int32_t pagesize);
```

Description

Set the size of the pages used to hold items in the database, in bytes. The minimum page size is 512 bytes, and the maximum page size is 64K bytes. If the page size is not explicitly set, one is selected based on the underlying filesystem I/O block size. The automatically selected size has a lower limit of 512 bytes and an upper limit of 16K bytes.

For information on tuning the Berkeley DB page size, see "Selecting a Page Size."

The DB→set_pagesize interface may only be used to configure Berkeley DB before the **DB→open** interface is called.

The DB→set_pagesize function returns a non-zero error value on failure and 0 on success.

Errors

- EINVAL   An invalid flag value or parameter was specified.

DB→set_paniccall

```
#include <db.h>

int
DB→set_paniccall(DB *db,
    void (*paniccall)(DB_ENV *, int errval));
```

Description

Errors can occur in the Berkeley DB library where the only solution is to shut down the application and run recovery. (For example, if Berkeley DB is unable to write log records to disk because there is insufficient disk space.) In these cases, the value DB_RUNRECOVERY is returned by Berkeley DB.

In these cases, it is also often simpler to shut down the application when such errors occur rather than to try to gracefully return up the stack. The DB→set_paniccall function is used to specify a function to be called when DB_RUNRECOVERY is about to be returned from a Berkeley DB method. When called, the **dbenv** argument will be a reference to the current environment, and the **errval** argument is the error value that would have been returned to the calling function.

For DB handles opened inside of Berkeley DB environments, calling the DB→set_paniccall function affects the entire environment and is equivalent to calling the **DBENV→set_paniccall** function.

The DB→set_paniccall interface may be used to configure Berkeley DB at any time during the life of the application.

The DB→set_paniccall function returns a non-zero error value on failure and 0 on success.

DB→set_q_extentsize

```
#include <db.h>

int
DB→set_q_extentsize(DB *db, u_int32_t extentsize);
```

Description

Set the size of the extents used to hold pages in a Queue database, specified as a number of pages. Each extent is created as a separate physical file. If no extent size is set, the default behavior is to create only a single underlying database file.

For information on tuning the extent size, see "Selecting an Extent Size."

The DB→set_q_extentsize interface may only be used to configure Berkeley DB before the **DB→open** interface is called.

The DB→set_q_extentsize function returns a non-zero error value on failure and 0 on success.

Errors

- EINVAL   An invalid flag value or parameter was specified.

  Called after **DB→open** was called.

DB→set_re_delim

```
#include <db.h>

int
DB→set_re_delim(DB *db, int re_delim);
```

Description

Set the delimiting byte used to mark the end of a record in the backing source file for the Recno access method.

This byte is used for variable length records if the **re_source** file is specified. If the **re_source** file is specified and no delimiting byte was specified, <newline> characters (that is, ASCII 0x0a) are interpreted as end-of-record markers.

The DB→set_re_delim interface may only be used to configure Berkeley DB before the **DB→open** interface is called.

The DB→set_re_delim function returns a non-zero error value on failure and 0 on success.

Errors

- EINVAL   An invalid flag value or parameter was specified.

  Called after **DB→open** was called.

DB→set_re_len

```
#include <db.h>

int
DB→set_re_len(DB *db, u_int32_t re_len);
```

Description

For the Queue access method, specify that the records are of length **re_len**.

For the Recno access method, specify that the records are fixed-length, not byte- delimited, and are of length **re_len**.

Any records added to the database that are less than **re_len** bytes long are automatically padded (see **DB→set_re_pad** for more information).

Any attempt to insert records into the database that are greater than **re_len** bytes long will cause the call to fail immediately and return an error.

The DB→set_re_len interface may only be used to configure Berkeley DB before the **DB→open** interface is called.

The DB→set_re_len function returns a non-zero error value on failure and 0 on success.

Errors

- EINVAL   An invalid flag value or parameter was specified.

  Called after **DB→open** was called.

DB→set_re_pad

```
#include <db.h>

int
DB→set_re_pad(DB *db, int re_pad);
```

Description

Set the padding character for short, fixed-length records for the Queue and Recno access methods.

If no pad character is specified, <space> characters (that is, ASCII 0x20) are used for padding.

The DB→set_re_pad interface may only be used to configure Berkeley DB before the **DB→open** interface is called.

The DB→set_re_pad function returns a non-zero error value on failure and 0 on success.

Errors

- EINVAL   An invalid flag value or parameter was specified.

  Called after **DB→open** was called.

DB→set_re_source

```
#include <db.h>

int
DB→set_re_source(DB *db, char *re_source);
```

Description

Set the underlying source file for the Recno access method. The purpose of the **re_source** value is to provide fast access and modification to databases that are normally stored as flat text files.

If the **re_source** field is set, it specifies an underlying flat text database file that is read to initialize a transient record number index. In the case of variable length records, the records are separated, as specified by **DB→set_re_delim**. For example, standard UNIX byte stream files can be interpreted as a sequence of variable length records separated by <newline> characters.

In addition, when cached data would normally be written back to the underlying database file (for example, the **DB→close** or **DB→sync** methods are called), the in-memory copy of the database will be written back to the **re_source** file.

By default, the backing source file is read lazily; that is, records are not read from the file until they are requested by the application. If multiple processes (not threads) are accessing a Recno database concurrently, and are either inserting or deleting records, the backing source file must be read in its entirety before more than a single process accesses the database, and only that process should specify the backing source file as part of the DB→open call. See the DB_SNAPSHOT flag for more information.

Reading and writing the backing source file specified by re_source cannot be transaction-protected because it involves filesystem operations that are not part of the Db transaction methodology. For this reason, if a temporary database is used to hold the records; that is, a NULL was specified as the **file** argument to **DB→open**, it is possible to lose the contents of the **re_source** file; for example, if the system crashes at the right instant. If a file is used to hold the database (that is, a file name was specified as the **file** argument to **DB→open**), normal database recovery on that file can be used to prevent information loss, although it is still possible that the contents of **re_source** will be lost if the system crashes.

The **re_source** file must already exist (but may be zero-length) when **DB→open** is called.

It is not an error to specify a read-only **re_source** file when creating a database, nor is it an error to modify the resulting database. However, any attempt to write the changes to the backing source file using either the **DB→sync** or **DB→close** functions will fail, of course. Specify the DB_NOSYNC flag to the **DB→close** function to stop it from attempting to write the changes to the backing file; instead, they will be silently discarded.

For all of the previous reasons, the **re_source** field is generally used to specify databases that are read-only for DB applications; and that are either generated on the fly by software tools or modified using a different mechanism—for example, a text editor.

The DB→set_re_source interface may only be used to configure Berkeley DB before the **DB→open** interface is called.

The DB→set_re_source function returns a non-zero error value on failure and 0 on success.

Errors

- EINVAL   An invalid flag value or parameter was specified.

    Called after **DB→open** was called.

DB→set_realloc

```
#include <db.h>

int
DB→set_realloc(DB *db,
    void *(*db_realloc_fcn)(void *ptr, size_t size));
```

Description

Set the realloc function used by the DB methods to allocate memory in which to return key/data items to the application.

The DB_DBT_REALLOC flag, when specified in the **DBT** object, will cause the DB methods to allocate and re-allocate memory which then becomes the responsibility of the calling application. See **DBT** for more information.

On systems where there may be multiple library versions of realloc (notably Windows NT), specifying the DB_DBT_REALLOC flag will fail because the DB library will allocate memory from a different heap than the application will use to free it. To avoid this problem, the DB→set_realloc function can be used to pass Berkeley DB a reference to the application's allocation routine, in which case it will be used to allocate the memory returned when the DB_DBT_REALLOC flag is set.

The function specified must match the calling conventions of the ANSI C X3.159-1989 (ANSI C) library routine of the same name.

The DB→set_realloc interface may only be used to configure Berkeley DB before the **DB→open** interface is called.

The DB→set_realloc function returns a non-zero error value on failure and 0 on success.

Errors

- EINVAL   An invalid flag value or parameter was specified.

DB→stat

```
#include <db.h>

int
DB→stat(DB *db,
    void *sp, void *(*db_malloc)(size_t), u_int32_t flags);
```

Description

The DB→stat function creates a statistical structure and copies a pointer to it into user-specified memory locations. Specifically, if **sp** is non-NULL, a pointer to the statistics for the database are copied into the memory location it references.

Statistical structures are created in allocated memory. If **db_malloc** is non-NULL, it is called to allocate the memory; otherwise, the library function **malloc**(3) is used. The function **db_malloc** must match the calling conventions of the **malloc**(3) library routine. Regardless, the caller is responsible for deallocating the returned memory. To deallocate returned memory, free the returned memory reference; references inside the returned memory do not need to be individually freed.

The **flags** parameter must be set to 0 or the following value:

- DB_CACHED_COUNTS   Return a cached count of the keys and records in a database. This flag makes it possible for applications to request an possibly approximate key and record count without incurring the performance penalty of traversing the entire database. The statistics information described for the access method **XX_nkeys** and **XX_ndata** fields that follow is filled in, but no other information is collected. If the cached information has never been set, the fields will be returned set to 0.

- DB_RECORDCOUNT   Return a count of the records in a Btree or Recno Access Method database. This flag makes it possible for applications to request a record count without incurring the performance penalty of traversing the entire database. The statistics information described for the **bt_nkeys** field that follows is filled in, but no other information is collected.

  This option is only available for Recno databases or Btree databases, in which the underlying database was created with the DB_RECNUM flag.

The DB→stat function may access all the pages in the database, incurring a severe performance penalty as well as possibly flushing the underlying buffer pool.

In the presence of multiple threads or processes accessing an active database, the information returned by DB→stat may be out-of-date.

If the database was not opened read-only and the DB_CACHED_COUNTS flag was not specified, the cached key and record numbers will be updated after the statistical information has been gathered.

The DB→stat function cannot be transaction- protected. For this reason, it should be called in a thread of control that has no open cursors or active transactions.

The DB→stat function returns a non-zero error value on failure and 0 on success.

Hash Statistics

In the case of a Hash database, the statistics are stored in a structure of type DB_HASH_STAT. The following fields will be filled in:

- u_int32_t hash_magic   Magic number that identifies the file as a Hash file.
- u_int32_t hash_version   The version of the Hash database.
- u_int32_t hash_nkeys   The number of unique keys in the database.
- u_int32_t hash_ndata   The number of key/data pairs in the database.]
- u_int32_t hash_pagesize   The underlying Hash database page (and bucket) size.
- u_int32_t hash_nelem   The estimated size of the hash table specified at database-creation time.
- u_int32_t hash_ffactor   The desired fill factor (number of items per bucket) specified at database- creation time.
- u_int32_t hash_buckets   The number of hash buckets.
- u_int32_t hash_free   The number of pages on the free list.
- u_int32_t hash_bfree   The number of bytes free on bucket pages.
- u_int32_t hash_bigpages   The number of big key/data pages.
- u_int32_t hash_big_bfree   The number of bytes free on big item pages.
- u_int32_t hash_overflows   The number of overflow pages (overflow pages are pages that contain items that did not fit in the main bucket page).
- u_int32_t hash_ovfl_free   The number of bytes free on overflow pages.
- u_int32_t hash_dup   The number of duplicate pages.
- u_int32_t hash_dup_free   The number of bytes free on duplicate pages.

Btree and Recno Statistics

In the case of a Btree or Recno database, the statistics are stored in a structure of type DB_BTREE_STAT. The following fields will be filled in:

- u_int32_t bt_magic   Magic number that identifies the file as a Btree database.M
- u_int32_t bt_version   The version of the Btree database.
- u_int32_t bt_nkeys   For the Btree Access Method, the number of unique keys in the database.

For the Recno Access Method, the number of records in the database.

- u_int32_t bt_ndata   For the Btree Access Method, the number of key/data pairs in the database.

For the Recno Access Method, the number of records in the database. If the database has been configured to not renumber records during deletion, the number of records will only reflect undeleted records.

- u_int32_t bt_pagesize   Underlying database page size.
- u_int32_t bt_minkey   The minimum keys per page.
- u_int32_t bt_re_len   The length of fixed-length records.
- u_int32_t bt_re_pad   The padding byte value for fixed-length records.
- u_int32_t bt_levels   Number of levels in the database.
- u_int32_t bt_int_pg   Number of database internal pages.
- u_int32_t bt_leaf_pg   Number of database leaf pages.
- u_int32_t bt_dup_pg   Number of database duplicate pages.
- u_int32_t bt_over_pg   Number of database overflow pages.
- u_int32_t bt_free   Number of pages on the free list.
- u_int32_t bt_int_pgfree   Number of bytes free in database internal pages.
- u_int32_t bt_leaf_pgfree   Number of bytes free in database leaf pages.
- u_int32_t bt_dup_pgfree   Number of bytes free in database duplicate pages.
- u_int32_t bt_over_pgfree   Number of bytes free in database overflow pages.

Queue Statistics

In the case of a Queue database, the statistics are stored in a structure of type DB_QUEUE_STAT. The following fields will be filled in:

- u_int32_t qs_magic   Magic number that identifies the file as a Queue file.
- u_int32_t qs_version   The version of the Queue file type.
- u_int32_t qs_nkeys   The number of records in the database.
- u_int32_t qs_ndata   The number of records in the database.
- u_int32_t qs_pagesize   Underlying database page size.
- u_int32_t qs_pages   Number of pages in the database.
- u_int32_t qs_re_len   The length of the records.
- u_int32_t qs_re_pad   The padding byte value for the records.
- u_int32_t qs_pgfree   Number of bytes free in database pages.
- u_int32_t qs_start   Start offset.
- u_int32_t qs_first_recno   First undeleted record in the database.
- u_int32_t qs_cur_recno   Last allocated record number in the database.

The DB→stat function returns a non-zero error value on failure and 0 on success.

Errors

The DB→stat function may fail and return a non-zero error for errors specified for other Berkeley DB and C library or system functions. If a catastrophic error has occurred, the DB→stat function may fail and return DB_RUNRECOVERY, in which case all subsequent Berkeley DB calls will fail in the same way.

DB→sync

```
#include <db.h>

int
DB→sync(DB *db, u_int32_t flags);
```

Description

The DB→sync function flushes any cached information to disk.

If the database is in memory only, the DB→sync function has no effect and will always succeed.

The **flags** parameter is currently unused, and must be set to 0.

It is important to understand that flushing cached information to disk only minimizes the window of opportunity for corrupted data. Although unlikely, it is possible for database corruption to happen if a system or application crash occurs while writing data to the database. To ensure that database corruption never occurs, applications must either use transactions and logging with automatic recovery; use logging and application-specific recovery; or edit a copy of the database, and, once all applications using the database have successfully called **DB→close**, atomically replace the original database with the updated copy.

The DB→sync function returns a non-zero error value on failure, 0 on success, and returns DB_INCOMPLETE if the underlying database still has dirty pages in the cache. (The only reason to return DB_INCOMPLETE is if another thread of control was writing pages in the underlying database file at the same time as the DB→sync function was being called. For this reason, a return of DB_INCOMPLETE can normally be ignored; or, in cases where it is a possible return value, there may be no reason to call DB→sync.)

Errors

The DB→sync function may fail and return a non-zero error for the following conditions:

 • EINVAL   An invalid flag value or parameter was specified.

The DB→sync function may fail and return a non-zero error for errors specified for other Berkeley DB and C library or system functions. If a catastrophic error has occurred, the DB→sync function may fail and return DB_RUNRECOVERY, in which case all subsequent Berkeley DB calls will fail in the same way.

DB→upgrade

```
#include <db.h>

int
DB→upgrade(DB *db, const char *file, u_int32_t flags);
```

Description

The DB→upgrade function upgrades all of the databases included in the file **file**, if necessary. If no upgrade is necessary, DB→upgrade always returns success.

Database upgrades are done in place and are destructive. For example, if pages need to be allocated and no disk space is available, the database may be left corrupted. Backups should be made before databases are upgraded. See "Upgrading Databases" for more information.

Unlike all other database operations, DB→upgrade may only be done on a system with the same byte-order as the database.

The **flags** parameter must be set to 0 or one of the following values:

- DB_DUPSORT   This flag is only meaningful when upgrading databases from releases before the Berkeley DB 3.1 release.

  As part of the upgrade from the Berkeley DB 3.0 release to the 3.1 release, the on-disk format of duplicate data items changed. To correctly upgrade the format requires applications to specify whether duplicate data items in the database are sorted or not. Specifying the DB_DUPSORT flag informs DB→upgrade that the duplicates are sorted; otherwise, they are assumed to be unsorted. Incorrectly specifying the value of this flag may lead to database corruption.

  Further, because the DB→upgrade function upgrades a physical file (including all the databases it contains), it is not possible to use DB→upgrade to upgrade files in which some of the databases it includes have sorted duplicate data items, and some of the databases it includes have unsorted duplicate data items. If the file does not have more than a single database, if the databases do not support duplicate data items, or if all the databases that support duplicate data items support the same style of duplicates (either sorted or unsorted), DB→upgrade will work correctly as long as the DB_DUPSORT flag is correctly specified. Otherwise, the file cannot be upgraded using DB→upgrade; it must be upgraded manually by dumping and reloading the databases.

The DB→upgrade function returns a non-zero error value on failure and 0 on success.

The DB→upgrade function is the underlying function used by the **db_upgrade** utility. See the **db_upgrade** utility source code for an example of using DB→upgrade in a IEEE/ANSI Std 1003.1 (POSIX) environment.

Environment Variables

- DB_HOME   If the **dbenv** argument to **db_create** was initialized using **DBENV→open**, the environment variable **DB_HOME** may be used as the path of the database environment home. Specifically, DB→upgrade is affected by the configuration value DB_DATA_DIR.

Errors

The DB→upgrade function may fail and return a non-zero error for the following conditions:

- EINVAL   An invalid flag value or parameter was specified.

  The database is not in the same byte-order as the system.

DB→verify

```
#include <db.h>

int
DB→verify(DB *db,
    const char *file, const char *database, FILE *outfile, u_int32_t flags);
```

Description

The DB→verify function verifies the integrity of all databases in the file specified by the file argument, and optionally outputs the databases' key/data pairs to a file stream.

The **flags** parameter must be set to 0 or one of the following values:

- DB_SALVAGE   Write the key/data pairs from all databases in the file to the file stream named in the **outfile** argument. The output format is the same as that specified for the **db_dump** utility, and can be used as input for the **db_load** utility.

  Because the key/data pairs are output in page order as opposed to the sort order used by **db_dump**, using DB→verify to dump key/data pairs normally produces less than optimal loads for Btree databases.

In addition, the following flags may be set by bitwise inclusively **OR**'ing them into the **flags** parameter:

- DB_AGGRESSIVE   Output all the key/data pairs in the file that can be found. By default, DB→verify does not assume corruption. For example, if a key/data pair on a page is marked as deleted, it is not then written to the output file. When DB_AGGRESSIVE is specified, corruption is assumed, and any key/data pair that can be found is written. In this case, key/data pairs that are corrupted or have been deleted may appear in the output (even if the file being salvaged is in no way corrupt), and the output will almost certainly require editing before being loaded into a database.

- DB_NOORDERCHK   Skip the database checks for btree and duplicate sort order and for hashing.

  The DB→verify function normally verifies that btree keys and duplicate items are correctly sorted, and hash keys are correctly hashed. If the file being verified contains multiple databases using differing sorting or hashing algorithms, some of them must necessarily fail database verification because only one sort order or hash function can be specified before DB→verify is called. To verify files with multiple databases having differing sorting orders or hashing functions, first perform verification of the file as a whole by using the DB_NOORDERCHK flag, and then individually verify the sort order and hashing function for each database in the file using the DB_ORDER-CHKONLY flag.

- DB_ORDERCHKONLY   Perform the database checks for btree and duplicate sort order and for hashing, skipped by DB_NOORDERCHK.

When this flag is specified, a **database** argument should also be specified, indicating the database in the physical file which is to be checked. This flag is only safe to use on databases that have already successfully been verified using DB→verify with the DB_NOORDERCHK flag set.

The database argument must be set to NULL except when the DB_ORDER-CHKONLY flag is set.

The DB→verify function returns a non-zero error value on failure, 0 on success, and DB_VERIFY_BAD if a database is corrupted. When the DB_SALVAGE flag is specified, the DB_VERIFY_BAD return means that all key/data pairs in the file may not have been successfully output.

The DB→verify function is the underlying function used by the **db_verify** utility. See the **db_verify** utility source code for an example of using DB→verify in a IEEE/ANSI Std 1003.1 (POSIX) environment.

Environment Variables

- DB_HOME   If the **dbenv** argument to **db_create** was initialized using **DBENV→open**, the environment variable **DB_HOME** may be used as the path of the database environment home. Specifically, DB→verify is affected by the configuration value DB_DATA_DIR.

Errors

The DB→verify function may fail and return a non-zero error for the following conditions:

- EINVAL   An invalid flag value or parameter was specified.

The DB→verify function may fail and return a non-zero error for errors specified for other Berkeley DB and C library or system functions. If a catastrophic error has occurred, the DB→verify function may fail and return DB_RUNRECOVERY, in which case all subsequent Berkeley DB calls will fail in the same way.

- DB_OLD_VERSION   The database cannot be upgraded by this version of the Berkeley DB software.

The DB→upgrade function may fail and return a non-zero error for errors specified for other Berkeley DB and C library or system functions. If a catastrophic error has occurred, the DB→upgrade function may fail and return DB_RUNRECOVERY, in which case all subsequent Berkeley DB calls will fail in the same way.

DBENV→close

```
#include <db.h>

int
DBENV→close(DB_ENV *dbenv, u_int32_t flags);
```

Description

The DBENV→close function closes the Berkeley DB environment, freeing any allocated resources and closing any underlying subsystems.

Calling DBENV→close does not imply closing any databases that were opened in the environment, and all databases opened in the environment should be closed before the environment is closed.

The **flags** parameter is currently unused, and must be set to 0.

Where the environment was initialized with the DB_INIT_LOCK flag, calling DBENV→close does not release any locks still held by the closing process, providing functionality for long-lived locks. Processes that want to have all their locks released can do so by issuing the appropriate **lock_vec** call.

Where the environment was initialized with the DB_INIT_MPOOL flag, calling DBENV→close implies calls to **memp_fclose** for any remaining open files in the memory pool that were returned to this process by calls to **memp_fopen**. It does not imply a call to **memp_fsync** for those files.

Where the environment was initialized with the DB_INIT_TXN flag, calling DBENV→close aborts any unresolved transactions. Applications should not depend on this behavior for transactions involving Berkeley DB databases; all such transactions should be explicitly resolved. The problem with depending on this semantic is that aborting an unresolved transaction involving database operations requires a database handle. Because the database handles should have been closed before calling DBENV→close, it will not be possible to abort the transaction, and recovery will have to be run on the Berkeley DB environment before further operations are done.

In multithreaded applications, only a single thread may call DBENV→close.

Once DBENV→close has been called, regardless of its return, the Berkeley DB environment handle may not be accessed again.

The DBENV→close function returns a non-zero error value on failure and 0 on success.

Errors

The DBENV→close function may fail and return a non-zero error for errors specified for other Berkeley DB and C library or system functions. If a catastrophic error has occurred, the DBENV→close function may fail and return DB_RUNRECOVERY, in which case all subsequent Berkeley DB calls will fail in the same way.

DBENV→err

```
#include <db.h>

void
DBENV→err(DB_ENV *dbenv, int error, const char *fmt, ...);

void
DBENV→errx(DB_ENV *dbenv, const char *fmt, ...);

void
DB→err(DB *db, int error, const char *fmt, ...);

void
DB→errx(DB *db, const char *fmt, ...);
```

Description

The DBENV→err, DBENV→errx, DB→err and DB→errx functions provide error-messaging functionality for applications written using the Berkeley DB library.

The DBENV→err function constructs an error message consisting of the following elements:

- **An optional prefix string.** If no error callback function has been set using the **DBENV→set_errcall** function, any prefix string specified using the **DBENV→set_errpfx** function, followed by two separating characters: a colon and a <space> character.

- **An optional printf-style message.** The supplied message **fmt**, if non-NULL, in which the ANSI C X3.159-1989 (ANSI C) printf function specifies how subsequent arguments are converted for output.

- **A separator.** Two separating characters: a colon and a <space> character.

- **A standard error string.** The standard system or Berkeley DB library error string associated with the **error** value, as returned by the **db_strerror** function.

This constructed error message is then handled as follows:

If an error callback function has been set (see **DB→set_errcall** and **DBENV→set_errcall**), that function is called with two arguments: any prefix string specified (see **DB→set_errpfx** and **DBENV→set_errpfx**) and the error message.

If a C library FILE ★ has been set (see **DB→set_errfile** and **DBENV→set_errfile**), the error message is written to that output stream.

If none of these output options has been configured, the error message is written to stderr, the standard error output stream.

The DBENV→errx and DB→errx functions perform identically to the DBENV→err and DB→err functions, except that they do not append the final separator characters and standard error string to the error message.

DBENV→open

```
#include <db.h>

int
DBENV→open(DB_ENV *, char *db_home, u_int32_t flags, int mode);
```

Description

The DBENV→open function is the interface for opening the Berkeley DB environment. It provides a structure for creating a consistent environment for processes using one or more of the features of Berkeley DB.

The **db_home** argument to DBENV→open (and file name resolution in general) is described in "Berkeley DB File Naming."

The **flags** argument specifies the subsystems that are initialized and how the application's environment affects Berkeley DB file naming, among other things.

The **flags** value must be set to 0 or by bitwise inclusively **OR**'ing together one or more of the following values.

Because there are a large number of flags that can be specified, they have been grouped together by functionality. The first group of flags indicates which of the Berkeley DB subsystems should be initialized:

- DB_JOINENV   Join an existing environment. This option allows applications to join an existing environment without knowing which Berkeley DB subsystems the environment supports.

- DB_INIT_CDB   Initialize locking for the **Berkeley DB Concurrent Data Store** product. In this mode, Berkeley DB provides multiple reader/single writer access. The only other subsystem that should be specified with the DB_INIT_CDB flag is DB_INIT_MPOOL.

- DB_INIT_LOCK   Initialize the locking subsystem. This subsystem should be used when multiple processes or threads are going to be reading and writing a Berkeley DB database, so that they do not interfere with each other. If all threads are accessing the database(s) read-only, locking is unnecessary. When the DB_INIT_LOCK flag is specified, it is usually necessary to run a deadlock detector, as well. See **db_deadlock** and **lock_detect** for more information.

- DB_INIT_LOG   Initialize the logging subsystem. This subsystem should be used when recovery from application or system failure is necessary. If the log region is being created and log files are already present, the log files are reviewed; subsequent log writes are appended to the end of the log, rather than overwriting current log entries.

- DB_INIT_MPOOL   Initialize the shared memory buffer pool subsystem. This subsystem should be used whenever an application is using any Berkeley DB access method.

- DB_INIT_TXN   Initialize the transaction subsystem. This subsystem should be used when recovery and atomicity of multiple operations are important. The DB_INIT_TXN flag implies the DB_INIT_LOG flag.

The second group of flags govern what recovery, if any, is performed when the environment is initialized:

- DB_RECOVER   Run normal recovery on this environment before opening it for normal use. If this flag is set, the DB_CREATE flag must also be set because the regions will be removed and re-created.

- DB_RECOVER_FATAL   Run catastrophic recovery on this environment before opening it for normal use. If this flag is set, the DB_CREATE flag must also be set because the regions will be removed and re-created.

A standard part of the recovery process is to remove the existing Berkeley DB environment and create a new one in which to perform recovery. If the thread of control performing recovery does not specify the correct region initialization information (for example, the correct memory pool cache size), the result can be an application running in an environment with incorrect cache and other subsystem sizes. For this reason, the thread of control performing recovery should specify correct configuration information before calling the DBENV→open function; or it should remove the environment after recovery is completed, leaving creation of the correctly sized environment to a subsequent call to DBENV→open.

All Berkeley DB recovery processing must be single-threaded; that is, only a single thread of control may perform recovery or access a Berkeley DB environment while recovery is being performed. Because it is not an error to specify DB_RECOVER for an environment for which no recovery is required, it is reasonable programming practice for the thread of control responsible for performing recovery and creating the environment to always specify the DB_CREATE and DB_RECOVER flags during startup.

The DBENV→open function returns successfully if DB_RECOVER or DB_RECOVER_FATAL is specified and no log files exist, so it is necessary to ensure that all necessary log files are present before running recovery. For further information, consult **db_archive** and **db_recover**.

The third group of flags govern file-naming extensions in the environment:

- DB_USE_ENVIRON   The Berkeley DB process' environment may be permitted to specify information to be used when naming files; see "Berkeley DB File Naming." Because permitting users to specify which files are used can create security problems, environment information will be used in file naming for all users only if the DB_USE_ENVIRON flag is set.

- DB_USE_ENVIRON_ROOT   The Berkeley DB process' environment may be permitted to specify information to be used when naming files; see "Berkeley DB File Naming." Because permitting users to specify which files are used can create security problems, if the DB_USE_ENVIRON_ROOT flag is set, environment information will be used for file naming only for users with appropriate permissions (for example, users with a user-ID of 0 on UNIX systems).

Finally, there are a few additional unrelated flags:

- DB_CREATE   Cause Berkeley DB subsystems to create any underlying files, as necessary.

- DB_LOCKDOWN   Lock shared Berkeley DB environment files and memory-mapped databases into memory.

- DB_PRIVATE   Specify that the environment will only be accessed by a single process (although that process may be multithreaded). This flag has two effects on the Berkeley DB environment. First, all underlying data structures are allocated from per-process memory instead of from shared memory that is potentially accessible to more than a single process. Second, mutexes are only configured to work between threads.

  This flag should not be specified if more than a single process is accessing the environment because it is likely to cause database corruption and unpredictable behavior. For example, if both a server application and the Berkeley DB utility **db_stat** are expected to access the environment, the DB_PRIVATE flag should not be specified.

- DB_SYSTEM_MEM   Allocate memory from system shared memory instead of from memory backed by the filesystem. See "Shared Memory Regions" for more information.

- DB_THREAD   Cause the DB_ENV handle returned by DBENV→open to be *free-threaded*; that is, usable by multiple threads within a single address space.

On UNIX systems or in IEEE/ANSI Std 1003.1 (POSIX) environments, all files created by Berkeley DB are created with mode **mode** (as described in **chmod**(2)), and modified by the process' umask value at the time of creation (see **umask**(2)). The group ownership of created files is based on the system and directory defaults, and is not further specified by Berkeley DB. If **mode** is 0, files are created readable and writable by both owner and group. On Windows systems, the mode argument is ignored.

The DBENV→open function returns a non-zero error value on failure and 0 on success.

Environment Variables

- DB_HOME   The environment variable **DB_HOME** may be used as the path of the database home, as described in "Berkeley DB File Naming."

Errors

The DBENV→open function may fail and return a non-zero error for the following conditions:

- EAGAIN   The shared memory region was locked and (repeatedly) unavailable.

- EINVAL   An invalid flag value or parameter was specified.

  The DB_THREAD flag was specified, and spinlocks are not implemented for this architecture.

  The DB_HOME or TMPDIR environment variables were set, but empty.

  An incorrectly formatted **NAME VALUE** entry or line was found.

- ENOSPC   HP-UX only: a previously created Berkeley DB environment for this process still exists.

The DBENV→open function may fail and return a non-zero error for errors specified for other Berkeley DB and C library or system functions. If a catastrophic error has occurred, the DBENV→open function may fail and return DB_RUNRECOVERY, in which case all subsequent Berkeley DB calls will fail in the same way.

DBENV→remove

```
#include <db.h>

int
DBENV→remove(DB_ENV *, char *db_home, u_int32_t flags);
```

Description

The DBENV→remove function destroys a Berkeley DB environment if it is not currently in use. The environment regions, including any backing files, are removed. Any log or database files and the environment directory are not removed.

The **db_home** argument to DBENV→remove is described in "Berkeley DB File Naming."

If there are processes that have called **DBENV→open** without calling **DBENV→close** (that is, there are processes currently using the environment), DBENV→remove will fail without further action unless the DB_FORCE flag is set, in which case DBENV→remove will attempt to remove the environment, regardless of any processes still using it.

The result of attempting to forcibly destroy the environment when it is in use is unspecified. Processes using an environment often maintain open file descriptors for shared regions within it. On UNIX systems, the environment removal will usually succeed, and processes that have already joined the region will continue to run in that region without change. However, processes attempting to join the environment will either fail or create new regions. On other systems in which the **unlink**(2) system call will fail if any process has an open file descriptor for the file (for example, Windows/NT), the region removal will fail.

Calling DBENV→remove should not be necessary for most applications because the Berkeley DB environment is cleaned up as part of normal database recovery procedures. However, applications may wish to call DBENV→remove as part of application shutdown to free up system resources. For example, if the DB_SYSTEM_MEM flag was specified to **DBENV→open**, it may be useful to call DBENV→remove in order to release system shared memory segments that have been allocated. Or, on architectures in which mutexes require allocation of underlying system resources, it may be useful to call DBENV→remove in order to release those resources. Alternatively, if recovery is not required because no database state is maintained across failures, and no system resources need to be released, it is possible to clean up an environment by simply removing all the Berkeley DB files in the database environment's directories.

The **flags** value must be set to 0 or by bitwise inclusively **OR**'ing together one or more of the following values.

- DB_FORCE   If the DB_FORCE flag is set, the environment is removed, regardless of any processes that may still using it, and no locks are acquired during this process. (Generally, the DB_FORCE flag is specified only when applications were unable to shut down cleanly, and when there is a risk that an application may have died holding a Berkeley DB lock.)

- DB_USE_ENVIRON   The Berkeley DB process' environment may be permitted to specify information to be used when naming files; see "Berkeley DB File Naming." Because permitting users to specify which files are used can create security problems, environment information will be used in file naming for all users only if the DB_USE_ENVIRON flag is set.

- DB_USE_ENVIRON_ROOT   The Berkeley DB process' environment may be permitted to specify information to be used when naming files; see "Berkeley DB File Naming." Because permitting users to specify which files are used can create security problems, if the DB_USE_ENVIRON_ROOT flag is set, environment information will be used for file naming only for users with appropriate permissions (for example, users with a user-ID of 0 on UNIX systems).

In multithreaded applications, only a single thread may call DBENV→remove.

A DB_ENV handle that has already been used to open an environment should not be used to call the DBENV→remove function; a new DB_ENV handle should be created for that purpose.

Once DBENV→remove has been called, regardless of its return, the Berkeley DB environment handle may not be accessed again.

The DBENV→remove function returns a non-zero error value on failure and 0 on success.

Errors

- EBUSY   The shared memory region was in use and the force flag was not set.

The DBENV→remove function may fail and return a non-zero error for errors specified for other Berkeley DB and C library or system functions. If a catastrophic error has occurred, the DBENV→remove function may fail and return DB_RUNRECOVERY, in which case all subsequent Berkeley DB calls will fail in the same way.

DBENV→set_cachesize

```
#include <db.h>

int
DBENV→set_cachesize(DB_ENV *dbenv,
    u_int32_t gbytes, u_int32_t bytes, int ncache);
```

Description

Set the size of the database's shared memory buffer pool; that is, the cache, to **gbytes** gigabytes plus **bytes**. The cache should be the size of the normal working data set of the application, with some small amount of additional memory for unusual situations. (Note: The working set is not the same as the number of simultaneously referenced pages, and should be quite a bit larger!)

The default cache size is 256KB, and may not be specified as less than 20KB. Any cache size less than 500MB is automatically increased by 25% to account for buffer pool overhead; cache sizes larger than 500MB are used as specified. For information on tuning the Berkeley DB cache size, see "Selecting a Cache Size."

It is possible to specify caches to Berkeley DB that are large enough so that they cannot be allocated contiguously on some architectures; for example, some releases of Solaris limit the amount of memory that may be allocated contiguously by a process. If **ncache** is 0 or 1, the cache will be allocated contiguously in memory. If it is greater than 1, the cache will be broken up into **ncache** equally sized, separate pieces of memory.

The DBENV→set_cachesize interface may only be used to configure Berkeley DB before the **DBENV→open** interface is called.

The DBENV→set_cachesize function returns a non-zero error value on failure and 0 on success.

The database environment's cache size may also be set using the environment's **DB_CONFIG** file. The syntax of the entry in that file is a single line with the string "set_cachesize", one or more whitespace characters, and the three arguments specified to this interface, separated by whitespace characters, for example, "set_cachesize 1 500 2". Because the **DB_CONFIG** file is read when the database environment is opened, it will silently overrule configuration done before that time.

Errors

- EINVAL   An invalid flag value or parameter was specified.

  Called after **DBENV→open** was called.

  The specified cache size was impossibly small.

DBENV→set_data_dir

```
#include <db.h>

int
DBENV→set_data_dir(DB_ENV *dbenv, const char *dir);
```

Description

Set the path of a directory to be used as the location of the access method database files. Paths specified to the **DB→open** function will be searched relative to this path. Paths set using this interface are additive, and specifying more than one will result in each specified directory being searched for database files. If any directories are specified, created database files will always be created in the first path specified.

If no database directories are specified, database files can exist only in the environment home directory. See "Berkeley DB File Naming" for more information.

For the greatest degree of recoverability from system or application failure, database files and log files should be located on separate physical devices.

The DBENV→set_data_dir interface may only be used to configure Berkeley DB before the **DBENV→open** interface is called.

The DBENV→set_data_dir function returns a non-zero error value on failure and 0 on success.

The database environment's data directory may also be set using the environment's **DB_CONFIG** file. The syntax of the entry in that file is a single line with the string "set_data_dir", one or more whitespace characters, and the directory name. Because the **DB_CONFIG** file is read when the database environment is opened, it will silently overrule configuration done before that time.

Errors

- EINVAL   An invalid flag value or parameter was specified.

   Called after **DBENV→open** was called.

DBENV→set_errcall

```
#include <db.h>

void
DBENV→set_errcall(DB_ENV *dbenv,
    void (*db_errcall_fcn)(const char *errpfx, char *msg));
```

Description

When an error occurs in the Berkeley DB library, a Berkeley DB error or an error return value is returned by the function. In some cases, however, the **errno** value may be insufficient to completely describe the cause of the error, especially during initial application debugging.

The DBENV→set_errcall function is used to enhance the mechanism for reporting error messages to the application. In some cases, when an error occurs, Berkeley DB will call **db_errcall_fcn** with additional error information. The function must be declared with two arguments: the first will be the prefix string (as previously set by **DB→set_errpfx** or **DBENV→set_errpfx**); the second will be the error message string. It is up to the **db_errcall_fcn** function to display the error message in an appropriate manner.

Alternatively, you can use the **DB→set_errfile** or **DBENV→set_errfile** functions to display the additional information via a C library FILE *.

This error-logging enhancement does not slow performance or significantly increase application size, and may be run during normal operation as well as during application debugging.

The DBENV→set_errcall interface may be used to configure Berkeley DB at any time during the life of the application.

DBENV→set_errfile

```
#include <db.h>

void
DBENV→set_errfile(DB_ENV *dbenv, FILE *errfile);
```

Description

When an error occurs in the Berkeley DB library, a Berkeley DB error or an error return value is returned by the function. In some cases, however, the **errno** value may be insufficient to completely describe the cause of the error, especially during initial application debugging.

The DBENV→set_errfile function is used to enhance the mechanism for reporting error messages to the application by setting a C library FILE * to be used for displaying additional Berkeley DB error messages. In some cases, when an error occurs, Berkeley DB will output an additional error message to the specified file reference.

The error message will consist of the prefix string and a colon (":") (if a prefix string was previously specified using **DB→set_errpfx** or **DBENV→set_errpfx**), an error string, and a trailing <newline> character.

This error-logging enhancement does not slow performance or significantly increase application size, and may be run during normal operation as well as during application debugging.

The DBENV→set_errfile interface may be used to configure Berkeley DB at any time during the life of the application.

DBENV→set_errpfx

```
#include <db.h>

void
DBENV→set_errpfx(DB_ENV *dbenv, const char *errpfx);
```

Description

Set the prefix string that appears before error messages issued by Berkeley DB.

The DBENV→set_errpfx function does not copy the memory referenced by the **errpfx** argument; rather, it maintains a reference to it. This allows applications to modify the error message prefix at any time without repeatedly calling DBENV→set_errpfx, but it means that the memory must be maintained until the handle is closed.

The DBENV→set_errpfx interface may be used to configure Berkeley DB at any time during the life of the application.

DBENV→set_feedback

```
#include <db.h>

int
DBENV→set_feedback(DB_ENV *,
    void (*db_feedback_fcn)(DB_ENV *, int opcode, int pct));
```

Description

Some operations performed by the Berkeley DB library can take non-trivial amounts of time. The DBENV→set_feedback function can be used by applications to monitor progress within these operations.

When an operation is likely to take a long time, Berkeley DB will call the specified callback function. This function must be declared with three arguments: The first will be a reference to the enclosing environment, the second will be a flag value, and the third will be the percent of the operation that has been completed, specified as an integer value between 0 and 100. It is up to the callback function to display this information in an appropriate manner.

The **opcode** argument may take on any of the following values:

* DB_RECOVER   The environment is being recovered.

The DBENV→set_feedback interface may be used to configure Berkeley DB at any time during the life of the application.

The DBENV→set_feedback function returns a non-zero error value on failure and 0 on success.

DBENV→set_flags

```
#include <db.h>

int
DBENV→set_flags(DB_ENV *dbenv, u_int32_t flags, int onoff);
```

Description

The **flags** value must be set to 0 or by bitwise inclusively **OR**'ing together one or more of the following values. If **onoff** is zero, the specified flags are cleared, otherwise they are set.

* DB_CDB_ALLDB   For Berkeley DB Concurrent Data Store applications, perform locking on an environment-wide basis rather than per-database. This flag may be used only to configure Berkeley DB before the **DBENV→open** interface is called.

- DB_NOMMAP   Copy read-only database files in this environment into the local cache instead of potentially mapping them into process memory (see the description of the **DBENV→set_mp_mmapsize** function for further information).

- DB_TXN_NOSYNC   Do not synchronously flush the log on transaction commit or prepare. This means that transactions exhibit the ACI (atomicity, consistency, and isolation) properties, but not D (durability); that is, database integrity will be maintained, but it is possible that some number of the most recently committed transactions may be undone during recovery.

  The number of transactions potentially at risk is governed by how often the log is checkpointed (see **db_checkpoint** for more information) and how many log updates can fit into the log buffer.

The DBENV→set_flags function returns a non-zero error value on failure and 0 on success.

The database environment's flag values may also be set using the environment's **DB_CONFIG** file. The syntax of the entry in that file is a single line with the string "set_flags", one or more whitespace characters, and the interface flag argument as a string; for example, "set_flags DB_TXN_NOSYNC". Because the **DB_CONFIG** file is read when the database environment is opened, it will silently overrule configuration done before that time.

Errors

- EINVAL   An invalid flag value or parameter was specified.

DBENV→set_lg_bsize

```
#include <db.h>

int
DBENV→set_lg_bsize(DB_ENV *dbenv, u_int32_t lg_bsize);
```

Description

Set the size of the in-memory log buffer, in bytes. By default, or if the value is set to 0, a size of 32K is used. The size of the log file (see **DBENV→set_lg_max**) must be at least four times the size of the the in-memory log buffer.

Log information is stored in-memory until the storage space fills up or transaction commit forces the information to be flushed to stable storage. In the presence of long-running transactions or transactions producing large amounts of data, larger buffer sizes can increase throughput.

The DBENV→set_lg_bsize interface may be used only to configure Berkeley DB before the **DBENV→open** interface is called.

The DBENV→set_lg_bsize function returns a non-zero error value on failure and 0 on success.

The database environment's log buffer size may also be set using the environment's **DB_CONFIG** file. The syntax of the entry in that file is a single line with the string "set_lg_bsize", one or more whitespace characters, and the size in bytes. Because the **DB_CONFIG** file is read when the database environment is opened, it will silently overrule configuration done before that time.

Errors

- EINVAL   An invalid flag value or parameter was specified.

  Called after **DBENV→open** was called.

  The size of the log file is less than four times the size of the in-memory log buffer.

DBENV→set_lg_dir

```
#include <db.h>

int
DBENV→set_lg_dir(DB_ENV *dbenv, const char *dir);
```

Description

The path of a directory to be used as the location of logging files. Log files created by the Log Manager subsystem will be created in this directory.

If no logging directory is specified, log files are created in the environment home directory. See "Berkeley DB File Naming" for more information.

For the greatest degree of recoverability from system or application failure, database files and log files should be located on separate physical devices.

The DBENV→set_lg_dir interface may be used only to configure Berkeley DB before the **DBENV→open** interface is called.

The DBENV→set_lg_dir function returns a non-zero error value on failure and 0 on success.

The database environment's logging directory may also be set using the environment's **DB_CONFIG** file. The syntax of the entry in that file is a single line with the string "set_lg_dir", one or more whitespace characters, and the directory name. Because the **DB_CONFIG** file is read when the database environment is opened, it will silently overrule configuration done before that time.

Errors

- EINVAL   An invalid flag value or parameter was specified.

  Called after **DBENV→open** was called.

DBENV→set_lg_max

```
#include <db.h>

int
DBENV→set_lg_max(DB_ENV *dbenv, u_int32_t lg_max);
```

Description

Set the maximum size of a single file in the log, in bytes. Because **DB_LSN** file offsets are unsigned four-byte values, the set value may not be larger than the maximum unsigned four-byte value. By default, or if the value is set to 0, a size of 10MB is used. The size of the log file must be at least four times the size of the in-memory log buffer (see **DBENV→set_lg_bsize**).

See "Log File Limits" for more information.

The DBENV→set_lg_max interface may be used only to configure Berkeley DB before the **DBENV→open** interface is called.

The DBENV→set_lg_max function returns a non-zero error value on failure and 0 on success.

The database environment's log file size may also be set using the environment's **DB_CONFIG** file. The syntax of the entry in that file is a single line with the string "set_lg_max", one or more whitespace characters, and the size in bytes. Because the **DB_CONFIG** file is read when the database environment is opened, it will silently overrule configuration done before that time.

Errors

- EINVAL　An invalid flag value or parameter was specified.

  Called after **DBENV→open** was called.

  The size of the log file is less than four times the size of the in-memory log buffer.

  The specified log file size was too large.

DBENV→set_lk_conflicts

```
#include <db.h>

int
DBENV→set_lk_conflicts(DB_ENV *dbenv,
    u_int8_t *conflicts, int nmodes);
```

Description

Set the locking conflicts matrix. The **conflicts** argument is an **nmodes** by **nmodes** array. A non-0 value for the array element indicates that requested_mode and held_mode conflict:

```
conflicts[requested_mode][held_mode]
```

The *not-granted* mode must be represented by 0.

If DBENV→set_lk_conflicts is never called, a standard conflicts array is used; see "Standard Lock Modes" for more information.

The DBENV→set_lk_conflicts interface may be used only to configure Berkeley DB before the **DBENV→open** interface is called.

The DBENV→set_lk_conflicts function returns a non-zero error value on failure and 0 on success.

Errors

- EINVAL   An invalid flag value or parameter was specified.

  Called after **DBENV→open** was called.

- ENOMEM   No memory was available to copy the conflicts array.

DBENV→set_lk_detect

```
#include <db.h>

int
DBENV→set_lk_detect(DB_ENV *dbenv, u_int32_t detect);
```

Description

Set if the deadlock detector is to be run whenever a lock conflict occurs, and specify which transaction should be aborted in the case of a deadlock. The specified value must be one of the following list:

- DB_LOCK_DEFAULT   Use the default policy as specified by **db_deadlock**.
- DB_LOCK_OLDEST   Abort the oldest transaction.
- DB_LOCK_RANDOM   Abort a random transaction involved in the deadlock.
- DB_LOCK_YOUNGEST   Abort the youngest transaction.

The DBENV→set_lk_detect interface may be used only to configure Berkeley DB before the **DBENV→open** interface is called.

The DBENV→set_lk_detect function returns a non-zero error value on failure and 0 on success.

The database environment's deadlock detector configuration may also be set using the environment's **DB_CONFIG** file. The syntax of the entry in that file is a single line with the string "set_lk_detect", one or more whitespace characters, and the interface **detect** argument as a string; for example, "set_lk_detect DB_LOCK_OLDEST". Because the **DB_CONFIG** file is read when the database environment is opened, it will silently overrule configuration done before that time.

Errors

- EINVAL   An invalid flag value or parameter was specified.

  Called after **DBENV→open** was called.

DBENV→set_lk_max

```
#include <db.h>

int
DBENV→set_lk_max(DB_ENV *dbenv, u_int32_t max);
```

Description

Note: The DBENV→set_lk_max function interface has been deprecated in favor of the DBENV→set_lk_max_locks, DBENV→set_lk_max_lockers, and DBENV→set_lk_max_objects functions. Please update your applications.

Set each of the maximum number of locks, lockers, and lock objects supported by the Berkeley DB lock subsystem to **max**. This value is used by **DBENV→open** to estimate how much space to allocate for various lock-table data structures. For specific information on configuring the size of the lock subsystem, see "Configuring Locking: Sizing the System."

The DBENV→set_lk_max interface may be used only to configure Berkeley DB before the **DBENV→open** interface is called.

The DBENV→set_lk_max function returns a non-zero error value on failure and 0 on success.

The database environment's maximum number of locks may also be set using the environment's **DB_CONFIG** file. The syntax of the entry in that file is a single line with the string "set_lk_max", one or more whitespace characters, and the number of locks. Because the **DB_CONFIG** file is read when the database environment is opened, it will silently overrule configuration done before that time.

Errors

- EINVAL   An invalid flag value or parameter was specified.

  Called after **DBENV→open** was called.

DBENV→set_lk_max_lockers

```
#include <db.h>

int
DBENV→set_lk_max_lockers(DB_ENV *dbenv, u_int32_t max);
```

Description

Set the maximum number of simultaneous locking entities supported by the Berkeley DB lock subsystem. This value is used by **DBENV→open** to estimate how much space to allocate for various lock-table data structures. The default value is 1000 lockers. For specific information on configuring the size of the lock subsystem, see "Configuring Locking: Sizing the System."

The DBENV→set_lk_max_lockers interface may be used only to configure Berkeley DB before the **DBENV→open** interface is called.

The DBENV→set_lk_max_lockers function returns a non-zero error value on failure and 0 on success.

The database environment's maximum number of lockers may also be set using the environment's **DB_CONFIG** file. The syntax of the entry in that file is a single line with the string "set_lk_max_lockers", one or more whitespace characters, and the number of lockers. Because the **DB_CONFIG** file is read when the database environment is opened, it will silently overrule configuration done before that time.

Errors

- EINVAL   An invalid flag value or parameter was specified.

  Called after **DBENV→open** was called.

DBENV→set_lk_max_locks

```
#include <db.h>

int
DBENV→set_lk_max_locks(DB_ENV *dbenv, u_int32_t max);
```

Description

Set the maximum number of locks supported by the Berkeley DB lock subsystem. This value is used by **DBENV→open** to estimate how much space to allocate for various lock-table data structures. The default value is 1000 locks. For specific information on configuring the size of the lock subsystem, see "Configuring Locking: Sizing the System."

The DBENV→set_lk_max_locks interface may be used only to configure Berkeley DB before the **DBENV→open** interface is called.

The DBENV→set_lk_max_locks function returns a non-zero error value on failure and 0 on success.

The database environment's maximum number of locks may also be set using the environment's **DB_CONFIG** file. The syntax of the entry in that file is a single line with the string "set_lk_max_locks", one or more whitespace characters, and the number of locks. Because the **DB_CONFIG** file is read when the database environment is opened, it will silently overrule configuration done before that time.

Errors

- EINVAL   An invalid flag value or parameter was specified.

  Called after **DBENV→open** was called.

DBENV→set_lk_max_objects

```
#include <db.h>

int
DBENV→set_lk_max_objects(DB_ENV *dbenv, u_int32_t max);
```

Description

Set the maximum number of simultaneously locked objects supported by the Berkeley DB lock subsystem. This value is used by **DBENV→open** to estimate how much space to allocate for various lock-table data structures. The default value is 1000 objects. For specific information on configuring the size of the lock subsystem, see "Configuring Locking: Sizing the System."

The DBENV→set_lk_max_objects interface may be used only to configure Berkeley DB before the **DBENV→open** interface is called.

The DBENV→set_lk_max_objects function returns a non-zero error value on failure and 0 on success.

The database environment's maximum number of objects may also be set using the environment's **DB_CONFIG** file. The syntax of the entry in that file is a single line with the string "set_lk_max_objects", one or more whitespace characters, and the number of objects. Because the **DB_CONFIG** file is read when the database environment is opened, it will silently overrule configuration done before that time.

Errors

- EINVAL   An invalid flag value or parameter was specified.

  Called after **DBENV→open** was called.

DBENV→set_mp_mmapsize

```
#include <db.h>

int
DBENV→set_mp_mmapsize(DB_ENV *dbenv, size_t mp_mmapsize);
```

Description

Files that are opened read-only in the pool (and that satisfy a few other criteria) are, by default, mapped into the process address space instead of being copied into the local cache.

This can result in better-than-usual performance because available virtual memory is normally much larger than the local cache, and page faults are faster than page copying on many systems. However, it can cause resource starvation in the presence of limited virtual memory, and it can result in immense process sizes in the presence of large databases.

Set the maximum file size, in bytes, for a file to be mapped into the process address space. If no value is specified, it defaults to 10MB.

The DBENV→set_mp_mmapsize interface may be used only to configure Berkeley DB before the **DBENV→open** interface is called.

The DBENV→set_mp_mmapsize function returns a non-zero error value on failure and 0 on success.

The database environment's maximum mapped file size may also be set using the environment's **DB_CONFIG** file. The syntax of the entry in that file is a single line with the string "set_mp_mmapsize", one or more whitespace characters, and the size in bytes. Because the **DB_CONFIG** file is read when the database environment is opened, it will silently overrule configuration done before that time.

Errors

- EINVAL   An invalid flag value or parameter was specified.

    Called after **DBENV→open** was called.

DBENV→set_paniccall

```
#include <db.h>

int
DBENV→set_paniccall(DB_ENV *dbenv,
    void (*paniccall)(DB_ENV *, int errval));
```

Description

Errors can occur in the Berkeley DB library where the only solution is to shut down the application and run recovery (for example, if Berkeley DB is unable to write log records to disk because there is insufficient disk space). In these cases, the value DB_RUNRECOVERY is returned by Berkeley DB.

In these cases, it is also often simpler to shut down the application when such errors occur rather than attempting to gracefully return up the stack. The DBENV→set_paniccall function is used to specify a function to be called when DB_RUNRECOVERY is about to be returned from a Berkeley DB method. When called, the **dbenv** argument will be a reference to the current environment, and the **errval** argument is the error value that would have been returned to the calling function.

The DBENV→set_paniccall interface may be used to configure Berkeley DB at any time during the life of the application.

The DBENV→set_paniccall function returns a non-zero error value on failure and 0 on success.

DBENV→set_recovery_init

```
#include <db.h>

int
DBENV→set_recovery_init(DB_ENV *,
    int (*db_recovery_init_fcn)(DB_ENV *));
```

Description

Applications installing application-specific recovery functions need to be called before Berkeley DB performs recovery so they may add their recovery functions to Berkeley DB's.

The DBENV→set_recovery_init function supports this functionality. The **db_recovery_init_fcn** function must be declared with one argument, a reference to the enclosing Berkeley DB environment. This function will be called after the **DBENV→open** has been called, but before recovery is started.

If the **db_recovery_init_fcn** function returns a non-zero value, no recovery will be performed, and **DBENV→open** will return the same value to its caller.

The DBENV→set_recovery_init interface may be used only to configure Berkeley DB before the **DBENV→open** interface is called.

The DBENV→set_recovery_init function returns a non-zero error value on failure and 0 on success.

Errors

- EINVAL   An invalid flag value or parameter was specified.

  Called after **DBENV→open** was called.

DBENV→set_server

```
#include <db.h>

int
DBENV→set_server(DB_ENV *dbenv, char *host,
    long cl_timeout, long sv_timeout, u_int32_t flags);
```

Description

Connects to the DB server on the indicated hostname and sets up a channel for communication.

The **cl_timeout** argument specifies the number of seconds the client should wait for results to come back from the server. Once the timeout has expired on any communication with the server, DB_NOSERVER will be returned. If this value is zero, a default timeout is used.

The **sv_timeout** argument specifies the number of seconds the server should allow a client connection to remain idle before assuming that the client is gone. Once that timeout has been reached, the server releases all resources associated with that client connection. Subsequent attempts by that client to communicate with the server result in DB_NOSERVER_ID, indicating that an invalid identifier has been given to the server. This value can be considered a hint to the server. The server may alter this value based on its own policies or allowed values. If this value is zero, a default timeout is used.

The **flags** parameter is currently unused, and must be set to 0.

When the DBENV→set_server function has been called, any subsequent calls to Berkeley DB library interfaces may return either DB_NOSERVER or DB_NOSERVER_ID.

The DBENV→set_server function returns a non-zero error value on failure and 0 on success.

Errors

- EINVAL   An invalid flag value or parameter was specified.

  dbenv_set_server

DBENV→set_shm_key

```
#include <db.h>

int
DBENV→set_shm_key(DB_ENV *dbenv, long shm_key);
```

Description

Specify a base segment ID for Berkeley DB environment shared memory regions created in system memory on VxWorks or systems supporting X/Open-style shared memory interfaces; for example, UNIX systems supporting **shmget**(2) and related System V IPC interfaces.

This base segment ID will be used when Berkeley DB shared memory regions are first created. It will be incremented a small integer value each time a new shared memory region is created; that is, if the base ID is 35, the first shared memory region created will have a segment ID of 35, and the next one will have a segment ID between 36 and 40 or so. A Berkeley DB environment always creates a master shared memory region; an additional shared memory region for each of the subsystems supported by the environment (Locking, Logging, Memory Pool, and Transaction); plus an additional shared memory region for each additional memory pool cache that is supported. Already existing regions with the same segment IDs will be removed. See "Shared Memory Regions" for more information.

The intent behind this interface is two-fold: without it, applications have no way to ensure that two Berkeley DB applications don't attempt to use the same segment IDs when creating different Berkeley DB environments. In addition, by using the same segment IDs each time the environment is created, previously created segments will be removed, and the set of segments on the system will not grow without bound.

The DBENV→set_shm_key interface may only be used to configure Berkeley DB before the **DBENV→open** interface is called.

The DBENV→set_shm_key function returns a non-zero error value on failure and 0 on success.

The database environment's base segment ID may also be set using the environment's **DB_CONFIG** file. The syntax of the entry in that file is a single line with the string "set_shm_key", one or more whitespace characters, and the ID. Because the **DB_CONFIG** file is read when the database environment is opened, it will silently overrule configuration done before that time.

Errors

- EINVAL   An invalid flag value or parameter was specified.

  Called after **DBENV→open** was called.

DBENV→set_tmp_dir

```
#include <db.h>

int
DBENV→set_tmp_dir(DB_ENV *dbenv, const char *dir);
```

Description

The path of a directory to be used as the location of temporary files. The files created to back in-memory access method databases will be created relative to this path. These temporary files can be quite large, depending on the size of the database.

If no directories are specified, the following alternatives are checked in the specified order. The first existing directory path is used for all temporary files.

1. The value of the environment variable **TMPDIR**.

2. The value of the environment variable **TEMP**.

3. The value of the environment variable **TMP**.

4. The value of the environment variable **TempFolder**.

5. The value returned by the GetTempPath interface.

6. The directory **/var/tmp**.

7. The directory **/usr/tmp**.

8. The directory **/temp**.

9. The directory **/tmp**.

10. The directory **C:/temp**.

11. The directory **C:/tmp**.

Note: environment variables are only checked if one of the DB_USE_ENVIRON or DB_USE_ENVIRON_ROOT flags were specified.

Note: the GetTempPath interface is only checked on Win/32 platforms.

The DBENV→set_tmp_dir interface may only be used to configure Berkeley DB before the **DBENV→open** interface is called.

The DBENV→set_tmp_dir function returns a non-zero error value on failure and 0 on success.

The database environment's temporary file directory may also be set using the environment's **DB_CONFIG** file. The syntax of the entry in that file is a single line with the string "set_tmp_dir", one or more whitespace characters, and the directory name. Because the **DB_CONFIG** file is read when the database environment is opened, it will silently overrule configuration done before that time.

Errors

- EINVAL   An invalid flag value or parameter was specified.

  Called after **DBENV→open** was called.

DBENV→set_tx_max

```
#include <db.h>

int
DBENV→set_tx_max(DB_ENV *dbenv, u_int32_t tx_max);
```

Description

Set the maximum number of active transactions that are supported by the environment. This value bounds the size of backing shared memory regions. Note that child transactions must be counted as active until their ultimate parent commits or aborts.

When there are more than the specified number of concurrent transactions, calls to **txn_begin** will fail (until some active transactions complete). If no value is specified, a default value of 20 is used.

The DBENV→set_tx_max interface may only be used to configure Berkeley DB before the **DBENV→open** interface is called.

The DBENV→set_tx_max function returns a non-zero error value on failure and 0 on success.

The database environment's maximum number of active transactions may also be set using the environment's **DB_CONFIG** file. The syntax of the entry in that file is a single line with the string "set_tx_max", one or more whitespace characters, and the number of trans-actions. Because the **DB_CONFIG** file is read when the database environment is opened, it will silently overrule configuration done before that time.

Errors

- EINVAL   An invalid flag value or parameter was specified.

  Called after **DBENV→open** was called.

DBENV→set_tx_recover

```
#include <db.h>

int
DBENV→set_tx_recover(DB_ENV *dbenv,
    int (*tx_recover)(DB_ENV *dbenv,
    DBT *log_rec, DB_LSN *lsn, db_recops op));
```

Description

Set the application's function to be called during transaction abort and recovery. This function must return 0 on success and either **errno** or a value outside of the Berkeley DB error name space on failure. It takes four arguments:

- dbenv   A Berkeley DB environment.
- log_rec   A log record.
- lsn   A log sequence number.
- op   One of the following values:

  - DB_TXN_BACKWARD_ROLL   The log is being read backward to determine which transactions have been committed and to abort those operations that were not; undo the operation described by the log record.

  - DB_TXN_FORWARD_ROLL   The log is being played forward; redo the operation described by the log record.

  - DB_TXN_ABORT   The log is being read backward during a transaction abort; undo the operation described by the log record.

The DBENV→set_tx_recover interface may only be used to configure Berkeley DB before the **DBENV→open** interface is called.

The DBENV→set_tx_recover function returns a non-zero error value on failure and 0 on success.

Errors

- EINVAL   An invalid flag value or parameter was specified.

  Called after **DBENV→open** was called.

DBENV→set_tx_timestamp

```
#include <db.h>

int
DBENV→set_tx_timestamp(DB_ENV *dbenv, time_t *timestamp);
```

Description

Recover to the time specified by **timestamp** rather than to the most current possible date. The **timestamp** argument should be the number of seconds since 0 hours, 0 minutes, 0 seconds, January 1, 1970, Coordinated Universal Time; that is, the Epoch.

Once a database environment has been upgraded to a new version of Berkeley DB involving a log format change (see "Upgrading Berkeley DB Installations"), it is no longer possible to recover to a specific time before that upgrade.

The DBENV→set_tx_timestamp interface may only be used to configure Berkeley DB before the **DBENV→open** interface is called.

The DBENV→set_tx_timestamp function returns a non-zero error value on failure and 0 on success.

Errors

- EINVAL   An invalid flag value or parameter was specified.

  It is not possible to recover to the specified time using the log files currently present in the environment.

DBENV→set_verbose

```
#include <db.h>

int
DBENV→set_verbose(DB_ENV *dbenv, u_int32_t which, int onoff);
```

Description

The DBENV→set_verbose function turns additional informational and debugging messages in the Berkeley DB message output on and off. If **onoff** is set to non-zero, the additional messages are output.

The **which** parameter must be set to one of the following values:

- DB_VERB_CHKPOINT   Display checkpoint location information when searching the log for checkpoints.
- DB_VERB_DEADLOCK   Display additional information when doing deadlock detection.
- DB_VERB_RECOVERY   Display additional information when performing recovery.
- DB_VERB_WAITSFOR   Display the waits-for table when doing deadlock detection.

The DBENV→set_verbose interface may be used to configure Berkeley DB at any time during the life of the application.

The DBENV→set_verbose function returns a non-zero error value on failure and 0 on success.

The database environment's verbosity may also be set using the environment's **DB_CONFIG** file. The syntax of the entry in that file is a single line with the string "set_verbose", one or more whitespace characters, and the interface **which** argument as a string; for example, "set_verbose DB_VERB_CHKPOINT". Because the **DB_CONFIG** file is read when the database environment is opened, it will silently overrule configuration done before that time.

Errors

- EINVAL   An invalid flag value or parameter was specified.

DBT

Key/Data Pairs

Storage and retrieval for the Berkeley DB access methods are based on key/data pairs. Both key and data items are represented by the DBT data structure. (*DBT* is a mnemonic for *data base thang*, and was used because no one could think of a reasonable name that wasn't already in use somewhere else.) Key and data byte strings may reference strings of zero length up to strings of essentially unlimited length. See "Database Limits" for more information.

```
typedef struct {
        void *data;
        u_int32_t size;
        u_int32_t ulen;
        u_int32_t dlen;
        u_int32_t doff;
        u_int32_t flags;
} DBT;
```

In order to ensure compatibility with future releases of Berkeley DB, all fields of the DBT structure that are not explicitly set should be initialized to nul bytes before the first time the structure is used. Do this by declaring the structure external or static, or by calling the C library routine **bzero**(3) or **memset**(3).

By default, the **flags** structure element is expected to be set to 0. In this default case, when the application is providing Berkeley DB a key or data item to store into the database, Berkeley DB expects the **data** structure element to point to a byte string of **size** bytes.

When returning a key/data item to the application, Berkeley DB will store into the **data** structure element a pointer to a byte string of **size** bytes, and the memory referenced by the pointer will be allocated and managed by Berkeley DB.

The elements of the DBT structure are defined as follows:

- void *data;   A pointer to a byte string.

- u_int32_t size;   The length of **data**, in bytes.

- u_int32_t ulen;   The size of the user's buffer (referenced by **data**), in bytes. This location is not written by the Berkeley DB functions.

  Note that applications can determine the length of a record by setting the **ulen** field to 0 and checking the return value in the **size** field. See the DB_DBT_USERMEM flag for more information.

- u_int32_t dlen;   The length of the partial record being read or written by the application, in bytes. See the DB_DBT_PARTIAL flag for more information.

- u_int32_t doff;   The offset of the partial record being read or written by the application, in bytes. See the DB_DBT_PARTIAL flag for more information.

- u_int32_t flags;   The **flags** value must be set to 0 or by bitwise inclusively **OR**'ing together one or more of the following values:

- DB_DBT_MALLOC   When this flag is set, Berkeley DB will allocate memory for the returned key or data item (using **malloc**(3), or the user-specified malloc function), and return a pointer to it in the **data** field of the key or data DBT structure. Because any allocated memory becomes the responsibility of the calling application, the caller must determine whether memory was allocated using the returned value of the **data** field.

  It is an error to specify more than one of DB_DBT_MALLOC, DB_DBT_REAL-LOC, and DB_DBT_USERMEM.

- DB_DBT_REALLOC   When this flag is set Berkeley DB will allocate memory for the returned key or data item (using **realloc**(3), or the user-specified realloc function), and return a pointer to it in the **data** field of the key or data DBT structure. Because any allocated memory becomes the responsibility of the calling application, the caller must determine whether memory was allocated using the returned value of the **data** field.

  DB_DBT_REALLOC is that the latter will call **realloc**(3) instead of **malloc**(3), so the allocated memory will be grown as necessary instead of the application doing repeated free/malloc calls.

  DB_DBT_MALLOC, DB_DBT_REALLOC, and DB_DBT_USERMEM.

- DB_DBT_USERMEM   The **data** field of the key or data structure must reference memory that is at least **ulen** bytes in length. If the length of the requested item is less than or equal to that number of bytes, the item is copied into the memory referenced by the **data** field. Otherwise, the **size** field is set to the length needed for the requested item, and the error ENOMEM is returned.

It is an error to specify more than one of DB_DBT_MALLOC, DB_DBT_REAL-LOC, and DB_DBT_USERMEM.

- DB_DBT_PARTIAL   Do partial retrieval or storage of an item. If the calling application is doing a get, the **dlen** bytes starting **doff** bytes from the beginning of the retrieved data record are returned as if they comprised the entire record. If any or all of the specified bytes do not exist in the record, the get is successful, and the existing bytes or nul bytes are returned.

For example, if the data portion of a retrieved record was 100 bytes, and a partial retrieval was done using a DBT having a **dlen** field of 20 and a **doff** field of 85, the get call would succeed, the **data** field would reference the last 15 bytes of the record, and the **size** field would be set to 15.

If the calling application is doing a put, the **dlen** bytes starting **doff** bytes from the beginning of the specified key's data record are replaced by the data specified by the **data** and **size** structure elements. If **dlen** is smaller than **size**, the record will grow; and if **dlen** is larger than **size**, the record will shrink. If the specified bytes do not exist, the record will be extended using nul bytes as necessary, and the put call will succeed.

It is an error to attempt a partial put using the **DB→put** function in a database that supports duplicate records. Partial puts in databases supporting duplicate records must be done using a **DBcursor→c_put** function.

It is an error to attempt a partial put with differing **dlen** and **size** values in Queue or Recno databases with fixed-length records.

For example, if the data portion of a retrieved record was 100 bytes, and a partial put was done using a DBT having a **dlen** field of 20, a **doff** field of 85, and a **size** field of 30, the resulting record would be 115 bytes in length, where the last 30 bytes would be those specified by the put call.

DB_LSN

```
#include <db.h>
```

Description

A **DB_LSN** is a **log sequence number**, which indicates a unique position in the log. The **DB_LSN** structure is completely opaque, and no application should ever need to look inside. **DB_LSN** structures are used by the Logging and Memory Pool subsystems.

DBcursor→c_close

```
#include <db.h>

int
DBcursor→c_close(DBC *cursor);
```

Description

The DBcursor→c_close function discards the cursor.

It is possible for the DBcursor→c_close function to return DB_LOCK_DEADLOCK, signaling that any enclosing transaction should be aborted. If the application is already intending to abort the transaction, this error should be ignored, and the application should proceed.

Once DBcursor→c_close has been called, regardless of its return, the cursor handle may not be used again.

The DBcursor→c_close function returns a non-zero error value on failure and 0 on success.

Errors

The DBcursor→c_close function may fail and return a non-zero error for the following conditions:

- DB_LOCK_DEADLOCK   The operation was selected to resolve a deadlock.
- EINVAL   An invalid flag value or parameter was specified.

    The cursor was previously closed.

The DBcursor→c_close function may fail and return a non-zero error for errors specified for other Berkeley DB and C library or system functions. If a catastrophic error has occurred, the DBcursor→c_close function may fail and return DB_RUNRECOVERY, in which case all subsequent Berkeley DB calls will fail in the same way.

DBcursor→c_count

```
#include <db.h>

int
DBC→c_count(DBC *cursor, db_recno_t *countp, u_int32_t flags);
```

Description

The DBcursor→c_count function returns a count of the number of duplicate data items for the key referenced by the cursor into the memory location referenced by **countp**. If the underlying database does not support duplicate data items, the call will still succeed and a count of 1 will be returned.

The **flags** parameter is currently unused, and must be set to 0.

If the **cursor** argument is not yet initialized, the DBcursor→c_count function will return EINVAL.

Otherwise, the DBcursor→c_count function returns a non-zero error value on failure and 0 on success.

Errors

The DBcursor→c_count function may fail and return a non-zero error for errors specified for other Berkeley DB and C library or system functions. If a catastrophic error has occurred, the DBcursor→c_count function may fail and return DB_RUNRECOVERY, in which case all subsequent Berkeley DB calls will fail in the same way.

DBcursor→c_del

```
#include <db.h>

int
DBcursor→c_del(DBC *cursor, u_int32_t flags);
```

Description

The DBcursor→c_del function deletes the key/data pair currently referenced by the cursor.

The **flags** parameter is currently unused, and must be set to 0.

The cursor position is unchanged after a delete, and subsequent calls to cursor functions expecting the cursor to reference an existing key will fail.

If the element has already been deleted, DBcursor→c_del will return DB_KEYEMPTY.

If the cursor is not yet initialized, the DBcursor→c_del function will return EINVAL.

Otherwise, the DBcursor→c_del function returns a non-zero error value on failure and 0 on success.

Errors

The DBcursor→c_del function may fail and return a non-zero error for the following conditions:

- DB_LOCK_DEADLOCK   The operation was selected to resolve a deadlock.
- EINVAL   An invalid flag value or parameter was specified.
- EPERM   Write attempted on read-only cursor when the DB_INIT_CDB flag was specified to **DBENV→open**.

The DBcursor→c_del function may fail and return a non-zero error for errors specified for other Berkeley DB and C library or system functions. If a catastrophic error has occurred, the DBcursor→c_del function may fail and return DB_RUNRECOVERY, in which case all subsequent Berkeley DB calls will fail in the same way.

DBcursor→c_dup

```
#include <db.h>

int
DBC→c_dup(DBC *cursor, DBC **cursorp, u_int32_t flags);
```

Description

The DBcursor→c_dup function creates a new cursor that uses the same transaction and locker ID as the original cursor. This is useful when an application is using locking and requires two or more cursors in the same thread of control.

The **flags** value must be set to 0 or by bitwise inclusively **OR**'ing together one or more of the following values.

- DB_POSITION   The newly created cursor is initialized to reference the same position in the database as the original cursor and hold the same locks. If the DB_POSITION flag is not specified, then the created cursor is uninitialized and will behave like a cursor newly created using **DB→cursor**.

When using the Berkeley DB Concurrent Data Store product, there can be only one active write cursor at a time. For this reason, attempting to duplicate a cursor for which the DB_WRITECURSOR flag was specified during creation will return an error.

If the **cursor** argument is not yet initialized, the DBcursor→c_dup function will return EINVAL.

Otherwise, the DBcursor→c_dup function returns a non-zero error value on failure and 0 on success.

Errors

The DBcursor→c_dup function may fail and return a non-zero error for the following conditions:

- EINVAL   An invalid flag value or parameter was specified.

  The **cursor** argument was created using the DB_WRITECURSOR flag in the Berkeley DB Concurrent Data Store product.

The DBcursor→c_dup function may fail and return a non-zero error for errors specified for other Berkeley DB and C library or system functions. If a catastrophic error has occurred, the DBcursor→c_dup function may fail and return DB_RUNRECOVERY, in which case all subsequent Berkeley DB calls will fail in the same way.

DBcursor→c_get

```
#include <db.h>

int
DBcursor→c_get(DBC *cursor,
    DBT *key, DBT *data, u_int32_t flags);
```

Description

The DBcursor→c_get function retrieves key/data pairs from the database. The address and length of the key are returned in the object referenced by **key** (except for the case of the DB_SET flag, in which the **key** object is unchanged), and the address and length of the data are returned in the object referenced by **data**.

Modifications to the database during a sequential scan will be reflected in the scan; that is, records inserted behind a cursor will not be returned while records inserted in front of a cursor will be returned.

In Queue and Recno databases, missing entries (that is, entries that were never explicitly created or that were created and then deleted) will be skipped during a sequential scan.

The **flags** parameter must be set to one of the following values:

- DB_CURRENT   Return the key/data pair currently referenced by the cursor.

    If the cursor key/data pair was deleted, DBcursor→c_get will return DB_KEYEMPTY.

    If the cursor is not yet initialized, the DBcursor→c_get function will return EINVAL.

- DB_FIRST, DB_LAST   The cursor is set to reference the first (last) key/data pair of the database, and that pair is returned. In the presence of duplicate key values, the first (last) data item in the set of duplicates is returned.

    If the database is a Queue or Recno database, DBcursor→c_get using the DB_FIRST (DB_LAST) flags will ignore any keys that exist but were never explicitly created by the application, or were created and later deleted.

    If the database is empty, DBcursor→c_get will return DB_NOTFOUND.

- DB_GET_BOTH   The DB_GET_BOTH flag is identical to the DB_SET flag, except that both the key and the data arguments must be matched by the key and data item in the database.

- DB_GET_RECNO   Return the record number associated with the cursor. The record number will be returned in **data**, as described in **DBT**. The **key** parameter is ignored.

    For DB_GET_RECNO to be specified, the underlying database must be of type Btree, and it must have been created with the DB_RECNUM flag.

- DB_JOIN_ITEM   Do not use the data value found in all of the cursors as a lookup key for the primary database, but simply return it in the key parameter instead. The data parameter is left unchanged.

For DB_JOIN_ITEM to be specified, the underlying cursor must have been returned from the **DB→join** function.

- DB_NEXT, DB_PREV   If the cursor is not yet initialized, DB_NEXT (DB_PREV) is identical to DB_FIRST (DB_LAST). Otherwise, the cursor is moved to the next (previous) key/data pair of the database, and that pair is returned. In the presence of duplicate key values, the value of the key may not change.

    If the database is a Queue or Recno database, DBcursor→c_get using the DB_NEXT (DB_PREV) flag will skip any keys that exist but were never explicitly created by the application or were created and later deleted.

    If the cursor is already on the last (first) record in the database, DBcursor→c_get will return DB_NOTFOUND.

- DB_NEXT_DUP   If the next key/data pair of the database is a duplicate record for the current key/data pair, the cursor is moved to the next key/data pair of the database, and that pair is returned. Otherwise, DBcursor→c_get will return DB_NOTFOUND.

    If the cursor is not yet initialized, the DBcursor→c_get function will return EINVAL.

- DB_NEXT_NODUP, DB_PREV_NODUP   If the cursor is not yet initialized, DB_NEXT_NODUP (DB_PREV_NODUP) is identical to DB_FIRST (DB_LAST). Otherwise, the cursor is moved to the next (previous) non-duplicate key/data pair of the database, and that pair is returned.

    If the database is a Queue or Recno database, DBcursor→c_get using the DB_NEXT_NODUP (DB_PREV_NODUP) flags will ignore any keys that exist but were never explicitly created by the application, or those that were created and later deleted.

    If no non-duplicate key/data pairs occur after (before) the cursor position in the database, DBcursor→c_get will return DB_NOTFOUND.

- DB_SET   Move the cursor to the specified key/data pair of the database, and return the datum associated with the given key.

    In the presence of duplicate key values, DBcursor→c_get will return the first data item for the given key.

    If the database is a Queue or Recno database, and the requested key exists but was never explicitly created by the application or was later deleted, DBcursor→c_get will return DB_KEYEMPTY.

    If no matching keys are found, DBcursor→c_get will return DB_NOTFOUND.

- DB_SET_RANGE   The DB_SET_RANGE flag is identical to the DB_SET flag, except that the key is returned as well as the data item; and, in the case of the Btree access method, the returned key/data pair is the smallest key greater than or equal to the specified key (as determined by the comparison function), permitting partial key matches and range searches.

- DB_SET_RECNO   Move the cursor to the specific numbered record of the database, and return the associated key/data pair. The **data** field of the specified **key** must be a pointer to a memory location from which a db_recno_t may be read, as described in **DBT**. This memory location will be read to determine the record to be retrieved.

For DB_SET_RECNO to be specified, the underlying database must be of type Btree, and it must have been created with the DB_RECNUM flag.

In addition, the following flag may be set by bitwise inclusively **OR**'ing it into the **flags** parameter:

- DB_RMW   Acquire write locks instead of read locks when doing the retrieval. Setting this flag can eliminate deadlock during a read-modify-write cycle by acquiring the write lock during the read part of the cycle so that another thread of control acquiring a read lock for the same item, in its own read-modify-write cycle, will not result in deadlock.

Otherwise, the DBcursor→c_get function returns a non-zero error value on failure and 0 on success.

If DBcursor→c_get fails for any reason, the state of the cursor will be unchanged.

Errors

The DBcursor→c_get function may fail and return a non-zero error for the following conditions:

- DB_LOCK_DEADLOCK   The operation was selected to resolve a deadlock.
- ENOMEM   There was insufficient memory to return the requested item.
- EINVAL   An invalid flag value or parameter was specified.

  The specified cursor was not currently initialized.

The DBcursor→c_get function may fail and return a non-zero error for errors specified for other Berkeley DB and C library or system functions. If a catastrophic error has occurred, the DBcursor→c_get function may fail and return DB_RUNRECOVERY, in which case all subsequent Berkeley DB calls will fail in the same way.

DBcursor→c_put

```
#include <db.h>

int
DBcursor→c_put(DBC *, DBT *key, DBT *data, u_int32_t flags);
```

Description

The DBcursor→c_put function stores key/data pairs into the database.

The **flags** parameter must be set to one of the following values:

- DB_AFTER   In the case of the Btree and Hash access methods, insert the data element as a duplicate element of the key referenced by the cursor. The new element appears immediately after the current cursor position. It is an error to specify DB_AFTER if the underlying Btree or Hash database does not support duplicate data items. The **key** parameter is ignored.

In the case of the Recno access method, it is an error to specify DB_AFTER if the underlying Recno database was not created with the DB_RENUMBER flag. If the DB_RENUMBER flag was specified, a new key is created, all records after the inserted item are automatically renumbered, and the key of the new record is returned in the structure referenced by the parameter **key**. The initial value of the **key** parameter is ignored. See **DB→open** for more information.

The DB_AFTER flag may not be specified to the Queue access method.

If the current cursor record has already been deleted and the underlying access method is Hash, DBcursor→c_put will return DB_NOTFOUND. If the underlying access method is Btree or Recno, the operation will succeed.

If the cursor is not yet initialized or if a duplicate sort function has been specified, the DBcursor→c_put function will return EINVAL.

- DB_BEFORE   In the case of the Btree and Hash access methods, insert the data element as a duplicate element of the key referenced by the cursor. The new element appears immediately before the current cursor position. It is an error to specify DB_BEFORE if the underlying Btree or Hash database does not support duplicate data items. The **key** parameter is ignored.

In the case of the Recno access method, it is an error to specify DB_BEFORE if the underlying Recno database was not created with the DB_RENUMBER flag. If the DB_RENUMBER flag was specified, a new key is created, the current record and all records after it are automatically renumbered, and the key of the new record is returned in the structure referenced by the parameter **key**. The initial value of the **key** parameter is ignored. See **DB→open** for more information.

The DB_BEFORE flag may not be specified to the Queue access method.

If the current cursor record has already been deleted and the underlying access method is Hash, DBcursor→c_put will return DB_NOTFOUND. If the underlying access method is Btree or Recno, the operation will succeed.

If the cursor is not yet initialized or if a duplicate sort function has been specified, DBcursor→c_put will return EINVAL.

- DB_CURRENT   Overwrite the data of the key/data pair referenced by the cursor with the specified data item. The **key** parameter is ignored.

If a duplicate sort function has been specified and the data item of the current referenced key/data pair does not compare equally to the **data** parameter, DBcursor→c_put will return EINVAL.

If the current cursor record has already been deleted and the underlying access method is Hash, DBcursor→c_put will return DB_NOTFOUND. If the underlying access method is Btree, Queue, or Recno, the operation will succeed.

If the cursor is not yet initialized, DBcursor→c_put will return EINVAL.

- DB_KEYFIRST   In the case of the Btree and Hash access methods, insert the specified key/data pair into the database.

If the underlying database supports duplicate data items, and if the key already exists in the database and a duplicate sort function has been specified, the inserted data item is added in its sorted location. If the key already exists in the database and no duplicate sort function has been specified, the inserted data item is added as the first of the data items for that key.

The DB_KEYFIRST flag may not be specified to the Queue or Recno access methods.

- DB_KEYLAST   In the case of the Btree and Hash access methods, insert the specified key/data pair into the database.

If the underlying database supports duplicate data items, and if the key already exists in the database and a duplicate sort function has been specified, the inserted data item is added in its sorted location. If the key already exists in the database, and no duplicate sort function has been specified, the inserted data item is added as the last of the data items for that key.

The DB_KEYLAST flag may not be specified to the Queue or Recno access methods.

- DB_NODUPDATA   In the case of the Btree and Hash access methods, insert the specified key/data pair into the database, unless it already exists in the database. If the key/data pair already appears in the database, DB_KEYEXIST is returned. The DB_NODUPDATA flag may only be specified if the underlying database has been configured to support sorted duplicate data items.

The DB_NODUPDATA flag may not be specified to the Queue or Recno access methods.

Otherwise, the DBcursor→c_put function returns a non-zero error value on failure and 0 on success.

If DBcursor→c_put fails for any reason, the state of the cursor will be unchanged. If DBcursor→c_put succeeds and an item is inserted into the database, the cursor is always positioned to reference the newly inserted item.

Errors

The DBcursor→c_put function may fail and return a non-zero error for the following conditions:

- DB_LOCK_DEADLOCK   The operation was selected to resolve a deadlock.
- EACCES   An attempt was made to modify a read-only database.
- EINVAL   An invalid flag value or parameter was specified.

The DB_BEFORE or DB_AFTER flags were specified, and the underlying access method is Queue.

An attempt was made to add a record to a fixed-length database that was too large to fit.

- EPERM   Write attempted on read-only cursor when the DB_INIT_CDB flag was specified to **DBENV→open**.

The DBcursor→c_put function may fail and return a non-zero error for errors specified for other Berkeley DB and C library or system functions. If a catastrophic error has occurred, the DBcursor→c_put function may fail and return DB_RUNRECOVERY, in which case all subsequent Berkeley DB calls will fail in the same way.

db_create

```
#include <db.h>

int
db_create(DB **dbp, DB_ENV *dbenv, u_int32_t flags);
```

Description

The db_create function creates a DB structure that is the handle for a Berkeley DB database. A pointer to this structure is returned in the memory referenced by **db**.

If the **dbenv** argument is NULL, the database is standalone; that is, it is not part of any Berkeley DB environment.

If the **dbenv** argument is not NULL, the database is created within the specified Berkeley DB environment. The database access methods automatically make calls to the other subsystems in Berkeley DB, based on the enclosing environment. For example, if the environment has been configured to use locking, the access methods will automatically acquire the correct locks when reading and writing pages of the database.

The **flags** parameter must be set to 0 or the following value:

- DB_XA_CREATE   Instead of creating a standalone database, create a database intended to be accessed via applications running under an X/Open conformant Transaction Manager. The database will be opened in the environment specified by the OPENINFO parameter of the GROUPS section of the ubbconfig file. See the "XA Resource Manager" chapter in the *Reference Guide* for more information.

The DB handle contains a special field, "app_private", which is declared as type "void ★". This field is provided for the use of the application program. It is initialized to NULL and is not further used by Berkeley DB in any way.

The db_create function returns a non-zero error value on failure and 0 on success.

Errors

The db_create function may fail and return a non-zero error for errors specified for other Berkeley DB and C library or system functions. If a catastrophic error has occurred, the db_create function may fail and return DB_RUNRECOVERY, in which case all subsequent Berkeley DB calls will fail in the same way.

db_env_create

```
#include <db.h>

int
db_env_create(DB_ENV **dbenvp, u_int32_t flags);
```

Description

The db_env_create function creates a DB_ENV structure that is the handle for a Berkeley DB environment. A pointer to this structure is returned in the memory referenced by **dbenvp**.

The **flags** parameter must be set to 0 or the following value:

- DB_CLIENT   Create a client environment to connect to a server.

  The DB_CLIENT flag indicates to the system that this environment is remote on a server. The use of this flag causes the environment methods to use functions that call a server instead of local functions. Prior to making any environment or database method calls, the application must call the **DBENV→set_server** function to establish the connection to the server.

The DB_ENV handle contains a special field, "app_private", which is declared as type "void ★". This field is provided for the use of the application program. It is initialized to NULL and is not further used by Berkeley DB in any way.

The db_env_create function returns a non-zero error value on failure and 0 on success.

Errors

The db_env_create function may fail and return a non-zero error for errors specified for other Berkeley DB and C library or system functions. If a catastrophic error has occurred, the db_env_create function may fail and return DB_RUNRECOVERY, in which case all subsequent Berkeley DB calls will fail in the same way.

db_env_set_func_close

```
#include <db.h>

int
db_env_set_func_close(int (*func_close)(int fd));
```

Description

Replace Berkeley DB calls to the IEEE/ANSI Std 1003.1 (POSIX) **close** function with **func_close**, which must conform to the standard interface.

The db_env_set_func_close interface affects the entire application, not a single database or database environment.

Although the db_env_set_func_close interface may be used to configure Berkeley DB at any time during the life of the application, it should normally be called before making any calls to the **db_env_create** or **db_create** functions.

The db_env_set_func_close function returns a non-zero error value on failure and 0 on success.

Errors

- EINVAL   An invalid flag value or parameter was specified.

db_env_set_func_dirfree

```
#include <db.h>

int
db_env_set_func_dirfree(void (*func_dirfree)(char **namesp, int cnt));
```

Description

The Berkeley DB library requires the cap ability to return any memory allocated as part of the routine that reads through a directory and creates a list of files that the directory contains (see **db_env_set_func_dirlist**). The **func_dirfree** argument must conform to the following interface:

```
int dirfree(char **namesp, int cnt);
```

The **namesp** and **cnt** arguments are the same values as were returned by the **db_env_set_func_dirlist** function.

The **func_dirfree** function must return the value of **errno** on failure and 0 on success.

The db_env_set_func_dirfree interface affects the entire application, not a single database or database environment.

Although the db_env_set_func_dirfree interface may be used to configure Berkeley DB at any time during the life of the application, it should normally be called before making any calls to the **db_env_create** or **db_create** functions.

The db_env_set_func_dirfree function returns a non-zero error value on failure and 0 on success.

Errors

- EINVAL   An invalid flag value or parameter was specified.

db_env_set_func_dirlist

```
#include <db.h>

int
db_env_set_func_dirlist(
    int (*func_dirlist)(const char *dir, char ***namesp, int *cntp));
```

Description

The Berkeley DB library requires the ability to read through a directory and create a list of files that the directory contains. The **func_dirlist** argument must conform to the following interface:

```
int dirlist(const char *dir, char ***namesp, int *cntp);
```

The **dir** argument is the name of the directory to be searched. The function must return a pointer to an array of nul-terminated file names in the memory location referenced by the argument **namesp**, and a count of the number of elements in the array in the memory location referenced by **cntp**.

The **func_dirlist** function must return the value of **errno** on failure and 0 on success.

The db_env_set_func_dirlist interface affects the entire application, not a single database or database environment.

Although the db_env_set_func_dirlist interface may be used to configure Berkeley DB at any time during the life of the application, it should normally be called before making any calls to the **db_env_create** or **db_create** functions.

The db_env_set_func_dirlist function returns a non-zero error value on failure and 0 on success.

Errors

- EINVAL   An invalid flag value or parameter was specified.

db_env_set_func_exists

```
#include <db.h>

int
db_env_set_func_exists(int (*func_exists)(const char *path, int *isdirp));
```

Description

The Berkeley DB library requires the ability to determine whether a file exists, and optionally, whether it is a file of type directory. The **func** argument must conform to the following interface:

```
int exists(const char *path, int *isdirp);
```

The **path** argument is the pathname of the file to be checked.

If the **isdirp** argument is non-NULL, it must be set to non-0 if **path** is a directory, and 0 if **path** is not a directory.

The **func_exists** function must return the value of **errno** on failure and 0 on success.

The db_env_set_func_exists interface affects the entire application, not a single database or database environment.

Although the db_env_set_func_exists interface may be used to configure Berkeley DB at any time during the life of the application, it should normally be called before making any calls to the **db_env_create** or **db_create** functions.

The db_env_set_func_exists function returns a non-zero error value on failure and 0 on success.

Errors

- EINVAL   An invalid flag value or parameter was specified.

db_env_set_func_free

```
#include <db.h>

int
db_env_set_func_free(void (*func_free)(void *ptr));
```

Description

Replace Berkeley DB calls to the ANSI C X3.159-1989 (ANSI C) standard **free** function with **func_free**, which must conform to the standard interface.

The db_env_set_func_free interface affects the entire application, not a single database or database environment.

Although the db_env_set_func_free interface may be used to configure Berkeley DB at any time during the life of the application, it should normally be called before making any calls to the **db_env_create** or **db_create** functions.

The db_env_set_func_free function returns a non-zero error value on failure and 0 on success.

Errors

- EINVAL   An invalid flag value or parameter was specified.

db_env_set_func_fsync

```
#include <db.h>

int
db_env_set_func_fsync(int (*func_fsync)(int fd));
```

Description

Replace Berkeley DB calls to the IEEE/ANSI Std 1003.1 (POSIX) **fsync** function with **func_fsync**, which must conform to the standard interface.

The db_env_set_func_fsync interface affects the entire application, not a single database or database environment.

Although the db_env_set_func_fsync interface may be used to configure Berkeley DB at any time during the life of the application, it should normally be called before making any calls to the **db_env_create** or **db_create** functions.

The db_env_set_func_fsync function returns a non-zero error value on failure and 0 on success.

Errors

• EINVAL   An invalid flag value or parameter was specified.

db_env_set_func_ioinfo

```
#include <db.h>

int
db_env_set_func_ioinfo(int (*func_ioinfo)(const char *path,
    int fd, u_int32_t *mbytesp, u_int32_t *bytesp, u_int32_t *iosizep));
```

Description

The Berkeley DB library requires the ability to determine the size and I/O characteristics of a file. The **func_ioinfo** argument must conform to the following interface:

```
int ioinfo(const char *path, int fd,
u_int32_t *mbytesp, u_int32_t *bytesp, u_int32_t *iosizep);
```

The **path** argument is the pathname of the file to be checked, and the **fd** argument is an open file descriptor on the file.

If the **mbytesp** and **bytesp** arguments are non-NULL, the **ioinfo** function must return in them the size of the file: the number of megabytes in the file into the memory location referenced by the **mbytesp** argument, and the number of bytes over and above that number of megabytes into the memory location referenced by the **bytesp** argument.

In addition, if the **iosizep** argument is non-NULL, the **ioinfo** function must return the optimum granularity for I/O operations to the file in the memory location referenced by it.

The **func_ioinfo** function must return the value of **errno** on failure and 0 on success.

The db_env_set_func_ioinfo interface affects the entire application, not a single database or database environment.

Although the db_env_set_func_ioinfo interface may be used to configure Berkeley DB at any time during the life of the application, it should normally be called before making any calls to the **db_env_create** or **db_create** functions.

The db_env_set_func_ioinfo function returns a non-zero error value on failure and 0 on success.

Errors

- EINVAL   An invalid flag value or parameter was specified.

db_env_set_func_malloc

```
#include <db.h>

int
db_env_set_func_malloc(void *(*func_malloc)(size_t size));
```

Description

Replace Berkeley DB calls to the ANSI C X3.159-1989 (ANSI C) standard **malloc** function with **func_malloc**, which must conform to the standard interface.

The db_env_set_func_malloc interface affects the entire application, not a single database or database environment.

Although the db_env_set_func_malloc interface may be used to configure Berkeley DB at any time during the life of the application, it should normally be called before making any calls to the **db_env_create** or **db_create** functions.

The db_env_set_func_malloc function returns a non-zero error value on failure and 0 on success.

Errors

- EINVAL   An invalid flag value or parameter was specified.

db_env_set_func_map

```
#include <db.h>

int
db_env_set_func_map(int (*func_map)(char *path,
    size_t len, int is_region, int is_rdonly, void **addr));
```

Description

The Berkeley DB library requires the ability to map a file into memory and to create shared memory regions (which may or may not be backed by files). The **func_map** argument must conform to the following interface:

```
int map(char *path, size_t len,
    int is_region, int is_rdonly, void **addr);
```

The **path** argument is the name of a file.

The **is_region** argument will be zero if the intention is to map a file into shared memory. In this case, the **map** function must map the first **len** bytes of the file into memory and return a pointer to the mapped location in the memory location referenced by the argument **addr**. The **is_rdonly** argument will be non-zero if the file is considered read-only by the caller.

The **is_region** argument will be non-zero if the memory is intended to be used as a shared memory region for synchronization between Berkeley DB threads/processes. In this case, the returned memory may be of any kind (for example, anonymous), but must be able to support semaphores. In this case, the **path** argument may be ignored (although future **map** calls using the same **path** must return the same memory), and the **is_rdonly** argument will always be zero.

The **func_map** function must return the value of **errno** on failure and 0 on success.

The db_env_set_func_map interface affects the entire application, not a single database or database environment.

Although the db_env_set_func_map interface may be used to configure Berkeley DB at any time during the life of the application, it should normally be called before making any calls to the **db_env_create** or **db_create** functions.

The db_env_set_func_map function returns a non-zero error value on failure and 0 on success.

Errors

- EINVAL   An invalid flag value or parameter was specified.

db_env_set_func_open

```
#include <db.h>

int
db_env_set_func_open(int (*func_open)(const char *path, int flags, int mode));
```

Description

Replace Berkeley DB calls to the IEEE/ANSI Std 1003.1 (POSIX) **open** function with **func_open**, which must conform to the standard interface.

The db_env_set_func_open interface affects the entire application, not a single database or database environment.

Although the db_env_set_func_open interface may be used to configure Berkeley DB at any time during the life of the application, it should normally be called before making any calls to the **db_env_create** or **db_create** functions.

The db_env_set_func_open function returns a non-zero error value on failure and 0 on success.

Errors

- EINVAL   An invalid flag value or parameter was specified.

db_env_set_func_read

```
#include <db.h>

int
db_env_set_func_read(ssize_t (*func_read)(int fd, void *buf, size_t nbytes));
```

Description

Replace Berkeley DB calls to the IEEE/ANSI Std 1003.1 (POSIX) **read** function with **func_read**, which must conform to the standard interface.

The db_env_set_func_read interface affects the entire application, not a single database or database environment.

Although the db_env_set_func_read interface may be used to configure Berkeley DB at any time during the life of the application, it should normally be called before making any calls to the **db_env_create** or **db_create** functions.

The db_env_set_func_read function returns a non-zero error value on failure and 0 on success.

Errors

- EINVAL   An invalid flag value or parameter was specified.

db_env_set_func_realloc

```
#include <db.h>

int
db_env_set_func_realloc(void *(*func_realloc)(void *ptr, size_t size));
```

Description

Replace Berkeley DB calls to the ANSI C X3.159-1989 (ANSI C) standard **realloc** function with **func_realloc**, which must conform to the standard interface.

The db_env_set_func_realloc interface affects the entire application, not a single database or database environment.

Although the db_env_set_func_realloc interface may be used to configure Berkeley DB at any time during the life of the application, it should normally be called before making any calls to the **db_env_create** or **db_create** functions.

The db_env_set_func_realloc function returns a non-zero error value on failure and 0 on success.

Errors

- EINVAL   An invalid flag value or parameter was specified.

db_env_set_func_rename

```
#include <db.h>

int
db_env_set_func_rename(int (*func_rename)(int fd));
```

Description

Replace Berkeley DB calls to the IEEE/ANSI Std 1003.1 (POSIX) **rename** function with **func_rename**, which must conform to the standard interface.

The db_env_set_func_rename interface affects the entire application, not a single database or database environment.

Although the db_env_set_func_rename interface may be used to configure Berkeley DB at any time during the life of the application, it should normally be called before making any calls to the **db_env_create** or **db_create** functions.

The db_env_set_func_rename function returns a non-zero error value on failure and 0 on success.

Errors

- EINVAL   An invalid flag value or parameter was specified.

db_env_set_func_seek

```
#include <db.h>

int
db_env_set_func_seek(int (*func_seek)(int fd, size_t pgsize,
    db_pgno_t pageno, u_int32_t relative, int rewind, int whence));
```

Description

The Berkeley DB library requires the ability to specify that a subsequent read from or write to a file will occur at a specific location in that file. The **func_seek** argument must conform to the following interface:

```
int seek(int fd, size_t pgsize, db_pgno_t pageno,
u_int32_t relative, int rewind, int whence);
```

The **fd** argument is an open file descriptor on the file.

The **seek** function must cause a subsequent read from or write to the file to occur at a byte offset specified by the calculation:

```
(pgsize * pageno) + relative
```

If **rewind** is non-zero, the byte offset is treated as a backward seek, not a forward one.

The **whence** argument specifies where in the file the byte offset is relative to, as described by the IEEE/ANSI Std 1003.1 (POSIX) **lseek** system call.

The **func_seek** function must return the value of **errno** on failure and 0 on success.

The db_env_set_func_seek interface affects the entire application, not a single database or database environment.

Although the db_env_set_func_seek interface may be used to configure Berkeley DB at any time during the life of the application, it should normally be called before making any calls to the **db_env_create** or **db_create** functions.

The db_env_set_func_seek function returns a non-zero error value on failure and 0 on success.

Errors

- EINVAL   An invalid flag value or parameter was specified.

db_env_set_func_sleep

```
#include <db.h>

int
db_env_set_func_sleep(int (*func_sleep)(u_long seconds, u_long microseconds));
```

Description

The Berkeley DB library requires the ability to cause a thread of control to suspend itself for a period of time, relinquishing control of the processor to any other waiting thread of control. The **func_sleep** argument must conform to the following interface:

```
int sleep(u_long seconds, u_long microseconds);
```

The **seconds** and **microseconds** arguments specify the amount of time to wait until the suspending thread of control should run again.

The **seconds** and **microseconds** arguments may not be normalized when the **sleep** function is called; that is, the **microseconds** argument may be greater than 1000000.

The **func_sleep** function must return the value of **errno** on failure and 0 on success.

The db_env_set_func_sleep interface affects the entire application, not a single database or database environment.

Although the db_env_set_func_sleep interface may be used to configure Berkeley DB at any time during the life of the application, it should normally be called before making any calls to the **db_env_create** or **db_create** functions.

The db_env_set_func_sleep function returns a non-zero error value on failure and 0 on success.

Errors

• EINVAL   An invalid flag value or parameter was specified.

db_env_set_func_unlink

```
#include <db.h>

int
db_env_set_func_unlink(int (*func_unlink)(const char *path));
```

Description

Replace Berkeley DB calls to the IEEE/ANSI Std 1003.1 (POSIX) **unlink** function with **func_unlink**, which must conform to the standard interface.

The db_env_set_func_unlink interface affects the entire application, not a single database or database environment.

Although the db_env_set_func_unlink interface may be used to configure Berkeley DB at any time during the life of the application, it should normally be called before making any calls to the **db_env_create** or **db_create** functions.

The db_env_set_func_unlink function returns a non-zero error value on failure and 0 on success.

Errors

- EINVAL   An invalid flag value or parameter was specified.

db_env_set_func_unmap

```
#include <db.h>

int
db_env_set_func_unmap(int (*func_unmap)(void *addr, size_t len));
```

Description

The Berkeley DB library requires the ability to unmap a file or shared memory region from memory. The **func_unmap** argument must conform to the following interface:

```
int unmap(void *addr, size_t len);
```

The **addr** argument is the argument returned by the **db_env_set_func_map** function when the file or region was mapped into memory, and the **len** argument is the same as the **len** argument specified to the **db_env_set_func_map** function when the file or region was mapped into memory.

The **func_unmap** function must return the value of **errno** on failure and 0 on success.

The db_env_set_func_unmap interface affects the entire application, not a single database or database environment.

Although the db_env_set_func_unmap interface may be used to configure Berkeley DB at any time during the life of the application, it should normally be called before making any calls to the **db_env_create** or **db_create** functions.

The db_env_set_func_unmap function returns a non-zero error value on failure and 0 on success.

Errors

- EINVAL   An invalid flag value or parameter was specified.

db_env_set_func_write

```
#include <db.h>

int
db_env_set_func_write(
    ssize_t (*func_write)(int fd, const void *buffer, size_t nbytes));
```

Description

Replace Berkeley DB calls to the IEEE/ANSI Std 1003.1 (POSIX) **write** function with **func_write**, which must conform to the standard interface.

The db_env_set_func_write interface affects the entire application, not a single database or database environment.

Although the db_env_set_func_write interface may be used to configure Berkeley DB at any time during the life of the application, it should normally be called before making any calls to the **db_env_create** or **db_create** functions.

The db_env_set_func_write function returns a non-zero error value on failure and 0 on success.

Errors

- EINVAL   An invalid flag value or parameter was specified.

db_env_set_func_yield

```
#include <db.h>

int
db_env_set_func_yield(int (*func_yield)(void));
```

Description

The Berkeley DB library requires the ability to yield the processor from the current thread of control to any other waiting threads of control. The **func_yield** argument must conform to the following interface:

```
int yield(void); .
```

The **func_yield** function must be able to cause the rescheduling of all participants in the current Berkeley DB environment, whether threaded or not. It may be incorrect to supply a thread **yield** function if more than a single process is operating in the Berkeley DB environment. This is because many thread-yield functions will not allow other processes to run, and the contested lock may be held by another process, not by another thread.

If no **func_yield** function is specified, or if the **yield** function returns an error, the function specified by the **db_env_set_func_sleep** entry will be used instead or subsequently; that is, if no **yield** function is specified, or if it is possible for the **yield** function to fail, the **sleep** function must cause the processor to reschedule any waiting threads of control for execution.

The **func_yield** function must return the value of **errno** on failure and 0 on success.

The db_env_set_func_yield interface affects the entire application, not a single database or database environment.

Although the db_env_set_func_yield interface may be used to configure Berkeley DB at any time during the life of the application, it should normally be called before making any calls to the **db_env_create** or **db_create** functions.

The db_env_set_func_yield function returns a non-zero error value on failure and 0 on success.

Errors

- EINVAL   An invalid flag value or parameter was specified.

DBENV→set_mutexlocks

```
#include <db.h>

int
DBENV→set_mutexlocks(DB_ENV *dbenv, int do_lock);
```

Description

Toggle mutex locks. Setting **do_lock** to a zero value causes Berkeley DB to grant all requested mutual exclusion mutexes without regard for their availability.

This functionality should never be used for any other purpose than debugging.

The DBENV→set_mutexlocks interface may be used to configure Berkeley DB at any time during the life of the application.

The DBENV→set_mutexlocks function returns a non-zero error value on failure and 0 on success.

db_env_set_pageyield

```
#include <db.h>

int
db_env_set_pageyield(int pageyield);
```

Description

Yield the processor whenever requesting a page from the cache. Setting **pageyield** to a non-zero value causes Berkeley DB to yield the processor any time a thread requests a page from the cache. This functionality should never be used for any other purpose than stress testing.

The db_env_set_pageyield interface affects the entire application, not a single database or database environment.

The db_env_set_pageyield interface may be used to configure Berkeley DB at any time during the life of the application.

The db_env_set_pageyield function returns a non-zero error value on failure and 0 on success.

Errors

- EINVAL   An invalid flag value or parameter was specified.

db_env_set_panicstate

```
#include <db.h>

int
db_env_set_panicstate(int panic);
```

Description

Toggle the Berkeley DB panic state. Setting **panic** to a non-zero value causes Berkeley DB to refuse attempts to call Berkeley DB functions with the DB_RUNRECOVERY error return.

The db_env_set_panicstate interface affects the entire application, not a single database or database environment.

The **db_env_set_pageyield** interface may be used to configure Berkeley DB at any time during the life of the application.

The db_env_set_panicstate function returns a non-zero error value on failure and 0 on success.

Errors

- EINVAL   An invalid flag value or parameter was specified.

db_env_set_region_init

```
#include <db.h>

int
db_env_set_region_init(int region_init);
```

Description

Page-fault shared regions into memory when initially creating or joining a Berkeley DB environment. In some applications, the expense of page-faulting the shared memory regions can affect performance; for example, when the page-fault occurs while holding a lock, other lock requests can convoy, and overall throughput may decrease. Setting **region_init** to a non-zero value specifies that shared regions be read or written, as appropriate, when the region is joined by the application. This forces the underlying virtual memory and file systems to instantiate both the necessary memory and the necessary disk space. This can also avoid out-of-disk space failures later on.

The db_env_set_region_init interface affects the entire application, not a single database or database environment.

Although the db_env_set_region_init interface may be used to configure Berkeley DB at any time during the life of the application, it should normally be called before making any calls to the **db_env_create** or **db_create** functions.

The db_env_set_region_init function returns a non-zero error value on failure and 0 on success.

The database environment's initial behavior with respect to shared memory regions may also be set using the environment's **DB_CONFIG** file. The syntax of the entry in that file is a single line with the string "set_region_init", one or more whitespace characters, and the string "1". Because the **DB_CONFIG** file is read when the database environment is opened, it will silently overrule configuration done before that time.

Errors

- EINVAL   An invalid flag value or parameter was specified.

db_env_set_tas_spins

```
#include <db.h>

int
db_env_set_tas_spins(u_int32_t tas_spins);
```

Description

Specify that test-and-set mutexes should spin **tas_spins** times without blocking. The value defaults to 1 on uniprocessor systems and to 50 times the number of processors on multiprocessor systems.

The db_env_set_tas_spins interface affects the entire application, not a single database or database environment.

Although the db_env_set_tas_spins interface may be used to configure Berkeley DB at any time during the life of the application, it should normally be called before making any calls to the **db_env_create** or **db_create** functions.

The db_env_set_tas_spins function returns a non-zero error value on failure and 0 on success.

The database environment's test-and-set spin count may also be set using the environment's **DB_CONFIG** file. The syntax of the entry in that file is a single line with the string "set_tas_spins", one or more whitespace characters, and the number of spins. Because the

DB_CONFIG file is read when the database environment is opened, it will silently overrule configuration done before that time.

Errors

- EINVAL   An invalid flag value or parameter was specified.

db_strerror

```
#include <db.h>

char *
db_strerror(int error);
```

Description

The db_strerror function returns an error message string corresponding to the error number **error**. This interface is a superset of the ANSI C X3.159-1989 (ANSI C) **strerror**(3) interface. If the error number **error** is greater than or equal to 0, then the string returned by the system interface **strerror**(3) is returned. If the error number is less than 0, an error string appropriate to the corresponding Berkeley DB library error is returned. See "Error Returns to Applications" for more information.

db_version

```
#include <db.h>

char *
db_version(int *major, int *minor, int *patch);
```

Description

The db_version function returns a pointer to a string containing Berkeley DB version information. If **major** is non-NULL, the major version of the Berkeley DB release is stored in the memory it references. If **minor** is non-NULL, the minor version of the Berkeley DB release is stored in the memory it references. If **patch** is non-NULL, the patch version of the Berkeley DB release is stored in the memory it references.

dbm/ndbm

```
#define DB_DBM_HSEARCH    1

#include <db.h>
typedef struct {
     char *dptr;
     int dsize;
} datum;
```

Dbm Functions

```
int
dbminit(char *file);

int
dbmclose();

datum
fetch(datum key);

int
store(datum key, datum content);

int
delete(datum key);

datum
firstkey(void);

datum
nextkey(datum key);
```

Ndbm Functions

```
DBM *
dbm_open(char *file, int flags, int mode);

void
dbm_close(DBM *db);

datum
dbm_fetch(DBM *db, datum key);

int
dbm_store(DBM *db, datum key, datum content, int flags);

int
dbm_delete(DBM *db, datum key);

datum
dbm_firstkey(DBM *db);

datum
dbm_nextkey(DBM *db);

int
dbm_error(DBM *db);

int
dbm_clearerr(DBM *db);
```

Description

The dbm interfaces to the Berkeley DB library are intended to provide high-performance implementations and source code compatibility for applications written to historic interfaces. They are not recommended for any other purpose. The historic dbm database format **is not supported**, and databases previously built using the real dbm libraries cannot be read by the Berkeley DB functions.

To compile dbm applications, replace the application's **#include** of the dbm or ndbm include file (for example, **#include <dbm.h>** or **#include <ndbm.h>**) with the following two lines:

```
#define DB_DBM_HSEARCH    1
#include <db.h>
```

Then, recompile. If the application attempts to load against a dbm library (for example, **–ldbm**), remove the library from the load line.

Key and **content** arguments are objects described by the **datum** typedef. A **datum** specifies a string of **dsize** bytes pointed to by **dptr**. Arbitrary binary data, as well as normal text strings, are allowed.

Dbm Functions

Before a database can be accessed, it must be opened by dbminit. This will open and/or create the database **file**.db. If created, the database file is created read/write by owner only (as described in **chmod**(2) and modified by the process' umask value at the time of creation (see **umask**(2)). The group ownership of created files is based on the system and directory defaults, and is not further specified by Berkeley DB.

A database may be closed, and any held resources released, by calling dbmclose.

Once open, the data stored under a key is accessed by fetch, and data is placed under a key by store. A key (and its associated contents) are deleted by delete. A linear pass through all keys in a database may be made, in an (apparently) random order, by using firstkey and nextkey. The firstkey function will return the first key in the database. The nextkey function will return the next key in the database.

The following code will traverse the data base:

```
for (key = firstkey();
    key.dptr != NULL; key = nextkey(key)) {
        ...
}
```

Ndbm Functions

Before a database can be accessed, it must be opened by dbm_open. This will open and/or create the database file **file.db**, depending on the flags parameter (see **open**(2)). If created, the database file is created with mode **mode** (as described in **chmod**(2)) and modified by the process' umask value at the time of creation (see **umask**(2)). The group ownership of created files is based on the system and directory defaults, and is not further specified by Berkeley DB.

Once open, the data stored under a key is accessed by dbm_fetch, and data is placed under a key by dbm_store. The **flags** field can be either **DBM_INSERT** or **DBM_REPLACE**. **DBM_INSERT** will only insert new entries into the database, and will not change an existing entry with the same key. **DBM_REPLACE** will replace an existing entry if it has the same key. A key (and its associated contents) are deleted by dbm_delete. A linear pass through all keys in a database may be made, in an (apparently) random order, by using dbm_firstkey and dbm_nextkey. The dbm_firstkey function will return the first key in the database. The dbm_nextkey function will return the next key in the database.

The following code will traverse the data base:

```
for (key = dbm_firstkey(db);
    key.dptr != NULL; key = dbm_nextkey(db)) {
    ...
}
```

Compatibility Notes

The historic dbm library created two underlying database files, traditionally named **file.dir** and **file.pag**. The Berkeley DB library creates a single database file named **file.db**. Applications that are aware of the underlying database file names may require additional source code modifications.

The historic dbminit interface required that the underlying **.dir** and **.pag** files already exist (empty databases were created by first manually creating zero-length **.dir** and **.pag** files). Applications that expect to create databases using this method may require additional source code modifications.

The historic dbm_dirfno and dbm_pagfno macros are supported, but will return identical file descriptors because there is only a single underlying file used by the Berkeley DB hashing access method. Applications using both file descriptors for locking may require additional source code modifications.

If applications using the dbm interface exits without first closing the database, it may lose updates because the Berkeley DB library buffers write to underlying databases. Such applications will require additional source code modifications to work correctly with the Berkeley DB library.

Dbm Diagnostics

The dbminit function returns –1 on failure, setting **errno**, and 0 on success.

The fetch function sets the **dptr** field of the returned **datum** to NULL on failure, setting **errno**, and returns a non-NULL **dptr** on success.

The store function returns –1 on failure, setting **errno**, and 0 on success.

The delete function returns –1 on failure, setting **errno**, and 0 on success.

The firstkey function sets the **dptr** field of the returned **datum** to NULL on failure, setting **errno**, and returns a non-NULL **dptr** on success.

The nextkey function sets the **dptr** field of the returned **datum** to NULL on failure, setting **errno**, and returns a non-NULL **dptr** on success.

Errors

The dbminit, fetch, store, delete, firstkey, and nextkey functions may fail and return a non-zero error for errors specified for other Berkeley DB and C library or system functions.

Ndbm Diagnostics

The dbm_close function returns non-zero when an error has occurred reading or writing the database.

The dbm_close function resets the error condition on the named database.

The dbm_open function returns NULL on failure, setting **errno**, and 0 on success.

The dbm_fetch function sets the **dptr** field of the returned **datum** to NULL on failure, setting **errno**, and returns a non-NULL **dptr** on success.

The dbm_store function returns -1 on failure, setting **errno**, 0 on success, and 1 if DBM_INSERT was set and the specified key already existed in the database.

The dbm_delete function returns -1 on failure, setting **errno**, and 0 on success.

The dbm_firstkey function sets the **dptr** field of the returned **datum** to NULL on failure, setting **errno**, and returns a non-NULL **dptr** on success.

The dbm_nextkey function sets the **dptr** field of the returned **datum** to NULL on failure, setting **errno**, and returns a non-NULL **dptr** on success.

The dbm_close function returns -1 on failure, setting **errno**, and 0 on success.

The dbm_close function returns -1 on failure, setting **errno**, and 0 on success.

Errors

The dbm_open, dbm_close, dbm_fetch, dbm_store, dbm_delete, dbm_firstkey, and dbm_nextkey functions may fail and return a non-zero error for errors specified for other Berkeley DB and C library or system functions.

hsearch

```
#define DB_DBM_HSEARCH    1
#include <db.h>

typedef enum {
        FIND, ENTER
} ACTION;

typedef struct entry {
        char *key;
        void *data;
} ENTRY;

ENTRY *
hsearch(ENTRY item, ACTION action);

int
hcreate(size_t nelem);

void
hdestroy(void);
```

Description

The hsearch interface to the Berkeley DB library is intended to provide a high-performance implementation and source code compatibility for applications written to the historic hsearch interface. It is not recommended for any other purpose.

To compile hsearch applications, replace the application's **#include** of the hsearch include file (for example, **#include <search.h>**) with the following two lines:

```
#define DB_DBM_HSEARCH    1
#include <db.h>
```

and recompile.

The hcreate function creates an in-memory database. The **nelem** argument is an estimation of the maximum number of key/data pairs that will be stored in the database.

The **hdestroy** function discards the database.

Database elements are structures of type **ENTRY**, which contain at least two fields: **key** and **data**. The field **key** is declared to be of type **char ***, and is the key used for storage and retrieval. The field **data** is declared to be of type **void ***, and is its associated data.

The hsearch function retrieves key/data pairs from, and stores key/data pairs into the database.

The **action** argument must be set to one of two values:

- ENTER   If the key does not already appear in the database, insert the key/data pair into the database. If the key already appears in the database, return a reference to an **ENTRY** structure referencing the existing key and its associated data element.

- FIND   Retrieve the specified key/data pair from the database.

Compatibility Notes

Historically, hsearch required applications to maintain the keys and data in the application's memory for as long as the **hsearch** database existed. Because Berkeley DB handles key and data management internally, there is no requirement that applications maintain local copies of key and data items, although the only effect of doing so should be the allocation of additional memory.

Hsearch Diagnostics

The **hcreate** function returns 0 on failure, setting **errno**, and non-zero on success.

The **hsearch** function returns a pointer to an ENTRY structure on success, and NULL, setting **errno**, if the **action** specified was FIND and the item did not appear in the database.

Errors

The hcreate function may fail and return a non-zero error for errors specified for other Berkeley DB and C library or system functions. If a catastrophic error has occurred, the hcreate function may fail and return DB_RUNRECOVERY, in which case all subsequent Berkeley DB calls will fail in the same way.

The hsearch function may fail and return a non-zero error for errors specified for other Berkeley DB and C library or system functions. If a catastrophic error has occurred, the hsearch function may fail and return DB_RUNRECOVERY, in which case all subsequent Berkeley DB calls will fail in the same way.

In addition, the **hsearch** function will fail, setting **errno** to 0, if the **action** specified was FIND and the item did not appear in the database.

lock_detect

```
#include <db.h>

int
lock_detect(DB_ENV *env,
    u_int32_t flags, u_int32_t atype, int *aborted);
```

Description

The lock_detect function runs one iteration of the deadlock detector. The deadlock detector traverses the lock table, and marks one of the participating transactions for abort for each deadlock it finds.

The **flags** value must be set to 0 or by bitwise inclusively **OR**'ing together one or more of the following values.

- DB_LOCK_CONFLICT   Only run the deadlock detector if a lock conflict has occurred since the last time that the deadlock detector was run.

The **atype** parameter specifies which transaction to abort in the case of deadlock. It must be set to one of possible arguments listed for the **DBENV→set_lk_detect** interface.

If the **aborted** parameter is non-NULL, the memory location it references will be set to the number of transactions aborted by the lock_detect function.

The lock_detect function is the underlying function used by the **db_deadlock** utility. See the **db_deadlock** utility source code for an example of using lock_detect in a IEEE/ANSI Std 1003.1 (POSIX) environment.

The lock_detect function returns a non-zero error value on failure and 0 on success.

Errors

The lock_detect function may fail and return a non-zero error for errors specified for other Berkeley DB and C library or system functions. If a catastrophic error has occurred, the lock_detect function may fail and return DB_RUNRECOVERY, in which case all subsequent Berkeley DB calls will fail in the same way.

lock_get

```
#include <db.h>

int
lock_get(DB_ENV *env, u_int32_t locker,
    u_int32_t flags, const DBT *obj,
    const db_lockmode_t lock_mode, DB_LOCK *lock);
```

Description

The lock_get function acquires a lock from the lock table, returning information about it in the **lock** argument.

The **locker** argument specified to lock_get is an unsigned 32-bit integer quantity. It represents the entity requesting or releasing the lock.

The **flags** value must be set to 0 or the following value:

- DB_LOCK_NOWAIT   If a lock cannot be granted because the requested lock conflicts with an existing lock, return immediately instead of waiting for the lock to become available.

The **obj** argument is an untyped byte string that specifies the object to be locked or released. Applications using the locking subsystem directly while also doing locking via the Berkeley DB access methods must take care not to inadvertently lock objects that happen to be equal to the unique file IDs used to lock files. See "Access Method Locking Conventions" for more information.

The **mode** argument is an index into the environment's lock conflict array. See **DBENV→set_lk_conflicts** and "Standard Lock Modes" for a description of that array.

The lock_get function may return the following value:

- DB_LOCK_NOTGRANTED   A lock was requested that could not be immediately granted and the **flags** parameter was set to DB_LOCK_NOWAIT.

Otherwise, the lock_get function returns a non-zero error value on failure and 0 on success.

Errors

The lock_get function may fail and return a non-zero error for the following conditions:

- DB_LOCK_DEADLOCK   The operation was selected to resolve a deadlock.
- EINVAL   An invalid flag value or parameter was specified.
- ENOMEM   The maximum number of locks has been reached.

The lock_get function may fail and return a non-zero error for errors specified for other Berkeley DB and C library or system functions. If a catastrophic error has occurred, the lock_get function may fail and return DB_RUNRECOVERY, in which case all subsequent Berkeley DB calls will fail in the same way.

lock_id

```
#include <db.h>

int
lock_id(DB_ENV *env, u_int32_t *idp);
```

Description

The lock_id function copies a locker ID, which is guaranteed to be unique in the specified lock table, into the memory location referenced by **idp**.

The lock_id function returns a non-zero error value on failure and 0 on success.

Errors

The lock_id function may fail and return a non-zero error for errors specified for other Berkeley DB and C library or system functions. If a catastrophic error has occurred, the lock_id function may fail and return DB_RUNRECOVERY, in which case all subsequent Berkeley DB calls will fail in the same way.

lock_put

```
#include <db.h>

int
lock_put(DB_ENV *env, DB_LOCK *lock);
```

Description

The lock_put function releases **lock** from the lock table.

The lock_put function returns a non-zero error value on failure and 0 on success.

Errors

The lock_put function may fail and return a non-zero error for the following conditions:

- EINVAL   An invalid flag value or parameter was specified.

The lock_put function may fail and return a non-zero error for errors specified for other Berkeley DB and C library or system functions. If a catastrophic error has occurred, the lock_put function may fail and return DB_RUNRECOVERY, in which case all subsequent Berkeley DB calls will fail in the same way.

lock_stat

```
#include <db.h>

int
lock_stat(DB_ENV *env,
DB_LOCK_STAT **statp, void *(*db_malloc)(size_t));
```

Description

The lock_stat function creates a statistical structure and copies a pointer to it into a user-specified memory location.

Statistical structures are created in allocated memory. If **db_malloc** is non-NULL, it is called to allocate the memory; otherwise, the library function **malloc**(3) is used. The function **db_malloc** must match the calling conventions of the **malloc**(3) library routine. Regardless, the caller is responsible for deallocating the returned memory. To deallocate returned memory, free the returned memory reference; references inside the returned memory do not need to be individually freed.

The lock region statistics are stored in a structure of type DB_LOCK_STAT. The following DB_LOCK_STAT fields will be filled in:

- u_int32_t st_lastid;   The last allocated lock ID.
- u_int32_t st_nmodes;   The number of lock modes.
- u_int32_t st_maxlocks;   The maximum number of locks possible.
- u_int32_t st_maxlockers;   The maximum number of lockers possible.
- u_int32_t st_maxobjects;   The maximum number of objects possible.
- u_int32_t st_nlocks;   The number of current locks.
- u_int32_t st_maxnlocks;   The maximum number of locks at any one time.
- u_int32_t st_nlockers;   The number of current lockers.
- u_int32_t st_maxnlockers;   The maximum number of lockers at any one time.
- u_int32_t st_nobjects;   The number of current objects.
- u_int32_t st_maxnobjects;   The maximum number of objects at any one time.
- u_int32_t st_nrequests;   The total number of locks requested.
- u_int32_t st_nreleases;   The total number of locks released.
- u_int32_t st_nnowaits;   The total number of lock requests that failed because DB_LOCK_NOWAIT was set.
- u_int32_t st_nconflicts;   The total number of locks not immediately available due to conflicts.
- u_int32_t st_ndeadlocks;   The number of deadlocks detected.
- u_int32_t st_regsize;   The size of the region.
- u_int32_t st_region_wait;   The number of times that a thread of control was forced to wait before obtaining the region lock.
- u_int32_t st_region_nowait;   The number of times that a thread of control was able to obtain the region lock without waiting.

The lock_stat function returns a non-zero error value on failure and 0 on success.

Errors

The lock_stat function may fail and return a non-zero error for errors specified for other Berkeley DB and C library or system functions. If a catastrophic error has occurred, the lock_stat function may fail and return DB_RUNRECOVERY, in which case all subsequent Berkeley DB calls will fail in the same way.

lock_vec

```
#include <db.h>

int
lock_vec(DB_ENV *env, u_int32_t locker, u_int32_t flags,
    DB_LOCKREQ list[], int nlist, DB_LOCKREQ **elistp);
```

Description

The lock_vec function atomically obtains and releases one or more locks from the lock table. The lock_vec function is intended to support acquisition or trading of multiple locks under one lock table semaphore, as is needed for lock coupling or in multigranularity locking for lock escalation.

The **locker** argument specified to lock_vec is an unsigned 32-bit integer quantity. It represents the entity requesting or releasing the lock.

The **flags** value must be set to 0 or the following value:

- DB_LOCK_NOWAIT   If a lock cannot be immediately granted because the requested lock conflicts with an existing lock, return instead of waiting for the lock to become available.

The **list** array provided to lock_vec is typedef'd as DB_LOCKREQ. A DB_LOCKREQ structure has at least the following fields, which must be initialized before calling lock_vec:

- lockop_t op;   The operation to be performed, which must be set to one of the following values:
  - DB_LOCK_GET   Get a lock, as defined by the values of **locker**, **obj**, and **mode**. Upon return from lock_vec, if the **lock** field is non-NULL, a reference to the acquired lock is stored there. (This reference is invalidated by any call to lock_vec or **lock_put** that releases the lock.)
  - DB_LOCK_PUT   The lock referenced by the contents of the **lock** field is released.
  - DB_LOCK_PUT_ALL   All locks held by the **locker** are released. (Any locks acquired as a part of the current call to lock_vec that appear after the DB_LOCK_PUT_ALL entry are not considered for this operation).
  - DB_LOCK_PUT_OBJ   All locks held on the object **obj** are released. The **mode** and **locker** parameters are ignored. Note that any locks acquired as a part of the current call to lock_vec that occur before the DB_LOCK_PUT_OBJ will also be released; those acquired afterward will not be released.

- const DBT obj;   An untyped byte string that specifies the object to be locked or released. Applications using the locking subsystem directly while also doing locking via the Berkeley DB access methods must take care not to inadvertently lock objects that happen to be equal to the unique file IDs used to lock files. See "Access Method Locking Conventions" for more information.
- const lockmode_t mode;   The lock mode, used as an index into the environment's lock conflict array. See **DBENV→set_lk_conflicts** and "Standard Lock Modes" for a description of that array.
- DB_LOCK lock;   A lock reference.

The **nlist** argument specifies the number of elements in the **list** array.

If any of the requested locks cannot be acquired, or any of the locks to be released cannot be released, the operations before the failing operation are guaranteed to have completed successfully, and lock_vec returns a non-zero value. In addition, if **elistp** is not NULL, it is set to point to the DB_LOCKREQ entry that was being processed when the error occurred.

The lock_vec function may return the following value:

- DB_LOCK_NOTGRANTED   A lock was requested that could not be immediately granted and the **flag** parameter was set to DB_LOCK_NOWAIT. In this case, if non-NULL, **elistp** identifies the request that was not granted.

Otherwise, the lock_vec function returns a non-zero error value on failure and 0 on success.

Errors

The lock_vec function may fail and return a non-zero error for the following conditions:

- DB_LOCK_DEADLOCK   The operation was selected to resolve a deadlock.
- EINVAL   An invalid flag value or parameter was specified.
- ENOMEM   The maximum number of locks has been reached.

The lock_vec function may fail and return a non-zero error for errors specified for other Berkeley DB and C library or system functions. If a catastrophic error has occurred, the lock_vec function may fail and return DB_RUNRECOVERY, in which case all subsequent Berkeley DB calls will fail in the same way.

log_archive

```
#include <db.h>

int
log_archive(DB_ENV *env, char *(*listp)[],
    u_int32_t flags, void *(*db_malloc)(size_t));
```

Description

The log_archive function creates a NULL-terminated array of log or database filenames, and copies a pointer to them into the user-specified memory location **listp**.

By default, log_archive returns the names of all of the log files that are no longer in use (for example, no longer involved in active transactions), and that may safely be archived for catastrophic recovery and then removed from the system. If there were no filenames to return, the memory location referenced by **listp** will be set to NULL.

Arrays of log filenames are created in allocated memory. If **db_malloc** is non-NULL, it is called to allocate the memory; otherwise, the library function **malloc**(3) is used. The function **db_malloc** must match the calling conventions of the **malloc**(3) library routine. Regardless, the caller is responsible for deallocating the returned memory. To deallocate returned memory, free the returned memory reference; references inside the returned memory do not need to be individually freed.

The **flags** value must be set to 0 or by bitwise inclusively **OR**'ing together one or more of the following values.

- DB_ARCH_ABS   All pathnames are returned as absolute pathnames, instead of relative to the database home directory.

- DB_ARCH_DATA   Return the database files that need to be archived in order to recover the database from catastrophic failure. If any of the database files have not been accessed during the lifetime of the current log files, log_archive will not include them in this list. It is also possible that some of the files referenced in the log have since been deleted from the system.

- DB_ARCH_LOG   Return all the log file names, regardless of whether or not they are in use.

The DB_ARCH_DATA and DB_ARCH_LOG flags are mutually exclusive.

See the **db_archive** manual page for more information on database archival procedures.

The log_archive function is the underlying function used by the **db_archive** utility. See the **db_archive** utility source code for an example of using log_archive in a IEEE/ANSI Std 1003.1 (POSIX) environment.

The log_archive function returns a non-zero error value on failure and 0 on success.

Bugs

In a threaded application (that is, one in which the environment was created with the DB_THREAD flag specified), calling log_archive with the DB_ARCH_DATA flag will fail, returning EINVAL. To work around this problem, reopen the log explicitly without specifying DB_THREAD. This restriction is expected to be removed in a future version of Berkeley DB.

Errors

The log_archive function may fail and return a non-zero error for the following conditions:

- EINVAL   An invalid flag value or parameter was specified.

  The log was corrupted.

The log_archive function may fail and return a non-zero error for errors specified for other Berkeley DB and C library or system functions. If a catastrophic error has occurred, the log_archive function may fail and return DB_RUNRECOVERY, in which case all subsequent Berkeley DB calls will fail in the same way.

log_compare

```
#include <db.h>

int
log_compare(const DB_LSN *lsn0, const DB_LSN *lsn1);
```

Description

The log_compare function allows the caller to compare two DB_LSN structures, returning 0 if they are equal, 1 if **lsn0** is greater than **lsn1**, and -1 if **lsn0** is less than **lsn1**.

log_file

```
#include <db.h>

int
log_file(DB_ENV *env,
const DB_LSN *lsn, char *namep, size_t len);
```

Description

The log_file function maps DB_LSN structures to file names, copying the name of the file containing the record named by **lsn** into the memory location referenced by **namep**.

The **len** argument is the length of the **namep** buffer in bytes. If **namep** is too short to hold the file name, log_file will return ENOMEM. (Log file names are normally quite short, on the order of 10 characters.)

This mapping of DB_LSN structures to files is needed for database administration. For example, a transaction manager typically records the earliest DB_LSN needed for restart, and the database administrator may want to archive log files to tape when they contain only DB_LSN entries before the earliest one needed for restart.

The log_file function returns a non-zero error value on failure and 0 on success.

Errors

The log_file function may fail and return a non-zero error for the following conditions:

- ENOMEM   The supplied buffer was too small to hold the log file name.

The log_file function may fail and return a non-zero error for errors specified for other Berkeley DB and C library or system functions. If a catastrophic error has occurred, the log_file function may fail and return DB_RUNRECOVERY, in which case all subsequent Berkeley DB calls will fail in the same way.

log_flush

```
#include <db.h>

int
log_flush(DB_ENV *env, const DB_LSN *lsn);
```

Description

The log_flush function guarantees that all log records whose DB_LSN values are less than or equal to the **lsn** argument have been written to disk. If **lsn** is NULL, all records in the log are flushed.

The log_flush function returns a non-zero error value on failure and 0 on success.

Errors

The log_flush function may fail and return a non-zero error for the following conditions:

- EINVAL   An invalid flag value or parameter was specified.

The log_flush function may fail and return a non-zero error for errors specified for other Berkeley DB and C library or system functions. If a catastrophic error has occurred, the log_flush function may fail and return DB_RUNRECOVERY, in which case all subsequent Berkeley DB calls will fail in the same way.

log_get

```
#include <db.h>

int
log_get(DB_ENV *env, DB_LSN *lsn, DBT *data, u_int32_t flags);
```

Description

The log_get function implements a cursor inside of the log, retrieving records from the log according to the **lsn** and **flags** arguments.

The data field of the **data** structure is set to the record retrieved, and the size field indicates the number of bytes in the record. See **DBT** for a description of other fields in the **data** structure. When multiple threads are using the DB_ENV handle concurrently, one of the DB_DBT_MALLOC, DB_DBT_REALLOC, or DB_DBT_USERMEM flags must be specified for any **DBT** used for data retrieval.

The **flags** argument must be set to exactly one of the following values:

- DB_CHECKPOINT   The last record written with the DB_CHECKPOINT flag specified to the **log_put** function is returned in the **data** argument. The **lsn** argument is overwritten with the **DB_LSN** of the record returned. If no record has been previously written with the DB_CHECKPOINT flag specified, the first record in the log is returned.

If the log is empty, the log_get function will return DB_NOTFOUND.

- DB_FIRST The first record from any of the log files found in the log directory is returned in the **data** argument. The **lsn** argument is overwritten with the **DB_LSN** of the record returned.

  If the log is empty, the log_get function will return DB_NOTFOUND.

- DB_LAST The last record in the log is returned in the **data** argument. The **lsn** argument is overwritten with the **DB_LSN** of the record returned.

  If the log is empty, the log_get function will return DB_NOTFOUND.

- DB_NEXT, DB_PREV The current log position is advanced to the next (previous) record in the log, and that record is returned in the **data** argument. The **lsn** argument is overwritten with the **DB_LSN** of the record returned.

  If the pointer has not been initialized via DB_FIRST, DB_LAST, DB_SET, DB_NEXT, or DB_PREV, log_get will return the first (last) record in the log. If the last (first) log record has already been returned or the log is empty, the log_get function will return DB_NOTFOUND.

  If the log was opened with the DB_THREAD flag set, calls to log_get with the DB_NEXT (DB_PREV) flag set will return EINVAL.

- DB_CURRENT Return the log record currently referenced by the log.

  The log_get function will return EINVAL if the log pointer has not been initialized via DB_FIRST, DB_LAST, DB_SET, DB_NEXT, or DB_PREV; or if the log was opened with the DB_THREAD flag set.

- DB_SET Retrieve the record specified by the **lsn** argument. If the specified **DB_LSN** is invalid (for example, it does not appear in the log), log_get will return EINVAL.

Otherwise, the log_get function returns a non-zero error value on failure and 0 on success.

Errors

The log_get function may fail and return a non-zero error for the following conditions:

- EINVAL An invalid flag value or parameter was specified.

  The DB_NEXT or DB_PREV flags were set and the log was opened with the DB_THREAD flag set.

  The DB_CURRENT flag was set and the log pointer had not yet been initialized.

  The DB_SET flag was set and the specified log sequence number does not exist.

The log_get function may fail and return a non-zero error for errors specified for other Berkeley DB and C library or system functions. If a catastrophic error has occurred, the log_get function may fail and return DB_RUNRECOVERY, in which case all subsequent Berkeley DB calls will fail in the same way.

log_put

```
#include <db.h>

int
log_put(DB_ENV *env,
    DB_LSN *lsn, const DBT *data, u_int32_t flags);
```

Description

The log_put function appends records to the log. The **DB_LSN** of the put record is returned in the **lsn** argument. The **flags** argument may be set to one of the following values:

- DB_CHECKPOINT   The log should write a checkpoint record, recording any information necessary to make the log structures recoverable after a crash.

- DB_CURLSN   The **DB_LSN** of the next record to be put is returned in the **lsn** argument.

- DB_FLUSH   The log is forced to disk after this record is written, guaranteeing that all records with **DB_LSN** values less than or equal to the one being put are on disk before this function returns (this function is most often used for a transaction commit; see **txn_commit** for more information).

  The caller is responsible for providing any necessary structure to **data**. (For example, in a write-ahead logging protocol, the application must understand what part of **data** is an operation code, what part is redo information, and what part is undo information. In addition, most transaction managers will store in **data** the **DB_LSN** of the previous log record for the same transaction, to support chaining back through the transaction's log records during undo.)

The log_put function returns a non-zero error value on failure and 0 on success.

Errors

The **log_flush** function may fail and return a non-zero error for the following conditions:

- EINVAL   An invalid flag value or parameter was specified.

  The record to be logged is larger than the maximum log record.

The log_put function may fail and return a non-zero error for errors specified for other Berkeley DB and C library or system functions. If a catastrophic error has occurred, the log_put function may fail and return DB_RUNRECOVERY, in which case all subsequent Berkeley DB calls will fail in the same way.

log_register

```
#include <db.h>

int
log_register(DB_ENV *env, DB *dbp, const char *name);
```

Description

The log_register function registers a file name with the specified Berkeley DB environment's log manager. The log manager records all file name mappings at each checkpoint so that a recovery process can identify the file to which a record in the log refers.

The **dbp** argument should be a reference to the DB structure being registered. The **name** argument should be a file name appropriate for opening the file in the environment during recovery.

The log_register function returns a non-zero error value on failure and 0 on success.

Errors

The log_register function may fail and return a non-zero error for the following conditions:

- EINVAL   An invalid flag value or parameter was specified.

The log_register function may fail and return a non-zero error for errors specified for other Berkeley DB and C library or system functions. If a catastrophic error has occurred, the log_register function may fail and return DB_RUNRECOVERY, in which case all subsequent Berkeley DB calls will fail in the same way.

log_stat

```
#include <db.h>

int
log_stat(DB_ENV *env,
    DB_LOG_STAT **spp, void *(*db_malloc)(size_t));
```

Description

The log_stat function creates a statistical structure and copies a pointer to it into a user-specified memory location.

Statistical structures are created in allocated memory. If **db_malloc** is non-NULL, it is called to allocate the memory; otherwise, the library function **malloc**(3) is used. The function **db_malloc** must match the calling conventions of the **malloc**(3) library routine. Regardless, the caller is responsible for deallocating the returned memory. To deallocate returned memory, free the returned memory reference; references inside the returned memory do not need to be individually freed.

The log region statistics are stored in a structure of type DB_LOG_STAT. The following DB_LOG_STAT fields will be filled in:

- u_int32_t st_magic;   The magic number that identifies a file as a log file.
- u_int32_t st_version;   The version of the log file type.
- u_int32_t st_regsize;   The size of the region.
- int st_mode;   The mode of any created log files.
- u_int32_t st_lg_bsize;   The in-memory log record cache size.
- u_int32_t st_lg_max;   The maximum size of any individual file comprising the log.
- u_int32_t st_w_mbytes;   The number of megabytes written to this log.
- u_int32_t st_w_bytes;   The number of bytes over and above **st_w_mbytes** written to this log.
- u_int32_t st_wc_mbytes;   The number of megabytes written to this log since the last checkpoint.
- u_int32_t st_wc_bytes;   The number of bytes over and above **st_wc_mbytes** written to this log since the last checkpoint.
- u_int32_t st_wcount;   The number of times the log has been written to disk.
- u_int32_t st_wcount_fill;   The number of times the log has been written to disk because the in-memory log record cache filled up.
- u_int32_t st_scount;   The number of times the log has been flushed to disk.
- u_int32_t st_cur_file;   The current log file number.
- u_int32_t st_cur_offset;   The byte offset in the current log file.
- u_int32_t st_region_wait;   The number of times that a thread of control was forced to wait before obtaining the region lock.
- u_int32_t st_region_nowait;   The number of times that a thread of control was able to obtain the region lock without waiting.

The log_stat function returns a non-zero error value on failure and 0 on success.

Errors

The log_stat function may fail and return a non-zero error for errors specified for other Berkeley DB and C library or system functions. If a catastrophic error has occurred, the log_stat function may fail and return DB_RUNRECOVERY, in which case all subsequent Berkeley DB calls will fail in the same way.

log_unregister

```
#include <db.h>

int
log_unregister(DB_ENV *env, DB *dbp);
```

Description

The log_unregister function function unregisters the file represented by the **dbp** parameter from the Berkeley DB environment's log manager.

The log_unregister function returns a non-zero error value on failure and 0 on success.

Errors

The log_unregister function may fail and return a non-zero error for the following conditions:

- EINVAL   An invalid flag value or parameter was specified.

The log_unregister function may fail and return a non-zero error for errors specified for other Berkeley DB and C library or system functions. If a catastrophic error has occurred, the log_unregister function may fail and return DB_RUNRECOVERY, in which case all subsequent Berkeley DB calls will fail in the same way.

memp_fclose

```
#include <db.h>

int
memp_fclose(DB_MPOOLFILE *mpf);
```

Description

The memp_fclose function closes the source file indicated by the DB_MPOOLFILE structure. Calling memp_fclose does not imply a call to **memp_fsync**; that is, no pages are written to the source file as as a result of calling memp_fclose.

In addition, if the DB_MPOOLFILE was temporary, any underlying files created for this DB_MPOOLFILE will be removed.

Once memp_fclose has been called, regardless of its return, the DB_MPOOLFILE handle may not be accessed again.

The memp_fclose function returns a non-zero error value on failure and 0 on success.

Errors

The memp_fclose function may fail and return a non-zero error for errors specified for other Berkeley DB and C library or system functions. If a catastrophic error has occurred, the memp_fclose function may fail and return DB_RUNRECOVERY, in which case all subsequent Berkeley DB calls will fail in the same way.

memp_fget

```
#include <db.h>

int
memp_fget(DB_MPOOLFILE *mpf,
    db_pgno_t *pgnoaddr, u_int32_t flags, void **pagep);
```

Description

The memp_fget function copies a pointer to the page with the page number specified by **pgnoaddr**, from the source file in the DB_MPOOLFILE, into the memory location referenced by **pagep**. If the page does not exist or cannot be retrieved, memp_fget will fail.

Page numbers begin at 0; that is, the first page in the file is page number 0, not page number 1.

The returned page is **size_t** type aligned.

The **flags** value must be set to 0 or by bitwise inclusively **OR**'ing together one or more of the following values.

- DB_MPOOL_CREATE   If the specified page does not exist, create it. In this case, the pgin function, if specified, is called.

- DB_MPOOL_LAST   Return the last page of the source file, and copy its page number to the location referenced by **pgnoaddr**.

- DB_MPOOL_NEW   Create a new page in the file, and copy its page number to the location referenced by **pgnoaddr**. In this case, the pgin function, if specified, is **not** called.

The DB_MPOOL_CREATE, DB_MPOOL_LAST, and DB_MPOOL_NEW flags are mutually exclusive.

Created pages have all their bytes set to 0, unless otherwise specified when the file was opened.

All pages returned by memp_fget will be retained (that is, *pinned*) in the pool until a subsequent call to **memp_fput**.

The memp_fget function returns a non-zero error value on failure and 0 on success.

Errors

The memp_fget function may fail and return a non-zero error for the following conditions:

- EAGAIN   The page reference count has overflowed. (This should never happen unless there's a bug in the application.)

- EINVAL   An invalid flag value or parameter was specified.

  The DB_MPOOL_NEW flag was set, and the source file was not opened for writing.

  More than one of DB_MPOOL_CREATE, DB_MPOOL_LAST, and DB_MPOOL_NEW was set.

- EIO   The requested page does not exist, and DB_MPOOL_CREATE was not set.

- ENOMEM   The cache is full, and no more pages will fit in the pool.

The memp_fget function may fail and return a non-zero error for errors specified for other Berkeley DB and C library or system functions. If a catastrophic error has occurred, the memp_fget function may fail and return DB_RUNRECOVERY, in which case all subsequent Berkeley DB calls will fail in the same way.

memp_fopen

```
#include <db.h>

int
memp_fopen(DB_ENV *env, char *file, u_int32_t flags,
    int mode, size_t pagesize, DB_MPOOL_FINFO *finfop,
    DB_MPOOLFILE **mpf);
```

Description

The memp_fopen function opens a file in the pool specified by the DB_ENV **env**, copying the DB_MPOOLFILE pointer representing it into the memory location referenced by **mpf**.

The **file** argument is the name of the file to be opened. If **file** is NULL, a private temporary file is created that cannot be shared with any other process (although it may be shared with other threads).

The **flags** and **mode** arguments specify how files will be opened and/or created if they do not already exist.

The **flags** value must be set to 0 or by bitwise inclusively **OR**'ing together one or more of the following values.

- DB_CREATE   Create any underlying files, as necessary. If the files do not already exist and the DB_CREATE flag is not specified, the call will fail.

- DB_NOMMAP   Always copy this file into the local cache instead of potentially mapping it into process memory (see the description of the **DBENV→set_mp_mmapsize** function for further information).

- DB_RDONLY   Open any underlying files for reading only. Any attempt to write the file using the pool functions will fail, regardless of the actual permissions of the file.

On UNIX systems, or in IEEE/ANSI Std 1003.1 (POSIX) environments, all files created by function memp_fopen are created with mode **mode** (as described in **chmod**(2)) and modified by the process' umask value at the time of creation (see **umask**(2)). The group ownership of created files is based on the system and directory defaults, and is not further specified by Berkeley DB. If **mode** is 0, files are created readable and writable by both owner and group. On Windows systems, the mode argument is ignored.

The **pagesize** argument is the size, in bytes, of the unit of transfer between the application and the pool, although it is not necessarily the unit of transfer between the pool and the source file.

Files opened in the pool may be further configured based on the **finfop** argument to memp_fopen (which is a pointer to a structure of type DB_MPOOL_FINFO). No references to the **finfop** structure are maintained by Berkeley DB, so it may be discarded when the memp_fopen function returns. In order to ensure compatibility with future releases of Berkeley DB, all fields of the DB_MPOOL_FINFO structure that are not explicitly set should be initialized to 0 before the first time the structure is used. Do this by declaring the structure external or static, or by calling the C library routine **bzero**(3) or **memset**(3).

The fields of the DB_MPOOL_FINFO structure used by memp_fopen are described as follows. If **finfop** is NULL or any of its fields are set to their default value, defaults appropriate for the system are used.

- int ftype;   The **ftype** field should be the same as a **ftype** argument previously specified to the **memp_register** function, unless no input or output processing of the file's pages are necessary, in which case it should be 0. (See the description of the **memp_register** function for more information.)

- DBT *pgcookie;   The **pgcookie** field contains the byte string that is passed to the **pgin** and **pgout** functions for this file, if any. If no **pgin** or **pgout** functions are specified, the **pgcookie** field should be NULL. (See the description of the **memp_register** function for more information.)

- u_int8_t *fileid;   The **fileid** field is a unique identifier for the file. If the **fileid** field is non-NULL, it must reference a DB_FILE_ID_LEN length array of bytes that will be used to uniquely identify the file.

  The mpool functions must be able to uniquely identify files in order that multiple processes wanting to share a file will correctly identify it in the pool.

  On most UNIX/POSIX systems, the **fileid** field will not need to be set, and the mpool functions will simply use the file's device and inode numbers for this purpose. On Windows systems, the mpool functions use the values returned by GetFileInformationByHandle() by default— these values are known to be constant between processes and over reboot in the case of NTFS (in which they are the NTFS MFT indexes).

On other filesystems (for example, FAT or NFS) these default values are not necessarily unique between processes or across system reboots. Applications wanting to maintain a shared memory buffer pool between processes or across system reboots, in which the pool contains pages from files stored on such filesystems, must specify a unique file identifier to the memp_fopen call, and each process opening or registering the file must provide the same unique identifier.

This should not be necessary for most applications. Specifically, it is not necessary if the memory pool is not shared between processes and is reinstantiated after each system reboot, if the application is using the Berkeley DB access methods instead of calling the pool functions explicitly, or if the files in the memory pool are stored on filesystems in which the default values as described previously are invariant between process and across system reboots.

- int32_t lsn_offset;   The **lsn_offset** field is the zero-based byte offset in the page of the page's log sequence number (LSN), or –1 if no LSN offset is specified. (See the description of the **memp_sync** function for more information.)

- u_int32_t clear_len;   The **clear_len** field is the number of initial bytes in a page that should be set to zero when the page is created as a result of the DB_MPOOL_CRE-ATE or DB_MPOOL_NEW flags being specified to **memp_fget**. If **finfop** is NULL or **clear_len** is 0, the entire page is cleared.

The memp_fopen function returns a non-zero error value on failure and 0 on success.

Errors

The memp_fopen function may fail and return a non-zero error for the following conditions:

- EINVAL   An invalid flag value or parameter was specified.

  The file has already been entered into the pool, and the **pagesize** value is not the same as when the file was entered into the pool, or the length of the file is not zero or a multiple of the **pagesize**.

  The DB_RDONLY flag was specified for an in-memory pool.

- ENOMEM   The maximum number of open files has been reached.

The memp_fopen function may fail and return a non-zero error for errors specified for other Berkeley DB and C library or system functions. If a catastrophic error has occurred, the memp_fopen function may fail and return DB_RUNRECOVERY, in which case all subsequent Berkeley DB calls will fail in the same way.

memp_fput

```
#include <db.h>

int
memp_fput(DB_MPOOLFILE *mpf, void *pgaddr, u_int32_t flags);
```

Description

The memp_fput function indicates that the page referenced by **pgaddr** can be evicted from the pool. The **pgaddr** argument must be an address previously returned by **memp_fget**.

The **flags** value must be set to 0 or by bitwise inclusively **OR**'ing together one or more of the following values.

- DB_MPOOL_CLEAN   Clear any previously set modification information (that is, don't bother writing the page back to the source file).

- DB_MPOOL_DIRTY   The page has been modified and must be written to the source file before being evicted from the pool.

- DB_MPOOL_DISCARD   The page is unlikely to be useful in the near future, and should be discarded before other pages in the pool.

The DB_MPOOL_CLEAN and DB_MPOOL_DIRTY flags are mutually exclusive.

The memp_fput function returns a non-zero error value on failure and 0 on success.

Errors

The memp_fput function may fail and return a non-zero error for the following conditions:

- EACCES   The DB_MPOOL_DIRTY flag was set and the source file was not opened for writing.

- EINVAL   An invalid flag value or parameter was specified.

  The **pgaddr** parameter does not reference a page returned by **memp_fget**.

  More than one of DB_MPOOL_CLEAN and DB_MPOOL_DIRTY flags was set.

The memp_fput function may fail and return a non-zero error for errors specified for other Berkeley DB and C library or system functions. If a catastrophic error has occurred, the memp_fput function may fail and return DB_RUNRECOVERY, in which case all subsequent Berkeley DB calls will fail in the same way.

memp_fset

```
#include <db.h>

int
memp_fset(DB_MPOOLFILE *mpf, void *pgaddr, u_int32_t flags);
```

Description

The memp_fset function sets the flags associated with the page referenced by **pgaddr** without unpinning it from the pool. The **pgaddr** argument must be an address previously returned by **memp_fget**.

The **flags** value must be set to 0 or by bitwise inclusively **OR**'ing together one or more of the following values.

- DB_MPOOL_CLEAN   Clear any previously set modification information (that is, don't bother writing the page back to the source file).
- DB_MPOOL_DIRTY   The page has been modified and must be written to the source file before being evicted from the pool.
- DB_MPOOL_DISCARD   The page is unlikely to be useful in the near future, and should be discarded before other pages in the pool.

The DB_MPOOL_CLEAN and DB_MPOOL_DIRTY flags are mutually exclusive.

The memp_fset function returns a non-zero error value on failure and 0 on success.

Errors

The memp_fset function may fail and return a non-zero error for the following conditions:

- EINVAL   An invalid flag value or parameter was specified.

The memp_fset function may fail and return a non-zero error for errors specified for other Berkeley DB and C library or system functions. If a catastrophic error has occurred, the memp_fset function may fail and return DB_RUNRECOVERY, in which case all subsequent Berkeley DB calls will fail in the same way.

memp_fsync

```
#include <db.h>

int
memp_fsync(DB_MPOOLFILE *mpf);
```

Description

The memp_fsync function writes all pages associated with the DB_MPOOLFILE, which were marked as modified using **memp_fput** or **memp_fset**, back to the source file. If any of the modified pages are also *pinned* (that is, currently referenced by this or another process), memp_fsync will ignore them.

The memp_fsync function returns a non-zero error value on failure, 0 on success, and returns DB_INCOMPLETE if there were pages that were modified, but that memp_fsync was unable to write immediately.

Errors

The memp_fsync function may fail and return a non-zero error for errors specified for other Berkeley DB and C library or system functions. If a catastrophic error has occurred, the memp_fsync function may fail and return DB_RUNRECOVERY, in which case all subsequent Berkeley DB calls will fail in the same way.

memp_register

```
#include <db.h>

int
memp_register(DB_ENV *env, int ftype,
    int (*pgin_fcn)(DB_ENV *, db_pgno_t pgno, void *pgaddr, DBT *pgcookie),
    int (*pgout_fcn)(DB_ENV *, db_pgno_t pgno, void *pgaddr, DBT *pgcookie));
```

Description

The memp_register function registers page-in and page-out functions for files of type **ftype** in the specified pool.

If the **pgin_fcn** function is non-NULL, it is called each time a page is read into the memory pool from a file of type **ftype**, or a page is created for a file of type **ftype** (see the DB_MPOOL_CREATE flag for the **memp_fget** function).

If the **pgout_fcn** function is non-NULL, it is called each time a page is written to a file of type **ftype**.

Both the **pgin_fcn** and **pgout_fcn** functions are called with a reference to the current environment, the page number, a pointer to the page being read or written, and any argument **pgcookie** that was specified to the **memp_fopen** function when the file was opened. The **pgin_fcn** and **pgout_fcn** functions should return 0 on success, and an applicable non-zero **errno** value on failure, in which case the shared memory pool interface routine (and, by extension, any Berkeley DB library function) calling it will also fail, returning that **errno** value.

The purpose of the memp_register function is to support processing when pages are entered into, or flushed from, the pool. A file type must be specified to make it possible for unrelated threads or processes that are sharing a pool, to evict each other's pages from the pool. During initialization, applications should call memp_register for each type of file requiring input or output processing that will be sharing the underlying pool. (No registry is necessary for the standard Berkeley DB access method types because **DB→open** registers them separately.)

If a thread or process does not call memp_register for a file type, it is impossible for it to evict pages for any file requiring input or output processing from the pool. For this reason, memp_register should always be called by each application sharing a pool for each type of file included in the pool, regardless of whether or not the application itself uses files of that type.

There are no standard values for **ftype**, **pgin_fcn**, **pgout_fcn**, and **pgcookie**, except that the **ftype** value for a file must be a non-zero positive number because negative numbers are reserved for internal use by the Berkeley DB library. For this reason, applications sharing a pool must coordinate their values among themselves.

The memp_register function returns a non-zero error value on failure and 0 on success.

Errors

The memp_register function may fail and return a non-zero error for errors specified for other Berkeley DB and C library or system functions. If a catastrophic error has occurred, the memp_register function may fail and return DB_RUNRECOVERY, in which case all subsequent Berkeley DB calls will fail in the same way.

memp_stat

```
#include <db.h>

int
memp_stat(DB_ENV *env, DB_MPOOL_STAT **gsp,
    DB_MPOOL_FSTAT *(*fsp)[], void *(*db_malloc)(size_t));
```

Description

The memp_stat function method creates statistical structures and copies pointers to them into user-specified memory locations. The statistics include the number of files participating in the pool, the active pages in the pool, and information about how effective the cache has been.

Statistical structures are created in allocated memory. If **db_malloc** is non-NULL, it is called to allocate the memory; otherwise, the library function **malloc**(3) is used. The function **db_malloc** must match the calling conventions of the **malloc**(3) library routine. Regardless, the caller is responsible for deallocating the returned memory. To deallocate returned memory, free the returned memory reference; references inside the returned memory do not need to be individually freed.

If **gsp** is non-NULL, the global statistics for the memory pool **mp** are copied into the memory location it references. The global statistics are stored in a structure of type DB_MPOOL_STAT.

The following DB_MPOOL_STAT fields will be filled in:

- size_t st_gbytes;   Gigabytes of cache (total cache size is st_gbytes + st_bytes).
- size_t st_bytes;   Bytes of cache (total cache size is st_gbytes + st_bytes).
- u_int32_t st_ncache;   Number of caches.
- u_int32_t st_regsize;   Individual cache size.
- u_int32_t st_cache_hit;   Requested pages found in the cache.
- u_int32_t st_cache_miss;   Requested pages not found in the cache.

- u_int32_t st_map;   Requested pages mapped into the process' address space (there is no available information about whether or not this request caused disk I/O, although examining the application page fault rate may be helpful).

- u_int32_t st_page_create;   Pages created in the cache.

- u_int32_t st_page_in;   Pages read into the cache.

- u_int32_t st_page_out;   Pages written from the cache to the backing file.

- u_int32_t st_ro_evict;   Clean pages forced from the cache.

- u_int32_t st_rw_evict;   Dirty pages forced from the cache.

- u_int32_t st_hash_buckets;   Number of hash buckets in buffer hash table.

- u_int32_t st_hash_searches;   Total number of buffer hash table lookups.

- u_int32_t st_hash_longest;   The longest chain ever encountered in buffer hash table lookups.

- u_int32_t st_hash_examined;   Total number of hash elements traversed during hash table lookups.

- u_int32_t st_page_clean;   Clean pages currently in the cache.

- u_int32_t st_page_dirty;   Dirty pages currently in the cache.

- u_int32_t st_page_trickle;   Dirty pages written using the **memp_trickle** interface.

- u_int32_t st_region_wait;   The number of times that a thread of control was forced to wait before obtaining the region lock.

- u_int32_t st_region_nowait;   The number of times that a thread of control was able to obtain the region lock without waiting.

If **fsp** is non-NULL, a pointer to a NULL-terminated variable length array of statistics for individual files, in the memory pool **mp**, is copied into the memory location it references. If no individual files currently exist in the memory pool, **fsp** will be set to NULL.

The per-file statistics are stored in structures of type DB_MPOOL_FSTAT. The following DB_MPOOL_FSTAT fields will be filled in for each file in the pool; that is, each element of the array:

- char *file_name;   The name of the file.

- size_t st_pagesize;   Page size in bytes.

- u_int32_t st_cache_hit;   Requested pages found in the cache.

- u_int32_t st_cache_miss;   Requested pages not found in the cache.

- u_int32_t st_map;   Requested pages mapped into the process' address space.

- u_int32_t st_page_create;   Pages created in the cache.

- u_int32_t st_page_in;   Pages read into the cache.

- u_int32_t st_page_out;   Pages written from the cache to the backing file.

The memp_stat function returns a non-zero error value on failure and 0 on success.

Errors

The memp_stat function may fail and return a non-zero error for the following conditions:

- EINVAL   An invalid flag value or parameter was specified.

The memp_stat function may fail and return a non-zero error for errors specified for other Berkeley DB and C library or system functions. If a catastrophic error has occurred, the memp_stat function may fail and return DB_RUNRECOVERY, in which case all subsequent Berkeley DB calls will fail in the same way.

memp_sync

```
#include <db.h>

int
memp_sync(DB_ENV *env, DB_LSN *lsn);
```

Description

The memp_sync function ensures that any modified pages in the pool with log sequence numbers less than the **lsn** argument are written to disk. If **lsn** is NULL, all modified pages in the pool are flushed.

The primary purpose of the memp_sync function is to enable a transaction manager to ensure, as part of a checkpoint, that all pages modified by a certain time have been written to disk. Pages in the pool that cannot be written back to disk immediately (for example, that are currently pinned) are written to disk as soon as it is possible to do so. The expected behavior of the Berkeley DB or other Transaction subsystem is to call the memp_sync function and then, if the return indicates that some pages could not be written immediately, to wait briefly and retry again with the same log sequence number until the memp_sync function returns that all pages have been written.

To support the memp_sync functionality, it is necessary that the pool functions know the location of the log sequence number on the page for each file type. This location should be specified when the file is opened using the **memp_fopen** function. It is not required that the log sequence number be aligned on the page in any way.

The memp_sync function returns a non-zero error value on failure and 0 on success; and returns DB_INCOMPLETE if there were pages that need to be written, but that memp_sync was unable to write immediately. In addition, if memp_sync returns success, the value of **lsn** will be overwritten with the largest log sequence number from any page that was written by memp_sync to satisfy this request.

Errors

The memp_sync function may fail and return a non-zero error for the following conditions:

- EINVAL   An invalid flag value or parameter was specified.

  The memp_sync function was called without logging having been initialized in the environment.

The memp_sync function may fail and return a non-zero error for errors specified for other Berkeley DB and C library or system functions. If a catastrophic error has occurred, the memp_sync function may fail and return DB_RUNRECOVERY, in which case all subsequent Berkeley DB calls will fail in the same way.

memp_trickle

```
#include <db.h>

int
memp_trickle(DB_ENV *env, int pct, int *nwrotep);
```

Description

The memp_trickle function ensures that at least **pct** percent of the pages in the shared memory pool are clean by writing dirty pages to their backing files. If the **nwrotep** argument is non-NULL, the number of pages that were written to reach the correct percentage is returned in the memory location it references.

The purpose of the memp_trickle function is to enable a memory pool manager to ensure that a page is always available for reading in new information without having to wait for a write.

The memp_trickle function returns a non-zero error value on failure and 0 on success.

Errors

The memp_trickle function may fail and return a non-zero error for the following conditions:

- EINVAL   An invalid flag value or parameter was specified.

The memp_trickle function may fail and return a non-zero error for errors specified for other Berkeley DB and C library or system functions. If a catastrophic error has occurred, the memp_trickle function may fail and return DB_RUNRECOVERY, in which case all subsequent Berkeley DB calls will fail in the same way.

txn_abort

```
#include <db.h>

int
txn_abort(DB_TXN *tid);
```

Description

The txn_abort function causes an abnormal termination of the transaction. The log is played backward, and any necessary recovery operations are initiated through the **recover** function specified to **DBENV→open**. After the log processing is completed, all locks held by the transaction are released. As is the case for **txn_commit**, applications that require strict two-phase locking should not explicitly release any locks.

In the case of nested transactions, aborting a parent transaction causes all children (unresolved or not) of the parent transaction to be aborted.

Once the txn_abort function returns, the DB_TXN handle may not be accessed again.

The txn_abort function returns a non-zero error value on failure and 0 on success.

Errors

The txn_abort function may fail and return a non-zero error for errors specified for other Berkeley DB and C library or system functions. If a catastrophic error has occurred, the txn_abort function may fail and return DB_RUNRECOVERY, in which case all subsequent Berkeley DB calls will fail in the same way.

txn_begin

```
#include <db.h>

int
txn_begin(DB_ENV *env, DB_TXN *parent,
    DB_TXN **tid, u_int32_t flags);
```

Description

The txn_begin method creates a new transaction in the environment and copies a pointer to a DB_TXN that uniquely identifies it into the memory referenced by **tid**.

If the **parent** argument is non-NULL, the new transaction will be a nested transaction, with the transaction indicated by **parent** as its parent. Transactions may be nested to any level.

The **flags** parameter must be set to 0 or one of the following values:

- DB_TXN_NOSYNC   Do not synchronously flush the log when this transaction commits or prepares. This means the transaction will exhibit the ACI (atomicity, consistency, and isolation) properties, but not D (durability); that is, database integrity will be maintained but it is possible that this transaction may be undone during recovery.

This behavior may be set for a Berkeley DB environment using the **DBENV→set_flags** interface. Any value specified in this interface overrides that setting.

- DB_TXN_NOWAIT   If a lock is unavailable for any Berkeley DB operation performed in the context of this transaction, return immediately instead of blocking on the lock. The error return in the case will be DB_LOCK_NOTGRANTED.

- DB_TXN_SYNC   Synchronously flush the log when this transaction commits or prepares. This means the transaction will exhibit all of the ACID (atomicity, consistency, isolation, and durability) properties.

  This behavior is the default for Berkeley DB environments unless the DB_TXN_NOSYNC flag was specified to the **DBENV→set_flags** interface. Any value specified in this interface overrides that setting.

Note: A transaction may not span threads; that is, each transaction must begin and end in the same thread, and each transaction may only be used by a single thread.

Note: Cursors may not span transactions; that is, each cursor must be opened and closed within a single transaction.

Note: A parent transaction may not issue any Berkeley DB operations— except for txn_begin, txn_abort, and txn_commit— while it has active child transactions (child transactions that have not yet been committed or aborted).

The txn_begin function returns a non-zero error value on failure and 0 on success.

Errors

The txn_begin function may fail and return a non-zero error for the following conditions:

- ENOMEM   The maximum number of concurrent transactions has been reached.

The txn_begin function may fail and return a non-zero error for errors specified for other Berkeley DB and C library or system functions. If a catastrophic error has occurred, the txn_begin function may fail and return DB_RUNRECOVERY, in which case all subsequent Berkeley DB calls will fail in the same way.

txn_checkpoint

```
#include <db.h>

int
txn_checkpoint(const DB_ENV *env,
    u_int32_t kbyte, u_int32_t min, u_int32_t flags);
```

Description

The txn_checkpoint function flushes the underlying memory pool, writes a checkpoint record to the log, and then flushes the log.

If either **kbyte** or **min** is non-zero, the checkpoint is done only if there has been activity since the last checkpoint, and either more than **min** minutes have passed since the last checkpoint or if more than **kbyte** kilobytes of log data have been written since the last checkpoint.

The **flags** parameter must be set to 0 or one of the following values:

- DB_FORCE   Force a checkpoint record, even if there has been no activity since the last checkpoint.

The txn_checkpoint function returns a non-zero error value on failure, 0 on success, and returns DB_INCOMPLETE if there were pages that needed to be written to complete the checkpoint but that **memp_sync** was unable to write immediately.

The txn_checkpoint function is the underlying function used by the **db_checkpoint** utility. See the **db_checkpoint** utility source code for an example of using txn_checkpoint in a IEEE/ANSI Std 1003.1 (POSIX) environment.

Errors

The txn_checkpoint function may fail and return a non-zero error for the following conditions:

- EINVAL   An invalid flag value or parameter was specified.

The txn_checkpoint function may fail and return a non-zero error for errors specified for other Berkeley DB and C library or system functions. If a catastrophic error has occurred, the txn_checkpoint function may fail and return DB_RUNRECOVERY, in which case all subsequent Berkeley DB calls will fail in the same way.

txn_commit

```
#include <db.h>

int
txn_commit(DB_TXN *tid, u_int32_t flags);
```

Description

The txn_commit function ends the transaction. In the case of nested transactions, if the transaction is a parent transaction, committing the parent transaction causes all unresolved children of the parent to be committed.

In the case of nested transactions, if the transaction is a child transaction, its locks are not released, but are acquired by its parent. Although the commit of the child transaction will succeed, the actual resolution of the child transaction is postponed until the parent transaction is committed or aborted; that is, if its parent transaction commits, it will be committed; and if its parent transaction aborts, it will be aborted.

The **flags** parameter must be set to 0 or one of the following values:

- DB_TXN_NOSYNC   Do not synchronously flush the log. This means the transaction will exhibit the ACI (atomicity, consistency, and isolation) properties, but not D (durability); that is, database integrity will be maintained, but it is possible that this transaction may be undone during recovery.

    This behavior may be set for a Berkeley DB environment using the **DBENV→set_flags** interface or for a single transaction using the **txn_begin** interface. Any value specified in this interface overrides both of those settings.

- DB_TXN_SYNC   Synchronously flush the log. This means the transaction will exhibit all of the ACID (atomicity, consistency, isolation, and durability) properties.

    This behavior is the default for Berkeley DB environments unless the DB_TXN_NOSYNC flag was specified to the **DBENV→set_flags** interface. This behavior may also be set for a single transaction using the **txn_begin** interface. Any value specified in this interface overrides both of those settings.

Once the txn_commit function returns, the DB_TXN handle may not be accessed again. If txn_commit encounters an error, the transaction and all child transactions of the transaction are aborted.

The txn_commit function returns a non-zero error value on failure and 0 on success.

Errors

The txn_commit function may fail and return a non-zero error for errors specified for other Berkeley DB and C library or system functions. If a catastrophic error has occurred, the txn_commit function may fail and return DB_RUNRECOVERY, in which case all subsequent Berkeley DB calls will fail in the same way.

txn_id

```
#include <db.h>

u_int32_t
txn_id(DB_TXN *tid);
```

Description

The txn_id function returns the unique transaction id associated with the specified transaction. Locking calls made on behalf of this transaction should use the value returned from txn_id as the locker parameter to the **lock_get** or **lock_vec** calls.

txn_prepare

```
#include <db.h>

int
txn_prepare(DB_TXN *tid);
```

Description

The txn_prepare function initiates the beginning of a two-phase commit.

In a distributed transaction environment, Berkeley DB can be used as a local transaction manager. In this case, the distributed transaction manager must send *prepare* messages to each local manager. The local manager must then issue a txn_prepare and await its successful return before responding to the distributed transaction manager. Only after the distributed transaction manager receives successful responses from all of its *prepare* messages should it issue any *commit* messages.

In the case of nested transactions, preparing a parent transaction causes all unresolved children of the parent transaction to be prepared.

The txn_prepare function returns a non-zero error value on failure and 0 on success.

Errors

The txn_prepare function may fail and return a non-zero error for errors specified for other Berkeley DB and C library or system functions. If a catastrophic error has occurred, the txn_prepare function may fail and return DB_RUNRECOVERY, in which case all subsequent Berkeley DB calls will fail in the same way.

txn_stat

```
#include <db.h>

int
txn_stat(DB_ENV *env,
    DB_TXN_STAT **statp, void *(*db_malloc)(size_t));
```

Description

The txn_stat function creates a statistical structure and copies a pointer to it into a user-specified memory location.

Statistical structures are created in allocated memory. If **db_malloc** is non-NULL, it is called to allocate the memory; otherwise, the library function **malloc**(3) is used. The function **db_malloc** must match the calling conventions of the **malloc**(3) library routine. Regardless, the caller is responsible for deallocating the returned memory. To deallocate returned memory, free the returned memory reference, references inside the returned memory do not need to be individually freed.

The transaction region statistics are stored in a structure of type DB_TXN_STAT. The following DB_TXN_STAT fields will be filled in:

- **DB_LSN** st_last_ckp; The LSN of the last checkpoint.

- **DB_LSN** st_pending_ckp; The LSN of any checkpoint that is currently in progress. If **st_pending_ckp** is the same as **st_last_ckp** there is no checkpoint in progress.

- time_t st_time_ckp; The time the last completed checkpoint finished (as the number of seconds since the Epoch, returned by the IEEE/ANSI Std 1003.1 (POSIX) **time** interface).

- u_int32_t st_last_txnid; The last transaction ID allocated.

- u_int32_t st_maxtxns; The maximum number of active transactions possible.

- u_int32_t st_nactive; The number of transactions that are currently active.

- u_int32_t st_maxnactive; The maximum number of active transactions at any one time.

- u_int32_t st_nbegins; The number of transactions that have begun.

- u_int32_t st_naborts; The number of transactions that have aborted.

- u_int32_t st_ncommits; The number of transactions that have committed.

- u_int32_t st_regsize; The size of the region.

- u_int32_t st_region_wait; The number of times that a thread of control was forced to wait before obtaining the region lock.

- u_int32_t st_region_nowait; The number of times that a thread of control was able to obtain the region lock without waiting.

- DB_TXN_ACTIVE ★ st_txnarray; A pointer to an array of **st_nactive** DB_TXN_ACTIVE structures, describing the currently active transactions. The following fields of the DB_TXN_ACTIVE structure will be filled in:

- u_int32_t txnid; The transaction ID of the transaction.

- u_int32_t parentid; The transaction ID of the parent transaction (or 0, if no parent).

- **DB_LSN** lsn; The log sequence number of the transaction-begin record.

The txn_stat function returns a non-zero error value on failure and 0 on success.

Errors

The txn_stat function may fail and return a non-zero error for errors specified for other Berkeley DB and C library or system functions. If a catastrophic error has occurred, the txn_stat function may fail and return DB_RUNRECOVERY, in which case all subsequent Berkeley DB calls will fail in the same way.

29

C++ API

Db

```
#include <db_cxx.h>

class Db {
public:
        Db(DbEnv *dbenv, u_int32_t flags);
        ~Db();
        ...
};
```

Description

This manual page describes the specific details of the Db class, which is the center of access method activity.

If no **dbenv** value is specified, the database is standalone; that is, it is not part of any Berkeley DB environment.

If a **dbenv** value is specified, the database is created within the specified Berkeley DB environment. The database access methods automatically make calls to the other subsystems in Berkeley DB based on the enclosing environment. For example, if the environment has been configured to use locking, the access methods will automatically acquire the correct locks when reading and writing pages of the database.

The **flags** value must be set to 0 or by bitwise inclusively **OR**'ing together one or more of the following values.

- DB_CXX_NO_EXCEPTIONS   The Berkeley DB C++ API supports two different error behaviors. By default, whenever an error occurs, an exception is thrown that encapsulates the error information. This generally allows for cleaner logic for transaction processing because a try block can surround a single transaction. However, if DB_CXX_NO_EXCEPTIONS is specified, exceptions are not thrown; instead, each individual function returns an error code.

    If **dbenv** is not null, this flag is ignored, and the error behavior of the specified environment is used instead.

- DB_XA_CREATE   Instead of creating a standalone database, create a database intended to be accessed via applications running under a X/Open conformant Transaction Manager. The database will be opened in the environment specified by the OPENINFO parameter of the GROUPS section of the ubbconfig file. See the "XA Resource Manager" chapter in the *Reference Guide* for more information.

Db::close

```
#include <db_cxx.h>

int
Db::close(u_int32_t flags);
```

Description

The Db::close method flushes any cached database information to disk, closes any open cursors, frees any allocated resources, and closes any underlying files. Because key/data pairs are cached in memory, failing to sync the file with the Db::close or **Db::sync** method may result in inconsistent or lost information.

The **flags** parameter must be set to 0 or the following value:

- DB_NOSYNC   Do not flush cached information to disk. The DB_NOSYNC flag is a dangerous option. It should only be set if the application is doing logging (with transactions) so that the database is recoverable after a system or application crash, or if the database is always generated from scratch after any system or application crash.

    It is important to understand that flushing cached information to disk only minimizes the window of opportunity for corrupted data. Although unlikely, it is possible for database corruption to happen if a system or application crash occurs while writing data to the database. To ensure that database corruption never occurs, applications must either use transactions and logging with automatic recovery, use logging and application-specific recovery, or edit a copy of the database; and once all applications using the database have successfully called Db::close, atomically replace the original database with the updated copy.

When multiple threads are using the Berkeley DB handle concurrently, only a single thread may call the Db::close method.

Once Db::close has been called, regardless of its return, the **Db** handle may not be accessed again.

The Db::close method either returns a non-zero error value or throws an exception that encapsulates a non-zero error value on failure, 0 on success, and returns DB_INCOMPLETE if the underlying database still has dirty pages in the cache. (The only reason to return DB_INCOMPLETE is if another thread of control was writing pages in the underlying database file at the same time as the Db::close method was called. For this reason, a return of DB_INCOMPLETE can normally be ignored; or in cases where it is a possible return value, the DB_NOSYNC option should probably have been specified.)

Errors

The Db::close method may fail and throw an exception or return a non-zero error for errors specified for other Berkeley DB and C library or system methods. If a catastrophic error has occurred, the Db::close method may fail and either return DB_RUNRECOVERY or throw an exception encapsulating DB_RUNRECOVERY, in which case all subsequent Berkeley DB calls will fail in the same way.

Db::cursor

```
#include <db_cxx.h>

int
Db::cursor(DbTxn *txnid, Dbc **cursorp, u_int32_t flags);
```

Description

The Db::cursor method creates a cursor and copies a pointer to it into the memory referenced by **cursorp**.

If the operation is to be transactionally protected, the **txnid** parameter is a transaction handle returned from **DbEnv::txn_begin**; otherwise, NULL.

To transaction-protect cursor operations, cursors must be opened and closed within the context of a transaction, and the **txnid** parameter specifies the transaction context in which the cursor may be used.

The **flags** value must be set to 0 or by bitwise inclusively **OR**'ing together one or more of the following values.

- DB_WRITECURSOR   Specify that the cursor will be used to update the database. This flag should only be set when the DB_INIT_CDB flag was specified to **DbEnv::open**.

The Db::cursor method either returns a non-zero error value or throws an exception that encapsulates a non-zero error value on failure, and returns 0 on success.

Errors

The Db::cursor method may fail and throw an exception or return a non-zero error for the following condition:

- EINVAL   An invalid flag value or parameter was specified.

The Db::cursor method may fail and throw an exception or return a non-zero error for errors specified for other Berkeley DB and C library or system methods. If a catastrophic error has occurred, the Db::cursor method may fail and either return DB_RUNRECOVERY or throw an exception encapsulating DB_RUNRECOVERY; in which case, all subsequent Berkeley DB calls will fail in the same way.

Db::del

```
#include <db_cxx.h>

int
Db::del(DbTxn *txnid, Dbt *key, u_int32_t flags);
```

Description

The Db::del method removes key/data pairs from the database. The key/data pair associated with the specified **key** is discarded from the database. In the presence of duplicate key values, all records associated with the designated key will be discarded.

If the operation is to be transactionally protected, the **txnid** parameter is a transaction handle returned from **DbEnv::txn_begin**; otherwise, NULL.

The **flags** parameter is currently unused, and must be set to 0.

The Db::del method either returns a non-zero error value; or throws an exception that encapsulates a non-zero error value on failure, 0 on success, and DB_NOTFOUND if the specified **key** did not exist in the file.

Errors

The Db::del method may fail and throw an exception or return a non-zero error for the following conditions:

- DB_LOCK_DEADLOCK   The operation was selected to resolve a deadlock.
- EACCES   An attempt was made to modify a read-only database.
- EINVAL   An invalid flag value or parameter was specified.

The Db::del method may fail and throw an exception or return a non-zero error for errors specified for other Berkeley DB and C library or system methods. If a catastrophic error has occurred, the Db::del method may fail and either return DB_RUNRECOVERY or throw an exception encapsulating DB_RUNRECOVERY, in which case all subsequent Berkeley DB calls will fail in the same way.

Db::fd

```
#include <db_cxx.h>

int
Db::fd(int *fdp);
```

Description

The Db::fd method copies a file descriptor representative of the underlying database into the memory referenced by **fdp**. A file descriptor referencing the same file will be returned to all processes that call **Db::open** with the same **file** argument. This file descriptor may be safely used as an argument to the **fcntl**(2) and **flock**(2) locking functions. The file descriptor is not necessarily associated with any of the underlying files actually used by the access method.

The Db::fd method only supports a coarse-grained form of locking. Applications should use the lock manager where possible.

The Db::fd method either returns a non-zero error value or throws an exception that encapsulates a non-zero error value on failure, and returns 0 on success.

Errors

The Db::fd method may fail and throw an exception or return a non-zero error for errors specified for other Berkeley DB and C library or system methods. If a catastrophic error has occurred, the Db::fd method may fail and either return DB_RUNRECOVERY or throw an exception encapsulating DB_RUNRECOVERY, in which case all subsequent Berkeley DB calls will fail in the same way.

Db::get

```
#include <db_cxx.h>

int
Db::get(DbTxn *txnid, Dbt *key, Dbt *data, u_int32_t flags);
```

Description

The Db::get method retrieves key/data pairs from the database. The address and length of the data associated with the specified **key** are returned in the structure referenced by **data**.

In the presence of duplicate key values, Db::get will return the first data item for the designated key. Duplicates are sorted by insert order except where this order has been overridden by cursor operations. **Retrieval of duplicates requires the use of cursor operations.** See **Dbc::get** for details.

If the operation is to be transactionally protected, the **txnid** parameter is a transaction handle returned from **DbEnv::txn_begin**; otherwise, NULL.

The **flags** parameter must be set to 0 or one of the following values:

- DB_CONSUME   Return the record number and data from the available record closest to the head of the queue, and delete the record. The cursor will be positioned on the deleted record. The record number will be returned in **key**, as described in **Dbt**.

The data will be returned in the **data** parameter. A record is available if it is not deleted and is not currently locked. The underlying database must be of type Queue for DB_CONSUME to be specified.

- DB_CONSUME_WAIT   The DB_CONSUME_WAIT flag is the same as the DB_CONSUME flag, except that if the Queue database is empty, the thread of control will wait until there is data in the queue before returning. The underlying database must be of type Queue for DB_CONSUME_WAIT to be specified.

- DB_GET_BOTH   Retrieve the key/data pair only if both the key and data match the arguments.

- DB_SET_RECNO   Retrieve the specified numbered key/data pair from a database. Upon return, both the **key** and **data** items will have been filled in; not just the data item, as is done for all other uses of the Db::get method.

  The **data** field of the specified **key** must be a pointer to a logical record number (that is, a **db_recno_t**). This record number determines the record to be retrieved.

  For DB_SET_RECNO to be specified, the underlying database must be of type Btree, and it must have been created with the DB_RECNUM flag.

In addition, the following flag may be set by bitwise inclusively **OR**'ing it into the **flags** parameter:

- DB_RMW   Acquire write locks instead of read locks when doing the retrieval. Setting this flag can eliminate deadlock during a read-modify-write cycle by acquiring the write lock during the read part of the cycle so that another thread of control acquiring a read lock for the same item, in its own read-modify-write cycle, will not result in deadlock.

  As the Db::get interface will not hold locks across Berkeley DB interface calls in non-transactional environments, the DB_RMW flag to the Db::get call is only meaningful in the presence of transactions.

If the database is a Queue or Recno database and the requested key exists, but was never explicitly created by the application or was later deleted, the Db::get method returns DB_KEYEMPTY.

Otherwise, if the requested key is not in the database, the Db::get function returns DB_NOTFOUND.

Otherwise, the Db::get method either returns a non-zero error value; or throws an exception that encapsulates a non-zero error value on failure, and returns 0 on success.

Errors

The Db::get method may fail and throw an exception or return a non-zero error for the following conditions:

- DB_LOCK_DEADLOCK   The operation was selected to resolve a deadlock.

- ENOMEM   There was insufficient memory to return the requested item.

- EINVAL   An invalid flag value or parameter was specified.

A record number of 0 was specified.

The DB_THREAD flag was specified to the **Db::open** method and none of the DB_DBT_MALLOC, DB_DBT_REALLOC or DB_DBT_USERMEM flags were set in the **Dbt**.

The Db::get method may fail and throw an exception or return a non-zero error for errors specified for other Berkeley DB and C library or system methods. If a catastrophic error has occurred, the Db::get method may fail and either return DB_RUNRECOVERY or throw an exception encapsulating DB_RUNRECOVERY, in which case all subsequent Berkeley DB calls will fail in the same way.

Db::get_byteswapped

```
#include <db_cxx.h>

int
Db::get_byteswapped(void) const;
```

Description

The Db::get_byteswapped method returns 0 if the underlying database files were created on an architecture of the same byte order as the current one, and 1 if they were not (that is, big-endian on a little-endian machine, or vice-versa). This field may be used to determine if application data needs to be adjusted for this architecture or not.

Db::get_type

```
#include <db_cxx.h>

DBTYPE
Db::get_type(void) const;
```

Description

The Db::get_type method returns the type of the underlying access method (and file format). It returns one of DB_BTREE, DB_HASH, DB_RECNO, or DB_QUEUE. This value may be used to determine the type of the database after a return from **Db::open** with the **type** argument set to DB_UNKNOWN.

Db::join

```
#include <db_cxx.h>

int
Db::join(Dbc **curslist, Dbc **dbcp, u_int32_t flags);
```

Description

The Db::join method creates a specialized cursor for use in performing joins on secondary indexes. For information on how to organize your data to use this functionality, see "Logical Join."

The **primary** argument contains the **Db** handle of the primary database, which is keyed by the data values found in entries in the **curslist**.

The **curslist** argument contains a NULL- terminated array of cursors. Each cursor must have been initialized to reference the key on which the underlying database should be joined. Typically, this initialization is done by a **Dbc::get** call with the DB_SET flag specified. Once the cursors have been passed as part of a **curslist**, they should not be accessed or modified until the newly created join cursor has been closed, or else inconsistent results may be returned.

Joined values are retrieved by doing a sequential iteration over the first cursor in the **curslist** argument and a nested iteration over each secondary cursor in the order they are specified in the **curslist** argument. This requires database traversals to search for the current datum in all the cursors after the first. For this reason, the best join performance normally results from sorting the cursors from the one that references the least number of data items to the one that references the most. By default, Db::join does this sort on behalf of its caller.

The **flags** parameter must be set to 0 or the following value:

- DB_JOIN_NOSORT   Do not sort the cursors based on the number of data items they reference. If the data are structured so that cursors with many data items also share many common elements, higher performance will result from listing those cursors before cursors with fewer data items; that is, a sort order other than the default. The DB_JOIN_NOSORT flag permits applications to perform join optimization prior to calling Db::join.

A newly created cursor is returned in the memory location referenced by **dbcp**, and supports only the **Dbc::get** and **dbc_close** cursor functions:

- **Dbc::get**   Iterates over the values associated with the keys to which each item in **curslist** was initialized. Any data value that appears in all items specified by the **curslist** argument is then used as a key into the **primary**, and the key/data pair found in the **primary** is returned.

  The **flags** parameter must be set to 0 or the following value:

  - DB_JOIN_ITEM   Do not use the data value found in all of the cursors as a lookup key for the **primary**; simply return it in the key parameter instead. The data parameter is left unchanged.

    In addition, the following flag may be set by bitwise inclusively **OR**'ing it into the **flags** parameter:

  - DB_RMW   Acquire write locks instead of read locks when doing the retrieval. Setting this flag can eliminate deadlock during a read-modify-write cycle by acquiring the write lock during the read part of the cycle so that another thread of control acquiring a read lock for the same item, in its own read-modify-write cycle, will not result in deadlock.

- **Dbc::close** Close the returned cursor and release all resources. (Closing the cursors in **curslist** is the responsibility of the caller.)

For the returned join cursor to be used in a transaction-protected manner, the cursors listed in **curslist** must have been created within the context of the same transaction.

The Db::join method either returns a non-zero error value; or throws an exception that encapsulates a non-zero error value on failure, and returns 0 on success.

Errors

The Db::join method may fail and throw an exception or return a non-zero error for the following condition:

- EINVAL An invalid flag value or parameter was specified.

  Cursor functions other than **Dbc::get** or **Dbc::close** were called.

The Db::join method may fail and throw an exception or return a non-zero error for errors specified for other Berkeley DB and C library or system methods. If a catastrophic error has occurred, the Db::join method may fail and either return DB_RUNRECOVERY or throw an exception encapsulating DB_RUNRECOVERY, in which case all subsequent Berkeley DB calls will fail in the same way.

Db::key_range

```
#include <db_cxx.h>

int
Db::key_range(DbTxn *txnid Dbt *key,
    DB_KEY_RANGE *key_range, u_int32_t flags);
```

Description

The Db::key_range method returns an estimate of the proportion of keys that are less than, equal to, and greater than the specified key. The underlying database must be of type Btree.

The information is returned in the **key_range** argument, which contains three elements of type double, **less**, **equal**, and **greater**. Values are in the range of 0 to 1; for example, if the field **less** is 0.05, that indicates that 5% of the keys in the database are less than the key argument. The value for **equal** will be zero if there is no matching key, and will be non-zero otherwise.

If the operation is to be transactionally protected, the **txnid** parameter is a transaction handle returned from **DbEnv::txn_begin**; otherwise, NULL. The Db::key_range method does not retain the locks it acquires for the life of the transaction, so estimates may not be repeatable.

The **flags** parameter is currently unused, and must be set to 0.

The Db::key_range method either returns a non-zero error value or throws an exception that encapsulates a non-zero error value on failure, and returns 0 on success.

Errors

The Db::key_range method may fail and throw an exception or return a non-zero error for the following conditions:

- DB_LOCK_DEADLOCK   The operation was selected to resolve a deadlock.
- EINVAL   An invalid flag value or parameter was specified.

   The underlying database was not of type Btree.

The Db::key_range method may fail and throw an exception or return a non-zero error for errors specified for other Berkeley DB and C library or system methods. If a catastrophic error has occurred, the Db::key_range method may fail and either return DB_RUNRECOVERY or throw an exception encapsulating DB_RUNRECOVERY, in which case all subsequent Berkeley DB calls will fail in the same way.

Db::open

```
#include <db_cxx.h>

int
Db::open(const char *file,
    const char *database, DBTYPE type, u_int32_t flags, int mode);
```

Description

The currently supported Berkeley DB file formats (or *access methods*) are Btree, Hash, Queue, and Recno. The Btree format is a representation of a sorted, balanced tree structure. The Hash format is an extensible, dynamic hashing scheme. The Queue format supports fast access to fixed-length records accessed sequentially or by logical record number. The Recno format supports fixed- or variable-length records, accessed sequentially or by logical record number, and optionally backed by a flat text file.

Storage and retrieval for the Berkeley DB access methods are based on key/data pairs, see **Dbt** for more information.

The Db::open interface opens the database represented by the **file** and **database** arguments for both reading and writing. The **file** argument is used as the name of an underlying file that will be used to back the database. The **database** argument is optional and allows applications to have multiple databases in a single file. Although no **database** argument needs to be specified, it is an error to attempt to open a second database in a **file** that was not initially created using a **database** name. Further, the **database** argument is not supported by the Queue format.

In-memory databases never intended to be preserved on disk may be created by setting both the **file** and **database** arguments to NULL. Note that in-memory databases can only ever be shared by sharing the single database handle that created them, in circumstances where doing so is safe.

The **type** argument is of type DBTYPE and must be set to one of DB_BTREE, DB_HASH, DB_QUEUE, DB_RECNO, or DB_UNKNOWN. If **type** is DB_UNKNOWN, the database must already exist and Db::open will automatically determine its type. The **Db::get_type** method may be used to determine the underlying type of databases opened using DB_UNKNOWN.

The **flags** and **mode** arguments specify how files will be opened and/or created if they do not already exist.

The **flags** value must be set to 0 or by bitwise inclusively **OR**'ing together one or more of the following values.

- DB_CREATE   Create any underlying files, as necessary. If the files do not already exist and the DB_CREATE flag is not specified, the call will fail.

- DB_EXCL   Return an error if the file already exists. Underlying filesystem primitives are used to implement this flag. For this reason, it is only applicable to the file and cannot be used to test if a database in a file already exists.

  The DB_EXCL flag is only meaningful when specified with the DB_CREATE flag.

- DB_NOMMAP   Do not map this database into process memory (see the description of the **DbEnv::set_mp_mmapsize** method for further information).

- DB_RDONLY   Open the database for reading only. Any attempt to modify items in the database will fail, regardless of the actual permissions of any underlying files.

- DB_THREAD   Cause the **Db** handle returned by Db::open to be *free-threaded*; that is, usable by multiple threads within a single address space.

- DB_TRUNCATE   Physically truncate the underlying file, discarding all previous databases it might have held. Underlying filesystem primitives are used to implement this flag. For this reason, it is only applicable to the file and cannot be used to discard databases within a file.

  The DB_TRUNCATE flag cannot be transaction- protected, and it is an error to specify it in a transaction protected environment.

On UNIX systems, or in IEEE/ANSI Std 1003.1 (POSIX) environments, all files created by the access methods are created with mode **mode** (as described in **chmod**(2)) and modified by the process' umask value at the time of creation (see **umask**(2)). The group ownership of created files is based on the system and directory defaults, and is not further specified by Berkeley DB. If **mode** is 0, files are created readable and writable by both owner and group. On Windows systems, the mode argument is ignored.

Calling Db::open is a reasonably expensive operation, and maintaining a set of open databases will normally be preferable to repeatedly opening and closing the database for each new query.

The Db::open method either returns a non-zero error value or throws an exception that encapsulates a non-zero error value on failure, and returns 0 on success.

Environment Variables

- DB_HOME   If the **dbenv** argument to **db_create** was initialized using **DbEnv::open**, the environment variable **DB_HOME** may be used as the path of the database environment home. Specifically, Db::open is affected by the configuration value DB_DATA_DIR.

- TMPDIR   If the **file** and **dbenv** arguments to Db::open are NULL, the environment variable **TMPDIR** may be used as a directory in which to create a temporary backing file.

Errors

The Db::open method may fail and throw an exception or return a non-zero error for the following conditions:

- DB_OLD_VERSION   The database cannot be opened without being first upgraded.

- EEXIST   DB_CREATE and DB_EXCL were specified and the file exists.

- EINVAL   An invalid flag value or parameter was specified (for example, unknown database type, page size, hash function, pad byte, byte order), or a flag value or parameter that is incompatible with the specified database.

  The DB_THREAD flag was specified, and spinlocks are not implemented for this architecture.

  The DB_THREAD flag was specified to Db::open, but was not specified to the **DbEnv::open** call for the environment in which the **Db** handle was created.

  A backing flat text file was specified with either the DB_THREAD flag or the provided database environment supports transaction processing.

- ENOEN

- A non-existent **re_source** file was specified.

The Db::open method may fail and throw an exception or return a non-zero error for errors specified for other Berkeley DB and C library or system methods. If a catastrophic error has occurred, the Db::open method may fail and either return DB_RUNRECOVERY or throw an exception encapsulating DB_RUNRECOVERY, in which case all subsequent Berkeley DB calls will fail in the same way.

Db::put

```
#include <db_cxx.h>

int
Db::put(DbTxn *txnid, Dbt *key, Dbt *data, u_int32_t flags);
```

Description

The Db::put method stores key/data pairs in the database. The default behavior of the Db::put function is to enter the new key/data pair, replacing any previously existing key if duplicates are disallowed, or adding a duplicate data item if duplicates are allowed. If the database supports duplicates, the Db::put method adds the new data value at the end of the duplicate set. If the database supports sorted duplicates, the new data value is inserted at the correct sorted location.

If the operation is to be transactionally protected, the **txnid** parameter is a transaction handle returned from **DbEnv::txn_begin**; otherwise, NULL.

The **flags** parameter must be set to 0 or one of the following values:

- DB_APPEND   Append the key/data pair to the end of the database. For the DB_APPEND flag to be specified, the underlying database must be a Queue or Recno database. The record number allocated to the record is returned in the specified **key**.

  There is a minor behavioral difference between the Recno and Queue access methods for the DB_APPEND flag. If a transaction enclosing a Db::put operation with the DB_APPEND flag aborts, the record number may be decremented (and later reallocated by a subsequent DB_APPEND operation) by the Recno access method, but will not be decremented or reallocated by the Queue access method.

- DB_NODUPDATA   In the case of the Btree and Hash access methods, enter the new key/data pair only if it does not already appear in the database. If the key/data pair already appears in the database, DB_KEYEXIST is returned. The DB_NODUPDATA flag may only be specified if the underlying database has been configured to support sorted duplicates.

  The DB_NODUPDATA flag may not be specified to the Queue or Recno access methods.

- DB_NOOVERWRITE   Enter the new key/data pair only if the key does not already appear in the database. If the key already appears in the database, DB_KEYEXIST is returned. Even if the database allows duplicates, a call to Db::put with the DB_NOOVERWRITE flag set will fail if the key already exists in the database.

Otherwise, the Db::put method either returns a non-zero error value or throws an exception that encapsulates a non-zero error value on failure, and returns 0 on success.

Errors

The Db::put method may fail and throw an exception or return a non-zero error for the following conditions:

- DB_LOCK_DEADLOCK The operation was selected to resolve a deadlock.
- EACCES An attempt was made to modify a read-only database.
- EINVAL An invalid flag value or parameter was specified.

  A record number of 0 was specified.

  An attempt was made to add a record to a fixed-length database that was too large to fit.

  An attempt was made to do a partial put.

- ENOSPC A btree exceeded the maximum btree depth (255).

The Db::put method may fail and throw an exception or return a non-zero error for errors specified for other Berkeley DB and C library or system methods. If a catastrophic error has occurred, the Db::put method may fail and either return DB_RUNRECOVERY or throw an exception encapsulating DB_RUNRECOVERY, in which case all subsequent Berkeley DB calls will fail in the same way.

Db::remove

```
#include <db_cxx.h>

int
Db::remove(const char *file, const char *database, u_int32_t flags);
```

Description

The Db::remove interface removes the database specified by the **file** and **database** arguments. If no **database** is specified, the underlying file represented by **file** is removed, incidentally removing all databases that it contained.

Applications should not remove databases that are currently in use. If an underlying file is being removed and logging is currently enabled in the database environment, no database in the file may be open when the Db::remove method is called. In particular, some architectures do not permit the removal of files with open handles. On these architectures, attempts to remove databases that are currently in use by any thread of control in the system will fail.

The **flags** parameter is currently unused, and must be set to 0.

Once Db::remove has been called, regardless of its return, the **Db** handle may not be accessed again.

The Db::remove method either returns a non-zero error value or throws an exception that encapsulates a non-zero error value on failure, and returns 0 on success.

Environment Variable

- DB_HOME   If the **dbenv** argument to **db_create** was initialized using **DbEnv::open**, the environment variable **DB_HOME** may be used as the path of the database environment home. Specifically, Db::remove is affected by the configuration value DB_DATA_DIR.

Errors

The Db::remove method may fail and throw an exception or return a non-zero error for the following condition:

- EINVAL   A database in the file is currently open.

The Db::remove method may fail and throw an exception or return a non-zero error for errors specified for other Berkeley DB and C library or system methods. If a catastrophic error has occurred, the Db::remove method may fail and either return DB_RUNRECOVERY or throw an exception encapsulating DB_RUNRECOVERY, in which case all subsequent Berkeley DB calls will fail in the same way.

Db::rename

```
#include <db_cxx.h>

int
Db::rename(const char *file, const char *database,
        const char *newname, u_int32_t flags);
```

Description

The Db::rename interface renames the database specified by the **file** and **database** arguments to **newname**. If no **database** is specified, the underlying file represented by **file** is renamed, incidentally renaming all databases that it contained.

Applications should not rename databases that are currently in use. If an underlying file is being renamed and logging is currently enabled in the database environment, no database in the file may be open when the Db::rename method is called. In particular, some architectures do not permit renaming files with open handles. On these architectures, attempts to rename databases that are currently in use by any thread of control in the system will fail.

The **flags** parameter is currently unused, and must be set to 0.

Once Db::rename has been called, regardless of its return, the **Db** handle may not be accessed again.

The Db::rename method either returns a non-zero error value or throws an exception that encapsulates a non-zero error value on failure, and returns 0 on success.

Environment Variables

- DB_HOME   If the **dbenv** argument to **db_create** was initialized using **DbEnv::open**, the environment variable **DB_HOME** may be used as the path of the database environment home. Specifically, Db::rename is affected by the configuration value DB_DATA_DIR.

Errors

The Db::rename method may fail and throw an exception, or return a non-zero error for the following conditions:

- EINVAL   A database in the file is currently open.

The Db::rename method may fail and throw an exception or return a non-zero error for errors specified for other Berkeley DB and C library or system methods. If a catastrophic error has occurred, the Db::rename method may fail and either return DB_RUNRECOVERY or throw an exception encapsulating DB_RUNRECOVERY, in which case all subsequent Berkeley DB calls will fail in the same way.

b::set_append_recno

```
#include <db_cxx.h>

int
Db::set_append_recno(
    int (*db_append_recno_fcn)(DB *dbp, Dbt *data, db_recno_t recno));
```

Description

When using the DB_APPEND option of the **Db::put** method, it may be useful to modify the stored data based on the generated key. If a callback method is specified using the Db::set_append_recno method, it will be called after the record number has been selected but before the data has been stored. The callback function must return 0 on success, and **errno** or a value outside of the Berkeley DB error name space on failure.

The called function must take three arguments: a reference to the enclosing database handle, the data **Dbt** to be stored, and the selected record number. The called function may then modify the data **Dbt**.

The Db::set_append_recno interface may only be used to configure Berkeley DB before the **Db::open** interface is called.

The Db::set_append_recno method either returns a non-zero error value or throws an exception that encapsulates a non-zero error value on failure, and returns 0 on success.

Db::set_bt_compare

```
#include <db_cxx.h>

extern "C" {
    typedef int (*bt_compare_fcn_type)(DB *, const DBT *, const DBT *);
};
int
Db::set_bt_compare(bt_compare_fcn_type bt_compare_fcn);
```

Description

Set the Btree key comparison function. The comparison function is called when it is necessary to compare a key specified by the application with a key currently stored in the tree. The first argument to the comparison function is the **Dbt** representing the application supplied key, the second is the current tree's key.

The comparison function must return an integer value less than, equal to, or greater than zero if the first key argument is considered to be respectively less than, equal to, or greater than the second key argument. In addition, the comparison function must cause the keys in the database to be *well-ordered*. The comparison function must correctly handle any key values used by the application (possibly including zero-length keys). In addition, when Btree key prefix comparison is being performed (see **Db::set_bt_prefix** for more information), the comparison routine may be passed a prefix of any database key. The **data** and **size** fields of the **Dbt** are the only fields that may be used for the purposes of this comparison, and no particular alignment of the memory referenced by the **data** field may be assumed.

If no comparison function is specified, the keys are compared lexically, with shorter keys collating before longer keys. The same comparison method must be used each time a particular Btree is opened.

The Db::set_bt_compare interface may only be used to configure Berkeley DB before the **Db::open** interface is called.

The Db::set_bt_compare method either returns a non-zero error value or throws an exception that encapsulates a non-zero error value on failure, and returns 0 on success.

Errors

- EINVAL An invalid flag value or parameter was specified.

  Called after **Db::open** was called.

Db::set_bt_minkey

```
#include <db_cxx.h>

int
Db::set_bt_minkey(u_int32_t bt_minkey);
```

Description

Set the minimum number of keys that will be stored on any single Btree page.

This value is used to determine which keys will be stored on overflow pages; that is, if a key or data item is larger than the underlying database page size divided by the **bt_minkey** value, it will be stored on overflow pages instead of within the page itself. The **bt_minkey** value specified must be at least 2; if **bt_minkey** is not explicitly set, a value of 2 is used.

The Db::set_bt_minkey interface may only be used to configure Berkeley DB before the **Db::open** interface is called.

The Db::set_bt_minkey method either returns a non-zero error value or throws an exception that encapsulates a non-zero error value on failure, and returns 0 on success.

Errors

- EINVAL   An invalid flag value or parameter was specified.

  Called after **Db::open** was called.

Db::set_bt_prefix

```
#include <db_cxx.h>

extern "C" {
    typedef size_t (*bt_prefix_fcn_type)(DB *, const DBT *, const DBT *);
};
int
Db::set_bt_prefix(bt_prefix_fcn_type bt_prefix_fcn);
```

Description

Set the Btree prefix function. The prefix function must return the number of bytes of the second key argument that would be required by the Btree key comparison function to determine the second key argument's ordering relationship with respect to the first key argument. If the two keys are equal, the key length should be returned. The prefix function must correctly handle any key values used by the application (possibly including zero-length keys). The **data** and **size** fields of the **Dbt** are the only fields that may be used for the purposes of this determination, and no particular alignment of the memory referenced by the **data** field may be assumed.

The prefix function is used to determine the amount by which keys stored on the Btree internal pages can be safely truncated without losing their uniqueness. See the "Btree Prefix Comparison" section of the *Reference Guide* for more details about how this works. The usefulness of this is data-dependent; but in some data sets, it can produce significantly reduced tree sizes and search times.

If no prefix function or key comparison function is specified by the application, a default lexical comparison function is used as the prefix function. If no prefix function is specified and a key comparison function is specified, no prefix function is used. It is an error to specify a prefix function without also specifying a key comparison function.

The Db::set_bt_prefix interface may only be used to configure Berkeley DB before the **Db::open** interface is called.

The Db::set_bt_prefix method either returns a non-zero error value or throws an exception that encapsulates a non-zero error value on failure, and returns 0 on success.

Errors

- EINVAL   An invalid flag value or parameter was specified.

  Called after **Db::open** was called.

Db::set_cachesize

```
#include <db_cxx.h>

int
Db::set_cachesize(u_int32_t gbytes, u_int32_t bytes, int ncache);
```

Description

Set the size of the database's shared memory buffer pool (that is, the cache) to **gbytes** gigabytes plus **bytes**. The cache should be the size of the normal working data set of the application, with some small amount of additional memory for unusual situations. (Note that the working set is not the same as the number of simultaneously referenced pages, and should be quite a bit larger!)

The default cache size is 256KB, and may not be specified as less than 20KB. Any cache size less than 500MB is automatically increased by 25% to account for buffer pool overhead; cache sizes larger than 500MB are used as specified. For information on tuning the Berkeley DB cache size, see "Selecting a Cache Size."

It is possible to specify caches to Berkeley DB that are large enough so that they cannot be allocated contiguously on some architectures; for example, some releases of Solaris limit the amount of memory that may be allocated contiguously by a process. If **ncache** is 0 or 1, the cache will be allocated contiguously in memory. If it is greater than 1, the cache will be broken up into **ncache** equally sized separate pieces of memory.

Because databases opened within Berkeley DB environments use the cache specified to the environment, it is an error to attempt to set a cache in a database created within an environment.

The Db::set_cachesize interface may only be used to configure Berkeley DB before the **Db::open** interface is called.

The Db::set_cachesize method either returns a non-zero error value or throws an exception that encapsulates a non-zero error value on failure, and returns 0 on success.

Errors

- EINVAL   An invalid flag value or parameter was specified.

  The specified cache size was impossibly small.

Db::set_dup_compare

```
#include <db_cxx.h>

extern "C" {
    typedef int (*dup_compare_fcn_type)(DB *, const DBT *, const DBT *);
};
int
Db::set_dup_compare(dup_compare_fcn_type dup_compare_fcn);
```

Description

Set the duplicate data item comparison function. The comparison function is called when it is necessary to compare a data item specified by the application with a data item currently stored in the tree. The first argument to the comparison function is the **Dbt** representing the application's data item, the second is the current tree's data item.

The comparison function must return an integer value less than, equal to, or greater than zero if the first data item argument is considered to be respectively less than, equal to, or greater than the second data item argument. In addition, the comparison function must cause the data items in the set to be *well-ordered*. The comparison function must correctly handle any data item values used by the application (possibly including zero-length data items). The **data** and **size** fields of the **Dbt** are the only fields that may be used for the purposes of this comparison, and no particular alignment of the memory referenced by the **data** field may be assumed.

If no comparison function is specified, the data items are compared lexically, with shorter data items collating before longer data items. The same duplicate data item comparison method must be used each time a particular Btree is opened.

The Db::set_dup_compare interface may only be used to configure Berkeley DB before the **Db::open** interface is called.

The Db::set_dup_compare method either returns a non-zero error value or throws an exception that encapsulates a non-zero error value on failure, and returns 0 on success.

Errors

- EINVAL   An invalid flag value or parameter was specified.

Db::set_errcall

```
#include <db_cxx.h>

void Db::set_errcall(
    void (*db_errcall_fcn)(const char *errpfx, char *msg));
```

Description

When an error occurs in the Berkeley DB library, an exception is thrown or an error return value is returned by the method. In some cases, however, the **errno** value may be insufficient to completely describe the cause of the error, especially during initial application debugging.

The Db::set_errcall method is used to enhance the mechanism for reporting error messages to the application. In some cases, when an error occurs, Berkeley DB will call **db_errcall_fcn** with additional error information. The function must be defined with two arguments; the first will be the prefix string (as previously set by **Db::set_errpfx** or **DbEnv::set_errpfx**), the second will be the error message string. It is up to the **db_errcall_fcn** method to display the error message in an appropriate manner.

Alternatively, you can use the **DbEnv::set_error_stream** method to display the additional information via an output stream, or the **Db::set_errfile** or **DbEnv::set_errfile** methods to display the additional information via a C library FILE *. You should not mix these approaches.

This error-logging enhancement does not slow performance or significantly increase application size, and may be run during normal operation as well as during application debugging.

For **Db** handles opened inside of Berkeley DB environments, calling the Db::set_errcall method affects the entire environment and is equivalent to calling the **DbEnv::set_errcall** method.

The Db::set_errcall interface may be used to configure Berkeley DB at any time during the life of the application.

Db::set_errfile

```
#include <db_cxx.h>

void Db::set_errfile(FILE *errfile);
```

Description

When an error occurs in the Berkeley DB library, an exception is thrown or an error return value is returned by the method. In some cases, however, the **errno** value may be insufficient to completely describe the cause of the error, especially during initial application debugging.

The Db::set_errfile method is used to enhance the mechanism for reporting error messages to the application by setting a C library FILE * to be used for displaying additional Berkeley DB error messages. In some cases, when an error occurs, Berkeley DB will output an additional error message to the specified file reference.

Alternatively, you can use the **DbEnv::set_error_stream** method to display the additional information via an output stream, or the **DbEnv::set_errcall** method to capture the additional error information in a way that does not use either output streams or C library FILE *'s. You should not mix these approaches.

The error message will consist of the prefix string and a colon (":") (if a prefix string was previously specified using **Db::set_errpfx** or **DbEnv::set_errpfx**), an error string, and a trailing <newline> character.

This error- logging enhancement does not slow performance or significantly increase application size, and may be run during normal operation as well as during application debugging.

For **Db** handles opened inside of Berkeley DB environments, calling the Db::set_errfile method affects the entire environment and is equivalent to calling the **DbEnv::set_errfile** method.

The Db::set_errfile interface may be used to configure Berkeley DB at any time during the life of the application.

Db::set_errpfx

```
#include <db_cxx.h>

void Db::set_errpfx(const char *errpfx);
```

Description

Set the prefix string that appears before error messages issued by Berkeley DB.

The Db::set_errpfx method does not copy the memory referenced by the **errpfx** argument; rather, it maintains a reference to it. This allows applications to modify the error message prefix at any time, without repeatedly calling Db::set_errpfx, but it means that the memory must be maintained until the handle is closed.

For **Db** handles opened inside of Berkeley DB environments, calling the Db::set_errpfx method affects the entire environment and is equivalent to calling the **DbEnv::set_errpfx** method.

The Db::set_errpfx interface may be used to configure Berkeley DB at any time during the life of the application.

Db::set_feedback

```
#include <db_cxx.h>

int
Db::set_feedback(
    void (*db_feedback_fcn)(DB *dbp, int opcode, int pct));
```

Description

Some operations performed by the Berkeley DB library can take non-trivial amounts of time. The Db::set_feedback method can be used by applications to monitor progress within these operations.

When an operation is likely to take a long time, Berkeley DB will call the specified callback method. This method must be declared with three arguments: The first will be a reference to the enclosing database handle, the second will be a flag value, and the third will be the percent of the operation that has been completed, specified as an integer value between 0 and 100. It is up to the callback method to display this information in an appropriate manner.

The **opcode** argument may take on any of the following values:

- DB_UPGRADE   The underlying database is being upgraded.
- DB_VERIFY   The underlying database is being verified.

The Db::set_feedback interface may be used to configure Berkeley DB at any time during the life of the application.

The Db::set_feedback method either returns a non-zero error value or throws an exception that encapsulates a non-zero error value on failure, and returns 0 on success.

Db::set_flags

```
#include <db_cxx.h>

int
Db::set_flags(u_int32_t flags);
```

Description

Calling Db::set_flags is additive; there is no way to clear flags.

The **flags** value must be set to 0 or by bitwise inclusively **OR**'ing together one or more of the following values.

Btree

The following flags may be specified for the Btree access method:

- DB_DUP   Permit duplicate data items in the tree; that is, insertion when the key of the key/data pair being inserted already exists in the tree will be successful. The ordering of duplicates in the tree is determined by the order of insertion, unless the ordering is otherwise specified by use of a cursor operation. It is an error to specify both DB_DUP and DB_RECNUM.
- DB_DUPSORT   Permit duplicate data items in the tree; that is, insertion when the key of the key/data pair being inserted already exists in the tree will be successful. The ordering of duplicates in the tree is determined by the duplicate comparison function. If the application does not specify a comparison function using the **Db::set_dup_compare** method, a default lexical comparison will be used. It is an error to specify both DB_DUPSORT and DB_RECNUM.
- DB_RECNUM   Support retrieval from the Btree using record numbers. For more information, see the DB_GET_RECNO flag to the **Db::get** and **Dbc::get** methods.

Logical record numbers in Btree databases are mutable in the face of record insertion or deletion. See the DB_RENUMBER flag in the Recno access method information for further discussion.

Maintaining record counts within a Btree introduces a serious point of contention, namely the page locations where the record counts are stored. In addition, the entire tree must be locked during both insertions and deletions, effectively single-threading the tree for those operations. Specifying DB_RECNUM can result in serious performance degradation for some applications and data sets.

It is an error to specify both DB_DUP and DB_RECNUM.

- DB_REVSPLITOFF   Turn off reverse splitting in the Btree. As pages are emptied in a database, the Berkeley DB Btree implementation attempts to coalesce empty pages into higher-level pages in order to keep the tree as small as possible and minimize tree search time. This can hurt performance in applications with cyclical data demands; that is, applications where the database grows and shrinks repeatedly. For example, because Berkeley DB does page-level locking, the maximum level of concurrency in a database of two pages is far smaller than that in a database of 100 pages, and so a database that has shrunk to a minimal size can cause severe deadlocking when a new cycle of data insertion begins.

Hash

The following flags may be specified for the Hash access method:

- DB_DUP   Permit duplicate data items in the tree; that is, insertion when the key of the key/data pair being inserted already exists in the tree will be successful. The ordering of duplicates in the tree is determined by the order of insertion, unless the ordering is otherwise specified by use of a cursor operation. It is an error to specify both DB_DUP and DB_RECNUM.

- DB_DUPSORT   Permit duplicate data items in the tree; that is, insertion when the key of the key/data pair being inserted already exists in the tree will be successful. The ordering of duplicates in the tree is determined by the duplicate comparison function. If the application does not specify a comparison function using the **Db::set_dup_compare** method, a default lexical comparison will be used. It is an error to specify both DB_DUPSORT and DB_RECNUM.

Queue

There are no additional flags that may be specified for the Queue access method.

Recno

The following flags may be specified for the Recno access method:

- DB_RENUMBER   Specifying the DB_RENUMBER flag causes the logical record numbers to be mutable and change as records are added to and deleted from the database. For example, the deletion of record number 4 causes records numbered 5 and greater to be renumbered downward by one. If a cursor was positioned to record number 4 before the deletion, it will reference the new record number 4, if any such record exists, after the deletion. If a cursor was positioned after record number 4 before the deletion, it will be shifted downward one logical record, continuing to reference the same record as it did before.

Using the **Db::put** or **Dbc::put** interfaces to create new records will cause the creation of multiple records if the record number is more than one greater than the largest record currently in the database. For example, creating record 28, when record 25 was previously the last record in the database, will create records 26 and 27 as well as 28. Attempts to retrieve records that were created in this manner will result in an error return of DB_KEYEMPTY.

If a created record is not at the end of the database, all records following the new record will be automatically renumbered upward by one. For example, the creation of a new record numbered 8 causes records numbered 8 and greater to be renumbered upward by one. If a cursor was positioned to record number 8 or greater before the insertion, it will be shifted upward one logical record, continuing to reference the same record as it did before.

For these reasons, concurrent access to a Recno database with the DB_RENUMBER flag specified may be largely meaningless, although it is supported.

- DB_SNAPSHOT   This flag specifies that any specified **re_source** file be read in its entirety when **Db::open** is called. If this flag is not specified, the **re_source** file may be read lazily.

The Db::set_flags interface may only be used to configure Berkeley DB before the **Db::open** interface is called.

The Db::set_flags method either returns a non-zero error value or throws an exception that encapsulates a non-zero error value on failure, and returns 0 on success.

Errors

- EINVAL   An invalid flag value or parameter was specified.

Db::set_h_ffactor

```
#include <db_cxx.h>
```

```
int
Db::set_h_ffactor(u_int32_t h_ffactor);
```

Description

Set the desired density within the hash table.

The density is an approximation of the number of keys allowed to accumulate in any one bucket, determining when the hash table grows or shrinks. If you know the average sizes of the keys and data in your dataset, setting the fill factor can enhance performance. A reasonable rule computing fill factor is to set it to

```
(pagesize - 32) / (average_key_size + average_data_size + 8)
```

If no value is specified, the fill factor will be selected dynamically as pages are filled.

The Db::set_h_ffactor interface may only be used to configure Berkeley DB before the **Db::open** interface is called.

The Db::set_h_ffactor method either returns a non-zero error value or throws an exception that encapsulates a non-zero error value on failure, and returns 0 on success.

Errors

- EINVAL   An invalid flag value or parameter was specified.

   Called after **Db::open** was called.

Db::set_h_hash

```
#include <db_cxx.h>

extern "C" {
     typedef u_int32_t (*h_hash_fcn_type)
             (DB *, const void *bytes, u_int32_t length);
};
int
Db::set_h_hash(h_hash_fcn_type h_hash_fcn);
```

Description

Set a user- defined hash method; if no hash method is specified, a default hash method is used. Because no hash method performs equally well on all possible data, the user may find that the built-in hash method performs poorly with a particular data set. User-specified hash functions must take a pointer to a byte string and a length as arguments, and return a value of type **u_int32_t**. The hash function must handle any key values used by the application (possibly including zero-length keys).

If a hash method is specified, **Db::open** will attempt to determine whether the hash method specified is the same as the one with which the database was created, and will fail if it detects that it is not.

The Db::set_h_hash interface may only be used to configure Berkeley DB before the **Db::open** interface is called.

The Db::set_h_hash method either returns a non-zero error value or throws an exception that encapsulates a non-zero error value on failure, and returns 0 on success.

Errors

- EINVAL   An invalid flag value or parameter was specified.

   Called after **Db::open** was called.

Db::set_h_nelem

```
#include <db_cxx.h>

int
Db::set_h_nelem(u_int32_t h_nelem);
```

Description

Set an estimate of the final size of the hash table.

If not set or set too low, hash tables will still expand gracefully as keys are entered, although a slight performance degradation may be noticed.

The Db::set_h_nelem interface may only be used to configure Berkeley DB before the **Db::open** interface is called.

The Db::set_h_nelem method either returns a non-zero error value or throws an exception that encapsulates a non-zero error value on failure, and returns 0 on success.

Errors

- EINVAL   An invalid flag value or parameter was specified.

   Called after **Db::open** was called.

Db::set_lorder

```
#include <db_cxx.h>

int
Db::set_lorder(int lorder);
```

Description

Set the byte order for integers in the stored database metadata. The number should represent the order as an integer; for example, big-endian order is the number 4,321; and little-endian order is the number 1,234. If **lorder** is not explicitly set, the host order of the machine where the Berkeley DB library was compiled is used.

The value of **lorder** is ignored except when databases are being created. If a database already exists, the byte order it uses is determined when the database is opened.

The access methods provide no guarantees about the byte ordering of the application data stored in the database, and applications are responsible for maintaining any necessary ordering.

The Db::set_lorder interface may only be used to configure Berkeley DB before the **Db::open** interface is called.

The Db::set_lorder method either returns a non-zero error value or throws an exception that encapsulates a non-zero error value on failure, and returns 0 on success.

Errors

- EINVAL   An invalid flag value or parameter was specified.

Db::set_malloc

```
#include <db_cxx.h>

extern "C" {
     typedef void *(*db_malloc_fcn_type)(size_t);
};
int
Db::set_malloc(db_malloc_fcn_type db_malloc);
```

Description

Set the allocation function used by the **Db** methods to allocate memory in which to return key/data items to the application.

The DB_DBT_MALLOC flag, when specified in the **Dbt** object, will cause the **Db** methods to allocate and reallocate memory, which then becomes the responsibility of the calling application. See **Dbt** for more information.

On systems in which there may be multiple library versions of malloc (notably Windows NT), specifying the DB_DBT_MALLOC flag will fail because the **Db** library will allocate memory from a different heap than the application will use to free it. To avoid this problem, the Db::set_malloc method can be used to pass Berkeley DB a reference to the application's allocation routine, in which case it will be used to allocate the memory returned when the DB_DBT_MALLOC flag is set.

The method specified must match the calling conventions of the ANSI C X3.159-1989 (ANSI C) library routine of the same name.

The Db::set_malloc interface may only be used to configure Berkeley DB before the **Db::open** interface is called.

The Db::set_malloc method either returns a non-zero error value or throws an exception that encapsulates a non-zero error value on failure, and returns 0 on success.

Errors

- EINVAL   An invalid flag value or parameter was specified.

Db::set_pagesize

```
#include <db_cxx.h>

int
Db::set_pagesize(u_int32_t pagesize);
```

Description

Set the size of the pages used to hold items in the database, in bytes. The minimum page size is 512 bytes, and the maximum page size is 64K bytes. If the page size is not explicitly set, one is selected based on the underlying filesystem I/O block size. The automatically selected size has a lower limit of 512 bytes and an upper limit of 16K bytes.

For information on tuning the Berkeley DB page size, see "Selecting a Page Size."

The Db::set_pagesize interface may only be used to configure Berkeley DB before the **Db::open** interface is called.

The Db::set_pagesize method either returns a non-zero error value or throws an exception that encapsulates a non-zero error value on failure, and returns 0 on success.

Errors

- EINVAL   An invalid flag value or parameter was specified.

Db::set_paniccall

```
#include <db_cxx.h>

int
Db::set_paniccall(
    void (*db_paniccall_fcn)(DbEnv *dbenv, int errval));
```

Description

Errors can occur in the Berkeley DB library where the only solution is to shut down the application and run recovery. (For example, if Berkeley DB is unable to write log records to disk because there is insufficient disk space.) In these cases, when the C++ error model has been configured so that the individual Berkeley DB methods return error codes (see **DbException** for more information), the value DB_RUNRECOVERY is returned by Berkeley DB methods.

In these cases, it is also often simpler to shut down the application when such errors occur rather than attempting to gracefully return up the stack. The Db::set_paniccall method is used to specify a method to be called when DB_RUNRECOVERY is about to be returned from a Berkeley DB method. When called, the **dbenv** argument will be a reference to the current environment, and the **errval** argument is the error value that would have been returned to the calling method.

For **Db** handles opened inside of Berkeley DB environments, calling the Db::set_paniccall method affects the entire environment and is equivalent to calling the **DbEnv::set_paniccall** method.

The Db::set_paniccall interface may be used to configure Berkeley DB at any time during the life of the application.

The Db::set_paniccall method either returns a non-zero error value or throws an exception that encapsulates a non-zero error value on failure, and returns 0 on success.

Db::set_q_extentsize

```
#include <db_cxx.h>

int
Db::set_q_extentsize(u_int32_t extentsize);
```

Description

Set the size of the extents used to hold pages in a Queue database, specified as a number of pages. Each extent is created as a separate physical file. If no extent size is set, the default behavior is to create only a single underlying database file.

For information on tuning the extent size, see "Selecting a Extent Size."

The Db::set_q_extentsize interface may only be used to configure Berkeley DB before the **Db::open** interface is called.

The Db::set_q_extentsize method either returns a non-zero error value or throws an exception that encapsulates a non-zero error value on failure, and returns 0 on success.

Errors

- EINVAL   An invalid flag value or parameter was specified.

  Called after **Db::open** was called.

Db::set_re_delim

```
#include <db_cxx.h>

int
Db::set_re_delim(int re_delim);
```

Description

Set the delimiting byte used to mark the end of a record in the backing source file for the Recno access method.

This byte is used for variable length records, if the **re_source** file is specified. If the **re_source** file is specified and no delimiting byte was specified, <newline> characters (that is, ASCII 0x0a) are interpreted as end-of-record markers.

The Db::set_re_delim interface may only be used to configure Berkeley DB before the **Db::open** interface is called.

The Db::set_re_delim method either returns a non-zero error value or throws an exception that encapsulates a non-zero error value on failure, and returns 0 on success.

Errors

- EINVAL   An invalid flag value or parameter was specified.

  Called after **Db::open** was called.

Db::set_re_len

```
#include <db_cxx.h>

int
Db::set_re_len(u_int32_t re_len);
```

Description

For the Queue access method, specify that the records are of length **re_len**.

For the Recno access method, specify that the records are fixed-length, not byte-delimited; and are of length **re_len**.

Any records added to the database that are less than **re_len** bytes long are automatically padded (see **Db::set_re_pad** for more information).

Any attempt to insert records into the database that are greater than **re_len** bytes long will cause the call to fail immediately and return an error.

The Db::set_re_len interface may only be used to configure Berkeley DB before the **Db::open** interface is called.

The Db::set_re_len method either returns a non-zero error value or throws an exception that encapsulates a non-zero error value on failure, and returns 0 on success.

Errors

- EINVAL   An invalid flag value or parameter was specified.

  Called after **Db::open** was called.

Db::set_re_pad

```
#include <db_cxx.h>

int
Db::set_re_pad(int re_pad);
```

Description

Set the padding character for short, fixed-length records for the Queue and Recno access methods.

If no pad character is specified, <space> characters (that is, ASCII 0x20) are used for padding.

The Db::set_re_pad interface may only be used to configure Berkeley DB before the **Db::open** interface is called.

The Db::set_re_pad method either returns a non-zero error value or throws an exception that encapsulates a non-zero error value on failure, and returns 0 on success.

Errors

• EINVAL   An invalid flag value or parameter was specified.

Called after **Db::open** was called.

Db::set_re_source

```
#include <db_cxx.h>

int
Db::set_re_source(char *re_source);
```

Description

Set the underlying source file for the Recno access method. The purpose of the **re_source** value is to provide fast access and modification to databases that are normally stored as flat text files.

If the **re_source** field is set, it specifies an underlying flat text database file that is read to initialize a transient record number index. In the case of variable length records, the records are separated as specified by **Db::set_re_delim**. For example, standard UNIX byte stream files can be interpreted as a sequence of variable length records separated by <newline> characters.

In addition, when cached data would normally be written back to the underlying database file (for example, the **Db::close** or **Db::sync** methods are called), the in-memory copy of the database will be written back to the **re_source** file.

By default, the backing source file is read lazily; that is, records are not read from the file until they are requested by the application. If multiple processes (not threads) are accessing a Recno database concurrently and either inserting or deleting records, the backing source file must be read in its entirety before more than a single process accesses the database, and only that process should specify the backing source file as part of the **Db::open** call. See the **DB_SNAPSHOT** flag for more information.

Reading and writing the backing source file specified by **re_source** cannot be transactionally protected because it involves filesystem operations that are not part of the Db transaction methodology. For this reason, if a temporary database is used to hold the records; that is, a NULL was specified as the **file** argument to **Db::open**, it is possible to lose the contents of the **re_source** file—for example, if the system crashes at the right instant. If a file is used to hold the database; that is, a file name was specified as the **file** argument to **Db::open**, normal database recovery on that file can be used to prevent information loss, although it is still possible that the contents of **re_source** will be lost if the system crashes.

The **re_source** file must already exist (but may be zero-length) when **Db::open** is called.

It is not an error to specify a read-only **re_source** file when creating a database, nor is it an error to modify the resulting database. However, any attempt to write the changes to the backing source file using either the **Db::sync** or **Db::close** methods will fail, of course. Specify the DB_NOSYNC flag to the **Db::close** method to stop it from attempting to write the changes to the backing file; instead, they will be silently discarded.

For all of these reasons, the **re_source** field is generally used to specify databases that are read-only for **Db** applications, and that are either generated on the fly by software tools or modified using a different mechanism; for example, a text editor.

The Db::set_re_source interface may only be used to configure Berkeley DB before the **Db::open** interface is called.

The Db::set_re_source method either returns a non-zero error value or throws an exception that encapsulates a non-zero error value on failure, and returns 0 on success.

Errors

- EINVAL   An invalid flag value or parameter was specified.

  Called after **Db::open** was called.

Db::set_realloc

```
#include <db_cxx.h>

extern "C" {
      typedef void *(*db_realloc_fcn_type)(void *, size_t);
};
int
Db::set_realloc(db_realloc_fcn_type db_realloc_fcn);
```

Description

Set the realloc function used by the **Db** methods to allocate memory in which to return key/data items to the application.

The DB_DBT_REALLOC flag, when specified in the **Dbt** object, will cause the **Db** methods to allocate and reallocate memory, which then becomes the responsibility of the calling application. See **Dbt** for more information.

On systems where there may be multiple library versions of realloc (notably Windows NT), specifying that the DB_DBT_REALLOC flag will fail because the **Db** library will allocate memory from a different heap than the application will use to free it. To avoid this problem, the Db::set_realloc method can be used to pass Berkeley DB a reference to the application's allocation routine, in which case it will be used to allocate the memory returned when the DB_DBT_REALLOC flag is set.

The method specified must match the calling conventions of the ANSI C X3.159-1989 (ANSI C) library routine of the same name.

The Db::set_realloc interface may only be used to configure Berkeley DB before the **Db::open** interface is called.

The Db::set_realloc method either returns a non-zero error value or throws an exception that encapsulates a non-zero error value on failure, and returns 0 on success.

Errors

- EINVAL   An invalid flag value or parameter was specified.

Db::stat

```
#include <db_cxx.h>

extern "C" {
    typedef void *(*db_malloc_fcn_type)(size_t);
};
int
Db::stat(void *sp, db_malloc_fcn_type db_malloc, u_int32_t flags);
```

Description

The Db::stat method creates a statistical structure and copies a pointer to it into user-specified memory locations. Specifically, if **sp** is non-NULL, a pointer to the statistics for the database are copied into the memory location it references.

Statistical structures are created in allocated memory. If **db_malloc** is non-NULL, it is called to allocate the memory; otherwise, the library function **malloc**(3) is used. The function **db_malloc** must match the calling conventions of the **malloc**(3) library routine. Regardless, the caller is responsible for deallocating the returned memory. To deallocate returned memory, free the returned memory reference; references inside the returned memory do not need to be individually freed.

The **flags** parameter must be set to 0 or the following value:

- DB_CACHED_COUNTS   Return a cached count of the keys and records in a database. This flag makes it possible for applications to request a possibly approximate key and record count without incurring the performance penalty of traversing the entire database. The statistics information described for the access method **XX_nkeys** and **XX_ndata** fields below is filled in, but no other information is collected. If the cached information has never been set, the fields will be returned set to 0.

- DB_RECORDCOUNT   Return a count of the records in a Btree or Recno Access Method database. This flag makes it possible for applications to request a record count without incurring the performance penalty of traversing the entire database. The statistics information described for the **bt_nkeys** field below is filled in, but no other information is collected.

  This option is only available for Recno databases or Btree databases where the underlying database was created with the DB_RECNUM flag.

The Db::stat method may access all the pages in the database, incurring a severe performance penalty, as well as possibly flushing the underlying buffer pool.

In the presence of multiple threads or processes accessing an active database, the information returned by Db::stat may be out-of-date.

If the database was not opened read-only and the DB_CACHED_COUNTS flag was not specified, the cached key and record numbers will be updated after the statistical information has been gathered.

The Db::stat method cannot be transaction-protected. For this reason, it should be called in a thread of control that has no open cursors or active transactions.

The Db::stat method either returns a non-zero error value or throws an exception that encapsulates a non-zero error value on failure, and returns 0 on success.

Hash Statistics

In the case of a Hash database, the statistics are stored in a structure of type DB_HASH_STAT. The following fields will be filled in:

- u_int32_t hash_magic;   Magic number that identifies the file as a Hash file.
- u_int32_t hash_version;   Version of the Hash database.
- u_int32_t hash_nkeys;   Number of unique keys in the database.
- u_int32_t hash_ndata;   Number of key/data pairs in the database.
- u_int32_t hash_pagesize;   Underlying Hash database page (and bucket) size.
- u_int32_t hash_nelem;   Estimated size of the hash table specified at database creation time.
- u_int32_t hash_ffactor;   Desired fill factor (number of items per bucket) specified at database creation time.
- u_int32_t hash_buckets;   Number of hash buckets.
- u_int32_t hash_free;   Number of pages on the free list.
- u_int32_t hash_bfree;   Number of bytes free on bucket pages.
- u_int32_t hash_bigpages;   Number of big key/data pages.
- u_int32_t hash_big_bfree;   Number of bytes free on big item pages.
- u_int32_t hash_overflows;   Number of overflow pages (overflow pages are pages that contain items that did not fit in the main bucket page).
- u_int32_t hash_ovfl_free;   Number of bytes free on overflow pages.
- u_int32_t hash_dup;   Number of duplicate pages.
- u_int32_t hash_dup_free;   Number of bytes free on duplicate pages.

Btree and Recno Statistics

In the case of a Btree or Recno database, the statistics are stored in a structure of type DB_BTREE_STAT. The following fields will be filled in:

- u_int32_t bt_magic;   Magic number that identifies the file as a Btree database.
- u_int32_t bt_version;   Version of the Btree database.
- u_int32_t bt_nkeys;   For the Btree Access Method, the number of unique keys in the database.

For the Recno Access Method, the number of records in the database.

- u_int32_t bt_ndata;   For the Btree Access Method, the number of key/data pairs in the database.

For the Recno Access Method, the number of records in the database. If the database has been configured to not renumber records during deletion, the number of records will only reflect undeleted records.

- u_int32_t bt_pagesize;   Underlying database page size.
- u_int32_t bt_minkey;   Minimum keys per page.

- u_int32_t bt_re_len; Length of fixed-length records.
- u_int32_t bt_re_pad; Padding byte value for fixed-length records.
- u_int32_t bt_levels; Number of levels in the database.
- u_int32_t bt_int_pg; Number of database internal pages.
- u_int32_t bt_leaf_pg; Number of database leaf pages.
- u_int32_t bt_dup_pg; Number of database duplicate pages.
- u_int32_t bt_over_pg; Number of database overflow pages.
- u_int32_t bt_free; Number of pages on the free list.
- u_int32_t bt_int_pgfree; Number of bytes free in database internal pages.
- u_int32_t bt_leaf_pgfree; Number of bytes free in database leaf pages.
- u_int32_t bt_dup_pgfree; Number of bytes free in database duplicate pages.
- u_int32_t bt_over_pgfree;Number of bytes free in database overflow pages.

Queue Statistics

In the case of a Queue database, the statistics are stored in a structure of type DB_QUEUE_STAT. The following fields will be filled in:

- u_int32_t qs_magic; Magic number that identifies the file as a Queue file.
- u_int32_t qs_version; Version of the Queue file type.
- u_int32_t qs_nkeys; Number of records in the database.
- u_int32_t qs_ndata; Number of records in the database.
- u_int32_t qs_pagesize; Underlying database page size.
- u_int32_t qs_pages; Number of pages in the database.
- u_int32_t qs_re_len; Length of the records.
- u_int32_t qs_re_pad; Padding byte value for the records.
- u_int32_t qs_pgfree; Number of bytes free in database pages.
- u_int32_t qs_start; Start offset.
- u_int32_t qs_first_recno; First undeleted record in the database.
- u_int32_t qs_cur_recno; Last allocated record number in the database.

The Db::stat method either returns a non-zero error value or throws an exception that encapsulates a non-zero error value on failure, and returns 0 on success.

Errors

The Db::stat method may fail and throw an exception or return a non-zero error for errors specified for other Berkeley DB and C library or system methods. If a catastrophic error has occurred, the Db::stat method may fail and either return DB_RUNRECOVERY or throw an exception encapsulating DB_RUNRECOVERY, in which case all subsequent Berkeley DB calls will fail in the same way.

Db::sync

```
#include <db_cxx.h>

int
Db::sync(u_int32_t flags);
```

Description

The Db::sync method flushes any cached information to disk.

If the database is in memory only, the Db::sync method has no effect and will always succeed.

The **flags** parameter is currently unused, and must be set to 0.

It is important to understand that flushing cached information to disk only minimizes the window of opportunity for corrupted data. Although unlikely, it is possible for database corruption to happen if a system or application crash occurs while writing data to the database. To ensure that database corruption never occurs, applications must either use transactions and logging with automatic recovery, use logging and application-specific recovery, or edit a copy of the database; and once all applications using the database have successfully called **Db::close**, atomically replace the original database with the updated copy.

The Db::sync method either returns a non-zero error value or throws an exception that encapsulates a non-zero error value on failure, 0 on success, and returns DB_INCOMPLETE if the underlying database still has dirty pages in the cache. (The only reason to return DB_INCOMPLETE is if another thread of control was writing pages in the underlying database file at the same time as the Db::sync method was being called. For this reason, a return of DB_INCOMPLETE can normally be ignored, or, in cases where it is a possible return value, there may be no reason to call Db::sync.)

Errors

The Db::sync method may fail and throw an exception or return a non-zero error for the following conditions:

- EINVAL   An invalid flag value or parameter was specified.

The Db::sync method may fail and throw an exception or return a non-zero error for errors specified for other Berkeley DB and C library or system methods. If a catastrophic error has occurred, the Db::sync method may fail and either return DB_RUNRECOVERY or throw an exception encapsulating DB_RUNRECOVERY, in which case all subsequent Berkeley DB calls will fail in the same way.

Db::upgrade

```
#include <db_cxx.h>

int
Db::upgrade(const char *file, u_int32_t flags);
```

Description

The Db::upgrade method upgrades all of the databases included in the file **file**, if necessary. If no upgrade is necessary, Db::upgrade always returns success.

Database upgrades are done in place and are destructive; for example, if pages need to be allocated and no disk space is available, the database may be left corrupted. Backups should be made before databases are upgraded. See "Upgrading Databases" for more information.

Unlike all other database operations, Db::upgrade may only be done on a system with the same byte-order as the database.

The **flags** parameter must be set to 0 or one of the following values:

- DB_DUPSORT   This flag is only meaningful when upgrading databases from releases before the Berkeley DB 3.1 release.

   As part of the upgrade from the Berkeley DB 3.0 release to the 3.1 release, the on-disk format of duplicate data items changed. To correctly upgrade the format requires that applications specify whether duplicate data items in the database are sorted or not. Specifying the DB_DUPSORT flag informs Db::upgrade that the duplicates are sorted; otherwise, they are assumed to be unsorted. Incorrectly specifying the value of this flag may lead to database corruption.

   Further, because the Db::upgrade method upgrades a physical file (including all of the databases it contains), it is not possible to use Db::upgrade to upgrade files where some of the databases it includes have sorted duplicate data items and some of the databases it includes have unsorted duplicate data items. If the file does not have more than a single database, if the databases do not support duplicate data items, or if all the databases that support duplicate data items support the same style of duplicates (either sorted or unsorted), Db::upgrade will work correctly as long as the DB_DUPSORT flag is correctly specified. Otherwise, the file cannot be upgraded using Db::upgrade and must be upgraded manually by dumping and reloading the databases.

The Db::upgrade method either returns a non-zero error value or throws an exception that encapsulates a non-zero error value on failure, and returns 0 on success.

Environment Variables

- DB_HOME   If the **dbenv** argument to **db_create** was initialized using **DbEnv::open**, the environment variable **DB_HOME** may be used as the path of the database environment home. Specifically, Db::upgrade is affected by the configuration value DB_DATA_DIR.

Errors

The Db::upgrade method may fail and throw an exception or return a non-zero error for the following conditions:

- EINVAL   An invalid flag value or parameter was specified.

  The database is not in the same byte-order as the system.

- DB_OLD_VERSION   The database cannot be upgraded by this version of the Berkeley DB software.

The Db::upgrade method may fail and throw an exception or return a non-zero error for errors specified for other Berkeley DB and C library or system methods. If a catastrophic error has occurred, the Db::upgrade method may fail and either return DB_RUNRECOVERY or throw an exception encapsulating DB_RUNRECOVERY, in which case all subsequent Berkeley DB calls will fail in the same way.

Db::verify

```
#include <db_cxx.h>

int
Db::verify(const char *file,
    const char *database, ostream *outfile, u_int32_t flags);
```

Description

The Db::verify method verifies the integrity of all databases in the file specified by the file argument, and optionally outputs the databases' key/data pairs to a file stream.

The **flags** parameter must be set to 0 or one of the following values:

- DB_SALVAGE   Write the key/data pairs from all databases in the file to the file stream named in the **outfile** argument. The output format is the same as that specified for the **db_dump** utility, and can be used as input for the **db_load** utility.

  Because the key/data pairs are output in page order as opposed to the sort order used by **db_dump**, using Db::verify to dump key/data pairs normally produces less than optimal loads for Btree databases.

In addition, the following flags may be set by bitwise inclusively **OR**'ing them into the **flags** parameter:

- DB_AGGRESSIVE   Output all the key/data pairs in the file that can be found. By default, Db::verify does not assume corruption. For example, if a key/data pair on a page is marked as deleted, it is not then written to the output file. When DB_AGGRESSIVE is specified, corruption is assumed, and any key/data pair that can be found is written. In this case, key/data pairs that are corrupted or have been deleted may appear in the output (even if the file being salvaged is in no way corrupt), and the output will almost certainly require editing before being loaded into a database.

- DB_NOORDERCHK   Skip the database checks for btree and duplicate sort order and for hashing.

The Db::verify method normally verifies that btree keys and duplicate items are correctly sorted and hash keys are correctly hashed. If the file being verified contains multiple databases using differing sorting or hashing algorithms, some of them must necessarily fail database verification as only one sort order or hash function can be specified before Db::verify is called. To verify files with multiple databases having differing sorting orders or hashing functions, first perform verification of the file as a whole by using the DB_NOORDERCHK flag and then individually verify the sort order and hashing function for each database in the file using the DB_ORDERCHKONLY flag.

- DB_ORDERCHKONLY   Perform the database checks for btree and duplicate sort order and for hashing, skipped by DB_NOORDERCHK.

  When this flag is specified, a database argument should also be specified, indicating the database in the physical file which is to be checked. This flag is only safe to use on databases that have already successfully been verified using Db::verify with the DB_NOORDERCHK flag set.

The database argument must be set to NULL, except when the DB_ORDERCHKONLY flag is set.

The Db::verify method either returns a non-zero error value or throws an exception that encapsulates a non-zero error value on failure, 0 on success, and DB_VERIFY_BAD if a database is corrupted. When the DB_SALVAGE flag is specified, the DB_VERIFY_BAD return means that all key/data pairs in the file may not have been successfully output.

Environment Variables

- DB_HOME   If the **dbenv** argument to **db_create** was initialized using **DbEnv::open**, the environment variable **DB_HOME** may be used as the path of the database environment home. Specifically, Db::verify is affected by the configuration value DB_DATA_DIR.

Errors

The Db::verify method may fail and throw an exception or return a non-zero error for the following conditions:

- EINVAL   An invalid flag value or parameter was specified.

The Db::verify method may fail and throw an exception or return a non-zero error for errors specified for other Berkeley DB and C library or system methods. If a catastrophic error has occurred, the Db::verify method may fail and either return DB_RUNRECOVERY or throw an exception encapsulating DB_RUNRECOVERY, in which case all subsequent Berkeley DB calls will fail in the same way.

DbEnv

```
#include <db_cxx.h>

class DbEnv {
public:
        DbEnv(u_int32 flags);
        ~DbEnv();
        ...
};
```

Description

This manual page describes the specific details of the DbEnv class, which is the center of the Berkeley DB environment.

The following **flags** value may be specified:

- DB_CLIENT   Create a client environment to connect to a server.

  The DB_CLIENT flag indicates to the system that this environment is remote on a server. The use of this flag causes the environment methods to use functions that call a server instead of local functions. Prior to making any environment or database method calls, the application must call the **DbEnv::set_server** function to establish the connection to the server.

- DB_CXX_NO_EXCEPTIONS   The Berkeley DB C++ API supports two different error behaviors. By default, whenever an error occurs, an exception is thrown that encapsulates the error information. This generally allows for cleaner logic for transaction processing because a try block can surround a single transaction. However, if DB_CXX_NO_EXCEPTIONS is specified, exceptions are not thrown, instead each individual function returns an error code.

DbEnv::close

```
#include <db_cxx.h>

DbEnv::close(u_int32_t flags);
```

Description

The DbEnv::close method closes the Berkeley DB environment, freeing any allocated resources and closing any underlying subsystems.

Calling DbEnv::close does not imply closing any databases that were opened in the environment, and all databases opened in the environment should be closed before the environment is closed.

The **flags** parameter is currently unused, and must be set to 0.

Where the environment was initialized with the DB_INIT_LOCK flag, calling DbEnv::close does not release any locks still held by the closing process, providing functionality for long-lived locks. Processes that wish to have all their locks released can do so by issuing the appropriate **DbEnv::lock_vec** call.

Where the environment was initialized with the DB_INIT_MPOOL flag, calling DbEnv::close implies calls to **DbMpoolFile::close** for any remaining open files in the memory pool that were returned to this process by calls to **DbMpoolFile::open**. It does not imply a call to **DbMpoolFile::sync** for those files.

Where the environment was initialized with the DB_INIT_TXN flag, calling DbEnv::close aborts any unresolved transactions. Applications should not depend on this behavior for transactions involving Berkeley DB databases, all such transactions should be explicitly resolved. The problem with depending on this semantic is that aborting an unresolved transaction involving database operations requires a database handle. As the database handles should have been closed before calling DbEnv::close, it will not be possible to abort the transaction, and recovery will have to be run on the Berkeley DB environment before further operations are done.

In multithreaded applications, only a single thread may call DbEnv::close.

Once DbEnv::close has been called, regardless of its return, the Berkeley DB environment handle may not be accessed again.

The DbEnv::close method either returns a non-zero error value or throws an exception that encapsulates a non-zero error value on failure, and returns 0 on success.

Errors

The DbEnv::close method may fail and throw an exception or return a non-zero error for errors specified for other Berkeley DB and C library or system methods. If a catastrophic error has occurred, the DbEnv::close method may fail and either return DB_RUNRECOVERY or throw an exception encapsulating DB_RUNRECOVERY, in which case all subsequent Berkeley DB calls will fail in the same way.

DbEnv::err

```
#include <db_cxx.h>

DbEnv::err(int error, const char *fmt, ...);

DbEnv::errx(const char *fmt, ...);

Db::err(int error, const char *fmt, ...);

Db::errx(const char *fmt, ...);
```

Description

The DbEnv::err, DbEnv::errx, Db::err, and Db::errx methods provide error-messaging functionality for applications written using the Berkeley DB library.

The DbEnv::err method constructs an error message consisting of the following elements:

- **An optional prefix string**   If no error callback method has been set using the **DbEnv::set_errcall** method, any prefix string specified using the **DbEnv::set_errpfx** method, followed by two separating characters: a colon and a <space> character.

- **An optional printf-style message**   The supplied message **fmt**, if non-NULL, where the ANSI C X3.159-1989 (ANSI C) printf function specifies how subsequent arguments are converted for output.

- **A separator**   Two separating characters: a colon and a <space> character.

- **A standard error string**   The standard system or Berkeley DB library error string associated with the **error** value, as returned by the **DbEnv::strerror** method.

This constructed error message is then handled as follows:

- If an error callback method has been set (see **Db::set_errcall** and **DbEnv::set_errcall**), that method is called with two arguments: any prefix string specified (see **Db::set_errpfx** and **DbEnv::set_errpfx**) and the error message.

- If a C library FILE * has been set (see **Db::set_errfile** and **DbEnv::set_errfile**), the error message is written to that output stream.

- If a C++ ostream has been set (see **DbEnv::set_error_stream**), the error message is written to that stream.

- If none of these output options has been configured, the error message is written to stderr, the standard error output stream.

The DbEnv::errx and Db::errx methods perform identically to the DbEnv::err and Db::err methods, except that they do not append the final separator characters and standard error string to the error message.

DbEnv::lock_detect

```
#include <db_cxx.h>

int
DbEnv::lock_detect(u_int32_t flags, u_int32_t atype, int *aborted);
```

Description

The DbEnv::lock_detect method runs one iteration of the deadlock detector. The deadlock detector traverses the lock table; and for each deadlock it finds, marks one of the participating transactions for abort.

The **flags** value must be set to 0 or by bitwise inclusively **OR**'ing together one or more of the following values.

- DB_LOCK_CONFLICT   Only run the deadlock detector if a lock conflict has occurred since the last time that the deadlock detector was run.

The **atype** parameter specifies which transaction to abort in the case of deadlock. It must be set to one of possible arguments listed for the **DbEnv::set_lk_detect** interface.

If the **aborted** parameter is non-NULL, the memory location it references will be set to the number of transactions aborted by the DbEnv::lock_detect method.

The DbEnv::lock_detect method either returns a non-zero error value or throws an exception that encapsulates a non-zero error value on failure, and returns 0 on success.

Errors

The DbEnv::lock_detect method may fail and throw an exception or return a non-zero error for errors specified for other Berkeley DB and C library or system methods. If a catastrophic error has occurred, the DbEnv::lock_detect method may fail and either return DB_RUNRECOVERY or throw an exception encapsulating DB_RUNRECOVERY, in which case all subsequent Berkeley DB calls will fail in the same way.

DbEnv::lock_get

```
#include <db_cxx.h>

int
DbEnv::lock_get(u_int32_t locker, u_int32_t flags,
    const Dbt *obj, const db_lockmode_t lock_mode, DbLock *lock);
```

Description

The DbEnv::lock_get method acquires a lock from the lock table, returning information about it in the **lock** argument.

The **locker** argument specified to DbEnv::lock_get is an unsigned 32-bit integer quantity. It represents the entity requesting or releasing the lock.

The **flags** value must be set to 0 or the following value:

- DB_LOCK_NOWAIT If a lock cannot be granted because the requested lock conflicts with an existing lock, return immediately instead of waiting for the lock to become available.

The **obj** argument is an untyped byte string that specifies the object to be locked or released. Applications using the locking subsystem directly while also doing locking via the Berkeley DB access methods must take care not to inadvertently lock objects that happen to be equal to the unique file IDs used to lock files. See "Access Method Locking Conventions" for more information.

The **mode** argument is an index into the environment's lock conflict array. See **DbEnv::set_lk_conflicts** and "Standard Lock Modes" for a description of that array.

The DbEnv::lock_get method may return or throw an exception encapsulating one of the following values:

DB_LOCK_NOTGRANTED

A lock was requested that could not be immediately granted and the flags parameter was set to DB_LOCK_NOWAIT.

Otherwise, the DbEnv::lock_get method either returns a non-zero error value or throws an exception that encapsulates a non-zero error value on failure, and returns 0 on success.

Errors

The DbEnv::lock_get method may fail and throw an exception or return a non-zero error for the following conditions:

- DB_LOCK_DEADLOCK   The operation was selected to resolve a deadlock.
- EINVAL   An invalid flag value or parameter was specified.
- ENOMEM   The maximum number of locks has been reached.

The DbEnv::lock_get method may fail and throw an exception or return a non-zero error for errors specified for other Berkeley DB and C library or system methods. If a catastrophic error has occurred, the DbEnv::lock_get method may fail and either return DB_RUNRECOVERY or throw an exception encapsulating DB_RUNRECOVERY, in which case all subsequent Berkeley DB calls will fail in the same way.

DbEnv::lock_id

```
#include <db_cxx.h>

int
DbEnv::lock_id(u_int32_t *idp);
```

Description

The DbEnv::lock_id method copies a locker ID, which is guaranteed to be unique in the specified lock table, into the memory location referenced by **idp**.

The DbEnv::lock_id method either returns a non-zero error value or throws an exception that encapsulates a non-zero error value on failure, and returns 0 on success.

Errors

The DbEnv::lock_id method may fail and throw an exception or return a non-zero error for errors specified for other Berkeley DB and C library or system methods. If a catastrophic error has occurred, the DbEnv::lock_id method may fail and either return DB_RUNRECOVERY or throw an exception encapsulating DB_RUNRECOVERY, in which case all subsequent Berkeley DB calls will fail in the same way.

DbEnv::lock_stat

```
#include <db_cxx.h>

extern "C" {
    typedef void *(*db_malloc_fcn_type)(size_t);
};
int
DbEnv::lock_stat(DB_LOCK_STAT **statp, db_malloc_fcn_type db_malloc);
```

Description

The DbEnv::lock_stat method creates a statistical structure and copies a pointer to it into a user-specified memory location.

Statistical structures are created in allocated memory. If **db_malloc** is non-NULL, it is called to allocate the memory; otherwise, the library function **malloc**(3) is used. The function **db_malloc** must match the calling conventions of the **malloc**(3) library routine. Regardless, the caller is responsible for deallocating the returned memory. To deallocate returned memory, free the returned memory reference, references inside the returned memory do not need to be individually freed.

The lock region statistics are stored in a structure of type DB_LOCK_STAT. The following DB_LOCK_STAT fields will be filled in:

- u_int32_t st_lastid; The last allocated lock ID.
- u_int32_t st_nmodes; The number of lock modes.
- u_int32_t st_maxlocks; The maximum number of locks possible.
- u_int32_t st_maxlockers; The maximum number of lockers possible.
- u_int32_t st_maxobjects; The maximum number of objects possible.
- u_int32_t st_nlocks; The number of current locks.
- u_int32_t st_maxnlocks; The maximum number of locks at any one time.
- u_int32_t st_nlockers; The number of current lockers.
- u_int32_t st_maxnlockers; The maximum number of lockers at any one time.
- u_int32_t st_nobjects; The number of current objects.
- u_int32_t st_maxnobjects; The maximum number of objects at any one time.
- u_int32_t st_nrequests; The total number of locks requested.
- u_int32_t st_nreleases; The total number of locks released.
- u_int32_t st_nnowaits; The total number of lock requests that failed because DB_LOCK_NOWAIT was set.
- u_int32_t st_nconflicts; The total number of locks not immediately available due to conflicts.
- u_int32_t st_ndeadlocks; The number of deadlocks detected.
- u_int32_t st_regsize; The size of the region.
- u_int32_t st_region_wait; The number of times that a thread of control was forced to wait before obtaining the region lock.
- u_int32_t st_region_nowait; The number of times that a thread of control was able to obtain the region lock without waiting.

The DbEnv::lock_stat method either returns a non-zero error value or throws an exception that encapsulates a non-zero error value on failure, and returns 0 on success.

Errors

The DbEnv::lock_stat method may fail and throw an exception or return a non-zero error for errors specified for other Berkeley DB and C library or system methods. If a catastrophic error has occurred, the DbEnv::lock_stat method may fail and either return DB_RUNRECOVERY or throw an exception encapsulating DB_RUNRECOVERY, in which case all subsequent Berkeley DB calls will fail in the same way.

DbEnv::lock_vec

```
#include <db_cxx.h>

int
DbEnv::lock_vec(u_int32_t locker, u_int32_t flags,
    DB_LOCKREQ list[], int nlist, DB_LOCKREQ **elistp);
```

Description

The DbEnv::lock_vec method atomically obtains and releases one or more locks from the lock table. The DbEnv::lock_vec method is intended to support acquisition or trading of multiple locks under one lock table semaphore, as is needed for lock coupling or in multi-granularity locking for lock escalation.

The **locker** argument specified to DbEnv::lock_vec is an unsigned 32-bit integer quantity. It represents the entity requesting or releasing the lock.

The **flags** value must be set to 0 or the following value:

- DB_LOCK_NOWAIT   If a lock cannot be immediately granted because the requested lock conflicts with an existing lock, return instead of waiting for the lock to become available.

The **list** array provided to DbEnv::lock_vec is typedef'd as DB_LOCKREQ. A DB_LOCKREQ structure has at least the following fields, which must be initialized before calling DbEnv::lock_vec:

- lockop_t op;   The operation to be performed, which must be set to one of the following values:

  - DB_LOCK_GET   Get a lock, as defined by the values of **locker**, **obj**, and **mode**. Upon return from DbEnv::lock_vec, if the **lock** field is non-NULL, a reference to the acquired lock is stored there. (This reference is invalidated by any call to DbEnv::lock_vec or **DbLock::put** that releases the lock.)

  - DB_LOCK_PUT   The lock referenced by the contents of the **lock** field is released.

  - DB_LOCK_PUT_ALL   All locks held by the **locker** are released. (Any locks acquired as a part of the current call to DbEnv::lock_vec that appear after the DB_LOCK_PUT_ALL entry are not considered for this operation).

  - DB_LOCK_PUT_OBJ   All locks held on the object **obj** are released. The **mode** and **locker** parameters are ignored. Note that any locks acquired as a part of the current call to DbEnv::lock_vec that occur before the DB_LOCK_PUT_OBJ will also be released; those acquired afterwards will not be released.

- const Dbt obj; An untyped byte string that specifies the object to be locked or released. Applications using the locking subsystem directly while also doing locking via the Berkeley DB access methods must take care not to inadvertently lock objects that happen to be equal to the unique file IDs used to lock files. See "Access Method Locking Conventions" for more information.

- const lockmode_t mode; The lock mode, used as an index into the environment's lock conflict array. See **DbEnv::set_lk_conflicts** and **Standard Lock Modes** for a description of that array.

- DB_LOCK lock; A lock reference.

The **nlist** argument specifies the number of elements in the **list** array.

If any of the requested locks cannot be acquired, or if any of the locks to be released cannot be released, the operations before the failing operation are guaranteed to have completed successfully, and DbEnv::lock_vec returns a non-zero value. In addition, if **elistp** is not NULL, it is set to point to the DB_LOCKREQ entry that was being processed when the error occurred.

The DbEnv::lock_vec method may return or throw an exception encapsulating one of the following values:

- DB_LOCK_NOTGRANTED A lock was requested that could not be immediately granted and the **flag** parameter was set to DB_LOCK_NOWAIT. In this case, if non-NULL, **elistp** identifies the request that was not granted.

Otherwise, the DbEnv::lock_vec method either returns a non-zero error value or throws an exception that encapsulates a non-zero error value on failure, and returns 0 on success.

Errors

The DbEnv::lock_vec method may fail and throw an exception or return a non-zero error for the following conditions:

- DB_LOCK_DEADLOCK The operation was selected to resolve a deadlock.

- EINVAL An invalid flag value or parameter was specified.

- ENOMEM The maximum number of locks has been reached.

The DbEnv::lock_vec method may fail and throw an exception or return a non-zero error for errors specified for other Berkeley DB and C library or system methods. If a catastrophic error has occurred, the DbEnv::lock_vec method may fail and either return DB_RUNRECOVERY or throw an exception encapsulating DB_RUNRECOVERY, in which case all subsequent Berkeley DB calls will fail in the same way.

DbEnv::log_archive

```
#include <db_cxx.h>

extern "C" {
        typedef void *(*db_malloc_fcn_type)(size_t);
};
int
DbEnv::log_archive(char *(*listp)[],
    u_int32_t flags, db_malloc_fcn_type db_malloc);
```

Description

The DbEnv::log_archive method creates a NULL-terminated array of log or database file names and copies a pointer to them into the user-specified memory location **listp**.

By default, DbEnv::log_archive returns the names of all of the log files that are no longer in use (for example, no longer involved in active transactions), and that may safely be archived for catastrophic recovery and then removed from the system. If there were no file names to return, the memory location referenced by **listp** will be set to NULL.

Arrays of log file names are created in allocated memory. If **db_malloc** is non-NULL, it is called to allocate the memory; otherwise, the library function **malloc**(3) is used. The function **db_malloc** must match the calling conventions of the **malloc**(3) library routine. Regardless, the caller is responsible for deallocating the returned memory. To deallocate returned memory, free the returned memory reference; references inside the returned memory do not need to be individually freed.

The **flags** value must be set to 0 or by bitwise inclusively **OR**'ing together one or more of the following values.

- DB_ARCH_ABS   All pathnames are returned as absolute pathnames, instead of relative to the database home directory.

- DB_ARCH_DATA   Return the database files that need to be archived in order to recover the database from catastrophic failure. If any of the database files have not been accessed during the lifetime of the current log files, DbEnv::log_archive will not include them in this list. It is also possible that some of the files referenced in the log have since been deleted from the system.

- DB_ARCH_LOG   Return all the log filenames, regardless of whether or not they are in use.

The DB_ARCH_DATA and DB_ARCH_LOG flags are mutually exclusive.

See the **db_archive** manual page for more information on database archival procedures.

The DbEnv::log_archive method either returns a non-zero error value or throws an exception that encapsulates a non-zero error value on failure, and returns 0 on success.

Bugs

In a threaded application (that is, one where the environment was created with the DB_THREAD flag specified), calling DbEnv::log_archive with the DB_ARCH_DATA flag will fail, returning EINVAL. To work around this problem, reopen the log explicitly without specifying DB_THREAD. This restriction is expected to be removed in a future version of Berkeley DB.

Errors

The DbEnv::log_archive method may fail and throw an exception or return a non-zero error for the following conditions:

- EINVAL   An invalid flag value or parameter was specified.

  The log was corrupted.

The DbEnv::log_archive method may fail and throw an exception or return a non-zero error for errors specified for other Berkeley DB and C library or system methods. If a catastrophic error has occurred, the DbEnv::log_archive method may fail and either return DB_RUNRECOVERY or throw an exception encapsulating DB_RUNRECOVERY, in which case all subsequent Berkeley DB calls will fail in the same way.

DbEnv::log_compare

```
#include <db_cxx.h>

static int
DbEnv::log_compare(const DbLsn *lsn0, const DbLsn *lsn1);
```

Description

The DbEnv::log_compare method allows the caller to compare two **DbLsn** objects, returning 0 if they are equal, 1 if **lsn0** is greater than **lsn1**, and -1 if **lsn0** is less than **lsn1**.

DbEnv::log_file

```
#include <db_cxx.h>

int
DbEnv::log_file(const DbLsn *lsn, char *namep, size_t len);
```

Description

The DbEnv::log_file method maps **DbLsn** objects to filenames, copying the name of the file containing the record named by **lsn** into the memory location referenced by **namep**.

The **len** argument is the length of the **namep** buffer in bytes. If **namep** is too short to hold the filename, DbEnv::log_file will return ENOMEM. (Log filenames are normally quite short—on the order of 10 characters.)

This mapping of **DbLsn** objects to files is needed for database administration. For example, a transaction manager typically records the earliest **DbLsn** needed for restart, and the database administrator may want to archive log files to tape when they contain only **DbLsn** entries before the earliest one needed for restart.

The DbEnv::log_file method either returns a non-zero error value or throws an exception that encapsulates a non-zero error value on failure, and returns 0 on success.

Errors

The DbEnv::log_file method may fail and throw an exception or return a non-zero error for the following conditions:

- ENOMEM   The supplied buffer was too small to hold the log file name.

The DbEnv::log_file method may fail and throw an exception or return a non-zero error for errors specified for other Berkeley DB and C library or system methods. If a catastrophic error has occurred, the DbEnv::log_file method may fail and either return DB_RUNRECOVERY or throw an exception encapsulating DB_RUNRECOVERY, in which case all subsequent Berkeley DB calls will fail in the same way.

DbEnv::log_flush

```
#include <db_cxx.h>

int
DbEnv::log_flush(const DbLsn *lsn);
```

Description

The DbEnv::log_flush method guarantees that all log records whose **DbLsn** values are less than or equal to the **lsn** argument have been written to disk. If **lsn** is NULL, all records in the log are flushed.

The DbEnv::log_flush method either returns a non-zero error value or throws an exception that encapsulates a non-zero error value on failure, and returns 0 on success.

Errors

The DbEnv::log_flush method may fail and throw an exception or return a non-zero error for the following conditions:

- EINVAL   An invalid flag value or parameter was specified.

The DbEnv::log_flush method may fail and throw an exception or return a non-zero error for errors specified for other Berkeley DB and C library or system methods. If a catastrophic error has occurred, the DbEnv::log_flush method may fail and either return DB_RUNRECOVERY or throw an exception encapsulating DB_RUNRECOVERY, in which case all subsequent Berkeley DB calls will fail in the same way.

DbEnv::log_get

```
#include <db_cxx.h>

int
DbEnv::log_get(DbLsn *lsn, Dbt *data, u_int32_t flags);
```

Description

The DbEnv::log_get method implements a cursor inside of the log, retrieving records from the log according to the **lsn** and **flags** arguments.

The data field of the **data** structure is set to the record retrieved, and the size field indicates the number of bytes in the record. See **Dbt** for a description of other fields in the **data** structure. When multiple threads are using the **DbEnv** handle concurrently, one of the DB_DBT_MALLOC, DB_DBT_REALLOC, or DB_DBT_USERMEM flags must be specified for any **Dbt** used for data retrieval.

The **flags** argument must be set to exactly one of the following values:

- DB_CHECKPOINT   The last record written with the DB_CHECKPOINT flag specified to the **DbEnv::log_put** method is returned in the **data** argument. The **lsn** argument is overwritten with the **DbLsn** of the record returned. If no record has been previously written with the DB_CHECKPOINT flag specified, the first record in the log is returned.

    If the log is empty, the DbEnv::log_get method will return DB_NOTFOUND.

- DB_FIRST   The first record from any of the log files found in the log directory is returned in the **data** argument. The **lsn** argument is overwritten with the **DbLsn** of the record returned.

    If the log is empty, the DbEnv::log_get method will return DB_NOTFOUND.

- DB_LAST   The last record in the log is returned in the **data** argument. The **lsn** argument is overwritten with the **DbLsn** of the record returned.

    If the log is empty, the DbEnv::log_get method will return DB_NOTFOUND.

- DB_NEXT, DB_PREV   The current log position is advanced to the next (previous) record in the log, and that record is returned in the **data** argument. The **lsn** argument is overwritten with the **DbLsn** of the record returned.

    If the pointer has not been initialized via DB_FIRST, DB_LAST, DB_SET, DB_NEXT, or DB_PREV, DbEnv::log_get will return the first (last) record in the log. If the last (first) log record has already been returned or the log is empty, the DbEnv::log_get method will return DB_NOTFOUND.

    If the log was opened with the DB_THREAD flag set, calls to DbEnv::log_get with the DB_NEXT (DB_PREV) flag set will return EINVAL.

- DB_CURRENT   Return the log record currently referenced by the log.

If the log pointer has not been initialized via DB_FIRST, DB_LAST, DB_SET, DB_NEXT, or DB_PREV, or if the log was opened with the DB_THREAD flag set, DbEnv::log_get will return EINVAL.

- DB_SET   Retrieve the record specified by the **lsn** argument. If the specified **DbLsn** is invalid (for example, does not appear in the log) DbEnv::log_get will return EINVAL.

Otherwise, the DbEnv::log_get method either returns a non-zero error value or throws an exception that encapsulates a non-zero error value on failure, and returns 0 on success.

Errors

The DbEnv::log_get method may fail and throw an exception or return a non-zero error for the following conditions:

- EINVAL   An invalid flag value or parameter was specified.

    The DB_NEXT or DB_PREV flags were set and the log was opened with the DB_THREAD flag set.

    The DB_CURRENT flag was set and the log pointer had not yet been initialized.

    The DB_SET flag was set and the specified log sequence number does not exist.

The DbEnv::log_get method may fail and throw an exception or return a non-zero error for errors specified for other Berkeley DB and C library or system methods. If a catastrophic error has occurred, the DbEnv::log_get method may fail and either return DB_RUNRECOVERY or throw an exception encapsulating DB_RUNRECOVERY, in which case all subsequent Berkeley DB calls will fail in the same way.

DbEnv::log_put

```
#include <db_cxx.h>

int
DbEnv::log_put(DbLsn *lsn, const Dbt *data, u_int32_t flags);
```

Description

The DbEnv::log_put method appends records to the log. The **DbLsn** of the put record is returned in the **lsn** argument. The **flags** argument may be set to one of the following values:

- DB_CHECKPOINT   The log should write a checkpoint record, recording any information necessary to make the log structures recoverable after a crash.

- DB_CURLSN   The **DbLsn** of the next record to be put is returned in the **lsn** argument.

- DB_FLUSH   The log is forced to disk after this record is written, guaranteeing that all records with **DbLsn** values less than or equal to the one being put are on disk before this function returns (this function is most often used for a transaction commit, see **DbTxn::commit** for more information).

The caller is responsible for providing any necessary structure to data. (For example, in a write-ahead logging protocol, the application must understand what part of data is an operation code, what part is redo information, and what part is undo information. In addition, most transaction managers will store in data the DbLsn of the previous log record for the same transaction, to support chaining back through the transaction's log records during undo.)

The DbEnv::log_put method either returns a non-zero error value or throws an exception that encapsulates a non-zero error value on failure, and returns 0 on success.

Errors

The **DbEnv::log_flush** method may fail and throw an exception or return a non-zero error for the following conditions:

- EINVAL   An invalid flag value or parameter was specified.

    The record to be logged is larger than the maximum log record.

The DbEnv::log_put method may fail and throw an exception or return a non-zero error for errors specified for other Berkeley DB and C library or system methods. If a catastrophic error has occurred, the DbEnv::log_put method may fail and either return DB_RUNRECOVERY or throw an exception encapsulating DB_RUNRECOVERY, in which case all subsequent Berkeley DB calls will fail in the same way.

DbEnv::log_register

```
#include <db_cxx.h>

int
DbEnv::log_register(Db *dbp, const char *name);
```

Description

The DbEnv::log_register method registers a filename with the specified Berkeley DB environment's log manager. The log manager records all filename mappings at each checkpoint so that a recovery process can identify the file to which a record in the log refers.

The **dbp** argument should be a reference to the **Db** object being registered. The **name** argument should be a filename appropriate for opening the file in the environment, during recovery.

The DbEnv::log_register method either returns a non-zero error value or throws an exception that encapsulates a non-zero error value on failure, and returns 0 on success.

Errors

The DbEnv::log_register method may fail and throw an exception or return a non-zero error for the following conditions:

- EINVAL   An invalid flag value or parameter was specified.

The DbEnv::log_register method may fail and throw an exception or return a non-zero error for errors specified for other Berkeley DB and C library or system methods. If a catastrophic error has occurred, the DbEnv::log_register method may fail and either return DB_RUNRECOVERY or throw an exception encapsulating DB_RUNRECOVERY, in which case all subsequent Berkeley DB calls will fail in the same way.

DbEnv::log_stat

```
#include <db_cxx.h>

extern "C" {
    typedef void *(*db_malloc_fcn_type)(size_t);
};
int
DbEnv::log_stat(DB_LOG_STAT **spp, db_malloc_fcn_type db_malloc);
```

Description

The DbEnv::log_stat method creates a statistical structure and copies a pointer to it into a user-specified memory location.

Statistical structures are created in allocated memory. If **db_malloc** is non-NULL, it is called to allocate the memory; otherwise, the library function **malloc**(3) is used. The function **db_malloc** must match the calling conventions of the **malloc**(3) library routine. Regardless, the caller is responsible for deallocating the returned memory. To deallocate returned memory, free the returned memory reference; references inside the returned memory do not need to be individually freed.

The log region statistics are stored in a structure of type DB_LOG_STAT. The following DB_LOG_STAT fields will be filled in:

- u_int32_t st_magic;   The magic number that identifies a file as a log file.
- u_int32_t st_version;   The version of the log file type.
- u_int32_t st_regsize;   The size of the region.
- int st_mode;   The mode of any created log files.
- u_int32_t st_lg_bsize;   The in-memory log record cache size.
- u_int32_t st_lg_max;   The maximum size of any individual file comprising the log.
- u_int32_t st_w_mbytes;   The number of megabytes written to this log.
- u_int32_t st_w_bytes;   The number of bytes over and above **st_w_mbytes** written to this log.
- u_int32_t st_wc_mbytes;   The number of megabytes written to this log since the last checkpoint.
- u_int32_t st_wc_bytes;   The number of bytes over and above **st_wc_mbytes** written to this log since the last checkpoint.
- u_int32_t st_wcount;   The number of times the log has been written to disk.
- u_int32_t st_wcount_fill;   The number of times the log has been written to disk because the in-memory log record cache filled up.

- u_int32_t st_scount; The number of times the log has been flushed to disk.

- u_int32_t st_cur_file; The current log file number.

- u_int32_t st_cur_offset; The byte offset in the current log file.

- u_int32_t st_region_wait; The number of times that a thread of control was forced to wait before obtaining the region lock.

- u_int32_t st_region_nowait; The number of times that a thread of control was able to obtain the region lock without waiting.

The DbEnv::log_stat method either returns a non-zero error value or throws an exception that encapsulates a non-zero error value on failure, and returns 0 on success.

Errors

The DbEnv::log_stat method may fail and throw an exception or return a non-zero error for errors specified for other Berkeley DB and C library or system methods. If a catastrophic error has occurred, the DbEnv::log_stat method may fail and either return DB_RUNRECOVERY or throw an exception encapsulating DB_RUNRECOVERY, in which case all subsequent Berkeley DB calls will fail in the same way.

DbEnv::log_unregister

```
#include <db_cxx.h>

int
DbEnv::log_unregister(int32_t DB *dbp);
```

Description

The DbEnv::log_unregister method function unregisters the file represented by the **dbp** parameter from the Berkeley DB environment's log manager.

The DbEnv::log_unregister method either returns a non-zero error value or throws an exception that encapsulates a non-zero error value on failure, and returns 0 on success.

Errors

The DbEnv::log_unregister method may fail and throw an exception or return a non-zero error for the following conditions:

- EINVAL An invalid flag value or parameter was specified.

The DbEnv::log_unregister method may fail and throw an exception or return a non-zero error for errors specified for other Berkeley DB and C library or system methods. If a catastrophic error has occurred, the DbEnv::log_unregister method may fail and either return DB_RUNRECOVERY or throw an exception encapsulating DB_RUNRECOVERY, in which case all subsequent Berkeley DB calls will fail in the same way.

DbEnv::memp_register

```
#include <db_cxx.h>
extern "C" {
    typedef int (*pgin_fcn_type)(DB_ENV *dbenv,
            db_pgno_t pgno, void *pgaddr, DBT *pgcookie);
    typedef int (*pgout_fcn_type)(DB_ENV *dbenv,
            db_pgno_t pgno, void *pgaddr, DBT *pgcookie);
};
int
DbEnv::memp_register(int ftype,
    pgin_fcn_type pgin_fcn, pgout_fcn_type pgout_fcn);
```

Description

The DbEnv::memp_register method registers page-in and page-out functions for files of type **ftype** in the specified pool.

If the **pgin_fcn** function is non-NULL, it is called each time a page is read into the memory pool from a file of type **ftype**, or a page is created for a file of type **ftype** (see the DB_MPOOL_CREATE flag for the **DbMpoolFile::get** method).

If the **pgout_fcn** function is non-NULL, it is called each time a page is written to a file of type **ftype**.

Both the **pgin_fcn** and **pgout_fcn** functions are called with a reference to the current environment, the page number, a pointer to the page being read or written, and any argument **pgcookie** that was specified to the **DbMpoolFile::open** function when the file was opened. The **pgin_fcn** and **pgout_fcn** functions should return 0 on success, and an applicable non-zero **errno** value on failure, in which case the shared memory pool interface routine (and, by extension, any Berkeley DB library function) calling it will also fail, returning that **errno** value.

The purpose of the DbEnv::memp_register function is to support processing when pages are entered into or flushed from the pool. A file type must be specified to make it possible for unrelated threads or processes that are sharing a pool to evict each other's pages from the pool. Applications should call DbEnv::memp_register, during initialization, for each type of file requiring input or output processing that will be sharing the underlying pool. (No registry is necessary for the standard Berkeley DB access method types, as **Db::open** registers them separately.)

If a thread or process does not call DbEnv::memp_register for a file type, it is impossible for it to evict pages for any file requiring input or output processing from the pool. For this reason, DbEnv::memp_register should always be called by each application sharing a pool for each type of file included in the pool, regardless of whether or not the application itself uses files of that type.

There are no standard values for **ftype**, **pgin_fcn**, **pgout_fcn**, and **pgcookie**, except that the **ftype** value for a file must be a non-zero positive number because negative numbers are reserved for internal use by the Berkeley DB library. For this reason, applications sharing a pool must coordinate their values amongst themselves.

The DbEnv::memp_register method either returns a non-zero error value or throws an exception that encapsulates a non-zero error value on failure, and returns 0 on success.

Errors

The DbEnv::memp_register method may fail and throw an exception or return a non-zero error for errors specified for other Berkeley DB and C library or system methods. If a catastrophic error has occurred, the DbEnv::memp_register method may fail and either return DB_RUNRECOVERY or throw an exception encapsulating DB_RUNRECOVERY, in which case all subsequent Berkeley DB calls will fail in the same way.

DbEnv::memp_stat

```
#include <db_cxx.h>
extern "C" {
    typedef void *(*db_malloc_fcn_type)(size_t);
};
int
DbEnv::memp_stat(DB_MPOOL_STAT **gsp,
    DB_MPOOL_FSTAT *(*fsp)[], db_malloc_fcn_type db_malloc);
```

Description

The DbEnv::memp_stat method method creates statistical structures and copies pointers to them into user-specified memory locations. The statistics include the number of files participating in the pool, the active pages in the pool, and information about how effective the cache has been.

Statistical structures are created in allocated memory. If **db_malloc** is non-NULL, it is called to allocate the memory; otherwise, the library function **malloc**(3) is used. The function **db_malloc** must match the calling conventions of the **malloc**(3) library routine. Regardless, the caller is responsible for deallocating the returned memory. To deallocate returned memory, free the returned memory reference; references inside the returned memory do not need to be individually freed.

If **gsp** is non-NULL, the global statistics for the memory pool **mp** are copied into the memory location it references. The global statistics are stored in a structure of type DB_MPOOL_STAT.

The following DB_MPOOL_STAT fields will be filled in:

- size_t st_gbytes;   Gigabytes of cache (total cache size is st_gbytes + st_bytes)
- size_t st_bytes;   Bytes of cache (total cache size is st_gbytes + st_bytes)
- u_int32_t st_ncache;   Number of caches.
- u_int32_t st_regsize;   Individual cache size.
- u_int32_t st_cache_hit;   Requested pages found in the cache.
- u_int32_t st_cache_miss;   Requested pages not found in the cache.
- u_int32_t st_map;   Requested pages mapped into the process' address space (there is no available information about whether or not this request caused disk I/O, although examining the application page fault rate may be helpful).
- u_int32_t st_page_create;   Pages created in the cache.
- u_int32_t st_page_in;   Pages read into the cache.

- u_int32_t st_page_out; Pages written from the cache to the backing file.

- u_int32_t st_ro_evict; Clean pages forced from the cache.

- u_int32_t st_rw_evict; Dirty pages forced from the cache.

- u_int32_t st_hash_buckets; Number of hash buckets in buffer hash table.

- u_int32_t st_hash_searches; Total number of buffer hash table lookups.

- u_int32_t st_hash_longest; The longest chain ever encountered in buffer hash table lookups.

- u_int32_t st_hash_examined; Total number of hash elements traversed during hash table lookups.

- u_int32_t st_page_clean; Clean pages currently in the cache.

- u_int32_t st_page_dirty; Dirty pages currently in the cache.

- u_int32_t st_page_trickle; Dirty pages written using the **DbEnv::memp_trickle** interface.

- u_int32_t st_region_wait; The number of times that a thread of control was forced to wait before obtaining the region lock.

- u_int32_t st_region_nowait; The number of times that a thread of control was able to obtain the region lock without waiting.

If **fsp** is non-NULL, a pointer to a NULL-terminated variable length array of statistics for individual files in the memory pool **mp** is copied into the memory location it references. If no individual files currently exist in the memory pool, **fsp** will be set to NULL.

The per-file statistics are stored in structures of type DB_MPOOL_FSTAT. The following DB_MPOOL_FSTAT fields will be filled in for each file in the pool; that is, each element of the array:

- char *file_name; Name of the file.

- size_t st_pagesize; Page size in bytes.

- u_int32_t st_cache_hit; Requested pages found in the cache.

- u_int32_t st_cache_miss; Requested pages not found in the cache.

- u_int32_t st_map; Requested pages mapped into the process' address space.

- u_int32_t st_page_create; Pages created in the cache.

- u_int32_t st_page_in; Pages read into the cache.

- u_int32_t st_page_out; Pages written from the cache to the backing file.

The DbEnv::memp_stat method either returns a non-zero error value or throws an exception that encapsulates a non-zero error value on failure, and returns 0 on success.

Errors

The DbEnv::memp_stat method may fail and throw an exception or return a non-zero error for the following conditions:

- EINVAL   An invalid flag value or parameter was specified.

The DbEnv::memp_stat method may fail and throw an exception or return a non-zero error for errors specified for other Berkeley DB and C library or system methods. If a catastrophic error has occurred, the DbEnv::memp_stat method may fail and either return DB_RUNRECOVERY or throw an exception encapsulating DB_RUNRECOVERY, in which case all subsequent Berkeley DB calls will fail in the same way.

DbEnv::memp_sync

```
#include <db_cxx.h>

int
DbEnv::memp_sync(DbLsn *lsn);
```

Description

The DbEnv::memp_sync method ensures that any modified pages in the pool with log sequence numbers less than the **lsn** argument are written to disk. If **lsn** is NULL, all modified pages in the pool are flushed.

The primary purpose of the DbEnv::memp_sync function is to enable a transaction manager to ensure, as part of a checkpoint, that all pages modified by a certain time have been written to disk. Pages in the pool that cannot be written back to disk immediately (for example, that are currently pinned) are written to disk as soon as it is possible to do so. The expected behavior of the Berkeley DB or other transaction subsystem is to call the DbEnv::memp_sync function and then, if the return indicates that some pages could not be written immediately, to wait briefly and retry again with the same log sequence number until the DbEnv::memp_sync function returns that all pages have been written.

To support the DbEnv::memp_sync functionality, it is necessary that the pool functions know the location of the log sequence number on the page for each file type. This location should be specified when the file is opened using the **DbMpoolFile::open** function. It is not required that the log sequence number be aligned on the page in any way.

The DbEnv::memp_sync method either returns a non-zero error value or throws an exception that encapsulates a non-zero error value on failure, 0 on success, and returns DB_INCOMPLETE if there were pages which need to be written but which DbEnv::memp_sync was unable to write immediately. In addition, if DbEnv::memp_sync returns success, the value of **lsn** will be overwritten with the largest log sequence number from any page that was written by DbEnv::memp_sync to satisfy this request.

Errors

The DbEnv::memp_sync method may fail and throw an exception or return a non-zero error for the following conditions:

- EINVAL   An invalid flag value or parameter was specified.

  ˙The DbEnv::memp_sync function was called without logging having been initialized in the environment.

The DbEnv::memp_sync method may fail and throw an exception or return a non-zero error for errors specified for other Berkeley DB and C library or system methods. If a catastrophic error has occurred, the DbEnv::memp_sync method may fail and either return DB_RUNRECOVERY or throw an exception encapsulating DB_RUNRECOVERY, in which case all subsequent Berkeley DB calls will fail in the same way.

DbEnv::memp_trickle

```
#include <db_cxx.h>

int
DbEnv::memp_trickle(int pct, int *nwrotep);
```

Description

The DbEnv::memp_trickle method ensures that at least **pct** percent of the pages in the shared memory pool are clean by writing dirty pages to their backing files. If the **nwrotep** argument is non-NULL, the number of pages that were written to reach the correct percentage is returned in the memory location it references.

The purpose of the DbEnv::memp_trickle function is to enable a memory pool manager to ensure that a page is always available for reading in new information without having to wait for a write.

The DbEnv::memp_trickle method either returns a non-zero error value or throws an exception that encapsulates a non-zero error value on failure, and returns 0 on success.

Errors

The DbEnv::memp_trickle method may fail and throw an exception or return a non-zero error for the following conditions:

- EINVAL   An invalid flag value or parameter was specified.

The DbEnv::memp_trickle method may fail and throw an exception or return a non-zero error for errors specified for other Berkeley DB and C library or system methods. If a catastrophic error has occurred, the DbEnv::memp_trickle method may fail and either return DB_RUNRECOVERY or throw an exception encapsulating DB_RUNRECOVERY, in which case all subsequent Berkeley DB calls will fail in the same way.

DbEnv::open

```
#include <db_cxx.h>

int
DbEnv::open(const char *db_home, u_int32_t flags, int mode);
```

Description

The DbEnv::open method is the interface for opening the Berkeley DB environment. It provides a structure for creating a consistent environment for processes using one or more of the features of Berkeley DB.

The **db_home** argument to DbEnv::open (and filename resolution in general) is described in "Berkeley DB File Naming."

The **flags** argument specifies the subsystems that are initialized and how the application's environment affects Berkeley DB file naming, among other things.

The **flags** value must be set to 0 or by bitwise inclusively **OR**'ing together one or more of the following values.

Because there are a large number of flags that can be specified, they have been grouped together by functionality. The first group of flags indicate which of the Berkeley DB subsystems should be initialized:

- DB_JOINENV   Join an existing environment. This option allows applications to join an existing environment without knowing which Berkeley DB subsystems the environment supports.

- DB_INIT_CDB   Initialize locking for the **Berkeley DB Concurrent Data Store** product. In this mode, Berkeley DB provides multiple reader/single writer access. The only other subsystem that should be specified with the DB_INIT_CDB flag is DB_INIT_MPOOL.

- DB_INIT_LOCK   Initialize the locking subsystem. This subsystem should be used when multiple processes or threads are going to be reading and writing a Berkeley DB database, so that they do not interfere with each other. If all threads are accessing the database(s) read-only, then locking is unnecessary. When the DB_INIT_LOCK flag is specified, it is usually necessary to run a deadlock detector, as well. See **db_deadlock** and **DbEnv::lock_detect** for more information.

- DB_INIT_LOG   Initialize the logging subsystem. This subsystem should be used when recovery from application or system failure is necessary. If the log region is being created and log files are already present, the log files are reviewed and subsequent log writes are appended to the end of the log, rather than overwriting current log entries.

- DB_INIT_MPOOL   Initialize the shared memory buffer pool subsystem. This subsystem should be used whenever an application is using any Berkeley DB access method.

- DB_INIT_TXN   Initialize the transaction subsystem. This subsystem should be used when recovery and atomicity of multiple operations are important. The DB_INIT_TXN flag implies the DB_INIT_LOG flag.

The second group of flags govern what recovery, if any, is performed when the environment is initialized:

- DB_RECOVER Run normal recovery on this environment before opening it for normal use. If this flag is set, the DB_CREATE flag must also be set since the regions will be removed and re-created.

- DB_RECOVER_FATAL Run catastrophic recovery on this environment before opening it for normal use. If this flag is set, the DB_CREATE flag must also be set since the regions will be removed and re-created.

A standard part of the recovery process is to remove the existing Berkeley DB environment and create a new one in which to perform recovery. If the thread of control performing recovery does not specify the correct region initialization information (for example, the correct memory pool cache size), the result can be an application running in an environment with incorrect cache and other subsystem sizes. For this reason, the thread of control performing recovery should either specify correct configuration information before calling the DbEnv::open method, or it should remove the environment after recovery is completed, leaving creation of the correctly sized environment to a subsequent call to DbEnv::open.

All Berkeley DB recovery processing must be single-threaded; that is, only a single thread of control may perform recovery or access a Berkeley DB environment while recovery is being performed. Because it is not an error to specify DB_RECOVER for an environment for which no recovery is required, it is reasonable programming practice for the thread of control responsible for performing recovery and creating the environment to always specify the DB_CREATE and DB_RECOVER flags during startup.

The DbEnv::open function returns successfully if DB_RECOVER or DB_RECOVER_FATAL is specified and no log files exist, so it is necessary to ensure that all necessary log files are present before running recovery. For further information, consult **db_archive** and **db_recover**.

The third group of flags govern file naming extensions in the environment:

- DB_USE_ENVIRON The Berkeley DB process' environment may be permitted to specify information to be used when naming files; see "Berkeley DB File Naming." Because permitting users to specify which files are used can create security problems, environment information will be used in file naming for all users only if the DB_USE_ENVIRON flag is set.

- DB_USE_ENVIRON_ROOT The Berkeley DB process' environment may be permitted to specify information to be used when naming files; see "Berkeley DB File Naming." Because permitting users to specify which files are used can create security problems, if the DB_USE_ENVIRON_ROOT flag is set, environment information will be used for file naming only for users with appropriate permissions (for example, users with a user-ID of 0 on UNIX systems).

Finally, there are a few additional unrelated flags:

- DB_CREATE Cause Berkeley DB subsystems to create any underlying files, as necessary.

- DB_LOCKDOWN   Lock shared Berkeley DB environment files and memory-mapped databases into memory.

- DB_PRIVATE   Specify that the environment will only be accessed by a single process (although that process may be multithreaded). This flag has two effects on the Berkeley DB environment. First, all underlying data structures are allocated from per-process memory instead of from shared memory that is potentially accessible to more than a single process. Second, mutexes are only configured to work between threads.

  This flag should not be specified if more than a single process is accessing the environment because it is likely to cause database corruption and unpredictable behavior. For example, if both a server application and the Berkeley DB utility **db_stat** are expected to access the environment, the DB_PRIVATE flag should not be specified.

- DB_SYSTEM_MEM   Allocate memory from system shared memory instead of from memory backed by the filesystem. See "Shared Memory Regions" for more information.

- DB_THREAD   Cause the **DbEnv** handle returned by DbEnv::open to be *free-threaded*; that is, usable by multiple threads within a single address space.

On UNIX systems, or in IEEE/ANSI Std 1003.1 (POSIX) environments, all files created by Berkeley DB are created with mode **mode** (as described in **chmod**(2)) and modified by the process' umask value at the time of creation (see **umask**(2)). The group ownership of created files is based on the system and directory defaults, and is not further specified by Berkeley DB. If **mode** is 0, files are created readable and writable by both owner and group. On Windows systems, the mode argument is ignored.

The DbEnv::open method either returns a non-zero error value or throws an exception that encapsulates a non-zero error value on failure, and returns 0 on success.

Environment Variables

- DB_HOME   The environment variable **DB_HOME** may be used as the path of the database home as described in "Berkeley DB File Naming."

Errors

The DbEnv::open method may fail and throw an exception or return a non-zero error for the following conditions:

- EAGAIN   The shared memory region was locked and (repeatedly) unavailable.

- EINVAL   An invalid flag value or parameter was specified.

  The DB_THREAD flag was specified and spinlocks are not implemented for this architecture.

  The DB_HOME or TMPDIR environment variables were set but empty.

  An incorrectly formatted **NAME VALUE** entry or line was found.

- ENOSPC   HP-UX only: a previously created Berkeley DB environment for this process still exists.

The DbEnv::open method may fail and throw an exception or return a non-zero error for errors specified for other Berkeley DB and C library or system methods. If a catastrophic error has occurred, the DbEnv::open method may fail and either return DB_RUNRECOVERY or throw an exception encapsulating DB_RUNRECOVERY, in which case all subsequent Berkeley DB calls will fail in the same way.

DbEnv::remove

```
#include <db_cxx.h>

int
DbEnv::remove(const char *db_home, u_int32_t flags);
```

Description

The DbEnv::remove method destroys a Berkeley DB environment if it is not currently in use. The environment regions, including any backing files, are removed. Any log or database files and the environment directory are not removed.

The **db_home** argument to DbEnv::remove is described in "Berkeley DB File Naming."

If there are processes that have called **DbEnv::open** without calling **DbEnv::close** (that is, there are processes currently using the environment), DbEnv::remove will fail without further action unless the DB_FORCE flag is set, in which case DbEnv::remove will attempt to remove the environment regardless of any processes still using it.

The result of attempting to forcibly destroy the environment when it is in use is unspecified. Processes using an environment often maintain open file descriptors for shared regions within it. On UNIX systems, the environment removal will usually succeed and processes that have already joined the region will continue to run in that region without change; however, processes attempting to join the environment will either fail or create new regions. On other systems (for example, Windows/NT) in which the **unlink**(2) system call will fail if any process has an open file descriptor for the file, the region removal will fail.

Calling DbEnv::remove should not be necessary for most applications because the Berkeley DB environment is cleaned up as part of normal database recovery procedures. However, applications may wish to call DbEnv::remove as part of application shutdown to free up system resources. For example, if the DB_SYSTEM_MEM flag was specified to **DbEnv::open**, it may be useful to call DbEnv::remove in order to release system shared memory segments that have been allocated. Or, on architectures where mutexes require allocation of underlying system resources, it may be useful to call DbEnv::remove in order to release those resources. Alternatively, if recovery is not required because no database state is maintained across failures and no system resources need to be released, it is possible to clean up an environment by simply removing all of the Berkeley DB files in the database environment's directories.

The **flags** value must be set to 0 or by bitwise inclusively **OR**'ing together one or more of the following values.

- DB_FORCE   If the DB_FORCE flag is set, the environment is removed regardless of any processes that may still using it, and no locks are acquired during this process. (Generally, the DB_FORCE flag is only specified when applications were unable to shut down cleanly, and there is a risk that an application may have died holding a Berkeley DB lock.)

- DB_USE_ENVIRON   The Berkeley DB process' environment may be permitted to specify information to be used when naming files; see "Berkeley DB File Naming." Because permitting users to specify which files are used can create security problems, environment information will be used in file naming for all users only if the DB_USE_ENVIRON flag is set.

- DB_USE_ENVIRON_ROOT   The Berkeley DB process' environment may be permitted to specify information to be used when naming files; see "Berkeley DB File Naming." Because permitting users to specify which files are used can create security problems, if the DB_USE_ENVIRON_ROOT flag is set, environment information will be used for file naming only for users with appropriate permissions (for example, users with a user-ID of 0 on UNIX systems).

In multithreaded applications, only a single thread may call DbEnv::remove.

A **DbEnv** handle that has already been used to open an environment should not be used to call the DbEnv::remove method; a new **DbEnv** handle should be created for that purpose.

Once DbEnv::remove has been called, regardless of its return, the Berkeley DB environment handle may not be accessed again.

The DbEnv::remove method either returns a non-zero error value or throws an exception that encapsulates a non-zero error value on failure, and returns 0 on success.

Errors

- EBUSY   The shared memory region was in use and the force flag was not set.

The DbEnv::remove method may fail and throw an exception or return a non-zero error for errors specified for other Berkeley DB and C library or system methods. If a catastrophic error has occurred, the DbEnv::remove method may fail and either return DB_RUNRECOVERY or throw an exception encapsulating DB_RUNRECOVERY, in which case all subsequent Berkeley DB calls will fail in the same way.

DbEnv::set_cachesize

```
#include <db_cxx.h>

int
DbEnv::set_cachesize(u_int32_t gbytes, u_int32_t bytes, int ncache);
```

Description

Set the size of the database's shared memory buffer pool; that is, the cache, to **gbytes** giga-bytes plus **bytes**. The cache should be the size of the normal working data set of the application, with some small amount of additional memory for unusual situations. (Note, the work-ing set is not the same as the number of simultaneously referenced pages, and should be quite a bit larger!)

The default cache size is 256KB, and may not be specified as less than 20KB. Any cache size less than 500MB is automatically increased by 25% to account for buffer pool overhead, cache sizes larger than 500MB are used, as specified. For information on tuning the Berkeley DB cache size, see "Selecting a Cache Size."

It is possible to specify caches to Berkeley DB that are large enough so that they cannot be allocated contiguously on some architectures; for example, some releases of Solaris limit the amount of memory that may be allocated contiguously by a process. If **ncache** is 0 or 1, the cache will be allocated contiguously in memory. If it is greater than 1, the cache will be broken up into **ncache** equally sized separate pieces of memory.

The DbEnv::set_cachesize interface may only be used to configure Berkeley DB before the **DbEnv::open** interface is called.

The DbEnv::set_cachesize method either returns a non-zero error value or throws an exception that encapsulates a non-zero error value on failure, and returns 0 on success.

The database environment's cache size may also be set using the environment's **DB_CONFIG** file. The syntax of the entry in that file is a single line with the string "set_cachesize", one or more whitespace characters, and the three arguments specified to this interface, separated by whitespace characters, for example, "set_cachesize 1 500 2". Because the **DB_CONFIG** file is read when the database environment is opened, it will silently overrule configuration done before that time.

Errors

- EINVAL   An invalid flag value or parameter was specified.

  Called after **DbEnv::open** was called.

  The specified cache size was impossibly small.

DbEnv::set_data_dir

```
#include <db_cxx.h>

int
DbEnv::set_data_dir(const char *dir);
```

Description

Set the path of a directory to be used as the location of the access method database files. Paths specified to the **Db::open** function will be searched relative to this path. Paths set using this interface are additive, and specifying more than one will result in each specified directory being searched for database files. If any directories are specified, created database files will always be created in the first path specified.

If no database directories are specified, database files can only exist in the environment home directory. See "Berkeley DB File Naming" for more information.

For the greatest degree of recoverability from system or application failure, database files and log files should be located on separate physical devices.

The DbEnv::set_data_dir interface may only be used to configure Berkeley DB before the **DbEnv::open** interface is called.

The DbEnv::set_data_dir method either returns a non-zero error value or throws an exception that encapsulates a non-zero error value on failure, and returns 0 on success.

The database environment's data directory may also be set using the environment's **DB_CONFIG** file. The syntax of the entry in that file is a single line with the string "set_data_dir", one or more whitespace characters, and the directory name. Because the **DB_CONFIG** file is read when the database environment is opened, it will silently overrule configuration done before that time.

Errors

- EINVAL   An invalid flag value or parameter was specified.

  Called after **DbEnv::open** was called.

DbEnv::set_errcall

```
#include <db_cxx.h>

void DbEnv::set_errcall(
    void (*db_errcall_fcn)(const char *errpfx, char *msg));
```

Description

When an error occurs in the Berkeley DB library, an exception is thrown or an error return value is returned by the method. In some cases, however, the **errno** value may be insufficient to completely describe the cause of the error, especially during initial application debugging.

The DbEnv::set_errcall method is used to enhance the mechanism for reporting error messages to the application. In some cases when an error occurs, Berkeley DB will call **db_errcall_fcn** with additional error information. The function must be defined with two arguments; the first will be the prefix string (as previously set by **Db::set_errpfx** or **DbEnv::set_errpfx**), the second will be the error message string. It is up to the **db_errcall_fcn** method to display the error message in an appropriate manner.

Alternatively, you can use the **DbEnv::set_error_stream** method to display the additional information via an output stream, or the **Db::set_errfile** or **DbEnv::set_errfile** methods to display the additional information via a C library FILE *. You should not mix these approaches.

This error-logging enhancement does not slow performance or significantly increase application size, and may be run during normal operation as well as during application debugging.

The DbEnv::set_errcall interface may be used to configure Berkeley DB at any time during the life of the application.

DbEnv::set_errfile

```
#include <db_cxx.h>

void DbEnv::set_errfile(FILE *errfile);
```

Description

When an error occurs in the Berkeley DB library, an exception is thrown or an error return value is returned by the method. In some cases, however, the **errno** value may be insufficient to completely describe the cause of the error, especially during initial application debugging.

The DbEnv::set_errfile method is used to enhance the mechanism for reporting error messages to the application by setting a C library FILE ★ to be used for displaying additional Berkeley DB error messages. In some cases, when an error occurs, Berkeley DB will output an additional error message to the specified file reference.

Alternatively, you can use the **DbEnv::set_error_stream** method to display the additional information via an output stream, or the **DbEnv::set_errcall** method to capture the additional error information in a way that does not use either output streams or C library FILE ★'s. You should not mix these approaches.

The error message will consist of the prefix string and a colon (":") (if a prefix string was previously specified using **Db::set_errpfx** or **DbEnv::set_errpfx**), an error string, and a trailing <newline> character.

This error-logging enhancement does not slow performance or significantly increase application size, and may be run during normal operation as well as during application debugging.

The DbEnv::set_errfile interface may be used to configure Berkeley DB at any time during the life of the application.

DbEnv::set_error_stream

```
#include <db_cxx.h>

void DbEnv::set_error_stream(class ostream*);
```

Description

When an error occurs in the Berkeley DB library, an exception is thrown or an **errno** value is returned by the method. In some cases, however, the **errno** value may be insufficient to completely describe the cause of the error, especially during initial application debugging.

The DbEnv::set_error_stream method is used to enhance the mechanism for reporting error messages to the application by setting the C++ ostream used for displaying additional Berkeley DB error messages. In some cases, when an error occurs, Berkeley DB will output an additional error message to the specified stream.

The error message will consist of the prefix string and a colon (":") (if a prefix string was previously specified using **DbEnv::set_errpfx**), an error string, and a trailing <newline> character.

Alternatively, you can use the **DbEnv::set_errfile** method to display the additional information via a C library FILE *, or the **DbEnv::set_errcall** method to capture the additional error information in a way that does not use either output streams or C library FILE *'s. You should not mix these approaches.

This error-logging enhancement does not slow performance or significantly increase application size, and may be run during normal operation as well as during application debugging.

DbEnv::set_errpfx

```
#include <db_cxx.h>

void DbEnv::set_errpfx(const char *errpfx);
```

Description

Set the prefix string that appears before error messages issued by Berkeley DB.

The DbEnv::set_errpfx method does not copy the memory referenced by the **errpfx** argument; rather, it maintains a reference to it. This allows applications to modify the error message prefix at any time without repeatedly calling DbEnv::set_errpfx, but means that the memory must be maintained until the handle is closed.

The DbEnv::set_errpfx interface may be used to configure Berkeley DB at any time during the life of the application.

DbEnv::set_feedback

```
#include <db_cxx.h>

int
DbEnv::set_feedback(
    void (*db_feedback_fcn)(DbEnv *, int opcode, int pct));
```

Description

Some operations performed by the Berkeley DB library can take non-trivial amounts of time. The DbEnv::set_feedback method can be used by applications to monitor progress within these operations.

When an operation is likely to take a long time, Berkeley DB will call the specified callback method. This method must be declared with three arguments: the first will be a reference to the enclosing environment; the second will be a flag value; and the third will be the percent of the operation that has been completed, specified as an integer value between 0 and 100. It is up to the callback method to display this information in an appropriate manner.

The **opcode** argument may take on any of the following values:

• DB_RECOVER   The environment is being recovered.

The DbEnv::set_feedback interface may be used to configure Berkeley DB at any time during the life of the application.

The DbEnv::set_feedback method either returns a non-zero error value or throws an exception that encapsulates a non-zero error value on failure, and returns 0 on success.

DbEnv::set_flags

```
#include <db_cxx.h>

int
DbEnv::set_flags(u_int32_t flags, int onoff);
```

Description

The **flags** value must be set to 0 or by bitwise inclusively **OR**'ing together one or more of the following values. If **onoff** is zero, the specified flags are cleared, otherwise they are set.

- DB_CDB_ALLDB   For Berkeley DB Concurrent Data Store applications, perform locking on an environment-wide basis rather than per-database. This flag may only be used to configure Berkeley DB before the **DbEnv::open** interface is called.

- DB_NOMMAP   Copy read-only database files in this environment into the local cache instead of potentially mapping them into process memory (see the description of the **DbEnv::set_mp_mmapsize** method for further information).

- DB_TXN_NOSYNC   Do not synchronously flush the log on transaction commit or prepare. This means that transactions exhibit the ACI (atomicity, consistency, and isolation) properties, but not D (durability); that is, database integrity will be maintained but it is possible that some number of the most recently committed transactions may be undone during recovery.

  The number of transactions potentially at risk is governed by how often the log is checkpointed (see **db_checkpoint** for more information) and how many log updates can fit into the log buffer.

The DbEnv::set_flags method either returns a non-zero error value or throws an exception that encapsulates a non-zero error value on failure, and returns 0 on success.

The database environment's flag values may also be set using the environment's **DB_CONFIG** file. The syntax of the entry in that file is a single line with the string "set_flags", one or more whitespace characters, and the interface flag argument as a string—for example, "set_flags DB_TXN_NOSYNC". Because the **DB_CONFIG** file is read when the database environment is opened, it will silently overrule configuration done before that time.

Errors

- EINVAL   An invalid flag value or parameter was specified.

DbEnv::set_lg_bsize

```
#include <db_cxx.h>

int
DbEnv::set_lg_bsize(u_int32_t lg_bsize);
```

Description

Set the size of the in-memory log buffer, in bytes. By default or if the value is set to 0, a size of 32K is used. The size of the log file (see **DbEnv::set_lg_max**) must be at least four times the size of the the in-memory log buffer.

Log information is stored in-memory until the storage space fills up or transaction commit forces the information to be flushed to stable storage. In the presence of long-running transactions or transactions producing large amounts of data, larger buffer sizes can increase throughput.

The DbEnv::set_lg_bsize interface may only be used to configure Berkeley DB before the **DbEnv::open** interface is called.

The DbEnv::set_lg_bsize method either returns a non-zero error value or throws an exception that encapsulates a non-zero error value on failure, and returns 0 on success.

The database environment's log buffer size may also be set using the environment's **DB_CONFIG** file. The syntax of the entry in that file is a single line with the string "set_lg_bsize", one or more whitespace characters, and the size in bytes. Because the **DB_CONFIG** file is read when the database environment is opened, it will silently overrule configuration done before that time.

Errors

- EINVAL   An invalid flag value or parameter was specified.

  Called after **DbEnv::open** was called.

  The size of the log file is less than four times the size of the in-memory log buffer.

DbEnv::set_lg_dir

```
#include <db_cxx.h>

int
DbEnv::set_lg_dir(const char *dir);
```

Description

The path of a directory to be used as the location of logging files. Log files created by the Log Manager subsystem will be created in this directory.

If no logging directory is specified, log files are created in the environment home directory. See "Berkeley DB File Naming" for more information.

For the greatest degree of recoverability from system or application failure, database files and log files should be located on separate physical devices.

The DbEnv::set_lg_dir interface may only be used to configure Berkeley DB before the **DbEnv::open** interface is called.

The DbEnv::set_lg_dir method either returns a non-zero error value or throws an exception that encapsulates a non-zero error value on failure, and returns 0 on success.

The database environment's logging directory may also be set using the environment's **DB_CONFIG** file. The syntax of the entry in that file is a single line with the string "set_lg_dir", one or more whitespace characters, and the directory name. Because the **DB_CONFIG** file is read when the database environment is opened, it will silently overrule configuration done before that time.

Errors

- EINVAL   An invalid flag value or parameter was specified.

  Called after **DbEnv::open** was called.

DbEnv::set_lg_max

```
#include <db_cxx.h>

int
DbEnv::set_lg_max(u_int32_t lg_max);
```

Description

Set the maximum size of a single file in the log, in bytes. Because **DbLsn** file offsets are unsigned 4-byte values, the set value may not be larger than the maximum unsigned 4-byte value. By default, or if the value is set to 0, a size of 10MB is used. The size of the log file must be at least 4 times the size of the in-memory log buffer (see **DbEnv::set_lg_bsize**).

See "Log File Limits" for more information.

The DbEnv::set_lg_max interface may only be used to configure Berkeley DB before the **DbEnv::open** interface is called.

The DbEnv::set_lg_max method either returns a non-zero error value or throws an exception that encapsulates a non-zero error value on failure, and returns 0 on success.

The database environment's log file size may also be set using the environment's **DB_CONFIG** file. The syntax of the entry in that file is a single line with the string "set_lg_max", one or more whitespace characters, and the size in bytes. Because the **DB_CONFIG** file is read when the database environment is opened, it will silently overrule configuration done before that time.

Errors

- EINVAL   An invalid flag value or parameter was specified.

    Called after **DbEnv::open** was called.

    The size of the log file is less than four times the size of the in-memory log buffer.

    The specified log file size was too large.

DbEnv::set_lk_conflicts

```
#include <db_cxx.h>

int
DbEnv::set_lk_conflicts(u_int8_t *conflicts, int nmodes);
```

Description

Set the locking conflicts matrix. The **conflicts** argument is an **nmodes** by **nmodes** array. A non-0 value for the following array element indicates that requested_mode and held_mode conflict:

```
conflicts[requested_mode][held_mode]
```

The *not-granted* mode must be represented by 0.

If DbEnv::set_lk_conflicts is never called, a standard conflicts array is used; see "Standard Lock Modes" for more information.

The DbEnv::set_lk_conflicts interface may only be used to configure Berkeley DB before the **DbEnv::open** interface is called.

The DbEnv::set_lk_conflicts method either returns a non-zero error value or throws an exception that encapsulates a non-zero error value on failure, and returns 0 on success.

Errors

- EINVAL   An invalid flag value or parameter was specified.

    Called after **DbEnv::open** was called.

- ENOMEM   No memory was available to copy the conflicts array.

DbEnv::set_lk_detect

```
#include <db_cxx.h>

int
DbEnv::set_lk_detect(u_int32_t detect);
```

Description

Set if the deadlock detector is to be run whenever a lock conflict occurs, and specify which transaction should be aborted in the case of a deadlock. The specified value must be one of the following list:

- DB_LOCK_DEFAULT   Use the default policy as specified by **db_deadlock**.

- DB_LOCK_OLDEST   Abort the oldest transaction.

- DB_LOCK_RANDOM   Abort a random transaction involved in the deadlock.

- DB_LOCK_YOUNGEST   Abort the youngest transaction.

The DbEnv::set_lk_detect interface may only be used to configure Berkeley DB before the **DbEnv::open** interface is called.

The DbEnv::set_lk_detect method either returns a non-zero error value or throws an exception that encapsulates a non-zero error value on failure, and returns 0 on success.

The database environment's deadlock detector configuration may also be set using the environment's **DB_CONFIG** file. The syntax of the entry in that file is a single line with the string "set_lk_detect", one or more whitespace characters, and the interface **detect** argument as a string; for example, "set_lk_detect DB_LOCK_OLDEST". Because the **DB_CONFIG** file is read when the database environment is opened, it will silently overrule configuration done before that time.

Errors

- EINVAL   An invalid flag value or parameter was specified.

    Called after **DbEnv::open** was called.

DbEnv::set_lk_max

```
#include <db_cxx.h>

int
DbEnv::set_lk_max(u_int32_t max);
```

Description

The DbEnv::set_lk_max method interface has been deprecated in favor of the DbEnv::set_lk_max_locks, DbEnv::set_lk_max_lockers, and DbEnv::set_lk_max_objects methods. Please update your applications.

Set each of the maximum number of locks, lockers, and lock objects supported by the Berkeley DB lock subsystem to **max**. This value is used by **DbEnv::open** to estimate how much space to allocate for various lock-table data structures. For specific information on configuring the size of the lock subsystem, see "Configuring Locking: Sizing the System."

The DbEnv::set_lk_max interface may only be used to configure Berkeley DB before the **DbEnv::open** interface is called.

The DbEnv::set_lk_max method either returns a non-zero error value or throws an exception that encapsulates a non-zero error value on failure, and returns 0 on success.

The database environment's maximum number of locks may also be set using the environment's **DB_CONFIG** file. The syntax of the entry in that file is a single line with the string "set_lk_max", one or more whitespace characters, and the number of locks. Because the **DB_CONFIG** file is read when the database environment is opened, it will silently overrule configuration done before that time.

Errors

- EINVAL   An invalid flag value or parameter was specified.

  Called after **DbEnv::open** was called.

DbEnv::set_lk_max_lockers

```
#include <db_cxx.h>

int
DbEnv::set_lk_max_lockers(u_int32_t max);
```

Description

Set the maximum number of simultaneous locking entities supported by the Berkeley DB Locking subsystem. This value is used by **DbEnv::open** to estimate how much space to allocate for various lock-table data structures. The default value is 1000 lockers. For specific information on configuring the size of the lock subsystem, see "Configuring Locking: Sizing the System."

The DbEnv::set_lk_max_lockers interface may only be used to configure Berkeley DB before the **DbEnv::open** interface is called.

The DbEnv::set_lk_max_lockers method either returns a non-zero error value or throws an exception that encapsulates a non-zero error value on failure, and returns 0 on success.

The database environment's maximum number of lockers may also be set using the environment's **DB_CONFIG** file. The syntax of the entry in that file is a single line with the string "set_lk_max_lockers", one or more whitespace characters, and the number of lockers. Because the **DB_CONFIG** file is read when the database environment is opened, it will silently overrule configuration done before that time.

Errors

- EINVAL   An invalid flag value or parameter was specified.

  Called after **DbEnv::open** was called.

DbEnv::set_lk_max_locks

```
#include <db_cxx.h>

int
DbEnv::set_lk_max_locks(u_int32_t max);
```

Description

Set the maximum number of locks supported by the Berkeley DB lock subsystem. This value is used by **DbEnv::open** to estimate how much space to allocate for various lock-table data structures. The default value is 1000 locks. For specific information on configuring the size of the lock subsystem, see "Configuring Locking: Sizing the System."

The DbEnv::set_lk_max_locks interface may only be used to configure Berkeley DB before the **DbEnv::open** interface is called.

The DbEnv::set_lk_max_locks method either returns a non-zero error value or throws an exception that encapsulates a non-zero error value on failure, and returns 0 on success.

The database environment's maximum number of locks may also be set using the environment's **DB_CONFIG** file. The syntax of the entry in that file is a single line with the string "set_lk_max_locks", one or more whitespace characters, and the number of locks. Because the **DB_CONFIG** file is read when the database environment is opened, it will silently overrule configuration done before that time.

Errors

- EINVAL   An invalid flag value or parameter was specified.

    Called after **DbEnv::open** was called.

DbEnv::set_lk_max_objects

```
#include <db_cxx.h>

int
DbEnv::set_lk_max_objects(u_int32_t max);
```

Description

Set the maximum number of simultaneously locked objects supported by the Berkeley DB Locking subsystem. This value is used by **DbEnv::open** to estimate how much space to allocate for various lock-table data structures. The default value is 1000 objects. For specific information on configuring the size of the lock subsystem, see "Configuring Locking: Sizing the System."

The DbEnv::set_lk_max_objects interface may only be used to configure Berkeley DB before the **DbEnv::open** interface is called.

The DbEnv::set_lk_max_objects method either returns a non-zero error value or throws an exception that encapsulates a non-zero error value on failure, and returns 0 on success.

The database environment's maximum number of objects may also be set using the environment's **DB_CONFIG** file. The syntax of the entry in that file is a single line with the string "set_lk_max_objects", one or more whitespace characters, and the number of objects. Because the **DB_CONFIG** file is read when the database environment is opened, it will silently overrule configuration done before that time.

Errors

- EINVAL   An invalid flag value or parameter was specified.

  Called after **DbEnv::open** was called.

DbEnv::set_mp_mmapsize

```
#include <db_cxx.h>

int
DbEnv::set_mp_mmapsize(size_t mp_mmapsize);
```

Description

Files that are opened read-only in the pool (and that satisfy a few other criteria) are, by default, mapped into the process address space instead of being copied into the local cache. This can result in better-than-usual performance because available virtual memory is normally much larger than the local cache, and page faults are faster than page- copying on many systems. However, in the presence of limited virtual memory, it can cause resource starvation; in the presence of large databases, it can result in immense process sizes.

Set the maximum file size, in bytes, for a file to be mapped into the process address space. If no value is specified, it defaults to 10MB.

The DbEnv::set_mp_mmapsize interface may only be used to configure Berkeley DB before the **DbEnv::open** interface is called.

The DbEnv::set_mp_mmapsize method either returns a non-zero error value or throws an exception that encapsulates a non-zero error value on failure, and returns 0 on success.

The database environment's maximum mapped file size may also be set using the environment's **DB_CONFIG** file. The syntax of the entry in that file is a single line with the string "set_mp_mmapsize", one or more whitespace characters, and the size in bytes. Because the **DB_CONFIG** file is read when the database environment is opened, it will silently overrule configuration done before that time.

Errors

- EINVAL   An invalid flag value or parameter was specified.

  Called after **DbEnv::open** was called.

DbEnv::set_mutexlocks

```
#include <db_cxx.h>

int
DbEnv::set_mutexlocks(int do_lock);
```

Description

Toggle mutex locks. Setting **do_lock** to a zero value causes Berkeley DB to grant all requested mutual exclusion mutexes without regard for their availability.

This functionality should never be used for any other purpose than debugging.

The DbEnv::set_mutexlocks interface may be used to configure Berkeley DB at any time during the life of the application.

The DbEnv::set_mutexlocks method either returns a non-zero error value or throws an exception that encapsulates a non-zero error value on failure, and returns 0 on success.

DbEnv::set_pageyield

```
#include <db_cxx.h>

static int
DbEnv::set_pageyield(int pageyield);
```

Description

Yield the processor whenever requesting a page from the cache. Setting **pageyield** to a non-zero value causes Berkeley DB to yield the processor any time a thread requests a page from the cache. This functionality should never be used for any other purpose than stress testing.

The DbEnv::set_pageyield interface affects the entire application, not a single database or database environment.

The DbEnv::set_pageyield interface may be used to configure Berkeley DB at any time during the life of the application.

The DbEnv::set_pageyield method either returns a non-zero error value or throws an exception that encapsulates a non-zero error value on failure, and returns 0 on success.

Errors

- EINVAL   An invalid flag value or parameter was specified.

DbEnv::set_paniccall

```
#include <db_cxx.h>

int
DbEnv::set_paniccall(void (*)(DbEnv *, int));
```

Description

Errors can occur in the Berkeley DB library where the only solution is to shut down the application and run recovery (for example, if Berkeley DB is unable to write log records to disk because there is insufficient disk space). In these cases, when the C++ error model has been configured so that the individual Berkeley DB methods return error codes (see **DbException** for more information), the value DB_RUNRECOVERY is returned by Berkeley DB methods.

In these cases, it is also often simpler to shut down the application when such errors occur rather than attempting to gracefully return up the stack. The DbEnv::set_paniccall method is used to specify a method to be called when DB_RUNRECOVERY is about to be returned from a Berkeley DB method. When called, the **dbenv** argument will be a reference to the current environment, and the **errval** argument is the error value that would have been returned to the calling method.

The DbEnv::set_paniccall interface may be used to configure Berkeley DB at any time during the life of the application.

The DbEnv::set_paniccall method either returns a non-zero error value or throws an exception that encapsulates a non-zero error value on failure, and returns 0 on success.

DbEnv::set_panicstate

```
#include <db_cxx.h>

static int
DbEnv::set_panicstate(int panic);
```

Description

Toggle the Berkeley DB panic state. Setting **panic** to a non-zero value causes Berkeley DB to refuse attempts to call Berkeley DB functions with the DB_RUNRECOVERY error return.

The DbEnv::set_panicstate interface affects the entire application, not a single database or database environment.

The **DbEnv::set_pageyield** interface may be used to configure Berkeley DB at any time during the life of the application.

The DbEnv::set_panicstate method either returns a non-zero error value or throws an exception that encapsulates a non-zero error value on failure, and returns 0 on success.

Errors

- EINVAL   An invalid flag value or parameter was specified.

DbEnv::set_recovery_init

```
#include <db_cxx.h>

int
DbEnv::set_recovery_init(int (*db_recovery_init_fcn)(DbEnv *));
```

Description

Applications installing application-specific recovery methods need to be called before Berkeley DB performs recovery so they may add their recovery methods to Berkeley DB's.

The DbEnv::set_recovery_init method supports this functionality. The **db_recovery_init_fcn** method must be declared with one argument, a reference to the enclosing Berkeley DB environment. This method will be called after the **DbEnv::open** has been called, but before recovery is started.

If the **db_recovery_init_fcn** method returns a non-zero value, no recovery will be performed, and **DbEnv::open** will return the same value to its caller.

The DbEnv::set_recovery_init interface may only be used to configure Berkeley DB before the **DbEnv::open** interface is called.

The DbEnv::set_recovery_init method either returns a non-zero error value or throws an exception that encapsulates a non-zero error value on failure, and returns 0 on success.

Errors

- EINVAL   An invalid flag value or parameter was specified.

   Called after **DbEnv::open** was called.

DbEnv::set_region_init

```
#include <db_cxx.h>

static int
DbEnv::set_region_init(int region_init);
```

Description

Page-fault shared regions into memory when initially creating or joining a Berkeley DB environment. In some applications, the expense of page-faulting the shared memory regions can affect performance; for example, when the page-fault occurs while holding a lock, other lock requests can convoy and overall throughput may decrease. Setting **region_init** to a non-zero value specifies that shared regions be read or written, as appropriate, when the region is joined by the application. This forces the underlying virtual memory and file systems to instantiate both the necessary memory and the necessary disk space. This can also avoid out-of-disk space failures later on.

The DbEnv::set_region_init interface affects the entire application, not a single database or database environment.

Although the DbEnv::set_region_init interface may be used to configure Berkeley DB at any time during the life of the application, it should normally be called before making any calls to the **db_env_create** or **db_create** methods.

The DbEnv::set_region_init method either returns a non-zero error value or throws an exception that encapsulates a non-zero error value on failure, and returns 0 on success.

The database environment's initial behavior with respect to shared memory regions may also be set using the environment's **DB_CONFIG** file. The syntax of the entry in that file is a single line with the string "set_region_init", one or more whitespace characters, and the string "1". Because the **DB_CONFIG** file is read when the database environment is opened, it will silently overrule configuration done before that time.

Errors

- EINVAL   An invalid flag value or parameter was specified.

DbEnv::set_server

```
#include <db_cxx.h>

int
DbEnv::set_server(char *host,
    long cl_timeout, long sv_timeout, u_int32_t flags);
```

Description

Connects to the DB server on the indicated hostname and sets up a channel for communication.

The **cl_timeout** argument specifies the number of seconds the client should wait for results to come back from the server. Once the timeout has expired on any communication with the server, DB_NOSERVER will be returned. If this value is zero, a default timeout is used.

The **sv_timeout** argument specifies the number of seconds the server should allow a client connection to remain idle before assuming that client is gone. Once that timeout has been reached, the server releases all resources associated with that client connection. Subsequent attempts by that client to communicate with the server result in DB_NOSERVER_ID indicating that an invalid identifier has been given to the server. This value can be considered a hint to the server. The server may alter this value, based on its own policies or allowed values. If this value is zero, a default timeout is used.

The **flags** parameter is currently unused, and must be set to 0.

When the DbEnv::set_server method has been called, any subsequent calls to Berkeley DB library interfaces may return either DB_NOSERVER or DB_NOSERVER_ID.

The DbEnv::set_server method either returns a non-zero error value or throws an exception that encapsulates a non-zero error value on failure, and returns 0 on success.

Errors

- EINVAL   An invalid flag value or parameter was specified.

```
#include <db_cxx.h>

int
DbEnv::set_shm_key(long shm_key);
```

Description

Specify a base segment ID for Berkeley DB environment shared memory regions created in system memory on VxWorks or systems supporting X/Open-style shared memory interfaces; for example, UNIX systems supporting **shmget**(2) and related System V IPC interfaces.

This base segment ID will be used when Berkeley DB shared memory regions are first created. It will be incremented a small integer value each time a new shared memory region is created; that is, if the base ID is 35, the first shared memory region created will have a segment ID of 35, and the next one will have a segment ID between 36 and 40 or so. A Berkeley DB environment always creates a master shared memory region, plus an additional shared memory region for each of the subsystems supported by the environment (Locking, Logging, Memory Pool, and Transaction), plus an additional shared memory region for each additional memory pool cache that is supported. Already existing regions with the same segment IDs will be removed. See "Shared Memory Regions" for more information.

The intent behind this interface is two-fold: Without it, applications have no way to ensure that two Berkeley DB applications won't attempt to use the same segment IDs when creating different Berkeley DB environments. In addition, by using the same segment IDs each time the environment is created, previously created segments will be removed, and the set of segments on the system will not grow without bound.

The DbEnv::set_shm_key interface may only be used to configure Berkeley DB before the **DbEnv::open** interface is called.

The DbEnv::set_shm_key method either returns a non-zero error value or throws an exception that encapsulates a non-zero error value on failure, and returns 0 on success.

The database environment's base segment ID may also be set using the environment's **DB_CONFIG** file. The syntax of the entry in that file is a single line with the string "set_shm_key", one or more whitespace characters, and the ID. Because the **DB_CONFIG** file is read when the database environment is opened, it will silently overrule configuration done before that time.

Errors

- EINVAL   An invalid flag value or parameter was specified.

  Called after **DbEnv::open** was called.

DbEnv::set_tas_spins

```
#include <db_cxx.h>

static int
DbEnv::set_tas_spins(u_int32_t tas_spins);
```

Description

Specify that test-and-set mutexes should spin **tas_spins** times without blocking. The value defaults to 1 on uniprocessor systems and to 50 times the number of processors on multiprocessor systems.

The DbEnv::set_tas_spins interface affects the entire application, not a single database or database environment.

Although the DbEnv::set_tas_spins interface may be used to configure Berkeley DB at any time during the life of the application, it should normally be called before making any calls to the **db_env_create** or **db_create** methods.

The DbEnv::set_tas_spins method either returns a non-zero error value or throws an exception that encapsulates a non-zero error value on failure, and returns 0 on success.

The database environment's test-and-set spin count may also be set using the environment's **DB_CONFIG** file. The syntax of the entry in that file is a single line with the string "set_tas_spins", one or more whitespace characters, and the number of spins. Because the **DB_CONFIG** file is read when the database environment is opened, it will silently overrule configuration done before that time.

Errors

- EINVAL   An invalid flag value or parameter was specified.

DbEnv::set_tmp_dir

```
#include <db_cxx.h>

int
DbEnv::set_tmp_dir(const char *dir);
```

Description

The path of a directory to be used as the location of temporary files. The files created to back in-memory access method databases will be created relative to this path. These temporary files can be quite large, depending on the size of the database.

If no directories are specified, the following alternatives are checked in the specified order. The first existing directory path is used for all temporary files.

1. The value of the environment variable **TMPDIR**.

2. The value of the environment variable **TEMP**.

3. The value of the environment variable **TMP**.

4. The value of the environment variable **TempFolder**.

5. The value returned by the GetTempPath interface.

6. The directory **/var/tmp**.

7. The directory **/usr/tmp**.

8. The directory **/temp**.

9. The directory **/tmp**.

10. The directory **C:/temp**.

11. The directory **C:/tmp**.

Environment variables are only checked if one of the DB_USE_ENVIRON or DB_USE_ENVIRON_ROOT flags were specified.

The GetTempPath interface is only checked on Win/32 platforms.

The DbEnv::set_tmp_dir interface may only be used to configure Berkeley DB before the **DbEnv::open** interface is called.

The DbEnv::set_tmp_dir method either returns a non-zero error value or throws an exception that encapsulates a non-zero error value on failure, and returns 0 on success.

The database environment's temporary file directory may also be set using the environment's **DB_CONFIG** file. The syntax of the entry in that file is a single line with the string "set_tmp_dir", one or more whitespace characters, and the directory name. Because the **DB_CONFIG** file is read when the database environment is opened, it will silently overrule configuration done before that time.

Errors

- EINVAL   An invalid flag value or parameter was specified.

  Called after **DbEnv::open** was called.

DbEnv::set_tx_max

```
#include <db_cxx.h>

int
DbEnv::set_tx_max(u_int32_t tx_max);
```

Description

Set the maximum number of active transactions that are supported by the environment. This value bounds the size of backing shared memory regions. Note that child transactions must be counted as active until their ultimate parent commits or aborts.

When there are more than the specified number of concurrent transactions, calls to **DbEnv::txn_begin** will fail (until some active transactions complete). If no value is specified, a default value of 20 is used.

The DbEnv::set_tx_max interface may only be used to configure Berkeley DB before the **DbEnv::open** interface is called.

The DbEnv::set_tx_max method either returns a non-zero error value or throws an exception that encapsulates a non-zero error value on failure, and returns 0 on success.

The database environment's maximum number of active transactions may also be set using the environment's **DB_CONFIG** file. The syntax of the entry in that file is a single line with the string "set_tx_max", one or more whitespace characters, and the number of transactions. Because the **DB_CONFIG** file is read when the database environment is opened, it will silently overrule configuration done before that time.

Errors

- EINVAL   An invalid flag value or parameter was specified.

    Called after **DbEnv::open** was called.

DbEnv::set_tx_recover

```
#include <db_cxx.h>

int
DbEnv::set_tx_recover(int (*)(DbEnv *dbenv,
    Dbt *log_rec, DbLsn *lsn, db_recops op));
```

Description

Set the application's method to be called during transaction abort and recovery. This method must return 0 on success, and either **errno** or a value outside of the Berkeley DB error name space on failure. It takes four arguments:

- dbenv   A Berkeley DB environment.
- log_rec   A log record.
- lsn   A log sequence number.
- op   One of the following values:
    - DB_TXN_BACKWARD_ROLL   The log is being read backward to determine which transactions have been committed; to abort those operations that were not, undo the operation described by the log record.
    - DB_TXN_FORWARD_ROLL   The log is being played forward; redo the operation described by the log record.
    - DB_TXN_ABORT   The log is being read backward during a transaction abort; undo the operation described by the log record.

The DbEnv::set_tx_recover interface may only be used to configure Berkeley DB before the **DbEnv::open** interface is called.

The DbEnv::set_tx_recover method either returns a non-zero error value or throws an exception that encapsulates a non-zero error value on failure, and returns 0 on success.

Errors

- EINVAL An invalid flag value or parameter was specified.

  Called after **DbEnv::open** was called.

DbEnv::set_tx_timestamp

```
#include <db_cxx.h>

int
DbEnv::set_tx_timestamp(time_t *timestamp);
```

Description

Recover to the time specified by **timestamp** rather than to the most current possible date. The **timestamp** argument should be the number of seconds since 0 hours, 0 minutes, 0 seconds, January 1, 1970, Coordinated Universal Time; that is, the Epoch.

Once a database environment has been upgraded to a new version of Berkeley DB involving a log format change (see "Upgrading Berkeley DB Installations"), it is no longer possible to recover to a specific time before that upgrade.

The DbEnv::set_tx_timestamp interface may only be used to configure Berkeley DB before the **DbEnv::open** interface is called.

The DbEnv::set_tx_timestamp method either returns a non-zero error value or throws an exception that encapsulates a non-zero error value on failure, and returns 0 on success.

Errors

- EINVAL An invalid flag value or parameter was specified.

  It is not possible to recover to the specified time using the log files currently present in the environment.

DbEnv::set_verbose

```
#include <db_cxx.h>

int
DbEnv::set_verbose(u_int32_t which, int onoff);
```

Description

The DbEnv::set_verbose method turns additional informational and debugging messages in the Berkeley DB message output on and off. If **onoff** is set to non-zero, the additional messages are output.

The **which** parameter must be set to one of the following values:

- DB_VERB_CHKPOINT   Display checkpoint location information when searching the log for checkpoints.
- DB_VERB_DEADLOCK   Display additional information when doing deadlock-detection.
- DB_VERB_RECOVERY   Display additional information when performing recovery.
- DB_VERB_WAITSFOR   Display the waits-for table when doing deadlock detection.

The DbEnv::set_verbose interface may be used to configure Berkeley DB at any time during the life of the application.

The DbEnv::set_verbose method either returns a non-zero error value or throws an exception that encapsulates a non-zero error value on failure, and returns 0 on success.

The database environment's verbosity may also be set using the environment's **DB_CONFIG** file. The syntax of the entry in that file is a single line with the string "set_verbose", one or more whitespace characters, and the interface **which** argument as a string, for example, "set_verbose DB_VERB_CHKPOINT". Because the **DB_CONFIG** file is read when the database environment is opened, it will silently overrule configuration done before that time.

Errors

- EINVAL   An invalid flag value or parameter was specified.

DbEnv::strerror

```
#include <db_cxx.h>

static char *
DbEnv::strerror(int error);
```

Description

The DbEnv::strerror method returns an error message string corresponding to the error number **error**. This interface is a superset of the ANSI C X3.159-1989 (ANSI C) **strerror**(3) interface. If the error number **error** is greater than or equal to 0, the string returned by the system interface **strerror**(3) is returned. If the error number is less than 0, an error string appropriate to the corresponding Berkeley DB library error is returned. See "Error Returns to Applications" for more information.

DbEnv::txn_begin

```
#include <db_cxx.h>

int
DbEnv::txn_begin(DbTxn *parent, DbTxn **tid, u_int32_t flags);
```

Description

The DbEnv::txn_begin method creates a new transaction in the environment and copies a pointer to a **DbTxn** that uniquely identifies it into the memory referenced by **tid**.

If the **parent** argument is non-NULL, the new transaction will be a nested transaction, with the transaction indicated by **parent** as its parent. Transactions may be nested to any level.

The **flags** parameter must be set to 0 or one of the following values:

- DB_TXN_NOSYNC   Do not synchronously flush the log when this transaction commits or prepares. This means the transaction will exhibit the ACI (atomicity, consistency, and isolation) properties, but not D (durability); that is, database integrity will be maintained, but it is possible that this transaction may be undone during recovery.

  This behavior may be set for a Berkeley DB environment using the **DbEnv::set_flags** interface. Any value specified in this interface overrides that setting.

- DB_TXN_NOWAIT   If a lock is unavailable for any Berkeley DB operation performed in the context of this transaction, return immediately instead of blocking on the lock. The error return in the case will be DB_LOCK_NOTGRANTED.

- DB_TXN_SYNC   Synchronously flush the log when this transaction commits or prepares. This means the transaction will exhibit all of the ACID (atomicity, consistency, isolation, and durability) properties.

  This behavior is the default for Berkeley DB environments, unless the DB_TXN_NOSYNC flag was specified to the **DbEnv::set_flags** interface. Any value specified in this interface overrides that setting.

A transaction may not span threads; that is, each transaction must begin and end in the same thread, and each transaction may only be used by a single thread.

Cursors may not span transactions; that is, each cursor must be opened and closed within a single transaction.

A parent transaction may not issue any Berkeley DB operations—except for **DbEnv::txn_begin, DbTxn::abort,** and **DbTxn::commit**—while it has active child transactions (child transactions that have not yet been committed or aborted).

The DbEnv::txn_begin method either returns a non-zero error value or throws an exception that encapsulates a non-zero error value on failure, and returns 0 on success.

Errors

The DbEnv::txn_begin method may fail and throw an exception or return a non-zero error for the following conditions:

- ENOMEM   The maximum number of concurrent transactions has been reached.

The DbEnv::txn_begin method may fail and throw an exception or return a non-zero error for errors specified for other Berkeley DB and C library or system methods. If a catastrophic error has occurred, the DbEnv::txn_begin method may fail and either return DB_RUNRECOVERY or throw an exception encapsulating DB_RUNRECOVERY, in which case all subsequent Berkeley DB calls will fail in the same way.

DbEnv::txn_checkpoint

```
#include <db_cxx.h>

int
DbEnv::txn_checkpoint(u_int32_t kbyte, u_int32_t min, u_int32_t flags) const;
```

Description

The DbEnv::txn_checkpoint method flushes the underlying memory pool, writes a checkpoint record to the log, and then flushes the log.

If either **kbyte** or **min** is non-zero, the checkpoint is only done if there has been activity since the last checkpoint and either more than **min** minutes have passed since the last checkpoint, or if more than **kbyte** kilobytes of log data have been written since the last checkpoint.

The **flags** parameter must be set to 0 or one of the following values:

DB_FORCE   Force a checkpoint record even if there has been no activity since the last checkpoint.

The DbEnv::txn_checkpoint method either returns a non-zero error value or throws an exception that encapsulates a non-zero error value on failure, 0 on success, and returns DB_INCOMPLETE if there were pages that needed to be written to complete the checkpoint but that **DbEnv::memp_sync** was unable to write immediately.

Errors

The DbEnv::txn_checkpoint method may fail and throw an exception or return a non-zero error for the following conditions:

- EINVAL   An invalid flag value or parameter was specified.

The DbEnv::txn_checkpoint method may fail and throw an exception or return a non-zero error for errors specified for other Berkeley DB and C library or system methods. If a catastrophic error has occurred, the DbEnv::txn_checkpoint method may fail and either return DB_RUNRECOVERY or throw an exception encapsulating DB_RUNRECOVERY, in which case all subsequent Berkeley DB calls will fail in the same way.

DbEnv::txn_stat

```
#include <db_cxx.h>

extern "C" {
    typedef void *(*db_malloc_fcn_type)(size_t);
};
int
DbEnv::txn_stat(DB_TXN_STAT **statp, db_malloc_fcn_type db_malloc);
```

Description

The DbEnv::txn_stat method creates a statistical structure and copies a pointer to it into a user-specified memory location.

Statistical structures are created in allocated memory. If **db_malloc** is non-NULL, it is called to allocate the memory; otherwise, the library function **malloc**(3) is used. The function **db_malloc** must match the calling conventions of the **malloc**(3) library routine. Regardless, the caller is responsible for deallocating the returned memory. To deallocate returned memory, free the returned memory reference, references inside the returned memory do not need to be individually freed.

The transaction region statistics are stored in a structure of type DB_TXN_STAT. The following DB_TXN_STAT fields will be filled in:

- **DbLsn** st_last_ckp;   The LSN of the last checkpoint.
- **DbLsn** st_pending_ckp;   The LSN of any checkpoint that is currently in progress. If **st_pending_ckp** is the same as **st_last_ckp** there is no checkpoint in progress.
- time_t st_time_ckp;   The time the last completed checkpoint finished (as the number of seconds since the Epoch, returned by the IEEE/ANSI Std 1003.1 (POSIX) **time** interface).
- u_int32_t st_last_txnid;   The last transaction ID allocated.
- u_int32_t st_maxtxns;   The maximum number of active transactions possible.
- u_int32_t st_nactive;   The number of transactions that are currently active.
- u_int32_t st_maxnactive;   The maximum number of active transactions at any one time.
- u_int32_t st_nbegins;   The number of transactions that have begun.
- u_int32_t st_naborts;   The number of transactions that have aborted.
- u_int32_t st_ncommits;   The number of transactions that have committed.
- u_int32_t st_regsize;   The size of the region.
- u_int32_t st_region_wait;   The number of times that a thread of control was forced to wait before obtaining the region lock.
- u_int32_t st_region_nowait;   The number of times that a thread of control was able to obtain the region lock without waiting.
- DB_TXN_ACTIVE * st_txnarray;   A pointer to an array of **st_nactive** DB_TXN_ACTIVE structures, describing the currently active transactions. The following fields of the DB_TXN_ACTIVE structure will be filled in:
    - u_int32_t txnid;   The transaction ID of the transaction.
    - u_int32_t parentid;   The transaction ID of the parent transaction (or 0, if no parent).
    - **DbLsn** lsn;   The log sequence number of the transaction-begin record.

The DbEnv::txn_stat method either returns a non-zero error value or throws an exception that encapsulates a non-zero error value on failure, and returns 0 on success.

Errors

The DbEnv::txn_stat method may fail and throw an exception or return a non-zero error for errors specified for other Berkeley DB and C library or system methods. If a catastrophic error has occurred, the DbEnv::txn_stat method may fail and either return DB_RUNRECOVERY or throw an exception encapsulating DB_RUNRECOVERY, in which case all subsequent Berkeley DB calls will fail in the same way.

DbEnv::version

```
#include <db_cxx.h>

static char *
DbEnv::version(int *major, int *minor, int *patch);
```

Description

The DbEnv::version method returns a pointer to a string containing Berkeley DB version information. If **major** is non-NULL, the major version of the Berkeley DB release is stored in the memory it references. If **minor** is non-NULL, the minor version of the Berkeley DB release is stored in the memory it references. If **patch** is non-NULL, the patch version of the Berkeley DB release is stored in the memory it references.

DbException

```
#include <db_cxx.h>

class DbException {
    DbException(int err);
    DbException(const char *description);
    DbException(const char *prefix, int err);
    DbException(const char *prefix1, const char *prefix2, int err);
};
```

Description

This manual page describes the DbException class and how it is used by the various Berkeley DB classes.

Most methods in the Berkeley DB classes return an int, but also throw an exception. This allows for two different error behaviors. By default, the Berkeley DB C++ API is configured to throw an exception whenever a serious error occurs. This generally allows for cleaner logic for transaction processing because a try block can surround a single transaction. Alternatively, Berkeley DB can be configured to not throw exceptions, and instead have the individual function return an error code, by setting the constructor flags for the Db and **DbEnv** objects.

A DbException object contains an informational string and an errno. The errno can be obtained by using **DbException::get_errno**. The informational string can be obtained by using **DbException::what**.

We expect in the future that this class will inherit from the standard class exception, but certain language implementation bugs currently prevent this on some platforms.

Some methods may return non-zero values without issuing an exception. This occurs in situations that are not normally considered an error, but when some informational status is returned. For example, **Db::get** returns DB_NOTFOUND when a requested key does not appear in the database.

DbException::get_errno

```
#include <db_cxx.h>

const int
DbException::get_errno();
```

Description

A DbException object contains an informational string and an errno. The errno can be obtained by using DbException::get_errno. The informational string can be obtained by using **DbException::what**.

DbException::what

```
#include <db_cxx.h>

virtual const char *
DbException::what() const;
```

Description

A DbException object contains an informational string and an errno. The errno can be obtained by using **DbException::get_errno**. The informational string can be obtained by using DbException::what.

DbLock

```
#include <db_cxx.h>

class DbLock {
public:
      DbLock();
      DbLock(const DbLock &);
      DbLock &operator = (const DbLock &);
      ~DbLock();
};
```

Description

The **DbEnv** lock methods and the DbLock class are used to provide general-purpose locking. Although designed to work with the other Db classes, they are also useful for more general locking purposes. Locks can be shared between processes.

In most cases, when multiple threads or processes are using locking, the deadlock detector, **db_deadlock** should be run.

DbLock::put

```
#include <db_cxx.h>

int
DbLock::put(DbEnv *env);
```

Description

The DbLock::put method releases **lock** from the lock table.

The DbLock::put method either returns a non-zero error value or throws an exception that encapsulates a non-zero error value on failure, and returns 0 on success.

Errors

The DbLock::put method may fail and throw an exception or return a non-zero error for the following conditions:

- EINVAL   An invalid flag value or parameter was specified.

The DbLock::put method may fail and throw an exception or return a non-zero error for errors specified for other Berkeley DB and C library or system methods. If a catastrophic error has occurred, the DbLock::put method may fail and either return DB_RUNRECOVERY or throw an exception encapsulating DB_RUNRECOVERY, in which case all subsequent Berkeley DB calls will fail in the same way.

DbLsn

```
#include <db_cxx.h>

class DbLsn { ... };
```

Description

A DbLsn is a **log sequence number** that is fully encapsulated. The class itself has no methods other than a default constructor, so there is no way for the user to manipulate its data directly. Methods always take a pointer to a DbLsn as an argument.

DbMpoolFile

```
#include <db_cxx.h>

class DbMpoolFile { ... };
```

Description

This manual page describes the specific details of the DbMpoolFile class.

The **DbEnv** memory pool methods and the DbMpoolFile class are the library interface that provide general-purpose, page-oriented buffer management of one or more files. Altlhough designed to work with the other Db classes, they are also useful for more general purposes. The memory pools are referred to in this document as simply *pools*.

Pools may be shared between processes. Pools are usually filled by pages from one or more files. Pages in the pool are replaced in LRU (least-recently-used) order, with each new page replacing the page that has been unused the longest. Pages retrieved from the pool using **DbMpoolFile::get** are *pinned* in the pool until they are returned to the control of the buffer pool using the **DbMpoolFile::put** method.

DbMpoolFile::close

```
#include <db_cxx.h>

int
DbMpoolFile::close();
```

Description

The DbMpoolFile::close method closes the source file indicated by the **DbMpoolFile** object. Calling DbMpoolFile::close does not imply a call to **DbMpoolFile::sync**; that is, no pages are written to the source file as a result of calling DbMpoolFile::close.

In addition, if the **DbMpoolFile** was temporary, any underlying files created for this **DbMpoolFile** will be removed.

Once DbMpoolFile::close has been called, regardless of its return, the **DbMpoolFile** handle may not be accessed again.

The DbMpoolFile::close method either returns a non-zero error value or throws an exception that encapsulates a non-zero error value on failure, and returns 0 on success.

Errors

The DbMpoolFile::close method may fail and throw an exception or return a non-zero error for errors specified for other Berkeley DB and C library or system methods. If a catastrophic error has occurred, the DbMpoolFile::close method may fail and either return DB_RUNRECOVERY or throw an exception encapsulating DB_RUNRECOVERY, in which case all subsequent Berkeley DB calls will fail in the same way.

DbMpoolFile::get

```
#include <db_cxx.h>

int
DbMpoolFile::get(db_pgno_t *pgnoaddr, u_int32_t flags, void **pagep);
```

Description

The DbMpoolFile::get method copies a pointer to the page with the page number specified by **pgnoaddr**, from the source file in the **DbMpoolFile**, into the memory location referenced by **pagep**. If the page does not exist or cannot be retrieved, DbMpoolFile::get will fail.

Page numbers begin at 0; that is, the first page in the file is page number 0, not page number 1.

The returned page is **size_t** type aligned.

The **flags** value must be set to 0 or by bitwise inclusively **OR**'ing together one or more of the following values.

- DB_MPOOL_CREATE   If the specified page does not exist, create it. In this case, the pgin method, if specified, is called.
- DB_MPOOL_LAST   Return the last page of the source file, and copy its page number to the location referenced by **pgnoaddr**.
- DB_MPOOL_NEW   Create a new page in the file, and copy its page number to the location referenced by **pgnoaddr**. In this case, the pgin method, if specified, is **not** called.

The DB_MPOOL_CREATE, DB_MPOOL_LAST, and DB_MPOOL_NEW flags are mutually exclusive.

Created pages have all their bytes set to 0, unless otherwise specified when the file was opened.

All pages returned by DbMpoolFile::get will be retained (that is, *pinned*), in the pool until a subsequent call to **DbMpoolFile::put**.

The DbMpoolFile::get method either returns a non-zero error value or throws an exception that encapsulates a non-zero error value on failure, and returns 0 on success.

Errors

The DbMpoolFile::get method may fail and throw an exception or return a non-zero error for the following conditions:

- EAGAIN   The page reference count has overflowed. (This should never happen unless there's a bug in the application.)
- EINVAL   An invalid flag value or parameter was specified.

  The DB_MPOOL_NEW flag was set, and the source file was not opened for writing.

  More than one of DB_MPOOL_CREATE, DB_MPOOL_LAST, and DB_MPOOL_NEW was set.
- EIO   The requested page does not exist, and DB_MPOOL_CREATE was not set.
- ENOMEM   The cache is full and no more pages will fit in the pool.

The DbMpoolFile::get method may fail and throw an exception or return a non-zero error for errors specified for other Berkeley DB and C library or system methods. If a catastrophic error has occurred, the DbMpoolFile::get method may fail and either return DB_RUNRECOVERY or throw an exception encapsulating DB_RUNRECOVERY, in which case all subsequent Berkeley DB calls will fail in the same way.

DbMpoolFile::open

```
#include <db_cxx.h>

static int
DbMpoolFile::open(DbEnv *env, const char *file, u_int32_t flags, int mode,
    size_t pagesize, DB_MPOOL_FINFO *finfop, DbMpoolFile **mpf);
```

Description

The DbMpoolFile::open method opens a file in the pool specified by the **DbEnv env**, copying the **DbMpoolFile** pointer representing it into the memory location referenced by **mpf**.

The **file** argument is the name of the file to be opened. If **file** is NULL, a private temporary file is created that cannot be shared with any other process (although it may be shared with other threads).

The **flags** and **mode** arguments specify the way files will be opened and/or created if they do not already exist.

The **flags** value must be set to 0 or by bitwise inclusively **OR**'ing together one or more of the following values.

- DB_CREATE   Create any underlying files, as necessary. If the files do not already exist and the DB_CREATE flag is not specified, the call will fail.

- DB_NOMMAP   Always copy this file into the local cache instead of potentially mapping it into process memory (see the description of the **DbEnv::set_mp_mmapsize** method for further information).

- DB_RDONLY   Open any underlying files for reading only. Any attempt to write the file using the pool functions will fail, regardless of the actual permissions of the file.

On UNIX systems, or in IEEE/ANSI Std 1003.1 (POSIX) environments, all files created by function DbMpoolFile::open are created with mode **mode** (as described in **chmod**(2)) and modified by the process' umask value at the time of creation (see **umask**(2)). The group ownership of created files is based on the system and directory defaults, and is not further specified by Berkeley DB. If **mode** is 0, files are created readable and writable by both owner and group. On Windows systems, the mode argument is ignored.

The **pagesize** argument is the size, in bytes, of the unit of transfer between the application and the pool, although it is not necessarily the unit of transfer between the pool and the source file.

Files opened in the pool may be further configured, based on the **finfop** argument to DbMpoolFile::open (which is a pointer to a structure of type DB_MPOOL_FINFO). No references to the **finfop** structure are maintained by Berkeley DB, so it may be discarded when the DbMpoolFile::open function returns. In order to ensure compatibility with future releases of Berkeley DB, all fields of the DB_MPOOL_FINFO structure that are not explicitly set should be initialized to 0 before the first time the structure is used. Do this by declaring the structure external or static, or by calling the C library routine **bzero**(3) or **memset**(3).

The fields of the DB_MPOOL_FINFO structure used by DbMpoolFile::open are described below. If **finfop** is NULL or any of its fields are set to their default value, defaults appropriate for the system are used.

- int ftype; The **ftype** field should be the same as a **ftype** argument previously specified to the **DbEnv::memp_register** function, unless no input or output processing of the file's pages are necessary, in which case it should be 0. (See the description of the **DbEnv::memp_register** function for more information.)

- DBT *pgcookie; The **pgcookie** field contains the byte string that is passed to the **pgin** and **pgout** functions for this file, if any. If no **pgin** or **pgout** functions are specified, the **pgcookie** field should be NULL. (See the description of the **DbEnv::memp_register** function for more information.)

- u_int8_t *fileid; The **fileid** field is a unique identifier for the file. If the **fileid** field is non-NULL, it must reference a DB_FILE_ID_LEN length array of bytes that will be used to uniquely identify the file.

    The mpool functions must be able to uniquely identify files so that multiple processes wanting to share a file will correctly identify it in the pool.

    On most UNIX/POSIX systems, the **fileid** field will not need to be set—the mpool functions will simply use the file's device and inode numbers for this purpose. On Windows systems, the mpool functions use the values returned by GetFileInformationByHandle() by default—these values are known to be constant between processes and over reboot in the case of NTFS (where they are the NTFS MFT indexes).

    On other filesystems (for example, FAT or NFS), these default values are not necessarily unique between processes or across system reboots. Applications wanting to maintain a shared memory buffer pool between processes or across system reboots, in which the pool contains pages from files stored on such filesystems, must specify a unique file identifier to the **DbMpoolFile::open** call, and each process opening or registering the file must provide the same unique identifier.

    This should not be necessary for most applications. Specifically, it is not necessary if the memory pool is not shared between processes and is reinstantiated after each system reboot, or the application is using the Berkeley DB access methods instead of calling the pool functions explicitly, or the files in the memory pool are stored on filesystems where the default values as described previously are invariant between process and across system reboots.

- int32_t lsn_offset;   The **lsn_offset** field is the zero-based byte offset in the page of the page's log sequence number (LSN), or -1 if no LSN offset is specified. (See the description of the **DbEnv::memp_sync** function for more information.)

- u_int32_t clear_len;   The **clear_len** field is the number of initial bytes in a page that should be set to zero when the page is created as a result of the DB_MPOOL_CRE-ATE or DB_MPOOL_NEW flags being specified to **DbMpoolFile::get**. If **finfop** is NULL or **clear_len** is 0, the entire page is cleared.

The DbMpoolFile::open method either returns a non-zero error value or throws an exception that encapsulates a non-zero error value on failure, and returns 0 on success.

Errors

The DbMpoolFile::open method may fail and throw an exception or return a non-zero error for the following conditions:

- EINVAL   An invalid flag value or parameter was specified.

  The file has already been entered into the pool, and the **pagesize** value is not the same as when the file was entered into the pool, or the length of the file is not zero or a multiple of the **pagesize**.

  The DB_RDONLY flag was specified for an in-memory pool.

- ENOMEM   The maximum number of open files has been reached.

The DbMpoolFile::open method may fail and throw an exception or return a non-zero error for errors specified for other Berkeley DB and C library or system methods. If a catastrophic error has occurred, the DbMpoolFile::open method may fail and either return DB_RUNRECOVERY or throw an exception encapsulating DB_RUNRECOVERY, in which case all subsequent Berkeley DB calls will fail in the same way.

DbMpoolFile::put

```
#include <db_cxx.h>

int
DbMpoolFile::put(void *pgaddr, u_int32_t flags);
```

Description

The DbMpoolFile::put method indicates that the page referenced by **pgaddr** can be evicted from the pool. The **pgaddr** argument must be an address previously returned by **DbMpoolFile::get**.

The **flags** value must be set to 0 or by bitwise inclusively **OR**'ing together one or more of the following values.

- DB_MPOOL_CLEAN   Clear any previously set modification information (that is, don't bother writing the page back to the source file).

- DB_MPOOL_DIRTY   The page has been modified and must be written to the source file before being evicted from the pool.

- DB_MPOOL_DISCARD   The page is unlikely to be useful in the near future, and should be discarded before other pages in the pool.

The DB_MPOOL_CLEAN and DB_MPOOL_DIRTY flags are mutually exclusive.

The DbMpoolFile::put method either returns a non-zero error value or throws an exception that encapsulates a non-zero error value on failure, and returns 0 on success.

Errors

The DbMpoolFile::put method may fail and throw an exception or return a non-zero error for the following conditions:

- EACCES   The DB_MPOOL_DIRTY flag was set and the source file was not opened for writing.

- EINVAL   An invalid flag value or parameter was specified.

  The **pgaddr** parameter does not reference a page returned by **DbMpoolFile::get**.

  More than one of DB_MPOOL_CLEAN and DB_MPOOL_DIRTY flags was set.

The DbMpoolFile::put method may fail and throw an exception or return a non-zero error for errors specified for other Berkeley DB and C library or system methods. If a catastrophic error has occurred, the DbMpoolFile::put method may fail and either return DB_RUNRECOVERY or throw an exception encapsulating DB_RUNRECOVERY, in which case all subsequent Berkeley DB calls will fail in the same way.

DbMpoolFile::set

```
#include <db_cxx.h>

int
DbMpoolFile::set(void *pgaddr, u_int32_t flags);
```

Description

The DbMpoolFile::set method sets the flags associated with the page referenced by **pgaddr** without unpinning it from the pool. The **pgaddr** argument must be an address previously returned by **DbMpoolFile::get**.

The **flags** value must be set to 0 or by bitwise inclusively **OR**'ing together one or more of the following values.

- DB_MPOOL_CLEAN   Clear any previously set modification information (that is, don't bother writing the page back to the source file).

- DB_MPOOL_DIRTY   The page has been modified and must be written to the source file before being evicted from the pool.

- DB_MPOOL_DISCARD   The page is unlikely to be useful in the near future, and should be discarded before other pages in the pool.

The DB_MPOOL_CLEAN and DB_MPOOL_DIRTY flags are mutually exclusive.

The DbMpoolFile::set method either returns a non-zero error value or throws an exception that encapsulates a non-zero error value on failure, and returns 0 on success.

Errors

The DbMpoolFile::set method may fail and throw an exception or return a non-zero error for the following conditions:

- EINVAL   An invalid flag value or parameter was specified.

The DbMpoolFile::set method may fail and throw an exception or return a non-zero error for errors specified for other Berkeley DB and C library or system methods. If a catastrophic error has occurred, the DbMpoolFile::set method may fail and either return DB_RUNRECOVERY or throw an exception encapsulating DB_RUNRECOVERY, in which case all subsequent Berkeley DB calls will fail in the same way.

DbMpoolFile::sync

```
#include <db_cxx.h>

int
DbMpoolFile::sync();
```

Description

The DbMpoolFile::sync method writes all pages associated with the **DbMpoolFile**, which were marked as modified using **DbMpoolFile::put** or **DbMpoolFile::set**, back to the source file. If any of the modified pages are also *pinned* (that is, currently referenced by this or another process), DbMpoolFile::sync will ignore them.

The DbMpoolFile::sync method either returns a non-zero error value or throws an exception that encapsulates a non-zero error value on failure, 0 on success, and returns DB_INCOMPLETE if there were pages which were modified but which DbMpoolFile::sync was unable to write immediately.

Errors

The DbMpoolFile::sync method may fail and throw an exception or return a non-zero error for errors specified for other Berkeley DB and C library or system methods. If a catastrophic error has occurred, the DbMpoolFile::sync method may fail and either return DB_RUNRECOVERY or throw an exception encapsulating DB_RUNRECOVERY, in which case all subsequent Berkeley DB calls will fail in the same way.

DbTxn

```
#include <db_cxx.h>

class DbTxn { ... };
```

Description

This manual page describes the specific details of the DbTxn class.

The **DbEnv** transaction methods and the DbTxn class provide transaction semantics. Full transaction support is provided by a collection of modules that provide interfaces to the services required for transaction processing. These services are recovery, concurrency control, and the management of shared data.

Transaction semantics can be applied to the access methods described in Db through method call parameters.

The model intended for transactional use (and the one that is used by the access methods) is write-ahead logging to record both before- and after-images. Locking follows a two-phase protocol, with all locks being released at transaction commit.

DbTxn::abort

```
#include <db_cxx.h>

int
DbTxn::abort();
```

Description

The DbTxn::abort method causes an abnormal termination of the transaction. The log is played backward, and any necessary recovery operations are initiated through the **recover** function specified to **DbEnv::open**. After the log processing is completed, all locks held by the transaction are released. As is the case for **DbTxn::commit**, applications that require strict two-phase locking should not explicitly release any locks.

In the case of nested transactions, aborting a parent transaction causes all children (unresolved or not) of the parent transaction to be aborted.

Once the DbTxn::abort method returns, the **DbTxn** handle may not be accessed again.

The DbTxn::abort method either returns a non-zero error value or throws an exception that encapsulates a non-zero error value on failure, and returns 0 on success.

Errors

The DbTxn::abort method may fail and throw an exception or return a non-zero error for errors specified for other Berkeley DB and C library or system methods. If a catastrophic error has occurred, the DbTxn::abort method may fail and either return DB_RUNRECOVERY or throw an exception encapsulating DB_RUNRECOVERY, in which case all subsequent Berkeley DB calls will fail in the same way.

DbTxn::commit

```
#include <db_cxx.h>

int
DbTxn::commit(u_int32_t flags);
```

Description

The DbTxn::commit method ends the transaction. In the case of nested transactions, if the transaction is a parent transaction, committing the parent transaction causes all unresolved children of the parent to be committed.

In the case of nested transactions, if the transaction is a child transaction, its locks are not released, but are acquired by its parent. Although the commit of the child transaction will succeed, the actual resolution of the child transaction is postponed until the parent transaction is committed or aborted; that is, if its parent transaction commits, it will be committed; if its parent transaction aborts, it will be aborted.

The **flags** parameter must be set to 0 or one of the following values:

- DB_TXN_NOSYNC   Do not synchronously flush the log. This means the transaction will exhibit the ACI (atomicity, consistency, and isolation) properties, but not D (durability); that is, database integrity will be maintained, but it is possible that this transaction may be undone during recovery.

  This behavior may be set for a Berkeley DB environment using the **DbEnv::set_flags** interface or for a single transaction using the **DbEnv::txn_begin** interface. Any value specified in this interface overrides both of those settings.

- DB_TXN_SYNC   Synchronously flush the log. This means the transaction will exhibit all of the ACID (atomicity, consistency, isolation, and durability) properties.

  This behavior is the default for Berkeley DB environments unless the DB_TXN_NOSYNC flag was specified to the **DbEnv::set_flags** interface. This behavior may also be set for a single transaction using the **DbEnv::txn_begin** interface. Any value specified in this interface overrides both of those settings.

Once the DbTxn::commit method returns, the **DbTxn** handle may not be accessed again. If DbTxn::commit encounters an error, the transaction and all child transactions of the transaction are aborted.

The DbTxn::commit method either returns a non-zero error value or throws an exception that encapsulates a non-zero error value on failure, and returns 0 on success.

Errors

The DbTxn::commit method may fail and throw an exception or return a non-zero error for errors specified for other Berkeley DB and C library or system methods. If a catastrophic error has occurred, the DbTxn::commit method may fail and either return DB_RUNRECOVERY or throw an exception encapsulating DB_RUNRECOVERY, in which case all subsequent Berkeley DB calls will fail in the same way.

DbTxn::id

```
#include <db_cxx.h>

u_int32_t
DbTxn::id();
```

Description

The DbTxn::id method returns the unique transaction id associated with the specified transaction. Locking calls made on behalf of this transaction should use the value returned from DbTxn::id as the locker parameter to the **DbEnv::lock_get** or **DbEnv::lock_vec** calls.

DbTxn::prepare

```
#include <db_cxx.h>

int
DbTxn::prepare();
```

Description

The DbTxn::prepare method initiates the beginning of a two-phase commit.

In a distributed transaction environment, Berkeley DB can be used as a local transaction manager. In this case, the distributed transaction manager must send *prepare* messages to each local manager. The local manager must then issue a DbTxn::prepare and await its successful return before responding to the distributed transaction manager. Only after the distributed transaction manager receives successful responses from all of its *prepare* messages should it issue any *commit* messages.

In the case of nested transactions, preparing a parent transaction causes all unresolved children of the parent transaction to be prepared.

The DbTxn::prepare method either returns a non-zero error value or throws an exception that encapsulates a non-zero error value on failure, and returns 0 on success.

Errors

The DbTxn::prepare method may fail and throw an exception or return a non-zero error for errors specified for other Berkeley DB and C library or system methods. If a catastrophic error has occurred, the DbTxn::prepare method may fail and either return DB_RUNRECOVERY or throw an exception encapsulating DB_RUNRECOVERY, in which case all subsequent Berkeley DB calls will fail in the same way.

Dbc

```
#include <db_cxx.h>

class Dbc { ... };
```

Description

This manual page describes the specific details of the Dbc class, which provides cursor support for the access methods in Db.

The Dbc functions are the library interface supporting sequential access to the records stored by the access methods of the Berkeley DB library. Cursors are created by calling the **Db::cursor** method which returns a pointer to a Dbc object.

Dbc::close

```
#include <db_cxx.h>

int
Dbc::close(void);
```

Description

The Dbc::close method discards the cursor.

It is possible for the Dbc::close method to return DB_LOCK_DEADLOCK, signaling that any enclosing transaction should be aborted. If the application is already intending to abort the transaction, this error should be ignored, and the application should proceed.

Once Dbc::close has been called, regardless of its return, the cursor handle may not be used again.

The Dbc::close method either returns a non-zero error value or throws an exception that encapsulates a non-zero error value on failure, and returns 0 on success.

Errors

The Dbc::close method may fail and throw an exception or return a non-zero error for the following conditions:

- DB_LOCK_DEADLOCK   The operation was selected to resolve a deadlock.

- EINVAL   An invalid flag value or parameter was specified.

  The cursor was previously closed.

The Dbc::close method may fail and throw an exception or return a non-zero error for errors specified for other Berkeley DB and C library or system methods. If a catastrophic error has occurred, the Dbc::close method may fail and either return DB_RUNRECOVERY or throw an exception encapsulating DB_RUNRECOVERY, in which case all subsequent Berkeley DB calls will fail in the same way.

This manual page describes the specific details of the Dbc class, which provides cursor support for the access methods in Db.

The Dbc functions are the library interface supporting sequential access to the records stored by the access methods of the Berkeley DB library. Cursors are created by calling the **Db::cursor** method which returns a pointer to a Dbc object.

Dbc::count

```
#include <db_cxx.h>

int
Dbc::count(db_recno_t *countp, u_int32_t flags);
```

Description

The Dbc::count method returns a count of the number of duplicate data items for the key referenced by the cursor into the memory location referenced by **countp**. If the underlying database does not support duplicate data items the call will still succeed and a count of 1 will be returned.

The **flags** parameter is currently unused, and must be set to 0.

If the **cursor** argument is not yet initialized, the Dbc::count method either returns EINVAL or throws an exception that encapsulates EINVAL.

Otherwise, the Dbc::count method either returns a non-zero error value or throws an exception that encapsulates a non-zero error value on failure, and returns 0 on success.

Errors

The Dbc::count method may fail and throw an exception or return a non-zero error for errors specified for other Berkeley DB and C library or system methods. If a catastrophic error has occurred, the Dbc::count method may fail and either return DB_RUNRECOVERY or throw an exception encapsulating DB_RUNRECOVERY, in which case all subsequent Berkeley DB calls will fail in the same way.

Dbc::del

```
#include <db_cxx.h>

int
Dbc::del(u_int32_t flags);
```

Description

The Dbc::del method deletes the key/data pair currently referenced by the cursor.

The **flags** parameter is currently unused, and must be set to 0.

The cursor position is unchanged after a delete, and subsequent calls to cursor functions expecting the cursor to reference an existing key will fail.

If the element has already been deleted, Dbc::del will return DB_KEYEMPTY.

If the cursor is not yet initialized, the Dbc::del method either returns EINVAL or throws an exception that encapsulates EINVAL.

Otherwise, the Dbc::del method either returns a non-zero error value or throws an exception that encapsulates a non-zero error value on failure, and returns 0 on success.

Errors

The Dbc::del method may fail and throw an exception or return a non-zero error for the following conditions:

- DB_LOCK_DEADLOCK   The operation was selected to resolve a deadlock.
- EINVAL   An invalid flag value or parameter was specified.

- EPERM   Write attempted on read-only cursor when the DB_INIT_CDB flag was specified to **DbEnv::open**.

The Dbc::del method may fail and throw an exception or return a non-zero error for errors specified for other Berkeley DB and C library or system methods. If a catastrophic error has occurred, the Dbc::del method may fail and either return DB_RUNRECOVERY or throw an exception encapsulating DB_RUNRECOVERY, in which case all subsequent Berkeley DB calls will fail in the same way.

Dbc::dup

```
#include <db_cxx.h>

int
Dbc::dup(Dbc **cursorp, u_int32_t flags);
```

Description

The Dbc::dup method creates a new cursor that uses the same transaction and locker ID as the original cursor. This is useful when an application is using locking and requires two or more cursors in the same thread of control.

The **flags** value must be set to 0 or by bitwise inclusively **OR**'ing together one or more of the following values.

- DB_POSITION   The newly created cursor is initialized to reference the same position in the database as the original cursor and hold the same locks. If the DB_POSITION flag is not specified, then the created cursor is uninitialized and will behave like a cursor newly created using **Db::cursor**.

When using the Berkeley DB Concurrent Data Store product, there can be only one active write cursor at a time. For this reason, attempting to duplicate a cursor for which the DB_WRITECURSOR flag was specified during creation will return an error.

If the **cursor** argument is not yet initialized, the Dbc::dup method either returns EINVAL or throws an exception that encapsulates EINVAL.

Otherwise, the Dbc::dup method either returns a non-zero error value or throws an exception that encapsulates a non-zero error value on failure, and returns 0 on success.

Errors

The Dbc::dup method may fail and throw an exception or return a non-zero error for the following conditions:

- EINVAL   An invalid flag value or parameter was specified.

  The **cursor** argument was created using the DB_WRITECURSOR flag in the Berkeley DB Concurrent Data Store product.

The Dbc::dup method may fail and throw an exception or return a non-zero error for errors specified for other Berkeley DB and C library or system methods. If a catastrophic error has occurred, the Dbc::dup method may fail and either return DB_RUNRECOVERY or throw an exception encapsulating DB_RUNRECOVERY, in which case all subsequent Berkeley DB calls will fail in the same way.

Dbc::get

```
#include <db_cxx.h>

int
Dbc::get(Dbt *key, Dbt *data, u_int32_t flags);
```

Description

The Dbc::get method retrieves key/data pairs from the database. The address and length of the key are returned in the object referenced by **key** (except for the case of the DB_SET flag, in which the **key** object is unchanged), and the address and length of the data are returned in the object referenced by **data**.

Modifications to the database during a sequential scan will be reflected in the scan; that is, records inserted behind a cursor will not be returned while records inserted in front of a cursor will be returned.

In Queue and Recno databases, missing entries (that is, entries that were never explicitly created or that were created and then deleted), will be skipped during a sequential scan.

The **flags** parameter must be set to one of the following values:

- DB_CURRENT   Return the key/data pair currently referenced by the cursor.

  If the cursor key/data pair was deleted, Dbc::get will return DB_KEYEMPTY.

  If the cursor is not yet initialized, the Dbc::get method either returns EINVAL or throws an exception that encapsulates EINVAL.

- DB_FIRST, DB_LAST   The cursor is set to reference the first (last) key/data pair of the database, and that pair is returned. In the presence of duplicate key values, the first (last) data item in the set of duplicates is returned.

  If the database is a Queue or Recno database, Dbc::get using the DB_FIRST (DB_LAST) flags will ignore any keys that exist but were never explicitly created by the application or were created and later deleted.

  If the database is empty, Dbc::get will return DB_NOTFOUND.

- DB_GET_BOTH   The DB_GET_BOTH flag is identical to the DB_SET flag, except that both the key and the data arguments must be matched by the key and data item in the database.

- DB_GET_RECNO   Return the record number associated with the cursor. The record number will be returned in **data** as described in **Dbt**. The **key** parameter is ignored.

  For DB_GET_RECNO to be specified, the underlying database must be of type Btree, and it must have been created with the DB_RECNUM flag.

- DB_JOIN_ITEM   Do not use the data value found in all of the cursors as a lookup key for the primary database, but simply return it in the key parameter instead. The data parameter is left unchanged.

For DB_JOIN_ITEM to be specified, the underlying cursor must have been returned from the **Db::join** method.

- DB_NEXT, DB_PREV   If the cursor is not yet initialized, DB_NEXT (DB_PREV) is identical to DB_FIRST (DB_LAST). Otherwise, the cursor is moved to the next (previous) key/data pair of the database, and that pair is returned. In the presence of duplicate key values, the value of the key may not change.

  If the database is a Queue or Recno database, Dbc::get using the DB_NEXT (DB_PREV) flag will skip any keys that exist but were never explicitly created by the application, or were created and later deleted.

  If the cursor is already on the last (first) record in the database, Dbc::get will return DB_NOTFOUND.

- DB_NEXT_DUP   If the next key/data pair of the database is a duplicate record for the current key/data pair, the cursor is moved to the next key/data pair of the database, and that pair is returned. Otherwise, Dbc::get will return DB_NOTFOUND.

  If the cursor is not yet initialized, the Dbc::get method either returns EINVAL or throws an exception that encapsulates EINVAL.

- DB_NEXT_NODUP, DB_PREV_NODUP   If the cursor is not yet initialized, DB_NEXT_NODUP (DB_PREV_NODUP) is identical to DB_FIRST (DB_LAST). Otherwise, the cursor is moved to the next (previous) non-duplicate key/data pair of the database, and that pair is returned.

  If the database is a Queue or Recno database, Dbc::get using the DB_NEXT_NODUP (DB_PREV_NODUP) flags will ignore any keys that exist but were never explicitly created by the application, or were created and later deleted.

  If no non-duplicate key/data pairs occur after (before) the cursor position in the database, Dbc::get will return DB_NOTFOUND.

- DB_SET   Move the cursor to the specified key/data pair of the database, and return the datum associated with the given key.

  In the presence of duplicate key values, Dbc::get will return the first data item for the given key.

  If the database is a Queue or Recno database and the requested key exists, but was never explicitly created by the application or was later deleted, Dbc::get will return DB_KEYEMPTY.

  If no matching keys are found, Dbc::get will return DB_NOTFOUND.

- DB_SET_RANGE   The DB_SET_RANGE flag is identical to the DB_SET flag, except that the key is returned as well as the data item; in the case of the Btree access method, the returned key/data pair is the smallest key greater than or equal to the specified key (as determined by the comparison method), permitting partial key matches and range searches.

- DB_SET_RECNO   Move the cursor to the specific numbered record of the database, and return the associated key/data pair. The **data** field of the specified **key** must be a pointer to a memory location from which a db_recno_t may be read, as described in **Dbt**. This memory location will be read to determine the record to be retrieved.

For DB_SET_RECNO to be specified, the underlying database must be of type Btree, and it must have been created with the DB_RECNUM flag.

In addition, the following flag may be set by bitwise inclusively **OR**'ing it into the **flags** parameter:

- DB_RMW   Acquire write locks instead of read locks when doing the retrieval. Setting this flag can eliminate deadlock during a read-modify-write cycle by acquiring the write lock during the read part of the cycle so that another thread of control acquiring a read lock for the same item, in its own read-modify-write cycle, will not result in deadlock.

Otherwise, the Dbc::get method either returns a non-zero error value or throws an exception that encapsulates a non-zero error value on failure, and returns 0 on success.

If Dbc::get fails for any reason, the state of the cursor will be unchanged.

Errors

The Dbc::get method may fail and throw an exception or return a non-zero error for the following conditions:

- DB_LOCK_DEADLOCK   The operation was selected to resolve a deadlock.
- ENOMEM   There was insufficient memory to return the requested item.
- EINVAL   An invalid flag value or parameter was specified.

  The specified cursor was not currently initialized.

The Dbc::get method may fail and throw an exception or return a non-zero error for errors specified for other Berkeley DB and C library or system methods. If a catastrophic error has occurred, the Dbc::get method may fail and either return DB_RUNRECOVERY or throw an exception encapsulating DB_RUNRECOVERY, in which case all subsequent Berkeley DB calls will fail in the same way.

Dbc::put

```
#include <db_cxx.h>

int
Dbc::put(Dbt *key, Dbt *data, u_int32_t flags);
```

Description

The Dbc::put method stores key/data pairs into the database.

The **flags** parameter must be set to one of the following values:

- DB_AFTER   In the case of the Btree and Hash access methods, insert the data element as a duplicate element of the key referenced by the cursor. The new element appears immediately after the current cursor position. It is an error to specify DB_AFTER if the underlying Btree or Hash database does not support duplicate data items. The **key** parameter is ignored.

In the case of the Recno access method, it is an error to specify DB_AFTER if the underlying Recno database was not created with the DB_RENUMBER flag. If the DB_RENUMBER flag was specified, a new key is created, all records after the inserted item are automatically renumbered, and the key of the new record is returned in the structure referenced by the parameter **key**. The initial value of the **key** parameter is ignored. See **Db::open** for more information.

The DB_AFTER flag may not be specified to the Queue access method.

If the current cursor record has already been deleted and the underlying access method is Hash, Dbc::put will return DB_NOTFOUND. If the underlying access method is Btree or Recno, the operation will succeed.

If the cursor is not yet initialized or a duplicate sort function has been specified, the Dbc::put function will return EINVAL.

- DB_BEFORE   In the case of the Btree and Hash access methods, insert the data element as a duplicate element of the key referenced by the cursor. The new element appears immediately before the current cursor position. It is an error to specify DB_BEFORE if the underlying Btree or Hash database does not support duplicate data items. The **key** parameter is ignored.

In the case of the Recno access method, it is an error to specify DB_BEFORE if the underlying Recno database was not created with the DB_RENUMBER flag. If the DB_RENUMBER flag was specified, a new key is created, the current record and all records after it are automatically renumbered, and the key of the new record is returned in the structure referenced by the parameter **key**. The initial value of the **key** parameter is ignored. See **Db::open** for more information.

The DB_BEFORE flag may not be specified to the Queue access method.

If the current cursor record has already been deleted and the underlying access method is Hash, Dbc::put will return DB_NOTFOUND. If the underlying access method is Btree or Recno, the operation will succeed.

If the cursor is not yet initialized or a duplicate sort function has been specified, Dbc::put will return EINVAL.

- DB_CURRENT   Overwrite the data of the key/data pair referenced by the cursor with the specified data item. The **key** parameter is ignored.

If a duplicate sort function has been specified and the data item of the current referenced key/data pair does not compare equally to the **data** parameter, Dbc::put will return EINVAL.

If the current cursor record has already been deleted and the underlying access method is Hash, Dbc::put will return DB_NOTFOUND. If the underlying access method is Btree, Queue, or Recno, the operation will succeed.

If the cursor is not yet initialized, Dbc::put will return EINVAL.

- DB_KEYFIRST   In the case of the Btree and Hash access methods, insert the specified key/data pair into the database.

If the underlying database supports duplicate data items, and if the key already exists in the database and a duplicate sort function has been specified, the inserted data item is added in its sorted location. If the key already exists in the database and no duplicate sort function has been specified, the inserted data item is added as the first of the data items for that key.

The DB_KEYFIRST flag may not be specified to the Queue or Recno access methods.

- DB_KEYLAST   In the case of the Btree and Hash access methods, insert the specified key/data pair into the database.

  If the underlying database supports duplicate data items, and if the key already exists in the database and a duplicate sort function has been specified, the inserted data item is added in its sorted location. If the key already exists in the database, and no duplicate sort function has been specified, the inserted data item is added as the last of the data items for that key.

  The DB_KEYLAST flag may not be specified to the Queue or Recno access methods.

- DB_NODUPDATA   In the case of the Btree and Hash access methods, insert the specified key/data pair into the database unless it already exists in the database. If the key/data pair already appears in the database, DB_KEYEXIST is returned. The DB_NODUPDATA flag may only be specified if the underlying database has been configured to support sorted duplicate data items.

  The DB_NODUPDATA flag may not be specified to the Queue or Recno access methods.

Otherwise, the Dbc::put method either returns a non-zero error value or throws an exception that encapsulates a non-zero error value on failure, and returns 0 on success.

If Dbc::put fails for any reason, the state of the cursor will be unchanged. If Dbc::put succeeds and an item is inserted into the database, the cursor is always positioned to reference the newly inserted item.

Errors

The Dbc::put method may fail and throw an exception or return a non-zero error for the following conditions:

- DB_LOCK_DEADLOCK   The operation was selected to resolve a deadlock.
- EACCES   An attempt was made to modify a read-only database.
- EINVAL   An invalid flag value or parameter was specified.

  The DB_BEFORE or DB_AFTER flags were specified, and the underlying access method is Queue.

  An attempt was made to add a record to a fixed-length database that was too large to fit.

- EPERM   Write attempted on read-only cursor when the DB_INIT_CDB flag was specified to **DbEnv::open**.

The Dbc::put method may fail and throw an exception or return a non-zero error for errors specified for other Berkeley DB and C library or system methods. If a catastrophic error has occurred, the Dbc::put method may fail and either return DB_RUNRECOVERY or throw an exception encapsulating DB_RUNRECOVERY, in which case all subsequent Berkeley DB calls will fail in the same way.

Dbt

```
#include <db_cxx.h>

class Dbt {
public:
        void *get_data()
        const; void set_data(void *);

        u_int32_t get_size() const;
        void set_size(u_int32_t);

        u_int32_t get_ulen() const;
        void set_ulen(u_int32_t);

        u_int32_t get_dlen() const;
        void set_dlen(u_int32_t);

        u_int32_t get_doff() const;
        void set_doff(u_int32_t);

        u_int32_t get_flags() const;
        void set_flags(u_int32_t);

        Dbt(void *data, size_t size);
        Dbt();
        Dbt(const Dbt &);
        Dbt &operator = (const Dbt &);
        ~Dbt();
};
```

Description

This manual page describes the specific details of the Dbt class, used to encode keys and data items in a database.

Key/Data Pairs

Storage and retrieval for the Db access methods are based on key/data pairs. Both key and data items are represented by Dbt objects. Key and data byte strings may reference strings of zero length up to strings of essentially unlimited length. See "Database Limits" for more information.

The Dbt class provides simple access to an underlying data structure, whose elements can be examined or changed using the **set_** or **get_** methods. The remainder of the manual page sometimes refers to these accesses using the underlying name; for example, simply **ulen** instead of Dbt::get_ulen and Dbt::set_ulen. Dbt can be subclassed, providing a way to associate with it additional data or references to other structures.

The constructors set all elements of the underlying structure to zero. The constructor with two arguments has the effect of setting all elements to zero except for the specified **data** and **size** elements.

In the case in which the **flags** structure element is set to 0, when the application is providing Berkeley DB a key or data item to store into the database, Berkeley DB expects the **data** object to point to a byte string of **size** bytes. When returning a key/data item to the application, Berkeley DB will store into the **data** object a pointer to a byte string of **size** bytes, and the memory referenced by the pointer will be allocated and managed by Berkeley DB.

The elements of the structure underlying the Dbt class are defined as follows:

- void *data;   A pointer to a byte string. This element is accessed using Dbt::get_data and Dbt::set_data, and may be initialized using one of the constructors.

- int offset;   The number of bytes offset into the **data** array to determine the portion of the array actually used. This element is accessed using Dbt::get_offset and Dbt::set_offset.

- u_int32_t size;   The length of **data**, in bytes. This element is accessed using Dbt::get_size and Dbt::set_size, and may be initialized using the constructor with two arguments.

- u_int32_t ulen;   The size of the user's buffer (referenced by **data**), in bytes. This location is not written by the Db methods.

  Note that applications can determine the length of a record by setting the **ulen** to 0 and checking the return value found in **size**. See the DB_DBT_USERMEM flag for more information.

  This element is accessed using Dbt::get_ulen and Dbt::set_ulen.

- u_int32_t dlen;   The length of the partial record being read or written by the application, in bytes. See the DB_DBT_PARTIAL flag for more information. This element is accessed using Dbt::get_dlen, and Dbt::set_dlen.

- u_int32_t doff;   The offset of the partial record being read or written by the application, in bytes. See the DB_DBT_PARTIAL flag for more information. This element is accessed using Dbt::get_doff and Dbt::set_doff.

- u_int32_t flags;

- This element is accessed using Dbt::get_flags and Dbt::set_flags.

  The **flags** value must be set to 0 or by bitwise inclusively **OR**'ing together one or more of the following values.

  - DB_DBT_MALLOC   When this flag is set Berkeley DB will allocate memory for the returned key or data item (using **malloc**(3) or the user-specified malloc method) and return a pointer to it in the **data** field of the key or data Dbt object. As any allocated memory becomes the responsibility of the calling application, the caller must determine if memory was allocated using the returned value of the **data** field.

    It is an error to specify more than one of DB_DBT_MALLOC, DB_DBT_REALLOC and DB_DBT_USERMEM.

- DB_DBT_REALLOC   When this flag is set Berkeley DB will allocate memory
  for the returned key or data item (using **realloc**(3) or the user-specified realloc
  method) and return a pointer to it in the **data** field of the key or data Dbt object.
  As any allocated memory becomes the responsibility of the calling application, the
  caller must determine if memory was allocated using the returned value of the
  data field.

  It is an error to specify more than one of DB_DBT_MALLOC,
  DB_DBT_REALLOC, and DB_DBT_USERMEM.

- DB_DBT_USERMEM   The **data** field of the key or data object must reference
  memory that is at least **ulen** bytes in length. If the length of the requested item is
  less than or equal to that number of bytes, the item is copied into the memory referenced by the **data** field. Otherwise, the **size** field is set to the length needed for
  the requested item, and the error ENOMEM is returned.

  It is an error to specify more than one of DB_DBT_MALLOC,
  DB_DBT_REALLOC and DB_DBT_USERMEM.

If DB_DBT_MALLOC or DB_DBT_REALLOC is specified, Berkeley DB allocates a
properly sized byte array to contain the data. This can be convenient if you know little
about the nature of the data, specifically the size of data in the database. However, if
your application makes repeated calls to retrieve keys or data, you may notice increased
garbage collection due to this allocation. If you know the maximum size of data you are
retrieving, you might decrease the memory burden and speed your application by allocating your own byte array and using DB_DBT_USERMEM. Even if you don't know
the maximum size, you can use this option and reallocate your array whenever your
retrieval API call returns an ENOMEM error or throws an exception encapsulating an
ENOMEM.

- DB_DBT_PARTIAL   Do partial retrieval or storage of an item. If the calling
  application is doing a get, the **dlen** bytes starting **doff** bytes from the beginning of
  the retrieved data record are returned as if they comprised the entire record. If any
  or all of the specified bytes do not exist in the record, the get is successful and the
  existing bytes or nul bytes are returned.

For example, if the data portion of a retrieved record was 100 bytes, and a partial
retrieval was done using a Dbt having a **dlen** field of 20 and a **doff** field of 85, the get
call would succeed, the **data** field would reference the last 15 bytes of the record, and
the **size** field would be set to 15.

If the calling application is doing a put, the **dlen** bytes starting **doff** bytes from the
beginning of the specified key's data record are replaced by the data specified by the
data and **size** objects. If **dlen** is smaller than **size**, the record will grow; if **dlen** is larger
than **size**, the record will shrink. If the specified bytes do not exist, the record will be
extended using nul bytes as necessary, and the put call will succeed.

It is an error to attempt a partial put using the **Db::put** method in a database that supports duplicate records. Partial puts in databases supporting duplicate records must be
done using a **Dbc** method.

It is an error to attempt a partial put with differing **dlen** and **size** values in Queue or Recno databases with fixed-length records.

For example, if the data portion of a retrieved record was 100 bytes, and a partial put was done using a Dbt having a **dlen** field of 20, a **doff** field of 85, and a **size** field of 30, the resulting record would be 115 bytes in length, where the last 30 bytes would be those specified by the put call.

30

Java API

Db

```
import com.sleepycat.db.*;

public class Db extends Object
{
        Db(DbEnv dbenv, int flags)
                throws DbException;
        ...
}
```

Description

This manual page describes the specific details of the Db class, which is the center of access method activity.

If no **dbenv** value is specified, the database is standalone; that is, it is not part of any Berkeley DB environment.

If a **dbenv** value is specified, the database is created within the specified Berkeley DB environment. The database access methods automatically make calls to the other subsystems in Berkeley DB based on the enclosing environment. For example, if the environment has been configured to use locking, then the access methods will automatically acquire the correct locks when reading and writing pages of the database.

The **flags** value must be set to 0 or by bitwise inclusively **OR**'ing together one or more of the following values.

- Db.DB_XA_CREATE   Instead of creating a standalone database, create a database intended to be accessed via applications running under a X/Open conformant Transaction Manager. The database will be opened in the environment specified by the OPENINFO parameter of the GROUPS section of the ubbconfig file. See "XA Resource Manager" in the *Reference Guide* for more information.

Db.close

```
import com.sleepycat.db.*;

public int close(int flags)
        throws DbException;
```

Description

The Db.close method flushes any cached database information to disk, closes any open cursors, frees any allocated resources, and closes any underlying files. Because key/data pairs are cached in memory, failing to sync the file with the Db.close or **Db.sync** method may result in inconsistent or lost information.

The **flags** parameter must be set to 0 or the following value:

- Db.DB_NOSYNC   Do not flush cached information to disk. The DB_NOSYNC flag is a dangerous option. It should only be set if the application is doing logging (with transactions) so that the database is recoverable after a system or application crash, or if the database is always generated from scratch after any system or application crash.

  It is important to understand that flushing cached information to disk only minimizes the window of opportunity for corrupted data. Although unlikely, it is possible for database corruption to happen if a system or application crash occurs while writing data to the database. To ensure that database corruption never occurs, applications must either use transactions and logging with automatic recovery, use logging and application-specific recovery, or edit a copy of the database. After all applications using the database have successfully called Db.close, they must also atomically replace the original database with the updated copy.

When multiple threads are using the Berkeley DB handle concurrently, only a single thread may call the Db.close method.

Once Db.close has been called, regardless of its return, the **Db** handle may not be accessed again.

The Db.close method throws an exception that encapsulates a non-zero error value on failure, and returns DB_INCOMPLETE if the underlying database still has dirty pages in the cache. (The only reason to return DB_INCOMPLETE is if another thread of control was writing pages in the underlying database file at the same time as the Db.close method was called. For this reason, a return of DB_INCOMPLETE can normally be ignored; or, in cases where it is a possible return value, the DB_NOSYNC option should probably have been specified.)

Errors

The Db.close method may fail and throw an exception for errors specified for other Berkeley DB and C library or system methods. If a catastrophic error has occurred, the Db.close method may fail and throw a **DbRunRecoveryException**, in which case all subsequent Berkeley DB calls will fail in the same way.

Db.cursor

```
import com.sleepycat.db.*;

public Dbc cursor(DbTxn txnid, int flags)
    throws DbException;
```

Description

The Db.cursor method creates a cursor.

If the operation is to be transactionally protected, the **txnid** parameter is a transaction handle returned from **DbEnv.txn_begin**, otherwise, null.

To transaction-protect cursor operations, cursors must be opened and closed within the context of a transaction, and the **txnid** parameter specifies the transaction context in which the cursor may be used.

The **flags** value must be set to 0 or by bitwise inclusively **OR**'ing together one or more of the following values.

- Db.DB_WRITECURSOR   Specify that the cursor will be used to update the database. This flag should **only** be set when the DB_INIT_CDB flag was specified to **DbEnv.open**.

The Db.cursor method throws an exception that encapsulates a non-zero error value on failure.

Errors

The Db.cursor method may fail and throw an exception encapsulating a non-zero error for the following conditions:

- EINVAL   An invalid flag value or parameter was specified.

The Db.cursor method may fail and throw an exception for errors specified for other Berkeley DB and C library or system methods. If a catastrophic error has occurred, the Db.cursor method may fail and throw a **DbRunRecoveryException**, in which case all subsequent Berkeley DB calls will fail in the same way.

Db.del

```
import com.sleepycat.db.*;

public int del(DbTxn txnid, Dbt key, int flags)
        throws DbException;
```

Description

The Db.del method removes key/data pairs from the database. The key/data pair associated with the specified **key** is discarded from the database. In the presence of duplicate key values, all records associated with the designated key will be discarded.

If the operation is to be transaction-protected, the **txnid** parameter is a transaction handle returned from **DbEnv.txn_begin**; otherwise, null.

The **flags** parameter is currently unused, and must be set to 0.

The Db.del method throws an exception that encapsulates a non-zero error value on failure, and DB_NOTFOUND if the specified **key** did not exist in the file.

Errors

The Db.del method may fail and throw an exception encapsulating a non-zero error for the following conditions:

- EACCES   An attempt was made to modify a read-only database.
- EINVAL   An invalid flag value or parameter was specified.

If the operation was selected to resolve a deadlock, the Db.del method will fail and throw a **DbDeadlockException** exception.

The Db.del method may fail and throw an exception for errors specified for other Berkeley DB and C library or system methods. If a catastrophic error has occurred, the Db.del method may fail and throw a **DbRunRecoveryException**, in which case all subsequent Berkeley DB calls will fail in the same way.

Db.fd

```
import com.sleepycat.db.*;

public int fd()
throws DbException;
```

Description

The Db.fd method returns a file descriptor representative of the underlying database. This method does not fit well into the Java framework, and may be removed in subsequent releases.

The Db.fd method throws an exception that encapsulates a non-zero error value on failure.

Errors

The Db.fd method may fail and throw an exception for errors specified for other Berkeley DB and C library or system methods. If a catastrophic error has occurred, the Db.fd method may fail and throw a **DbRunRecoveryException**, in which case all subsequent Berkeley DB calls will fail in the same way.

Db.get

```
import com.sleepycat.db.*;

public int get(DbTxn txnid, Dbt key, Dbt data, int flags)
    throws DbException;
```

Description

The Db.get method retrieves key/data pairs from the database. The byte array and length of the data associated with the specified **key** are returned in the structure referenced by **data**.

In the presence of duplicate key values, Db.get will return the first data item for the designated key. Duplicates are sorted by insert order, except where this order has been overridden by cursor operations. **Retrieval of duplicates requires the use of cursor operations.** See **Dbc.get** for details.

If the operation is to be transaction-protected, the **txnid** parameter is a transaction handle returned from **DbEnv.txn_begin**; otherwise, null.

The **flags** parameter must be set to 0 or one of the following values:

- Db.DB_CONSUME   Return the record number and data from the available record closest to the head of the queue, and delete the record. The cursor will be positioned on the deleted record. The record number will be returned in **key**, as described in **Dbt**. The data will be returned in the **data** parameter. A record is available if it is not deleted and is not currently locked. The underlying database must be of type Queue for Db.DB_CONSUME to be specified.

- Db.DB_CONSUME_WAIT   The Db.DB_CONSUME_WAIT flag is the same as the Db.DB_CONSUME flag, except that if the Queue database is empty, the thread of control will wait until there is data in the queue before returning. The underlying database must be of type Queue for Db.DB_CONSUME_WAIT to be specified.

- Db.DB_GET_BOTH   Retrieve the key/data pair only if both the key and data match the arguments.

- Db.DB_SET_RECNO   Retrieve the specified numbered key/data pair from a database. Upon return, both the **key** and **data** items will have been filled in, not just the data item as is done for all other uses of the Db.get method.

  The **data** field of the specified **key** must be a byte array large enough to hold a logical record number (that is, an int). This record number determines the record to be retrieved.

  For Db.DB_SET_RECNO to be specified, the underlying database must be of type Btree, and it must have been created with the DB_RECNUM flag.

In addition, the following flag may be set by bitwise inclusively **OR**'ing it into the **flags** parameter:

- Db.DB_RMW   Acquire write locks instead of read locks when doing the retrieval. Setting this flag can eliminate deadlock during a read-modify-write cycle by acquiring the write lock during the read part of the cycle so that another thread of control acquiring a read lock for the same item, in its own read-modify-write cycle, will not result in deadlock.

  Because the Db.get interface will not hold locks across Berkeley DB interface calls in non-transactional environments, the DB_RMW flag to the Db.get call is only meaningful in the presence of transactions.

If the database is a Queue or Recno database, and the requested key exists, but was never explicitly created by the application or was later deleted, the Db.get method returns DB_KEYEMPTY.

Otherwise, if the requested key is not in the database, the Db.get function returns DB_NOTFOUND.

Otherwise, the Db.get method throws an exception that encapsulates a non-zero error value on failure.

Errors

The Db.get method may fail and throw an exception encapsulating a non-zero error for the following conditions:

- EINVAL   An invalid flag value or parameter was specified.

  A record number of 0 was specified.

  The DB_THREAD flag was specified to the **Db.open** method, and none of the DB_DBT_MALLOC, DB_DBT_REALLOC or DB_DBT_USERMEM flags were set in the **Dbt**.

If the operation was selected to resolve a deadlock, the Db.get method will fail and throw a **DbDeadlockException** exception.

If the requested item could not be returned due to insufficient memory, the Db.get method will fail and throw a **DbMemoryException** exception.

The Db.get method may fail and throw an exception for errors specified for other Berkeley DB and C library or system methods. If a catastrophic error has occurred, the Db.get method may fail and throw a **DbRunRecoveryException**, in which case all subsequent Berkeley DB calls will fail in the same way.

Db.get_byteswapped

```
import com.sleepycat.db.*;

public boolean get_byteswapped();
```

Description

The Db.get_byteswapped method returns false if the underlying database files were created on an architecture of the same byte order as the current one, and true if they were not (that is, big-endian on a little-endian machine or vice versa). This field may be used to determine whether application data needs to be adjusted for this architecture or not.

Db.get_type

```
import com.sleepycat.db.*;

public int get_type();
```

Description

The Db.get_type method returns the type of the underlying access method (and file format). It returns one of Db.DB_BTREE, Db.DB_HASH, Db.DB_RECNO, or Db.DB_QUEUE. This value may be used to determine the type of the database after a return from **Db.open** with the **type** argument set to Db.DB_UNKNOWN.

Db.join

```
import com.sleepycat.db.*;

public Dbc join(Dbc curslist[], int flags)
     throws DbException;
```

Description

The Db.join method creates a specialized cursor for use in performing joins on secondary indexes. For information on how to organize your data to use this functionality, see "Logical Join."

The **primary** argument contains the **Db** handle of the primary database, which is keyed by the data values found in entries in the **curslist**.

The **curslist** argument contains a null- terminated array of cursors. Each cursor must have been initialized to reference the key on which the underlying database should be joined. Typically, this initialization is done by a **Dbc.get** call with the DB_SET flag specified. Once the cursors have been passed as part of a **curslist**, they should not be accessed or modified until the newly created join cursor has been closed, or else inconsistent results may be returned.

Joined values are retrieved by doing a sequential iteration over the first cursor in the **curslist** argument, and a nested iteration over each secondary cursor in the order they are specified in the **curslist** argument. This requires database traversals to search for the current datum in all the cursors after the first. For this reason, the best join performance normally results from sorting the cursors from the one that references the least number of data items to the one that references the most. By default, Db.join does this sort on behalf of its caller.

The **flags** parameter must be set to 0 or the following value:

- Db.DB_JOIN_NOSORT   Do not sort the cursors based on the number of data items they reference. If the data are structured so that cursors with many data items also share many common elements, higher performance will result from listing those cursors before cursors with fewer data items; that is, a sort order other than the default. The Db.DB_JOIN_NOSORT flag permits applications to perform join optimization prior to calling Db.join.

The returned cursor supports only the **Dbc.get** and **dbc_close** cursor functions:

- **Dbc.get**   Iterates over the values associated with the keys to which each item in **curslist** was initialized. Any data value that appears in all items specified by the **curslist** argument is then used as a key into the **primary**, and the key/data pair found in the **primary** is returned.

  The **flags** parameter must be set to 0 or the following value:

  - Db.DB_JOIN_ITEM   Do not use the data value found in all of the cursors as a lookup key for the **primary**, but simply return it in the key parameter instead. The data parameter is left unchanged.

  In addition, the following flag may be set by bitwise inclusively **OR**'ing it into the **flags** parameter:

  - Db.DB_RMW   Acquire write locks instead of read locks when doing the retrieval. Setting this flag can eliminate deadlock during a read-modify-write cycle by acquiring the write lock during the read part of the cycle so that another thread of control acquiring a read lock for the same item, in its own read-modify-write cycle, will not result in deadlock.

- **Dbc.close**   Close the returned cursor and release all resources. (Closing the cursors in **curslist** is the responsibility of the caller.)

For the returned join cursor to be used in a transaction- protected manner, the cursors listed in **curslist** must have been created within the context of the same transaction.

The Db.join method throws an exception that encapsulates a non-zero error value on failure.

Errors

The Db.join method may fail and throw an exception encapsulating a non-zero error for the following conditions:

- EINVAL   An invalid flag value or parameter was specified.

  Cursor functions other than **Dbc.get** or **Dbc.close** were called.

The Db.join method may fail and throw an exception for errors specified for other Berkeley DB and C library or system methods. If a catastrophic error has occurred, the Db.join method may fail and throw a **DbRunRecoveryException**, in which case all subsequent Berkeley DB calls will fail in the same way.

Db.key_range

```
import com.sleepycat.db.*;

public void key_range(DbTxn txnid
      Dbt key, DbKeyRange key_range, int flags)
      throws DbException;
```

Description

The Db.key_range method returns an estimate of the proportion of keys that are less than, equal to, and greater than the specified key. The underlying database must be of type Btree.

The information is returned in the **key_range** argument, which contains three elements of type double, **less**, **equal,** and **greater**. Values are in the range of 0 to 1; for example, if the field **less** is 0.05, it indicates that 5% of the keys in the database are less than the key argument. The value for **equal** will be zero if there is no matching key and non-zero otherwise.

If the operation is to be transaction-protected, the **txnid** parameter is a transaction handle returned from **DbEnv.txn_begin**; otherwise, null. The Db.key_range method does not retain the locks it acquires for the life of the transaction, so estimates may not be repeatable.

The **flags** parameter is currently unused, and must be set to 0.

The Db.key_range method throws an exception that encapsulates a non-zero error value on failure.

Errors

The Db.key_range method may fail and throw an exception encapsulating a non-zero error for the following conditions:

- EINVAL   An invalid flag value or parameter was specified.

    The underlying database was not of type Btree.

If the operation was selected to resolve a deadlock, the Db.key_range method will fail and throw a **DbDeadlockException** exception.

The Db.key_range method may fail and throw an exception for errors specified for other Berkeley DB and C library or system methods. If a catastrophic error has occurred, the Db.key_range method may fail and throw a **DbRunRecoveryException**, in which case all subsequent Berkeley DB calls will fail in the same way.

Db.open

```
import com.sleepycat.db.*;
import java.io.FileNotFoundException;

public void open(String file,
    String database, int type, int flags, int mode)
      throws DbException, FileNotFoundException;
```

Description

The currently supported Berkeley DB file formats (or *access methods*) are Btree, Hash, Queue, and Recno. The Btree format is a representation of a sorted, balanced tree structure. The Hash format is an extensible, dynamic hashing scheme. The Queue format supports fast access to fixed-length records accessed sequentially or by logical record number. The Recno format supports fixed- or variable-length records, accessed sequentially or by logical record number, and optionally backed by a flat text file.

Storage and retrieval for the Berkeley DB access methods are based on key/data pairs; see **Dbt** for more information.

The Db.open interface opens the database represented by the **file** and **database** arguments for both reading and writing. The **file** argument is used as the name of an underlying file that will be used to back the database. The **database** argument is optional and allows applications to have multiple databases in a single file. Although no **database** argument needs to be specified, it is an error to attempt to open a second database in a **file** that was not initially created using a **database** name. Further, the **database** argument is not supported by the Queue format.

In-memory databases never intended to be preserved on disk may be created by setting both the **file** and **database** arguments to null. Note that in-memory databases can only ever be shared by sharing the single database handle that created them, in circumstances where doing so is safe.

The **type** argument is of type int, and must be set to one of Db.DB_BTREE, Db.DB_HASH, Db.DB_QUEUE, Db.DB_RECNO, or Db.DB_UNKNOWN. If **type** is Db.DB_UNKNOWN, the database must already exist, and Db.open will automatically determine its type. The **Db.get_type** method may be used to determine the underlying type of databases opened using Db.DB_UNKNOWN.

The **flags** and **mode** arguments specify the way files will be opened and/or created if they do not already exist.

The **flags** value must be set to 0 or by bitwise inclusively **OR**'ing together one or more of the following values.

- Db.DB_CREATE   Create any underlying files, as necessary. If the files do not already exist and the DB_CREATE flag is not specified, the call will fail.

- Db.DB_EXCL   Return an error if the file already exists. Underlying filesystem primitives are used to implement this flag. For this reason, it is only applicable to the file and cannot be used to test whether a database in a file already exists.

    The Db.DB_EXCL flag is only meaningful when specified with the Db.DB_CREATE flag.

- Db.DB_NOMMAP   Do not map this database into process memory (see the description of the **DbEnv.set_mp_mmapsize** method for further information).

- Db.DB_RDONLY   Open the database for reading only. Any attempt to modify items in the database will fail, regardless of the actual permissions of any underlying files.

- Db.DB_THREAD   Cause the **Db** handle returned by Db.open to be *free-threaded*; that is, usable by multiple threads within a single address space.

  Threading is always assumed in the Java API, so no special flags are required, and Berkeley DB functions will always behave as if the DB_THREAD flag were specified.

- Db.DB_TRUNCATE   Physically truncate the underlying file, discarding all previous databases it might have held. Underlying filesystem primitives are used to implement this flag. For this reason, it is only applicable to the file and cannot be used to discard databases within a file.

  The Db.DB_TRUNCATE flag cannot be transaction- protected, and it is an error to specify it in a transaction protected environment.

On UNIX systems, or in IEEE/ANSI Std 1003.1 (POSIX) environments, all files created by the access methods are created with mode **mode** (as described in **chmod**(2)) and modified by the process' umask value at the time of creation (see **umask**(2)). The group ownership of created files is based on the system and directory defaults, and it is not further specified by Berkeley DB. If **mode** is 0, files are created readable and writable by both owner and group. On Windows systems, the mode argument is ignored.

Calling Db.open is a reasonably expensive operation, and maintaining a set of open databases will normally be preferable to repeatedly opening and closing the database for each new query.

The Db.open method throws an exception that encapsulates a non-zero error value on failure.

Environment Variables

- DB_HOME   If the **dbenv** argument to **db_create** was initialized using **DbEnv.open**, the environment variable **DB_HOME** may be used as the path of the database environment home. Specifically, Db.open is affected by the configuration value DB_DATA_DIR.

- TMPDIR   If the **file** and **dbenv** arguments to Db.open are null, the environment variable **TMPDIR** may be used as a directory in which to create a temporary backing file.

Errors

The Db.open method may fail and throw an exception encapsulating a non-zero error for the following conditions:

- Db.DB_OLD_VERSION   The database cannot be opened without being first upgraded.

- EEXIST   DB_CREATE and DB_EXCL were specified and the file exists.

- EINVAL   An invalid flag value or parameter was specified (for example, unknown database type, page size, hash function, pad byte, byte order) or a flag value or parameter that is incompatible with the specified database.

The DB_THREAD flag was specified, and spinlocks are not implemented for this architecture.

The DB_THREAD flag was specified to Db.open, but was not specified to the **DbEnv.open** call for the environment in which the **Db** handle was created.

A backing flat text file was specified with either the DB_THREAD flag or the provided database environment supports transaction processing.

- ENOENT   A nonexistent **re_source** file was specified.

The Db.open method may fail and throw an exception for errors specified for other Berkeley DB and C library or system methods. If a catastrophic error has occurred, the Db.open method may fail and throw a **DbRunRecoveryException**, in which case all subsequent Berkeley DB calls will fail in the same way.

Db.put

```
import com.sleepycat.db.*;

public int put(DbTxn txnid, Dbt key, Dbt data, int flags)
    throws DbException;
```

Description

The Db.put method stores key/data pairs in the database. The default behavior of the Db.put function is to enter the new key/data pair, replacing any previously existing key if duplicates are disallowed, or adding a duplicate data item if duplicates are allowed. If the database supports duplicates, the Db.put method adds the new data value at the end of the duplicate set. If the database supports sorted duplicates, the new data value is inserted at the correct sorted location.

If the operation is to be transaction-protected, the **txnid** parameter is a transaction handle returned from **DbEnv.txn_begin**; otherwise, null.

The **flags** parameter must be set to 0 or one of the following values:

- Db.DB_APPEND   Append the key/data pair to the end of the database. For the Db.DB_APPEND flag to be specified, the underlying database must be a Queue or Recno database. The record number allocated to the record is returned in the specified **key**.

  There is a minor behavioral difference between the Recno and Queue access methods for the Db.DB_APPEND flag. If a transaction enclosing a Db.put operation with the Db.DB_APPEND flag aborts, the record number may be decremented (and later reallocated by a subsequent Db.DB_APPEND operation) by the Recno access method, but will not be decremented or re-allocated by the Queue access method.

- Db.DB_NODUPDATA   In the case of the Btree and Hash access methods, enter the new key/data pair only if it does not already appear in the database. If the key/data pair already appears in the database, DB_KEYEXIST is returned. The Db.DB_NODUPDATA flag may only be specified if the underlying database has been configured to support sorted duplicates.

The Db.DB_NODUPDATA flag may not be specified to the Queue or Recno access methods.

- Db.DB_NOOVERWRITE   Enter the new key/data pair only if the key does not already appear in the database. If the key already appears in the database, DB_KEYEXIST is returned. Even if the database allows duplicates, a call to Db.put with the Db.DB_NOOVERWRITE flag set will fail if the key already exists in the database.

Otherwise, the Db.put method throws an exception that encapsulates a non-zero error value on failure.

Errors

The Db.put method may fail and throw an exception encapsulating a non-zero error for the following conditions:

- EACCES   An attempt was made to modify a read-only database.
- EINVAL   An invalid flag value or parameter was specified.

  A record number of 0 was specified.

  An attempt was made to add a record to a fixed-length database that was too large to fit.

  An attempt was made to do a partial put.

- ENOSPC   A btree exceeded the maximum btree depth (255).

If the operation was selected to resolve a deadlock, the Db.put method will fail and throw a **DbDeadlockException** exception.

The Db.put method may fail and throw an exception for errors specified for other Berkeley DB and C library or system methods. If a catastrophic error has occurred, the Db.put method may fail and throw a **DbRunRecoveryException**, in which case all subsequent Berkeley DB calls will fail in the same way.

Db.remove

```
import com.sleepycat.db.*;
import java.io.FileNotFoundException;

public void remove(String file, String database, int flags)
    throws DbException, FileNotFoundException;
```

Description

The Db.remove interface removes the database specified by the **file** and **database** arguments. If no **database** is specified, the underlying file represented by **file** is removed, incidentally removing all databases that it contained.

Applications should not remove databases that are currently in use. If an underlying file is being removed and logging is currently enabled in the database environment, no database in the file may be open when the Db.remove method is called. In particular, some architectures do not permit the removal of files with open handles. On these architectures, attempts to remove databases that are currently in use by any thread of control in the system will fail.

The **flags** parameter is currently unused, and must be set to 0.

Once Db.remove has been called, regardless of its return, the **Db** handle may not be accessed again.

The Db.remove method throws an exception that encapsulates a non-zero error value on failure.

Environment Variables

- DB_HOME If the **dbenv** argument to **db_create** was initialized using **DbEnv.open** the environment variable **DB_HOME** may be used as the path of the database environment home. Specifically, Db.remove is affected by the configuration value DB_DATA_DIR.

Errors

The Db.remove method may fail and throw an exception encapsulating a non-zero error for the following conditions:

- EINVAL A database in the file is currently open.

If the file or directory does not exist, the Db.remove method will fail and throw a FileNotFoundException exception.

The Db.remove method may fail and throw an exception for errors specified for other Berkeley DB and C library or system methods. If a catastrophic error has occurred, the Db.remove method may fail and throw a **DbRunRecoveryException**, in which case all subsequent Berkeley DB calls will fail in the same way.

Db.rename

```
import com.sleepycat.db.*;
import java.io.FileNotFoundException;

public void rename(String file, String database, String newname, int flags)
     throws DbException, FileNotFoundException;
```

Description

The Db.rename interface renames the database specified by the **file** and **database** arguments to **newname**. If no **database** is specified, the underlying file represented by **file** is renamed, incidentally renaming all databases that it contained.

Applications should not rename databases that are currently in use. If an underlying file is being renamed and logging is currently enabled in the database environment, no database in the file may be open when the Db.rename method is called. In particular, some architectures do not permit renaming files with open handles. On these architectures, attempts to rename databases that are currently in use by any thread of control in the system will fail.

The **flags** parameter is currently unused, and must be set to 0.

Once Db.rename has been called, regardless of its return, the **Db** handle may not be accessed again.

The Db.rename method throws an exception that encapsulates a non-zero error value on failure.

Environment Variables

- DB_HOME   If the **dbenv** argument to **db_create** was initialized using **DbEnv.open**, the environment variable **DB_HOME** may be used as the path of the database environment home. Specifically, Db.rename is affected by the configuration value DB_DATA_DIR.

Errors

The Db.rename method may fail and throw an exception encapsulating a non-zero error for the following conditions:

- EINVAL   A database in the file is currently open.

If the file or directory does not exist, the Db.rename method will fail and throw a FileNotFoundException exception.

The Db.rename method may fail and throw an exception for errors specified for other Berkeley DB and C library or system methods. If a catastrophic error has occurred, the Db.rename method may fail and throw a **DbRunRecoveryException**, in which case all subsequent Berkeley DB calls will fail in the same way.

Db.set_append_recno

```
import com.sleepycat.db.*;

public interface DbAppendRecno
{
        public abstract void db_append_recno(Db db, Dbt data, int recno);
            throws DbException;
}
public class Db
{
        public void set_append_recno(DbAppendRecno db_append_recno)
            throws DbException;
        ...
}
```

Description

When using the DB_APPEND option of the **Db.put** method, it may be useful to modify the stored data based on the generated key. If a callback method is specified using the Db.set_append_recno method, it will be called after the record number has been selected, but before the data has been stored. The callback function must throw a **DbException** object to encapsulate the error on failure. That object will be thrown to caller of **Db.put**.

The called function must take three arguments: a reference to the enclosing database handle, the data **Dbt** to be stored, and the selected record number. The called function may then modify the data **Dbt**.

The Db.set_append_recno interface may only be used to configure Berkeley DB before the **Db.open** interface is called.

The Db.set_append_recno method throws an exception that encapsulates a non-zero error value on failure.

Db.set_bt_compare

```
import com.sleepycat.db.*;

public interface DbBtreeCompare
{
        public abstract int bt_compare(Db db, Dbt dbt1, Dbt dbt2);
}
public class Db
{
        public void set_bt_compare(DbBtreeCompare bt_compare)
                throws DbException;
        ...
}
```

Description

Set the Btree key comparison function. The comparison function is called when it is necessary to compare a key specified by the application with a key currently stored in the tree. The first argument to the comparison function is the **Dbt** representing the application supplied key, the second is the current tree's key.

The comparison function must return an integer value less than, equal to, or greater than zero if the first key argument is considered to be respectively less than, equal to, or greater than the second key argument. In addition, the comparison function must cause the keys in the database to be *well-ordered*. The comparison function must correctly handle any key values used by the application (possibly including zero-length keys). In addition, when Btree key prefix comparison is being performed (see **Db.set_bt_prefix** for more information), the comparison routine may be passed a prefix of any database key. The **data** and **size** fields of the **Dbt** are the only fields that may be used for the purposes of this comparison, and no particular alignment of the memory referenced by the **data** field may be assumed.

If no comparison function is specified, the keys are compared lexically, with shorter keys collating before longer keys. The same comparison method must be used each time a particular Btree is opened.

The Db.set_bt_compare interface may only be used to configure Berkeley DB before the **Db.open** interface is called.

The Db.set_bt_compare method throws an exception that encapsulates a non-zero error value on failure.

Errors

- EINVAL   An invalid flag value or parameter was specified.

  Called after **Db.open** was called.

Db.set_bt_minkey

```
import com.sleepycat.db.*;

public int set_bt_minkey(int bt_minkey)
     throws DbException;
```

Description

Set the minimum number of keys that will be stored on any single Btree page.

This value is used to determine which keys will be stored on overflow pages; that is, if a key or data item is larger than the underlying database page size divided by the **bt_minkey** value, it will be stored on overflow pages instead of within the page itself. The **bt_minkey** value specified must be at least 2; if **bt_minkey** is not explicitly set, a value of 2 is used.

The Db.set_bt_minkey interface may only be used to configure Berkeley DB before the **Db.open** interface is called.

The Db.set_bt_minkey method throws an exception that encapsulates a non-zero error value on failure.

Errors

- EINVAL   An invalid flag value or parameter was specified.

  Called after **Db.open** was called.

Db.set_bt_prefix

```
import com.sleepycat.db.*;

public interface DbBtreePrefix
{
     public abstract int bt_prefix(Db db, Dbt dbt1, Dbt dbt2);
}
public class Db
{
     public void set_bt_prefix(DbBtreePrefix bt_prefix)
          throws DbException;
     ...
}
```

Description

Set the Btree prefix function. The prefix function must return the number of bytes of the second key argument that would be required by the Btree key comparison function to determine the second key argument's ordering relationship with respect to the first key argument. If the two keys are equal, the key length should be returned. The prefix function must correctly handle any key values used by the application (possibly including zero-length keys). The **data** and **size** fields of the **Dbt** are the only fields that may be used for the purposes of this determination, and no particular alignment of the memory referenced by the **data** field may be assumed.

The prefix function is used to determine the amount by which keys stored on the Btree internal pages can be safely truncated without losing their uniqueness. See the "Btree Prefix Comparison" section of the *Reference Guide* for more details about how this works. The usefulness of this is data- dependent, but can produce significantly reduced tree sizes and search times in some data sets.

If no prefix function or key comparison function is specified by the application, a default lexical comparison function is used as the prefix function. If no prefix function is specified and a key comparison function is specified, no prefix function is used. It is an error to specify a prefix function without also specifying a key comparison function.

The Db.set_bt_prefix interface may only be used to configure Berkeley DB before the **Db.open** interface is called.

The Db.set_bt_prefix method throws an exception that encapsulates a non-zero error value on failure.

Errors

- EINVAL   An invalid flag value or parameter was specified.

  Called after **Db.open** was called.

Db.set_cachesize

```
import com.sleepycat.db.*;

public int set_cachesize(int gbytes, int bytes, int ncache)
    throws DbException;
```

Description

Set the size of the database's shared memory buffer pool—that is, the cache—to **gbytes** gigabytes plus **bytes**. The cache should be the size of the normal working data set of the application, with some small amount of additional memory for unusual situations. (Note: The working set is not the same as the number of simultaneously referenced pages, and should be quite a bit larger!)

The default cache size is 256KB, and may not be specified as less than 20KB. Any cache size less than 500MB is automatically increased by 25% to account for buffer pool overhead; cache sizes larger than 500MB are used as specified. For information on tuning the Berkeley DB cache size, see "Selecting a Cache Size."

It is possible to specify caches to Berkeley DB that are large enough so that they cannot be allocated contiguously on some architectures. For example, some releases of Solaris limit the amount of memory that may be allocated contiguously by a process. If **ncache** is 0 or 1, the cache will be allocated contiguously in memory. If it is greater than 1, the cache will be broken up into **ncache** equally sized separate pieces of memory.

Because databases opened within Berkeley DB environments use the cache specified to the environment, it is an error to attempt to set a cache in a database created within an environment.

The Db.set_cachesize interface may only be used to configure Berkeley DB before the **Db.open** interface is called.

The Db.set_cachesize method throws an exception that encapsulates a non-zero error value on failure.

Errors

- EINVAL   An invalid flag value or parameter was specified.

    The specified cache size was impossibly small.

Db.set_dup_compare

```
import com.sleepycat.db.*;

public interface DbDupCompare
{
        public abstract int dup_compare(Db db, Dbt dbt1, Dbt dbt2);
}
public class Db
{
        public void set_dup_compare(DbDupCompare dup_compare)
                throws DbException;
        ...
}
```

Description

Set the duplicate data item comparison function. The comparison function is called when it is necessary to compare a data item specified by the application with a data item currently stored in the tree. The first argument to the comparison function is the **Dbt** representing the application's data item, the second is the current tree's data item.

The comparison function must return an integer value less than, equal to, or greater than zero if the first data item argument is considered to be respectively less than, equal to, or greater than the second data item argument. In addition, the comparison function must cause the data items in the set to be *well-ordered*. The comparison function must correctly handle any data item values used by the application (possibly including zero-length data items). The **data** and **size** fields of the **Dbt** are the only fields that may be used for the purposes of this comparison, and no particular alignment of the memory referenced by the **data** field may be assumed.

If no comparison function is specified, the data items are compared lexically, with shorter data items collating before longer data items. The same duplicate data item comparison method must be used each time a particular Btree is opened.

The Db.set_dup_compare interface may only be used to configure Berkeley DB before the **Db.open** interface is called.

The Db.set_dup_compare method throws an exception that encapsulates a non-zero error value on failure.

Errors

- EINVAL   An invalid flag value or parameter was specified.

Db.set_errcall

```
import com.sleepycat.db.*;

public interface DbErrcall
{
      public abstract void errcall(String errpfx, String msg);
}
public class Db
{
      public void set_errcall(DbErrcall errcall);
      ...
}
```

Description

When an error occurs in the Berkeley DB library, an exception is thrown. In some cases, however, the **errno** value may be insufficient to completely describe the cause of the error, especially during initial application debugging.

The Db.set_errcall method is used to enhance the mechanism for reporting error messages to the application. The **DbEnv.set_errcall** method must be called with a single object argument. The object's class must implement the DbErrcall interface. In some cases, when an error occurs, Berkeley DB will invoke the object's errcall() method with two arguments: The first is the prefix string (as previously set by **Db.set_errpfx** or **DbEnv.set_errpfx**), and the second is an error message string. It is up to this method to display the message in an appropriate manner.

Alternatively, you can use the **DbEnv.set_error_stream** method to display the additional information via an output stream. You should not mix these approaches.

This error-logging enhancement does not slow performance or significantly increase application size, and may be run during normal operation as well as during application debugging.

For **Db** handles opened inside of Berkeley DB environments, calling the Db.set_errcall method affects the entire environment and is equivalent to calling the **DbEnv.set_errcall** method.

The Db.set_errcall interface may be used to configure Berkeley DB at any time during the life of the application.

Db.set_errpfx

```
import com.sleepycat.db.*;

public void set_errpfx(String errpfx);
```

Description

Set the prefix string that appears before error messages issued by Berkeley DB.

For **Db** handles opened inside of Berkeley DB environments, calling the Db.set_errpfx method affects the entire environment and is equivalent to calling the **DbEnv.set_errpfx** method.

The Db.set_errpfx interface may be used to configure Berkeley DB at any time during the life of the application.

Db.set_feedback

```
import com.sleepycat.db.*;

public interface DbFeedback
{
        public abstract void db_feedback(Db db, int opcode, int pct);
}
public class Db
{
        public void set_feedback(DbFeedback db_feedback)
             throws DbException;
        ...
}
```

Description

Some operations performed by the Berkeley DB library can take non-trivial amounts of time. The Db.set_feedback method can be used by applications to monitor progress within these operations.

When an operation is likely to take a long time, Berkeley DB will call the specified callback method. This method must be declared with three arguments: The first will be a reference to the enclosing database handle; the second will be a flag value; and the third will be the percent of the operation that has been completed, specified as an integer value between 0 and 100. It is up to the callback method to display this information in an appropriate manner.

The **opcode** argument may take on any of the following values:

- Db.DB_UPGRADE   The underlying database is being upgraded.
- Db.DB_VERIFY   The underlying database is being verified.

The Db.set_feedback interface may be used to configure Berkeley DB at any time during the life of the application.

The Db.set_feedback method throws an exception that encapsulates a non-zero error value on failure.

Db.set_flags

```
import com.sleepycat.db.*;

public void set_flags(int flags)
        throws DbException;
```

Description

Calling Db.set_flags is additive, there is no way to clear flags.

The **flags** value must be set to 0 or by bitwise inclusively **OR**'ing together one or more of the following values.

Btree

The following flags may be specified for the Btree access method:

- Db.DB_DUP   Permit duplicate data items in the tree; that is, insertion when the key of the key/data pair being inserted already exists in the tree will be successful. The ordering of duplicates in the tree is determined by the order of insertion, unless the ordering is otherwise specified by use of a cursor operation. It is an error to specify both Db.DB_DUP and Db.DB_RECNUM.

- Db.DB_DUPSORT   Permit duplicate data items in the tree; that is, insertion when the key of the key/data pair being inserted already exists in the tree will be successful. The ordering of duplicates in the tree is determined by the duplicate comparison function. A default lexical comparison will be used. It is an error to specify both Db.DB_DUPSORT and Db.DB_RECNUM.

- Db.DB_RECNUM   Support retrieval from the Btree using record numbers. For more information, see the DB_GET_RECNO flag to the **Db.get** and **Dbc.get** methods.

  Logical record numbers in Btree databases are mutable in the face of record insertion or deletion. See the DB_RENUMBER flag in the Recno access method information for further discussion.

Maintaining record counts within a Btree introduces a serious point of contention, namely the page locations where the record counts are stored. In addition, the entire tree must be locked during both insertions and deletions, effectively single-threading the tree for those operations. Specifying DB_RECNUM can result in serious performance degradation for some applications and data sets.

It is an error to specify both DB_DUP and DB_RECNUM.

- Db.DB_REVSPLITOFF   Turn off reverse splitting in the Btree. As pages are emptied in a database, the Berkeley DB Btree implementation attempts to coalesce empty pages into higher-level pages in order to keep the tree as small as possible and minimize tree search time. This can hurt performance in applications with cyclical data demands; that is, applications where the database grows and shrinks repeatedly. For example, because Berkeley DB does page-level locking, the maximum level of concurrency in a database of two pages is far smaller than that in a database of 100 pages, so a database that has shrunk to a minimal size can cause severe deadlocking when a new cycle of data insertion begins.

Hash

The following flags may be specified for the Hash access method:

- Db.DB_DUP   Permit duplicate data items in the tree; that is, insertion when the key of the key/data pair being inserted already exists in the tree will be successful. The ordering of duplicates in the tree is determined by the order of insertion, unless the ordering is otherwise specified by use of a cursor operation. It is an error to specify both Db.DB_DUP and Db.DB_RECNUM.

- Db.DB_DUPSORT   Permit duplicate data items in the tree; that is, insertion when the key of the key/data pair being inserted already exists in the tree will be successful. The ordering of duplicates in the tree is determined by the duplicate comparison function. A default lexical comparison will be used. It is an error to specify both Db.DB_DUPSORT and Db.DB_RECNUM.

Queue

There are no additional flags that may be specified for the Queue access method.

Recno

The following flags may be specified for the Recno access method:

- Db.DB_RENUMBER   Specifying the DB_RENUMBER flag causes the logical record numbers to be mutable, and change as records are added to and deleted from the database. For example, the deletion of record number 4 causes records numbered 5 and greater to be renumbered downward by one. If a cursor was positioned to record number 4 before the deletion, it will reference the new record number 4 (if any such record exists) after the deletion. If a cursor was positioned after record number 4 before the deletion, it will be shifted downward one logical record, continuing to reference the same record as it did before.

Using the **Db.put** or **Dbc.put** interfaces to create new records will cause the creation of multiple records if the record number is more than one greater than the largest record currently in the database. For example, creating record 28, when record 25 was previously the last record in the database, will create records 26 and 27 as well as record 28. Attempts to retrieve records that were created in this manner will result in an error return of DB_KEYEMPTY.

If a created record is not at the end of the database, all records following the new record will be automatically renumbered upward by one. For example, the creation of a new record number 8 causes records numbered 8 and greater to be renumbered upward by one. If a cursor was positioned to record number 8 or greater before the insertion, it will be shifted upward one logical record, continuing to reference the same record as it did before.

For these reasons, concurrent access to a Recno database with the Db.DB_RENUMBER flag specified may be largely meaningless, although it is supported.

- Db.DB_SNAPSHOT   This flag specifies that any specified **re_source** file be read in its entirety when **Db.open** is called. If this flag is not specified, the **re_source** file may be read lazily.

The Db.set_flags interface may only be used to configure Berkeley DB before the **Db.open** interface is called.

The Db.set_flags method throws an exception that encapsulates a non-zero error value on failure.

Errors

- EINVAL   An invalid flag value or parameter was specified.

Db.set_h_ffactor

```
import com.sleepycat.db.*;

public void set_h_ffactor(int h_ffactor)
     throws DbException;
```

Description

Set the desired density within the hash table.

The density is an approximation of the number of keys allowed to accumulate in any one bucket, determining when the hash table grows or shrinks. If you know the average sizes of the keys and data in your dataset, setting the fill factor can enhance performance. A reasonable rule computing fill factor is to set it to the following:

```
(pagesize - 32) / (average_key_size + average_data_size + 8)
```

If no value is specified, the fill factor will be selected dynamically as pages are filled.

The Db.set_h_ffactor interface may only be used to configure Berkeley DB before the **Db.open** interface is called.

The Db.set_h_ffactor method throws an exception that encapsulates a non-zero error value on failure.

Errors

- EINVAL   An invalid flag value or parameter was specified.

    Called after **Db.open** was called.

Db.set_h_hash

```
import com.sleepycat.db.*;

public interface DbHash
{
        public abstract int hash(Db db, byte[] data, int len);
}
public class Db
{
        public void set_h_hash(DbHash h_hash)
                throws DbException;
        ...
}
```

Description

Set a user-defined hash method; if no hash method is specified, a default hash method is used. Because no hash method performs equally well on all possible data, the user may find that the built-in hash method performs poorly with a particular data set. User-specified hash functions must take a pointer to a byte string and a length as arguments, and return a value of type **int**. The hash function must handle any key values used by the application (possibly including zero-length keys).

If a hash method is specified, **Db.open** will attempt to determine whether the hash method specified is the same as the one with which the database was created, and will fail if it detects that it is not.

The Db.set_h_hash interface may only be used to configure Berkeley DB before the **Db.open** interface is called.

The Db.set_h_hash method throws an exception that encapsulates a non-zero error value on failure.

Errors

- EINVAL   An invalid flag value or parameter was specified.

    Called after **Db.open** was called.

Db.set_h_nelem

```
import com.sleepycat.db.*;

public void set_h_nelem(int h_nelem)
    throws DbException;
```

Description

Set an estimate of the final size of the hash table.

If not set or set too low, hash tables will still expand gracefully as keys are entered, although a slight performance degradation may be noticed.

The Db.set_h_nelem interface may only be used to configure Berkeley DB before the **Db.open** interface is called.

The Db.set_h_nelem method throws an exception that encapsulates a non-zero error value on failure.

Errors

- EINVAL   An invalid flag value or parameter was specified.

  Called after **Db.open** was called.

Db.set_lorder

```
import com.sleepycat.db.*;

public void set_lorder(int lorder)
    throws DbException;
```

Description

Set the byte order for integers in the stored database metadata. The number should represent the order as an integer. For example, big-endian order is the number 4,321, and little-endian order is the number 1,234. If **lorder** is not explicitly set, the host order of the machine where the Berkeley DB library was compiled is used.

The value of **lorder** is ignored except when databases are being created. If a database already exists, the byte order it uses is determined when the database is opened.

The access methods provide no guarantees about the byte-ordering of the application data stored in the database, and applications are responsible for maintaining any necessary ordering.

The Db.set_lorder interface may only be used to configure Berkeley DB before the **Db.open** interface is called.

The Db.set_lorder method throws an exception that encapsulates a non-zero error value on failure.

Errors

- EINVAL   An invalid flag value or parameter was specified.

Db.set_pagesize

```
import com.sleepycat.db.*;

public void set_pagesize(long pagesize)
    throws DbException;
```

Description

Set the size of the pages used to hold items in the database, in bytes. The minimum page size is 512 bytes, and the maximum page size is 64K bytes. If the page size is not explicitly set, one is selected based on the underlying filesystem I/O block size. The automatically selected size has a lower limit of 512 bytes and an upper limit of 16K bytes.

For information on tuning the Berkeley DB page size, see "Selecting a Page Size."

The Db.set_pagesize interface may only be used to configure Berkeley DB before the **Db.open** interface is called.

The Db.set_pagesize method throws an exception that encapsulates a non-zero error value on failure.

Errors

- EINVAL   An invalid flag value or parameter was specified.

Db.set_q_extentsize

```
import com.sleepycat.db.*;

public void set_q_extentsize(int extentsize)
    throws DbException;
```

Description

Set the size of the extents used to hold pages in a Queue database, specified as a number of pages. Each extent is created as a separate physical file. If no extent size is set, the default behavior is to create only a single underlying database file.

For information on tuning the extent size, see "Selecting an Extent Size."

The Db.set_q_extentsize interface may only be used to configure Berkeley DB before the **Db.open** interface is called.

The Db.set_q_extentsize method throws an exception that encapsulates a non-zero error value on failure.

Errors

• EINVAL An invalid flag value or parameter was specified.

Called after **Db.open** was called.

Db.set_re_delim

```
import com.sleepycat.db.*;

public void set_re_delim(int re_delim)
    throws DbException;
```

Description

Set the delimiting byte used to mark the end of a record in the backing source file for the Recno access method.

This byte is used for variable length records if the **re_source** file is specified. If the **re_source** file is specified and no delimiting byte was specified, <newline> characters (that is, ASCII 0x0a) are interpreted as end-of-record markers.

The Db.set_re_delim interface may only be used to configure Berkeley DB before the **Db.open** interface is called.

The Db.set_re_delim method throws an exception that encapsulates a non-zero error value on failure.

Errors

• EINVAL An invalid flag value or parameter was specified.

Called after **Db.open** was called.

Db.set_re_len

```
import com.sleepycat.db.*;

public void set_re_len(int re_len)
    throws DbException;
```

Description

For the Queue access method, specify that the records are of length **re_len**.

For the Recno access method, specify that the records are fixed-length, not byte-delimited, and are of length **re_len**.

Any records added to the database that are less than **re_len** bytes long are automatically padded (see **Db.set_re_pad** for more information).

Any attempt to insert records into the database that are greater than **re_len** bytes long will cause the call to fail immediately and return an error.

The Db.set_re_len interface may only be used to configure Berkeley DB before the **Db.open** interface is called.

The Db.set_re_len method throws an exception that encapsulates a non-zero error value on failure.

Errors

- EINVAL   An invalid flag value or parameter was specified.

  Called after **Db.open** was called.

Db.set_re_pad

```
import com.sleepycat.db.*;

public void set_re_pad(int re_pad)
    throws DbException;
```

Description

Set the padding character for short, fixed-length records for the Queue and Recno access methods.

If no pad character is specified, <space> characters (that is, ASCII 0x20) are used for padding.

The Db.set_re_pad interface may only be used to configure Berkeley DB before the **Db.open** interface is called.

The Db.set_re_pad method throws an exception that encapsulates a non-zero error value on failure.

Errors

- EINVAL   An invalid flag value or parameter was specified.

  Called after **Db.open** was called.

Db.set_re_source

```
import com.sleepycat.db.*;

public void set_re_source(String re_source)
    throws DbException;
```

Description

Set the underlying source file for the Recno access method. The purpose of the **re_source** value is to provide fast access and modification to databases that are normally stored as flat text files.

If the **re_source** field is set, it specifies an underlying flat text database file that is read to initialize a transient record number index. In the case of variable length records, the records are separated as specified by **Db.set_re_delim**. For example, standard UNIX byte stream files can be interpreted as a sequence of variable length records separated by <newline> characters.

In addition, when cached data would normally be written back to the underlying database file (for example, when the **Db.close** or **Db.sync** methods are called), the in-memory copy of the database will be written back to the **re_source** file.

By default, the backing source file is read lazily; that is, records are not read from the file until they are requested by the application. If multiple processes (not threads) are accessing a Recno database concurrently and are either inserting or deleting records, the backing source file must be read in its entirety before more than a single process accesses the database, and only that process should specify the backing source file as part of the Db.open call. See the **DB_SNAPSHOT** flag for more information.

Reading and writing the backing source file specified by **re_source** cannot be transaction-protected because it involves filesystem operations that are not part of the Db transaction methodology. For this reason, if a temporary database is used to hold the records; that is, a null was specified as the **file** argument to **Db.open**; it is possible to lose the contents of the **re_source** file—for example, if the system crashes at the right instant. If a file is used to hold the database, that is, if a file name was specified as the **file** argument to **Db.open**, normal database recovery on that file can be used to prevent information loss, although it is still possible that the contents of **re_source** will be lost if the system crashes.

The **re_source** file must already exist (but may be zero-length) when **Db.open** is called.

It is not an error to specify a read-only **re_source** file when creating a database, nor is it an error to modify the resulting database. However, any attempt to write the changes to the backing source file using either the **Db.sync** or **Db.close** methods will fail, of course. Specify the DB_NOSYNC flag to the **Db.close** method to stop it from attempting to write the changes to the backing file; instead, they will be silently discarded.

For all of these reasons, the **re_source** field is generally used to specify databases that are read-only for **Db** applications, and that are either generated on the fly by software tools or modified using a different mechanism—for example, a text editor.

The Db.set_re_source interface may only be used to configure Berkeley DB before the **Db.open** interface is called.

The Db.set_re_source method throws an exception that encapsulates a non-zero error value on failure.

Errors

- EINVAL An invalid flag value or parameter was specified.

  Called after **Db.open** was called.

Db.stat

```
import com.sleepycat.db.*;

public Object Db.stat(int flags);
```

Description

The Db.stat method creates a statistical structure and fills it with statistics for the database.

Statistical structures are created in allocated memory. If **db_malloc** is non-NULL, it is called to allocate the memory; otherwise, the library function **malloc**(3) is used. The function **db_malloc** must match the calling conventions of the **malloc**(3) library routine. Regardless, the caller is responsible for deallocating the returned memory. To deallocate returned memory, free the returned memory reference; references inside the returned memory do not need to be individually freed.

The **flags** parameter must be set to 0 or the following value:

- Db.DB_CACHED_COUNTS   Return a cached count of the keys and records in a database. This flag makes it possible for applications to request an possibly approximate key and record count without incurring the performance penalty of traversing the entire database. The statistics information described for the access method **XX_nkeys** and **XX_ndata** fields as follows is filled-in, but no other information is collected. If the cached information has never been set, the fields will be returned set to 0.

- Db.DB_RECORDCOUNT   Return a count of the records in a Btree or Recno Access Method database. This flag makes it possible for applications to request a record count without incurring the performance penalty of traversing the entire database. The statistics information described for the **bt_nkeys** field below is filled in, but no other information is collected.

  This option is only available for Recno databases or Btree databases in which the underlying database was created with the DB_RECNUM flag.

The Db.stat method may access all the pages in the database, incurring a severe performance penalty as well as possibly flushing the underlying buffer pool.

In the presence of multiple threads or processes accessing an active database, the information returned by Db.stat may be out-of-date.

If the database was not opened read-only and the Db.DB_CACHED_COUNTS flag was not specified, the cached key and record numbers will be updated after the statistical information has been gathered.

The Db.stat method cannot be transaction-protected. For this reason, it should be called in a thread of control that has no open cursors or active transactions.

The Db.stat method throws an exception that encapsulates a non-zero error value on failure.

Hash Statistics

In the case of a Hash database, the statistics are returned in an instance of DbHashStat. The following data fields are available from DbHashStat:

- public int hash_magic;   The magic number that identifies the file as a Hash file.
- public int hash_version;   The version of the Hash database.
- public int hash_nkeys;   The number of unique keys in the database.
- public int hash_ndata;   The number of key/data pairs in the database.]
- public int hash_pagesize;   The underlying Hash database page (and bucket) size.
- public int hash_nelem;   The estimated size of the hash table specified at database creation time.
- public int hash_ffactor;   The desired fill factor (number of items per bucket) specified at database- creation time.
- public int hash_buckets;   The number of hash buckets.
- public int hash_free;   The number of pages on the free list.
- public int hash_bfree;   The number of bytes free on bucket pages.
- public int hash_bigpages;   The number of big key/data pages.
- public int hash_big_bfree;   The number of bytes free on big item pages.
- public int hash_overflows;   The number of overflow pages (overflow pages are pages that contain items that did not fit in the main bucket page).
- public int hash_ovfl_free;   The number of bytes free on overflow pages.
- public int hash_dup;   The number of duplicate pages.
- public int hash_dup_free;   The number of bytes free on duplicate pages.

Btree and Recno Statistics

In the case of a Btree or Recno database, the statistics are returned in an instance of DbBtreeStat. The following data fields are available from DbBtreeStat:

- public int bt_magic;   The magic number that identifies the file as a Btree database.
- public int bt_version;   The version of the Btree database.
- public int bt_nkeys;   For the Btree Access Method, the number of unique keys in the database.

  For the Recno Access Method, the number of records in the database.
- public int bt_ndata;   For the Btree Access Method, the number of key/data pairs in the database.

  For the Recno Access Method, the number of records in the database. If the database has been configured to not renumber records during deletion, the number of records will only reflect undeleted records.
- public int bt_pagesize;   Underlying database page size.
- public int bt_minkey;   The minimum keys per page.

- public int bt_re_len;   The length of fixed-length records.
- public int bt_re_pad;   The padding byte value for fixed-length records.
- public int bt_levels;   The number of levels in the database.
- public int bt_int_pg;   The number of database internal pages.
- public int bt_leaf_pg;   The number of database leaf pages.
- public int bt_dup_pg;   The number of database duplicate pages.
- public int bt_over_pg;   The number of database overflow pages.
- public int bt_free;   The number of pages on the free list.
- public int bt_int_pgfree;   The number of bytes free in database internal pages.
- public int bt_leaf_pgfree;   The number of bytes free in database leaf pages.
- public int bt_dup_pgfree;   The number of bytes free in database duplicate pages.
- public int bt_over_pgfree;   The number of bytes free in database overflow pages.

Queue Statistics

In the case of a Queue database, the statistics are returned in an instance of DbQueueStat. The following data fields are available from DbQueueStat:

- public int qs_magic;   The magic number that identifies the file as a Queue file.
- public int qs_version;   The version of the Queue file type.
- public int qs_nkeys;   The number of records in the database.
- public int qs_ndata;   The number of records in the database.
- public int qs_pagesize;   The underlying database page size.
- public int qs_pages;   The number of pages in the database.
- public int qs_re_len;   The length of the records.
- public int qs_re_pad;   The padding byte value for the records.
- public int qs_pgfree;   The number of bytes free in database pages.
- public int qs_start;   The start offset.
- public int qs_first_recno;   The first undeleted record in the database.
- public int qs_cur_recno;   The last allocated record number in the database.

The Db.stat method throws an exception that encapsulates a non-zero error value on failure.

Errors

The Db.stat method may fail and throw an exception for errors specified for other Berkeley DB and C library or system methods. If a catastrophic error has occurred, the Db.stat method may fail and throw a **DbRunRecoveryException**, in which case all subsequent Berkeley DB calls will fail in the same way.

Db.sync

```
import com.sleepycat.db.*;

public int sync(int flags)
        throws DbException;
```

Description

The Db.sync method flushes any cached information to disk.

If the database is in memory only, the Db.sync method has no effect and will always succeed.

The **flags** parameter is currently unused, and must be set to 0.

It is important to understand that flushing cached information to disk only minimizes the window of opportunity for corrupted data. Although unlikely, it is possible for database corruption to happen if a system or application crash occurs while writing data to the database. To ensure that database corruption never occurs, applications must either use transactions and logging with automatic recovery; use logging and application-specific recovery; or edit a copy of the database, and, once all applications using the database have successfully called **Db.close**, atomically replace the original database with the updated copy.

The Db.sync method throws an exception that encapsulates a non-zero error value on failure, and returns DB_INCOMPLETE if the underlying database still has dirty pages in the cache. (The only reason to return DB_INCOMPLETE is if another thread of control was writing pages in the underlying database file at the same time as the Db.sync method was being called. For this reason, a return of DB_INCOMPLETE can normally be ignored; or, in cases where it is a possible return value, there may be no reason to call Db.sync.)

Errors

The Db.sync method may fail and throw an exception encapsulating a non-zero error for the following conditions:

- EINVAL   An invalid flag value or parameter was specified.

The Db.sync method may fail and throw an exception for errors specified for other Berkeley DB and C library or system methods. If a catastrophic error has occurred, the Db.sync method may fail and throw a **DbRunRecoveryException**, in which case all subsequent Berkeley DB calls will fail in the same way.

Db.upgrade

```
import com.sleepycat.db.*;

public void upgrade(String file, int flags)
        throws DbException;
```

Description

The Db.upgrade method upgrades all of the databases included in the file **file**, if necessary. If no upgrade is necessary, Db.upgrade always returns success.

Database upgrades are done in place and are destructive; for example, if pages need to be allocated and no disk space is available, the database may be left corrupted. Backups should be made before databases are upgraded. See "Upgrading Databases" for more information.

Unlike all other database operations, Db.upgrade may only be done on a system with the same byte-order as the database.

The **flags** parameter must be set to 0 or one of the following values:

- Db.DB_DUPSORT   This flag is only meaningful when upgrading databases from releases before the Berkeley DB 3.1 release.

  As part of the upgrade from the Berkeley DB 3.0 release to the 3.1 release, the on-disk format of duplicate data items changed. To correctly upgrade the format requires applications to specify whether duplicate data items in the database are sorted or not. Specifying the Db.DB_DUPSORT flag informs Db.upgrade that the duplicates are sorted; otherwise, they are assumed to be unsorted. Incorrectly specifying the value of this flag may lead to database corruption.

  Further, because the Db.upgrade method upgrades a physical file (including all the databases it contains), it is not possible to use Db.upgrade to upgrade files where some of the databases it includes have sorted duplicate data items, and some of the databases it includes have unsorted duplicate data items. If the file does not have more than a single database, if the databases do not support duplicate data items, or if all the databases that support duplicate data items support the same style of duplicates (either sorted or unsorted), Db.upgrade will work correctly as long as the Db.DB_DUPSORT flag is correctly specified. Otherwise, the file cannot be upgraded using Db.upgrade, and must be upgraded manually by dumping and reloading the databases.

The Db.upgrade method throws an exception that encapsulates a non-zero error value on failure.

Environment Variables

- DB_HOME   If the **dbenv** argument to **db_create** was initialized using **DbEnv.open**, the environment variable **DB_HOME** may be used as the path of the database environment home. Specifically, Db.upgrade is affected by the configuration value DB_DATA_DIR.

Errors

The Db.upgrade method may fail and throw an exception encapsulating a non-zero error for the following conditions:

- EINVAL   An invalid flag value or parameter was specified.

  The database is not in the same byte-order as the system.

- Db.DB_OLD_VERSION   The database cannot be upgraded by this version of the Berkeley DB software.

The Db.upgrade method may fail and throw an exception for errors specified for other Berkeley DB and C library or system methods. If a catastrophic error has occurred, the Db.upgrade method may fail and throw a **DbRunRecoveryException**, in which case all subsequent Berkeley DB calls will fail in the same way.

Db.verify

```
import com.sleepycat.db.*;

public void verify(String file,
    String database, java.io.OutputStream outfile, int flags)
        throws DbException;
```

Description

The Db.verify method verifies the integrity of all databases in the file specified by the file argument, and optionally outputs the databases' key/data pairs to a file stream.

The **flags** parameter must be set to 0 or one of the following values:

- Db.DB_SALVAGE   Write the key/data pairs from all databases in the file to the file stream named in the **outfile** argument. The output format is the same as that specified for the **db_dump** utility, and can be used as input for the **db_load** utility.

  Because the key/data pairs are output in page order as opposed to the sort order used by **db_dump**, using Db.verify to dump key/data pairs normally produces less-than-optimal loads for Btree databases.

In addition, the following flags may be set by bitwise inclusively **OR**'ing them into the **flags** parameter:

- Db.DB_AGGRESSIVE   Output **all** the key/data pairs in the file that can be found. By default, Db.verify does not assume corruption. For example, if a key/data pair on a page is marked as deleted, it is not then written to the output file. When Db.DB_AGGRESSIVE is specified, corruption is assumed, and any key/data pair that can be found is written. In this case, key/data pairs that are corrupted or have been deleted may appear in the output (even if the file being salvaged is in no way corrupt), and the output will almost certainly require editing before being loaded into a database.

- Db.DB_NOORDERCHK   Skip the database checks for btree and duplicate sort order and for hashing.

  The Db.verify method normally verifies that btree keys and duplicate items are correctly sorted, and hash keys are correctly hashed. If the file being verified contains multiple databases using differing sorting or hashing algorithms, some of them must necessarily fail database verification because only one sort order or hash function can be specified before Db.verify is called. To verify files with multiple databases having differing sorting orders or hashing functions, first perform verification of the file as a whole by using the Db.DB_NOORDERCHK flag; then individually verify the sort order and hashing function for each database in the file using the Db.DB_ORDERCHKONLY flag.

- Db.DB_ORDERCHKONLY   Perform the database checks for btree and duplicate sort order and for hashing; skipped by Db.DB_NOORDERCHK.

  When this flag is specified, a **database** argument should also be specified, indicating the database in the physical file that is to be checked. This flag is only safe to use on databases that have already successfully been verified using Db.verify with the Db.DB_NOORDERCHK flag set.

The database argument must be set to null except when the Db.DB_ORDERCHKONLY flag is set.

The Db.verify method throws an exception that encapsulates a non-zero error value on failure, and DB_VERIFY_BAD if a database is corrupted. When the Db.DB_SALVAGE flag is specified, the DB_VERIFY_BAD return means that all key/data pairs in the file may not have been successfully output.

Environment Variables

- DB_HOME   If the **dbenv** argument to **db_create** was initialized using **DbEnv.open** the environment variable **DB_HOME** may be used as the path of the database environment home. Specifically, Db.verify is affected by the configuration value DB_DATA_DIR.

Errors

The Db.verify method may fail and throw an exception encapsulating a non-zero error for the following conditions:

- EINVAL   An invalid flag value or parameter was specified.

The Db.verify method may fail and throw an exception for errors specified for other Berkeley DB and C library or system methods. If a catastrophic error has occurred, the Db.verify method may fail and throw a **DbRunRecoveryException**, in which case all subsequent Berkeley DB calls will fail in the same way.

DbDeadlockException

```
import com.sleepycat.db.*;

public class DbDeadlockException extends DbException { ... }
```

Description

This manual page describes the DbDeadlockException class and how it is used by the various Db★ classes.

A DbDeadlockException is thrown when multiple threads competing for a lock are deadlocked. One of the threads' transactions is selected for termination, and a DbDeadlockException is thrown to that thread.

See **DbEnv.set_lk_detect** for more information.

DbEnv

```
import com.sleepycat.db.*;

public class DbEnv extends Object
{
      public DbEnv(int flags);
      ...
}
```

Description

This manual page describes the specific details of the DbEnv class, which is the center of the Berkeley DB environment.

The following **flags** value may be specified:

• Db.DB_CLIENT   Create a client environment to connect to a server.

The Db.DB_CLIENT flag indicates to the system that this environment is remote on a server. The use of this flag causes the environment methods to use functions that call a server instead of local functions. Prior to making any environment or database method calls, the application must call the **DbEnv.set_server** function to establish the connection to the server.

DbEnv.close

```
import com.sleepycat.db.*;

public void close(int flags)
      throws DbException;
```

Description

The DbEnv.close method closes the Berkeley DB environment, freeing any allocated resources and closing any underlying subsystems.

Calling DbEnv.close does not imply closing any databases that were opened in the environment, and all databases opened in the environment should be closed before the environment is closed.

The **flags** parameter is currently unused, and must be set to 0.

Where the environment was initialized with the DB_INIT_LOCK flag, calling DbEnv.close does not release any locks still held by the closing process, providing functionality for long-lived locks.

Where the environment was initialized with the DB_INIT_MPOOL flag, calling DbEnv.close implies calls to **DbMpoolFile.close** for any remaining open files in the memory pool that were returned to this process by calls to **DbMpoolFile.open**. It does not imply a call to **DbMpoolFile.sync** for those files.

Where the environment was initialized with the DB_INIT_TXN flag, calling DbEnv.close aborts any unresolved transactions. Applications should not depend on this behavior for transactions involving Berkeley DB databases, all such transactions should be explicitly resolved. The problem with depending on this semantic is that aborting an unresolved transaction involving database operations requires a database handle. Because the database handles should have been closed before calling DbEnv.close, it will not be possible to abort the transaction and recovery will have to be run on the Berkeley DB environment before further operations are done.

In multithreaded applications, only a single thread may call DbEnv.close.

Once DbEnv.close has been called, the Berkeley DB environment handle may not be accessed again, regardless of its return.

The DbEnv.close method throws an exception that encapsulates a non-zero error value on failure.

Errors

The DbEnv.close method may fail and throw an exception for errors specified for other Berkeley DB and C library or system methods. If a catastrophic error has occurred, the DbEnv.close method may fail and throw a **DbRunRecoveryException**, in which case all subsequent Berkeley DB calls will fail in the same way.

DbEnv.get_version_major

```
import com.sleepycat.db.*;

public static int get_version_major();
public static int get_version_minor();
public static int get_version_patch();
public static String get_version_string();
```

Description

These methods return version information about the underlying Berkeley DB software. Berkeley DB is released with a major, minor and patch number, which is returned by DbEnv.get_version_major, DbEnv.get_version_minor, and DbEnv.get_version_patch. A verbose version of this information, suitable for display, is returned by DbEnv.get_version_string.

DbEnv.lock_detect

```
import com.sleepycat.db.*;

public int lock_detect(int flags, int atype)
     throws DbException;
```

Description

The DbEnv.lock_detect method runs one iteration of the deadlock detector. The deadlock detector traverses the lock table; for each deadlock it finds, it marks one of the participating transactions for abort.

The **flags** value must be set to 0 or by bitwise inclusively **OR**'ing together one or more of the following values.

- Db.DB_LOCK_CONFLICT   Only run the deadlock detector if a lock conflict has occurred since the last time that the deadlock detector was run.

The **atype** parameter specifies which transaction to abort in the case of deadlock. It must be set to one of possible arguments listed for the **DbEnv.set_lk_detect** interface.

The DbEnv.lock_detect method returns the number of transactions aborted.

The DbEnv.lock_detect method throws an exception that encapsulates a non-zero error value on failure.

Errors

The DbEnv.lock_detect method may fail and throw an exception for errors specified for other Berkeley DB and C library or system methods. If a catastrophic error has occurred, the DbEnv.lock_detect method may fail and throw a **DbRunRecoveryException**, in which case all subsequent Berkeley DB calls will fail in the same way.

DbEnv.lock_get

```
import com.sleepycat.db.*;

public DbLock lock_get(int locker,
        int flags, Dbt obj, int lock_mode)
        throws DbException;
```

Description

The DbEnv.lock_get method acquires a lock from the lock table, returning information about it in a DbLock object.

The **locker** argument specified to DbEnv.lock_get is an unsigned 32-bit integer quantity. It represents the entity requesting or releasing the lock.

The **flags** value must be set to 0 or the following value:

- Db.DB_LOCK_NOWAIT

If a lock cannot be granted because the requested lock conflicts with an existing lock, return immediately instead of waiting for the lock to become available.

The **obj** argument is an untyped byte string that specifies the object to be locked or released. Applications using the Locking subsystem directly while also doing locking via the Berkeley DB access methods must take care not to inadvertently lock objects that happen to be equal to the unique file IDs used to lock files. See "Access Method Locking Conventions" for more information.

The **mode** argument is an index into the environment's lock conflict array. See **DbEnv.set_lk_conflicts** and "Standard Lock Modes" for a description of that array.

The DbEnv.lock_get method may throw an exception encapsulating one of the following values:

- Db.DB_LOCK_NOTGRANTED   A lock was requested that could not be immediately granted and the flags parameter was set to DB_LOCK_NOWAIT.

Otherwise, the DbEnv.lock_get method throws an exception that encapsulates a non-zero error value on failure.

Errors

The DbEnv.lock_get method may fail and throw an exception encapsulating a non-zero error for the following conditions:

- EINVAL   An invalid flag value or parameter was specified.

- ENOMEM   The maximum number of locks has been reached.

If the operation was selected to resolve a deadlock, the DbEnv.lock_get method will fail and throw a **DbDeadlockException** exception.

The DbEnv.lock_get method may fail and throw an exception for errors specified for other Berkeley DB and C library or system methods. If a catastrophic error has occurred, the DbEnv.lock_get method may fail and throw a **DbRunRecoveryException**, in which case all subsequent Berkeley DB calls will fail in the same way.

DbEnv.lock_id

```
import com.sleepycat.db.*;

public int lock_id()
     throws DbException;
```

Description

The DbEnv.lock_id method returns a locker ID, which is guaranteed to be unique in the specified lock table.

The DbEnv.lock_id method throws an exception that encapsulates a non-zero error value on failure.

Errors

The DbEnv.lock_id method may fail and throw an exception for errors specified for other Berkeley DB and C library or system methods. If a catastrophic error has occurred, the DbEnv.lock_id method may fail and throw a **DbRunRecoveryException**, in which case all subsequent Berkeley DB calls will fail in the same way.

DbEnv.lock_stat

```
import com.sleepycat.db.*;

public DbLockStat lock_stat()
    throws DbException;
```

Description

The DbEnv.lock_stat method creates a DbLockStat object encapsulating a statistical structure. The lock region statistics are stored in a DbLockStat object. The following data fields are available from the DbLockStat object:

Statistical structures are created in allocated memory. If **db_malloc** is non-NULL, it is called to allocate the memory; otherwise, the library function **malloc**(3) is used. The function **db_malloc** must match the calling conventions of the **malloc**(3) library routine. Regardless, the caller is responsible for deallocating the returned memory. To deallocate returned memory, free the returned memory reference; references inside the returned memory do not need to be individually freed.

The lock region statistics are stored in a structure of type DB_LOCK_STAT. The following DB_LOCK_STAT fields will be filled in:

- public int st_lastid;   The last allocated lock ID.
- public int st_nmodes;   The number of lock modes.
- public int st_maxlocks;   The maximum number of locks possible.
- public int st_maxlockers;   The maximum number of lockers possible.
- public int st_maxobjects;   The maximum number of objects possible.
- public int st_nlocks;   The number of current locks.
- public int st_maxnlocks;   The maximum number of locks at any one time.
- public int st_nlockers;   The number of current lockers.
- public int st_maxnlockers;   The maximum number of lockers at any one time.
- public int st_nobjects;   The number of current objects.
- public int st_maxnobjects;   The maximum number of objects at any one time.
- public int st_nrequests;   The total number of locks requested.
- public int st_nreleases;   The total number of locks released.
- public int st_nnowaits;   The total number of lock requests that failed because DB_LOCK_NOWAIT was set.

- public int st_nconflicts;   The total number of locks not immediately available due to conflicts.

- public int st_ndeadlocks;   The number of deadlocks detected.

- public int st_regsize;   The size of the region.

- public int st_region_wait;   The number of times that a thread of control was forced to wait before obtaining the region lock.

- public int st_region_nowait;   The number of times that a thread of control was able to obtain the region lock without waiting.

The DbEnv.lock_stat method throws an exception that encapsulates a non-zero error value on failure.

Errors

The DbEnv.lock_stat method may fail and throw an exception for errors specified for other Berkeley DB and C library or system methods. If a catastrophic error has occurred, the DbEnv.lock_stat method may fail and throw a **DbRunRecoveryException**, in which case all subsequent Berkeley DB calls will fail in the same way.

DbEnv.lock_vec

```
import com.sleepycat.db.*;
```

Description

A DbEnv.lock_vec method is not available in the Berkeley DB Java API.

DbEnv.log_archive

```
import com.sleepycat.db.*;

public String[] log_archive(int flags)
    throws DbException;
```

Description

The DbEnv.log_archive method returns an array of log or database filenames.

By default, DbEnv.log_archive returns the names of all of the log files that are no longer in use (for example, no longer involved in active transactions), and that may safely be archived for catastrophic recovery and then removed from the system. If there were no filenames to return, the memory location referenced by **listp** will be set to null.

The **flags** value must be set to 0 or by bitwise inclusively **OR**'ing together one or more of the following values.

- Db.DB_ARCH_ABS   All pathnames are returned as absolute pathnames, instead of relative to the database home directory.

- Db.DB_ARCH_DATA   Return the database files that need to be archived in order to recover the database from catastrophic failure. If any of the database files have not been accessed during the lifetime of the current log files, DbEnv.log_archive will not include them in this list. It is also possible that some of the files referenced in the log have since been deleted from the system.

- Db.DB_ARCH_LOG   Return all the log filenames, regardless of whether or not they are in use.

The Db.DB_ARCH_DATA and Db.DB_ARCH_LOG flags are mutually exclusive.

See the **db_archive** manual page for more information on database- archival procedures.

The DbEnv.log_archive method throws an exception that encapsulates a non-zero error value on failure.

Bugs

In a threaded application (that is, one in which the environment was created with the DB_THREAD flag specified), calling DbEnv.log_archive with the DB_ARCH_DATA flag will fail, returning EINVAL. To work around this problem, reopen the log explicitly without specifying DB_THREAD. This restriction is expected to be removed in a future version of Berkeley DB.

Errors

The DbEnv.log_archive method may fail and throw an exception encapsulating a non-zero error for the following conditions:

- EINVAL   An invalid flag value or parameter was specified.

    The log was corrupted.

The DbEnv.log_archive method may fail and throw an exception for errors specified for other Berkeley DB and C library or system methods. If a catastrophic error has occurred, the DbEnv.log_archive method may fail and throw a **DbRunRecoveryException**, in which case all subsequent Berkeley DB calls will fail in the same way.

DbEnv.log_compare

```
import com.sleepycat.db.*;

public static int log_compare(DbLsn lsn0, DbLsn lsn1);
```

Description

The DbEnv.log_compare method allows the caller to compare two **DbLsn** objects, returning 0 if they are equal, 1 if **lsn0** is greater than **lsn1**, and –1 if **lsn0** is less than **lsn1**.

DbEnv.log_file

```
import com.sleepycat.db.*;

public String log_file(DbLsn lsn)
    throws DbException;
```

Description

The DbEnv.log_file method maps **DbLsn** objects to filenames, returning the name of the file containing the record named by **lsn**.

The **len** argument is the length of the **namep** buffer in bytes. If **namep** is too short to hold the filename, DbEnv.log_file will return ENOMEM. (Log filenames are normally quite short; on the order of 10 characters.)

This mapping of **DbLsn** objects to files is needed for database administration. For example, a transaction manager typically records the earliest **DbLsn** needed for restart, and the database administrator may want to archive log files to tape when they contain only **DbLsn** entries before the earliest one needed for restart.

The DbEnv.log_file method throws an exception that encapsulates a non-zero error value on failure.

Errors

The DbEnv.log_file method may fail and throw an exception encapsulating a non-zero error for the following conditions:

- ENOMEM   The supplied buffer was too small to hold the log file name.

The DbEnv.log_file method may fail and throw an exception for errors specified for other Berkeley DB and C library or system methods. If a catastrophic error has occurred, the DbEnv.log_file method may fail and throw a **DbRunRecoveryException**, in which case all subsequent Berkeley DB calls will fail in the same way.

DbEnv.log_flush

```
import com.sleepycat.db.*;

public void log_flush(DbLsn lsn)
    throws DbException;
```

Description

The DbEnv.log_flush method guarantees that all log records whose **DbLsn** values are less than or equal to the **lsn** argument have been written to disk. If **lsn** is null, all records in the log are flushed.

The DbEnv.log_flush method throws an exception that encapsulates a non-zero error value on failure.

Errors

The DbEnv.log_flush method may fail and throw an exception encapsulating a non-zero error for the following conditions:

- EINVAL   An invalid flag value or parameter was specified.

The DbEnv.log_flush method may fail and throw an exception for errors specified for other Berkeley DB and C library or system methods. If a catastrophic error has occurred, the DbEnv.log_flush method may fail and throw a **DbRunRecoveryException**, in which case all subsequent Berkeley DB calls will fail in the same way.

DbEnv.log_get

```
import com.sleepycat.db.*;

public void log_get(DbLsn lsn, Dbt data, int flags)
        throws DbException;
```

Description

The DbEnv.log_get method implements a cursor inside of the log, retrieving records from the log according to the **lsn** and **flags** arguments.

The data field of the **data** structure is set to the record retrieved and the size field indicates the number of bytes in the record. See **Dbt** for a description of other fields in the **data** structure. When multiple threads are using the **DbEnv** handle concurrently, one of the DB_DBT_MALLOC, DB_DBT_REALLOC, or DB_DBT_USERMEM flags must be specified for any **Dbt** used for data retrieval.

The **flags** argument must be set to exactly one of the following values:

- Db.DB_CHECKPOINT   The last record written with the DB_CHECKPOINT flag specified to the **DbEnv.log_put** method is returned in the **data** argument. The **lsn** argument is overwritten with the **DbLsn** of the record returned. If no record has been previously written with the DB_CHECKPOINT flag specified, the first record in the log is returned.

  If the log is empty, the DbEnv.log_get method will return DB_NOTFOUND.

- Db.DB_FIRST   The first record from any of the log files found in the log directory is returned in the **data** argument. The **lsn** argument is overwritten with the **DbLsn** of the record returned.

If the log is empty, the DbEnv.log_get method will return DB_NOTFOUND.

- Db.DB_LAST   The last record in the log is returned in the **data** argument. The **lsn** argument is overwritten with the **DbLsn** of the record returned.

  If the log is empty, the DbEnv.log_get method will return DB_NOTFOUND.

- Db.DB_NEXT, Db.DB_PREV   The current log position is advanced to the next (previous) record in the log and that record is returned in the **data** argument. The **lsn** argument is overwritten with the **DbLsn** of the record returned.

  If the pointer has not been initialized via DB_FIRST, DB_LAST, DB_SET, DB_NEXT, or DB_PREV, DbEnv.log_get will return the first (last) record in the log. If the last (first) log record has already been returned or the log is empty, the DbEnv.log_get method will return DB_NOTFOUND.

  If the log was opened with the DB_THREAD flag set, calls to DbEnv.log_get with the DB_NEXT (DB_PREV) flag set will return EINVAL.

- Db.DB_CURRENT   Return the log record currently referenced by the log.

  If the log pointer has not been initialized via DB_FIRST, DB_LAST, DB_SET, DB_NEXT, or DB_PREV, or if the log was opened with the DB_THREAD flag set, DbEnv.log_get will return EINVAL.

- Db.DB_SET   Retrieve the record specified by the **lsn** argument. If the specified **DbLsn** is invalid (for example, does not appear in the log) DbEnv.log_get will return EINVAL.

Otherwise, the DbEnv.log_get method throws an exception that encapsulates a non-zero error value on failure.

Errors

The DbEnv.log_get method may fail and throw an exception encapsulating a non-zero error for the following conditions:

- EINVAL   An invalid flag value or parameter was specified.

  The DB_NEXT or DB_PREV flags were set and the log was opened with the DB_THREAD flag set.

  The DB_CURRENT flag was set and the log pointer had not yet been initialized.

  The DB_SET flag was set and the specified log sequence number does not exist.

The DbEnv.log_get method may fail and throw an exception for errors specified for other Berkeley DB and C library or system methods. If a catastrophic error has occurred, the DbEnv.log_get method may fail and throw a **DbRunRecoveryException**, in which case all subsequent Berkeley DB calls will fail in the same way.

DbEnv.log_put

```
import com.sleepycat.db.*;

public void log_put(DbLsn lsn, Dbt data, int flags)
    throws DbException;
```

Description

The DbEnv.log_put method appends records to the log. The **DbLsn** of the put record is returned in the **lsn** argument. The **flags** argument may be set to one of the following values:

- Db.DB_CHECKPOINT   The log should write a checkpoint record, recording any information necessary to make the log structures recoverable after a crash.

- Db.DB_CURLSN   The **DbLsn** of the next record to be put is returned in the **lsn** argument.

- Db.DB_FLUSH   The log is forced to disk after this record is written, guaranteeing that all records with **DbLsn** values less than or equal to the one being put are on disk before this function returns (this function is most often used for a transaction commit; see **DbTxn.commit** for more information).

  The caller is responsible for providing any necessary structure to **data**. (For example, in a write-ahead logging protocol, the application must understand what part of **data** is an operation code, what part is redo information, and what part is undo information. In addition, most transaction managers will store in **data** the **DbLsn** of the previous log record for the same transaction, to support chaining back through the transaction's log records during undo.)

The DbEnv.log_put method throws an exception that encapsulates a non-zero error value on failure.

Errors

The **DbEnv.log_flush** method may fail and throw an exception encapsulating a non-zero error for the following conditions:

- EINVAL   An invalid flag value or parameter was specified.

  The record to be logged is larger than the maximum log record.

The DbEnv.log_put method may fail and throw an exception for errors specified for other Berkeley DB and C library or system methods. If a catastrophic error has occurred, the DbEnv.log_put method may fail and throw a **DbRunRecoveryException**, in which case all subsequent Berkeley DB calls will fail in the same way.

DbEnv.log_register

```
import com.sleepycat.db.*;

public int log_register(Db dbp, String name)
    throws DbException;
```

Description

The DbEnv.log_register method registers a filename with the specified Berkeley DB environment's log manager. The log manager records all filename mappings at each checkpoint so that a recovery process can identify the file to which a record in the log refers.

The **dbp** argument should be a reference to the **Db** object being registered. The **name** argument should be a filename appropriate for opening the file in the environment, during recovery.

The DbEnv.log_register method throws an exception that encapsulates a non-zero error value on failure.

Errors

The DbEnv.log_register method may fail and throw an exception encapsulating a non-zero error for the following conditions:

- EINVAL   An invalid flag value or parameter was specified.

The DbEnv.log_register method may fail and throw an exception for errors specified for other Berkeley DB and C library or system methods. If a catastrophic error has occurred, the DbEnv.log_register method may fail and throw a **DbRunRecoveryException**, in which case all subsequent Berkeley DB calls will fail in the same way.

DbEnv.log_stat

```
import com.sleepycat.db.*;

public DbLogStat log_stat()
    throws DbException;
```

Description

The DbEnv.log_stat method creates a DbLogStat object encapsulating a statistical structure. The log region statistics are stored in a DbLogStat object. The following data fields are available from the DbLogStat object:

Statistical structures are created in allocated memory. If **db_malloc** is non-NULL, it is called to allocate the memory; otherwise, the library function **malloc**(3) is used. The function **db_malloc** must match the calling conventions of the **malloc**(3) library routine. Regardless, the caller is responsible for deallocating the returned memory. To deallocate returned memory, free the returned memory reference, references inside the returned memory do not need to be individually freed.

The log region statistics are stored in a structure of type DB_LOG_STAT. The following DB_LOG_STAT fields will be filled in:

- public int st_magic;   The magic number that identifies a file as a log file.
- public int st_version;   The version of the log file type.
- public int st_regsize;   The size of the region.

- public int st_mode;   The mode of any created log files.

- public int st_lg_bsize;   The in-memory log record cache size.

- public int st_lg_max;   The maximum size of any individual file comprising the log.

- public int st_w_mbytes;   The number of megabytes written to this log.

- public int st_w_bytes;   The number of bytes over and above **st_w_mbytes** written to this log.

- public int st_wc_mbytes;   The number of megabytes written to this log since the last checkpoint.

- public int st_wc_bytes;   The number of bytes over and above **st_wc_mbytes** written to this log since the last checkpoint.

- public int st_wcount;   The number of times the log has been written to disk.

- public int st_wcount_fill;   The number of times the log has been written to disk because the in-memory log record cache filled up.

- public int st_scount;   The number of times the log has been flushed to disk.

- public int st_cur_file;   The current log file number.

- public int st_cur_offset;   The byte offset in the current log file.

- public int st_region_wait;   The number of times that a thread of control was forced to wait before obtaining the region lock.

- public int st_region_nowait;   The number of times that a thread of control was able to obtain the region lock without waiting.

The DbEnv.log_stat method throws an exception that encapsulates a non-zero error value on failure.

Errors

The DbEnv.log_stat method may fail and throw an exception for errors specified for other Berkeley DB and C library or system methods. If a catastrophic error has occurred, the DbEnv.log_stat method may fail and throw a **DbRunRecoveryException**, in which case all subsequent Berkeley DB calls will fail in the same way.

DbEnv.log_unregister

```
import com.sleepycat.db.*;

public void log_unregister(Db dbp)
        throws DbException;
```

Description

The DbEnv.log_unregister method function unregisters the file represented by the **dbp** parameter from the Berkeley DB environment's log manager.

The DbEnv.log_unregister method throws an exception that encapsulates a non-zero error value on failure.

Errors

The DbEnv.log_unregister method may fail and throw an exception encapsulating a non-zero error for the following conditions:

- EINVAL   An invalid flag value or parameter was specified.

The DbEnv.log_unregister method may fail and throw an exception for errors specified for other Berkeley DB and C library or system methods. If a catastrophic error has occurred, the DbEnv.log_unregister method may fail and throw a **DbRunRecoveryException**, in which case all subsequent Berkeley DB calls will fail in the same way.

DbEnv.memp_register

```
import com.sleepycat.db.*;
```

Description

A DbEnv.memp_register method is not available in the Berkeley DB Java API.

DbEnv.memp_stat

```
import com.sleepycat.db.*;

public DbMpoolStat memp_stat()
    throws DbException;

public DbMpoolFStat[] memp_fstat()
    throws DbException;
```

Description

The DbEnv.memp_stat and **DbEnv.memp_fstat** method create statistical structures and return to the caller. The statistics include the number of files participating in the pool, the active pages in the pool, and information about how effective the cache has been.

The DbEnv.memp_stat method creates a DbMpoolStat object containing global statistics. The following data fields are available:

- public long st_gbytes;   Gigabytes of cache (total cache size is st_gbytes + st_bytes).
- public long st_bytes;   Bytes of cache (total cache size is st_gbytes + st_bytes).
- public int st_ncache;   Number of caches.
- public int st_regsize;   Individual cache size.
- public int st_cache_hit;   Requested pages found in the cache.
- public int st_cache_miss;   Requested pages not found in the cache.
- public int st_map;   Requested pages mapped into the process' address space (there is no available information about whether or not this request caused disk I/O, although examining the application page fault rate may be helpful).
- public int st_page_create;   Pages created in the cache.

- public int st_page_in;   Pages read into the cache.

- public int st_page_out;   Pages written from the cache to the backing file.

- public int st_ro_evict;   Clean pages forced from the cache.

- public int st_rw_evict;   Dirty pages forced from the cache.

- public int st_hash_buckets;   Number of hash buckets in the buffer hash table.

- public int st_hash_searches;   Total number of buffer hash table lookups.

- public int st_hash_longest;   Longest chain ever encountered in buffer hash table lookups.

- public int st_hash_examined;   Total number of hash elements traversed during hash table lookups.

- public int st_page_clean;   Clean pages currently in the cache.

- public int st_page_dirty;   Dirty pages currently in the cache.

- public int st_page_trickle;   Dirty pages written using the **DbEnv.memp_trickle** interface.

- public int st_region_wait;   Number of times that a thread of control was forced to wait before obtaining the region lock.

- public int st_region_nowait;   Number of times that a thread of control was able to obtain the region lock without waiting.

The **DbEnv.memp_fstat** method creates an array of DbMpoolFStat objects containing statistics for individual files in the pool. Each DbMpoolFStat object contains statistics for an individual DbMpoolFile. The following data fields are available for each DbMpoolFStat object:

- public string file_name;   Name of the file.

- public long st_pagesize;   Page size in bytes.

- public int st_cache_hit;   Requested pages found in the cache.

- public int st_cache_miss;   Requested pages not found in the cache.

- public int st_map;   Requested pages mapped into the process' address space.

- public int st_page_create;   Pages created in the cache.

- public int st_page_in;   Pages read into the cache.

- public int st_page_out;   Pages written from the cache to the backing file.

The DbEnv.memp_stat method throws an exception that encapsulates a non-zero error value on failure.

Errors

The DbEnv.memp_stat method may fail and throw an exception encapsulating a non-zero error for the following conditions:

- EINVAL   An invalid flag value or parameter was specified.

The DbEnv.memp_stat method may fail and throw an exception for errors specified for other Berkeley DB and C library or system methods. If a catastrophic error has occurred, the DbEnv.memp_stat method may fail and throw a **DbRunRecoveryException**, in which case all subsequent Berkeley DB calls will fail in the same way.

DbEnv.memp_sync

```
import com.sleepycat.db.*;
```

Description

A DbEnv.memp_sync method is not available in the Berkeley DB Java API.

DbEnv.memp_trickle

```
import com.sleepycat.db.*;

public int memp_trickle(int pct)
       throws DbException;
```

Description

The DbEnv.memp_trickle method ensures that at least **pct** percent of the pages in the shared memory pool are clean by writing dirty pages to their backing files. The number of pages that were written to reach the correct percentage is returned.

The purpose of the DbEnv.memp_trickle function is to enable a memory pool manager to ensure that a page is always available for reading in new information without having to wait for a write.

The DbEnv.memp_trickle method throws an exception that encapsulates a non-zero error value on failure.

Errors

The DbEnv.memp_trickle method may fail and throw an exception encapsulating a non-zero error for the following conditions:

- EINVAL   An invalid flag value or parameter was specified.

The DbEnv.memp_trickle method may fail and throw an exception for errors specified for other Berkeley DB and C library or system methods. If a catastrophic error has occurred, the DbEnv.memp_trickle method may fail and throw a **DbRunRecoveryException**, in which case all subsequent Berkeley DB calls will fail in the same way.

DbEnv.open

```
import com.sleepycat.db.*;
import java.io.FileNotFoundException;

public void open(String db_home, int flags, int mode)
    throws DbException, FileNotFoundException;
```

Description

The DbEnv.open method is the interface for opening the Berkeley DB environment. It provides a structure for creating a consistent environment for processes using one or more of the features of Berkeley DB.

The **db_home** argument to DbEnv.open (and filename resolution in general) is described in "Berkeley DB File Naming."

The **flags** argument specifies the subsystems that are initialized and how the application's environment affects Berkeley DB file naming, among other things.

The **flags** value must be set to 0 or by bitwise inclusively **OR**'ing together one or more of the following values.

Because there are a large number of flags that can be specified, they have been grouped together by functionality. The first group of flags indicates which of the Berkeley DB subsystems should be initialized:

- Db.DB_JOINENV   Join an existing environment. This option allows applications to join an existing environment without knowing which Berkeley DB subsystems the environment supports.

- Db.DB_INIT_CDB   Initialize locking for the **Berkeley DB Concurrent Data Store** product. In this mode, Berkeley DB provides multiple reader/single writer access. The only other subsystem that should be specified with the Db.DB_INIT_CDB flag is Db.DB_INIT_MPOOL.

- Db.DB_INIT_LOCK   Initialize the Locking subsystem. This subsystem should be used when multiple processes or threads will be reading and writing a Berkeley DB database, so that they do not interfere with each other. If all threads are accessing the database(s) read-only, then locking is unnecessary. When the Db.DB_INIT_LOCK flag is specified, it is usually necessary to run a deadlock detector, as well. See **db_deadlock** and **DbEnv.lock_detect** for more information.

- Db.DB_INIT_LOG   Initialize the Logging subsystem, which should be used when recovery from application or system failure is necessary. If the log region is being created and log files are already present, the log files are reviewed and subsequent log writes are appended to the end of the log, rather than overwriting current log entries.

- Db.DB_INIT_MPOOL   Initialize the shared Memory Buffer Pool subsystem. This subsystem should be used whenever an application is using any Berkeley DB access method.

- Db.DB_INIT_TXN   Initialize the Transaction subsystem. This subsystem should be used when recovery and atomicity of multiple operations are important. The Db.DB_INIT_TXN flag implies the Db.DB_INIT_LOG flag.

The second group of flags govern what recovery, if any, is performed when the environment is initialized:

- Db.DB_RECOVER   Run normal recovery on this environment before opening it for normal use. If this flag is set, the DB_CREATE flag must also be set because the regions will be removed and re-created.
- Db.DB_RECOVER_FATAL   Run catastrophic recovery on this environment before opening it for normal use. If this flag is set, the DB_CREATE flag must also be set because the regions will be removed and re-created.

A standard part of the recovery process is to remove the existing Berkeley DB environment and create a new one in which to perform recovery. If the thread of control performing recovery does not specify the correct region initialization information (for example, the correct memory pool cache size), the result can be an application running in an environment with incorrect cache and other subsystem sizes. For this reason, the thread of control performing recovery should either specify correct configuration information before calling the DbEnv.open method, or it should remove the environment after recovery is completed—leaving creation of the correctly sized environment to a subsequent call to DbEnv.open.

All Berkeley DB recovery processing must be single-threaded; that is, only a single thread of control may perform recovery or access a Berkeley DB environment while recovery is being performed. Because it is not an error to specify Db.DB_RECOVER for an environment for which no recovery is required, it is reasonable programming practice for the thread of control responsible for performing recovery and creating the environment to always specify the Db.DB_CREATE and Db.DB_RECOVER flags during startup.

The DbEnv.open function returns successfully if Db.DB_RECOVER or Db.DB_RECOVER_FATAL is specified and no log files exist, so it is necessary to ensure that all necessary log files are present before running recovery. For further information, consult **db_archive** and **db_recover**.

The third group of flags govern file-naming extensions in the environment:

- Db.DB_USE_ENVIRON   The Berkeley DB process' environment may be permitted to specify information to be used when naming files; see "Berkeley DB File Naming." Because permitting users to specify which files are used can create security problems, environment information will be used in file naming for all users only if the DB_USE_ENVIRON flag is set.
- Db.DB_USE_ENVIRON_ROOT   The Berkeley DB process' environment may be permitted to specify information to be used when naming files; see "Berkeley DB File Naming." Because permitting users to specify which files are used can create security problems; if the DB_USE_ENVIRON_ROOT flag is set, environment information will be used for file naming only for users with appropriate permissions (for example, users with a user-ID of 0 on UNIX systems).

Finally, there are a few additional unrelated flags:

- Db.DB_CREATE   Cause Berkeley DB subsystems to create any underlying files, as necessary.

- Db.DB_LOCKDOWN   Lock shared Berkeley DB environment files and memory-mapped databases into memory.

- Db.DB_PRIVATE   Specify that the environment will only be accessed by a single process (although that process may be multithreaded). This flag has two effects on the Berkeley DB environment. First, all underlying data structures are allocated from per-process memory instead of from shared memory that is potentially accessible to more than a single process. Second, mutexes are only configured to work between threads.

    This flag should not be specified if more than a single process is accessing the environment because it is likely to cause database corruption and unpredictable behavior. For example, if both a server application and the Berkeley DB utility **db_stat** are expected to access the environment, the Db.DB_PRIVATE flag should not be specified.

- Db.DB_SYSTEM_MEM   Allocate memory from system shared memory instead of from memory backed by the filesystem. See "Shared Memory Regions" for more information.

- Db.DB_THREAD   Cause the **DbEnv** handle returned by DbEnv.open to be *free-threaded*, that is, usable by multiple threads within a single address space.

    Threading is always assumed in the Java API, so no special flags are required, and Berkeley DB functions will always behave as if the Db.DB_THREAD flag was specified.

On UNIX systems, or in IEEE/ANSI Std 1003.1 (POSIX) environments, all files created by Berkeley DB are created with mode **mode** (as described in **chmod**(2)) and modified by the process' umask value at the time of creation (see **umask**(2)). The group ownership of created files is based on the system and directory defaults, and is not further specified by Berkeley DB. If **mode** is 0, files are created readable and writable by both owner and group. On Windows systems, the mode argument is ignored.

The DbEnv.open method throws an exception that encapsulates a non-zero error value on failure.

Environment Variables

- DB_HOME   The environment variable **DB_HOME** may be used as the path of the database home as described in "Berkeley DB File Naming."

Errors

The DbEnv.open method may fail and throw an exception encapsulating a non-zero error for the following conditions:

- EAGAIN   The shared memory region was locked and (repeatedly) unavailable.

- EINVAL   An invalid flag value or parameter was specified.

The Db.DB_THREAD flag was specified, and spinlocks are not implemented for this architecture.

The DB_HOME or TMPDIR environment variables were set but empty.

An incorrectly formatted **NAME VALUE** entry or line was found.

- ENOSPC   HP-UX only: a previously created Berkeley DB environment for this process still exists.

If the file or directory does not exist, the DbEnv.open method will fail and throw a FileNotFoundException exception.

The DbEnv.open method may fail and throw an exception for errors specified for other Berkeley DB and C library or system methods. If a catastrophic error has occurred, the DbEnv.open method may fail and throw a **DbRunRecoveryException**, in which case all subsequent Berkeley DB calls will fail in the same way.

DbEnv.remove

```
import com.sleepycat.db.*;
import java.io.FileNotFoundException;

public void remove(String db_home, int flags)
    throws DbException, FileNotFoundException;
```

Description

The DbEnv.remove method destroys a Berkeley DB environment, if it is not currently in use. The environment regions, including any backing files, are removed. Any log or database files and the environment directory are not removed.

The **db_home** argument to DbEnv.remove is described in "Berkeley DB File Naming."

If there are processes that have called **DbEnv.open** without calling **DbEnv.close** (that is, there are processes currently using the environment), DbEnv.remove will fail without further action, unless the DB_FORCE flag is set, in which case DbEnv.remove will attempt to remove the environment regardless of any processes still using it.

The result of attempting to forcibly destroy the environment when it is in use is unspecified. Processes using an environment often maintain open file descriptors for shared regions within it. On UNIX systems, the environment removal will usually succeed, and processes that have already joined the region will continue to run in that region without change; however, processes attempting to join the environment will either fail or create new regions. On other systems (for example, Windows/NT), in which the **unlink**(2) system call will fail if any process has an open file descriptor for the file, the region removal will fail.

Calling DbEnv.remove should not be necessary for most applications because the Berkeley DB environment is cleaned up as part of normal database recovery procedures. However, applications may wish to call DbEnv.remove as part of application shutdown to free up system resources. For example, if the DB_SYSTEM_MEM flag was specified to **DbEnv.open**, it may be useful to call DbEnv.remove in order to release system- shared memory segments that have been allocated. Or, on architectures in which mutexes require allocation of underlying system resources, it may be useful to call DbEnv.remove in order to release those resources. Alternatively, if recovery is not required because no database state is maintained across failures, and no system resources need to be released, it is possible to clean up an environment by simply removing all of the Berkeley DB files in the database environment's directories.

The **flags** value must be set to 0 or by bitwise inclusively **OR**'ing together one or more of the following values.

- Db.DB_FORCE   If the DB_FORCE flag is set, the environment is removed, regardless of any processes that may still using it, and no locks are acquired during this process. (Generally, the DB_FORCE flag is only specified when applications were unable to shut down cleanly, and there is a risk that an application may have died holding a Berkeley DB lock.)

- Db.DB_USE_ENVIRON   The Berkeley DB process' environment may be permitted to specify information to be used when naming files; see "Berkeley DB File Naming." Because permitting users to specify which files are used can create security problems, environment information will be used in file naming for all users only if the DB_USE_ENVIRON flag is set.

- Db.DB_USE_ENVIRON_ROOT   The Berkeley DB process' environment may be permitted to specify information to be used when naming files; see "Berkeley DB File Naming." Because permitting users to specify which files are used can create security problems, if the DB_USE_ENVIRON_ROOT flag is set, environment information will be used for file naming only for users with appropriate permissions (for example, users with a user-ID of 0 on UNIX systems).

In multithreaded applications, only a single thread may call DbEnv.remove.

A **DbEnv** handle that has already been used to open an environment should not be used to call the DbEnv.remove method; a new **DbEnv** handle should be created for that purpose.

Once DbEnv.remove has been called, regardless of its return, the Berkeley DB environment handle may not be accessed again.

The DbEnv.remove method throws an exception that encapsulates a non-zero error value on failure.

Errors

- EBUSY   The shared memory region was in use and the force flag was not set.

If the file or directory does not exist, the DbEnv.remove method will fail and throw a FileNotFoundException exception.

The DbEnv.remove method may fail and throw an exception for errors specified for other Berkeley DB and C library or system methods. If a catastrophic error has occurred, the DbEnv.remove method may fail and throw a **DbRunRecoveryException**, in which case all subsequent Berkeley DB calls will fail in the same way.

DbEnv.set_cachesize

```
import com.sleepycat.db.*;

public int set_cachesize(int gbytes, int bytes, in ncache)
     throws DbException;
```

Description

Set the size of the database's shared memory buffer pool; that is, the cache, to **gbytes** giga-bytes plus **bytes**. The cache should be the size of the normal working data set of the application, with some small amount of additional memory for unusual situations. (Note: The working set is not the same as the number of simultaneously referenced pages, and should be quite a bit larger!)

The default cache size is 256KB, and may not be specified as less than 20KB. Any cache size less than 500MB is automatically increased by 25% to account for buffer pool overhead; cache sizes larger than 500MB are used as specified. For information on tuning the Berkeley DB cache size, see "Selecting a Cache Size."

It is possible to specify caches to Berkeley DB that are large enough so that they cannot be allocated contiguously on some architectures; for example, some releases of Solaris limit the amount of memory that may be allocated contiguously by a process. If **ncache** is 0 or 1, the cache will be allocated contiguously in memory. If it is greater than 1, the cache will be broken up into **ncache** equally sized separate pieces of memory.

The DbEnv.set_cachesize interface may only be used to configure Berkeley DB before the **DbEnv.open** interface is called.

The DbEnv.set_cachesize method throws an exception that encapsulates a non-zero error value on failure.

The database environment's cache size may also be set using the environment's **DB_CONFIG** file. The syntax of the entry in that file is a single line with the string "set_cachesize", one or more whitespace characters, and the three arguments specified to this interface, separated by whitespace characters; for example, "set_cachesize 1 500 2". Because the **DB_CONFIG** file is read when the database environment is opened, it will silently overrule configuration done before that time.

Errors

- **EINVAL**
- An invalid flag value or parameter was specified.

  Called after **DbEnv.open** was called.

  The specified cache size was impossibly small.

DbEnv.set_data_dir

```
import com.sleepycat.db.*;

public void set_data_dir(String dir)
        throws DbException;
```

Description

Set the path of a directory to be used as the location of the access method database files. Paths specified to the **Db.open** function will be searched relative to this path. Paths set using this interface are additive, and specifying more than one will result in each specified directory being searched for database files. If any directories are specified, created database files will always be created in the first path specified.

If no database directories are specified, database files can only exist in the environment home directory. See "Berkeley DB File Naming" for more information.

For the greatest degree of recoverability from system or application failure, database files and log files should be located on separate physical devices.

The DbEnv.set_data_dir interface may only be used to configure Berkeley DB before the **DbEnv.open** interface is called.

The DbEnv.set_data_dir method throws an exception that encapsulates a non-zero error value on failure.

The database environment's data directory may also be set using the environment's **DB_CONFIG** file. The syntax of the entry in that file is a single line with the string "set_data_dir", one or more whitespace characters, and the directory name. Because the **DB_CONFIG** file is read when the database environment is opened, it will silently overrule configuration done before that time.

Errors

- EINVAL An invalid flag value or parameter was specified.

  Called after **DbEnv.open** was called.

DbEnv.set_errcall

```
import com.sleepycat.db.*;

public interface DbErrcall
{
      public abstract void errcall(String errpfx, String msg);
}
public class DbEnv
{
       public void set_errcall(DbErrcall errcall);
       ...
}
```

Description

When an error occurs in the Berkeley DB library, an exception is thrown. In some cases, however, the **errno** value may be insufficient to completely describe the cause of the error, especially during initial application debugging.

The DbEnv.set_errcall method is used to enhance the mechanism for reporting error messages to the application. The DbEnv.set_errcall method must be called with a single object argument. The object's class must implement the DbErrcall interface. In some cases, when an error occurs, Berkeley DB will invoke the object's errcall() method with two arguments: The first is the prefix string (as previously set by **Db.set_errpfx** or **DbEnv.set_errpfx**), and the second is an error message string. It is up to this method to display the message in an appropriate manner.

Alternatively, you can use the **DbEnv.set_error_stream** method to display the additional information via an output stream. You should not mix these approaches.

This error-logging enhancement does not slow performance or significantly increase application size, and may be run during normal operation as well as during application debugging.

The DbEnv.set_errcall interface may be used to configure Berkeley DB at any time during the life of the application.

DbEnv.set_error_stream

```
import com.sleepycat.db.*;

public void Db.Env.set_error_stream(OutputStream s)
     throws DbException
```

Description

When an error occurs in the Berkeley DB library, an exception is thrown. In some cases, however, the **errno** value may be insufficient to completely describe the cause of the error, especially during initial application debugging.

The DbEnv.set_error_stream method is used to enhance the mechanism for reporting error messages to the application by setting a OutputStream to be used for displaying additional Berkeley DB error messages. In some cases, when an error occurs, Berkeley DB will output an additional error message to the specified stream.

The error message will consist of the prefix string and a colon (":") (if a prefix string was previously specified using **DbEnv.set_errpfx**), an error string, and a trailing <newline> character.

Alternatively, you can use the **DbEnv.set_errcall** method to capture the additional error information in a way that does not use output streams. You should not mix these approaches.

This error-logging enhancement does not slow performance or significantly increase application size, and may be run during normal operation as well as during application debugging.

DbEnv.set_errpfx

```
import com.sleepycat.db.*;

public void set_errpfx(String errpfx);
```

Description

Set the prefix string that appears before error messages issued by Berkeley DB.

The DbEnv.set_errpfx interface may be used to configure Berkeley DB at any time during the life of the application.

DbEnv.set_feedback

```
import com.sleepycat.db.*;

public interface DbEnvFeedback
{
        public abstract void db_feedback(DbEnv dbenv, int opcode, int pct);
}
public class DbEnv
{
        public void set_feedback(DbEnvFeedback db_feedback)
                throws DbException;
        ...
}
```

Description

Some operations performed by the Berkeley DB library can take non-trivial amounts of time. The DbEnv.set_feedback method can be used by applications to monitor progress within these operations.

When an operation is likely to take a long time, Berkeley DB will call the specified callback method. This method must be declared with three arguments: The first is a reference to the enclosing environment, the second is a flag value, and the third is the percent of the operation that has been completed— specified as an integer value between 0 and 100. It is up to the callback method to display this information in an appropriate manner.

The **opcode** argument may take on any of the following values:

- Db.DB_RECOVER   The environment is being recovered.

The DbEnv.set_feedback interface may be used to configure Berkeley DB at any time during the life of the application.

The DbEnv.set_feedback method throws an exception that encapsulates a non-zero error value on failure.

DbEnv.set_flags

```
import com.sleepycat.db.*;

public void set_flags(int flags, int onoff)
    throws DbException;
```

Description

The **flags** value must be set to 0 or by bitwise inclusively **OR**'ing together one or more of the following values. If **onoff** is zero, the specified flags are cleared; otherwise, they are set.

- Db.DB_CDB_ALLDB   For Berkeley DB Concurrent Data Store applications, perform locking on an environment-wide basis rather than per-database. This flag may only be used to configure Berkeley DB before the **DbEnv.open** interface is called.

- Db.DB_NOMMAP   Copy read-only database files in this environment into the local cache instead of potentially mapping them into process memory (see the description of the **DbEnv.set_mp_mmapsize** method for further information).

- Db.DB_TXN_NOSYNC   Do not synchronously flush the log on transaction commit or prepare. This means that transactions exhibit the ACI (atomicity, consistency, and isolation) properties, but not D (durability); that is, database integrity will be maintained but it is possible that some number of the most recently committed transactions may be undone during recovery.

    The number of transactions potentially at risk is governed by how often the log is checkpointed (see **db_checkpoint** for more information) and how many log updates can fit into the log buffer.

The DbEnv.set_flags method throws an exception that encapsulates a non-zero error value on failure.

The database environment's flag values may also be set using the environment's **DB_CONFIG** file. The syntax of the entry in that file is a single line with the string "set_flags", one or more whitespace characters, and the interface flag argument as a string; for example, "set_flags DB_TXN_NOSYNC". Because the **DB_CONFIG** file is read when the database environment is opened, it will silently overrule configuration done before that time.

Errors

- EINVAL   An invalid flag value or parameter was specified.

DbEnv.set_lg_bsize

```
import com.sleepycat.db.*;

public void set_lg_bsize(int lg_bsize)
    throws DbException;
```

Description

Set the size of the in-memory log buffer, in bytes. By default, or if the value is set to 0, a size of 32K is used. The size of the log file (see **DbEnv.set_lg_max**) must be at least four times the size of the the in-memory log buffer.

Log information is stored in-memory until the storage space fills up or transaction commit forces the information to be flushed to stable storage. In the presence of long-running transactions or transactions producing large amounts of data, larger buffer sizes can increase throughput.

The DbEnv.set_lg_bsize interface may only be used to configure Berkeley DB before the **DbEnv.open** interface is called.

The DbEnv.set_lg_bsize method throws an exception that encapsulates a non-zero error value on failure.

The database environment's log buffer size may also be set using the environment's **DB_CONFIG** file. The syntax of the entry in that file is a single line with the string "set_lg_bsize", one or more whitespace characters, and the size in bytes. Because the **DB_CONFIG** file is read when the database environment is opened, it will silently overrule configuration done before that time.

Errors

- EINVAL   An invalid flag value or parameter was specified.

  Called after **DbEnv.open** was called.

  The size of the log file is less than 4 times the size of the in-memory log buffer.

DbEnv.set_lg_dir

```
import com.sleepycat.db.*;

public void set_lg_dir(String dir)
       throws DbException;
```

Description

The path of a directory to be used as the location of logging files. Log files created by the Log Manager subsystem will be created in this directory.

If no logging directory is specified, log files are created in the environment home directory. See "Berkeley DB File Naming" for more information.

For the greatest degree of recoverability from system or application failure, database files and log files should be located on separate physical devices.

The DbEnv.set_lg_dir interface may only be used to configure Berkeley DB before the **DbEnv.open** interface is called.

The DbEnv.set_lg_dir method throws an exception that encapsulates a non-zero error value on failure.

The database environment's logging directory may also be set using the environment's **DB_CONFIG** file. The syntax of the entry in that file is a single line with the string "set_lg_dir", one or more whitespace characters, and the directory name. Because the **DB_CONFIG** file is read when the database environment is opened, it will silently overrule configuration done before that time.

Errors

- EINVAL   An invalid flag value or parameter was specified.

    Called after **DbEnv.open** was called.

DbEnv.set_lg_max

```
import com.sleepycat.db.*;

public void set_lg_max(int lg_max)
    throws DbException;
```

Description

Set the maximum size of a single file in the log, in bytes. Because **DbLsn** file offsets are unsigned four-byte values, the set value may not be larger than the maximum unsigned four-byte value. By default, or if the value is set to 0, a size of 10MB is used. The size of the log file must be at least four times the size of the in-memory log buffer (see **DbEnv.set_lg_bsize**).

See "Log File Limits" for more information.

The DbEnv.set_lg_max interface may only be used to configure Berkeley DB before the **DbEnv.open** interface is called.

The DbEnv.set_lg_max method throws an exception that encapsulates a non-zero error value on failure.

The database environment's log file size may also be set using the environment's **DB_CONFIG** file. The syntax of the entry in that file is a single line with the string "set_lg_max", one or more whitespace characters, and the size in bytes. Because the **DB_CONFIG** file is read when the database environment is opened, it will silently overrule configuration done before that time.

Errors

- EINVAL   An invalid flag value or parameter was specified.

    Called after **DbEnv.open** was called.

    The size of the log file is less than four times the size of the in-memory log buffer.

    The specified log file size was too large.

DbEnv.set_lk_conflicts

```
import com.sleepycat.db.*;

public void set_lk_conflicts(byte[][] conflicts)
    throws DbException;
```

Description

Set the locking conflicts matrix. A non-0 value for the following array element indicates that requested_mode and held_mode conflict:

```
conflicts[requested_mode][held_mode]
```

The *not-granted* mode must be represented by 0.

If DbEnv.set_lk_conflicts is never called, a standard conflicts array is used; see "Standard Lock Modes" for more information..

The DbEnv.set_lk_conflicts interface may only be used to configure Berkeley DB before the **DbEnv.open** interface is called.

The DbEnv.set_lk_conflicts method throws an exception that encapsulates a non-zero error value on failure.

Errors

- EINVAL   An invalid flag value or parameter was specified.

  Called after **DbEnv.open** was called.

- ENOMEM   No memory was available to copy the conflicts array.

DbEnv.set_lk_detect

```
import com.sleepycat.db.*;

public void set_lk_detect(int detect)
    throws DbException;
```

Description

Set if the deadlock detector is to be run whenever a lock conflict occurs, and specify which transaction should be aborted in the case of a deadlock. The specified value must be one of the following list:

- Db.DB_LOCK_DEFAULT   Use the default policy as specified by **db_deadlock**.
- Db.DB_LOCK_OLDEST   Abort the oldest transaction.
- Db.DB_LOCK_RANDOM   Abort a random transaction involved in the deadlock.
- Db.DB_LOCK_YOUNGEST   Abort the youngest transaction.

The DbEnv.set_lk_detect interface may only be used to configure Berkeley DB before the **DbEnv.open** interface is called.

The DbEnv.set_lk_detect method throws an exception that encapsulates a non-zero error value on failure.

The database environment's deadlock detector configuration may also be set using the environment's **DB_CONFIG** file. The syntax of the entry in that file is a single line with the string "set_lk_detect", one or more whitespace characters, and the interface **detect** argument as a string; for example, "set_lk_detect DB_LOCK_OLDEST". Because the **DB_CONFIG** file is read when the database environment is opened, it will silently overrule configuration done before that time.

Errors

- EINVAL   An invalid flag value or parameter was specified.

  Called after **DbEnv.open** was called.

DbEnv.set_lk_max

```
import com.sleepycat.db.*;

public void set_lk_max(int max)
        throws DbException;
```

Description

The **DbEnv.set_lk_max** method interface has been deprecated in favor of the **DbEnv.set_lk_max_locks, DbEnv.set_lk_max_lockers,** and **DbEnv.set_lk_max_objects** methods. Please update your applications.

Set each of the maximum number of locks, lockers, and lock objects supported by the Berkeley DB Locking subsystem to **max**. This value is used by **DbEnv.open** to estimate how much space to allocate for various lock-table data structures. For specific information on configuring the size of the lock subsystem, see "Configuring Locking: Sizing the System."

The DbEnv.set_lk_max interface may only be used to configure Berkeley DB before the **DbEnv.open** interface is called.

The DbEnv.set_lk_max method throws an exception that encapsulates a non-zero error value on failure.

The database environment's maximum number of locks may also be set using the environment's **DB_CONFIG** file. The syntax of the entry in that file is a single line with the string "set_lk_max", one or more whitespace characters, and the number of locks. Because the **DB_CONFIG** file is read when the database environment is opened, it will silently overrule configuration done before that time.

Errors

- EINVAL   An invalid flag value or parameter was specified.

  Called after **DbEnv.open** was called.

DbEnv.set_lk_max_lockers

```
import com.sleepycat.db.*;

public void set_lk_max_lockers(int max)
        throws DbException;
```

Description

Set the maximum number of simultaneous locking entities supported by the Berkeley DB Locking subsystem. This value is used by **DbEnv.open** to estimate how much space to allocate for various lock-table data structures. The default value is 1000 lockers. For specific information on configuring the size of the lock subsystem, see "Configuring Locking: Sizing the System."

The DbEnv.set_lk_max_lockers interface may only be used to configure Berkeley DB before the **DbEnv.open** interface is called.

The DbEnv.set_lk_max_lockers method throws an exception that encapsulates a non-zero error value on failure.

The database environment's maximum number of lockers may also be set using the environment's **DB_CONFIG** file. The syntax of the entry in that file is a single line with the string "set_lk_max_lockers", one or more whitespace characters, and the number of lockers. Because the **DB_CONFIG** file is read when the database environment is opened, it will silently overrule configuration done before that time.

Errors

- EINVAL   An invalid flag value or parameter was specified.

  Called after **DbEnv.open** was called.

DbEnv.set_lk_max_locks

```
import com.sleepycat.db.*;

public void set_lk_max_locks(int max)
        throws DbException;
```

Description

Set the maximum number of locks supported by the Berkeley DB Locking subsystem. This value is used by **DbEnv.open** to estimate how much space to allocate for various lock-table data structures. The default value is 1000 locks. For specific information on configuring the size of the Locking subsystem, see "Configuring Locking: Sizing the System."

The DbEnv.set_lk_max_locks interface may only be used to configure Berkeley DB before the **DbEnv.open** interface is called.

The DbEnv.set_lk_max_locks method throws an exception that encapsulates a non-zero error value on failure.

The database environment's maximum number of locks may also be set using the environment's **DB_CONFIG** file. The syntax of the entry in that file is a single line with the string "set_lk_max_locks", one or more whitespace characters, and the number of locks. Because the **DB_CONFIG** file is read when the database environment is opened, it will silently overrule configuration done before that time.

Errors

- EINVAL   An invalid flag value or parameter was specified.

  Called after **DbEnv.open** was called.

DbEnv.set_lk_max_objects

```
import com.sleepycat.db.*;

public void set_lk_max_objects(int max)
     throws DbException;
```

Description

Set the maximum number of simultaneously locked objects supported by the Berkeley DB Locking subsystem. This value is used by **DbEnv.open** to estimate how much space to allocate for various lock-table data structures. The default value is 1000 objects. For specific information on configuring the size of the lock subsystem, see "Configuring Locking: Sizing the System."

The DbEnv.set_lk_max_objects interface may only be used to configure Berkeley DB before the **DbEnv.open** interface is called.

The DbEnv.set_lk_max_objects method throws an exception that encapsulates a non-zero error value on failure.

The database environment's maximum number of objects may also be set using the environment's **DB_CONFIG** file. The syntax of the entry in that file is a single line with the string "set_lk_max_objects", one or more whitespace characters, and the number of objects. Because the **DB_CONFIG** file is read when the database environment is opened, it will silently overrule configuration done before that time.

Errors

- EINVAL An invalid flag value or parameter was specified.

  Called after **DbEnv.open** was called.

DbEnv.set_mp_mmapsize

```
import com.sleepycat.db.*;

public void set_mp_mmapsize(long mmapsize)
    throws DbException;
```

Description

Files that are opened read-only in the pool (and that satisfy a few other criteria) are, by default, mapped into the process address space instead of being copied into the local cache. This can result in better-than-usual performance because available virtual memory is normally much larger than the local cache, and page faults are faster than page copying on many systems. However, in the presence of limited virtual memory it can cause resource starvation, and in the presence of large databases, it can result in immense process sizes.

Set the maximum file size, in bytes, for a file to be mapped into the process address space. If no value is specified, it defaults to 10MB.

The DbEnv.set_mp_mmapsize interface may only be used to configure Berkeley DB before the **DbEnv.open** interface is called.

The DbEnv.set_mp_mmapsize method throws an exception that encapsulates a non-zero error value on failure.

The database environment's maximum mapped file size may also be set using the environment's **DB_CONFIG** file. The syntax of the entry in that file is a single line with the string "set_mp_mmapsize", one or more whitespace characters, and the size in bytes. Because the **DB_CONFIG** file is read when the database environment is opened, it will silently overrule configuration done before that time.

Errors

- EINVAL An invalid flag value or parameter was specified.

  Called after **DbEnv.open** was called.

DbEnv.set_mutexlocks

```
import com.sleepycat.db.*;

public void set_mutexlocks(int do_lock)
    throws DbException;
```

Description

Toggle mutex locks. Setting **do_lock** to a false value causes Berkeley DB to grant all requested mutual exclusion mutexes without regard for their availability.

This functionality should never be used for any other purpose than debugging.

The DbEnv.set_mutexlocks interface may be used to configure Berkeley DB at any time during the life of the application.

The DbEnv.set_mutexlocks method throws an exception that encapsulates a non-zero error value on failure.

DbEnv.set_pageyield

```
import com.sleepycat.db.*;

static int
DbEnv.set_pageyield(int pageyield);
    throws DbException;
```

Description

Yield the processor whenever requesting a page from the cache. Setting **pageyield** to a true value causes Berkeley DB to yield the processor any time a thread requests a page from the cache. This functionality should never be used for any other purpose than stress testing.

The DbEnv.set_pageyield interface affects the entire application, not a single database or database environment.

The DbEnv.set_pageyield interface may be used to configure Berkeley DB at any time during the life of the application.

The DbEnv.set_pageyield method throws an exception that encapsulates a non-zero error value on failure.

Errors

- EINVAL   An invalid flag value or parameter was specified.

DbEnv.set_panicstate

```
import com.sleepycat.db.*;

static int
DbEnv.set_panicstate(int panic);
    throws DbException;
```

Description

Toggle the Berkeley DB panic state. Setting **panic** to a true value causes Berkeley DB to refuse attempts to call Berkeley DB functions with the DB_RUNRECOVERY error return.

The DbEnv.set_panicstate interface affects the entire application, not a single database or database environment.

The **DbEnv.set_pageyield** interface may be used to configure Berkeley DB at any time during the life of the application.

The DbEnv.set_panicstate method throws an exception that encapsulates a non-zero error value on failure.

Errors

- EINVAL   An invalid flag value or parameter was specified.

DbEnv.set_recovery_init

```
import com.sleepycat.db.*;

public interface DbRecoveryInit
{
        public abstract int db_recovery_init_fcn(DbEnv dbenv);
}
public class DbEnv
{
        public void set_recovery_init(DbRecoveryInit db_recovery_init_fcn)
                throws DbException;
        ...
}
```

Description

Applications installing application-specific recovery methods need to be called before Berkeley DB performs recovery so they may add their recovery methods to Berkeley DB's.

The DbEnv.set_recovery_init method supports this functionality. The **db_recovery_init_fcn** method must be declared with one argument, a reference to the enclosing Berkeley DB environment. This method will be called after the **DbEnv.open** has been called, but before recovery is started.

If the **db_recovery_init_fcn** method returns a non-zero value, no recovery will be performed and **DbEnv.open** will return the same value to its caller.

The DbEnv.set_recovery_init interface may only be used to configure Berkeley DB before the **DbEnv.open** interface is called.

The DbEnv.set_recovery_init method throws an exception that encapsulates a non-zero error value on failure.

Errors

- EINVAL   An invalid flag value or parameter was specified.

  Called after **DbEnv.open** was called.

DbEnv.set_region_init

```
import com.sleepycat.db.*;

static int
DbEnv.set_region_init(int region_init);
    throws DbException;
```

Description

Page-fault shared regions into memory when initially creating or joining a Berkeley DB environment. In some applications, the expense of page-faulting the shared memory regions can affect performance; for example, when the page-fault occurs while holding a lock, other lock requests can convoy, and overall throughput may decrease. Setting **region_init** to a true value specifies that shared regions be read or written, as appropriate, when the region is joined by the application. This forces the underlying virtual memory and file systems to instantiate both the necessary memory and the necessary disk space. This can also avoid out-of-disk space failures later on.

The DbEnv.set_region_init interface affects the entire application, not a single database or database environment.

Although the DbEnv.set_region_init interface may be used to configure Berkeley DB at any time during the life of the application, it should normally be called before making any calls to the **db_env_create** or **db_create** methods.

The DbEnv.set_region_init method throws an exception that encapsulates a non-zero error value on failure.

The database environment's initial behavior with respect to shared memory regions may also be set using the environment's **DB_CONFIG** file. The syntax of the entry in that file is a single line with the string "set_region_init", one or more whitespace characters, and the string "1". Because the **DB_CONFIG** file is read when the database environment is opened, it will silently overrule configuration done before that time.

Errors

- EINVAL   An invalid flag value or parameter was specified.

DbEnv.set_server

```
import com.sleepycat.db.*;

public void set_server(String host,
    long cl_timeout, long sv_timeout, int flags)
        throws DbException;
```

Description

Connects to the DB server on the indicated hostname and sets up a channel for communication.

The **cl_timeout** argument specifies the number of seconds the client should wait for results to come back from the server. Once the timeout has expired on any communication with the server, Db.DB_NOSERVER will be returned. If this value is zero, a default timeout is used.

The **sv_timeout** argument specifies the number of seconds the server should allow a client connection to remain idle before assuming that client is gone. Once that timeout has been reached, the server releases all resources associated with that client connection. Subsequent attempts by that client to communicate with the server result in Db.DB_NOSERVER_ID, indicating that an invalid identifier has been given to the server. This value can be considered a hint to the server. The server may alter this value based on its own policies or allowed values. If this value is zero, a default timeout is used.

The **flags** parameter is currently unused, and must be set to 0.

When the DbEnv.set_server method has been called, any subsequent calls to Berkeley DB library interfaces may return either DB_NOSERVER or DB_NOSERVER_ID.

The DbEnv.set_server method throws an exception that encapsulates a non-zero error value on failure.

Errors

- EINVAL   An invalid flag value or parameter was specified.

    dbenv_set_server

DbEnv.set_shm_key

```
import com.sleepycat.db.*;

public void set_shm_key(long shm_key)
    throws DbException;
```

Description

Specify a base segment ID for Berkeley DB environment shared memory regions created in system memory on VxWorks or systems supporting X/Open-style shared memory interfaces; for example, UNIX systems supporting **shmget**(2) and related System V IPC interfaces.

This base segment ID will be used when Berkeley DB shared memory regions are first created. It will be incremented a small integer value each time a new shared memory region is created; that is, if the base ID is 35, the first shared memory region created will have a segment ID of 35, and the next one will have a segment ID between 36 and 40 or so. A Berkeley DB environment always creates a master shared memory region, plus an additional shared memory region for each of the subsystems supported by the environment (Locking, Logging, Memory Pool, and Transaction), plus an additional shared memory region for each additional memory pool cache that is supported. Already existing regions with the same segment IDs will be removed. See "Shared Memory Regions" for more information.

The intent behind this interface is two-fold: Without it, applications have no way to ensure that two Berkeley DB applications don't attempt to use the same segment IDs when creating different Berkeley DB environments. In addition, by using the same segment IDs each time the environment is created, previously created segments will be removed, and the set of segments on the system will not grow without bound.

The DbEnv.set_shm_key interface may only be used to configure Berkeley DB before the **DbEnv.open** interface is called.

The DbEnv.set_shm_key method throws an exception that encapsulates a non-zero error value on failure.

The database environment's base segment ID may also be set using the environment's **DB_CONFIG** file. The syntax of the entry in that file is a single line with the string "set_shm_key", one or more whitespace characters, and the ID. Because the **DB_CONFIG** file is read when the database environment is opened, it will silently overrule configuration done before that time.

Errors

- EINVAL   An invalid flag value or parameter was specified.

  Called after **DbEnv.open** was called.

DbEnv.set_tas_spins

```
import com.sleepycat.db.*;

static int
DbEnv.set_tas_spins(u_int32_t tas_spins);
    throws DbException;
```

Description

Specify that test-and-set mutexes should spin **tas_spins** times without blocking. The value defaults to 1 on uniprocessor systems, and to 50 times the number of processors on multi-processor systems.

The DbEnv.set_tas_spins interface affects the entire application, not a single database or database environment.

Although the DbEnv.set_tas_spins interface may be used to configure Berkeley DB at any time during the life of the application, it should normally be called before making any calls to the **db_env_create** or **db_create** methods.

The DbEnv.set_tas_spins method throws an exception that encapsulates a non-zero error value on failure.

The database environment's test-and-set spin count may also be set using the environment's **DB_CONFIG** file. The syntax of the entry in that file is a single line with the string "set_tas_spins", one or more whitespace characters, and the number of spins. Because the **DB_CONFIG** file is read when the database environment is opened, it will silently overrule configuration done before that time.

Errors

- EINVAL   An invalid flag value or parameter was specified.

```
DbEnv.set_tmp_dir
```
```
import com.sleepycat.db.*;

public void set_tmp_dir(String dir)
     throws DbException;
```

Description

The path of a directory to be used as the location of temporary files. The files created to back in-memory access method databases will be created relative to this path. These temporary files can be quite large, depending on the size of the database.

If no directories are specified, the following alternatives are checked in the specified order. The first existing directory path is used for all temporary files.

1. The value of the environment variable **TMPDIR**
2. The value of the environment variable **TEMP**
3. The value of the environment variable **TMP**
4. The value of the environment variable **TempFolder**
5. The value returned by the GetTempPath interface
6. The directory **/var/tmp**
7. The directory **/usr/tmp**
8. The directory **/temp**
9. The directory **/tmp**
10. The directory **C:/temp**
11. The directory **C:/tmp**

Environment variables are only checked if one of the DB_USE_ENVIRON or DB_USE_ENVIRON_ROOT flags was specified.

The GetTempPath interface is only checked on Win/32 platforms.

The DbEnv.set_tmp_dir interface may only be used to configure Berkeley DB before the **DbEnv.open** interface is called.

The DbEnv.set_tmp_dir method throws an exception that encapsulates a non-zero error value on failure.

The database environment's temporary file directory may also be set using the environment's **DB_CONFIG** file. The syntax of the entry in that file is a single line with the string "set_tmp_dir", one or more whitespace characters, and the directory name. Because the **DB_CONFIG** file is read when the database environment is opened, it will silently overrule configuration done before that time.

Errors

- EINVAL   An invalid flag value or parameter was specified.

  Called after **DbEnv.open** was called.

DbEnv.set_tx_max

```
import com.sleepycat.db.*;

public void set_tx_max(int tx_max)
    throws DbException;
```

Description

Set the maximum number of active transactions that are supported by the environment. This value bounds the size of backing shared memory regions. Note that child transactions must be counted as active until their ultimate parent commits or aborts.

When there are more than the specified number of concurrent transactions, calls to **DbEnv.txn_begin** will fail (until some active transactions complete). If no value is specified, a default value of 20 is used.

The DbEnv.set_tx_max interface may only be used to configure Berkeley DB before the **DbEnv.open** interface is called.

The DbEnv.set_tx_max method throws an exception that encapsulates a non-zero error value on failure.

The database environment's maximum number of active transactions may also be set using the environment's **DB_CONFIG** file. The syntax of the entry in that file is a single line with the string "set_tx_max", one or more whitespace characters, and the number of transactions. Because the **DB_CONFIG** file is read when the database environment is opened, it will silently overrule configuration done before that time.

Errors

- EINVAL   An invalid flag value or parameter was specified.

  Called after **DbEnv.open** was called.

DbEnv.set_tx_recover

```
import com.sleepycat.db.*;

public interface DbTxnRecover
{
    public abstract int tx_recover(DbEnv dbenv, Dbt log_rec, DbLsn lsn, int op);
}
public class DbEnv
{
    public void set_tx_recover(DbTxnRecover tx_recover)
        throws DbException;
    ...
}
```

Description

Set the application's method to be called during transaction abort and recovery. This method must return 0 on success and either **errno** or a value outside of the Berkeley DB error name space on failure. It takes four arguments:

- dbenv   A Berkeley DB environment.
- log_rec   A log record.
- lsn   A log sequence number.
- op   One of the following values:
  - Db.DB_TXN_BACKWARD_ROLL   The log is being read backward to determine which transactions have been committed and to abort those operations that were not; undo the operation described by the log record.
  - Db.DB_TXN_FORWARD_ROLL   The log is being played forward; redo the operation described by the log record.
  - Db.DB_TXN_ABORT   The log is being read backward during a transaction abort; undo the operation described by the log record.

The DbEnv.set_tx_recover interface may only be used to configure Berkeley DB before the **DbEnv.open** interface is called.

The DbEnv.set_tx_recover method throws an exception that encapsulates a non-zero error value on failure.

Errors

- EINVAL   An invalid flag value or parameter was specified.

  Called after **DbEnv.open** was called.

DbEnv.set_tx_timestamp

```
import com.sleepycat.db.*;

public void set_tx_timestamp(java.util.Date timestamp)
    throws DbException;
```

Description

Recover to the time specified by **timestamp** rather than to the most current possible date. Note that only the seconds (not the milliseconds) of the **timestamp** are used.

Once a database environment has been upgraded to a new version of Berkeley DB involving a log format change (see "Upgrading Berkeley DB Installations"), it is no longer possible to recover to a specific time before that upgrade.

The DbEnv.set_tx_timestamp interface may only be used to configure Berkeley DB before the **DbEnv.open** interface is called.

The DbEnv.set_tx_timestamp method throws an exception that encapsulates a non-zero error value on failure.

Errors

- EINVAL   An invalid flag value or parameter was specified.

  It is not possible to recover to the specified time using the log files currently present in the environment.

DbEnv.set_verbose

```
import com.sleepycat.db.*;

public int set_verbose(u_int32_t which, boolean onoff);
```

Description

The DbEnv.set_verbose method turns additional informational and debugging messages in the Berkeley DB message output on and off. If **onoff** is set to true, the additional messages are output.

The **which** parameter must be set to one of the following values:

- Db.DB_VERB_CHKPOINT   Display checkpoint location information when searching the log for checkpoints.
- Db.DB_VERB_DEADLOCK   Display additional information when doing deadlock detection.
- Db.DB_VERB_RECOVERY   Display additional information when performing recovery.
- Db.DB_VERB_WAITSFOR   Display the waits-for table when doing deadlock detection.

The DbEnv.set_verbose interface may be used to configure Berkeley DB at any time during the life of the application.

The DbEnv.set_verbose method throws an exception that encapsulates a non-zero error value on failure.

The database environment's verbosity may also be set using the environment's **DB_CONFIG** file. The syntax of the entry in that file is a single line with the string "set_verbose", one or more whitespace characters, and the interface **which** argument as a string; for example, "set_verbose DB_VERB_CHKPOINT". Because the **DB_CONFIG** file is read when the database environment is opened, it will silently overrule configuration done before that time.

Errors

- EINVAL   An invalid flag value or parameter was specified.

DbEnv.strerror

```
import com.sleepycat.db.*;

public static String strerror(int errcode);
```

Description

The DbEnv.strerror method returns an error message string corresponding to the error number **error**. This interface is a superset of the ANSI C X3.159-1989 (ANSI C) **strerror**(3) interface. If the error number **error** is greater than or equal to 0, the string returned by the system interface **strerror**(3) is returned. If the error number is less than 0, an error string appropriate to the corresponding Berkeley DB library error is returned. See "Error Returns to Applications" for more information.

DbEnv.txn_begin

```
import com.sleepycat.db.*;

public DbTxn txn_begin(DbTxn parent, int flags)
        throws DbException;
```

Description

The DbEnv.txn_begin method creates a new transaction in the environment and returns a **DbTxn** that uniquely identifies it.

If the **parent** argument is non-null, the new transaction will be a nested transaction, with the transaction indicated by **parent** as its parent. Transactions may be nested to any level.

The **flags** parameter must be set to 0 or one of the following values:

- Db.DB_TXN_NOSYNC   Do not synchronously flush the log when this transaction commits or prepares. This means the transaction will exhibit the ACI (atomicity, consistency, and isolation) properties, but not D (durability); that is, database integrity will be maintained, but it is possible that this transaction may be undone during recovery.

  This behavior may be set for a Berkeley DB environment using the **DbEnv.set_flags** interface. Any value specified in this interface overrides that setting.

- Db.DB_TXN_NOWAIT   If a lock is unavailable for any Berkeley DB operation performed in the context of this transaction, return immediately instead of blocking on the lock. The error return in the case will be DB_LOCK_NOTGRANTED.

- Db.DB_TXN_SYNC   Synchronously flush the log when this transaction commits or prepares. This means the transaction will exhibit all of the ACID (atomicity, consistency, and isolation and durability) properties.

  This behavior is the default for Berkeley DB environments unless the DB_TXN_NOSYNC flag was specified to the **DbEnv.set_flags** interface. Any value specified in this interface overrides that setting.

A transaction may not span threads; that is, each transaction must begin and end in the same thread, and each transaction may only be used by a single thread.

Cursors may not span transactions; that is, each cursor must be opened and closed within a single transaction.

A parent transaction may not issue any Berkeley DB operations, except for **DbEnv.txn_begin**, **DbTxn.abort**, and **DbTxn.commit**; although it has active child transactions (child transactions that have not yet been committed or aborted).

The DbEnv.txn_begin method throws an exception that encapsulates a non-zero error value on failure.

Errors

The DbEnv.txn_begin method may fail and throw an exception encapsulating a non-zero error for the following conditions:

- ENOMEM   The maximum number of concurrent transactions has been reached.

The DbEnv.txn_begin method may fail and throw an exception for errors specified for other Berkeley DB and C library or system methods. If a catastrophic error has occurred, the DbEnv.txn_begin method may fail and throw a **DbRunRecoveryException**, in which case all subsequent Berkeley DB calls will fail in the same way.

DbEnv.txn_checkpoint

```
import com.sleepycat.db.*;

int
public int txn_checkpoint(int kbyte, int min, int flags)
        throws DbException;
```

Description

The DbEnv.txn_checkpoint method flushes the underlying memory pool, writes a check-point record to the log, and then flushes the log.

If either **kbyte** or **min** is non-zero, the checkpoint is only done if there has been activity since the last checkpoint, and either more than **min** minutes have passed since the last checkpoint or more than **kbyte** kilobytes of log data have been written since the last checkpoint.

The **flags** parameter must be set to 0 or one of the following values:

- Db.DB_FORCE   Force a checkpoint record even if there has been no activity since the last checkpoint.

The DbEnv.txn_checkpoint method throws an exception that encapsulates a non-zero error value on failure, and returns DB_INCOMPLETE if there were pages that needed to be written to complete the checkpoint but that **DbEnv.memp_sync** was unable to write immediately.

Errors

The DbEnv.txn_checkpoint method may fail and throw an exception encapsulating a non-zero error for the following conditions:

- EINVAL   An invalid flag value or parameter was specified.

The DbEnv.txn_checkpoint method may fail and throw an exception for errors specified for other Berkeley DB and C library or system methods. If a catastrophic error has occurred, the DbEnv.txn_checkpoint method may fail and throw a **DbRunRecoveryException**, in which case all subsequent Berkeley DB calls will fail in the same way.

DbEnv.txn_stat

```
import com.sleepycat.db.*;

public DbTxnStat txn_stat()
throws DbException;
```

Description

The DbEnv.txn_stat method creates a DbTxnStat object encapsulating a statistical structure. The transaction region statistics are stored in a DbTxnStat object. The following data fields are available from the DbTxnStat object:

Statistical structures are created in allocated memory. If **db_malloc** is non-NULL, it is called to allocate the memory; otherwise, the library function **malloc**(3) is used. The function **db_malloc** must match the calling conventions of the **malloc**(3) library routine. Regardless, the caller is responsible for deallocating the returned memory. To deallocate returned memory, free the returned memory reference; references inside the returned memory do not need to be individually freed.

The transaction region statistics are stored in a structure of type DB_TXN_STAT. The following DB_TXN_STAT fields will be filled in:

- public **DbLsn** st_last_ckp;   The LSN of the last checkpoint.
- public **DbLsn** st_pending_ckp;   The LSN of any checkpoint that is currently in progress. If **st_pending_ckp** is the same as **st_last_ckp**, there is no checkpoint in progress.
- public long st_time_ckp;   The time the last completed checkpoint finished (as the number of seconds since the Epoch, returned by the IEEE/ANSI Std 1003.1 (POSIX) **time** interface).
- public int st_last_txnid;   The last transaction ID allocated.
- public int st_maxtxns;   The maximum number of active transactions possible.
- public int st_nactive;   The number of transactions that are currently active.
- public int st_maxnactive;   The maximum number of active transactions at any one time.
- public int st_nbegins;   The number of transactions that have begun.
- public int st_naborts;   The number of transactions that have aborted.

- public int st_ncommits;   The number of transactions that have committed.
- public int st_regsize;   The size of the region.
- public int st_region_wait;   The number of times that a thread of control was forced to wait before obtaining the region lock.
- public int st_region_nowait;   The number of times that a thread of control was able to obtain the region lock without waiting.
- public Active st_txnarray[];   The array of active transactions. Each element of the array is an object of type DbTxnStat.Active, a top-level inner class, that has the following fields:
  - public int txnid;   The Transaction ID.
  - public DbLsn lsn;   The LSN of the begin record.

The DbEnv.txn_stat method throws an exception that encapsulates a non-zero error value on failure.

Errors

The DbEnv.txn_stat method may fail and throw an exception for errors specified for other Berkeley DB and C library or system methods. If a catastrophic error has occurred, the DbEnv.txn_stat method may fail and throw a **DbRunRecoveryException**, in which case all subsequent Berkeley DB calls will fail in the same way.

DbException

```
import com.sleepycat.db.*;

public class DbException extends Exception { ... }
```

Description

This manual page describes the DbException class and how it is used by the various Berkeley DB classes.

Most methods in the Berkeley DB classes throw an exception when an error occurs. A DbException object contains an informational string and an errno. The errno can be obtained using **DbException.get_errno**. Because DbException inherits from the java.Exception, the string portion is available using toString().

Some methods may return non-zero values without issuing an exception. This occurs in situations that are not normally considered an error, but when some informational status is returned. For example, **Db.get** returns DB_NOTFOUND when a requested key does not appear in the database.

DbException.get_errno

```
import com.sleepycat.db.*;

public int get_errno();
```

Description

Most methods in the Db classes throw an exception when an error occurs. A DbException object contains an informational string and an errno. The errno can be obtained using DbException.get_errno. Because DbException inherits from the java.Exception, the string portion is available using toString().

DbLock

```
import com.sleepycat.db.*;

public class DbLock extends Object { ... }
```

Description

The **DbEnv** lock methods and the DbLock class are used to provide general-purpose locking. Although designed to work with the other Db classes, they are also useful for more general locking purposes. Locks can be shared between processes.

In most cases, when multiple threads or processes are using locking, the deadlock detector, **db_deadlock** should be run.

DbLock.put

```
import com.sleepycat.db.*;

public native void put(DbEnv env)
        throws DbException;
```

Description

The DbLock.put method releases **lock** from the lock table.

The DbLock.put method throws an exception that encapsulates a non-zero error value on failure.

Errors

The DbLock.put method may fail and throw an exception encapsulating a non-zero error for the following conditions:

- EINVAL   An invalid flag value or parameter was specified.

The DbLock.put method may fail and throw an exception for errors specified for other Berkeley DB and C library or system methods. If a catastrophic error has occurred, the DbLock.put method may fail and throw a **DbRunRecoveryException**, in which case all subsequent Berkeley DB calls will fail in the same way.

DbLsn

```
import com.sleepycat.db.*;

public class DbLsn extends Object { ... }
```

Description

A DbLsn is a **log sequence number** that is fully encapsulated. The class itself has no methods, other than a default constructor, so there is no way for the user to manipulate its data directly.

DbMemoryException

```
import com.sleepycat.db.*;

public class DbMemoryException extends DbException { ... }
```

Description

This manual page describes the DbMemoryException class and how it is used by the various Db★ classes.

A DbMemoryException is thrown when there is insufficient memory to complete an operation.

This may or may not be recoverable. An example of where it would be recoverable is during a **Db.get** or **Dbc.get** operation with the **Dbt** flags set to DB_DBT_USERMEM.

DbMpoolFile.close

```
import com.sleepycat.db.*;
```

Description

A DbMpoolFile.close method is not available in the Berkeley DB Java API.

DbMpoolFile.get

```
import com.sleepycat.db.*;
```

Description

A DbMpoolFile.get method is not available in the Berkeley DB Java API.

DbMpoolFile.open

```
import com.sleepycat.db.*;
```

Description

A DbMpoolFile.open method is not available in the Berkeley DB Java API.

DbMpoolFile.put

```
import com.sleepycat.db.*;
```

Description

A DbMpoolFile.put method is not available in the Berkeley DB Java API.

DbMpoolFile.set

```
import com.sleepycat.db.*;
```

Description

A DbMpoolFile.set method is not available in the Berkeley DB Java API.

DbMpoolFile.sync

```
import com.sleepycat.db.*;
```

Description

A DbMpoolFile.sync method is not available in the Berkeley DB Java API.

DbRunRecoveryException

```
import com.sleepycat.db.*;

public class DbRunRecoveryException extends DbException { ... }
```

Description

This manual page describes the DbRunRecoveryException class and how it is used by the various Db* classes.

Errors can occur in the Berkeley DB library where the only solution is to shut down the application and run recovery (for example, if Berkeley DB is unable to write log records to disk because there is insufficient disk space). When a fatal error occurs in Berkeley DB, methods will throw a DbRunRecoveryException, at which point all subsequent database calls will also fail in the same way. When this occurs, recovery should be performed.

DbTxn

```
import com.sleepycat.db.*;

public class DbTxn extends Object { ... }
```

Description

This manual page describes the specific details of the DbTxn class.

The **DbEnv** transaction methods and the DbTxn class provide transaction semantics. Full transaction support is provided by a collection of modules that provide interfaces to the services required for transaction processing. These services are recovery, concurrency control, and the management of shared data.

Transaction semantics can be applied to the access methods described in Db through method call parameters.

The model intended for transactional use (and the one that is used by the access methods) is write-ahead logging to record both before- and after-images. Locking follows a two-phase protocol with all locks being released at transaction commit.

DbTxn.abort

```
import com.sleepycat.db.*;

public void abort()
       throws DbException;
```

Description

The DbTxn.abort method causes an abnormal termination of the transaction. The log is played backward, and any necessary recovery operations are initiated through the **recover** function specified to **DbEnv.open**. After the log processing is completed, all locks held by the transaction are released. As is the case for **DbTxn.commit**, applications that require strict two-phase locking should not explicitly release any locks.

In the case of nested transactions, aborting a parent transaction causes all children (unresolved or not) of the parent transaction to be aborted.

Once the DbTxn.abort method returns, the **DbTxn** handle may not be accessed again.

The DbTxn.abort method throws an exception that encapsulates a non-zero error value on failure.

Errors

The DbTxn.abort method may fail and throw an exception for errors specified for other Berkeley DB and C library or system methods. If a catastrophic error has occurred, the DbTxn.abort method may fail and throw a **DbRunRecoveryException**, in which case all subsequent Berkeley DB calls will fail in the same way.

DbTxn.commit

```
import com.sleepycat.db.*;

public void commit(u_int32_t flags)
        throws DbException;
```

Description

The DbTxn.commit method ends the transaction. In the case of nested transactions, if the transaction is a parent transaction, committing the parent transaction causes all unresolved children of the parent to be committed.

In the case of nested transactions, if the transaction is a child transaction, its locks are not released, but are acquired by its parent. Although the commit of the child transaction will succeed, the actual resolution of the child transaction is postponed until the parent transaction is committed or aborted; that is, if its parent transaction commits, it will be committed, and if its parent transaction aborts, it will be aborted.

The **flags** parameter must be set to 0 or one of the following values:

- Db.DB_TXN_NOSYNC   Do not synchronously flush the log. This means the transaction will exhibit the ACI (atomicity, consistency, and isolation) properties, but not D (durability); that is, database integrity will be maintained, but it is possible that this transaction may be undone during recovery.

  This behavior may be set for a Berkeley DB environment using the **DbEnv.set_flags** interface or for a single transaction using the **DbEnv.txn_begin** interface. Any value specified in this interface overrides both of those settings.

- Db.DB_TXN_SYNC   Synchronously flush the log. This means the transaction will exhibit all of the ACID (atomicity, consistency, isolation, and durability) properties.

  This behavior is the default for Berkeley DB environments unless the DB_TXN_NOSYNC flag was specified to the **DbEnv.set_flags** interface. This behavior may also be set for a single transaction using the **DbEnv.txn_begin** interface. Any value specified in this interface overrides both of those settings.

Once the DbTxn.commit method returns, the **DbTxn** handle may not be accessed again. If DbTxn.commit encounters an error, the transaction and all child transactions of the transaction are aborted.

The DbTxn.commit method throws an exception that encapsulates a non-zero error value on failure.

Errors

The DbTxn.commit method may fail and throw an exception for errors specified for other Berkeley DB and C library or system methods. If a catastrophic error has occurred, the DbTxn.commit method may fail and throw a **DbRunRecoveryException**, in which case all subsequent Berkeley DB calls will fail in the same way.

DbTxn.id

```
import com.sleepycat.db.*;

public int id()
      throws DbException;
```

Description

The DbTxn.id method returns the unique transaction id associated with the specified transaction. Locking calls made on behalf of this transaction should use the value returned from DbTxn.id as the locker parameter to the **DbEnv.lock_get** or **DbEnv.lock_vec** calls.

DbTxn.prepare

```
import com.sleepycat.db.*;

public void prepare()
      throws DbException;
```

Description

The DbTxn.prepare method initiates the beginning of a two-phase commit.

In a distributed transaction environment, Berkeley DB can be used as a local transaction manager. In this case, the distributed transaction manager must send *prepare* messages to each local manager. The local manager must then issue a DbTxn.prepare and await its successful return before responding to the distributed transaction manager. Only after the distributed transaction manager receives successful responses from all of its *prepare* messages should it issue any *commit* messages.

In the case of nested transactions, preparing a parent transaction causes all unresolved children of the parent transaction to be prepared.

The DbTxn.prepare method throws an exception that encapsulates a non-zero error value on failure.

Errors

The DbTxn.prepare method may fail and throw an exception for errors specified for other Berkeley DB and C library or system methods. If a catastrophic error has occurred, the DbTxn.prepare method may fail and throw a **DbRunRecoveryException**, in which case all subsequent Berkeley DB calls will fail in the same way.

Dbc

```
import com.sleepycat.db.*;

public class Dbc extends Object { ... }
```

Description

This manual page describes the specific details of the Dbc class, which provides cursor support for the access methods in Db.

The Dbc functions are the library interface supporting sequential access to the records stored by the access methods of the Berkeley DB library. Cursors are created by calling the **Db.cursor** method which returns a Dbc object.

Dbc.close

```
import com.sleepycat.db.*;

public void close()
    throws DbException;
```

Description

The Dbc.close method discards the cursor.

It is possible for the Dbc.close method to return DB_LOCK_DEADLOCK, signaling that any enclosing transaction should be aborted. If the application is already intending to abort the transaction, this error should be ignored, and the application should proceed.

Once Dbc.close has been called, regardless of its return, the cursor handle may not be used again.

The Dbc.close method throws an exception that encapsulates a non-zero error value on failure.

Errors

The Dbc.close method may fail and throw an exception encapsulating a non-zero error for the following conditions:

- EINVAL   An invalid flag value or parameter was specified.

  The cursor was previously closed.

If the operation was selected to resolve a deadlock, the Dbc.close method will fail and throw a **DbDeadlockException** exception.

The Dbc.close method may fail and throw an exception for errors specified for other Berkeley DB and C library or system methods. If a catastrophic error has occurred, the Dbc.close method may fail and throw a **DbRunRecoveryException**, in which case all subsequent Berkeley DB calls will fail in the same way.

Dbc.count

```
import com.sleepycat.db.*;

public int count(int flags)
    throws DbException;
```

Description

The Dbc.count method returns a count of the number of duplicate data items for the key referenced by the cursor. If the underlying database does not support duplicate data items, the call will still succeed and a count of 1 will be returned.

The **flags** parameter is currently unused, and must be set to 0.

If the **cursor** argument is not yet initialized, the Dbc.count method throws an exception that encapsulates EINVAL.

Otherwise, the Dbc.count method throws an exception that encapsulates a non-zero error value on failure.

Errors

The Dbc.count method may fail and throw an exception for errors specified for other Berkeley DB and C library or system methods. If a catastrophic error has occurred, the Dbc.count method may fail and throw a **DbRunRecoveryException**, in which case all subsequent Berkeley DB calls will fail in the same way.

Dbc.del

```
import com.sleepycat.db.*;

public int del(int flags)
    throws DbException;
```

Description

The Dbc.del method deletes the key/data pair currently referenced by the cursor.

The **flags** parameter is currently unused, and must be set to 0.

The cursor position is unchanged after a delete, and subsequent calls to cursor functions expecting the cursor to reference an existing key will fail.

If the element has already been deleted, Dbc.del will return DB_KEYEMPTY.

If the cursor is not yet initialized, the Dbc.del method throws an exception that encapsulates EINVAL.

Otherwise, the Dbc.del method throws an exception that encapsulates a non-zero error value on failure.

Errors

The Dbc.del method may fail and throw an exception encapsulating a non-zero error for the following conditions:

- EINVAL   An invalid flag value or parameter was specified.
- EPERM   Write attempted on read-only cursor when the DB_INIT_CDB flag was specified to DbEnv.open.

If the operation was selected to resolve a deadlock, the Dbc.del method will fail and throw a **DbDeadlockException** exception.

The Dbc.del method may fail and throw an exception for errors specified for other Berkeley DB and C library or system methods. If a catastrophic error has occurred, the Dbc.del method may fail and throw a **DbRunRecoveryException**, in which case all subsequent Berkeley DB calls will fail in the same way.

Dbc.dup

```
import com.sleepycat.db.*;

public Dbc dup(int flags)
        throws DbException;
```

Description

The Dbc.dup method creates a new cursor that uses the same transaction and locker ID as the original cursor. This is useful when an application is using locking and requires two or more cursors in the same thread of control.

The **flags** value must be set to 0 or by bitwise inclusively **OR**'ing together one or more of the following values.

- Db.DB_POSITION   The newly created cursor is initialized to reference the same position in the database as the original cursor and hold the same locks. If the Db.DB_POSITION flag is not specified, the created cursor is uninitialized and will behave like a cursor newly created using **Db.cursor**.

When using the Berkeley DB Concurrent Data Store product, there can be only one active write cursor at a time. For this reason, attempting to duplicate a cursor for which the DB_WRITECURSOR flag was specified during creation will return an error.

If the **cursor** argument is not yet initialized, the Dbc.dup method throws an exception that encapsulates EINVAL.

Otherwise, the Dbc.dup method throws an exception that encapsulates a non-zero error value on failure.

Errors

The Dbc.dup method may fail and throw an exception encapsulating a non-zero error for the following conditions:

- EINVAL   An invalid flag value or parameter was specified.

  The **cursor** argument was created using the DB_WRITECURSOR flag in the Berkeley DB Concurrent Data Store product.

The Dbc.dup method may fail and throw an exception for errors specified for other Berkeley DB and C library or system methods. If a catastrophic error has occurred, the Dbc.dup method may fail and throw a **DbRunRecoveryException**, in which case all subsequent Berkeley DB calls will fail in the same way.

Dbc.get

```
import com.sleepycat.db.*;

public int get(Dbt key, Dbt data, int flags)
     throws DbException;
```

Description

The Dbc.get method retrieves key/data pairs from the database. The byte array and length of the key are returned in the object referenced by **key** (except for the case of the Db.DB_SET flag, where the **key** object is unchanged), and the byte array and length of the data are returned in the object referenced by **data**.

Modifications to the database during a sequential scan will be reflected in the scan; that is, records inserted behind a cursor will not be returned, whereas records inserted in front of a cursor will be returned.

In Queue and Recno databases, missing entries (that is, entries that were never explicitly created or that were created and then deleted) will be skipped during a sequential scan.

The **flags** parameter must be set to one of the following values:

- Db.DB_CURRENT   Return the key/data pair currently referenced by the cursor.

  If the cursor key/data pair was deleted, Dbc.get will return DB_KEYEMPTY.

  If the cursor is not yet initialized, the Dbc.get method throws an exception that encapsulates EINVAL.

- Db.DB_FIRST, Db.DB_LAST   The cursor is set to reference the first (last) key/data pair of the database, and that pair is returned. In the presence of duplicate key values, the first (last) data item in the set of duplicates is returned.

  If the database is a Queue or Recno database, Dbc.get using the Db.DB_FIRST (Db.DB_LAST) flags will ignore any keys that exist, but were never explicitly created by the application or were created and later deleted.

  If the database is empty, Dbc.get will return DB_NOTFOUND.

- Db.DB_GET_BOTH   The Db.DB_GET_BOTH flag is identical to the Db.DB_SET flag, except that both the key and the data arguments must be matched by the key and data item in the database.

- Db.DB_GET_RECNO   Return the record number associated with the cursor. The record number will be returned in **data**, as described in **Dbt**. The **key** parameter is ignored.

  For Db.DB_GET_RECNO to be specified, the underlying database must be of type Btree, and it must have been created with the DB_RECNUM flag.

- Db.DB_JOIN_ITEM   Do not use the data value found in all of the cursors as a lookup key for the primary database, but simply return it in the key parameter instead. The data parameter is left unchanged.

  For Db.DB_JOIN_ITEM to be specified, the underlying cursor must have been returned from the **Db.join** method.

- Db.DB_NEXT, Db.DB_PREV   If the cursor is not yet initialized, Db.DB_NEXT (Db.DB_PREV) is identical to Db.DB_FIRST (Db.DB_LAST). Otherwise, the cursor is moved to the next (previous) key/data pair of the database, and that pair is returned. In the presence of duplicate key values, the value of the key may not change.

  If the database is a Queue or Recno database, Dbc.get using the Db.DB_NEXT (Db.DB_PREV) flag will skip any keys that exist but were never explicitly created by the application or were created and later deleted.

  If the cursor is already on the last (first) record in the database, Dbc.get will return DB_NOTFOUND.

- Db.DB_NEXT_DUP   If the next key/data pair of the database is a duplicate record for the current key/data pair, the cursor is moved to the next key/data pair of the database, and that pair is returned. Otherwise, Dbc.get will return DB_NOTFOUND.

  If the cursor is not yet initialized, the Dbc.get method throws an exception that encapsulates EINVAL.

- Db.DB_NEXT_NODUP, Db.DB_PREV_NODUP   If the cursor is not yet initialized, Db.DB_NEXT_NODUP (Db.DB_PREV_NODUP) is identical to Db.DB_FIRST (Db.DB_LAST). Otherwise, the cursor is moved to the next (previous) non-duplicate key/data pair of the database, and that pair is returned.

  If the database is a Queue or Recno database, Dbc.get using the Db.DB_NEXT_NODUP (Db.DB_PREV_NODUP) flags will ignore any keys that exist, but were never explicitly created by the application or were created and later deleted.

  If no non-duplicate key/data pairs occur after (before) the cursor position in the database, Dbc.get will return DB_NOTFOUND.

- Db.DB_SET   Move the cursor to the specified key/data pair of the database, and return the datum associated with the given key.

  In the presence of duplicate key values, Dbc.get will return the first data item for the given key.

  If the database is a Queue or Recno database and the requested key exists, but was never explicitly created by the application or was later deleted, Dbc.get will return DB_KEYEMPTY.

  If no matching keys are found, Dbc.get will return DB_NOTFOUND.

- Db.DB_SET_RANGE   The Db.DB_SET_RANGE flag is identical to the Db.DB_SET flag, except that the key is returned as well as the data item; and, in the case of the Btree access method, the returned key/data pair is the smallest key greater than or equal to the specified key (as determined by the comparison method), permitting partial key matches and range searches.

- Db.DB_SET_RECNO   Move the cursor to the specific numbered record of the database, and return the associated key/data pair. The **data** field of the specified **key** must be a byte array containing a record number, as described in **Dbt**. This determines the record to be retrieved.

  For Db.DB_SET_RECNO to be specified, the underlying database must be of type Btree, and it must have been created with the DB_RECNUM flag.

In addition, the following flag may be set by bitwise inclusively **OR**'ing it into the **flags** parameter:

- Db.DB_RMW   Acquire write locks instead of read locks when doing the retrieval. Setting this flag can eliminate deadlock during a read-modify-write cycle by acquiring the write lock during the read part of the cycle so that another thread of control acquiring a read lock for the same item, in its own read-modify-write cycle, will not result in deadlock.

Otherwise, the Dbc.get method throws an exception that encapsulates a non-zero error value on failure.

If Dbc.get fails for any reason, the state of the cursor will be unchanged.

Errors

The Dbc.get method may fail and throw an exception encapsulating a non-zero error for the following conditions:

- EINVAL   An invalid flag value or parameter was specified.

  The specified cursor was not currently initialized.

If the operation was selected to resolve a deadlock, the Dbc.get method will fail and throw a **DbDeadlockException** exception.

If the requested item could not be returned due to insufficient memory, the Dbc.get method will fail and throw a **DbMemoryException** exception.

The Dbc.get method may fail and throw an exception for errors specified for other Berkeley DB and C library or system methods. If a catastrophic error has occurred, the Dbc.get method may fail and throw a **DbRunRecoveryException**, in which case all subsequent Berkeley DB calls will fail in the same way.

Dbc.put

```
import com.sleepycat.db.*;

public void put(Dbt key, Dbt data, int flags)
        throws DbException;
```

Description

The Dbc.put method stores key/data pairs into the database.

The **flags** parameter must be set to one of the following values:

- Db.DB_AFTER   In the case of the Btree and Hash access methods, insert the data element as a duplicate element of the key referenced by the cursor. The new element appears immediately after the current cursor position. It is an error to specify Db.DB_AFTER if the underlying Btree or Hash database does not support duplicate data items. The **key** parameter is ignored.

In the case of the Recno access method, it is an error to specify Db.DB_AFTER if the underlying Recno database was not created with the DB_RENUMBER flag. If the DB_RENUMBER flag was specified, a new key is created, all records after the inserted item are automatically renumbered, and the key of the new record is returned in the structure referenced by the parameter **key**. The initial value of the **key** parameter is ignored. See **Db.open** for more information.

The Db.DB_AFTER flag may not be specified to the Queue access method.

If the current cursor record has already been deleted and the underlying access method is Hash, Dbc.put will return DB_NOTFOUND. If the underlying access method is Btree or Recno, the operation will succeed.

If the cursor is not yet initialized or a duplicate sort function has been specified, the Dbc.put function will return EINVAL.

- Db.DB_BEFORE   In the case of the Btree and Hash access methods, insert the data element as a duplicate element of the key referenced by the cursor. The new element appears immediately before the current cursor position. It is an error to specify Db.DB_BEFORE if the underlying Btree or Hash database does not support duplicate data items. The **key** parameter is ignored.

In the case of the Recno access method, it is an error to specify Db.DB_BEFORE if the underlying Recno database was not created with the DB_RENUMBER flag. If the DB_RENUMBER flag was specified, a new key is created, the current record and all records after it are automatically renumbered, and the key of the new record is returned in the structure referenced by the parameter **key**. The initial value of the **key** parameter is ignored. See **Db.open** for more information.

The Db.DB_BEFORE flag may not be specified to the Queue access method.

If the current cursor record has already been deleted and the underlying access method is Hash, Dbc.put will return DB_NOTFOUND. If the underlying access method is Btree or Recno, the operation will succeed.

If the cursor is not yet initialized or a duplicate sort function has been specified, Dbc.put will return EINVAL.

- Db.DB_CURRENT   Overwrite the data of the key/data pair referenced by the cursor with the specified data item. The **key** parameter is ignored.

If a duplicate sort function has been specified and the data item of the current referenced key/data pair does not compare equally to the **data** parameter, Dbc.put will return EINVAL.

If the current cursor record has already been deleted and the underlying access method is Hash, Dbc.put will return DB_NOTFOUND. If the underlying access method is Btree, Queue, or Recno, the operation will succeed.

If the cursor is not yet initialized, Dbc.put will return EINVAL.

- Db.DB_KEYFIRST   In the case of the Btree and Hash access methods, insert the specified key/data pair into the database.

If the underlying database supports duplicate data items, and if the key already exists in the database and a duplicate sort function has been specified, the inserted data item is added in its sorted location. If the key already exists in the database and no duplicate sort function has been specified, the inserted data item is added as the first of the data items for that key.

The Db.DB_KEYFIRST flag may not be specified to the Queue or Recno access methods.

- Db.DB_KEYLAST   In the case of the Btree and Hash access methods, insert the specified key/data pair into the database.

   If the underlying database supports duplicate data items, and if the key already exists in the database and a duplicate sort function has been specified, the inserted data item is added in its sorted location. If the key already exists in the database, and no duplicate sort function has been specified, the inserted data item is added as the last of the data items for that key.

   The Db.DB_KEYLAST flag may not be specified to the Queue or Recno access methods.

- Db.DB_NODUPDATA   In the case of the Btree and Hash access methods, insert the specified key/data pair into the database unless it already exists in the database. If the key/data pair already appears in the database, DB_KEYEXIST is returned. The Db.DB_NODUPDATA flag may only be specified if the underlying database has been configured to support sorted duplicate data items.

   The Db.DB_NODUPDATA flag may not be specified to the Queue or Recno access methods.

Otherwise, the Dbc.put method throws an exception that encapsulates a non-zero error value on failure.

If Dbc.put fails for any reason, the state of the cursor will be unchanged. If Dbc.put succeeds and an item is inserted into the database, the cursor is always positioned to reference the newly inserted item.

Errors

The Dbc.put method may fail and throw an exception encapsulating a non-zero error for the following conditions:

- EACCES   An attempt was made to modify a read-only database.
- EINVAL   An invalid flag value or parameter was specified.

   The Db.DB_BEFORE or Db.DB_AFTER flags were specified, and the underlying access method is Queue.

   An attempt was made to add a record to a fixed-length database that was too large to fit.

- EPERM   Write attempted on read-only cursor when the DB_INIT_CDB flag was specified to **DbEnv.open**.

If the operation was selected to resolve a deadlock, the Dbc.put method will fail and throw a **DbDeadlockException** exception.

The Dbc.put method may fail and throw an exception for errors specified for other Berkeley DB and C library or system methods. If a catastrophic error has occurred, the Dbc.put method may fail and throw a **DbRunRecoveryException**, in which case all subsequent Berkeley DB calls will fail in the same way.

Dbt

```java
import com.sleepycat.db.*;

public class Dbt extends Object
{
    public Dbt(byte[] data);
    public Dbt(byte[] data, int off, int len);

    public void set_data(byte[] data);
    public byte[] get_data();

    public void set_offset(int off);
    public int get_offset();

    public int get_size();
    public void set_size(int size);

    public int get_ulen();
    public void set_ulen(int ulen);

    public int get_dlen();
    public void set_dlen(int dlen);

    public int get_doff();
    public void set_doff(int doff);

    public int get_flags();
    public void set_flags(int flags);

    public void set_recno_key_data(int recno);
    public int get_recno_key_data();
}
```

Description

This manual page describes the specific details of the Dbt class, which is used to encode keys and data items in a database.

Key/Data Pairs

Storage and retrieval for the Db access methods are based on key/data pairs. Both key and data items are represented by Dbt objects. Key and data byte strings may reference strings of zero length up to strings of essentially unlimited length. See "Database Limits" for more information.

The Dbt class provides simple access to an underlying data structure, whose elements can be examined or changed using the **set_** or **get_** methods. The remainder of the manual page sometimes refers to these accesses using the underlying name; for example, simply **ulen** instead of Dbt.get_ulen and Dbt.set_ulen. Dbt can be subclassed, providing a way to associate with it additional data, or references to other structures.

The constructors set all elements of the underlying structure to zero. The constructor with one argument has the effect of setting all elements to zero except for the specified **data** and **size** elements. The constructor with three arguments has the additional effect of only using the portion of the array specified by the size and offset.

For the case in which the **flags** structure element is set to 0 when being provided a key or data item by the application, the Berkeley DB package expects the **data** object to be set to a byte array of **size** bytes. When returning a key/data item to the application, the Berkeley DB package will store into the **data** object a byte array of **size** bytes. During a get operation, one of the Db.DB_DBT_MALLOC, Db.DB_DBT_REALLOC, or Db.DB_DBT_USERMEM flags must be specified.

The elements of the structure underlying the Dbt class are defined as follows:

- byte[] data;   A byte array containing the data. This element is accessed using Dbt.get_data and Dbt.set_data, and may be initialized using one of the constructors. Note that the array data is not copied immediately, but only when the Dbt is used.

- int offset;   The number of bytes offset into the **data** array to determine the portion of the array actually used. This element is accessed using Dbt.get_offset and Dbt.set_offset. Although Java normally maintains proper alignment of byte arrays, the set_offset method can be used to specify unaligned addresses. Unaligned address accesses that are not supported by the underlying hardware may be reported as an exception, or may stop the running Java program.

- int size;   The length of **data**, in bytes. This element is accessed using Dbt.get_size and Dbt.set_size, and may be initialized implicitly to the length of the data array with the constructor having one argument.

- int ulen;   The size of the user's buffer (referenced by **data**), in bytes. This location is not written by the Db methods.

    Note that applications can determine the length of a record by setting the **ulen** to 0 and checking the return value found in **size**. See the Db.DB_DBT_USERMEM flag for more information.

    This element is accessed using Dbt.get_ulen and Dbt.set_ulen.

- int dlen;   The length of the partial record being read or written by the application, in bytes. See the Db.DB_DBT_PARTIAL flag for more information. This element is accessed using Dbt.get_dlen and Dbt.set_dlen.

- int doff;   The offset of the partial record being read or written by the application, in bytes. See the Db.DB_DBT_PARTIAL flag for more information. This element is accessed using Dbt.get_doff and Dbt.set_doff.

- int flags;   This element is accessed using Dbt.get_flags and Dbt.set_flags.

The **flags** value must be set by bitwise inclusively **OR**'ing together one or more of the following values.

- Db.DB_DBT_MALLOC   When this flag is set, Berkeley DB will allocate memory for the returned key or data item, and return a byte array containing the data in the **data** field of the key or data Dbt object.

  If Db.DB_DBT_MALLOC is specified, Berkeley DB allocates a properly sized byte array to contain the data. This can be convenient if you know little about the nature of the data, specifically the size of data in the database. However, if your application makes repeated calls to retrieve keys or data, you may notice increased garbage collection due to this allocation. If you know the maximum size of data you are retrieving, you might decrease the memory burden and speed your application by allocating your own byte array and using Db.DB_DBT_USERMEM. Even if you don't know the maximum size, you can use this option and reallocate your array whenever your retrieval API call throws a **DbMemoryException**.

  It is an error to specify more than one of Db.DB_DBT_MALLOC, Db.DB_DBT_REALLOC, and Db.DB_DBT_USERMEM.

- Db.DB_DBT_REALLOC   When this flag is set, Berkeley DB will return the data in the **data** field of the key or data Dbt object, reusing the existing byte array if it is large enough, or allocating a new one of the appropriate size.

  It is an error to specify more than one of Db.DB_DBT_MALLOC, Db.DB_DBT_REALLOC, and Db.DB_DBT_USERMEM.

- Db.DB_DBT_USERMEM   The **data** field of the key or data object must reference memory that is at least **ulen** bytes in length. If the length of the requested item is less than or equal to that number of bytes, the item is copied into the memory referenced by the **data** field. Otherwise, the **size** field is set to the length needed for the requested item, and the error ENOMEM is returned.

  If Db.DB_DBT_USERMEM is specified, the data field of the Dbt must be set to an appropriately sized byte array.

  It is an error to specify more than one of Db.DB_DBT_MALLOC, Db.DB_DBT_REALLOC, and Db.DB_DBT_USERMEM.

If Db.DB_DBT_MALLOC or Db.DB_DBT_REALLOC is specified, Berkeley DB allocates a properly sized byte array to contain the data. This can be convenient if you know little about the nature of the data, specifically the size of data in the database. However, if your application makes repeated calls to retrieve keys or data, you may notice increased garbage collection due to this allocation. If you know the maximum size of data you are retrieving, you might decrease the memory burden and speed your application by allocating your own byte array and using Db.DB_DBT_USERMEM. Even if you don't know the maximum size, you can use this option and reallocate your array whenever your retrieval API call throws a **DbMemoryException**.

- Db.DB_DBT_PARTIAL   Do partial retrieval or storage of an item. If the calling application is doing a get, the **dlen** bytes starting **doff** bytes from the beginning of the retrieved data record are returned as if they comprised the entire record. If any or all of the specified bytes do not exist in the record, the get is successful, and the existing bytes or nul bytes are returned.

For example, if the data portion of a retrieved record was 100 bytes, and a partial retrieval was done using a Dbt having a **dlen** field of 20 and a **doff** field of 85, the get call would succeed, the **data** field would reference the last 15 bytes of the record, and the **size** field would be set to 15.

If the calling application is doing a put, the **dlen** bytes starting **doff** bytes from the beginning of the specified key's data record are replaced by the data specified by the **data** and **size** objects. If **dlen** is smaller than **size**, the record will grow; if **dlen** is larger than **size**, the record will shrink. If the specified bytes do not exist, the record will be extended using nul bytes as necessary, and the put call will succeed.

It is an error to attempt a partial put using the **Db.put** method in a database that supports duplicate records. Partial puts in databases supporting duplicate records must be done using a **Dbc** method.

It is an error to attempt a partial put with differing **dlen** and **size** values in Queue or Recno databases with fixed-length records.

For example, if the data portion of a retrieved record was 100 bytes, and a partial put was done using a Dbt having a **dlen** field of 20, a **doff** field of 85, and a **size** field of 30, the resulting record would be 115 bytes in length, where the last 30 bytes would be those specified by the put call.

31

Tcl APIs

berkdb dbremove

```
berkdb dbremove
      [-env env]
      [--]
      file
      [database]
```

Description

Remove the Berkeley DB database specified by the database name **file** and [database] name arguments. If no **database** is specified, the physical file represented by **file** is removed, incidentally removing all databases that it contained.

No reference count of database use is maintained by Berkeley DB. Applications should not remove databases that are currently in use.

The options are as follows:

- -env env   If an **-env** argument is given, the database in the specified Berkeley DB environment is removed.

- —   Mark the end of the command arguments.

The **berkdb dbremove** command returns 0 on success, and in the case of error, a Tcl error is thrown.

berkdb dbrename

```
berkdb rename
      [-env env]
      [--]
      file
      [database
      newname]
```

Description

Renames the Berkeley DB database specified by the database name **file** and [database] name arguments to the new name given. If no **database** is specified, the physical file represented by **file** is renamed.

No reference count of database use is maintained by Berkeley DB. Applications should not rename databases that are currently in use.

The options are as follows:

- -env env   If a **-env** argument is given, the database in the specified Berkeley DB environment is renamed.

- —   Mark the end of the command arguments.

The **berkdb dbrename** command returns 0 on success, and in the case of error, a Tcl error is thrown.

berkdb env

```
berkdb env
      [-cachesize {gbytes bytes ncache}]
      [-create]
      [-data_dir dirname]
      [-errfile filename]
      [-home directory]
      [-log_dir dirname]
      [-mode mode]
      [-private]
      [-recover]
      [-recover_fatal]
      [-shm_key shmid]
      [-system_mem]
      [-tmp_dir dirname]
      [-txn [nosync]]
      [-txn_max max]
      [-use_environ]
      [-use_environ_root]
```

Description

The **berkdb env** command opens and optionally creates a database environment. The returned environment handle is bound to a Tcl command of the form **envN**, where N is an integer starting at 0 (for example, env0 and env1). It is through this Tcl command that the script accesses the environment methods. The command automatically initializes the Shared Memory Buffer Pool subsystem. This subsystem is used whenever the application is using any Berkeley DB access method.

The options are as follows:

- -cachesize {gbytes bytes ncache}   Set the size of the database's shared memory buffer pool (that is, the cache) to **gbytes** gigabytes plus **bytes**. The cache should be the size of the normal working data set of the application, with some small amount of additional memory for unusual situations. (Note: The working set is not the same as the number of simultaneously referenced pages, and should be quite a bit larger!)

  The default cache size is 256KB, and may not be specified as less than 20KB. Any cache size less than 500MB is automatically increased by 25% to account for buffer pool overhead; cache sizes larger than 500MB are used as specified.

  It is possible to specify caches to Berkeley DB that are large enough so that they cannot be allocated contiguously on some architectures; for example, some releases of Solaris limit the amount of memory that may be allocated contiguously by a process. If **ncache** is 0 or 1, the cache will be allocated contiguously in memory. If it is greater than 1, the cache will be broken up into **ncache** equally sized separate pieces of memory.

  For information on tuning the Berkeley DB cache size, see "Selecting a Cache Size."

- -create   Cause Berkeley DB subsystems to create any underlying files, as necessary.

- -data_dir dirname   Specify the environment's data directory as described in "Berkeley DB File Naming."

- -errfile filename   When an error occurs in the Berkeley DB library, a Berkeley DB error or an error return value is returned by the function. In some cases, however, the errno value may be insufficient to completely describe the cause of the error especially during initial application debugging.

  The **-errfile** argument is used to enhance the mechanism for reporting error messages to the application by specifying a file to be used for displaying additional Berkeley DB error messages. In some cases, when an error occurs, Berkeley DB will output an additional error message to the specified file reference.

  The error message will consist of the environment command name (for example, env0) and a colon (":"), an error string, and a trailing <newline> character.

  This error- logging enhancement does not slow performance or significantly increase application size, and may be run during normal operation as well as during application debugging.

- -home directory   The **-home** argument is described in "Berkeley DB File Naming."

- -log_dir dirname   Specify the environment's logging file directory as described in "Berkeley DB File Naming."

- -mode mode   On UNIX systems, or in IEEE/ANSI Std 1003.1 (POSIX) environments, all files created by Berkeley DB are created with mode **mode** (as described in **chmod**(2)) and modified by the process' umask value at the time of creation (see **umask**(2)). The group ownership of created files is based on the system and directory defaults, and is not further specified by Berkeley DB. If **mode** is 0, files are created readable and writable by both owner and group. On Windows systems, the mode argument is ignored.

- -private   Specify that the environment will only be accessed by a single process (although that process may be multithreaded). This flag has two effects on the Berkeley DB environment. First, all underlying data structures are allocated from per-process memory instead of from shared memory that is potentially accessible to more than a single process. Second, mutexes are only configured to work between threads.

  This flag should not be specified if more than a single process is accessing the environment because it is likely to cause database corruption and unpredictable behavior; for example, if both a server application and the Berkeley DB utility **db_stat** will access the environment, the **-private** option should not be specified.

- -recover   Run normal recovery on this environment before opening it for normal use. If this flag is set, the **-create** option must also be set because the regions will be removed and re-created.

- -recover_fatal   Run catastrophic recovery on this environment before opening it for normal use. If this flag is set, the **-create** option must also be set since the regions will be removed and re-created.

- -shm_key key   Specify a base segment ID for Berkeley DB environment shared memory regions created in system memory on systems supporting X/Open-style shared memory interfaces, e.g., UNIX systems supporting shmget(2) and related System V IPC interfaces. See "Shared Memory Regions" for more information.

- -system_mem   Allocate memory from system shared memory instead of memory backed by the filesystem. See "Shared Memory Regions" for more information.

- -tmp_dir dirname   Specify the environment's tmp directory, as described in "Berkeley DB File Naming."

- -txn [nosync]   Initialize the Transaction subsystem. This subsystem is used when recovery and atomicity of multiple operations and recovery are important. The **-txn** option implies the initialization of the logging and locking subsystems as well.

  If the optional **nosync** argument is specified, the log will not be synchronously flushed on transaction commit or prepare. This means that transactions exhibit the ACI (atomicity, consistency, and isolation) properties, but not D (durability); that is, database integrity will be maintained, but it is possible that some number of the most recently committed transactions may be undone during recovery instead of being redone.

  The number of transactions that are potentially at risk is governed by how often the log is checkpointed (see **db_checkpoint** for more information) and how many log updates can fit on a single log page.

- -txn_max max   Set the maximum number of simultaneous transactions that are supported by the environment, which bounds the size of backing files. When there are more than the specified number of concurrent transactions, calls to *env* **txn** will fail (until some active transactions complete).

- -use_environ   The Berkeley DB process' environment may be permitted to specify information to be used when naming files; see "Berkeley DB File Naming." Because permitting users to specify which files are used can create security problems, environment information will be used in file naming for all users only if the **–use_environ** flag is set.

- -use_environ_root   The Berkeley DB process' environment may be permitted to specify information to be used when naming files; see "Berkeley DB File Naming." Because permitting users to specify which files are used can create security problems, if the **–use_environ_root** flag is set, environment information will be used for file naming only for users with appropriate permissions (for example, users with a user-ID of 0 on IEEE/ANSI Std 1003.1 (POSIX) systems).

The **berkdb env** command returns an environment handle on success.

In the case of error, a Tcl error is thrown.

berkdb envremove

```
berkdb envremove
       [-data_dir directory]
       [-force]
       [-home directory]
       [-log_dir directory]
       [-tmp_dir directory]
       [-use_environ]
       [-use_environ_root]
```

Description

Remove a Berkeley DB environment.

The options are as follows:

- -data_dir dirname   Specify the environment's data directory, as described in "Berkeley DB File Naming."

- -force   If there are processes that have called **berkdb env** without calling *env* **close** (that is, there are processes currently using the environment), **berkdb envremove** will fail without further action, unless the **–force** flag is set, in which case **berkdb envremove** will attempt to remove the environment regardless of any processes still using it.

- -home directory   The **–home** argument is described in "Berkeley DB File Naming."

- -log_dir dirname   Specify the environment's log directory, as described in "Berkeley DB File Naming."

- -tmp_dir dirname   Specify the environment's tmp directory, as described in "Berkeley DB File Naming."

- -use_environ   The Berkeley DB process' environment may be permitted to specify information to be used when naming files; see "Berkeley DB File Naming." Because permitting users to specify which files are used can create security problems, environment information will be used in file naming for all users only if the **-use_environ** flag is set.

- -use_environ_root   The Berkeley DB process' environment may be permitted to specify information to be used when naming files; see "Berkeley DB File Naming." Because permitting users to specify which files are used can create security problems, if the **-use_environ_root** flag is set, environment information will be used for file naming only for users with appropriate permissions (for example, users with a user-ID of 0 on IEEE/ANSI Std 1003.1 (POSIX) systems).

The **berkdb envremove** command returns 0 on success, and in the case of error, a Tcl error is thrown.

berkdb open

```
berkdb open
        [-btree | -hash | -recno | -queue | -unknown]
        [-cachesize {gbytes bytes ncache}]
        [-create]
        [-delim delim]
        [-dup]
        [-dupsort]
        [-env env]
        [-errfile filename]
        [-excl]
        [-extent size]
        [-ffactor density]
        [-len len]
        [-mode mode]
        [-nelem size]
        [-pad pad]
        [-pagesize pagesize]
        [-rdonly]
        [-recnum]
        [-renumber]
        [-snapshot]
        [-source file]
        [-truncate]
        [-upgrade]
        [--]
        [file [database]]
```

Description

The **berkdb open** command opens and optionally creates a database. The returned database handle is bound to a Tcl command of the form **dbN**, where N is an integer starting at 0 (for example, db0 and db1). It is through this Tcl command that the script accesses the database methods.

The options are as follows:

- -btree   Open/create a database of type Btree. The Btree format is a representation of a sorted, balanced tree structure.

- -hash   Open/create a database of type Hash. The Hash format is an extensible, dynamic hashing scheme.

- -queue   Open/create a database of type Queue. The Queue format supports fast access to fixed-length records accessed by sequentially or logical record number.

- -recno   Open/create a database of type Recno. The Recno format supports fixed- or variable-length records, accessed sequentially or by logical record number, and optionally retrieved from a flat text file.

- -unknown   The database is of an unknown type, and must already exist.

- -cachesize {gbytes bytes ncache}   Set the size of the database's shared memory buffer pool (that is, the cache) to **gbytes** gigabytes plus **bytes**. The cache should be the size of the normal working data set of the application, with some small amount of additional memory for unusual situations. (Note: The working set is not the same as the number of simultaneously referenced pages, and should be quite a bit larger!)

  The default cache size is 256KB, and may not be specified as less than 20KB. Any cache size less than 500MB is automatically increased by 25% to account for buffer pool overhead; cache sizes larger than 500MB are used as specified.

  It is possible to specify caches to Berkeley DB that are large enough so that they cannot be allocated contiguously on some architectures; for example, some releases of Solaris limit the amount of memory that may be allocated contiguously by a process. If ncache is 0 or 1, the cache will be allocated contiguously in memory. If it is greater than 1, the cache will be broken up into ncache equally sized separate pieces of memory.

  For information on tuning the Berkeley DB cache size, see "Selecting a Cache Size."

  Because databases opened within Berkeley DB environments use the cache specified to the environment, it is an error to attempt to set a cache in a database created within an environment.

- -create   Create any underlying files, as necessary. If the files do not already exist and the **-create** argument is not specified, the call will fail.

- -delim delim   Set the delimiting byte used to mark the end of a record in the backing source file for the Recno access method.

  This byte is used for variable length records if the -source argument file is specified. If the -source argument file is specified and no delimiting byte was specified, <newline> characters (that is, ASCII 0x0a) are interpreted as end-of-record markers.

- -dup   Permit duplicate data items in the tree; that is, insertion when the key of the key/data pair being inserted already exists in the tree will be successful. The ordering of duplicates in the tree is determined by the order of insertion unless the ordering is otherwise specified by use of a cursor or a duplicate comparison function.

  It is an error to specify both **-dup and -recnum**.

- -dupsort   Sort duplicates within a set of data items. A default lexical comparison will be used. Specifying that duplicates are to be sorted changes the behavior of the *db* **put** operation as well as the *dbc* **put** operation when the **-keyfirst**, **-keylast** and **-current** options are specified.

- -env env   If no **-env** argument is given, the database is standalone; that is, it is not part of any Berkeley DB environment.

  If a **-env** argument is given, the database is created within the specified Berkeley DB environment. The database access methods automatically make calls to the other subsystems in Berkeley DB, based on the enclosing environment. For example, if the environment has been configured to use locking, the access methods will automatically acquire the correct locks when reading and writing pages of the database.

- -errfile filename   When an error occurs in the Berkeley DB library, a Berkeley DB error or an error return value is returned by the function. In some cases, however, the errno value may be insufficient to completely describe the cause of the error especially during initial application debugging.

  The **-errfile** argument is used to enhance the mechanism for reporting error messages to the application by specifying a file to be used for displaying additional Berkeley DB error messages. In some cases, when an error occurs, Berkeley DB will output an additional error message to the specified file reference.

  The error message will consist of a Tcl command name and a colon (":"), an error string, and a trailing <newline> character. If the database was opened in an environment, the Tcl command name will be the environment name (for example, env0); otherwise, it will be the database command name (for example, db0).

  This error- logging enhancement does not slow performance or significantly increase application size, and may be run during normal operation as well as during application debugging.

  For database handles opened inside of Berkeley DB environments, specifying the **-errfile** argument affects the entire environment and is equivalent to specifying the same argument to the **berkdb env** command.

- -excl   Return an error if the file already exists. Underlying filesystem primitives are used to implement this flag. For this reason, it is only applicable to the physical database file and cannot be used to test if a database in a file already exists.

- -extent size   Set the size of the extents of the Queue database; the size is specified as the number of pages in an extent. Each extent is created as a separate physical file. If no extent size is set, the default behavior is to create only a single underlying database file.

  For information on tuning the extent size, see "Selecting an Extent Size."

- -ffactor density   Set the desired density within the hash table. The density is an approximation of the number of keys allowed to accumulate in any one bucket

- -len len   For the Queue access method, specify that the records are of length **len**.

  For the Recno access method, specify that the records are fixed-length, not byte-delimited, and are of length **len**.

Any records added to the database that are less than **len** bytes long are automatically padded (see the **-pad** argument for more information).

Any attempt to insert records into the database that are greater than **len** bytes long will cause the call to fail immediately and return an error.

- -mode mode On UNIX systems, or in IEEE/ANSI Std 1003.1 (POSIX) environments, all files created by the access methods are created with mode **mode** (as described in **chmod**(2)) and modified by the process' umask value at the time of creation (see **umask**(2)). The group ownership of created files is based on the system and directory defaults, and is not further specified by Berkeley DB. If **mode** is 0, files are created readable and writable by both owner and group. On Windows systems, the mode argument is ignored.

- -nelem size Set an estimate of the final size of the hash table.

If not set or set too low, hash tables will still expand gracefully as keys are entered, although a slight performance degradation may be noticed.

- -pad pad Set the padding character for short, fixed-length records for the Queue and Recno access methods.

If no pad character is specified, <space> characters (that is, ASCII 0x20) are used for padding.

- -pagesize pagesize Set the size of the pages used to hold items in the database, in bytes. The minimum page size is 512 bytes, and the maximum page size is 64K bytes. If the page size is not explicitly set, one is selected based on the underlying filesystem I/O block size. The automatically selected size has a lower limit of 512 bytes and an upper limit of 16K bytes.

For information on tuning the Berkeley DB page size, see "Selecting a Page Size."

- -rdonly Open the database for reading only. Any attempt to modify items in the database will fail, regardless of the actual permissions of any underlying files.

- -recnum Support retrieval from the Btree using record numbers.

Logical record numbers in Btree databases are mutable in the face of record insertion or deletion. See the **-renumber** argument for further discussion.

Maintaining record counts within a Btree introduces a serious point of contention, namely the page locations where the record counts are stored. In addition, the entire tree must be locked during both insertions and deletions, effectively single-threading the tree for those operations. Specifying **-recnum** can result in serious performance degradation for some applications and data sets.

It is an error to specify both **-dup** and **-recnum**.

- -renumber Specifying the **-renumber** argument causes the logical record numbers to be mutable, and change as records are added to and deleted from the database. For example, the deletion of record number 4 causes records numbered 5 and greater to be renumbered downward by one. If a cursor was positioned to record number 4 before the deletion, it will reference the new record number 4, if any such record exists, after the deletion. If a cursor was positioned after record number 4 before the deletion, it will be shifted downward one logical record, continuing to reference the same record as it did before.

Using the *db* **put** or *dbc* **put** interfaces to create new records will cause the creation of multiple records if the record number is more than one greater than the largest record currently in the database. For example, creating record 28 when record 25 was previously the last record in the database, will create records 26 and 27 as well as 28.

If a created record is not at the end of the database, all records following the new record will be automatically renumbered upward by one. For example, the creation of a new record numbered 8 causes records numbered 8 and greater to be renumbered upward by one. If a cursor was positioned to record number 8 or greater before the insertion, it will be shifted upward one logical record, continuing to reference the same record as it did before.

For these reasons, concurrent access to a Recno database with the **-renumber** flag specified may be largely meaningless, although it is supported.

- -snapshot   This argument specifies that any specified **-source** file be read in its entirety when the database is opened. If this argument is not specified, the **-source** file may be read lazily.

- -source file   Set the underlying source file for the Recno access method. The purpose of the **-source** file is to provide fast access and modification to databases that are normally stored as flat text files.

If the **-source** argument is give, it specifies an underlying flat text database file that is read to initialize a transient record number index. In the case of variable length records, the records are separated as specified by **-delim**. For example, standard UNIX byte stream files can be interpreted as a sequence of variable length records separated by <newline> characters.

In addition, when cached data would normally be written back to the underlying database file (for example, the *db* **close** or *db* **sync** commands are called), the in-memory copy of the database will be written back to the **-source** file.

By default, the backing source file is read lazily, that is, records are not read from the file until they are requested by the application. If multiple processes (not threads) are accessing a Recno database concurrently and either inserting or deleting records, the backing source file must be read in its entirety before more than a single process accesses the database, and only that process should specify the backing source argument as part of the berkdb open call. See the -**snapshot** argument for more information.

Reading and writing the backing source file specified by -**source** cannot be transaction- protected because it involves filesystem operations that are not part of the Berkeley DB transaction methodology. For this reason, if a temporary database is used to hold the records (that is, no **file** argument was specified to the **berkdb open** call), it is possible to lose the contents of the -**file** file; for example, if the system crashes at the right instant. If a file is used to hold the database that is, a file name was specified as the **file** argument to **berkdb open**), normal database recovery on that file can be used to prevent information loss, although it is still possible that the contents of -**source** will be lost if the system crashes.

The **-source** file must already exist (but may be zero-length) when **berkdb open** is called.

It is not an error to specify a read-only **-source** file when creating a database, nor is it an error to modify the resulting database. However, any attempt to write the changes to the backing source file using either the *db* **close** or *db* **sync** commands will fail, of course. Specify the **-nosync** argument to the *db* **close** command will stop it from attempting to write the changes to the backing file; instead, they will be silently discarded.

For all of the previous reasons, the **-source** file is generally used to specify databases that are read-only for Berkeley DB applications, and that are either generated on- the-fly by software tools or modified using a different mechanism; for example, a text editor.

- -truncate   Physically truncate the underlying file, discarding all previous databases it might have held. Underlying filesystem primitives are used to implement this flag. For this reason, it is only applicable to the physical file and cannot be used to discard databases within a file.

  The **-truncate** argument cannot be transaction-protected, and it is an error to specify it in a transaction protected environment.

- -upgrade   Upgrade the database represented by **file**, if necessary.

  Note: Database upgrades are done in place and are destructive; for example, if pages need to be allocated and no disk space is available, the database may be left corrupted. Backups should be made before databases are upgraded. See "Upgrading Databases" for more information.

- —   Mark the end of the command arguments.

- file   The name of a single physical file on disk that will be used to back the database.

- database   The **database** argument allows applications to have multiple databases inside of a single physical file. This is useful when the databases are both numerous and reasonably small, in order to avoid creating a large number of underlying files. It is an error to attempt to open a second database file that was not initially created using a **database** name.

The **berkdb open** command returns a database handle on success.

In the case of error, a Tcl error is thrown.

berkdb version

```
berkdb version
     [-string]
```

Description

Return a list of the form {major minor patch} for the major, minor and patch levels of the underlying Berkeley DB release.

The options are as follows:

- -string   Return a string with formatted Berkeley DB version information.

In the case of error, a Tcl error is thrown.

db close

```
db close
     [-nosync]
```

Description

The *db* **close** command flushes any cached database information to disk, closes any open cursors, frees any allocated resources, and closes any underlying files. Because key/data pairs are cached in memory, failing to sync the file with the *db* **close** or *db* **sync** command may result in inconsistent or lost information.

The options are as follows:

- -nosync   Do not flush cached information to disk.

  The -nosync flag is a dangerous option. It should only be set if the application is doing logging (with transactions) so that the database is recoverable after a system or application crash, or if the database is always generated from scratch after any system or application crash.

  It is important to understand that flushing cached information to disk only minimizes the window of opportunity for corrupted data. Although unlikely, it is possible for database corruption to happen if a system or application crash occurs while writing data to the database. To ensure that database corruption never occurs, applications must either use transactions and logging with automatic recovery, use logging and application-specific recovery, or edit a copy of the database; and after all applications using the database have successfully called *db* **close**, atomically replace the original database with the updated copy.

After *db* **close** has been called, regardless of its return, the DB handle may not be accessed again.

The *db* **close** command returns 0 on success, and in the case of error, a Tcl error is thrown.

dbc close

```
dbc close
```

Description

The *dbc* **close** command discards the cursor.

After *dbc* **close** has been called, regardless of its return, the cursor handle may not be used again.

The *dbc* **close** command returns 0 on success, and in the case of error, a Tcl error is thrown.

db count

```
db count key
```

Description

The *db* **count** command returns a count of the number of duplicate data items for the key given. If the key does not exist, a value of 0 is returned. If there are no duplicates, or if the database does not support duplicates but a key/data pair exists, a value of 1 is returned. If an error occurs, a Berkeley DB error message is returned or a Tcl error is thrown.

db cursor

```
db cursor
     [-txn txnid]
```

Description

The *db* **cursor** command creates a database cursor. The returned cursor handle is bound to a Tcl command of the form **dbN.cX**, where X is an integer starting at 0 (for example, db0.c0 and db0.c1). It is through this Tcl command that the script accesses the cursor methods.

The options are as follows:

- -txn txnid   If the file is being accessed under transaction protection, the **txnid** parameter is a transaction handle returned from *env* **txn**.

In the case of error, a Tcl error is thrown.

db del

```
db del
     [-glob]
     [-txn txnid]
     key
```

Description

The *db* **del** command removes key/data pairs from the database.

In the presence of duplicate key values, all records associated with the designated key will be discarded.

The options are as follows:

- -glob   The specified key is a wildcard pattern, and all keys matching that pattern are discarded from the database. The pattern is a simple wildcard; any characters after the wildcard character are ignored.

- -txn txnid   If the file is being accessed under transaction protection, the **txnid** parameter is a transaction handle returned from *env* **txn**.

The *db* **del** command returns 0 on success, and in the case of error, a Tcl error is thrown.

dbc del

```
dbc del
```

Description

The *dbc* **del** command deletes the key/data pair currently referenced by the cursor.

The cursor position is unchanged after a delete, and subsequent calls to cursor commands expecting the cursor to reference an existing key will fail.

The *dbc* **del** command returns 0 on success, and in the case of error, a Tcl error is thrown.

dbc dup

```
dbc dup
    [-position]
```

Description

The *dbc* **dup** command duplicates the cursor, creates a new cursor that uses the same transaction and locker ID as the original cursor. This is useful when an application is using locking and requires two or more cursors in the same thread of control.

The options are as follows:

- -position   The newly created cursor is initialized to reference the same position in the database as the original cursor and hold the same locks. If the **-position** flag is not specified, the created cursor is uninitialized and will behave like a cursor newly created using the *db* **cursor** command.

The *dbc* **dup** command returns 0 on success, and in the case of error, a Tcl error is thrown.

db get

```
db get
    [-consume]
    [-consume_wait]
    [-glob]
    [-partial {doff dlen}]
    [-recno]
    [-rmw]
    [-txn txnid]
    key
db get
    -get_both
    [-partial {doff dlen}]
    [-rmw]
    [-txn txnid]
    key data
```

Description

The *db* **get** command returns key/data pairs from the database.

In the presence of duplicate key values, *db* **get** will return all duplicate items. Duplicates are sorted by insert order except where this order has been overridden by cursor operations.

The options are as follows:

- -consume   Return the record number and data from the available record closest to the head of the queue, and delete the record. The cursor will be positioned on the deleted record. A record is available if it is not deleted and is not currently locked. The underlying database must be of type Queue for **-consume** to be specified.

- -consume_wait   The same as the **-consume** flag, except that if the Queue database is empty, the thread of control will wait until there is data in the queue before returning. The underlying database must be of type Queue for **-consume_wait** to be specified.

- -get_both key data   Retrieve the key/data pair only if both the key and data match the arguments.

- -glob   Return all keys matching the given key, where the key is a simple wildcard pattern. Where it is used, it replaces the use of the key with the given pattern of a set of keys. Any characters after the wildcard character are ignored. For example, in a database of last names, the command "db0 get Jones" will return all occurrences of "Jones" in the database, and the command "db0 get -glob Jo★" will return both "Jones" and "Johnson" from the database. The command "db0 get -glob ★" will return all the key/data pairs in the database.

- -partial {doff dlen}   The **dlen** bytes starting **doff** bytes from the beginning of the retrieved data record are returned as if they comprised the entire record. If any or all of the specified bytes do not exist in the record, the command is successful, and the existing bytes or 0 bytes are returned.

- -recno   Retrieve the specified numbered key/data pair from a database. For **-recno** to be specified, the specified key must be a record number; and the underlying database must be of type Recno or Queue, or of type Btree that was created with the **-recnum** option.

- -rmw   Acquire write locks instead of read locks when doing the retrieval. Setting this flag may decrease the likelihood of deadlock during a read-modify-write cycle by immediately acquiring the write lock during the read part of the cycle so that another thread of control acquiring a read lock for the same item, in its own read-modify-write cycle, will not result in deadlock.

  Because the *db* **get** command will not hold locks across Berkeley DB interface calls in nontransactional environments, the **-rmw** argument to the *db* **get** call is only meaningful in the presence of transactions.

- -txn txnid   If the file is being accessed under transaction protection, the **txnid** parameter is a transaction handle returned from *env* **txn**.

If the underlying database is a Queue or Recno database, the given key will be interpreted by Tcl as an integer. For all other database types, the key is interpreted by Tcl as a byte array, unless indicated by a given option.

A list of key/data pairs is returned. In the error case that no matching key exists, an empty list is returned. In all other cases, a Tcl error is thrown.

---

dbc get

```
dbc get
      [-current]
      [-first]
      [-get_recno]
      [-join_item]
      [-last]
      [-next]
      [-nextdup]
      [-nextnodup]
      [-partial {offset length}]
      [-prev]
      [-prevnodup]
      [-rmw]
dbc get
      [-partial {offset length}]
      [-rmw]
      [-set]
      [-set_range]
      [-set_recno]
      key
dbc get
      -get_both
      [-partial {offset length}]
      [-rmw]
      key data
```

Description

The *dbc* **get** command returns a list of {key value} pairs, except in the case of the **-get_recno** and **-join_item** options. In the case of the **-get_recno** option, *dbc* **get** returns a list of the record numbers. In the case of the **-join_item** option, *dbc* **get** returns a list containing the joined key.

The options are as follows:

- -current   Return the key/data pair currently referenced by the cursor.

   If the cursor key/data pair was deleted, *dbc* **get** will return an empty list.

- -first   The cursor is set to reference the first key/data pair of the database, and that pair is returned. In the presence of duplicate key values, the first data item in the set of duplicates is returned.

   If the database is a Queue or Recno database, *dbc* **get** using the **-first** option will skip any keys that exist but were never explicitly created by the application, or were created and later deleted.

If the database is empty, *dbc* **get** will return an empty list.

- -last   The cursor is set to reference the last key/data pair of the database, and that pair is returned. In the presence of duplicate key values, the last data item in the set of duplicates is returned.

  If the database is a Queue or Recno database, *dbc* **get** using the **-last** option will skip any keys that exist but were never explicitly created by the application, or were created and later deleted.

  If the database is empty, *dbc* **get** will return an empty list.

- -next   If the cursor is not yet initialized, the **-next** option is identical to **-first**.

  Otherwise, the cursor is moved to the next key/data pair of the database, and that pair is returned. In the presence of duplicate key values, the value of the key may not change.

  If the database is a Queue or Recno database, *dbc* **get** using the **-next** option will skip any keys that exist but were never explicitly created by the application, or were created and later deleted.

  If the cursor is already on the last record in the database, *dbc* **get** will return an empty list.

- -nextdup   If the next key/data pair of the database is a duplicate record for the current key/data pair, the cursor is moved to the next key/data pair of the database, and that pair is returned. Otherwise, *dbc* **get** will return an empty list.

- -nextnodup   If the cursor is not yet initialized, the **-nextnodup** option is identical to **-first**.

  Otherwise, the cursor is moved to the next non-duplicate key/data pair of the database, and that pair is returned.

  If no non-duplicate key/data pairs occur after the cursor position in the database, *dbc* **get** will return an empty list.

- -prev   If the cursor is not yet initialized, **-prev** is identical to **-last**.

  Otherwise, the cursor is moved to the previous key/data pair of the database, and that pair is returned. In the presence of duplicate key values, the value of the key may not change.

  If the database is a Queue or Recno database, *dbc* **get** using the **-prev** flag will skip any keys that exist but were never explicitly created by the application, or were created and later deleted.

  If the cursor is already on the first record in the database, *dbc* **get** will return an empty list.

- -prevnodup   If the cursor is not yet initialized, the **-prevnodup** option is identical to **-last**.

  Otherwise, the cursor is moved to the previous non-duplicate key/data pair of the database, and that pair is returned.

  If no non-duplicate key/data pairs occur before the cursor position in the database, *dbc* **get** will return an empty list.

- -set Move the cursor to the specified key/data pair of the database, and return the datum associated with the given key.

  In the presence of duplicate key values, *dbc* **get** will return the first data item for the given key.

  If the database is a Queue or Recno database and the requested key exists, but was never explicitly created by the application or was later deleted, *dbc* **get** will return an empty list.

  If no matching keys are found, *dbc* **get** will return an empty list.

- -set_range The **-set_range** option is identical to the **-set** option, except that the key is returned as well as the data item, and, in the case of the Btree access method, the returned key/data pair is the smallest key greater than or equal to the specified key (as determined by the comparison function), permitting partial key matches and range searches.

- -get_both The **-get_both** option is identical to the **-set** option, except that both the key and the data arguments must be matched by the key and data item in the database.

  For **-get_both** to be specified, the underlying database must be of type Btree or Hash.

- -set_recno Move the cursor to the specific numbered record of the database, and return the associated key/data pair. The key must be a record number.

  For the **-set_recno** option to be specified, the underlying database must be of type Btree, and it must have been created with the **-recnum** option.

- -get_recno Return a list of the record number associated with the current cursor position. No key argument should be specified.

  For **-get_recno** to be specified, the underlying database must be of type Btree, and it must have been created with the **-recnum** option.

- -join_item Do not use the data value found in all the cursors as a lookup key for the primary database, but simply return it in the key parameter instead. The data parameter is left unchanged.

  For **-join_item** to be specified, the cursor must have been created by the *db* **join** command.

- -partial {offset length} The **dlen** bytes starting **doff** bytes from the beginning of the retrieved data record are returned as if they comprised the entire record. If any or all the specified bytes do not exist in the record, the command is successful and the existing bytes or 0 bytes are returned.

- -rmw Acquire write locks instead of read locks when doing the retrieval. Setting this flag may decrease the likelihood of deadlock during a read-modify-write cycle by immediately acquiring the write lock during the read part of the cycle so that another thread of control acquiring a read lock for the same item, in its own read-modify-write cycle, will not result in deadlock.

If a key is specified, and if the underlying database is a Queue or Recno database, the given key will be interpreted by Tcl as an integer. For all other database types, the key is interpreted by Tcl as a byte array, unless indicated by a given option.

In the normal error case of attempting to retrieve a key that does not exist an empty list is returned.

In the case of error, a Tcl error is thrown.

db get_join

```
db get_join
    [-txn txnid]
    {db key}
    {db key}
    ...
```

Description

The *db* **get_join** command performs the cursor operations required to join the specified keys and returns a list of joined {key data} pairs. See "**Logical Join**" for more information on the underlying requirements for joining.

The options are as follows:

- -txn txnid   If the file is being accessed under transaction protection, the **txnid** parameter is a transaction handle returned from *env* **txn**.

In the case of error, a Tcl error is thrown.

db get_type

```
db get_type
```

Description

The *db* **get_type** command returns the underlying database type, returning one of "btree", "hash", "queue" or "recno".

In the case of error, a Tcl error is thrown.

db is_byteswapped

```
db is_byteswapped
```

Description

The *db* **is_byteswapped** command returns 0 if the underlying database files were created on an architecture of the same byte order as the current one, and 1 if they were not (that is, big-endian on a little-endian machine, or vice versa). This value may be used to determine whether application data needs to be adjusted for this architecture or not.

In the case of error, a Tcl error is thrown.

db join

```
db join
      db.cX
      db.cY
      db.cZ
      ...
```

Description

The *db* **join** command joins the specified cursors and returns a cursor handle that can be used to iterate through the joined {key data} pairs. The returned cursor handle is bound to a Tcl command of the form **dbN.cX**, where X is an integer starting at 0 (for example, db0.c0 and db0.c1). It is through this Tcl command that the script accesses the cursor methods.

The returned join cursor has limited cursor functionality, and only the *dbc* **get** and *dbc* **close** commands will succeed.

See "Logical Join" for more information on the underlying requirements for joining.

In a transaction-protected environment, all the cursors listed must have been created within the same transaction.

In the case of error, a Tcl error is thrown.

db put

```
db put
      -append
      [-partial {doff dlen}]
      [-txn txnid]
      data
db put
      [-nooverwrite]
      [-partial {doff dlen}]
      [-txn txnid]
      key data
```

Description

The *db* **put** command stores the specified key/data pair into the database.

The options are as follows:

- -append   Append the data item to the end of the database. For the **–append** option to be specified, the underlying database must be a Queue or Recno database. The record number allocated to the record is returned on success.

- -nooverwrite   Enter the new key/data pair only if the key does not already appear in the database.

- -partial {doff dlen}   The **dlen** bytes starting **doff** bytes from the beginning of the specified key's data record are replaced by the data specified by the data and size structure elements. If **dlen** is smaller than the length of the supplied data, the record will grow; if **dlen** is larger than the length of the supplied data, the record will shrink. If the specified bytes do not exist, the record will be extended using nul bytes as necessary, and the *db* **put** call will succeed.

  It is an error to attempt a partial put using the *db* **put** command in a database that supports duplicate records. Partial puts in databases supporting duplicate records must be done using a *dbc* **put** command.

  It is an error to attempt a partial put with differing **dlen** and supplied data length values in Queue or Recno databases with fixed-length records.

- -txn txnid   If the file is being accessed under transaction protection, the **txnid** parameter is a transaction handle returned from *env* **txn**.

The *db* **put** command returns either 0 or a record number for success (the record number is returned if the **–append** option was specified). If an error occurs, a Berkeley DB error message is returned or a Tcl error is thrown.

If the underlying database is a Queue or Recno database, then the given key will be interpreted by Tcl as an integer. For all other database types, the key is interpreted by Tcl as a byte array.

db stat

```
db stat
     [-recordcount]
```

Description

The *db* **stat** command returns a list of name/value pairs comprising the statistics of the database.

The options are as follows:

- -recordcount   Return the number of records in the database. The **–recordcount** option may only be specified for Recno databases, or Btree databases where the underlying database was created with the **–recnum** option.

In the case of error, a Tcl error is thrown.

db sync

```
db sync
```

Description

The *db* **sync** command function flushes any database cached information to disk.

See *db* **close** for a discussion of Berkeley DB and cached data.

The *db* **sync** command returns 0 on success, and in the case of error, a Tcl error is thrown.

dbc put

```
dbc put
      [-after]
      [-before]
      [-current]
      [-partial {doff dlen}]
      data
dbc put
      [-keyfirst]
      [-keylast]
      [-partial {doff dlen}]
      key data
```

Description

The *dbc* **put** command stores the specified key/data pair into the database.

The options are as follows:

- -after   In the case of the Btree and Hash access methods, insert the data element as a duplicate element of the key referenced by the cursor. The new element appears immediately after the current cursor position. It is an error to specify **-after** if the underlying Btree or Hash database was not created with the **-dup** option. No key argument should be specified.

    In the case of the Recno access method, it is an error to specify the **-after** option if the underlying Recno database was not created with the **-renumber** option. If the **-renumber** option was specified, a new key is created, all records after the inserted item are automatically renumbered, and the key of the new record is returned in the structure referenced by the parameter key. The initial value of the key parameter is ignored. See **berkdb open** for more information.

    In the case of the Queue access method, it is always an error to specify **-after**.

    If the current cursor record has already been deleted, and the underlying access method is Hash, *dbc* **put** will throw a Tcl error. If the underlying access method is Btree or Recno, the operation will succeed.

- -before   In the case of the Btree and Hash access methods, insert the data element as a duplicate element of the key referenced by the cursor. The new element appears immediately before the current cursor position. It is an error to specify **-before** if the underlying Btree or Hash database was not created with the **-dup** option. No key argument should be specified.

    In the case of the Recno access method, it is an error to specify **-before** if the underlying Recno database was not created with the **-before** option. If the **-before** option was specified, a new key is created, the current record and all records after it are automatically renumbered, and the key of the new record is returned in the structure referenced by the parameter key. The initial value of the key parameter is ignored. See **berkdb open** for more information.

In the case of the Queue access method, it is always an error to specify **-before**.

If the current cursor record has already been deleted and the underlying access method is Hash, *dbc* **put** will throw a Tcl error. If the underlying access method is Btree or Recno, the operation will succeed.

- -current   Overwrite the data of the key/data pair referenced by the cursor with the specified data item. No key argument should be specified.

  If the **-dupsort** option was specified to **berkdb open** and the data item of the current referenced key/data pair does not compare equally to the data parameter, *dbc* **put** will throw a Tcl error.

  If the current cursor record has already been deleted and the underlying access method is Hash, *dbc* **put** will throw a Tcl error. If the underlying access method is Btree, Queue, or Recno, the operation will succeed.

- -keyfirst   In the case of the Btree and Hash access methods, insert the specified key/data pair into the database.

  If the key already exists in the database, and the **-dupsort** option was specified to **berkdb open**, the inserted data item is added in its sorted location. If the key already exists in the database, and the **-dupsort** option was not specified, the inserted data item is added as the first of the data items for that key.

  The **-keyfirst** option may not be specified to the Queue or Recno access methods.

- -keylast   In the case of the Btree and Hash access methods, insert the specified key/data pair into the database.

  If the key already exists in the database, and the **-dupsort** option was specified to **berkdb open**, the inserted data item is added in its sorted location. If the key already exists in the database, and the **-dupsort** option was not specified, the inserted data item is added as the last of the data items for that key.

  The **-keylast** option may not be specified to the Queue or Recno access methods.

- -partial {doff dlen}   The **dlen** bytes starting **doff** bytes from the beginning of the specified key's data record are replaced by the data specified by the data and size structure elements. If **dlen** is smaller than the length of the supplied data, the record will grow; and if **dlen** is larger than the length of the supplied data, the record will shrink. If the specified bytes do not exist, the record will be extended using nul bytes as necessary, and the *dbc* **put** call will succeed.

  It is an error to attempt a partial put using the *dbc* **put** command in a database that supports duplicate records. Partial puts in databases supporting duplicate records must be done using a *dbc* **put** command.

  It is an error to attempt a partial put with differing **dlen** and supplied data length values in Queue or Recno databases with fixed-length records.

If a key is specified, and if the underlying database is a Queue or Recno database, the given key will be interpreted by Tcl as an integer. For all other database types, the key is interpreted by Tcl as a byte array.

If *dbc* **put** fails for any reason, the state of the cursor will be unchanged. If *dbc* **put** succeeds and an item is inserted into the database, the cursor is always positioned to reference the newly inserted item.

The *dbc* **put** command returns 0 on success, and in the case of error, a Tcl error is thrown.

env close

```
env close
```

Description

Close the Berkeley DB environment, freeing any allocated resources and closing any underlying subsystems.

This does not imply closing any databases that were opened in the environment.

Where the environment was initialized with the **-lock** option, calling *env* **close** does not release any locks still held by the closing process, providing functionality for long-lived locks.

Once *env* **close** has been called, the **env** handle may not be accessed again.

The *env* **close** command returns 0 on success, and in the case of error, a Tcl error is thrown.

env txn

```
env txn
      [-nosync]
      [-nowait]
      [-parent txnid]
      [-sync]
```

Description

The *env* **txn** command begins a transaction. The returned transaction handle is bound to a Tcl command of the form **env.txnX**, where X is an integer starting at 0 (for example, env0.txn0 and env0.txn1). It is through this Tcl command that the script accesses the transaction methods.

The options are as follows:

• -nosync   Do not synchronously flush the log when this transaction commits or prepares. This means the transaction will exhibit the ACI (atomicity, consistency, and isolation) properties, but not D (durability); that is, database integrity will be maintained, but it is possible that this transaction may be undone during recovery instead of being redone.

This behavior may be set for an entire Berkeley DB environment as part of the **berkdb env** interface.

- -nowait If a lock is unavailable for any Berkeley DB operation performed in the context of this transaction, throw a Tcl error immediately instead of blocking on the lock.

- -parent txnid Create the new transaction as a nested transaction, with the specified transaction indicated as its parent. Transactions may be nested to any level.

- -sync Synchronously flush the log when this transaction commits or prepares. This means the transaction will exhibit all of the ACID (atomicity, consistency, isolation, and durability) properties.

  This behavior is the default for Berkeley DB environments unless the **-nosync** option was specified to the **berkdb env** interface.

The *env* **txn** command returns a transaction handle on success.

In the case of error, a Tcl error is thrown.

txn abort

```
txn abort
```

Description

The *txn* **abort** command causes an abnormal termination of the transaction.

The log is played backward, and any necessary recovery operations are performed. After recovery is completed, all locks held by the transaction are acquired by the parent transaction in the case of a nested transaction, or released in the case of a non-nested transaction. As is the case for *txn* **commit**, applications that require strict two-phase locking should not explicitly release any locks.

In the case of nested transactions, aborting the parent transaction causes all children of that transaction to be aborted.

After *txn* **abort** has been called, regardless of its return, the **txn** handle may not be accessed again.

The *txn* **abort** command returns 0 on success, and in the case of error, a Tcl error is thrown.

txn commit

```
txn commit
     [-nosync]
     [-sync]
```

Description

The *txn* **commit** command ends the transaction.

In the case of nested transactions, if the transaction is a parent transaction with unresolved (neither committed or aborted) child transactions, the child transactions are aborted and the commit of the parent will succeed.

In the case of nested transactions, if the transaction is a child transaction, its locks are not released, but are acquired by its parent. Although the commit of the child transaction will succeed, the actual resolution of the child transaction is postponed until the parent transaction is committed or aborted; that is, if its parent transaction commits, it will be committed, and if its parent transaction aborts, it will be aborted.

If the **-nosync** option is not specified, a commit log record is written and flushed to disk, as are all previously written log records.

The options are as follows:

- -nosync   Do not synchronously flush the log. This means the transaction will exhibit the ACI (atomicity, consistency, and isolation) properties, but not D (durability); that is, database integrity will be maintained, but it is possible that this transaction may be undone during recovery instead of being redone.

  This behavior may be set for an entire Berkeley DB environment as part of the **berkdb env** interface.

- -sync   Synchronously flush the log. This means the transaction will exhibit all of the ACID (atomicity, consistency, isolation, and durability) properties.

  This behavior is the default for Berkeley DB environments unless the **-nosync** option was specified to the **berkdb env** or *env* **txn** interfaces.

After *txn* **commit** has been called, regardless of its return, the **txn** handle may not be accessed again. If *txn* **commit** encounters an error, this transaction and all child transactions of this transaction are aborted.

The *txn* **commit** command returns 0 on success, and in the case of error, a Tcl error is thrown.

32

Supporting Utilities

berkeley_db_svc

```
berkeley_db_svc [-Vv] [-h home]
    [-I seconds] [-L file] [-t seconds] [-T seconds]
```

Description

The berkeley_db_svc utility is the Berkeley DB RPC server.

The options are as follows:

- **-h** Add the specified home directory to the list of allowed home directories that can be specified by the client. The home directory should be an absolute pathname. The last component of each home directory specified must be unique because that is how clients specify which database environment they wish to join.

  Recovery will be run on each specified environment before the server begins accepting requests from clients. For this reason, only one copy of the server program should ever be run at any time because recovery must always be single-threaded.

- **-I** Set the default idle timeout for client environments to the specified number of seconds. The default timeout is 24 hours.

- **-L** Log the execution of the berkeley_db_svc utility to the specified file in the following format, where ### is the process ID, and the date is the time the utility was started.

```
berkeley_db_svc: ### Wed Jun 15 01:23:45 EDT 1995
```

This file will be removed if the berkeley_db_svc utility exits gracefully.

- **-t**   Set the default timeout for client resources (idle transactions and cursors) to the specified number of seconds. When the timeout expires, if the resource is a transaction, it is aborted; if the resource is a cursor, it is closed. The default timeout is 5 minutes.

- **-T**   Set the maximum timeout allowed for client resources. The default timeout is 20 minutes. If a client application requests a server timeout greater than the maximum timeout set for this server, the client's timeout will be capped at the maximum timeout value.

- **-V**   Write the version number to the standard output and exit.

- **-v**   Run in verbose mode.

The berkeley_db_svc utility uses a Berkeley DB environment (as described for the **-h** option, the environment variable **DB_HOME**, or because the utility was run in a directory containing a Berkeley DB environment). In order to avoid environment corruption when using a Berkeley DB environment, berkeley_db_svc should always be given the chance to detach from the environment and exit gracefully. To cause berkeley_db_svc to release all environment resources and exit cleanly, send it an interrupt signal (SIGINT).

The berkeley_db_svc utility exits 0 on success, and >0 if an error occurs.

Environment Variables

- DB_HOME   If the **-h** option is not specified and the environment variable DB_HOME is set, it is used as the path of the database home, as described in **DBENV→open**.

See Also

berkeley_db_svc, **db_archive**, **db_checkpoint**, **db_deadlock**, **db_dump**, **db_load**, **db_recover**, **db_stat**, **db_upgrade**, and **db_verify**.

db_archive

```
db_archive [-alsVv] [-h home]
```

Description

The db_archive utility writes the pathnames of log files that are no longer in use (for example, no longer involved in active transactions), to the standard output, one pathname per line. These log files should be written to backup media to provide for recovery in the case of catastrophic failure (which also requires a snapshot of the database files), but they may then be deleted from the system to reclaim disk space.

The options are as follows:

- **-a**   Write all pathnames as absolute pathnames, instead of relative to the database home directories.

- **-h**   Specify a home directory for the database environment; by default, the current working directory is used.

- **-l**   Write out the pathnames of all of the database log files, whether or not they are involved in active transactions.

- **-s**   Write the pathnames of all the database files that need to be archived in order to recover the database from catastrophic failure. If any of the database files have not been accessed during the lifetime of the current log files, db_archive will not include them in this output.

   It is possible that some of the files referenced in the log have since been deleted from the system. In this case, db_archive will ignore them. When **db_recover** is run, any files referenced in the log that are not present during recovery are assumed to have been deleted and will not be recovered.

- **-V**   Write the version number to the standard output, and exit.

- **-v**   Run in verbose mode, listing the checkpoints in the log files as they are reviewed.

The db_archive utility uses a Berkeley DB environment (as described for the **-h** option, the environment variable **DB_HOME**, or because the utility was run in a directory containing a Berkeley DB environment). In order to avoid environment corruption when using a Berkeley DB environment, db_archive should always be given the chance to detach from the environment and exit gracefully. To cause db_archive to release all environment resources and exit cleanly, send it an interrupt signal (SIGINT).

The db_archive utility exits 0 on success, and >0 if an error occurs.

Environment Variables

- DB_HOME   If the **-h** option is not specified and the environment variable DB_HOME is set, it is used as the path of the database home, as described in **DBENV→open**.

See Also

berkeley_db_svc, db_archive, **db_checkpoint**, **db_deadlock**, **db_dump**, **db_load**, **db_recover**, **db_stat**, **db_upgrade**, and **db_verify**.

db_checkpoint

```
db_checkpoint [-1Vv]
    [-h home] [-k kbytes] [-L file] [-p min]
```

Description

The db_checkpoint utility is a daemon process that monitors the database log, and periodically calls **txn_checkpoint** to checkpoint it.

The options are as follows:

- **-1**   Checkpoint the log once, regardless of whether or not there has been activity since the last checkpoint and then exit.

- **-h**   Specify a home directory for the database environment; by default, the current working directory is used.

- **-k**   Checkpoint the database at least as often as every **kbytes** of log file are written.

- **-L**   Log the execution of the db_checkpoint utility to the specified file in the following format, where ### is the process ID, and the date is the time the utility was started.

  `db_checkpoint: ### Wed Jun 15 01:23:45 EDT 1995`

  This file will be removed if the db_checkpoint utility exits gracefully.

- **-p**   Checkpoint the database at least every **min** minutes if there has been any activity since the last checkpoint.

- **-V**   Write the version number to the standard output and exit.

- **-v**   Write the time of each checkpoint attempt to the standard output.

At least one of the **-1**, **-k**, and **-p** options must be specified.

The db_checkpoint utility uses a Berkeley DB environment (as described for the **-h** option, the environment variable **DB_HOME**, or because the utility was run in a directory containing a Berkeley DB environment). In order to avoid environment corruption when using a Berkeley DB environment, db_checkpoint should always be given the chance to detach from the environment and exit gracefully. To cause db_checkpoint to release all environment resources and exit cleanly, send it an interrupt signal (SIGINT).

The db_checkpoint utility does not attempt to create the Berkeley DB shared memory regions if they do not already exist. The application that creates the region should be started first, and once the region is created, the db_checkpoint utility should be started.

The db_checkpoint utility exits 0 on success, and >0 if an error occurs.

Environment Variables

- DB_HOME   If the **-h** option is not specified and the environment variable DB_HOME is set, it is used as the path of the database home, as described in **DBENV→open**.

See Also

berkeley_db_svc, **db_archive**, db_checkpoint, **db_deadlock**, **db_dump**, **db_load**, **db_recover**, **db_stat**, **db_upgrade**, and **db_verify**.

db_deadlock

```
db_deadlock [-Vvw]
    [-a o | y] [-h home] [-L file] [-t sec]
```

Description

The db_deadlock utility traverses the database lock structures, and aborts a lock request each time it detects a deadlock. By default, a random lock request is chosen to be aborted. This utility should be run as a background daemon, or the underlying Berkeley DB deadlock detection interfaces should be called in some other way, whenever there are multiple threads or processes accessing a database and at least one of them is modifying it.

The options are as follows:

- **-a** When a deadlock is detected, abort the oldest (o) lock request or the youngest (y) lock request.

- **-h** Specify a home directory for the database environment; by default, the current working directory is used.

- **-L** Log the execution of the db_deadlock utility to the specified file in the following format, where ### is the process ID, and the date is the time the utility was started.

    ```
    db_deadlock: ### Wed Jun 15 01:23:45 EDT 1995
    ```

    This file will be removed if the db_deadlock utility exits gracefully.

- **-t** Initiate a pass over the database locks at least every **sec** seconds.

- **-V** Write the version number to the standard output and exit.

- **-v** Run in verbose mode, generating messages each time the detector runs.

- **-w** Make a single pass over the database locks every time a process is forced to wait for a lock.

At least one of the **-t** and **-w** options must be specified.

The db_deadlock utility uses a Berkeley DB environment (as described for the **-h** option, the environment variable **DB_HOME**, or because the utility was run in a directory containing a Berkeley DB environment). In order to avoid environment corruption when using a Berkeley DB environment, db_deadlock should always be given the chance to detach from the environment and exit gracefully. To cause db_deadlock to release all environment resources and exit cleanly, send it an interrupt signal (SIGINT).

The db_deadlock utility does not attempt to create the Berkeley DB shared memory regions if they do not already exist. The application which creates the region should be started first, and then, once the region is created, the db_deadlock utility should be started.

The db_deadlock utility exits 0 on success, and >0 if an error occurs.

Environment Variables

- DB_HOME   If the **-h** option is not specified and the environment variable DB_HOME is set, it is used as the path of the database home, as described in **DBENV→open**.

See Also

berkeley_db_svc, **db_archive**, **db_checkpoint**, db_deadlock, **db_dump**, **db_load**, **db_recover**, **db_stat**, **db_upgrade**, and **db_verify**.

db_dump

```
db_dump [-klNpRrV] [-d ahr]
        [-f output] [-h home] [-s database] file
db_dump185 [-p] [-f output] file
```

Description

The db_dump utility reads the database file **file** and writes it to the standard output using a portable flat-text format understood by the **db_load** utility. The argument **file** must be a file produced using the Berkeley DB library functions.

The **db_dump185** utility is similar to the db_dump utility, except that it reads databases in the format used by Berkeley DB versions 1.85 and 1.86.

The options are as follows:

- **-d**   Dump the specified database in a format helpful for debugging the Berkeley DB library routines.

- a   Display all information.

- h   Display only page headers.

- r   Do not display the free-list or pages on the free list. This mode is used by the recovery tests.

  The output format of the -d option is not standard and may change, without notice, between releases of the Berkeley DB library.

- **-f**   Write to the specified **file** instead of to the standard output.

- **-h**   Specify a home directory for the database environment; by default, the current working directory is used.

- **-k**   Dump record numbers from Queue and Recno databases as keys.

- **-l**   List the databases stored in the file.

- **-N**   Do not acquire shared region locks while running. Other problems, such as potentially fatal errors in Berkeley DB, will be ignored as well. This option is intended only for debugging errors, and should not be used under any other circumstances.

- **-p** If characters in either the key or data items are printing characters (as defined by **isprint**(3)), use printing characters in **file** to represent them. This option permits users to use standard text editors and tools to modify the contents of databases.

  Note: different systems may have different notions about what characters are considered *printing characters*, and databases dumped in this manner may be less portable to external systems.

- **-R** Aggressively salvage data from a possibly corrupt file. The **-R** flag differs from the **-r** option in that it will return all possible data from the file at the risk of also returning already deleted or otherwise nonsensical items. Data dumped in this fashion will almost certainly have to be edited by hand or other means before the data is ready for reload into another database

- **-r** Salvage data from a possibly corrupt file. When used on a uncorrupted database, this option should return equivalent data to a normal dump, but most likely in a different order.

- **-s** Specify a single database to dump. If no database is specified, all databases in the database file are dumped.

- **-V** Write the version number to the standard output, and exit.

Dumping and reloading Hash databases that use user-defined hash functions will result in new databases that use the default hash function. Although using the default hash function may not be optimal for the new database, it will continue to work correctly.

Dumping and reloading Btree databases that use user-defined prefix or comparison functions will result in new databases that use the default prefix and comparison functions. In this case, it is quite likely that the database will be damaged beyond repair, permitting neither record storage nor retrieval.

The only available workaround for either case is to modify the sources for the **db_load** utility to load the database using the correct hash, prefix, and comparison functions.

The **db_dump185** utility may not be available on your system because it is not always built when the Berkeley DB libraries and utilities are installed. If you are unable to find it, see your system administrator for further information.

The db_dump and **db_dump185** utility output formats are documented in the "Dump Output Formats" section of the *Reference Guide*.

The db_dump utility may be used with a Berkeley DB environment (as described for the **-h** option, the environment variable **DB_HOME**, or because the utility was run in a directory containing a Berkeley DB environment). In order to avoid environment corruption when using a Berkeley DB environment, db_dump should always be given the chance to detach from the environment and exit gracefully. To cause db_dump to release all environment resources and exit cleanly, send it an interrupt signal (SIGINT).

When using an Berkeley DB database environment, the db_dump utility does not configure for any kind of database locking, so it should not be used with active Berkeley DB environments. If db_dump is used in an active database environment, corruption may result.

The db_dump utility exits 0 on success, and >0 if an error occurs.

The **db_dump185** utility exits 0 on success, and >0 if an error occurs.

Environment Variables

- DB_HOME   If the **-h** option is not specified and the environment variable DB_HOME is set, it is used as the path of the database home, as described in **DBENV→open**.

See Also

berkeley_db_svc, **db_archive**, **db_checkpoint**, **db_deadlock**, db_dump, **db_load**, **db_recover**, **db_stat**, **db_upgrade**, and **db_verify**.

db_load

```
db_load [-nTV] [-c name=value] [-f file]
   [-h home] [-t btree | hash | queue | recno] file
```

Description

The db_load utility reads from the standard input and loads it into the database **file**. The database **file** is created if it does not already exist.

The input to db_load must be in the output format specified by the **db_dump** utility, utilities, or as specified for the **-T** below.

The options are as follows:

- **-c**   Specify configuration options ignoring any value they may have based on the input. The command-line format is **name=value**. See " Supported Keywords for a list of supported words for the **-c** option.

- **-f**   Read from the specified **input** file instead of from the standard input.

- **-h**   Specify a home directory for the database environment.

  If a home directory is specified, the database environment is opened using the DB_INIT_LOCK, DB_INIT_LOG, DB_INIT_MPOOL, DB_INIT_TXN, and DB_USE_ENVIRON flags to **DBENV→open**. (This means that db_load can be used to load data into databases while they are in use by other processes.) If the **DBENV→open** call fails, or if no home directory is specified, the database is still updated, but the environment is ignored; for example, no locking is done.

- **-n**   Do not overwrite existing keys in the database when loading into an already existing database. If a key/data pair cannot be loaded into the database for this reason, a warning message is displayed on the standard error output, and the key/data pair are skipped.

- **-T**   The **-T** option allows non-Berkeley DB applications to easily load text files into databases.

If the database to be created is of type Btree or Hash, or the keyword **keys** is specified as set, the input must be paired lines of text, where the first line of the pair is the key item, and the second line of the pair is its corresponding data item. If the database to be created is of type Queue or Recno and the keywork **keys** is not set, the input must be lines of text, where each line is a new data item for the database.

A simple escape mechanism, where newline and backslash (\) characters are special, is applied to the text input. Newline characters are interpreted as record separators. Backslash characters in the text will be interpreted in one of two ways: If the backslash character precedes another backslash character, the pair will be interpreted as a literal backslash. If the backslash character precedes any other character, the two characters following the backslash will be interpreted as a hexadecimal specification of a single character; for exmple, \0a is a newline character in the ASCII character set.

For this reason, any backslash or newline characters that naturally occur in the text input must be escaped to avoid misinterpretation by db_load.

If the **-T** option is specified, the underlying access method type must be specified using the **-t** option.

- **-t** Specify the underlying access method. If no **-t** option is specified, the database will be loaded into a database of the same type as was dumped; for example, a Hash database will be created if a Hash database was dumped.

  Btree and Hash databases may be converted from one to the other. Queue and Recno databases may be converted from one to the other. If the **-k** option was specified on the call to **db_dump** then Queue and Recno databases may be converted to Btree or Hash, with the key being the integer record number.

- **-V** Write the version number to the standard output and exit.

The db_load utility may be used with a Berkeley DB environment (as described for the **-h** option, the environment variable **DB_HOME**, or because the utility was run in a directory containing a Berkeley DB environment). In order to avoid environment corruption when using a Berkeley DB environment, db_load should always be given the chance to detach from the environment and exit gracefully. To cause db_load to release all environment resources and exit cleanly, send it an interrupt signal (SIGINT).

The db_load utility exits 0 on success, 1 if one or more key/data pairs were not loaded into the database because the key already existed, and >1 if an error occurs.

Examples

The db_load utility can be used to load text files into databases. For example, the following command loads the standard UNIX */etc/passwd* file into a database, with the login name as the key item and the entire password entry as the data item:

```
awk -F: '{print $1; print $0}' < /etc/passwd |
    sed 's/\\/\\\\/g' | db_load -T -t hash passwd.db
```

Note that backslash characters naturally occurring in the text are escaped to avoid interpretation as escape characters by db_load.

Environment Variables

- DB_HOME   If the **-h** option is not specified and the environment variable DB_HOME is set, it is used as the path of the database home, as described in **DBENV→open**.

Supported Keywords

The following keywords are supported for the **-c** command-line option to the db_load utility. See **DB→open** for further discussion of these keywords and what values should be specified.

The parenthetical listing specifies how the value part of the **name=value** pair is interpreted. Items listed as (boolean) expect value to be **1** (set) or **0** (unset). Items listed as (number) convert value to a number. Items listed as (string) use the string value without modification.

- bt_minkey (number)   The minimum number of keys per page.
- database (string)   The database to load.
- db_lorder (number)   The byte order for integers in the stored database metadata.
- db_pagesize (number)   The size of pages used for nodes in the tree, in bytes.
- duplicates (boolean)   The value of the DB_DUP flag.
- dupsort (boolean)   The value of the DB_DUPSORT flag.
- h_ffactor (number)   The density within the Hash database.
- h_nelem (number)   The size of the Hash database.
- keys (boolean)   Specify whether keys are present for Queue or Recno databases.
- re_len (number)   Specify fixed-length records of the specified length.
- re_pad (string)   Specify the fixed-length record pad character.
- recnum (boolean)   The value of the DB_RECNUM flag.
- renumber (boolean)   The value of the DB_RENUMBER flag.

See Also

berkeley_db_svc, **db_archive**, **db_checkpoint**, **db_deadlock**, **db_dump**, db_load, **db_recover**, **db_stat**, **db_upgrade**, and **db_verify**.

db_printlog

```
db_printlog [-NV] [-h home]
```

Description

The db_printlog utility is a debugging utility that dumps Berkeley DB log files in a human-readable format.

The options are as follows:

- **-h** Specify a home directory for the database environment; by default, the current working directory is used.

- **-N** Do not acquire shared region locks while running. Other problems, such as potentially fatal errors in Berkeley DB, will be ignored as well. This option is intended only for debugging errors and should not be used under any other circumstances.

- **-V** Write the version number to the standard output and exit.

For more information on the db_printlog output and using it to debug applications, see "Reviewing Berkeley DB Log Files."

The db_printlog utility uses a Berkeley DB environment (as described for the **-h** option, the environment variable **DB_HOME**, or because the utility was run in a directory containing a Berkeley DB environment). In order to avoid environment corruption when using a Berkeley DB environment, db_printlog should always be given the chance to detach from the environment and exit gracefully. To cause db_printlog to release all environment resources and exit cleanly, send it an interrupt signal (SIGINT).

The db_printlog utility exits 0 on success, and >0 if an error occurs.

Environment Variables

- DB_HOME If the **-h** option is not specified and the environment variable DB_HOME is set, it is used as the path of the database home, as described in **DBENV→open**.

See Also

berkeley_db_svc, **db_archive**, **db_checkpoint**, **db_deadlock**, **db_dump**, **db_load**, **db_recover**, **db_stat**, **db_upgrade**, and **db_verify**.

db_recover

```
db_recover [-cVv] [-h home] [-t [[CC]YY]MMDDhhmm[.SS]]]
```

Description

The db_recover utility must be run after an unexpected application, Berkeley DB, or system failure to restore the database to a consistent state. All committed transactions are guaranteed to appear after db_recover has run, and all uncommitted transactions will be completely undone.

The options are as follows:

- **-c** Perform catastrophic recovery instead of normal recovery.

- **-h** Specify a home directory for the database environment; by default, the current working directory is used.

- **-t** Recover to the time specified rather than to the most current possible date. The timestamp argument should be in the form [[CC]YY]MMDDhhmm[.SS], where each pair of letters represents the following:

  - CC The first two digits of the year (the century).

  - YY The second two digits of the year. If "YY" is specified, but "CC" is not, a value for "YY" between 69 and 99 results in a "YY" value of 19. Otherwise, a "YY" value of 20 is used.

  - MM The month of the year, from 1 to 12.

  - DD The day of the month, from 1 to 31.

  - hh The hour of the day, from 0 to 23.

  - mm The minute of the hour, from 0 to 59.

  - SS The second of the minute, from 0 to 61.

  If the "CC" and "YY" letter pairs are not specified, the values default to the current year. If the "SS" letter pair is not specified, the value defaults to 0.

- **-V** Write the version number to the standard output and exit.

- **-v** Run in verbose mode.

In the case of catastrophic recovery, an archival copy—or *snapshot*—of all database files must be restored along with all of the log files written since the database file snapshot was made. (If disk space is a problem, log files may be referenced by symbolic links). For further information on creating a database snapshot, see "Archival Procedures." For further information on performing recovery, see "Recovery Procedures."

If the failure was not catastrophic, the files present on the system at the time of failure are sufficient to perform recovery.

If log files are missing, db_recover will identify the missing log file(s) and fail, in which case the missing log files need to be restored and recovery performed again.

The db_recover utility uses a Berkeley DB environment (as described for the **-h** option, the environment variable **DB_HOME**, or because the utility was run in a directory containing a Berkeley DB environment). In order to avoid environment corruption when using a Berkeley DB environment, db_recover should always be given the chance to detach from the environment and exit gracefully. To cause db_recover to release all environment resources and exit cleanly, send it an interrupt signal (SIGINT).

The db_recover utility exits 0 on success, and >0 if an error occurs.

Environment Variables

- DB_HOME

  - If the **-h** option is not specified and the environment variable DB_HOME is set, it is used as the path of the database home, as described in **DBENV→open**.

See Also

berkeley_db_svc, **db_archive**, **db_checkpoint**, **db_deadlock**, **db_dump**, **db_load**, **db_recover**, **db_stat**, **db_upgrade**, and **db_verify**.

---

db_stat

```
db_stat [-celmNtV]
    [-C Acfhlmo] [-d file [-s database]] [-h home] [-M Ahlm]
```

Description

The db_stat utility displays statistics for Berkeley DB environments.

The options are as follows:

- **-C** Display internal information about the lock region. (The output from this option is often both voluminous and meaningless, and is intended only for debugging.)

  - A Display all information.

  - c Display lock conflict matrix.

  - f Display lock and object free lists.

  - l Display lockers within hash chains.

  - m Display region memory information.

  - o Display objects within hash chains.

- **-c** Display lock region statistics as described in **lock_stat**.

- **-d** Display database statistics for the specified file, as described in **DB→stat**.

If the database contains multiple databases and the **-s** flag is not specified, the statistics are for the internal database that describes the other databases the file contains, and not for the file as a whole.

- **-e** Display current environment statistics.

- **-h** Specify a home directory for the database environment; by default, the current working directory is used.

- **-l** Display log region statistics as described in **log_stat**.

- **-M** Display internal information about the shared memory buffer pool. (The output from this option is often both voluminous and meaningless, and is intended only for debugging.)

  - A Display all information.

  - h Display buffers within hash chains.

  - l Display buffers within LRU chains.

  - m Display region memory information.

- **-m** Display shared memory buffer pool statistics, as described in **memp_stat**.

- **-N**   Do not acquire shared region locks while running. Other problems, such as potentially fatal errors in Berkeley DB, will be ignored as well. This option is intended only for debugging errors and should not be used under any other circumstances.

- **-s**   Display statistics for the specified database contained in the file specified with the **-d** flag.

- **-t**   Display transaction region statistics, as described in **txn_stat**.

- **-V**   Write the version number to the standard output and exit.

Only one set of statistics is displayed for each run, and the last option specifying a set of statistics takes precedence.

Values smaller than 10 million are generally displayed without any special notation. Values larger than 10 million are normally displayed as **<number>M**.

The db_stat utility may be used with a Berkeley DB environment (as described for the **-h** option, the environment variable **DB_HOME**, or because the utility was run in a directory containing a Berkeley DB environment). In order to avoid environment corruption when using a Berkeley DB environment, db_stat should always be given the chance to detach from the environment and exit gracefully. To cause db_stat to release all environment resources and exit cleanly, send it an interrupt signal (SIGINT).

The db_stat utility exits 0 on success, and >0 if an error occurs.

Environment Variables

- DB_HOME   If the **-h** option is not specified and the environment variable DB_HOME is set, it is used as the path of the database home, as described in **DBENV→open**.

See Also

berkeley_db_svc, **db_archive**, **db_checkpoint**, **db_deadlock**, **db_dump**, **db_load**, **db_recover**, db_stat, **db_upgrade**, and **db_verify**.

db_upgrade

```
db_upgrade [-NsV] [-h home] file ...
```

Description

The db_upgrade utility upgrades the Berkeley DB version of one or more files and the databases they contain to the current release version.

The options are as follows:

- **-h** Specify a home directory for the database environment; by default, the current working directory is used.

- **-N** Do not acquire shared region locks while running. Other problems, such as potentially fatal errors in Berkeley DB, will be ignored as well. This option is intended only for debugging errors and should not be used under any other circumstances.

- **-s** This flag is only meaningful when upgrading databases from releases before the Berkeley DB 3.1 release.

  As part of the upgrade from the Berkeley DB 3.0 release to the 3.1 release, the on-disk format of duplicate data items changed. To correctly upgrade the format requires that applications specify whether duplicate data items in the database are sorted or not. Specifying the **-s** flag means that the duplicates are sorted; otherwise, they are assumed to be unsorted. Incorrectly specifying the value of this flag may lead to database corruption.

  Because the db_upgrade utility upgrades a physical file (including all the databases it contains), it is not possible to use db_upgrade to upgrade files where some of the databases it includes have sorted duplicate data items, and some of the databases it includes have unsorted duplicate data items. If the file does not have more than a single database, if the databases do not support duplicate data items, or if all the databases that support duplicate data items support the same style of duplicates (either sorted or unsorted), db_upgrade will work correctly as long as the **-s** flag is correctly specified. Otherwise, the file cannot be upgraded using db_upgrade, and must be upgraded manually using the **db_dump** and **db_load** utilities.

- **-V** Write the version number to the standard output and exit.

It is important to realize that Berkeley DB database upgrades are done in place, and so are potentially destructive. This means that if the system crashes during the upgrade procedure, or if the upgrade procedure runs out of disk space, the databases may be left in an inconsistent and unrecoverable state. See "Upgrading Databases" for more information.

The db_upgrade utility may be used with a Berkeley DB environment (as described for the **-h** option, the environment variable **DB_HOME**, or because the utility was run in a directory containing a Berkeley DB environment). In order to avoid environment corruption when using a Berkeley DB environment, db_upgrade should always be given the chance to detach from the environment and exit gracefully. To cause db_upgrade to release all environment resources and exit cleanly, send it an interrupt signal (SIGINT).

The db_upgrade utility exits 0 on success, and >0 if an error occurs.

Environment Variables

- DB_HOME If the **-h** option is not specified and the environment variable DB_HOME is set, it is used as the path of the database home, as described in **DBENV→open**.

See Also

berkeley_db_svc, db_archive, db_checkpoint, db_deadlock, db_dump, db_load, db_recover, db_stat, db_upgrade, and **db_verify.**

db_verify

```
db_verify [-NqV] [-h home] file ...
```

Description

The db_verify utility verifies the structure of one or more files and the databases they contain.

The options are as follows:

- **-h** Specify a home directory for the database environment; by default, the current working directory is used.

- **-N** Do not acquire shared region locks while running. Other problems, such as potentially fatal errors in Berkeley DB, will be ignored as well. This option is intended only for debugging errors and should not be used under any other circumstances.

- **-q** Suppress the printing of any error descriptions, simply exit success or failure.

- **-V** Write the version number to the standard output, and exit.

If the file being verified contains databases using non-default comparison or hashing functions, the db_verify utility may not be used for verification, as it will likely always return failure. Such files must be verified explicitly, using the **DB→verify** function, after setting the correct comparison or hashing functions.

The db_verify utility may be used with a Berkeley DB environment (as described for the **-h** option, the environment variable **DB_HOME**, or because the utility was run in a directory containing a Berkeley DB environment). In order to avoid environment corruption when using a Berkeley DB environment, db_verify should always be given the chance to detach from the environment and exit gracefully. To cause db_verify to release all environment resources and exit cleanly, send it an interrupt signal (SIGINT).

The db_verify utility exits 0 on success, and >0 if an error occurs.

Environment Variables

- DB_HOME If the **-h** option is not specified and the environment variable DB_HOME is set, it is used as the path of the database home, as described in **DBENV→open.**

See Also

berkeley_db_svc, db_archive, db_checkpoint, db_deadlock, db_dump, db_load, db_recover, db_stat, db_upgrade, and db_verify.

Index

Symbols

\ (backslash characters), dump output formats, 188

2PL (two-phase locking), 10, 151

A

aborting transactions, defined, 93

absolute pathnames (filename resolution), 80

access methods. *See also* data access
architecture support for, 69-70
Btree, 31
compared to Hash access method, 32-33
DB→set_flags function, 266
DB→stat function, 277-278
Db.set_flags method, 510-511
Db.stat method, 520-521
Db::set_flags method, 395-396
Db::stat method, 407-408
disk space requirements, 62-63
lock-coupling, 154
maximum depth, 62
minimum keys per page, 40
page locks, 149
prefix comparison routines, 39-40
record numbers, 40
renumbering records, 44-45
sort routines, 37, 39
byte order, selecting, 37
cache size, selecting, 36-37
closing databases, 51
database cursors, 52
closing, 58
deleting records, 54
duplicating, 54
item counts, 58
retrieving records, 52-53
stability, 58-59
storing records, 53-54

database file size limitations, 62
database statistics, 51
deleting records, 50
error return values, 67
flushing database cache, 51
Hash, 31
compared to Btree access method, 32-33
DB→set_flags function, 266-267
DB→stat function, 277
Db.set_flags method, 511
Db.stat method, 520
Db::set_flags method, 396
Db::stat method, 407
disk space requirements, 63, 65
page fill factor, 41
page locks, 149
specifying hash function, 41
table size, 42
key size limitations, 62
key/data pairs, 308-310
locking conventions, 152-154
logical joins, 54-58
logical record numbers, 34
memory allocation, 37
opening databases, 47-48
multiple databases in one file, 48-49
page size, selecting, 35
as part of architecture, 71
partial record storage and retrieval, 65-66
Queue, 32
compared to Recno access method, 33-34
DB→set_flags function, 267
DB→stat function, 278
Db.set_flags method, 511
Db.stat method, 521
Db::set_flags method, 396
Db::stat method, 408
extent size, 43
padding records, 43
page locks, 149, 152
record length, 42

Recno, 32
  backing source files, 43-44
  compared to Queue access method, 33-34
  DB→set_flags function, 267
  DB→stat function, 277-278
  Db.set_flags method, 511-512
  Db.stat method, 520-521
  Db::set_flags method, 396-397
  Db::stat method, 407-408
  locks, 154
  padding records, 43
  page locks, 149
  record delimiters, 42
  record length, 42
  renumbering records, 44-45
recoverability, 70
retrieved key/data permanence, 61
retrieving records, 50
selecting, 32
storing records, 50
upgrading databases, 49
verifying and salvaging databases, 59

ACID properties (transactions), 5

AIX, building Berkeley DB for (troubleshooting), 212-213

allocating memory, 37

APIs, 72. *See also* **interfaces**
  C programming language. *See* C API
  C++ programming language. *See* C++ API
  dbm/ndbm, 73
  hsearch, 73
  Java. *See* Java API
  Perl, 74
  Tcl. *See* Tcl API

application-specific logging and recovery, 139
  automatically generated functions, 140-143
  defining application-specific operations, 139-140
  nonconformant logging, 143-144

applications
  concurrent applications, locks, 151
  converting to run in XA, 129
  debugging, 191-192
    compile-time configuration options, 192
    list of common errors, 197-199
    log files, 193-197
    run-time errors, 193

multithreaded, support for, 134-135
non-Berkeley DB applications
  Locking subsystem, 158-159
  transactions, 170-171
signal-handling, 131
  error return values, 132-133
transactional applications
  archival procedures, 115-117
  atomicity, 92, 103-106
  Berkeley DB recoverability, 121-123
  cursors, 107-108, 110
  databases, opening, 98-100
  deadlock avoidance, 92, 102-103
  deadlock detection, 111, 113
  environment infrastructure, 111
  environment, opening, 95-98
  filesystem operations' effect on recovery, 120-121
  log file removal, 117, 119
  nested transactions, 110-111
  performing checkpoints, 113, 115
  recoverability, 92, 100, 102
  recovery procedures, 119-120
  recovery process overview, 139
  repeatable reads, 92, 106-107
  throughput, 123-125
transactional support structure, 93-95
upgrading, 231-233

architecture
  access method support, 69-70
  access methods, 71
  Berkeley DB library, 71
  Locking subsystem, 71
  Logging subsystem, 71
  memory pool, 71
  programmatic APIs, 72-73
  programming model, 72
  scripting languages, 74
  subsystems' independent use, 72
  supporting utilities, 75
  Transaction subsystem, 70-71

archival procedures in transactional applications, 115-117

atomicity (transactions), 5, 92, 103-106

autoconf options, configuring Berkeley DB, 202-204

B

backing source files (Recno access method), 43-44

backslash characters (\), dump output formats, 188

backups, hot, 6, 11. *See also* archival procedures

berkdb dbremove command, 591

berkdb dbrename command, 592

berkdb env command, 593-595

berkdb envremove command, 595-596

berkdb open command, 596-601

berkdb version command, 601

Berkeley DB
  building for UNIX, 201-202
    troubleshooting, 209-218
  building for VxWorks, 225-227
    programming notes, 227
    troubleshooting, 228-229
  building for Win32, 219-222
    programming notes, 223-224
    troubleshooting, 224
  configuring with Tuxedo System, 128-129
  configuring for UNIX
    compile or load options, 205
    GNU autoconf options, 202-204
  data access services, 9-10
  data management services, 10-11
  data type support, 12
  defined, 8-9
  design of, 11
  developer services, 15-16
  distribution contents, 16
  dynamic shared libraries for UNIX, 207-208
  installing for UNIX, 206
  libraries, independence of, 201
  list of directories, 239-240
  products available, 16-17
  recoverability in transactional applications, 121-123
  resources for further information, 241-242
  runtime configuration, 144-145
  runtime environments, 16
  technical papers on, 241

  test suite
    running under UNIX, 208-209
    running under Win32, 222-223
  what it is not, 11-12
    network databases, 13
    object-oriented databases, 13
    relational databases, 12-13
    servers, 14
  whether to use, 14-15

Berkeley DB Concurrent Data Store product, 17

Berkeley DB Data Store product, 17

Berkeley DB installations, upgrading, 231-233

Berkeley DB library, 71. *See also* architecture
  compatibility with UNIX interfaces, 138
  independence of, 201
  version information, 138

Berkeley DB Transactional Data Store product, 17

berkeley_db_svc utility, 74, 175-176, 617-618

BLOBs (binary large objects), 12

Btree access method, 31
  advantages of, 10
  compared to Hash access method, 32-33
  DB→set_flags function, 266
  DB→stat function, 277-278
  Db.set_flags method, 510-511
  Db.stat method, 520-521
  Db::set_flags method, 395-396
  Db::stat method, 407-408
  disk space requirements, 62-63
  lock-coupling, 154
  maximum depth, 62
  minimum keys per page, 40
  page-fill factor, 63
  page locks, 149
  prefix comparison routines, 39-40
  record numbers, 40
  renumbering records, 44-45
  sort routines, 37, 39

buffer pool, as part of architecture, 71

bugs, log_archive function, 348

building Berkeley DB
for UNIX, 201-202
troubleshooting, 209-218
for VxWorks, 225-227
programming notes, 227
troubleshooting, 228-229
for Win32, 219-222
programming notes, 223-224
troubleshooting, 224

buildtms utility, 128

byte order, selecting, 37

C

C API, 73
DB→close function, 245-246
DB→cursor function, 246-247
DB→del function, 247
DB→fd function, 248
DB→get function, 248-250
DB→get_byteswapped function, 250
DB→get_type function, 250
DB→join function, 251-252
DB→key_range function, 252-253
DB→open function, 253-255
DB→put function, 255-256
DB→remove function, 257
DB→rename function, 258
DB→set_append_recno function, 259
DB→set_bt_compare function, 259-260
DB→set_bt_minkey function, 260
DB→set_bt_prefix function, 261
DB→set_cachesize function, 261-262
DB→set_dup_compare function, 262-263
DB→set_errcall function, 263
DB→set_errfile function, 264
DB→set_errpfx function, 264-265
DB→set_feedback function, 265
DB→set_flags function, 265-267
DB→set_h_ffactor function, 268
DB→set_h_hash function, 268-269
DB→set_h_nelem function, 269
DB→set_lorder function, 269-270
DB→set_malloc function, 270
DB→set_pagesize function, 271
DB→set_paniccall function, 271-272
DB→set_q_extentsize function, 272
DB→set_realloc function, 275-276

DB→set_re_delim function, 272-273
DB→set_re_len function, 273
DB→set_re_pad function, 273-274
DB→set_re_source function, 274-275
DB→stat function, 276-277, 279
DB→sync function, 279
DB→upgrade function, 280-281
DB→verify function, 281-282
DBcursor→c_close function, 311
DBcursor→c_count function, 311-312
DBcursor→c_del function, 312
DBcursor→c_dup function, 313
DBcursor→c_get function, 314-316
DBcursor→c_put function, 316-319
DBENV→close function, 283
DBENV→err function, 284
DBENV→open function, 285-288
DBENV→remove function, 288-289
DBENV→set_cachesize function, 290
DBENV→set_data_dir function, 290-291
DBENV→set_errcall function, 291-292
DBENV→set_errfile function, 292
DBENV→set_errpfx function, 292
DBENV→set_feedback function, 293
DBENV→set_flags function, 293-294
DBENV→set_lg_bsize function, 294-295
DBENV→set_lg_dir function, 295
DBENV→set_lg_max function, 296
DBENV→set_lk_conflicts function,
296-297
DBENV→set_lk_detect function, 297-298
DBENV→set_lk_max function, 298
DBENV→set_lk_max_lockers
function, 299
DBENV→set_lk_max_locks function,
299-300
DBENV→set_lk_max_objects
function, 300
DBENV→set_mp_mmapsize
function, 300-301
DBENV→set_mutexlocks function, 333
DBENV→set_paniccall function, 301-302
DBENV→set_recovery_init function, 302
DBENV→set_server function, 302-303
DBENV→set_shm_key function, 303-304
DBENV→set_tmp_dir function, 304-305
DBENV→set_tx_max function, 305-306
DBENV→set_tx_recover function, 306
DBENV→set_tx_timestamp function, 307
DBENV→set_verbose function, 307-308

Dbm interface, 337-338
  compatibility notes, 339
  diagnostics, 339
  functions, 337-338
db_create function, 319
db_env_create function, 320
db_env_set_func_close function, 320-321
db_env_set_func_dirfree function, 321
db_env_set_func_dirlist function, 322
db_env_set_func_exists function, 322-323
db_env_set_func_free function, 323
db_env_set_func_fsync function, 324
db_env_set_func_ioinfo function, 324-325
db_env_set_func_malloc function, 325
db_env_set_func_map function, 326
db_env_set_func_open function, 327
db_env_set_func_read function, 327
db_env_set_func_realloc function, 328
db_env_set_func_rename function, 328
db_env_set_func_seek function, 329
db_env_set_func_sleep function, 330
db_env_set_func_unlink function, 330-331
db_env_set_func_unmap function, 331
db_env_set_func_write function, 332
db_env_set_func_yield function, 332-333
db_env_set_pageyield function, 333-334
db_env_set_panicstate function, 334
db_env_set_region_init function, 334-335
db_env_set_tas_spins function, 335-336
DB_LSN structure, 310
db_strerror function, 336
db_version function, 336
hsearch interface, 341
  compatibility notes, 341
  diagnostics, 341-342
key/data pairs, 308-310
lock_detect function, 342
lock_get function, 343
lock_id function, 344
lock_put function, 344
lock_stat function, 345-346
lock_vec function, 346-347
log_archive function, 348-349
log_compare function, 349
log_file function, 349
log_flush function, 350
log_get function, 350-351
log_put function, 352
log_register function, 353
log_stat function, 353-354

log_unregister function, 355
memp_fclose function, 355-356
memp_fget function, 356-357
memp_fopen function, 357-359
memp_fput function, 360
memp_fset function, 361
memp_fsync function, 361-362
memp_register function, 362-363
memp_stat function, 363-365
memp_sync function, 365-366
memp_trickle function, 366
name spaces, 136-137
Ndbm interface
  diagnostics, 340
  functions, 337-339
txn_abort function, 367
txn_begin function, 367-368
txn_checkpoint function, 368-369
txn_commit function, 369-370
txn_id function, 370
txn_prepare function, 371
txn_stat function, 371-372

C++ API, 73
Db class, 373-374
Db::close method, 374-375
Db::cursor method, 375-376
Db::del method, 376
Db::fd method, 377
Db::get method, 377-379
Db::get_byteswapped method, 379
Db::get_type method, 379
Db::join method, 380-381
Db::key_range method, 381-382
Db::open method, 382-384
Db::put method, 385-386
Db::remove method, 386-387
Db::rename method, 387-388
Db::set_append_recno method, 388
Db::set_bt_compare method, 389
Db::set_bt_minkey method, 390
Db::set_bt_prefix method, 390-391
Db::set_cachesize method, 391-392
Db::set_dup_compare method, 392
Db::set_errcall method, 393
Db::set_errfile method, 393-394
Db::set_errpfx method, 394
Db::set_feedback method, 394-395
Db::set_flags method, 395-397
Db::set_h_ffactor method, 397-398
Db::set_h_hash method, 398

Db::set_h_nelem method, 399
Db::set_lorder method, 399-400
Db::set_malloc method, 400
Db::set_pagesize method, 401
Db::set_paniccall method, 401
Db::set_q_extentsize method, 402
Db::set_realloc method, 405
Db::set_re_delim method, 402
Db::set_re_len method, 403
Db::set_re_pad method, 403-404
Db::set_re_source method, 404-405
Db::stat method, 406-409
Db::sync method, 409
Db::upgrade method, 410-411
Db::verify method, 411-412
Dbc class, 476
Dbc::close method, 477
Dbc::count method, 478
Dbc::del method, 478-479
Dbc::dup method, 479-480
Dbc::get method, 480-482
Dbc::put method, 482-485
DbEnv class, 413
DbEnv::close method, 413-414
DbEnv::err method, 414-415
DbEnv::lock_detect method, 415-416
DbEnv::lock_get method, 416-417
DbEnv::lock_id method, 417
DbEnv::lock_stat method, 418-419
DbEnv::lock_vec method, 419-420
DbEnv::log_archive method, 421-422
DbEnv::log_compare method, 422
DbEnv::log_file method, 422-423
DbEnv::log_flush method, 423
DbEnv::log_get method, 424-425
DbEnv::log_put method, 425-426
DbEnv::log_register method, 426-427
DbEnv::log_stat method, 427-428
DbEnv::log_unregister method, 428
DbEnv::memp_register method, 429-430
DbEnv::memp_stat method, 430-432
DbEnv::memp_sync method, 432-433
DbEnv::memp_trickle method, 433
DbEnv::open method, 434-437
DbEnv::remove method, 437-438
DbEnv::set_cachesize method, 438-439
DbEnv::set_data_dir method, 439-440
DbEnv::set_errcall method, 440
DbEnv::set_errfile method, 441
DbEnv::set_error_stream method, 441-442

DbEnv::set_errpfx method, 442
DbEnv::set_feedback method, 442-443
DbEnv::set_flags method, 443
DbEnv::set_lg_bsize method, 444
DbEnv::set_lg_dir method, 444-445
DbEnv::set_lg_max method, 445-446
DbEnv::set_lk_conflicts method, 446
DbEnv::set_lk_detect method, 447
DbEnv::set_lk_max method, 447-448
DbEnv::set_lk_max_lockers method, 448
DbEnv::set_lk_max_locks method, 449
DbEnv::set_lk_max_objects method,
    449-450
DbEnv::set_mp_mmapsize method, 450
DbEnv::set_mutexlocks method, 451
DbEnv::set_pageyield method, 451
DbEnv::set_paniccall method, 452
DbEnv::set_panicstate method, 452
DbEnv::set_recovery_init method, 453
DbEnv::set_region_init method, 453-454
DbEnv::set_server method, 454-455
DbEnv::set_shm_key method, 455
DbEnv::set_tas_spins method, 456
DbEnv::set_tmp_dir method, 456-457
DbEnv::set_tx_max method, 457-458
DbEnv::set_tx_recover method, 458-459
DbEnv::set_tx_timestamp method, 459
DbEnv::set_verbose method, 459-460
DbEnv::strerror method, 460
DbEnv::txn_begin method, 461
DbEnv::txn_checkpoint method, 462
DbEnv::txn_stat method, 463-464
DbEnv::version method, 464
DbException class, 464-465
DbException::get_errno method, 465
DbException::what method, 465
DbLock class, 465
DbLock::put method, 466
DbLsn class, 466
DbMpoolFile class, 467
DbMpoolFile::close method, 467
DbMpoolFile::get method, 468-469
DbMpoolFile::open method, 469-471
DbMpoolFile::put method, 471-472
DbMpoolFile::set method, 472-473
DbMpoolFile::sync method, 473
Dbt class, 485
    key/data pairs, 485-488
DbTxn class, 474
DbTxn::abort method, 474

DbTxn::commit method, 475
DbTxn::id method, 476
DbTxn::prepare method, 476
including for Win32 platforms, 220

cache, flushing records from, 51

cache size, selecting, 36-37

catastrophic recovery (transactional applications), 120

checkpoints, performing in transactional applications, 113, 115

choosing. *See* **selecting**

classes
Db, 373-374, 489-490
Dbc, 476, 578
DbDeadlockException, 525
DbEnv, 413, 526
DbException, 464-465, 571
DbLock, 465, 572
DbLsn, 466, 573
DbMemoryException, 573
DbMpoolFile, 467
DbRunRecoveryException, 574
Dbt, 485, 586-589
    key/data pairs, 485-488
DbTxn, 474, 575

CLASSPATH environment variable (Java API), 178

clearing structures, 23

client program, RPC support, 174-175

client-server model, Berkeley DB library, 72

client-server protocols, RPC support, 173-174
client program, 174-175
server program, 175-176

clients in database management systems, 8

closing
cursors, 58
databases, 28-29, 51

commands
berkdb dbremove, 591
berkdb dbrename, 592
berkdb env, 593-595
berkdb envremove, 595-596
berkdb open, 596-601

berkdb version, 601
db close, 602
db count, 603
db cursor, 603
db del, 603
db get, 604-606
db get_join, 609
db get_type, 609
db is_byteswapped, 609
db join, 610
db put, 610-611
db stat, 611
db sync, 611
dbc close, 602
dbc del, 604
dbc dup, 604
dbc get, 606-609
dbc put, 612-614
env close, 614
env txn, 614-615
load, 182
package, 182
in Tcl API, 182-183
txn abort, 615
txn commit, 615-616

committing transactions, defined, 93

comparison routines (Btree access method), 37, 39
prefix comparison routines, 39-40

compatibility
Berkeley DB library with UNIX interfaces, 138
Dbm interface, 339
hsearch interface, 341
Java API, 178-179

compile-time configuration options, 205
debugging applications, 192

compiling Tcl API with certain version, 185

concurrency, defined, 5

concurrent applications, locks, 151

Concurrent Data Store, locking conventions, 87, 154-155

concurrent read-write access, 87-89

configuration
Berkeley DB
    with Tuxedo System, 128-129
    for UNIX, 202-205

Locking subsystem, 156-158
Logging subsystem, 162
Memory Pool subsystem, 166
run-time configuration, 144-145
Transaction subsystem, 169-170

configuration files, file naming, 80

configuration options, debugging applications, 192

conflict matrix (Locking subsystem), 150

consistency (transactions), 5

converting applications to run in XA, 129

copying databases, 137-138

creating environment, 78-79

cursors, 52
closing, 58
deleting records with, 54
duplicating, 54
item counts, 58
logical joins, 54-58
retrieving records with, 52-53
stability, 58-59
storing records with, 53-54
in transactional applications, 107-108, 110
in transactions, limits on, 169
locking, 151, 153
renumbering records, 44-45
write cursors, forbidding multiple, 88

D

data access. *See also* **access methods**
in Berkeley DB, 9-10
defined, 4

data management
in Berkeley DB, 10-11
defined, 5-6

data types, Berkeley DB support for, 12

database management systems
clients and servers, 8
data access, 4
data management, 5-6
defined, 4
network databases, 7-8, 13
object-oriented databases, 7, 13
relational databases, 6, 12-13

selecting, 4
servers, 14

database records. *See* **records**

database systems theory, references on, 242

databases
adding elements to, 22-24
archival procedures in transactional applications, 115-117
closing, 28-29, 51
copying, 137-138
cursors, 52
closing, 58
deleting records with, 54
duplicating, 54
item counts, 58
logical joins, 54-58
retrieving records with, 52-53
stability, 58-59
storing records with, 53-54
disk space requirements, 62
Btree access method, 62-63
Hash access method, 63, 65
dumping, 187-188
output formats, 188-189
file size limitations, 62
flushing records from cache, 51
key size limitations, 62
loading text into, 189
opening, 21-22, 47-48
multiple databases in one file, 48-49
for transactional applications, 98-100
within environment, 84
removing elements from, 26, 28
retrieving elements from, 25-26
statistics, 51
upgrading, 49
verifying and salvaging, 59

Db class, 373-374, 489-490

db close command, 602

db count command, 603

db cursor command, 603

db del command, 603

db get command, 604-606

db get_join command, 609

db get_type command, 609

db is_byteswapped command, 609

db join command, 610

DB object handle, 136

db put command, 610-611

db stat command, 611

db sync command, 611

DB→close function, 28-29, 51, 245-246

DB→cursor function, 52, 246-247

DB→del function, 26, 28, 50, 247

DB→err function, 21-22, 67

DB→errx function, 21, 67

DB→fd function, 248

DB→get function, 25-26, 41, 50, 248-250
  concurrent read locks, 88

DB→get_byteswapped function, 250

DB→get_type function, 250

DB→join function, 55-56, 251-252

DB→key_range function, 252-253

DB→open function, 21-22, 47-48,
  253-255

DB→put function, 22-24, 50, 255-256

DB→remove function, 121, 257

DB→rename function, 121, 258

DB→set_append_recno function, 259

DB→set_bt_compare function, 37,
  259-260

DB→set_bt_minkey function, 40, 260

DB→set_bt_prefix function, 39, 261

DB→set_cachesize function, 36, 166,
  261-262

DB→set_dup_compare function, 262-263

DB→set_errcall function, 263

DB→set_errfile function, 264

DB→set_errpfx function, 67, 264-265

DB→set_feedback function, 265

DB→set_flags function, 40, 265-267

DB→set_h_ffactor function, 41, 268

DB→set_h_hash function, 41, 268-269

DB→set_h_nelem function, 42, 269

DB→set_lorder function, 37, 269-270

DB→set_malloc function, 37, 270

DB→set_pagesize function, 35, 149, 271

DB→set_paniccall function, 271-272

DB→set_q_extentsize function, 272

DB→set_realloc function, 37, 275-276

DB→set_re_delim function, 42, 272-273

DB→set_re_len function, 43, 273

DB→set_re_pad function, 43, 273-274

DB→set_re_source function, 43, 274-275

DB→stat function, 51, 276-277, 279

DB→sync function, 279
  building Berkeley DB for VxWorks, 227

DB→upgrade function, 49, 280-281

DB→verify function, 59, 281-282

Db.close method, 490-491

Db.cursor method, 491

Db.del method, 492

Db.fd method, 492-493

Db.get method, 493-494

Db.get_byteswapped method, 495

Db.get_type method, 495

Db.join method, 495-496

Db.key_range method, 497

Db.open method, 498-500

Db.put method, 500-501

Db.remove method, 501-502

Db.rename method, 502-503

Db.set_append_recno method, 504

Db.set_bt_compare method, 504-505

Db.set_bt_minkey method, 505

Db.set_bt_prefix method, 506

Db.set_cachesize method, 506-507

Db.set_dup_compare method, 507-508

Db.set_errcall method, 508-509

Db.set_errpfx method, 509

Db.set_feedback method, 509-510

Db.set_flags method, 510-512

Db.set_h_ffactor method, 512-513

Db.set_h_hash method, 513

Db.set_h_nelem method, 514

Db.set_lorder method, 514–515

Db.set_pagesize method, 515

Db.set_q_extentsize method, 515–516

Db.set_re_delim method, 516

Db.set_re_len method, 516–517

Db.set_re_pad method, 517

Db.set_re_source method, 517–518

Db.stat method, 519–521

Db.sync method, 522

Db.upgrade method, 523–524

Db.verify method, 524–525

Db::close method, 374–375

Db::cursor method, 375–376

Db::del method, 376

Db::fd method, 377

Db::get method, 377–379

Db::get_byteswapped method, 379

Db::get_type method, 379

Db::join method, 380–381

Db::key_range method, 381–382

Db::open method, 382–384

Db::put method, 385–386

Db::remove method, 386–387

Db::rename method, 387–388

Db::set_append_recno method, 388

Db::set_bt_compare method, 389

Db::set_bt_minkey method, 390

Db::set_bt_prefix method, 390–391

Db::set_cachesize method, 391–392

Db::set_dup_compare method, 392

Db::set_errcall method, 393

Db::set_errfile method, 393–394

Db::set_errpfx method, 394

Db::set_feedback method, 394–395

Db::set_flags method, 395–397

Db::set_h_ffactor method, 397–398

Db::set_h_hash method, 398

Db::set_h_nelem method, 399

Db::set_lorder method, 399–400

Db::set_malloc method, 400

Db::set_pagesize method, 401

Db::set_paniccall method, 401

Db::set_q_extentsize method, 402

Db::set_realloc method, 405

Db::set_re_delim method, 402

Db::set_re_len method, 403

Db::set_re_pad method, 403–404

Db::set_re_source method, 404–405

Db::stat method, 406–409

Db::sync method, 409

Db::upgrade method, 410–411

Db::verify method, 411–412

Dbc class, 476, 578

dbc close command, 602

dbc del command, 604

dbc dup command, 604

dbc get command, 606–609

DBC object handle, 136

dbc put command, 612–614

Dbc.close method, 578

Dbc.count method, 579

Dbc.del method, 579–580

Dbc.dup method, 580

Dbc.get method, 581–583

Dbc.put method, 583–586

Dbc::close method, 477

Dbc::count method, 478

Dbc::del method, 478–479

Dbc::dup method, 479–480

Dbc::get method, 480–482

Dbc::put method, 482–485

DBcursor→c_close function, 58, 311

DBcursor→c_count function, 58, 311–312

DBcursor→c_del function, 54, 312

DBcursor→c_dup function, 54, 313

DBcursor→c_get function, 41, 45, 52–53, 314–316

DBcursor→c_put function, 53–54, 316–319

DbDeadlockException class, 525

DbEnv class, 413, 526

DBENV→close function, 94, 283

DBENV→err function, 85, 193, 284

DBENV→errx function, 85, 193

DBENV→open function, 78-79, 285-288
  environment initialization, 87
  environment recovery, 94
  file naming, 79
  shared memory regions, 83-84
  transactional applications, 95

DBENV→remove function, 162, 166, 288-289

DBENV→set_cachesize function, 166, 290

DBENV→set_data_dir function, 80, 290-291

DBENV→set_errcall function, 193, 291-292

DBENV→set_errfile function, 193, 292

DBENV→set_errpfx function, 85, 193, 292

DBENV→set_feedback function, 293

DBENV→set_flags function, 166, 169, 293-294

DBENV→set_lg_bsize function, 162, 294-295

DBENV→set_lg_dir function, 80, 295

DBENV→set_lg_max function, 162, 296

DBENV→set_lk_conflicts function, 157, 296-297

DBENV→set_lk_detect function, 156, 297-298

DBENV→set_lk_max function, 298

DBENV→set_lk_max_lockers function, 157, 299

DBENV→set_lk_max_locks function, 157, 299-300

DBENV→set_lk_max_objects function, 157, 300

DBENV→set_mp_mmapsize function, 166, 300-301

DBENV→set_mutexlocks function, 333

DBENV→set_paniccall function, 133, 301-302

DBENV→set_recovery_init function, 302

DBENV→set_server function, 174-175, 302-303

DBENV→set_shm_key function, 303-304

DBENV→set_tmp_dir function, 80, 304-305

DBENV→set_tx_max function, 170, 305-306

DBENV→set_tx_recover function, 170, 306

DBENV→set_tx_timestamp function, 307

DBENV→set_verbose function, 191, 193, 307-308

DbEnv.close method, 526-527

DbEnv.get_version_major method, 527

DbEnv.lock_detect method, 528

DbEnv.lock_get method, 528-529

DbEnv.lock_id method, 529-530

DbEnv.lock_stat method, 530-531

DbEnv.lock_vec method, 531

DbEnv.log_archive method, 531-532

DbEnv.log_compare method, 533

DbEnv.log_file method, 533

DbEnv.log_flush method, 533-534

DbEnv.log_get method, 534-535

DbEnv.log_put method, 536

DbEnv.log_register method, 537

DbEnv.log_stat method, 537-538

DbEnv.log_unregister method, 538-539

DbEnv.memp_fstat method, 540

DbEnv.memp_register method, 539

DbEnv.memp_stat method, 539-541

DbEnv.memp_sync method, 541

DbEnv.memp_trickle method, 541

DbEnv.open method, 542-545

DbEnv.remove method, 545-546

DbEnv.set_cachesize method, 547

DbEnv.set_data_dir method, 548

DbEnv.set_errcall method, 549

DbEnv.set_error_stream method, 549

DbEnv.set_errpfx method, 550

DbEnv.set_feedback method, 550

DbEnv.set_flags method, 551

DbEnv.set_lg_bsize method, 552

DbEnv.set_lg_dir method, 552-553

DbEnv.set_lg_max method, 553

DbEnv.set_lk_conflicts method, 554

DbEnv.set_lk_detect method, 554-555

DbEnv.set_lk_max method, 555-556

DbEnv.set_lk_max_lockers method, 556

DbEnv.set_lk_max_locks method, 557

DbEnv.set_lk_max_objects method, 557-558

DbEnv.set_mp_mmapsize method, 558

DbEnv.set_mutexlocks method, 559

DbEnv.set_pageyield method, 559

DbEnv.set_panicstate method, 559-560

DbEnv.set_recovery_init method, 560

DbEnv.set_region_init method, 561

DbEnv.set_server method, 561-562

DbEnv.set_shm_key method, 562-563

DbEnv.set_tas_spins method, 563-564

DbEnv.set_tmp_dir method, 564-565

DbEnv.set_tx_max method, 565

DbEnv.set_tx_recover method, 566

DbEnv.set_tx_timestamp method, 566-567

DbEnv.set_verbose method, 567

DbEnv.strerror method, 568

DbEnv.txn_begin method, 568-569

DbEnv.txn_checkpoint method, 569-570

DbEnv.txn_stat method, 570-571

DbEnv::close method, 413-414

DbEnv::err method, 414-415

DbEnv::lock_detect method, 415-416

DbEnv::lock_get method, 416-417

DbEnv::lock_id method, 417

DbEnv::lock_stat method, 418-419

DbEnv::lock_vec method, 419-420

DbEnv::log_archive method, 421-422

DbEnv::log_compare method, 422

DbEnv::log_file method, 422-423

DbEnv::log_flush method, 423

DbEnv::log_get method, 424-425

DbEnv::log_put method, 425-426

DbEnv::log_register method, 426-427

DbEnv::log_stat method, 427-428

DbEnv::log_unregister method, 428

DbEnv::memp_register method, 429-430

DbEnv::memp_stat method, 430-432

DbEnv::memp_sync method, 432-433

DbEnv::memp_trickle method, 433

DbEnv::open method, 434-437

DbEnv::remove method, 437-438

DbEnv::set_cachesize method, 438-439

DbEnv::set_data_dir method, 439-440

DbEnv::set_errcall method, 440

DbEnv::set_errfile method, 441

DbEnv::set_error_stream method, 441-442

DbEnv::set_errpfx method, 442

DbEnv::set_feedback method, 442-443

DbEnv::set_flags method, 443

DbEnv::set_lg_bsize method, 444

DbEnv::set_lg_dir method, 444-445

DbEnv::set_lg_max method, 445-446

DbEnv::set_lk_conflicts method, 446

DbEnv::set_lk_detect method, 447

DbEnv::set_lk_max method, 447-448

DbEnv::set_lk_max_lockers method, 448

DbEnv::set_lk_max_locks method, 449

DbEnv::set_lk_max_objects method, 449-450

DbEnv::set_mp_mmapsize method, 450

DbEnv::set_mutexlocks method, 451

DbEnv::set_pageyield method, 451

DbEnv::set_paniccall method, 452

DbEnv::set_panicstate method, 452

DbEnv::set_recovery_init method, 453

DbEnv::set_region_init method, 453–454

DbEnv::set_server method, 454–455

DbEnv::set_shm_key method, 455

DbEnv::set_tas_spins method, 456

DbEnv::set_tmp_dir method, 456–457

DbEnv::set_tx_max method, 457–458

DbEnv::set_tx_recover method, 458–459

DbEnv::set_tx_timestamp method, 459

DbEnv::set_verbose method, 459–460

DbEnv::strerror method, 460

DbEnv::txn_begin method, 461

DbEnv::txn_checkpoint method, 462

DbEnv::txn_stat method, 463–464

DbEnv::version method, 464

DbException class, 180, 464–465, 571

DbException.get_errno method, 572

DbException::get_errno method, 465

DbException::what method, 465

DbLock class, 465, 572

DbLock.put method, 572–573

DbLock::put method, 466

DbLsn class, 466, 573

Dbm interface, 73, 337–338
 compatibility notes, 339
 diagnostics, 339
 functions, 337–338

DbMemoryException class, 573

DbMpoolFile class, 467

DbMpoolFile.close method, 573

DbMpoolFile.get method, 573

DbMpoolFile.open method, 574

DbMpoolFile.put method, 574

DbMpoolFile.set method, 574

DbMpoolFile.sync method, 574

DbMpoolFile::close method, 467

DbMpoolFile::get method, 468–469

DbMpoolFile::open method, 469–471

DbMpoolFile::put method, 471–472

DbMpoolFile::set method, 472–473

DbMpoolFile::sync method, 473

DbRunRecoveryException class, 574

Dbt class, 485, 586–589
 key/data pairs, 485–488

DBT data structure, key/data pairs,
 308–310

DBTs (database thangs), 20

DbTxn class, 474, 575

DbTxn.abort method, 575

DbTxn.commit method, 576

DbTxn.id method, 577

DbTxn.prepare method, 577

DbTxn::abort method, 474

DbTxn::commit method, 475

DbTxn::id method, 476

DbTxn::prepare method, 476

db_archive utility, 74, 116–118, 618–619

db_checkpoint utility, 74, 113, 620

DB_CONFIG, file naming, 80

db_create function, 21, 84, 136, 319
 RPC support, 173

db_deadlock utility, 74, 112, 155, 621

db_dump utility, 74, 187–189, 622–624

db_dump185 utility, 187–188
 output formats, 188–189
 troubleshooting, 211

DB_ENV object handle, 135

db_env_create function, 78–79, 135, 320
 RPC support, 173

db_env_set_func_close function, 320–321

db_env_set_func_dirfree function, 321

db_env_set_func_dirlist function, 322

db_env_set_func_exists function, 322–323

db_env_set_func_free function, 323

db_env_set_func_fsync function, 324

db_env_set_func_ioinfo function, 324–325

db_env_set_func_malloc function, 325

db_env_set_func_map function, 326

db_env_set_func_open function, 327

db_env_set_func_read function, 327

db_env_set_func_realloc function, 328

db_env_set_func_rename function, 328

db_env_set_func_seek function, 329

db_env_set_func_sleep function, 330

db_env_set_func_unlink function, 330-331

db_env_set_func_unmap function, 331

db_env_set_func_write function, 332

db_env_set_func_yield function, 332-333

db_env_set_pageyield function, 333-334

db_env_set_panicstate function, 334

db_env_set_region_init function, 334-335

db_env_set_tas_spins function, 335-336

DB_FIRST flag, 45

DB_GET_RECNO flag, 41

DB_HOME environment variable, 134
   file naming, 79
   filename resolution, 81

DB_KEYEMPTY flag, 45, 132

DB_KEYEXIST flag, 24

db_load utility, 75, 189, 624-626

DB_LOCK_DEADLOCK error return
   value, 102, 133

DB_LOCK_NOTGRANTED error
   return value, 133

DB_LSN structure, 310

DB_MPOOLFILE object handle, 136

DB_NOOVERWRITE flag, 24

DB_NOTFOUND flag, 21, 132

db_printlog utility, 75, 626-627
   debugging applications, 193-197

DB_RECNUM flag, 40

db_recover utility, 75, 119-120, 627-628

DB_RUNRECOVERY error return
   value, 133

DB_SET_RECNO flag, 41

db_stat utility, 36-37, 75, 629-630

db_strerror function, 67, 85, 336

DB_TXN object handle, 135

db_upgrade utility, 75, 630-631

db_verify utility, 75, 632

db_version function, 336

db_xa_switch functions, 127

deadlocks
   avoiding, 155-156
      with Concurrent Data Store, 87
      configuring locking system, 156-158
      transaction threads of control, 169
      with transactional applications, 92,
         102-103
   defined, 93, 147
   detecting in transactional applications,
      111, 113

debugging applications, 191-192. *See also*
troubleshooting
   compile-time configuration options, 192
   list of common errors, 197-199
   log files, 193-197
   run-time errors, 193

deleting. *See* removing

delimiting bytes (Recno access
method), 42

design of Berkeley DB, 11

developer services, 15-16

diagnostics
   Dbm interface, 339
   hsearch interface, 341-342
   Ndbm interface, 340

directories
   in Berkeley DB distribution, 239-240
   home directory, 77

directory tree (Java API), 177

—disable-bigfile configuration option
(GNU autoconf), 202

disk space requirements, 62
   Btree access method, 62-63
   Hash access method, 63, 65

distribution contents of Berkeley DB, 16

dumping databases, 187-188
   output formats, 188-189

duplicating cursors, 54

durability (transactions), 5

dynamic shared libraries for UNIX,
207-208

E

embedded database library, defined, 9

—enable-compat185 configuration option (GNU autoconf), 202

—enable-cxx configuration option (GNU autoconf), 202

—enable-debug configuration option (GNU autoconf), 192, 202

—enable-debug_rop configuration option (GNU autoconf), 203

—enable-debug_wop configuration option (GNU autoconf), 203

—enable-diagnostic configuration option (GNU autoconf), 192, 203

—enable-dump185 configuration option (GNU autoconf), 203

—enable-dynamic configuration option (GNU autoconf), 203

—enable-java configuration option (GNU autoconf), 203

—enable-posixmutexes configuration option (GNU autoconf), 204

—enable-rpc configuration option (GNU autoconf), 204

—enable-shared configuration option (GNU autoconf), 204

—enable-tcl configuration option (GNU autoconf), 204

—enable-test configuration option (GNU autoconf), 204

—enable-uimutexes configuration option (GNU autoconf), 204

—enable-umrw configuration option (GNU autoconf), 192, 204

env close command, 614

env txn command, 614–615

environment
  creating, 78-79
  defined, 77
  error message support, 85
  file naming structure, 79-80
  file permissions, 82
  filename resolution, 80, 82
  home directory, 77
    infrastructure for transactional applications, 111
      archival procedures, 115-117
      deadlock detection, 111, 113
      log file removal, 117, 119
      performing checkpoints, 113, 115
      recovery procedures, 119-120
    opening
      databases within, 84
      for transactional applications, 95, 97-98
    permissions, 82
    recovery, 94
    remote filesystems, 84
    shared memory regions, 83-84
    sharing, 77
    temporary backing files (security), 82-83

environment variables
  Berkeley DB library, 134
  berkeley_db_svc utility, 618
  CLASSPATH (Java API), 178
  DB→open function, 254
  DB→remove function, 257
  DB→rename function, 258
  DB→upgrade function, 280
  DB→verify function, 282
  Db.open method, 499
  Db.remove method, 502
  Db.rename method, 503
  Db.upgrade method, 523
  Db.verify method, 525
  Db::open method, 384
  Db::remove method, 387
  Db::rename method, 388
  Db::upgrade method, 410
  Db::verify method, 412
  DBENV→open function, 287
  DbEnv.open method, 544
  DbEnv::open method, 436
  db_archive utility, 619
  db_checkpoint utility, 620
  db_deadlock utility, 622
  db_dump utility, 624
  DB_HOME
    file naming, 79
    filename resolution, 81
  db_load utility, 626
  db_printlog utility, 627
  db_recovery utility, 628
  db_stat utility, 630
  db_upgrade utility, 631

db_verify utility, 632
LD_LIBRARY_PATH (Java API), 178
security, 82

errno global variable (error return values), 132

errno values, defined, 20

error handling, Tcl API, 183–184

error messages, environment support for, 85

error return values, 67, 132
DB_KEYEMPTY, 132
DB_LOCK_DEADLOCK, 133
DB_LOCK_NOTGRANTED, 133
DB_NOTFOUND, 132
DB_RUNRECOVERY, 133
defined, 20–21

errors
DB→close function, 246
DB→cursor function, 247
DB→del function, 247
DB→fd function, 248
DB→get function, 249
DB→join function, 252
DB→key_range function, 253
DB→open function, 255
DB→put function, 256
DB→remove function, 257
DB→rename function, 258
DB→set_bt_compare function, 260
DB→set_bt_minkey function, 260
DB→set_bt_prefix function, 261
DB→set_cachesize function, 262
DB→set_dup_compare function, 263
DB→set_flags function, 267
DB→set_h_ffactor function, 268
DB→set_h_hash function, 269
DB→set_h_nelem function, 269
DB→set_lorder function, 270
DB→set_malloc function, 270
DB→set_pagesize function, 271
DB→set_q_extentsize function, 272
DB→set_realloc function, 276
DB→set_re_delim function, 273
DB→set_re_len function, 273
DB→set_re_pad function, 274
DB→set_re_source function, 275
DB→stat function, 279
DB→sync function, 279

DB→upgrade function, 281
DB→verify function, 282
Db.close method, 491
Db.cursor method, 491
Db.del method, 492
Db.fd method, 493
Db.get method, 494
Db.join method, 496
Db.key_range method, 497
Db.open method, 499
Db.put method, 501
Db.remove method, 502
Db.rename method, 503
Db.set_bt_compare method, 505
Db.set_bt_minkey method, 505
Db.set_bt_prefix method, 506
Db.set_cachesize method, 507
Db.set_dup_compare method, 508
Db.set_flags method, 512
Db.set_h_ffactor method, 513
Db.set_h_hash method, 513
Db.set_h_nelem method, 514
Db.set_lorder method, 515
Db.set_pagesize method, 515
Db.set_q_extentsize method, 516
Db.set_re_delim method, 516
Db.set_re_len method, 517
Db.set_re_pad method, 517
Db.set_re_source method, 518
Db.stat method, 521
Db.sync method, 522
Db.upgrade method, 523
Db.verify method, 525
Db::close method, 375
Db::cursor method, 376
Db::del method, 376
Db::fd method, 377
Db::get method, 378
Db::join method, 381
Db::key_range method, 382
Db::open method, 384
Db::put method, 386
Db::remove method, 387
Db::rename method, 388
Db::set_bt_compare method, 389
Db::set_bt_minkey method, 390
Db::set_bt_prefix method, 391
Db::set_cachesize method, 392
Db::set_dup_compare method, 392
Db::set_flags method, 397

Db::set_h_ffactor method, 398
Db::set_h_hash method, 398
Db::set_h_nelem method, 399
Db::set_lorder method, 400
Db::set_malloc method, 400
Db::set_pagesize method, 401
Db::set_q_extentsize method, 402
Db::set_realloc method, 405
Db::set_re_delim method, 402
Db::set_re_len method, 403
Db::set_re_pad method, 404
Db::set_re_source method, 405
Db::stat method, 408
Db::sync method, 409
Db::upgrade method, 411
Db::verify method, 412
Dbc.close method, 578
Dbc.count method, 579
Dbc.del method, 579
Dbc.dup method, 580
Dbc.get method, 583
Dbc.put method, 585
Dbc::close method, 477
Dbc::count method, 478
Dbc::del method, 478
Dbc::dup method, 479
Dbc::get method, 482
Dbc::put method, 484
DBcursor→c_close function, 311
DBcursor→c_count function, 312
DBcursor→c_del function, 312
DBcursor→c_dup function, 313
DBcursor→c_get function, 316
DBcursor→c_put function, 318
DBENV→close function, 283
DBENV→open function, 287
DBENV→remove function, 289
DBENV→set_cachesize function, 290
DBENV→set_data_dir function, 291
DBENV→set_flags function, 294
DBENV→set_lg_bsize function, 295
DBENV→set_lg_dir function, 295
DBENV→set_lg_max function, 296
DBENV→set_lk_conflicts function, 297
DBENV→set_lk_detect function, 298
DBENV→set_lk_max function, 298
DBENV→set_lk_max_lockers
  function, 299
DBENV→set_lk_max_locks function, 300
DBENV→set_lk_max_objects
  function, 300

DBENV→set_mp_mmapsize function, 301
DBENV→set_recovery_init function, 302
DBENV→set_server function, 303
DBENV→set_shm_key function, 304
DBENV→set_tmp_dir function, 305
DBENV→set_tx_max function, 306
DBENV→set_tx_recover function, 306
DBENV→set_tx_timestamp function, 307
DBENV→set_verbose function, 308
DbEnv.close method, 527
DbEnv.lock_detect method, 528
DbEnv.lock_get method, 529
DbEnv.lock_id method, 530
DbEnv.lock_stat method, 531
DbEnv.log_archive method, 532
DbEnv.log_file method, 533
DbEnv.log_flush method, 534
DbEnv.log_get method, 535
DbEnv.log_put method, 536
DbEnv.log_register method, 537
DbEnv.log_stat method, 538
DbEnv.log_unregister method, 539
DbEnv.memp_stat method, 540
DbEnv.memp_trickle method, 541
DbEnv.open method, 544-545
DbEnv.remove method, 546
DbEnv.set_cachesize method, 547
DbEnv.set_data_dir method, 548
DbEnv.set_flags method, 551
DbEnv.set_lg_bsize method, 552
DbEnv.set_lg_dir method, 553
DbEnv.set_lg_max method, 553
DbEnv.set_lk_conflicts method, 554
DbEnv.set_lk_detect method, 555
DbEnv.set_lk_max method, 556
DbEnv.set_lk_max_lockers method, 556
DbEnv.set_lk_max_locks method, 557
DbEnv.set_lk_max_objects method, 558
DbEnv.set_mp_mmapsize method, 558
DbEnv.set_pageyield method, 559
DbEnv.set_panicstate method, 560
DbEnv.set_recovery_init method, 560
DbEnv.set_region_init method, 561
DbEnv.set_server method, 562
DbEnv.set_shm_key method, 563
DbEnv.set_tas_spins method, 564
DbEnv.set_tmp_dir method, 565
DbEnv.set_tx_max method, 565
DbEnv.set_tx_recover method, 566
DbEnv.set_tx_timestamp method, 567

DbEnv.set_verbose method, 567
DbEnv.txn_begin method, 569
DbEnv.txn_checkpoint method, 570
DbEnv.txn_stat method, 571
DbEnv::close method, 414
DbEnv::lock_detect method, 416
DbEnv::lock_get method, 417
DbEnv::lock_id method, 417
DbEnv::lock_stat method, 419
DbEnv::lock_vec method, 420
DbEnv::log_archive method, 422
DbEnv::log_file method, 423
DbEnv::log_flush method, 423
DbEnv::log_get method, 425
DbEnv::log_put method, 426
DbEnv::log_register method, 426
DbEnv::log_stat method, 428
DbEnv::log_unregister method, 428
DbEnv::memp_register method, 430
DbEnv::memp_stat method, 432
DbEnv::memp_sync method, 433
DbEnv::memp_trickle method, 433
DbEnv::open method, 436
DbEnv::remove method, 438
DbEnv::set_cachesize method, 439
DbEnv::set_data_dir method, 440
DbEnv::set_flags method, 443
DbEnv::set_lg_bsize method, 444
DbEnv::set_lg_dir method, 445
DbEnv::set_lg_max method, 446
DbEnv::set_lk_conflicts method, 446
DbEnv::set_lk_detect method, 447
DbEnv::set_lk_max method, 448
DbEnv::set_lk_max_lockers method, 448
DbEnv::set_lk_max_locks method, 449
DbEnv::set_lk_max_objects, 450
DbEnv::set_mp_mmapsize method, 450
DbEnv::set_pageyield method, 451
DbEnv::set_panicstate method, 452
DbEnv::set_recovery_init method, 453
DbEnv::set_region_init method, 454
DbEnv::set_server method, 455
DbEnv::set_shm_key method, 455
DbEnv::set_tas_spins method, 456
DbEnv::set_tmp_dir method, 457
DbEnv::set_tx_max method, 458
DbEnv::set_tx_recover method, 459
DbEnv::set_tx_timestamp method, 459
DbEnv::set_verbose method, 460
DbEnv::txn_begin method, 461

DbEnv::txn_checkpoint method, 462
DbEnv::txn_stat method, 464
DbLock.put method, 572
DbLock::put method, 466
Dbm interface, 339
DbMpoolFile::close method, 467
DbMpoolFile::get method, 468
DbMpoolFile::open method, 471
DbMpoolFile::put method, 472
DbMpoolFile::set method, 473
DbMpoolFile::sync method, 473
DbTxn.abort method, 575
DbTxn.commit method, 576
DbTxn.prepare method, 577
DbTxn::abort method, 474
DbTxn::commit method, 475
DbTxn::prepare method, 476
db_create function, 319
db_env_create function, 320
db_env_set_func_close function, 321
db_env_set_func_dirfree function, 321
db_env_set_func_dirlist function, 322
db_env_set_func_exists function, 323
db_env_set_func_free function, 323
db_env_set_func_fsync function, 324
db_env_set_func_ioinfo function, 325
db_env_set_func_malloc function, 325
db_env_set_func_map function, 326
db_env_set_func_open function, 327
db_env_set_func_read function, 327
db_env_set_func_realloc function, 328
db_env_set_func_rename function, 328
db_env_set_func_seek function, 329
db_env_set_func_sleep function, 330
db_env_set_func_unlink function, 331
db_env_set_func_unmap function, 331
db_env_set_func_write function, 332
db_env_set_func_yield function, 333
db_env_set_pageyield function, 334
db_env_set_panicstate function, 334
db_env_set_region_init function, 335
db_env_set_tas_spins function, 336
DB_LOCK_DEADLOCK (transactional
    applications), 102
hsearch interface, 341–342
lock_detect function, 342
lock_get function, 343
lock_id function, 344
lock_put function, 344
lock_stat function, 346

lock_vec function, 347
log_archive function, 348
log_file function, 349
log_flush function, 350
log_get function, 351
log_put function, 352
log_register function, 353
log_stat function, 354
log_unregister function, 355
memp_fclose function, 356
memp_fget function, 357
memp_fopen function, 359
memp_fput function, 360
memp_fset function, 361
memp_fsync function, 362
memp_register function, 363
memp_stat function, 365
memp_sync function, 366
memp_trickle function, 366
Ndbm interface, 340
run-time errors, debugging
   applications, 193
txn_abort function, 367
txn_begin function, 368
txn_checkpoint function, 369
txn_commit function, 370
txn_prepare function, 371
txn_stat function, 372

exceptions (Java API), 179

extent size (Queue access method), 43

F

file histories, extracting from log
files, 196

file naming structure
filename resolution, 80, 82
role of environment in, 79-80

file permissions, 82

filenames (log files), limits on usage,
162-163

filesystem operations, effect on recovery,
120-121

filesystems, name spaces, 137

finalization of objects (Java API), 179

fixed mode (logical record numbers), 34

fixed-length records
padding records, 43
record length, 42

flags
DB_FIRST, 45
DB_GET_RECNO, 41
DB_KEYEMPTY, 45
DB_KEYEXIST, 24
DB_NOOVERWRITE, 24
DB_NOTFOUND, 21
DB_RECNUM, 40
DB_SET_RECNO, 41

flat-text backing source files (Recno
access method), 43-44

flushing records from cache, 51

free-threaded handles, defined, 92

FreeBSD, building Berkeley DB for
(troubleshooting), 213

functions. *See also* **interfaces; methods**
application-specific logging and recovery,
   140-144
DB→close, 28-29, 51, 245-246
DB→cursor, 52, 246-247
DB→del, 26, 28, 50, 247
DB→err, 21-22, 67
DB→errx, 21, 67
DB→fd, 248
DB→get, 25-26, 41, 50, 88, 248-250
DB→get_byteswapped, 250
DB→get_type, 250
DB→join, 55-56, 251-252
DB→key_range, 252-253
DB→open, 21-22, 47-48, 253-255
DB→put, 22-24, 50, 255-256
DB→remove, 121, 257
DB→rename, 121, 258
DB→set_append_recno, 259
DB→set_bt_compare, 37, 259-260
DB→set_bt_minkey, 40, 260
DB→set_bt_prefix, 39, 261
DB→set_cachesize, 36, 166, 261-262
DB→set_dup_compare, 262-263
DB→set_errcall, 263
DB→set_errfile, 264
DB→set_errpfx, 67, 264-265
DB→set_feedback, 265
DB→set_flags, 40, 265-267
DB→set_h_ffactor, 41, 268

DB→set_h_hash, 41, 268-269
DB→set_h_nelem, 42, 269
DB→set_lorder, 37, 269-270
DB→set_malloc, 37, 270
DB→set_pagesize, 35, 149, 271
DB→set_paniccall, 271-272
DB→set_q_extentsize, 272
DB→set_realloc, 37, 275-276
DB→set_re_delim, 42, 272-273
DB→set_re_len, 43, 273
DB→set_re_pad, 43, 273-274
DB→set_re_source, 43, 274-275
DB→stat, 51, 276-277, 279
DB→sync, 227, 279
DB→upgrade, 49, 280-281
DB→verify, 59, 281-282
DBcursor→c_close, 58, 311
DBcursor→c_count, 58, 311-312
DBcursor→c_del, 54, 312
DBcursor→c_dup, 54, 313
DBcursor→c_get, 41, 45, 52-53, 314-316
DBcursor→c_put, 53-54, 316-319
DBENV→close, 94, 283
DBENV→err, 85, 193, 284
DBENV→errx, 85, 193
DBENV→open, 78-79, 285-288
  environment initialization, 87
  environment recovery, 94
  file naming, 79
  shared memory regions, 83-84
  transactional applications, 95
DBENV→remove, 162, 166, 288-289
DBENV→set_cachesize, 166, 290
DBENV→set_data_dir, 80, 290-291
DBENV→set_errcall, 193, 291-292
DBENV→set_errfile, 193, 292
DBENV→set_errpfx, 85, 193, 292
DBENV→set_feedback, 293
DBENV→set_flags, 166, 169, 293-294
DBENV→set_lg_bsize, 162, 294-295
DBENV→set_lg_dir, 80, 295
DBENV→set_lg_max, 162, 296
DBENV→set_lk_conflicts, 157, 296-297
DBENV→set_lk_detect, 156, 297-298
DBENV→set_lk_max, 298
DBENV→set_lk_max_lockers, 157, 299
DBENV→set_lk_max_locks, 157, 299-300
DBENV→set_lk_max_objects, 157, 300
DBENV→set_mp_mmapsize, 166, 300-301
DBENV→set_mutexlocks, 333
DBENV→set_paniccall, 133, 301-302

DBENV→set_recovery_init, 302
DBENV→set_server, 174-175, 302-303
DBENV→set_shm_key, 303-304
DBENV→set_tmp_dir, 80, 304-305
DBENV→set_tx_max, 170, 305-306
DBENV→set_tx_recover, 170, 306
DBENV→set_tx_timestamp, 307
DBENV→set_verbose, 191, 193, 307-308
Dbm interface, 337-338
db_create, 21, 84, 136, 173, 319
db_env_create, 78-79, 135, 173, 320
db_env_set_func_close, 320-321
db_env_set_func_dirfree, 321
db_env_set_func_dirlist, 322
db_env_set_func_exists, 322-323
db_env_set_func_free, 323
db_env_set_func_fsync, 324
db_env_set_func_ioinfo, 324-325
db_env_set_func_malloc, 325
db_env_set_func_map, 326
db_env_set_func_open, 327
db_env_set_func_read, 327
db_env_set_func_realloc, 328
db_env_set_func_rename, 328
db_env_set_func_seek, 329
db_env_set_func_sleep, 330
db_env_set_func_unlink, 330-331
db_env_set_func_unmap, 331
db_env_set_func_write, 332
db_env_set_func_yield, 332-333
db_env_set_pageyield, 333-334
db_env_set_panicstate, 334
db_env_set_region_init, 334-335
db_env_set_tas_spins, 335-336
db_strerror, 67, 85, 336
db_version, 336
db_xa_switch functions, 127
lock_detect, 112, 147, 155, 342
lock_get, 148, 170, 343
lock_id, 148, 344
lock_put, 148, 344
lock_stat, 148, 345-346
lock_vec, 148, 346-347
log_archive, 162, 348-349
log_compare, 162, 349
log_file, 162, 349
log_flush, 162, 350
log_get, 161, 350-351
log_put, 161, 170, 352
log_register, 162, 353
log_stat, 162, 353-354

log_unregister, 162, 355
memp_fclose, 136, 165, 355-356
memp_fget, 165, 356-357
memp_fopen, 165, 357-359
memp_fput, 165, 360
memp_fset, 165, 361
memp_fsync, 165, 361-362
memp_register, 166, 362-363
memp_stat, 166, 363-365
memp_sync, 165-166, 365-366
memp_trickle, 166, 366
Ndbm interface, 337-339
txn_abort, 135, 167, 170, 173, 367
txn_begin, 135, 167, 170, 173, 367-368
txn_checkpoint, 113, 168, 368-369
txn_commit, 135, 168, 170, 173, 369-370
txn_id, 168, 370
txn_prepare, 171, 371
txn_stat, 168, 371-372

G-H

GNU autoconf options, configuring
Berkeley DB, 202-204

handles, list of, 135-136

Hash access method, 31
compared to Btree access method, 32-33
DB→set_flags function, 266-267
DB→stat function, 277
Db.set_flags method, 511
Db.stat method, 520
Db::set_flags method, 396
Db::stat method, 407
disk space requirements, 63, 65
page-fill factor, 41, 63-64
page locks, 149
specifying hash function, 41
table size, 42

hash function, specifying, 41

hash tables, advantages of, 10

home directory, 77

hot backups, defined, 6, 11

HP-UX, building Berkeley DB for
(troubleshooting), 214-215

hsearch interface, 73, 341
compatibility notes, 341
diagnostics, 341-342

I

I/O processes, performance
considerations, 35

implictly created records, 45

indexes (secondary), logical joins, 54-58

initialization function, application-
specific logging and recovery, 142

initializing subsystems, environment
creation, 78

inserting elements in databases, 22-24

installing
Berkeley DB
for UNIX, 206
upgrades, 231-233
Tcl API as a Tcl package, 181-182

interfaces. See also APIs; functions
Dbm, 337-338
compatibility notes, 339
diagnostics, 339
hsearch, 341
compatibility notes, 341
diagnostics, 341-342
Ndbm, diagnostics, 340
run-time configuration, 144-145

IRIX, building Berkeley DB for
(troubleshooting), 215

isolation (transactions), 5

J

Java API, 73, 177-178
CLASSPATH environment variable, 178
compatibility issues, 178-179
Db class, 489-490
Db.close method, 490-491
Db.cursor method, 491
Db.del method, 492
Db.fd method, 492-493
Db.get method, 493-494
Db.get_byteswapped method, 495
Db.get_type method, 495
Db.join method, 495-496
Db.key_range method, 497
Db.open method, 498-500
Db.put method, 500-501
Db.remove method, 501-502

Db.rename method, 502-503
Db.set_append_recno method, 504
Db.set_bt_compare method, 504-505
Db.set_bt_minkey method, 505
Db.set_bt_prefix method, 506
Db.set_cachesize method, 506-507
Db.set_dup_compare method, 507-508
Db.set_errcall method, 508-509
Db.set_errpfx method, 509
Db.set_feedback method, 509-510
Db.set_flags method, 510-512
Db.set_h_ffactor method, 512-513
Db.set_h_hash method, 513
Db.set_h_nelem method, 514
Db.set_lorder method, 514-515
Db.set_pagesize method, 515
Db.set_q_extentsize method, 515-516
Db.set_re_delim method, 516
Db.set_re_len method, 516-517
Db.set_re_pad method, 517
Db.set_re_source method, 517-518
Db.stat method, 519-521
Db.sync method, 522
Db.upgrade method, 523-524
Db.verify method, 524-525
Dbc class, 578
Dbc.close method, 578
Dbc.count method, 579
Dbc.del method, 579-580
Dbc.dup method, 580
Dbc.get method, 581-583
Dbc.put method, 583-586
DbDeadlockException class, 525
DbEnv class, 526
DbEnv.close method, 526-527
DbEnv.get_version_major method, 527
DbEnv.lock_detect method, 528
DbEnv.lock_get method, 528-529
DbEnv.lock_id method, 529-530
DbEnv.lock_stat method, 530-531
DbEnv.lock_vec method, 531
DbEnv.log_archive method, 531-532
DbEnv.log_compare method, 533
DbEnv.log_file method, 533
DbEnv.log_flush method, 533-534
DbEnv.log_get method, 534-535
DbEnv.log_put method, 536
DbEnv.log_register method, 537
DbEnv.log_stat method, 537-538
DbEnv.log_unregister method, 538-539

DbEnv.memp_fstat method, 540
DbEnv.memp_register method, 539
DbEnv.memp_stat method, 539-541
DbEnv.memp_sync method, 541
DbEnv.memp_trickle method, 541
DbEnv.open method, 542-545
DbEnv.remove method, 545-546
DbEnv.set_cachesize method, 547
DbEnv.set_data_dir method, 548
DbEnv.set_errcall method, 549
DbEnv.set_error_stream method, 549
DbEnv.set_errpfx method, 550
DbEnv.set_feedback method, 550
DbEnv.set_flags method, 551
DbEnv.set_lg_bsize method, 552
DbEnv.set_lg_dir method, 552-553
DbEnv.set_lg_max method, 553
DbEnv.set_lk_conflicts method, 554
DbEnv.set_lk_detect method, 554-555
DbEnv.set_lk_max method, 555-556
DbEnv.set_lk_max_lockers method, 556
DbEnv.set_lk_max_locks method, 557
DbEnv.set_lk_max_objects method,
   557-558
DbEnv.set_mp_mmapsize method, 558
DbEnv.set_mutexlocks method, 559
DbEnv.set_pageyield method, 559
DbEnv.set_panicstate method, 559-560
DbEnv.set_recovery_init method, 560
DbEnv.set_region_init method, 561
DbEnv.set_server method, 561-562
DbEnv.set_shm_key method, 562-563
DbEnv.set_tas_spins method, 563-564
DbEnv.set_tmp_dir method, 564-565
DbEnv.set_tx_max method, 565
DbEnv.set_tx_recover method, 566
DbEnv.set_tx_timestamp method, 566-567
DbEnv.set_verbose method, 567
DbEnv.strerror method, 568
DbEnv.txn_begin method, 568-569
DbEnv.txn_checkpoint method, 569-570
DbEnv.txn_stat method, 570-571
DbException class, 180, 571
DbException.get_errno method, 572
DbLock class, 572
DbLock.put method, 572-573
DbLsn class, 573
DbMemoryException class, 573
DbMpoolFile.close method, 573
DbMpoolFile.get method, 573
DbMpoolFile.open method, 574

DbMpoolFile.put method, 574
DbMpoolFile.set method, 574
DbMpoolFile.sync method, 574
DbRunRecoveryException class, 574
Dbt class, 586-589
DbTxn class, 575
DbTxn.abort method, 575
DbTxn.commit method, 576
DbTxn.id method, 577
DbTxn.prepare method, 577
directory tree, 177
exceptions, 179
finalization of objects, 179
including for Win32 platforms, 221
LD_LIBRARY_PATHenvironment
    variable, 178
programming overview, 179-180

joins, logical, 54-58

K-L

key/data pairs, 308-310
Dbt class, 485-488, 586-589
defined, 20

keys, size limitations, 62

keywords, db_load utility, 626

**LD_LIBRARY_PATH environment
variable (Java API), 178**

**length of records (Recno and Queue
access methods), 42**

library. *See* **Berkeley DB library**

**Linux, building Berkeley DB for
(troubleshooting), 216**

load command, 182

**load options, configuring
Berkeley DB, 205**

loading
Tcl API, 182
text into databases, 189

locality of reference, defined, 32

lock-coupling, 149, 154

locking
in Berkeley DB, 15
concurrent read-write access, 87-89
performance considerations, page size, 35
two-phase locking, 10

Locking subsystem, 71, 147-148
access method conventions, 152-154
Concurrent Data Store, 154-155
conflict matrix, 150
deadlock avoidance, 155-156
    configuring locking system, 156-158
non-Berkeley DB applications, 158-159
page locks, 149
with transactions, 151
without transactions, 151

lock_detect function, 112, 147, 155, 342

lock_get function, 148, 170, 343

lock_id function, 148, 344

lock_put function, 148, 344

lock_stat function, 148, 345-346

lock_vec function, 148, 346-347

log filenames, limits on usage, 162-163

log files
application-specific logging and
    recovery, 139
    automatically generated functions, 140-143
    defining application-specific operations,
    139-140
    nonconformant logging, 143-144
archival procedures in transactional
    applications, 115-117
debugging applications, 193-197
performing checkpoints in transactional
    applications, 113, 115
removing in transactional applications,
    117, 119

**log function (application-specific logging
and recovery), 141**

log sequence numbers (LSNs), 161, 193

logging
in Berkeley DB, 15
write-ahead logging, 10

Logging subsystem, 71, 161-162
configuring, 162
limits on log file usage, 162-163

logical joins, 54-58

logical record numbers, 34
Btree access method, 40
Queue access method compared to Recno
    access method, 34
renumbering, 44-45

log_archive function, 162, 348–349

log_compare function, 162, 349

log_file function, 162, 349

log_flush function, 162, 350

log_get function, 161, 350–351

log_put function, 161, 170, 352

log_register function, 162, 353

log_stat function, 162, 353–354

log_unregister function, 162, 355

LSNs (log sequence numbers), 161, 193

M

major version number, defined, 138

memory
database key size limitations, 62
retrieved key/data permanence, 61
shared memory regions, 83–84

memory allocation, 37

memory pool, as part of architecture, 71

Memory Pool subsystem, 165–166

memp_fclose function, 136, 165, 355–356

memp_fget function, 165, 356–357

memp_fopen function, 165, 357–359

memp_fput function, 165, 360

memp_fset function, 165, 361

memp_fsync function, 165, 361–362

memp_register function, 166, 362–363

memp_stat function, 166, 363–365

memp_sync function, 165–166, 365–366

memp_trickle function, 166, 366

metadata pages, Btree access method
compared to Hash access method, 33

methods. See also functions
Db.close, 490–491
Db.cursor, 491
Db.del, 492
Db.fd, 492–493
Db.get, 493–494
Db.get_byteswapped, 495
Db.get_type, 495
Db.join, 495–496

Db.key_range, 497
Db.open, 498–500
Db.put, 500–501
Db.remove, 501–502
Db.rename, 502–503
Db.set_append_recno, 504
Db.set_bt_compare, 504–505
Db.set_bt_minkey, 505
Db.set_bt_prefix, 506
Db.set_cachesize, 506–507
Db.set_dup_compare, 507–508
Db.set_errcall, 508–509
Db.set_errpfx, 509
Db.set_feedback, 509–510
Db.set_flags, 510–512
Db.set_h_ffactor, 512–513
Db.set_h_hash, 513
Db.set_h_nelem, 514
Db.set_lorder, 514–515
Db.set_pagesize, 515
Db.set_q_extentsize, 515–516
Db.set_re_delim, 516
Db.set_re_len, 516–517
Db.set_re_pad, 517
Db.set_re_source, 517–518
Db.stat, 519–521
Db.sync, 522
Db.upgrade, 523–524
Db.verify, 524–525
Db::close, 374–375
Db::cursor, 375–376
Db::del, 376
Db::fd, 377
Db::get, 377–379
Db::get_byteswapped, 379
Db::get_type, 379
Db::join, 380–381
Db::key_range, 381–382
Db::open, 382–384
Db::put, 385–386
Db::remove, 386–387
Db::rename, 387–388
Db::set_append_recno, 388
Db::set_bt_compare, 389
Db::set_bt_minkey, 390
Db::set_bt_prefix, 390–391
Db::set_cachesize, 391–392
Db::set_dup_compare, 392
Db::set_errcall, 393
Db::set_errfile, 393–394

Db::set_errpfx, 394
Db::set_feedback, 394-395
Db::set_flags, 395-397
Db::set_h_ffactor, 397-398
Db::set_h_hash, 398
Db::set_h_nelem, 399
Db::set_lorder, 399-400
Db::set_malloc, 400
Db::set_pagesize, 401
Db::set_paniccall, 401
Db::set_q_extentsize, 402
Db::set_realloc, 405
Db::set_re_delim, 402
Db::set_re_len, 403
Db::set_re_pad, 403-404
Db::set_re_source, 404-405
Db::stat, 406-409
Db::sync, 409
Db::upgrade, 410-411
Db::verify, 411-412
Dbc.close, 578
Dbc.count, 579
Dbc.del, 579-580
Dbc.dup, 580
Dbc.get, 581-583
Dbc.put, 583-586
Dbc::close, 477
Dbc::count, 478
Dbc::del, 478-479
Dbc::dup, 479-480
Dbc::get, 480-482
Dbc::put, 482-485
DbEnv.close, 526-527
DbEnv.get_version_major, 527
DbEnv.lock_detect, 528
DbEnv.lock_get, 528-529
DbEnv.lock_id, 529-530
DbEnv.lock_stat, 530-531
DbEnv.lock_vec, 531
DbEnv.log_archive, 531-532
DbEnv.log_compare, 533
DbEnv.log_file, 533
DbEnv.log_flush, 533-534
DbEnv.log_get, 534-535
DbEnv.log_put, 536
DbEnv.log_register, 537
DbEnv.log_stat, 537-538
DbEnv.log_unregister, 538-539
DbEnv.memp_fstat, 540
DbEnv.memp_register, 539

DbEnv.memp_stat, 539-541
DbEnv.memp_sync, 541
DbEnv.memp_trickle, 541
DbEnv.open, 542-545
DbEnv.remove, 545-546
DbEnv.set_cachesize, 547
DbEnv.set_data_dir, 548
DbEnv.set_errcall, 549
DbEnv.set_error_stream, 549
DbEnv.set_errpfx, 550
DbEnv.set_feedback, 550
DbEnv.set_flags, 551
DbEnv.set_lg_bsize, 552
DbEnv.set_lg_dir, 552-553
DbEnv.set_lg_max, 553
DbEnv.set_lk_conflicts, 554
DbEnv.set_lk_detect, 554-555
DbEnv.set_lk_max, 555-556
DbEnv.set_lk_max_lockers, 556
DbEnv.set_lk_max_locks, 557
DbEnv.set_lk_max_objects, 557-558
DbEnv.set_mp_mmapsize, 558
DbEnv.set_mutexlocks, 559
DbEnv.set_pageyield, 559
DbEnv.set_panicstate, 559-560
DbEnv.set_recovery_init, 560
DbEnv.set_region_init, 561
DbEnv.set_server, 561-562
DbEnv.set_shm_key, 562-563
DbEnv.set_tas_spins, 563-564
DbEnv.set_tmp_dir, 564-565
DbEnv.set_tx_max, 565
DbEnv.set_tx_recover, 566
DbEnv.set_tx_timestamp, 566-567
DbEnv.set_verbose, 567
DbEnv.strerror, 568
DbEnv.txn_begin, 568-569
DbEnv.txn_checkpoint, 569-570
DbEnv.txn_stat, 570-571
DbEnv::close, 413-414
DbEnv::err, 414-415
DbEnv::lock_detect, 415-416
DbEnv::lock_get, 416-417
DbEnv::lock_id, 417
DbEnv::lock_stat, 418-419
DbEnv::lock_vec, 419-420
DbEnv::log_archive, 421-422
DbEnv::log_compare, 422
DbEnv::log_file, 422-423
DbEnv::log_flush, 423

DbEnv::log_get, 424–425
DbEnv::log_put, 425–426
DbEnv::log_register, 426–427
DbEnv::log_stat, 427–428
DbEnv::log_unregister, 428
DbEnv::memp_register, 429–430
DbEnv::memp_stat, 430–432
DbEnv::memp_sync, 432–433
DbEnv::memp_trickle, 433
DbEnv::open, 434–437
DbEnv::remove, 437–438
DbEnv::set_cachesize, 438–439
DbEnv::set_data_dir, 439–440
DbEnv::set_errcall, 440
DbEnv::set_errfile, 441
DbEnv::set_error_stream, 441–442
DbEnv::set_errpfx, 442
DbEnv::set_feedback, 442–443
DbEnv::set_flags, 443
DbEnv::set_lg_bsize, 444
DbEnv::set_lg_dir, 444–445
DbEnv::set_lg_max, 445–446
DbEnv::set_lk_conflicts, 446
DbEnv::set_lk_detect, 447
DbEnv::set_lk_max, 447–448
DbEnv::set_lk_max_lockers, 448
DbEnv::set_lk_max_locks, 449
DbEnv::set_lk_max_objects, 449–450
DbEnv::set_mp_mmapsize, 450
DbEnv::set_mutexlocks, 451
DbEnv::set_pageyield, 451
DbEnv::set_paniccall, 452
DbEnv::set_panicstate, 452
DbEnv::set_recovery_init, 453
DbEnv::set_region_init, 453–454
DbEnv::set_server, 454–455
DbEnv::set_shm_key, 455
DbEnv::set_tas_spins, 456
DbEnv::set_tmp_dir, 456–457
DbEnv::set_tx_max, 457–458
DbEnv::set_tx_recover, 458–459
DbEnv::set_tx_timestamp, 459
DbEnv::set_verbose, 459–460
DbEnv::strerror, 460
DbEnv::txn_begin, 461
DbEnv::txn_checkpoint, 462
DbEnv::txn_stat, 463–464
DbEnv::version, 464
DbException.get_errno, 572
DbException::get_errno, 465

DbException::what, 465
DbLock.put, 572–573
DbLock::put, 466
DbMpoolFile.close, 573
DbMpoolFile.get, 573
DbMpoolFile.open, 574
DbMpoolFile.put, 574
DbMpoolFile.set, 574
DbMpoolFile.sync, 574
DbMpoolFile::close, 467
DbMpoolFile::get, 468–469
DbMpoolFile::open, 469–471
DbMpoolFile::put, 471–472
DbMpoolFile::set, 472–473
DbMpoolFile::sync, 473
DbTxn.abort, 575
DbTxn.commit, 576
DbTxn.id, 577
DbTxn.prepare, 577
DbTxn::abort, 474
DbTxn::commit, 475
DbTxn::id, 476
DbTxn::prepare, 476

minimum keys per page (Btree access method), 40

minor version number, defined, 138

multiple databases, opening in one file, 48–49

multithreaded applications, support for, 134–135

mutable mode (logical record numbers), 34

mutable record numbers, renumbering, 44–45

N

name spaces
    C language, 136–137
    copying databases, 137–138
    filesystem, 137
naming files
    filename resolution, 80, 82
    role of environment in structure of, 79–80
Ndbm interface, 73
    diagnostics, 340
    functions, 337–339

nested transactions, 110-111

network databases, 7-8, 13

NFS-mounted filesystems, warning about, 84

non-Berkeley DB applications
Locking subsystem, 158-159
transactions, 170-171

nul bytes, 24

O-P

object handles
defined, 20
list of, 135-136

object-oriented databases, 7, 13

open source, defined, 9

opening
databases, 21-22, 47-48
multiple databases in one file, 48-49
for transactional applications, 98-100
within environment, 84
environment for transactional applications, 95-98

OSF/1, building Berkeley DB for (troubleshooting), 216

output formats, dumping databases, 188-189

overflow records, defined, 35

overwriting data, avoiding, 24

package command, 182

packages (Tcl), installing Tcl API as, 181-182

padding records (Recno and Queue access methods), 43

page cache management, 15

page histories, extracting from log files, 196

page locks, 149

page size, selecting, 35

page-fill factor
Btree access method, 63
Hash access method, 41, 63-64

partial records, storage and retrieval, 65-66

patch number, defined, 138

pathnames, absolute (filename resolution), 80

performance considerations
I/O processes, page size, 35
locking, page size, 35
transaction throughput, 123-125

performing checkpoints in transactional applications, 113, 115

Perl scripting language, 74

permanence, retrieved key/data items, 61

permissions, 82

pointer traversal (network databases), 7

prefix comparison routines (Btree access method), 39-40

primary keys (logical joins), 54-58

print function (application-specific logging and recovery), 142

programmatic APIs. *See* APIs

programming model, Berkeley DB library, 72

Q-R

Queue access method, 32
compared to Recno access method, 33-34
DB→set_flags function, 267
DB→stat function, 278
Db.set_flags method, 511
Db.stat method, 521
Db::set_flags method, 396
Db::stat method, 408
extent size, 43
padding records, 43
page locks, 149, 152
record length, 42

queues, advantages of, 10

read function (application-specific logging and recovery), 141

read locks, concurrent, 88

read-write access, concurrent, 87-89

Recno access method, 32
backing source files, 43-44
compared to Queue access method, 33-34
DB→set_flags function, 267
DB→stat function, 277-278
Db.set_flags method, 511-512
Db.stat method, 520-521
Db::set_flags method, 396-397
Db::stat method, 407-408
locks, 154
padding records, 43
page locks, 149
record delimiters, 42
record length, 42
renumbering records, 44-45

record delimiters (Recno access method), 42

record length (Recno and Queue access methods), 42

record types (log files), 194-195

record-number-based storage, advantages of, 10

records
defined, 4
deleting, 50
with cursors, 54
flushing from cache, 51
implicitly created, 45
logical record numbers, 34
Btree access method, 40
Queue access method compared to Recno access method, 34
renumbering, 44-45
network databases, 7
overflow records, defined, 35
padding (Recno and Queue access methods), 43
partial records, storage and retrieval, 65-66
relational databases, 6
retrieving, 50
with cursors, 52-53
storing, 50
with cursors, 53-54

recoverability
of Berkeley DB in transactional applications, 121-123
environment creation, 79
Transaction subsystem, 70
transactional applications, 92, 100, 102

recovery
application-specific logging and recovery, 139
automatically generated functions, 140-143
defining application-specific operations, 139-140
nonconformant logging, 143-144
defined, 5, 93
in transactional applications, 93-94
filesystem operations' effect on, 120-121
XA Resource Manager, 130

recovery function (application-specific logging and recovery), 142

recovery procedures in transactional applications, 119-120

recovery process, implementation overview, 139

references
Berkeley DB background information, 242
database systems theory, 242
technical papers on Berkeley DB, 241

relational databases, 6, 12-13

remote filesystems, environment, 84

Remote Procedure Call Protocol. *See* **RPC support**

removing
elements from databases, 26, 28
files, effect on transactional application recovery, 121
log files in transactional applications, 117, 119
records, 50
with cursors, 54

renaming files, effect on transactional application recovery, 121

renumbering records, 44-45

repeatable reads (transactional applications), 92, 106-107

requirements, disk space, 62
Btree access method, 62-63
Hash access method, 63, 65

resolution of file names, 80, 82

Resource Manager (XA support), 127-128
combining with non-XA transactions, 130
configuring Berkeley DB with Tuxedo, 128-129

converting applications to run under, 129
recovery, 130

retrieved key/data items, permanence, 61

retrieving
elements from databases, 25-26
partial records, 65-66
records, 50
with cursors, 52-53

RPC stubs, 14

RPC support, 173-174
client program, 174-175
server program, 175-176

run-time configuration, 144-145

**run-time errors, debugging
applications, 193**

running Berkeley DB test suite, 235-236
under UNIX, 208-209
under Win32, 222-223

**runtime environments for
Berkeley DB, 16**

S

salvaging databases, 59

scalability of Berkeley DB, 9

schema, defined, 12

**SCO, building Berkeley DB for
(troubleshooting), 216**

scripting languages, 74

secondary indexes (logical joins), 54-58

security
environment variables, 82
permissions, 82
temporary backing files, 82-83

selecting
access methods, 32
*Hash access method compared to Btree access
method, 32-33*
*Queue access method compared to Recno
access method, 33-34*
byte order, 37
cache size, 36-37
database management systems, 4
page size, 35

server program, RPC support, 175-176

servers, 8, 14

shared libraries for UNIX, 207-208

shared memory regions, 83-84

sharing environment, 77

signal-handling, 131
error return values, 132
DB_KEYEMPTY, 132
DB_LOCK_DEADLOCK, 133
DB_LOCK_NOTGRANTED, 133
DB_NOTFOUND, 132
DB_RUNRECOVERY, 133

size
Btree maximum depth, 62
of cache, selecting, 36-37
database file size limitations, 62
disk space requirements, 62
Btree access method, 62-63
Hash access method, 63, 65
of extents (Queue access method), 43
key size limitations, 62
of pages, selecting, 35
of tables (Hash access method), 42

sizing Locking subsystem, 157-158

**Solaris, building Berkeley DB for
(troubleshooting), 216-218**

**sort routines (Btree access method),
37, 39**

special error values, defined, 21

**SQL (Structured Query Language),
defined, 6**

stability of cursors, 58-59

**standalone application model
(Berkeley DB library), 72**

statistics (databases), 51

storing records, 50
partial records, 65-66
with cursors, 53-54

**Structured Query Language (SQL),
defined, 6**

structures, clearing, 23

**subsystem initialization, environment
creation, 78**

**SunOS, building Berkeley DB for
(troubleshooting), 218**

system or application failure, defined, 93

T

table size (Hash access method), 42

Tcl API, 181
  berkdb dbremove command, 591
  berkdb dbrename command, 592
  berkdb env command, 593-595
  berkdb envremove command, 595-596
  berkdb open command, 596-601
  berkdb version command, 601
  commands in, 182-183
  compiling with certain version, 185
  db close command, 602
  db count command, 603
  db cursor command, 603
  db del command, 603
  db get command, 604-606
  db get_join command, 609
  db get_type command, 609
  db is_byteswapped command, 609
  db join command, 610
  db put command, 610-611
  db stat command, 611
  db sync command, 611
  dbc close command, 602
  dbc del command, 604
  dbc dup command, 604
  dbc get command, 606-609
  dbc put command, 612-614
  env close command, 614
  env txn command, 614-615
  error handling, 183-184
  including for Win32 platforms, 221-222
  installing as a Tcl package, 181-182
  loading, 182
  programming overview, 183
  running Berkeley DB test suite under
    Win32, 222-223
  troubleshooting, 185
  txn abort command, 615
  txn commit command, 615-616

Tcl scripting language, 74

technical papers on Berkeley DB, 241

temporary backing files (security), 82-83

**temporary files (environmental
  variables), 134**

test suite (Berkeley DB)
  running, 235-236
    under UNIX, 208-209
    under Win32, 222-223
  troubleshooting, 237

text, loading into databases, 189

**threads, support for multithreaded
  applications, 134-135**

threads of control
  defined, 92
  transactions, 169

throughput of transactions, 123-125

timeouts (berkeley_db_svc utility), 175

**Tornado 2.0, building Berkeley DB for
  VxWorks, 225-227**

trailing nul bytes, 24

**transaction histories, extracting from log
  files, 196**

transaction IDs, limits on usage, 168-169

Transaction subsystem, 70-71, 167-168
  configuring, 169-170
  cursor limits, 169
  limits on usage, 168-169
  non-Berkeley DB applications, 170-171
  threads of control, 169

transactions
  aborting, 93
  application structure, 93-95
  atomicity, 92, 103-106
  in Berkeley DB, 15
  Berkeley DB recoverability, 121-123
  committing, 93
  cursors, 107-108, 110
  databases, opening, 98-100
  deadlocks
    avoiding, 92, 102-103
    defined, 93
  defined, 5, 92
  environment, opening, 95, 97-98
  environment infrastructure, 111
    archival procedures, 115-117
    deadlock detection, 111, 113
    log file removal, 117, 119
    performing checkpoints, 113, 115
    recovery procedures, 119-120
  extracting from log files, 196

filesystem operations, effect on recovery, 120-121

free-threaded handles, defined, 92
    locking with, 151
    locking without, 151
    nested transactions, 110-111
    reasons for using, 92
    recoverability, 92-93, 100, 102, 139
    repeatable reads, 92, 106-107
    system or application failure, defined, 93
    thread of control, 92, 169
    throughput, 123-125
    XA support, 130

trees. *See* **Btree access method**

troubleshooting. *See also* **debugging applications**
    building Berkeley DB for UNIX, 209-212
        AIX, 212-213
        FreeBSD, 213
        HP-UX, 214-215
        IRIX, 215
        Linux, 216
        OSF/1, 216
        SCO, 216
        Solaris, 216-218
        SunOS, 218
        Ultrix, 218
    building Berkeley DB for VxWorks, 228-229
    building Berkeley DB for Win32, 224
    concurrent read-write access, 88-89
    DbException (Java API), 180
    db_dump185 utility, 211
    Tcl API, 185
    test suite, 237

tuples, defined, 6

Tuxedo System, configuring Berkeley DB with, 128-129

two-phase locking, 10, 151

txn abort command, 615

txn commit command, 615-616

txn_abort function, 135, 167, 170, 173, 367

txn_begin function, 135, 167, 170, 173, 367-368

txn_checkpoint function, 113, 168, 368-369

txn_commit function, 135, 168, 170, 173, 369-370

txn_id function, 168, 370

txn_prepare function, 171, 371

txn_stat function, 168, 371-372

U–V

Ultrix, building Berkeley DB for (troubleshooting), 218

UNIX
    Berkeley DB library compatibility with, 138
    building Berkeley DB for, 201-202
        troubleshooting, 209-218
    configuring Berkeley DB for
        compile or load options, 205
        GNU autoconf options, 202-204
    dynamic shared libraries, 207-208
    installing Berkeley DB for, 206
    running Berkeley DB test suite under, 208-209

upgrading
    Berkeley DB installations, 231-233
    databases, 49

utilities
    berkeley_db_svc, 74, 175-176, 617-618
    buildtms, 128
    db_archive, 74, 116-118, 618-619
    db_checkpoint, 74, 113, 620
    db_deadlock, 74, 112, 155, 621
    db_dump, 74, 187-189, 622-624
    db_dump185, 187-188
        output formats, 188-189
        troubleshooting, 211
    db_load, 75, 189, 624-626
    db_printlog, 75, 626-627
        debugging applications, 193-197
    db_recover, 75, 119-120, 627-628
    db_stat, 75, 36-37, 629-630
    db_upgrade, 75, 630-631
    db_verify, 75, 632

variable-length records (record delimiters), 42

variables. *See* **environment variables**

verifying databases, 59

version information, Berkeley DB library, 138

versions of Tcl API, compiling, 185

Visual C++ 5.0, building Berkeley DB for Win32, 220

Visual C++ 6.0, building Berkeley DB for Win32, 219-220

VxWorks, building Berkeley DB for, 225-227
  programming notes, 227
  troubleshooting, 228-229

W-Z

Win32
  building Berkeley DB for, 219-222
    programming notes, 223-224
    troubleshooting, 224
  running Berkeley DB test suite under, 222-223

—with-tcl=DIR configuration option (GNU autoconf), 204

write cursors, forbidding multiple, 88

write-ahead logging, 10, 100

XA Resource Manager, 127-128
  combining with non-XA transactions, 130
  configuring Berkeley DB with Tuxedo, 128-129
  converting applications to run under, 129
  recovery, 130

HOW TO CONTACT US

VISIT OUR WEB SITE

WWW.NEWRIDERS.COM

On our web site, you'll find information about our other books, authors, tables of contents, and book errata. You will also find information about book registration and how to purchase our books, both domestically and internationally.

EMAIL US

Contact us at: **nrfeedback@newriders.com**

- If you have comments or questions about this book
- To report errors that you have found in this book
- If you have a book proposal to submit or are interested in writing for New Riders
- If you are an expert in a computer topic or technology and are interested in being a technical editor who reviews manuscripts for technical accuracy

Contact us at: **nreducation@newriders.com**

- If you are an instructor from an educational institution who wants to preview New Riders books for classroom use. Email should include your name, title, school, department, address, phone number, office days/hours, text in use, and enrollment, along with your request for desk/examination copies and/or additional information.

Contact us at: **nrmedia@newriders.com**

- If you are a member of the media who is interested in reviewing copies of New Riders books. Send your name, mailing address, and email address, along with the name of the publication or Web site you work for.

BULK PURCHASES/CORPORATE SALES

If you are interested in buying 10 or more copies of a title or want to set up an account for your company to purchase directly from the publisher at a substantial discount, contact us at 800-382-3419 or email your contact information to corpsales@pearsontechgroup.com. A sales representative will contact you with more information.

WRITE TO US

New Riders Publishing
201 W. 103rd St.
Indianapolis, IN 46290-1097

CALL/FAX US

Toll-free (800) 571-5840
If outside U.S. (317) 581-3500
Ask for New Riders
FAX: (317) 581-4663

New Riders

RELATED NEW RIDERS TITLES

ISBN: 073570998X
US $39.99

Embedded Linux

John Lombardo

Embedded Linux provides the reader the information needed to design, develop, and debug an embedded Linux appliance. It explores why Linux is a great choice for an embedded application and what to look for when choosing hardware.

ISBN: 0735710430
US $49.99

Advanced Linux Programming

Code Sourcery, LLC

An in-depth guide to programming Linux from the most recognized leaders in the Open Source community, this book is the ideal reference for Linux programmers who are reasonably skilled in the C programming language and who are in need of a book that covers the Linux C library (glibc).

ISBN: 0735710201
1152 pages
US $49.99

Inside XML

Steven Holzner

Inside XML is a foundation book that covers both the Microsoft and non-Microsoft approach to XML programming. It covers in detail the hot aspects of XML, such as, DTD's vs. XML Schemas, CSS, XSL, XSLT, Xlinks, Xpointers, XHTML, RDF, CDF, parsing XML in Perl and Java, and much more.

ISBN 0735710910
416 pages
US $34.99

Python Essential Reference, Second Editio

David Beazley

Python Essential Reference, Seco Edition, concisely describes th Python programming language and its large library of standar modules—collectively known the Python programming envir ment. It is arranged into four major parts. First, a brief tuto and introduction is presented, then an informal language refe ence covers lexical convention functions, statements, control flow, datatypes, classes, and ex cution models. The third secti covers the Python library, and final section covers the Pythor API that is used to write Pytho extensions. This book is is high focused and clearly provides t things a reader needs to know best utilize Python.

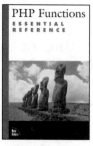

ISBN 0-7357-0970-X
500 pages
US $39.99

PHP Functions Essential Reference

The *PHP Essential Reference* is simple, clear and authoritative function reference that clarifie and expands upon PHP's existi documentation. The *PHP Esse Reference* will help the reader write effective code that make full use of the rich variety of functions available in PHP.

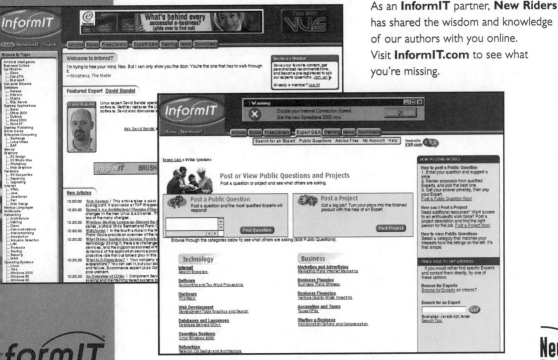

Colophon

The Sphinx of Giza featured on the cover of this book serves two purposes: It is in keeping with the images chosen for all of our Landmark series books, and more importantly it symbolizes the feline representation associated with Sleepycat Software.

Designed to have the head of a king and the body of a lion, this architecturally amazing monument stands taller than a six-story building, and it is as long as a city block. It is believed that the 4th dynasty king, Khafre, commissioned the monument. Its majesty was captured by award-winning photographer Hisham Ibrahim.

This book was written using standard text editors emacs and vi. Text files were post-processed with the UNIX m4 utility to create HTML files, which were converted by New Riders to Microsoft Word and laid out in QuarkXPress. The font used for the body text is Bembo and MCPdigital. It was printed on 50# Husky Offset Smooth paper at R.R. Donnelley & Sons in Crawfordsville, Indiana. Prepress consisted of PostScript computer-to-plate technology (filmless process). The cover was printed at Moore Langen Printing in Terre Haute, Indiana, on Carolina, coated on one side.